THE PROSPECTS OF INTERNATIONAL TRADE REGULATION

From fragmentation to coherence

For a long time, the GATT led a life of its own as a self-contained regime. The evolution from tariff to non-tariff barriers brought about increasing overlaps with other regulatory areas. WTO rules increasingly interface with other areas of law and policy, including environmental protection, agricultural policies, labour standards, investment, human rights and regional integration.

Against this backdrop, this book examines fragmentation in international trade regulation across a wide array of regulatory fields. To this end, it uses a conceptually coherent theoretical framework which is based on the effort to bring about greater coherence among different policy goals and fields, and thus to embed the multilateral trading system within the broader framework of international economics, law and relations. It will appeal to those interested in a forward-looking discussion of the most pressing issues of the international trade agenda. This book is the result of a four-year project run at the Swiss National Centre for Competence in Research – Trade Regulation (NCCR), which is financed by the Swiss National Science Foundation.

THOMAS COTTIER is Managing Director of the World Trade Institute and Professor of Law at the University of Bern.

PANAGIOTIS DELIMATSIS is Associate Professor of Law and Member of the Tilburg Law and Economics Center (TILEC) at Tilburg University, the Netherlands. He is also a senior research fellow at the World Trade Institute of the University of Bern.

THE PROSPECTS OF INTERNATIONAL TRADE REGULATION

From fragmentation to coherence

Edited by

THOMAS COTTIER

and

PANAGIOTIS DELIMATSIS

CAMBRIDGE
UNIVERSITY PRESS

CAMBRIDGE UNIVERSITY PRESS
Cambridge, New York, Melbourne, Madrid, Cape Town,
Singapore, São Paulo, Delhi, Tokyo, Mexico City

Cambridge University Press
The Edinburgh Building, Cambridge CB2 8RU, UK

Published in the United States of America by Cambridge University Press, New York

www.cambridge.org
Information on this title: www.cambridge.org/9781107004870

First published 2011

Printed in the United Kingdom at the University Press, Cambridge

A catalogue record for this publication is available from the British Library

Library of Congress Cataloguing in Publication data
The prospects of international trade regulation : from fragmentation to coherence / edited by
Thomas Cottier, Panagiotis Delimatsis.
p. cm.
Includes index.
ISBN 978-1-107-00487-0 (hardback)
1. Foreign trade regulation. I. Cottier, Thomas. II. Delimatsis, Panagiotis.
K3943.P76 2011
343′.087 – dc22 2010049073

ISBN 978-1-107-00487-0 Hardback

CONTENTS

FIGURES

TABLES

CONTRIBUTORS

PHILIPP AERNI is Senior Research Fellow at the World Trade Institute, University of Bern and the Institute for Environmental Decisions, ETH Zurich, Switzerland

KLAUS ARMINGEON is Professor of International Relations at the University of Bern, Switzerland

RICHARD BALDWIN is Professor of Economics at the Graduate Institute of International and Development Studies, Geneva, Switzerland

ERNST BALTENSPERGER is Professor of Economics at the University of Bern, Switzerland

HANNAH BARGAWI is Research Officer at the Centre for Development Policy and Research at the School of Oriental and African Studies (SOAS), University of London, United Kingdom

SUSETTE BIBER-KLEMM is Senior Research Fellow at the World Trade Institute, University of Bern, Switzerland

BERTRAM BOIE is Research Fellow at the World Trade Institute, University of Bern, Switzerland

YVES BONZON is a PhD student at the University of Lausanne Law Faculty, Switzerland

ELVA BOVA is a PhD student in Economics at the School of Oriental and African Studies (SOAS), University of London, United Kingdom

MICHAEL BURKARD is Research Fellow at the World Trade Institute, University of Bern, Switzerland

MIRA BURRI-NENOVA is Senior Research Fellow at the World Trade Institute and Lecturer in Law at the University of Bern, Switzerland

THERESA CARPENTER is Executive Director of the Centre for Trade and Economic Integration at the Graduate Institute of International and Development Studies, Geneva, Switzerland

JULIEN CHAISSE is Assistant Professor, Faculty of Law, Chinese University of Hong Kong, China

BARNALI CHOUDHURY is Assistant Professor of Law at Charleston School of Law, Canada

THOMAS COTTIER is Professor of Law at the University of Bern and Managing Director of the World Trade Institute, University of Bern, Switzerland

PANAGIOTIS DELIMATSIS is Associate Professor of Law at Tilburg University, the Netherlands, and Senior Research Fellow at the World Trade Institute, University of Bern, Switzerland

NICOLAS DIEBOLD is an Associate at Froriep Renggli, Zurich, Switzerland

MANFRED ELSIG is Assistant Professor of International Relations, World Trade Institute, University of Bern, Switzerland

BENNO FERRARINI is Senior Research Fellow at the World Trade Institute, University of Bern, Switzerland

MARINA FOLTEA is Research Fellow at the World Trade Institute, University of Bern, Switzerland

KATJA GEHNE is Senior Research Fellow at the World Trade Institute, University of Bern, Switzerland

CHRISTOPH BEAT GRABER is Professor of Law and Head of i-call (International Communications and Art Law Lucerne) Research Centre at the University of Lucerne, Switzerland

PHILIPPE GUGLER is Professor of Economics at the University of Fribourg, Switzerland

CHRISTIAN HÄBERLI is Senior Consultant at the World Trade Institute, University of Bern, Switzerland

NILS HERGER is Senior Research Fellow at the World Trade Institute and a Lecturer in Economics at the University of Bern and the Study Center Gerzensee, Switzerland

SIMONE HERI is Research Assistant at DEZA (Swiss Agency for Development and Cooperation) and the International Commission of Jurists, Bern and Geneva, Switzerland

FRANZISKA HUMBERT is Policy Advisor on Labour Rights at Oxfam, Berlin, Germany

SUFIAN JUSOH is Research Fellow at the World Trade Institute, University of Bern, Switzerland

BARIS KARAPINAR is Senior Research Fellow at the World Trade Institute, University of Bern, Switzerland

CHRISTINE KAUFMANN is Professor of International Law, University of Zurich, Switzerland

GARBA MALUMFASHI is a PhD student at the Centre for Energy, Petroleum and Mineral Law and Policy (CEPMLP), University of Dundee, United Kingdom

SOFYA MATTEOTTI-BERKUTOVA is Research Fellow at the World Trade Institute, University of Bern, Switzerland

THOMAS MESSERLI is Research Fellow at the Graduate Institute of International and Development Studies, Geneva, Switzerland

KAROLINA MILEWICZ is Senior Research Fellow at the World Trade Institute, University of Bern, Switzerland

MARTÍN MOLINUEVO is Research Fellow at the World Trade Institute, University of Bern, Switzerland

KRISTA NADAKAVUKAREN SCHEFER is Assistant Professor of International Law at the University of Basel, Switzerland

OLGA NARTOVA is Senior Research Fellow at the World Trade Institute, University of Bern, Switzerland

SUSAN NEWMAN is Senior Researcher in Corporate Strategy and Industrial Development, University of the Witwatersrand, South Africa

MARION PANIZZON is Assistant Professor of Law at the World Trade Institute, University of Bern, Switzerland

TETYANA PAYOSOVA is Research Fellow at the Institute of International and European Economic Law, University of Bern, Switzerland

SIMONE PETER is Senior Research Assistant at the Law Faculty, University of Basel, Switzerland

ANNE PETERS is Professor of International Law at the University of Basel, Switzerland

PIERRE SAUVÉ is Vice-Managing Director and Director of Studies at the World Trade Institute, University of Bern, Switzerland

JOËLLE DE SÉPIBUS is Senior Research Fellow of the World Trade Institute and Lecturer in International and European Law on Climate Change at the University of Bern, Switzerland

THOMAS STEINER is a lawyer and an Affiliated Member of i-call (International Communications and Art Law Lucerne) Research Centre at the University of Lucerne, Switzerland

MICHELANGELO TEMMERMAN is Research Fellow at the World Trade Institute, University of Bern, Switzerland

SADEQ Z. BIGDELI is Research Fellow at the World Trade Institute, University of Bern, Switzerland

ANDREAS ZIEGLER is Professor of Law at the University of Lausanne, Switzerland

PREFACE AND ACKNOWLEDGEMENTS

Fragmentation and coherence in international trade regulation are the core theme of this volume. For a long time, the General Agreement on Tariffs and Trade (GATT) led a life of its own in a self-contained regime. The evolution from tariff to non-tariff barriers brought about increasing overlaps with other regulatory areas, partly pertaining to core areas of domestic regulation. World Trade Organization (WTO) rules increasingly have an impact on other areas of law and policy, including environmental protection, agricultural and regional policies, labour standards, investment, human rights, culture and regional integration. Vice versa, other regulatory areas have an impact on trade rules. The process has resulted in tensions and challenges to the multilateral trading system with which the WTO has been confronted since its inception in 1995. Against this backdrop, this book offers an attempt to examine fragmentation in international trade regulation across a wide array of regulatory fields through the lens of a conceptually coherent theoretical framework. The effort to bring about greater coherence among different policy goals and fields, and thus to embed the multilateral trading system within the larger framework of international economics, law and international relations is the common thread connecting all chapters of this book and the proposals for reform which they submit.

The Swiss National Centre for Competence in Research on 'International Trade Regulation – From Fragmentation to Coherence' (NCCR Trade Regulation), financed by the Swiss National Science Foundation (SNF), is an international research network that was set up at the World Trade Institute (WTI) of the University of Bern, Switzerland, in 2005. It completed the first phase of its research in 2009 based on twelve individual projects dealing with a broad array of topics, ranging from the constitutionalisation of international law and decision-making in the WTO, regional integration, agriculture and commodities, human rights, services, finance, and intellectual property, to energy, biotechnology and information technology. The twelve projects comprise law, economics and international relations and put a clear accent on those issues that do not form part of the current trade agenda. The underlying rationale has been that academia has a key role to play in identifying, analysing and offering innovative policy and rule-making solutions to pressing challenges in modern trade diplomacy. This volume presents the research questions and synthesises the most significant achievements and innovative elements of our research output in the first four years of the NCCR Trade Regulation.

During its first four years, the NCCR Trade Regulation research team, comprising more than 60 researchers, tested its methodology and research outcomes at workshops, conferences and seminars organised in Switzerland and abroad. Several formal and informal rounds of discussions on the twelve chapters of this book were organised at the WTI, the most recent of which consisted of a peer-review process during the NCCR Annual Conference in 2009. Several contributions include suggestions for specific amendments to various provisions or parts of the relevant WTO agreements. This was possible because of the open approach that we adopted, encouraging work in research groups rather than individualist scholarship. The overwhelming majority of the contributions were drafted in a manner that reflects joint thinking and effort by both experienced, renowned trade experts and junior-level researchers, reflecting the knowledge-transfer philosophy of the NCCR Trade Regulation research network. In addition, all contributions resulted from interdisciplinary work, especially between lawyers and political scientists, and, to a lesser extent, economists.

This book is the contribution of the NCCR Trade Regulation as an academic institution to conceptualising the regulatory debates of the future, and, in particular, elucidating the value-related choices at stake. Taking into account theoretical insights from law, economics and political science and without any pre-existing bias against fragmentation per se, the NCCR Trade Regulation has aimed to develop innovative, concrete policy recommendations that reflect a better balance between economic and other regulatory objectives in fields where international trade rules interact with other types of rules. This book will become indispensable reading for regulators, trade negotiators, practitioners and academics. This is not only because of the handy structure that it adopts, but also because this book is forward-looking, as it also proposes a post-Doha agenda, suggesting the most pressing avenues that the international trade agenda should pursue beyond the current Doha Development Agenda.

We are indebted to the research teams and authors of this book who graciously agreed to revise their contributions several times to ensure optimum results by accommodating the suggestions of the editors and their colleagues. We are indebted to the external participants at conferences and workshops who were willing to share their knowledge. In particular, we would like to thank the NCCR Review Panel members for their insightful comments and suggestions throughout the duration of the project. We are grateful to Claudia Opitz-Belakhal and Dominique Foray for chairing the Panel, and to Keith Maskus, Geertrui van Overwalle, Debra Steger and Christian Tietje, as well as Patrick Low, Anthony McGrew, John Odell and Hélène Ruiz Fabri for their valuable contributions in assessing the work and offering guidance. We thank Thomas Griessen for servicing the Panel and the process on behalf of the SNF. We are grateful to the NCCR Research Council members and, notably, Professor John Jackson and Gary Hufbauer for guidance and advice. The editors wish to express their gratitude to Susan Brown for thoughtful and careful coordination and management of this ambitious project. The work of Susan Kaplan assisted by Jane Müller is acknowledged. They had to meet short deadlines and cope with manifold requests from the editors. The organisation of the conferences and workshops during which the chapters included in this book were discussed would not have been feasible without the active involvement of Margrit Vetter, Gaby Hofer, Piia Pappinen, Christian Steiger and François Rossé. Finally, we would like to thank the Swiss National Science Foundation and the Ecoscientia Foundation for their financial support and their trust throughout the project. Without their support, this book would not have seen the light of day.

Our sincere thanks are due to Cambridge University Press and especially to Finola O'Sullivan for her commitment to the finalisation of this book. For the same reason, we would like to thank Richard Woodham for his dedication and patience.

THOMAS COTTIER
PANAGIOTIS DELIMATSIS

TABLE OF CASES

1. International Court of Justice

Legality of the Use by a State of Nuclear Weapons in Armed Conflict, Advisory Opinion [1996] ICJ Reports 66

Oil Platforms (*Islamic Republic of Iran* v. *United States of America*) [2003] ICJ Reports 161.

Corfu Channel case (*United Kingdom* v. *Albania*), Merits [1949] ICJ Reports 2.

Nuclear Tests case (*New Zealand* v. *France*) [1974] ICJ Reports 457

2. Court of Justice (EU)

6/64, *Costa* v. *ENEL* [1964] ECR 1141

120/78, *Rewe-Zentrale AG* v. *Bundesmonopolverwaltung für Branntwein* [1979] ECR 649

302/86, *Commission* v. *Kingdom of Denmark* [1988] ECR 4607

C-6/90 and C-9/90, *Francovich* v. *Italy* [1991] ECR I-5357

C-393/92, *Almelo and Others* [1994] ECR I-1477

C-46/93 and C-48/93, *Brasserie du Pêcheur SA* v. *Germany* and *R.* v. *Secretary of State for Transport, ex-parte Factortame Ltd and others* [1996] ECR I-1029.

C-34/95, *Konsumentombudsmannen (KO)* v. *De Agostini* [1997] ECR I-3843

C-112/00, *Eugen Schmidberger, Internationale Transporte und Planzüge* v. *Republik Österreich* [2003] ECR I-5659

C-402/05P and C-415/05P, *Yassin Abdullah Kadi and Al Barakaat International Foundation* v. *Council of the European Union and Commission of the European Communities* [2008] ECR I-6351

3. General Court (EU)

T-174/00, *Biret International SA* v. *Council* [2002] ECR II-17

T-387/04, *EnBW Energie Baden-Württemberg AG* v. *Commission* [2007] ECR II-1195

4. European Patent Office (EPO)

EPO, Opposition Division, *Edinburgh University*, EP 0 695 351, not published; appeal withdrawn

EPO, Technical Board of Appeal, *Wisconsin Alumni Research Foundations*, T 1374/04

Technical Board of Appeal to the European Patent Office, *Brassica*, T 0083/05, 22 May 2007 (Appeal pending before the Enlarged Board of Appeal, case number G2/07

5. WTO Panels and Appellate Body

Appellate Body Report, *Argentina – Safeguard Measures on Imports of Footwear*, WT/DS121/AB/R, adopted 12 January 2000, DSR 2000:I, 515 (*Argentina – Footwear (EC)*)

Panel Report, *Argentina – Measures Affecting the Export of Bovine Hides and Import of Finished Leather*, WT/DS155/R and Corr.1, adopted 16 February 2001, DSR 2001:V, 1779 (*Argentina – Hides and Leather*)

Appellate Body Report, *Australia – Measures Affecting Importation of Salmon*, WT/DS18/AB/R, adopted 6 November 1998, DSR 1998:VIII, 3327 (*Australia – Salmon*)

Panel Report, *Australia – Measures Affecting Importation of Salmon*, WT/DS18/R and Corr.1, adopted 6 November 1998, as modified by Appellate Body Report WT/DS18/AB/R, DSR 1998:VIII, 3407 (*Australia – Salmon*)

Appellate Body Report, *Canada – Measures Affecting the Export of Civilian Aircraft*, WT/DS70/AB/R, adopted 20 August 1999, DSR 1999:III, 1377 (*Canada – Aircraft*)

Panel Report, *Canada – Measures Affecting the Export of Civilian Aircraft*, WT/DS70/R, adopted 20 August 1999, as upheld by Appellate Body Report WT/DS70/AB/R, DSR 1999:IV, 1443 (*Canada – Aircraft*)

Panel Report, *Canada – Certain Measures Affecting the Automotive Industry*, WT/DS139/R, WT/DS142/R, adopted 19 June 2000, modified by Appellate Body Report, WT/DS139/AB/R, WT/DS142/AB/R, DSR 2000:VII, 3043 (*Canada – Autos*)

Appellate Body Report, *Canada – Continued Suspension of Obligations in the EC – Hormones Dispute*, WT/DS321/AB/R, adopted 14 November 2008 (*Canada – Continued Suspension*)

Panel Report, *Canada – Continued Suspension of Obligations in the Hormones Dispute*, WT/DS321/R, adopted 14 November 2008 (*Canada – Continued Suspension*)

Appellate Body Report, *Canada – Measures Affecting the Importation of Milk and the Exportation of Dairy Products*, WT/DS103/AB/R, WT/DS113/AB/R and Corr.1, adopted 27 October 1999, DSR 1999:V, 2057 (*Canada – Dairy*)

Appellate Body Report, *Canada – Certain Measures Concerning Periodicals*, WT/DS31/AB/R, adopted 30 July 1997, DSR 1997:I, 449 (*Canada – Periodicals*)

Panel Report, *Canada – Certain Measures Concerning Periodicals*, WT/DS31/R and Corr.1, adopted 30 July 1997, as modified by the Appellate Body Report, WT/DS31/AB/R, DSR 1997:I, 481 (*Canada – Periodicals*)

Panel Report, *Canada – Patent Protection of Pharmaceutical Products*, WT/DS114/R, adopted 7 April 2000, DSR 2000:V, 2289 (*Canada – Pharmaceutical Patents*)

Panel Report, *China – Measures Affecting Trading Rights and Distribution Services for Certain Publications and Audiovisual Entertainment Products*, WT/DS363/R, adopted 12 August 2009 (*China – Audiovisual Products*)

Appellate Body Report, *China – Measures Affecting Trading Rights and Distribution Services for Certain Publications and Audiovisual Entertainment Products*, WT/DS363/AB/R, adopted 21 December 2009 (*China – Audiovisual Products*)

Appellate Body Report, *Dominican Republic – Measures Affecting the Importation and Internal Sale of Cigarettes*, WT/DS302/AB/R, adopted 19 May 2005, DSR 2005:XV, 7367 (*Dominican Republic – Import and Sale of Cigarettes*)

Appellate Body Report, *European Communities – Measures Affecting Asbestos and Asbestos-Containing Products*, WT/DS135/AB/R, adopted 5 April 2001, DSR 2001:VII, 3243 (*EC – Asbestos*)

Appellate Body Report, *European Communities – Regime for the Importation, Sale and Distribution of Bananas*, WT/DS27/AB/R, adopted 25 September 1997, DSR 1997:II, 591 (*EC – Bananas III*)

Panel Report, *European Communities – Regime for the Importation, Sale and Distribution of Bananas, Complaint by Ecuador*, WT/DS27/R/ECU, adopted 25 September 1997, WT/DS27/AB/R, DSR 1997:III, 1085 (*EC – Bananas III (Ecuador)*)

Panel Report, *European Communities – Regime for the Importation, Sale and Distribution of Bananas, Complaint by the United States*, WT/DS27/R/USA, adopted 25 September 1997, modified by Appellate Body Report, WT/DS27/AB/R, DSR 1997:II, 943 (*EC – Bananas III (US)*)

Panel Report, *European Communities – Measures Affecting the Approval and Marketing of Biotech Products*, WT/DS291/R, WT/DS292/R, WT/DS293/R, Add.1 to Add.9, and Corr.1, adopted 21 November 2006, DSR 2006:III-VIII (*EC – Biotech*)

Appellate Body Report, *EC Measures Concerning Meat and Meat Products (Hormones)*, WT/DS26/AB/R, WT/DS48/AB/R, adopted 13 February 1998, DSR 1998:I, 135 (*EC – Hormones*)

Panel Report, *EC Measures Concerning Meat and Meat Products (Hormones), Complaint by the United States*, WT/DS26/R/USA, adopted 13 February 1998, as modified by Appellate Body Report WT/DS26/AB/R, WT/DS48/AB/R, DSR 1998:III, 699 (*EC – Hormones (US)*)

Appellate Body Report, *European Communities – Trade Description of Sardines*, WT/DS231/AB/R, adopted 23 October 2002, DSR 2002:VIII, 3359 (*EC – Sardines*)

Appellate Body Report, *European Communities – Conditions for the Granting of Tariff Preferences to Developing Countries*, WT/DS246/AB/R, adopted 20 April 2004, DSR 2004:III, 925 (*EC – Tariff Preferences*)

Panel Report, *European Communities – Conditions for the Granting of Tariff Preferences to Developing Countries*, WT/DS246/R, adopted 20 April 2004, as modified by Appellate Body Report WT/DS/246/AB/R, DSR 2004:III, 1009 (*EC – Tariff Preferences*)

Panel Report, *India – Measures Affecting the Automotive Sector*, WT/DS146/R, WT/DS175/R and Corr.1, adopted 5 April 2002, DSR 2002:V, 1827 (*India – Autos*)

Appellate Body Report, *India – Quantitative Restrictions on Imports of Agricultural, Textile and Industrial Products*, WT/DS90/AB/R, adopted 22 September 1999, DSR 1999:IV, 1763 (*India – Quantitative Restrictions*)

Panel Report, *India – Quantitative Restrictions on Imports of Agricultural, Textile and Industrial Products*, WT/DS90/R, adopted 22 September 1999, as upheld by Appellate Body Report WT/DS90/AB/R, DSR 1999:V, 1799 (*India – Quantitative Restrictions*)

Appellate Body Report, *India – Patent Protection for Pharmaceutical and Agricultural Chemical Products*, WT/DS50/AB/R, adopted 16 January 1998, DSR 1998:I, 9 (*India – Patents (US)*)

Appellate Body Report, *Japan – Taxes on Alcoholic Beverages*, WT/DS8/AB/R, WT/DS10/AB/R, WT/DS11/AB/R, adopted 1 November 1996, DSR 1996:I, 97 (*Japan – Alcoholic Beverages*)

Panel Report, *Japan – Measures Affecting Consumer Photographic Film and Paper*, WT/DS44/R, adopted 22 April 1998, DSR 1998:IV, 1179 (*Japan – Film*)

Appellate Body Report, *Korea – Measures Affecting Imports of Fresh, Chilled and Frozen Beef*, WT/DS161/AB/R, WT/DS169/AB/R, adopted 10 January 2001, DSR 2001:I, 5 (*Korea – Beef*)

Panel Report, *Korea – Measures Affecting Imports of Fresh, Chilled and Frozen Beef*, WT/DS161/R, WT/DS169/R, adopted 10 January 2001, as modified by Appellate Body Report, WT/DS161/AB/R, WT/DS169/AB/R, DSR 2001:I, 59 (*Korea – Beef*)

Appellate Body Report, *Korea – Definitive Safeguard Measure on Imports of Certain Dairy Products*, WT/DS98/AB/R, adopted 12 January 2000, DSR 2000:I, 3 (*Korea – Dairy*)

Panel Report, *Mexico – Measures Affecting Telecommunications Services*, WT/DS204/R, adopted 1 June 2004, DSR 2004:IV, 1537 (*Mexico – Telecoms*)

Appellate Body Report, *United States – Continued Suspension of Obligations in the EC – Hormones Dispute*, WT/DS320/AB/R, adopted 14 November 2008 (*US – Continued Suspension*)

Panel Report, *United States – Continued Suspension of Obligations in the Hormones Dispute*, WT/DS320/R, circulated 31 March 2008 (*US – Continued Suspension*)

Appellate Body Report, *United States – Measures Affecting the Cross-Border Supply of Gambling and Betting Services*, WT/DS285/AB/R, adopted 20 April 2005, DSR 2005:XII, 5663 (Corr.1, DSR 2006:XII, 5475) (*US – Gambling*)

Panel Report, *United States – Measures Affecting the Cross-Border Supply of Gambling and Betting Services*, WT/DS285/R, adopted 20 April 2005, as modified by Appellate Body Report WT/DS285/AB/R, DSR 2005:XII, 5797 (*US – Gambling*)

Appellate Body Report, *United States – Standards for Reformulated and Conventional Gasoline*, WT/DS2/AB/R, adopted 20 May 1996, DSR 1996:I, 3 (*US – Gasoline*)

6. GATT

7. European Court of Human Rights (ECtHR)

Matthews v. *the United Kingdom*, No 24833/94, ECHR 1999-I 361
Behrami and Behrami v. *France* and *Saramati* v. *France, Germany and Norway* (dec.) (Grand Chamber), Joined App. Nos. 71412/01 and 78166/01, 2 May 2007

8. European Commission of Human Rights

Lawless v. *Ireland* (App no 332/57) (1959), Report of the Commission

9. NAFTA

In the Matter of Cross-Border Trucking Services, USA-MEX-98–2008–01, 6 February 2001
Feldman v. *Mexico,* ICSID Case No. ARB(AF)/99/1 (NAFTA), Award on Merits, 16 December 2002
S.D. Myers, Inc. v. *Canada,* UNCITRAL (NAFTA), First Partial Award, 13 November 2000
Occidental Exploration and Production Company v. *Ecuador*, LCIA Case No. UN3467, Final Award, 1 July 2004

10. Other Abritration

Trail Smelter (US v. *Canada),* Award II (1941) 3 UNRIAA 1905

11. Domestic Courts

(a) United States

Asahi Metal Industry Co. v. *Superior Court of California* 480 US 102 (1987)
John Moore v. *the Regents of the University of California (et al.)*, 9 July 1990, No S006987, 51 Cal. 3d 120.
International Shoe Co. v. *Washington* 326 US 310 (1945)
Madey v. *Duke University* 307 F.3d 1351 (Fed. Cir. 2002)
Metro-Goldwyn-Mayer Studios, Inc. v. *Grokster, Ltd.*, 125 S. Ct. 2764 (2005)
Sony Corp. of America v. *Universal City Studios, Inc.*, 464 US. 417 (1984)

(b) Canada

Harvard College v. *Canada (Commissioner of Patents)*, 5 December 2002, 4 Supreme Court Reports (Canada) 45 (2002)

ABBREVIATIONS

AB	Appellate Body
ALALC	Asociación Latinoamericana de Libre Comercio
ALOP	appropriate level of protection
AnGR	animal genetic resources
AoA	Agreement on Agriculture
APEC	Asia-Pacific Economic Cooperation
ASCM	Agreement on Subsidies and Countervailing Measures
ASEAN	Association of South-East Asian Nations
ATC	Agreement on Textiles and Clothing
BIS	Bank for International Settlements
BIT	bilateral investment treaty
BMMA	bilateral migration management agreements
BOP	balance of payments
BRIC	Brazil, Russia, India and China
CACM	Central American Common Market
CAFTA	United States–Dominican Republic–Central America Free Trade Agreement
CARICOM	Caribbean Community
CBD	Convention on Biological Diversity
CC	Creative Commons
CCD	Convention on Cultural Diversity
CDSF	Contingency Debt Sustainability Framework
CER	closer economic relations
CEMAC	Communauté économique et monétaire de l'Afrique Centrale
CFI	Court of First Instance of the European Communities
CIS	Commonwealth of Independent States
COMESA	Common Market for Eastern and Southern Africa
COMTRADE database	United Nations Commodity Trade Statistics Database
CPI	consumer price index
CPIA	country policy and institutional assessment

CPC	central product classification
CSR	corporate social responsibility
CTG	Council for Trade in Goods
CTS	consolidated tariff schedules
CUSFTA	Canada–US Free Trade Agreement
DDA	Doha Development Agenda
DDR	Doha Development Round
DRM	digital rights management
DSU	Dispute Settlement Understanding
EC	European Communities
ECCAS	Economic Community of Central African States
ECHR	European Convention on Human Rights
ECJ	European Court of Justice
ECT	Energy Charter Treaty
ECOWAS	Economic Community Of West African States
ECSC	European Coal and Steel Community
ECtHR	European Court of Human Rights
EEA	European Economic Area
EEC	European Union emissions trading scheme
EFTA	European Free Trade Agreement
EGE	European Group on Ethics in Science and New Technologies
EPA	Economic Partnership Agreement
EPO	European Patent Office
EU	European Union
EU ETS	European Union Emission Trading System
FAO	Food and Agriculture Organization of the United Nations
FDI	foreign direct investment
FET	fair and equitable treatment
FSA	Financial Services Authority
FTA	free trade agreement
GAPP	Generally Accepted Practices and Principles
GATT	General Agreement on Tariffs and Trade
GATS	General Agreement on Trade in Services
GDP	gross domestic product
GHG	greenhouse gas
GI	geographical indication
GM	genetically modified
GMO	genetically modified organism
GPA	Agreement on Government Procurement
GPP	green public procurement
GSP	Generalized System of Preferences

HIPC	heavily indebted poor countries
HRIA	human rights impact assessments
HRS	household responsibility system
HS	Harmonized Commodity Description and Coding System (HS Nomenclature)
HUGO	Human Genome Organisation
IAASTD	International Assessment of Agricultural Knowledge, Science and Technology for Development
ICA	International Commodity Agreements
ICJ	International Court of Justice
ICSID	International Centre for Settlement of Investment Disputes
ICTSD	International Centre for Trade and Sustainable Development
IDA	International Development Association
IEA	International Energy Agency
IIA	International Investment Arrangements
ILO	International Labour Organization
IMF	International Monetary Fund
IOE	International Organisation of Employers
IOM	International Organization for Migration
IO	international organisation
IP	Individual Project
IPCC	Intergovernmental Panel on Climate Change
IPPC	International Plant Protection Convention
IPR	intellectual property rights
ITA	WTO Information Technology Agreement
ITU	International Telecommunications Union
IWG	International Working Group
LAIA	Asociación Latinoamericana de Integración (the Latin American Integration Association)
LDCs	least developed countries
LICs	low-income countries
LMO	living modified organisms
MA	multilateral agreement
MAI	multilateral agreement on investment
MEA	multilateral environmental agreements
MERCOSUR	Regional Trade Agreement among Argentina, Brazil, Paraguay and Uruguay founded in 1991 by the Treaty of Asunción
MFN	most-favoured nation
MNE	multinational enterprise
MONP	Movement of Natural Persons

NAFTA	North American Free Trade Agreement
NAP	national allocation plan
NCCR	National Centre of Competence in Research
NFIDC	net food-importing developing countries
NGO	non-governmental organisation
NOPEC	No Oil Producing and Exporting Cartels Act of 2007
NT	national treatment
NYBOT	New York Board of Trade
OECD	Organisation for Economic Co-operation and Development
OIE	World Organisation for Animal Health
OPEC	Organization of the Petroleum Exporting Countries
PECS	Pan-European Cumulation System
PFI	Policy Framework for Investment
PIC	prior informed consent
PPM	process and production method
PPP	public–private partnership
PTA	preferential trade agreement
RE	renewable energy
ROO	rules of origin
RTA	regional trade agreement
R&D	research and development
SADC	South African Development Community
SCE	state-controlled entities
SCM	WTO Agreement on Subsidies and Countervailing Measures
SIA	Sustainability Impact Assessment
SME	small and medium-sized enterprises
SOE	state-owned enterprises
SPS Agreement	Agreement on the Application of Sanitary and Phytosanitary Measures
STABEX	Système de Stabilisation des Recettes d'Exportation
SWF	sovereign wealth funds
S&D	special and differential treatment
TBT Agreement	Agreement on Technical Barriers to Trade
TEC	Transatlantic Economic Council
TFEU	Treaty on the Functioning of the European Union
TNC	transnational companies
TRIMs	Agreement on Trade-Related Investment Measures
TRIPS	Agreement on Trade-Related Aspects of Intellectual Property Rights
TPRM	Trade Policy Review Mechanism

TSE	total support estimate
UCC	user created content
UDHR	Universal Declaration of Human Rights
UNCPC	United Nations Provisional Central Product Classification
UNCTAD	United Nations Conference on Trade and Development
UNESCO	United Nations Educational, Scientific and Cultural Organization
UNEP	United Nations Environment Programme
UNFCCC	United Nations Framework Convention on Climate Change
UNHCHR	Office of the High Commissioner for Human Rights
UR	Uruguay Round
VAR	vector autoregression
VCLT	Vienna Convention on the Law of Treaties
WAEMU	West African Economic and Monetary Union
WCO	World Customs Organization
WGTI	Working Group on Trade and Investment
WHO	World Health Organization
WIPO	World Intellectual Property Organization
WSIS	World Summit on the Information Society
WTO	World Trade Organization

Introduction

Fragmentation and coherence in international trade regulation: analysis and conceptual foundations

THOMAS COTTIER, PANAGIOTIS DELIMATSIS, KATJA GEHNE AND TETYANA PAYOSOVA*

KEY MESSAGES

- Fragmentation in international law is due to the specificity of the international order: there is no sovereign entity to govern but there are dynamics of cooperation and coordination between states and private actors, creating diverse regimes and poles of governance, of law, legal standards and jurisdiction. These dynamics are accelerating in times of globalisation with regulatory challenges reaching beyond territorial boundaries.
- Fragmentation of law and different regimes can be both useful and detrimental, depending upon specific regulatory constellations. Efforts to create greater coherence are required where fragmentation impairs the effectiveness, efficiency and legitimacy of law and the operation of the basic principles and values at stake.
- The process of moving from fragmentation to coherence implies neither centralisation nor uniformity. Different regimes need different concepts of governance. The traditional national state and related constitutional model of governance do not address the specificities of the post-national constellation.
- The research projects of Phase I of the NCCR did not set out from an agreed and shared regulatory theory. They pursued the goal of contributing to the debate on the basis of their own ideas and different methodologies in economics, international relations and law.
- Challenges and phenomena in international economic law are beyond the reach of the old nation state concept. The analysis of WTO jurisprudence shows that existing rules of treaty interpretation and coordination are not able to bring about

* We would like to thank Keith Maskus, Geertrui van Overwalle, Debra Steger and Christian Tietje for thoughtful remarks and inspiring suggestions. Remaining errors are the authors' own.

coherence to a sufficient degree. New models provide useful guidance with a view to creating coherence, moving from contractual to constitutional structures in international law.

- The model of multilayered governance offers an appropriate framework. Combining positivist traditions of legal theory and principle theory, it expands the process of constitutionalisation of international law to the overall legal order, defining the operation of different layers of governance horizontally and vertically. The nation state remains of key importance, but assumes the role of an intermediary and no longer that of an exclusive power.

A. The challenges of fragmentation

International trade in goods and services pertains to most internationalised areas of human activity. Specialisation, division of labour and longstanding policies of trade liberalisation since the end of World War II enhanced trade flows and interdependence of nations in an unprecedented manner. Globalisation reached a new generation. Due to new technologies allowing worldwide communication and transport, transnational markets and international relations have progressed dramatically over recent decades, demanding regulation beyond national borders.[1] As a corollary, trade regulation spearheaded new developments in international law and moved centre stage. The General Agreement on Tariffs and Trade (GATT) and, subsequently, the World Trade Organization (WTO) developed a sophisticated body of trade rules amounting to some 42,000 pages of law, comprising agreements and schedules of commitments of more than 150 members. In addition, numerous bilateral and regional trade agreements have emerged, creating an additional layer of preferential rules in addition to the principles and rules of the WTO. Domestic trade policy and law add to the panoply of sources and considerations to be taken into account. In Europe, regionalisation entered a period of supranational legal integration, building a new constitutional order, primarily in trade, before turning to include other policy areas. The European experience demonstrates that enhanced integration through trade liberalisation and non-discrimination, in the long run, needs to go hand in hand with integration of other policy areas under a common umbrella. In global relations, this is part of a larger challenge facing international law and relations.

1 A. von Bogdandy, 'Globalization and Europe: How to Square Democracy, Globalization, and International Law' (2004) 15(5) *European Journal of International Law* 885, at 888.

The unprecedented development of international trade regulation takes place formally within the body of international law, in particular treaty law. It shares the traits of contractual arrangements, entered into by sovereign nations. Rules and principles are specifically aimed at trade liberalisation and trade regulation. They follow the traditions of functionalism inherent to international law and specialised international organisations. They do not encompass per se other public policy areas, such as defence, health, natural resources, education, culture or related areas of international law, such as the law of the sea, investment protection, and the protection of human rights or of the environment. International agreements, including those pertaining to trade, live parallel lives. They follow their own rules, jurisdictions and dispute settlement mechanisms to the extent they are available at all.

As a result, the body of law is highly fragmented in line with the contractual nature of international law. All too often, coordination and coherence have to be based upon the application of exceptions. Such fragmentation raises practical problems of coordinating different policy areas horizontally in international law and in domestic law. It raises problems of vertical coordination in fine-tuning the relations of international and domestic law. It calls for practical coordination between the multilateral framework and preferential agreements. Principally, it raises problems of coordination with other international regimes.

WTO law constitutes only one of many international regimes. All these regimes exist in what is commonly termed a 'normative jungle'.[2] They remain essentially without proper coordination. There is no common institutional mechanism that can bring about coherence in their negotiation, application and/or interpretation, even though they all operate within the general international law system. National constitutional legal systems provide such an all-encompassing institutional framework that also safeguards the fundamental values of society. Globalisation assails these systems; they remain only one factor in today's complicated regulatory network. The challenge today is to find coherent regulatory solutions of good sustainable governance in a multilayered governmental environment. These solutions have to take account of economic and political realities. Coherence can only be achieved if trade regulation is tailored to the political and social constellations in which it is to be applied. Strengthened cooperation and coordination among players and regimes,

2 A. Lindroos, 'Addressing Norm Conflicts in a Fragmented Legal System: The Doctrine of *Lex Specialis*' (2005) 74 *Nordic Journal of International Law* 27.

which may simultaneously compete for regulatory authority,[3] can play an important role here.

WTO rules increasingly impinge upon other areas of law and policy, including environmental protection, agricultural and regional policies, labour standards, investment, human rights and culture. By the same token, international rules such as those relating to human rights or environmental protection can have a chilling effect on trade, particularly when trade barriers are used as a 'stick' to induce a certain type of behaviour.[4] Additionally, trade impediments can be the inevitable corollary of state policies aimed at attaining non-economic objectives.[5] In the realm of trade regulation, the phenomenon of fragmentation (with a potentially negative connotation) is articulated mainly through two different strands which affect each other and interact in manifold ways: first, fragmentation is the result of collisions or horizontal overlaps among regimes of sometimes equal force in terms of membership, such as the United Nations (UN), United Nations Environment Programme (UNEP) or the human rights special regimes. Collisions of this type also include conflicts between the canons agreed multilaterally within the WTO and the rules that emerge at the periphery by means of manifold preferential trade agreements (PTAs). The proliferation of such agreements creates political and economic tensions, further compounding fragmentation within the multilateral trading system. Fragmentation can also occur vertically in the form of collisions among different levels of governance. Here, one would also be bound to include soft-law norms, typically adopted by non-state actors.

Horizontal fragmentation implies the risk of clashes between diverse and competing ethical rationales, goals and norms. Here, a simple conflict of rules could imply a deep conflict of differing ethical backgrounds and values. If the systems promote a specific issue or value, the system that 'wins' the conflict is doing so at the expense of the others' objectives (e.g. conflicting norms of the trade and environment regimes). Which

3 J. Trachtman, *The Economic Structure of International Law* (Harvard University Press, 2008), p. 206.

4 P. Delimatsis, *International Trade in Services and Domestic Regulations – Necessity, Transparency, and Regulatory Diversity* (Oxford University Press, 2007); also J. Trachtman, 'Institutional Linkage: Transcending "Trade and . . . "' (2002) 96(1) *American Journal of International Law* 77.

5 P. Delimatsis, 'Determining the Necessity of Domestic Regulations in Services – The Best is Yet to Come' (2008) 19(2) *European Journal of International Law* 365.

criteria for conflict resolution should be applied in those cases?[6] Which regime should prevail? Who should decide? A similar, but subtly different situation occurs with regard to *vertical* fragmentation. Diverse layers of governance likewise comprise competing ethical rationales in terms of cultural, traditional and societal backgrounds. This is why a conflict of law and principles can also be laden with deep value conflicts, as, for example, when a societal conviction rejects aspects of conflicting trade law obligations for market access, as was the case in *EC – Hormones*. This may lead to frictions between international governance and its societal basis.[7]

The question arises as to what extent the WTO needs to take into account other regimes (horizontally), or (vertically) at which governance level authority should be allocated. Which perspective should prevail? Under what circumstances should, for instance, WTO panels defer to national preferences in a WTO context?

Both horizontal and vertical lines of fragmentation carry the potential for conflicts of jurisdiction, when specialised regimes include autonomous dispute settlement and law enforcement mechanisms. For instance, the complexity of the relationship between environmental and trade rules was highlighted in the *Chile – Swordfish* case. The case, which related to a controversy between the EU and Chile over swordfish fisheries in the South Pacific and landing of swordfish in Chilean ports, was brought before both the International Tribunal for the Law of the Sea and the WTO.[8]

Overlapping legal regimes provoke legal uncertainty regarding the competences of dispute settlement bodies, mainly when adjudication in each case could occur under different regimes pursuing different objectives. Practice has shown that opposing parties have the possibility to call upon different dispute settlement organs or choose a competent body according to their interests (forum shopping) horizontally (under different regimes),[9] carrying the risk of differing legal

6 J. Pauwelyn, *Conflict of Norms in Public International Law: How WTO Law Relates to Other Rules of International Law* (Cambridge University Press, 2003).

7 G. Teubner, 'Societal Constitutionalism: Alternatives to State Centered Constitutional Theory?', in C. Joerges, I.-J. Sand and G. Teubner (eds.), *Transnational Governance and Constitutionalism* (Hart Publishing, 2004), pp. 3–28.

8 The parties to the dispute later agreed to suspend proceedings in both courts.

9 G. Hafner, 'Risks Ensuing from Fragmentation of International Law', in *Official Records of the General Assembly, Fifty-fifth Session*, Supplement No. 10 (A/55/10), Annex, pp. 143–150, at p. 148 (available at: http://untreaty.un.org/ilc/reports/2000/repfra.htm).

outcomes.[10] Vertically, national courts may defy or fail to comply with international decisions. States may ultimately be called upon to comply with one system and at the same time violate the other, or vice versa,[11] a situation which not only compromises legal security, but also the effectiveness, efficiency and, indeed, survival of the 'losing' system.

Against this backdrop, the present volume is a first attempt to examine fragmentation in international trade regulation across a wide array of different regulatory fields and specialised trade regimes. The twelve individual projects (IPs) supported and funded by the National Centre of Competence in Research (NCCR) of the Swiss National Research Foundation, hosted at the World Trade Institute of the University of Bern, Switzerland, and which are discussed and summarised in this volume share the common trait of exploring fragmentation and seeking greater coherence in their respective fields. In doing so, researchers in the first phase of the project (2005–2009) faced a number of challenges. Firstly, the debate on fragmentation and coherence is controversial. There is no uniform and accepted doctrine which could be applied and pursued across the board. Secondly, the debate is mainly prominent in law, and less so in international relations or in economics. At the outset, a working hypothesis was agreed that, for our purposes, coherence does not necessarily strive for, nor amount to harmonisation, uniformity or centralisation. Rather, coherence entails multilateral, regional and unilateral regulations alike which would allow for tensions and competition between different and competing policy goals and rule-making fora. The fundamental challenge is thus a matter of defining suitable relationships between different regulatory areas and levels in a rational manner, combining them with adequate procedures and institutional mechanisms to facilitate interaction and efficient governance, while enhancing predictability and legal certainty.

Rational relationships need to be developed among different regulatory areas and regimes at the international level, but also between different layers of governance. Taking into account theoretical insights from the disciplines of law, economics and political science, the purpose of the NCCR has been to develop innovative, concrete policy

10 See for examples, M. Koskenniemi, 'Fragmentation of International Law: Difficulties Arising from the Diversification and Expansion of International Law', Report of the Study Group of the International Law Commission, United Nations, International Law Commission, A/CN.4/L.682, para. 10.

11 Hafner, above n 9, p. 147.

recommendations that reflect a better balance between economic and other regulatory objectives in a series of fields where international trade rules interact with other types of rules and thus elucidate the current '*dialogue de sourds*' that exists among several issue-areas affecting trade. In this respect, we found in several instances that, for want of anything better, fragmentation in the sense of regulatory decentralisation may entail inherently coherent solutions that ultimately lead to more efficient regulation of trade issues. Thus, in certain areas of trade regulation, such as services, allocation of regulatory authority at the regional level may prove to generate outcomes superior to those produced to date at the WTO level. Thus, instead of any one-size-fits-all recommendations, this volume takes a careful look at the peculiarities of the regulated areas without any pre-existing bias against fragmentation per se.

The chapters of this volume essentially confirm this view. They share the goals of improving horizontal or vertical policy coordination. They do not present a uniform theory or perception of fragmentation and coherence in international economics, international relations and law. They deal with the problem of fragmentation and coherence in their own ways, addressing the topic directly or indirectly. Different traits can be identified. The process of constitutionalisation of international law studied in IP 1 seeks to bring about a better framework, allowing for enhanced coherence by leaving traditional contractual relations behind. Its analytical and normative aspirations are tested against the insights of political science which explores the relationship of nations and international organisations and its decision-making processes within the framework of the principal–agent theory in IP 2. Efforts to improve coordination of the multilateral framework and regional or preferential trade agreements were at the heart of research in IP 3, culminating in proposals for long-term multilateralisation of preferential agreements. The coordination of trade and human rights in IP 4 essentially reflects a constitutionalist approach in the area of human rights as well as fundamental principles of non-discrimination. Research on agriculture in IP 5 focuses on coordinating different horizontal policy goals, including access to food, and dealing with imbalances between developing and developed countries caused by persistent protectionism. Research on trade and energy within IP 6 squares two hitherto separate horizontal policy areas and explores the changes required in WTO law in order to bring about more efficient and sustainable energy production. IP 7 interfaces trade and culture, in particular the impact of and on new media. It is here that doubts as to greater coherence loom large. The work of IP 8 focused on several areas of multilateral and preferential regulation of services. Work on services suggests that fragmentation of regulating services, understood as decentralisation of decision-making, may lead to higher levels of liberalisation and increased global welfare. At the same time, multilateral shaping of rules and principles appears to be the best policy choice. IP 9 builds upon the theory of multilayered governance in addressing biotechnology. It is an example as to how centralisation and decentralisation within a particular topic need to be combined with a view to achieving optimal results. IP 10 addresses selected topics on financial regulation and trade, identifying the beneficial effects of decentralisation of regulatory authority in the field with manifold organisations regulating sometimes overlapping areas. This chapter concludes with a brief review of the current credit crunch and the needs to address contagion and to further financial development are identified as the biggest challenges to international financial regulation. IP 11 tackled selected issues in trade and investment, including problems relating to sovereign wealth funds and the challenges of reverse investment flows, while identifying a creeping trend towards regulating investment flows beyond the national level. Finally, IP 12 addresses, from an economic perspective, production and trade in commodities in selected African countries. It sets out policies which may bring greater benefits to the countries concerned, albeit without addressing the problem specifically in terms of fragmentation and coherence.

Overall, the first phase of the project is characterised by a bottom-up and inductive approach to the problem of fragmentation and coherence. Important and interesting proposals are put forward for achieving a reasonable relationship between different horizontal policy goals, and shaping relations between the international system and domestic polities. Concrete legal text amending extant WTO provisions or proposing new ones is proposed in several chapters. Additionally, a doctrine of multilayered governance is gradually emerging within the NCCR project and will be discussed below. The results achieved reflect the challenges facing a research community which is still geared towards individual research and agendas, and has not yet adopted a proper interdisciplinary approach which is keen to absorb, and learn from, research results produced in related areas. The lack of a common understanding and methodology in law, international relations and economics was apparent during the first phase of the project. The challenges of fragmentation thus not only relate to substance, but equally to a widely fragmented culture in the scientific community. The main, long-term benefit of the NCCR project perhaps consists of bringing about a new generation of researchers who were trained and are willing, within the enduring constraints of a conservative and highly fragmented academic establishment, to interact with other disciplines and work towards common and shared goals.[12] The task still lies ahead. With this in mind, we turn to the foundations and expound the theories of fragmentation and coherence in international law, in particular trade regulation, and in legal and constitutional theory. We hope that insights achieved so far may offer further guidance in further work on the topic during the second and third phases of the NCCR project and stimulate similar research worldwide.

B. Fragmentation in international law

International law consists of diverse polycentric legal systems eclipsing the former Westphalian system of nation states.[13] The post-war propensity towards accelerated cooperation has led to intensive inter-state treaty-making and the emergence of autonomous legal orders beyond the nation state model. The phenomenon is not limited to international trade. Issues such as terrorism, international crime, migration and poverty, or environmental threats can no longer be dealt with at the national level alone.[14] The state's task of governance has become intrinsically linked to a multi-power-driven complex of global action and specialised regimes.[15]

From the point of view of international norms and regulation, the dynamics of legal subsystems lead not only to diverse issue-oriented and specialised regimes of *substantive* norms, but also to fragmented authority at different levels of governance.[16] In the first case, this creates the

12 See T. Cottier, 'Challenges Ahead in International Economic Law' (2009) 12(1) *Journal of International Economic Law* 3.

13 S.-D. Krasner, 'Compromising Westphalia', in D. Held and A. McGrew (eds.), *The Global Transformations Reader. An Introduction to the Globalization Debate*, 3rd edition (Cambridge University Press, 2002), pp. 124 *et seq.*

14 J. Pauwelyn, *Fragmentation of International Law*, Max Planck Encyclopedia of Public International Law (Oxford University Press, 2008), available at: www.mpepil.com/subscriber_article?id=/epil/entries/law-9780199231690-e1406, para. 10.

15 J. Whitman, *The Limits of Global Governance* (Routledge, 2005), p. 17; U. Beck, 'What is Globalization?', in D. Held and A. McGrew (eds.), *The Global Transformations Reader. An Introduction to the Globalization Debate*, 3rd edn (Cambridge University Press, 2002), pp. 99–103, at pp. 101 *et seq.*

16 T. Broude, 'Fragmentation(s) of International Law: On Normative Integration as Authority Allocation', in T. Broude and Y. Shany (eds.), *The Shifting Allocation of Authority in International Law: Considering Sovereignty, Supremacy and Subsidiarity* (Hart Publishing, 2008), pp. 99–120.

problem of choice of law among conflicting norms of equivalent status resulting from the myriad regimes.[17] In the latter case, fragmentation problems can be viewed as institutional challenges associated with the allocation of jurisdiction along horizontal, vertical and functional dimensions.[18]

While the diverse issue-oriented systems are integrated as regimes, they form a scattered landscape of law consisting of competing objectives and overlapping in scope. Typically, such regimes have their own preferred idiom, special ethos and structural bias.[19] There is no centralised power to coordinate the regimes and assure their legal and authoritative coherence.[20] The United Nations has not been able to assume this function successfully. In addition, the consensus-based post-war approach towards international relations suffers from a sort of sclerosis due to competition for influence in areas that may overlap. Each system seeks to be self-contained, which generates the tendency to steer clear of addressing possible conflicts with other regimes.[21] Reasons for this include the fear that integration of substantive norms from other regimes requires complex authority-integrating solutions, some of which may lead to a loss of authority.[22] The implementing organs of most of these regimes claim jurisdiction and legitimacy which is superior to other regimes[23] whenever jurisdictional conflict is nascent, thereby nourishing concerns about conflicting jurisprudence and forum shopping.[24] Thus, coordination of the regimes does not occur as naturally and is not as interest-driven

17 A. Fischer-Lescano and G. Teubner, 'Regime-Collisions: The Vain Search for Legal Unity in the Fragmentation of Global Law' (2004) 25 *Michigan Journal of International Law* 999, at 1018.

18 Trachtman, above n 3.

19 M. Koskenniemi, 'The Politics of International Law – 20 Years Later' (2009) 20(1) *European Journal of International Law* 7, at 9.

20 B. Kingsbury, 'Foreword: Is the Proliferation of International Courts and Tribunals a Systemic Problem?' (1999) 31 *New York University Journal of International Law and Politics* 679, at 681.

21 But see Art. 311 of the United Nations Convention on the Law of the Sea.

22 Broude, above n 16.

23 R. Howse, 'Adjudicative Legitimacy and Treaty Interpretation in International Trade Law – The Early Years of WTO Jurisprudence', in J. Weiler (ed.), *The EU, the WTO and the NAFTA: Towards a Common Law of International Trade* (Oxford University Press, 2000), pp. 35–69.

24 N. Matz-Lück, 'Promoting the Unity of International Law: Standard-Setting by International Tribunals', in D. König, P.-T. Stoll, V. Röben and N. Matz-Lück (eds.), *International Law Today: New Challenges and the Need for Reform?* (Berlin: Springer, 2008), pp. 99–212, at p. 102.

as cooperation on the issue-oriented specialised fields. Nor is authority integration a feasible option for the time being.[25]

Besides these inter-state dynamics, non-state actors seeking to regulate their private affairs through soft-law rules that serve as standards for transnational communities have gained importance within the interplay of fragmented islands of international law.[26] Global governance gaps motivate private action where there is a need for coordination or in response to societal needs.[27] In an increasingly complex and diversified world with an inconceivable pace of technological advance, the traditional state has neither the resources nor the savvy to regulate efficiently in all areas. Conceding part of its powers to the private community can allow acting and reacting to take place more efficiently and swiftly.[28] This transformation of the previously rigid public versus private divide brings about a redistribution of power and influence, adding to fragmentation of the law: there is a private law regime developing beyond the spheres and control of sovereign law-making.[29] Today's traditional inter-state rules are hardly able to capture these activities.[30] The issue of whether and under which conditions rules created within these transnational networks play a role or can prevail over national or international law is one of the manifold open questions.[31]

All these phenomena raise questions as to the overall coherence and consistency of international law. The issue became a prime concern among international law scholars.[32] However, if one considers the legal sources upon which international law is created, its fragmentation along the lines of uncoordinated and issue-tailored fields of law is nothing new or

25 Cf. Broude, above n 16; Y. Shany, *The Competing Jurisdiction of International Courts and Tribunals* (Oxford University Press, 2003), p. 114.

26 See, generally, K. W. Abbott and D. Snidal, 'Hard and Soft Law in International Governance' (2000) 54(3) *International Organization* 421.

27 P. Muchlinski, 'Global Bukowina Examined: Viewing the Multinational Enterprise as a Transnational Law-making Community', in G. Teubner (ed.), *Global Law Without A State* (Dartmouth, 1997), pp. 79–107.

28 H. Spruyt, *The Sovereign State and its Competitors* (Princeton University Press, 1994).

29 Also G. Teubner, 'Global Bukowina: Legal Pluralism in the World Society', in G. Teubner (ed.), *Global Law Without a State* (Dartmouth, 1997), pp. 3–28.

30 C. Donnelly, *Delegation of Governmental Power to Private Parties – A Comparative Perspective* (Oxford University Press, 2007).

31 G. Teubner and P. Korth, 'Two Kinds of Legal Pluralism: Collision of Laws in the Double Fragmentation of World Society', in M. Young (ed.), *Regime Interaction in International Law: Theoretical and Practical Challenges* (forthcoming), at p. 9.

32 B. Simma, 'Universality of International Law from the Perspective of a Practitioner' (2009) 20(2) *European Journal of International Law* 265, at 270.

surprising.[33] Absent a global legislator, international law has always been shaped on the basis of states organising themselves at a bilateral, regional or multilateral level in different issue-fields.[34] Uncertainty about applicable law and jurisdiction, interest-driven law application and forum shopping could pose threats to the integrity of a decentralised international legal order, endangering the authority and credibility of international law. It is in this vein that international judges and scholars have raised their voices to call attention to alarming signs of fragmented international law.[35] On the other hand, some scholars see the growing complexity of international law as an indicator for the social richness of a globalising world, of the international system's liveliness and dynamics.[36] We return to this debate below. At this point we note that states and tribunals face complex challenges. The coexistence of different legal regimes and the need to coordinate them horizontally and vertically is a prime concern in contemporary law. WTO dispute settlement is a prominent example in this respect. Among the different regimes in international law, it has been strongly exposed to these challenges. The experience is of general interest and informs other areas of international law.

C. Fragmentation in WTO dispute settlement

Fragmentation of international trade regulation has drawn little attention to date in academic literature. One can identify two relevant debates which nevertheless do not fully exhaust our understanding of fragmentation: the first is the so-called 'trade and . . . ' debate relating to the boundaries of the WTO.[37] The second is concerned with the proliferation of preferential trade agreements (PTAs) and the concomitant challenges raised in terms of jurisdiction, applicable law, or state obligations.[38] The

33 J. Pauwelyn, 'Bridging Fragmentation and Unity: International Law as a Universe of Inter-connected Islands' (2004) 25 *Michigan Journal of International Law* 903.

34 Koskenniemi, above n 10, para. 5.

35 Hafner, above n 9, p. 144; I. Brownlie, 'Problems Concerning the Unity of International Law', in P. L. Zanardi *et al.* (eds.), *International Law at the Time of its Codification, Essays in Honour of R. Ago*, vol. II (Giuffrè, 1987), p. 156.

36 Pauwelyn, above n 14, para. 17; Koskenniemi, above n 10, para. 222. M. Koskenniemi and P. Leino, 'Fragmentation of International Law? Postmodern Anxieties' (2002) 15 *Leiden Journal of International Law* 553, at 575; A. Peters, 'Die Zukunft der Völkerrechtswissenschaft: Wider den epistemischen Nationalismus' (2007) 67 *Zeitschrift für ausländisches öffentliches Recht und Völkerrecht* 721.

37 See the special issue in the *American Journal of International Law* (2002) 96 (1).

38 L. Bartels and F. Ortino (eds.), *Regional Trade Agreements and the WTO* (Oxford University Press, 2006).

NCCR bottom-up approach allows us to identify, both theoretically and empirically, instances of fragmented regulation and to examine avenues and possibilities for eliminating harmful inconsistencies. Such avenues may be found within the WTO, or outside it. Most importantly, they constitute the trade agenda of the twenty-first century and point to those issues that need to be tackled, if more appropriate even outside the WTO. In this sense, our method is functional rather than institutional. Based on these considerations, a review of the relevant WTO case law and practice vis-à-vis non-WTO international law appears to be apposite.

I. WTO law coordination

Formally, the WTO dispute settlement system is a self-contained regime in that it establishes its autonomous rules, ranging from dispute initiation to enforcement of countermeasures.[39] However, the Appellate Body clarified early on that WTO law should not be read in 'clinical isolation from public international law'.[40] To date, the only non-WTO treaty to which the WTO adjudicating bodies refer systematically is the Vienna Convention on the Law of Treaties (VCLT) and most prominently its customary rules on treaty interpretation, that is, Articles 31 and 32.[41] The WTO adjudicating bodies are bound to apply these customary rules pursuant to Article 3:2 Dispute Settlement Understanding (DSU).[42] For our purposes, an important corollary of the VCLT rules of interpretation is the interpretive principle of effectiveness (*ut res magis valeat quam pereat/effet utile*) which stipulates that interpretation must give meaning and effect to all the terms of the treaty.[43] This principle calls for interpretation in a way that does not reduce parts of the WTO Treaty 'to redundancy or inutility'.[44] It does not, however, call upon the WTO adjudicator to apply non-WTO law on an equal footing.

Furthermore, the WTO judicial system being inherently incomplete, non-WTO law has been consistently used to fill gaps relating to important procedural questions such as the allocation of the burden of

39 cf. Koskenniemi, above n 10, pp. 71, 100; J. Pauwelyn, 'The Role of Public International Law in the WTO: How Far Can We Go?' (2001) 95 *American Journal of International Law* 535, at 539.

40 Appellate Body Report, *US – Gasoline*, p. 16.

41 M. Lennard, 'Navigating by the Stars: Interpreting the WTO Agreements' (2002) 5 *Journal of International Economic Law* 17.

42 Appellate Body Report, *US – Gasoline*, p. 16; and Appellate Body Report, *Japan – Alcoholic Beverages II*, p. 10.

43 Appellate Body Report, *US – Gasoline*, p. 21.

44 Appellate Body Report, *Korea – Dairy*, para. 81.

proof;[45] legal standing;[46] temporal/retroactive application of treaties;[47] and representation before panels.[48] Thus, administration of substantive law at the WTO is made through recourse to rules and principles developed under general international law.[49] By the same token, the WTO judiciary has made extensive reference to (and, in part, use of) general principles of (international) law such as good faith and *abus de droit* or *in dubio mitius.*

Admittedly, frequent cross-referencing to customary rules of treaty interpretation and general principles of law as well as references to the relevant case law of the International Court of Justice (ICJ) enhances the legitimacy of the WTO dispute settlement system and of its judiciary in adjudicating competing values.[50] Unitary discourse can be particularly helpful in cases where rules outside the regime may reflect legitimate concerns or internationally recognised ethical positions.[51]

However, what about other international agreements and generally non-WTO rules? At the outset, a distinction is to be made between agreements to which several WTO agreements refer and agreements that are not explicitly mentioned in any WTO agreement. The former, by way of the explicit reference to them in a given WTO agreement, become direct and autonomous sources of law in WTO dispute settlement proceedings. This is the case, for instance, of the major international intellectual property conventions.[52] Under this category, equal mention should be made of the privileged role that the Agreement on Technical Barriers to Trade (TBT Agreement) and the Agreement on the Application of Sanitary and Phytosanitary Measures (SPS Agreement) reserve for international standardisation bodies.[53] This type of applied subsidiarity or 'legal outsourcing' leads to an awkward constellation: the application of voluntary semi-private standards can be accepted more easily for WTO dispute

45 Appellate Body Report, *US – Wool Shirts and Blouses*, p. 14.

46 Appellate Body Report, *EC – Bananas III*, para. 133.

47 Appellate Body Report, *Brazil – Desiccated Coconut*, p. 15.

48 Appellate Body Report, *EC – Bananas III*, para. 10.

49 J. Cameron and K. Gray, 'Principles of International Law in the WTO Dispute Settlement Body' (2001) 50 *International and Comparative Law Quarterly* 248; also: A. Mitchell, *Legal Principles in WTO Disputes* (Cambridge University Press, 2008).

50 R. Howse, 'From Politics to Technocracy – and Back Again: The Fate of the Multilateral Trading Regime' (2002) 96(1) *American Journal of International Law* 94, at 110.

51 B. Simma and D. Pulkowski, 'Of Planets and the Universe: Self-Contained Regimes in International Law' (2006) 17(3) *The European Journal of International Law* 483–529, at 511.

52 See, for instance, Panel Report, *US – Section 110(5) Copyright Act*, paras. 6.17–6.18.

53 Art. 2 TBT and Art. 5 SPS.

settlement purposes than, for instance, in an international treaty protecting human rights or establishing labour standards.

Non-WTO legal instruments can also be implicitly incorporated, e.g. the second paragraph of item (k), Annex I to the Subsidies Agreement.[54] Similarly, in *EC – Bananas III*, the WTO judiciary decided that it had competence to assess the Lomé Convention, agreed on by the EC and the African, Caribbean and Pacific Group of States (ACP countries), because the signatories had been granted a waiver by the WTO General Council. The WTO judicial review was established once the waiver effectively incorporated the Lomé Convention into a WTO agreement.[55]

Other than the instruments explicitly or implicitly referred to in the WTO Treaty and its Annexes, no unanimity exists regarding the role of international law in the WTO. Seemingly, the only exception to this statement is the Harmonized Commodity Description and Coding System ('Harmonized System') of the World Customs Organization for which the Appellate Body accepted that it constitutes context within the meaning of Article 31:3(a) VCLT.[56] Controversy enters the discussion once it becomes focused on which non-WTO rules (other multilateral treaties? preferential agreements? bilateral agreements?) and under what conditions (agreements binding on all WTO Members? binding only on the parties to the dispute?) could be relevant for WTO adjudication purposes.

With respect to customs, it was suggested that, in the absence of any clause in the WTO agreements excluding customary international law, the latter is relevant.[57] With respect to customary law, two examples are worth giving at this point. The first, an evocative example of incomplete application of international customary law within the WTO, relates to state responsibility rules on countermeasures.[58] However, retroactive remedies, while being customary law, have not found their place in the WTO proceedings, since for the calculation of damages in the WTO the end of the implementation period is pertinent.[59] The second example relates

54 Cf. Panel Report, *Brazil – Aircraft (21.5 – Canada II)*, paras. 5.80–5.91.

55 Panel Report, *EC – Bananas III*, paras. 7.95, 7.97; Appellate Body Report, *EC – Bananas III*, paras. 167, 169.

56 Appellate Body Report, *EC – Chicken Cuts*, para. 199.

57 Panel Report, *Korea – Government Procurement*, para. 7.96. This is, however, the only explicit reference in the WTO case law.

58 Decision of the Arbitrator, *US – FSC (22.6 – US)*, paras. 5.58 *et seq.*

59 Again, *restitutio in integrum* is granted where restitution is possible, for instance, in the case of illegal subsidies (*Australia – Automotive Leather II*) and unlawfully imposed anti-dumping duties (*Guatemala – Cement II*); but see G. Marceau, 'WTO Dispute Settlement and Human Rights' (2002) 13 *European Journal of International Law* 753, at 766.

to the precautionary principle[60] and its treatment by the WTO judiciary in the *EC – Hormones* case. Interestingly, the Appellate Body contended that this principle can be regarded as a general principle of customary international *environmental* law, but probably not as a principle of *general* or customary international law.[61]

Academic opinion over the role of non-WTO law for purposes of WTO adjudication is divided. First, there are scholars who argue that non-WTO law should be applicable and sometimes even prevail over WTO rules, for instance, when the responding party successfully invokes a defence from the non-WTO law *corpus*.[62] Thus, a trade restriction otherwise inconsistent with WTO law can be justified through reference to rights given by other treaties, for instance the Kyoto Protocol of the United Nations Framework Convention on Climate Change (UNFCCC). A central premise of this approach is that, whereas the DSU limits the jurisdiction of the WTO judiciary to claims of violation of WTO agreements, it does not exclude reference to other international law rules when *interpreting* WTO provisions (absence of 'contracting out').[63]

An alternative opinion has been expressed by a second group of scholars who have emphatically suggested that the WTO adjudicating bodies are to apply as substantive law WTO law only, that is, the 'covered agreements' in accordance with the DSU.[64] Article 7 DSU implies as much by essentially specifying the applicable law, that is, the covered agreements. At the most, non-WTO law can be regarded as a *factual* matter in order to interpret the applicable WTO provisions, for instance, under Articles 31:3(c) or 32 of the Vienna Convention.[65]

60 See Art. 15 of the Rio Declaration on Environment and Development.

61 Appellate Body Report, *EC – Hormones*, paras. 123–125.

62 Most prominently, Pauwelyn, above n 6.

63 Pauwelyn, above n 39, at 560; also L. Bartels, *Applicable Law Before International Courts and Tribunals* (Oxford University Press, 2010, forthcoming). See also Panel Report, *Korea – Government Procurement*, para. 7.101, fn 755.

64 J. Trachtman, 'The Domain of WTO Dispute Resolution' (1999) 40 *Harvard International Law Journal* 333.

65 G. Marceau, 'A Call for Coherence in International Law' (1999) 33 *Journal of World Trade* 87, at 128, 131; G. Marceau, 'Fragmentation in International Law: The Relationship Between WTO Law and General International Law – A Few Comments from a WTO Perspective' (2006) 17 *Finnish Yearbook of International Law* 31; J. Trachtman, 'The World Trading System, the International Legal System and Multilevel Choice' (2006) 12(4) *European Law Journal* 469, at 483; also P. Mavroidis, 'No Outsourcing of Law? WTO Law as Practiced by WTO Courts' (2008) 102(3) *American Journal of International Law* 421; also Pauwelyn, above n 39, at 572.

It is safe to say that the absence in the DSU of any express reference to international law other than the one relating to customary rules of interpretation does not necessarily mean that such law does not have a role to play in WTO adjudication. Additionally, just as in other regimes, in the WTO there is a presumption in favour of exhaustive regulation of a given subject matter, which potentially has spill-overs in, or could be settled by, other regimes, within the WTO.[66] Once WTO jurisdiction based upon the relevant WTO agreements is established, the application of norms originating in sources other than the WTO offers an important contribution towards bringing about greater coherence between different regimes.

WTO case law has not yet shed light on the appropriate approach to follow. In *US – Shrimp*, the Appellate Body used 'modern international conventions and declarations' to interpret the GATT, in particular the concept of 'exhaustible natural resources' of Article XX(g). In the compliance ruling, the Appellate Body noted that such international agreements can assist in identifying a wide consensus on certain facts (for instance, are sea turtles an exhaustible resource?) and thus in correctly establishing the meaning of Article XX(g). By adopting an evolutionary (and, from an international law perspective, a unitary) approach, the Appellate Body largely neglected the relevant negotiating history of the GATT and instead found that 'exhaustible natural resources' include both finite resources (such as oil) and biological resources (such as sea turtles). Importantly, the Appellate Body referred to non-WTO law which does *not* bind all WTO Members. Arguably, then, whenever the WTO judiciary feels that the non-WTO rules invoked embody legitimate concerns or internationally recognised ethical positions preferably backed by a sufficient degree of consensus among WTO Members, it will apply them, even if not *all* WTO Members are also parties to the other agreement.[67]

More recently, the *EC – Biotech* Panel, taking issue with the approach just described, denied considering the Cartagena Biosafety Protocol as relevant for DSU purposes. In interpreting Article 31:3(c) VCLT, the Panel contended that this provision requires that all WTO Members

66 D. M. McRae, 'The WTO in International Law: Tradition Continued or New Frontier?' (2000) 3(1) *Journal of International Economic Law* 27.

67 Simma and Pulkowski, above n 51, at 511. Also cf. Appellate Body Report, *EC – Chicken Cuts*, para. 199; also Appellate Body Report, *US – FSC (21.5 – EC)*; Appellate Body Report, *EC – Asbestos*, paras. 114, 135.

have to be members to another agreement for that agreement to qualify as a 'relevant rule of international law applicable in the relations between the parties'.[68]

This result may be applauded for being likely to result in a coherent application of the WTO law across the WTO membership,[69] but it is doubtful whether it produces equally coherent results from an international law viewpoint.[70] At the very least, it is submitted that applying the Protocol to the parties to the dispute who were also parties to the Protocol (viz. the EU, Argentina and Canada) would allow for more coherence in interpreting public international law as a whole so far as these specific countries are concerned. It is unclear why the Protocol should not be regarded as applicable law by the WTO adjudicating bodies so that the WTO obligations of these parties are determined in the light of the obligations that they subsequently undertake in other fora.[71] A different approach seems to lead to an undesirable delinking of the WTO from other branches of international law and appears to allow specific countries to avoid their obligations depending on the forum chosen, thereby increasing the chances for extensive forum shopping.

Non-WTO law can also be looked at to determine the appropriate *application*, rather than interpretation of a given WTO provision.[72] According to the Appellate Body, a non-WTO instrument is not thereby converted into an autonomous legal standard, but is merely evidence of non-comparable, and potentially discriminatory treatment of non-signatories.[73] In *US – Shrimp (21.5 – Malaysia)*, the Appellate Body agreed with the Panel that regional fishing arrangements negotiated by the United States demonstrated the good faith efforts of that Member to protect sea turtles. Hence, reliance even on regional arrangements or standards

68 Panel Report, *EC – Biotech*, paras. 7.67–7.71; also R. Howse and H. Horn, 'European Communities – Measures Affecting the Approval and Marketing of Biotech Products' (2009) 8(1) *World Trade Review* 49.

69 Cf. F. Roessler, 'Comment: Mexico – Tax Measures on Soft Drinks and Other Beverages' (2009) 8(1) *World Trade Review* 25, at 27.

70 See also B. McGrady, 'Fragmentation of International Law or "Systemic Integration" of Treaty Regimes: EC – Biotech Products and the Proper Interpretation of Article 31(3)(c) of the Vienna Convention on the Law of Treaties' (2008) 42 (4) *Journal of World Trade* 589.

71 See, along these lines, Panel Report, *US – Shrimp (21.5 – Malaysia)*, para. 5.57.

72 Cf. Appellate Body Report, *US – Shrimp*, para. 172. Also D. Palmeter and P. Mavroidis, *Dispute Settlement in the World Trade Organization – Practice and Procedure*, 2nd edn (Cambridge University Press, 2004), 74.

73 Appellate Body Report, *US – Shrimp (Art. 21.5 – Malaysia)*, para. 130.

may provide a de facto presumption of good faith, as warranted by Article XX.[74]

II. The role of bilateral and regional agreements

This type of agreement has largely been used as a supplementary means of interpretation within the meaning of Article 32 VCLT. In the majority of the cases, the WTO adjudicating bodies have only implicitly suggested so.[75]

In the GATT years, the Arbitrator in *EC – Article XXVIII* clarified that such agreements are to be considered if the following criteria are met: (1) a close connection exists between the bilateral agreement and the GATT; (2) the Agreement is consistent with the GATT objectives; and (3) both signatories request recourse to the GATT arbitration procedures.[76] In the WTO era, as demonstrated in *EC – Poultry*, the first criterion is of particular importance. In that case, both the Panel and the Appellate Body decided to use as a supplementary means of interpretation a bilateral agreement between the EC and Brazil, the Oilseeds Agreement, in order to determine the EC obligations under the WTO agreements vis-à-vis Brazil.[77] In *Turkey – Textiles*, the Panel rejected Turkey's argument that its bilateral customs union agreement with the EC obliged Turkey to act in a given manner.[78] More recently, the *Korea – Commercial Vessels* Panel used a bilateral agreement between the EC and Korea to elucidate several factual matters in the dispute.[79]

The role of bilateral agreements has also been examined in relation to the right of initiating dispute settlement proceedings under the WTO. In *Argentina – Poultry*, the respondent contended that the Protocol of Olivos, agreed under MERCOSUR, prevented Brazil from referring to the WTO a case which had already been decided by a MERCOSUR Ad Hoc Arbitral Tribunal. First, Argentina argued that Brazil's decision to bring a case successively before different fora constitutes conduct which contradicts

74 M. Cossy and G. Marceau, 'Institutional Challenges to Enhance Policy Co-ordination – How WTO Rules Could be Utilised to Meet Climate Objectives?', in T. Cottier, O. Nartova and S. Z. Bigdeli (eds.), *International Trade Regulation and the Mitigation of Climate Change* (Cambridge University Press, 2009), pp. 371–394, at p. 384.

75 See also Koskenniemi, above n 10, p. 225. Mavroidis proposes that such agreements be considered as historical context pursuant to Art. 31:2 VCLT. See Mavroidis, above n 65.

76 Award by the Arbitrator, *EC – Article XXVIII*, BISD 37S/80, at 84.

77 Appellate Body Report, *EC – Poultry*, para. 83.

78 Panel Report, *Turkey – Textiles*, paras. 9.178, 9.182.

79 Panel Report, *Korea – Commercial Vessels*, para. 7.130.

the principle of good faith. Second, Argentina invoked the principle of estoppel, which provides that if one party has been induced to act in reliance on the assurances of another party, in such a way that it would be prejudiced were the other party later to change its position, such a change in position is 'estopped', i.e. it is precluded.[80] Third, in Argentina's view, Article 31:3(c) is alternatively applicable, thereby requiring that the Panel be bound by earlier rulings within MERCOSUR relating to the measure at stake.[81]

As to the first argument, the Panel referred to the ruling of the Appellate Body in *US – Offset Act (Byrd Amendment)* finding that absence of good faith is a valid argument in DSU proceedings,[82] but applied a fairly narrow reading of it.[83] Second, the Panel, without ruling on the application of the principle of estoppel, agreed with a finding by an unadopted GATT Panel Report that estoppel cannot be invoked unless there is 'express, or in exceptional cases implied consent of the complaining parties'.[84] In addition, a decisive background element in the decision of the Panel was that the Protocol of Olivos had not entered into force. The wording of the Panel in this respect seems to suggest that, had the Protocol entered into force, the outcome may have been different.[85] In *EC – Export Subsidies on Sugar*, however, the Appellate Body failed to fully examine the proper concept of estoppel as determined by the ICJ case law[86] and, for all practical purposes, confirmed the essentially unlimited possibility for Members to bring an action before the WTO regardless of their conduct elsewhere. The Appellate Body did, however, point to the responsible behaviour that Articles 3:7 and 3:10 DSU require from Members.[87] Finally, with respect to Article 31:3(c) VCLT, the Panel noted that the rules of the VCLT are concerned with the interpretation of the WTO Agreements and cannot be understood to require that a given WTO provision be applied in a particular way which would be in line, in this case, with the ruling delivered by the MERCOSUR tribunal.

80 Panel Report, *Guatemala – Cement II*, para. 8.23; also Panel Report, *EC – Asbestos*, para. 8.60 referring to the ICJ decision on *North Sea Continental Shelf*, Reports of Judgments 1969, p. 26, para. 30.

81 Panel Report, *Argentina – Poultry*, para. 7.18.

82 Appellate Body Report, *US – Offset Act (Byrd Amendment)*, paras. 297–8.

83 In *EC – Export Subsidies on Sugar*, the Appellate Body approved the panel's decision to examine good faith and the principle of estoppel together.

84 GATT Panel Report, *EEC – Bananas I*, 3 June 1993, DS32/R, para. 361.

85 Panel Report, *Argentina – Poultry*, para. 7.38.

86 See, for instance, the *Nuclear Tests* case (*New Zealand* v. *France*) (1973–1977, I.C.J.).

87 See Appellate Body Report, *Export Subsidies on Sugar*, para. 312.

In *US – FSC*, the panel rejected the US argument that footnote 59 of the SCM Agreement required that the EU resort to alternative tax fora, including bilateral tax treaties before having recourse to the WTO dispute settlement.[88] In *Mexico – Soft Drinks*, the US filed a complaint against a discriminatory tax on soft drinks imposed by Mexico. This measure was in essence a countermeasure that Mexico implemented due to the unwillingness of the US to agree on the establishment of a NAFTA tribunal and in order to induce the US to comply with its NAFTA obligations. Mexico called upon the WTO judiciary to decline jurisdiction in favour of the Chapter 20 Arbitral Panel under NAFTA. Both the panel and the Appellate Body rejected the Mexican claim. The Appellate Body confirmed that panels have the right to determine the existence (Kompetenz-Kompetenz)[89] and the scope of their jurisdiction.[90] The Appellate Body followed a rather rigid, decontextualised syllogism which refers to the 'comprehensive nature' of Members' right to resort to the WTO dispute settlement system and the fact that Members are 'entitled' to a ruling by a Panel once their jurisdiction is established according to the relevant DSU provisions.[91] Importantly, however, it left the door wide open for speculation when it denied expressing any views as to the possible existence of legal impediments (such as the Protocol of Olivos in the *Argentina – Poultry* case) which preclude a WTO panel from hearing it. It bears mention that the Appellate Body, in note 86 of its report, referred to the panel finding in *Argentina – Poultry* regarding the relevance of the entry into force of the pertinent regional agreement, thereby implying that the WTO judiciary could decline jurisdiction in a case of a regional agreement incorporating a rule of mandatory choice of adjudicative forum.[92]

The second important issue that the WTO judiciary addressed in *Mexico – Soft Drinks* related to the interpretation of Article XX(d). More specifically, Mexico sought to justify the measure by arguing that it was necessary to secure the compliance *of the US* with its obligations under *NAFTA*. The Appellate Body found that this provision cannot be construed so as to encompass *international* countermeasures seeking to secure

88 Panel Report, *US – FSC*, para. 7.19.

89 Cf. *Nottebohm* case (*Liechtenstein* v. *Guatemala*), 1953 I.C.J. Reports 7, 119 (21 March).

90 Appellate Body Report, *Mexico – Soft Drinks*, para. 45.

91 Cf. Broude, above n 16; C. Henckels, 'Overcoming Jurisdictional Isolationism at the WTO–FTA Nexus: A Potential Approach for the WTO' (2008) 19(3) *European Journal of International Law* 571.

92 Also W. Davey and A. Sapir, 'The *Soft Drinks* Case: The WTO and Regional Agreements' (2009) 8(1) *World Trade Review* 5, at 11–12.

compliance of *another* WTO Member with its *international* obligations.[93] Crucially, the Appellate Body emphasised that Mexico's argument would allow circumvention of Articles XXIII:2 GATT and 22–23 DSU.[94] However, from this statement it would be erroneous in our view to draw a general conclusion that the WTO judiciary rejected the use of non-WTO law as a defence to justify state conduct that was otherwise WTO-inconsistent.

Lastly, the *India – Autos* panel discussed the legal relevance of bilateral mutually agreed solutions and their role in subsequent dispute settlement proceedings. India asserted that the mutually agreed solution between the parties should be interpreted as limiting the procedural rights of the EC. To determine the legal effect of such an agreement, the Panel went on to undertake a fairly thorough, but strictly textual analysis of the scope of this agreement before concluding that it did not regulate the same matter.[95] This is yet another example of a norm-fragmenting technique that courts use to avoid (arguably, artificially) inter-institutional conflicts.[96] We deal with this issue in the next section.

III. Decisions by regional international tribunals and res judicata

The proliferation of international tribunals makes procedural and substantive overlaps all the more likely, especially because courts will rarely declare *forum non conveniens*. In the presence of a valid legal basis referring to the relevant legal provision of a given PTA, the regional tribunal will not decline jurisdiction in favour of the WTO judiciary.[97] However, under certain circumstances, a multilateral forum may be considered as the most efficient solution from a global welfare perspective.[98] From the viewpoint of procedural efficiency and expedited delivery of rulings, the WTO also seems to have compelling advantages.[99] For instance, cases such as *Canada – Periodicals*, *Mexico – Soft Drinks*, or the *Softwood*

93 Appellate Body Report, *Mexico – Soft Drinks*, para. 75.

94 *Ibid.*, para. 77.

95 Panel Report, *India – Autos*, paras. 7.105 *et seq.*

96 Cf. Y. Shany, 'Similarity in the Eye of the Beholder: Revisiting the Application of Rules Governing Jurisdictional Conflicts in the Lauder/CME Cases', in A. Rovine (ed.), *Contemporary Issues in International Arbitration and Mediation* (Martinus Nijhoff, 2008), p. 119.

97 E.-U. Petersmann, 'Justice as Conflict Resolution: Proliferation, Fragmentation, and Decentralization of Dispute Settlement in International Trade' (2006) 27 *University of Pennsylvania Journal of International Economic Law* 273.

98 Cf. Roessler, above n 69.

99 See W. Davey, 'Dispute Settlement in the WTO and RTAs: A Comment', in Bartels and Ortino (eds.), above n 38, pp. 345–349.

Lumber saga provide ample evidence of weaknesses in NAFTA when it comes to dispute settlement.

From our previous discussion and in what follows it becomes clear that WTO panels are not bound by rulings delivered by regional courts and will claim jurisdiction regardless of whether the essence of a given dispute was decided elsewhere.[100] In other words, the principle *ne bis in idem* is not applicable in this context. This is so because, formally speaking, each tribunal will apply different legal provisions to the same facts.[101] Worse, based on the same facts, tribunals can reach conflicting verdicts.

US – Softwood Lumber is illustrative of the current situation, as it relates to an issue that was raised before both the WTO judiciary and the NAFTA dispute settlement proceedings, leading to conflicting rulings.[102] This is a long-lasting dispute between the US and Canada, culminating in May 2002, over the imposition by the US of duties on imports of Canadian softwood lumber based on the argument that the US lumber industry was threatened with material injury due to dumped and subsidised imports of Canadian lumber. Similar facts were brought under both NAFTA and the WTO. Most strikingly, in 2005, whereas a WTO panel accepted the US finding that continued imports of Canadian lumber threatened to cause material injury to the US relevant industry, a NAFTA Chapter 19 panel had earlier found unanimously against the US, as did a NAFTA extraordinary Challenge Committee confirming the panel's ruling. In essence, whereas NAFTA panels that dealt with the relevant cases all ruled against the US antidumping and countervailing practices, some WTO panels ruled in favour (more recently, the *US – Softwood Lumber VI (21.5 – Canada)* panel).[103] In 2006, Canada and the US concluded the Softwood Lumber Agreement in which the US pledged to return US$ 4 billion of the total US$ 5.3 billion. Canada in return would essentially control its softwood lumber exports to the US (if necessary, through an export tax). The Agreement provides that disputes are to be brought before the London Court of International Arbitration (LCIA).

According to Article 2005 NAFTA, a forum can be chosen at the discretion of the *complainant*. Preference is given to NAFTA proceedings in

100 Panel Report, *Argentina – Poultry*, para. 7.41.

101 See also n 96 and the accompanying text. Also K. Kwak and G. Marceau, 'Overlaps and Conflicts of Jurisdiction between the World Trade Organization and Regional Trade Agreements' in Bartels and Ortino (eds.), above n 38, pp. 469–70.

102 See also J. Pauwelyn, 'Adding Sweeteners to Softwood Lumber: The WTO–NAFTA "Spaghetti Bowl" is Cooking' (2007) 9(1) *Journal of International Economic Law* 197.

103 This ruling was overturned by the Appellate Body. See Appellate Body Report, *US – Softwood Lumber VI (21.5 – Canada)*.

cases involving environmental, SPS, or standards-related measures. This provision further stipulates that, once procedures have been initiated in either forum,[104] the forum selected must be used *to the exclusion of the other.* Did Canada or the US violate their NAFTA obligations by pursuing proceedings before both fora? This is a thorny subject, and relates to the concept of *res judicata.* For this concept to apply there should be established identity of (1) parties; (2) subject matter; and (3) legal claims.[105] While the first and the second element may be met under certain circumstances, the third is unlikely ever to be met when the overlapping proceedings take place in different fora. Even so, it is striking that no sign of taking cognisance of the other forum's analysis is traceable.

A second issue that bears mention here relates to the role of rulings by regional courts. In *Brazil – Tyres*, the dispute arose out of certain measures that adversely affected EC exports of retreaded tyres to Brazil. Brazil claimed that the measures were part and parcel of a comprehensive public policy to protect public health. However, imports of retreaded tyres from other MERCOSUR countries were exempted, after a ruling delivered by a MERCOSUR panel against Brazil (MERCOSUR exemption). The Panel regarded the MERCOSUR ruling as a reasonable basis to enact the MERCOSUR exemption and thus found that the ensuing discrimination was not arbitrary.[106] Nonetheless, the Appellate Body disagreed, as the MERCOSUR exemption and the relevant Brazilian court injunctions and the ensuing discrimination went against the objective pursued by Brazil.[107] The Appellate Body further appeared to consider as decisive the fact that, during the MERCOSUR arbitral proceedings, Brazil did not consider it necessary to invoke Article 50(d) of the treaty of Montevideo, which is the corresponding provision of Article XX(b). Thus, the Appellate Body reached the conclusion that no actual conflict exists between the two legal texts.

IV. Some tentative concluding remarks

It appears that the role of non-WTO rules in the WTO context is far from settled, particularly due to the ever-increasing emergence of specialised regimes which are aimed at satisfying the contemporary needs of our society such as addressing global warming, protecting biodiversity

104 Importantly, Art. 2005:7 NAFTA clarifies that no actual establishment of a panel is necessary; the *request* for such establishment suffices.

105 Panel Report, *India – Autos*, para. 7.66.

106 Panel Report, *Brazil – Tyres*, para. 7.281.

107 Appellate Body Report, *Brazil – Tyres*, paras. 228, 246.

or shielding indigenous communities and their traditional cultural expressions. Nevertheless, there are some observations that can already be made at this stage.

First, international law is built upon the principle of good faith[108] and the presumption that states, when they conclude agreements, do keep in mind the obligations that they have undertaken in other fora and thus will avoid agreements which would lead to breaching their obligations deriving from other agreements. Arguably, Article 3:10 DSU equally incorporates this obligation for WTO Members.[109] This implies that real conflicts should not arise and international obligations of a state can be interpreted in a way that accommodates all obligations of a given state in a harmonious manner. In addition, whereas no provision of WTO law limits Members' rights to bring an action before the WTO judiciary,[110] Members are invited to avoid forum shopping or manipulation of the several possibilities for adjudication that their participation in diverse regimes gives them.

Second, the VCLT does not offer adequate solutions allowing for the 'defragmentation' of international trade regulation.[111] In addition, it appears that the DSU meant to bring into the WTO realm only 'customary rules of *interpretation* of public international law'.[112] An erroneous application of this provision can also result in peculiar legal constructions which may prove harmful to inter-state and inter-regime relations overall. The *EC – Biotech* Panel Report, in which the Panel refused to look into the Cartagena Biosafety Protocol because not *all* WTO Members were parties to it, is a case in point.

Appellate Body case law appears to point in the opposite direction. In *EC – Chicken Cuts*, the Appellate Body looked at the Harmonized System to determine whether it constituted context within the meaning of Article 31:2(a) VCLT. Contrary to the argumentation of the *EC – Biotech* Panel, to validate this, the Appellate Body examined whether the parties *to the dispute at hand* were signatories of the Harmonised System.[113]

108 See, generally, M. Panizzon, *Good Faith in the Jurisprudence of the WTO* (Hart Publishing, 2006).

109 Cf. Appellate Body report, *US – FSC*, para. 166.

110 Cf. Appellate Body Report, *EC – Export Subsidies on Sugar*, para. 312.

111 Also J. Neumann, *Die Koordination des WTO-Rechts mit anderen völkerrechtlichen Ordnungen: Konflikte des materiellen Rechts und Konkurrenzen der Streitbeilegung* (Duncker & Humblot, 2002). See, *contra*, Mavroidis, above n 65.

112 Lennard, above n 41, at 41.

113 Appellate Body Report, *EC – Chicken Cuts*, para. 196 and fn 377; cf. also Appellate Body Report, *EC – Computer Equipment*, para. 89.

Nor do the other, in theory, relevant principles of *lex specialis* or *lex posterior* provide handy solutions to contemporary problems. Regarding *lex specialis*, in a multilateral international legal system of increasing functional specialisation, identifying the prevailing *lex specialis* becomes a daunting task.[114] As to *lex posterior*, it is not always clear how to substantiate a claim that later commitments are to prevail over earlier ones, notably in the absence of identity of parties.[115]

Third, while the ever-increasing judicialisation of international relations through the establishment of several tribunals is regarded as inducing fragmentation of international law, the proliferation of courts may actually have the opposite effect: that states increasingly have recourse to peaceful means to resolve their disputes and that judicial control of state acts, coupled with the creation of loose communication networks among judicial bodies, can at least achieve the important objective of avoiding armed conflicts in international relations.[116] For our study on international trade regulation the same goes for inter-regional law and the courts that it establishes.

D. Conceptual responses to fragmentation

There have been various propositions in legal doctrine to deal with the problem of fragmentation in international law, inter alia, a hierarchical system of judicial competences with the ICJ as a coordinator, the ICJ supervising the consistency of international treaty making,[117] or global structures channelling governance fields and identifying points of intersectional cooperation.[118] Of the many approaches for dealing with the issue we will confine the discussion to two main lines of thought in the fragmentation discourse:

1. a hermeneutical approach, upon existing law of conflict resolution, as principally anchored in the VCLT, equally reflected in WTO jurisprudence discussed above; and

114 Simma and Pulkowski, above n 51, at 489.

115 Cf. Koskenniemi, above n 10, pp. 116–117.

116 R. Higgins, 'The ICJ, the ECJ and the Integrity of International Law' (2003) 52 *International and Comparative Law Quarterly* 1, 18.

117 G. Hafner, 'Pros and Cons Ensuing from Fragmentation of International Law' (2004) 25(4) *Michigan Journal of International Law* 849, at 861 *et seq.*

118 R. Wolfrum and N. Matz, 'Conflicts in International Environmental Law' (Springer, 2003), pp. 159 *et seq.*

2. a constitutionalist approach referring to the benchmark of a system-model of governance.

We will use these as a basis upon which to present the NCCR trade regulation's approach of multilayered governance, which can be described as a model between the two schools. Against this backdrop, we will examine fundamental critiques of a legal approach to the fragmentation of international law.

I. The hermeneutical approach: systemic legal reasoning and policy coordination

A hermeneutical approach to dealing with the fragmentation of international law focuses on established methods of interpretation to mitigate incoherencies. This approach relies upon the positive framework of existing international law. It is mainly advocated by the ILC-study group in its report.[119] From this point of view, the fragmentation problem of international law is not 'so much about fragmentation and coherence but about consistent law making and legal reasoning'.[120] Thus, the problem of fragmentation occurs mainly because specialised law-making and institution-building 'tend to take place with a relative ignorance of legislative and institutional activities in the adjoining fields' and 'of general principles and practices of international law'. In this regard, the ILC study group, based on the VCLT and traditional principles of law interpretation, analysed a set of rules regarding the resolution of conflicts of norms as they may occur in international law; among them the rules of *lex specialis* and *lex posterior*, as well as structures of hierarchy and a general principle of 'systemic integration' that seeks to avoid or mitigate conflicts through integrative law interpretation.[121] In the same spirit, some scholars have proposed cooperative governance models and coordination between organs of overlapping regimes and mutual expert advice.[122] Along similar lines a 'fall-back' principle as a 'gene-therapy against excessive fragmentation' has been promoted. It demands reliance on general international

119 Koskenniemi, above n 10, para. 20. 120 *Ibid.*, para. 28.

121 See for an overview: Conclusions of the Work of the Study Group on the Fragmentation of International Law: Difficulties Arising from the Diversification and Expansion of International Law, United Nations, 2006; for an in-depth discussion of the subject see also Pauwelyn, above n 65.

122 Neumann, above n 111; N. Matz, *Wege zur Koordinierung völkerrechtlicher Verträge* (Springer, 2005).

law when questions are not explicitly addressed in a treaty.[123] Conflicts of systems and jurisdictions are not necessarily deemed to be problematic but to have a positive side effect: such competition of systems could favour the 'winning' of the best system or the best interpretation of the case, and thus add to rather than compromise the quality of international law.[124]

Against this backdrop, fragmentation of the substance of international law seems harmless. The unity of international law has always been a chimera. Unity – or the constitutionalist reading of international law – is, to some extent, an academic artefact. Thus, deviation from this concept does not constitute a cause for concern but rather it realistically reflects 'the differing pursuits and preferences that actors in a pluralistic (global) society have'.[125] The emergence of new 'branches' of law, novel types of treaties or clusters of treaties is a feature of the social complexity of a globalising world. Warning voices referring to the loss of unity of international law and of its capability to deal with the growing complexity of the international fragmented system thus have no reason for concern.

The analysis of WTO case law above indicates that this approach to coordination and coherence, essentially relying upon interpretation, is able to reduce tensions and bring about practical coordination to some extent, but cannot overcome basic conflicts and the overall fragmentation of the international system. In particular, the problems caused by fragmented systems of jurisdiction and dispute settlement cannot successfully and satisfactorily be addressed within the framework of positive law and the rules on international treaties embodied in the VCLT. These issues call for breaking free from the contractual approach and lead into constitutional models.

II. The constitutionalist approach: systemic governance order and common values

International constitutionalist approaches go beyond mere interpretation of particular norms. They conceive the international order as a comprehensive system of law constituting a legal framework of cosmopolitan values and internationally agreed standards of international governance. Yet, international constitutionalism does not necessarily presume or imply the existence of a homogeneous international societal order, nor is there necessarily a vision of a world state.

123 Pauwelyn, above n 14, para. 29.

124 Pauwelyn, above n 65, at 916.

125 Koskenniemi, above n 10, para. 222.

The first constitutionalist models regarding the international order emerged in the 1920s, conceiving international law as a comprehensive legal system of different interrelated and mutually supportive legal orders (so-called 'German constitutionalism').[126] Marked by World War II and the experience of totalitarianism, German international constitutionalism put an emphasis on issues of morality and justice as guardrails and benchmarks for national law and policies based on principles of natural law and justice. International law was responsible for looking after fundamental human morality and combating inhuman behaviour of individuals and states. International law became a main guarantor against failures of the nation state. This moral perception of international law was fuelled by commonly agreed foundations of 'world order treaties', most importantly the UN Charter and the Universal Declaration of Human Rights, providing international benchmarks for moral standards.[127]

The constitutionalist idea as it emerged in the eighteenth and nineteenth centuries has been closely connected, conceptually speaking, to the political order of the nation state.[128] Historically, through the philosophical stream of the enlightenment period of the eighteenth century, the concepts of modern constitutionalism and the nation state developed simultaneously. The nation state emerged after the Peace of Westphalia as an integral political unity based on a people, a territory and a governing power. The concept led to a clear division between a nation state's societal order, steered by a political power bound by common values and a hierarchical legal system of 'law and order' and the international political order and its contractual relations, free from 'society', 'governance' or 'morality', as a mode of coexistence with other states.[129] This changed at the end of World War II with the establishment of the UN, the Bretton Woods system and GATT. With the emergence of international organisations, elements of international constitutional structures were identified in regard to shared public interests, the individual's position in international law, and institutionalisation through specialised regimes, such

126 H. Kelsen, *Reine Rechtslehre* (Verlag Österreich, 2000), p. 115; see for an overview A. von Bogdandy, 'Constitutionalism in International Law. Comment on a Proposal from Germany' (2006) 47(1) *Harvard International Law Journal* 223.

127 See for further explanation P.-M. Dupuy, 'A Doctrinal Debate in the Globalization Era: On the "Fragmentation" of International Law' (2007) 1 *European Journal of Legal Studies*, available at: www.ejls.eu/1/4UK.pdf.

128 T. Cottier and M. Hertig, 'The Prospects of 21st Century Constitutionalism' (2003) 7 *Max Planck Yearbook of United Nations Law* 261, at 265.

129 *Ibid.*, p. 265 *et seq.*

as the UN, UNCLOS, the WTO, or the international investment regime (ICC, ICSID).

Describing the current landscape of constitutionalist theory relating to the international level is not an easy task as demonstrated by the work undertaken in IP 1 within the NCCR. It was difficult to distinguish aspects of modern constitutionalism from the basis of a nation state model which today still leads to confusion in discussions on the elements of international constitutionalism or decentralised models of multilayered governance. The very notion of 'constitutionalism' let alone its applicability to the international order is subject to a fierce debate.[130] Some conceive constitutionalism as inextricably linked to the nation state, as a people and a culturally homogeneous society is considered to be a precondition for a (democratic) constitutional order.[131] Some call for decoupling the constitutional concept from the *finalité* of a state model as governance structure and instead hold that constitutional principles and values, such as democracy, the rule of law, or human rights, should be adequately observed on the level of international governance.[132] Constitutional principles would then be fundamental boundaries to international governance.[133] Some observe a 'partial outsourcing' of constitutional functions to the international order[134] and perceive international organisations like the WTO as regimes that reinforce national constitutional tasks (e.g. protection of the environment and protection of human rights).[135] Others classify

130 See for an overview of definitions and conceptions A. Peters, 'Compensatory Constitutionalism: The Function and Potential of Fundamental International Norms and Structures' (2006) 19 *Leiden Journal of International Law* 579, at 580 *et seq.*

131 See for discussion A. Peters, 'The Constitutionalist Reconstruction of International Law: Pros and Cons', National Centre of Competence in Research (NCCR) Workshop, 'Compensatory Constitutionalism: Opportunities and Impediments', Hotel Bernerhof Kandersteg, 12.01.2007.

132 *Ibid.*

133 See for example with regard to the balance of powers principle, C. Möllers, *Die drei Gewalten* (Velbrück, 2008).

134 G. Biaggini, 'Die Idee der Verfassung – Neuausrichtung im Zeitalter der Globalisierung?' (2000) 119 *Zeitschrift für Schweizerisches Recht* 445–476.

135 See with regard to the WTO legal order and its positive effect on individual freedoms E-U. Petersmann, 'National Constitutions, Foreign Trade and European Community Law' (1992) 3 *European Journal of International Law* 1 *et seq.*; P.-T. Stoll, 'Freihandel und Verfassung. Einzelstaatliche Gewährleistung und die konstitutionelle Funktion der Welthandelsordnung (GATT/WTO)' (1997) 57 *Zeitschrift für ausländisches öffentliches Recht und Völkerrecht* 83, 86; for a critical analysis M. Krajewski, *Verfassungsperspektiven und Legitimation des Rechts der Welthandelsorganisation (WTO)* (Duncker und Humblot, 2001); P. Alston, 'Resisting the Merger and Acquisition of Human Rights by Trade Law:

treaties of international organisations that institutionalise international policy structures as 'constitutions', providing the international order with islands of different coexisting micro-constitutionalist orders.[136]

In sum, regarding the constitutionalist debate, there is no agreed type of constitutionalism, but different concepts with differing priorities and functions coexist in the literature. Generally speaking, a constitutionalist approach aims at achieving coherence through establishing a clear system of political order, governance and normative values, whereas the hermeneutic approach focuses on a technically coherent system with regard to competing legal regimes.[137] Analysing the international legal order in constitutionalist terms often means referring to a certain model of constitutionalist content representing a 'basic', 'good' or 'effective' order. The fragmented landscape of international law is compared with this guiding model. As a result, there are optimistic and pessimistic constitutionalist perceptions of international fragmentation. Optimists see the constitutionalist model as a visionary way to address the fragmentation problem, whereas the pessimists come to the conclusion, that according to current experience, international constitutionalism does not exist and has no potential to develop in the real world. The latter perspective leaves the international order to its problematic state of fragmentation, promotes the defence of national orders and values, and calls for international norm generation and fragmentation to be opposed. An intermediate view denies the constitutional nature of the WTO, but argues, within the framework of embedded liberalism, for greater coherence[138] or seeks to import principles of administrative law, in particular relating to transparency and

A Reply to Petersmann' (2002) 13 *European Journal of International Law* 815; S. A. Aaronson, *Trade Imbalance. The Struggle to Weigh Human Rights Concerns in Trade Policymaking* (Cambridge University Press, 2008).

136 For an overview Cottier and Hertig, above n 128, at 277 *et seq.*; B. Fassbender, 'The United Nations Charter as the Constitution of the International Community' (Martinus Nijhoff, 2009); with regard to the WTO see D. Cass, *The Constitutionalization of the World Trade Organization. Legitimacy, Democracy, and Community in the International Trading System* (Oxford University Press, 2005); concerning micro-constitutionalism see Peters, above n 130, at 593 *et seq.*; also see A. Peters, 'Membership in the Global Constitutional Community', in J. Klabbers, A. Peters and D. Ulfstein, *The Constitutionalization of International Law* (Oxford University Press, 2009), pp. 153–261, at pp. 201 *et seq.*

137 Pauwelyn, above n 14, para. 15.

138 R. Howse and K. Nicolaidis, 'Legitimacy through "Higher Law"? Why Constitutionalizing the WTO is a Step Too Far', in T. Cottier and P. C. Mavroidis, *The Role of the Judge in International Trade Regulation* (University of Michigan Press, 2006), pp. 307–348, at pp. 312 *et seq.*

fairness, from domestic legal orders into the realm of international law and the World Trade Organization.[139]

As to the WTO legal order, there has been a fundamental debate about its constitutionalist character and functions.[140] While some see the WTO as contributing to the protection and enforcement of the constitutional values of peaceful coexistence and cooperation, such as non-discrimination, equal opportunity, liberty, freedom of information, and transparency,[141] others warn about the absence of core constitutionalist elements, such as democratic participation, and the constitutionalist concept inappropriately legitimising the WTO system through a one-sided constitutionalist notion.[142] Some scholars have concentrated on shedding light on certain aspects of constitutionalist functions, such as the lack of democratic legitimacy and negative impacts on human rights, or, the positive influence of the WTO order on liberty or economic rights. Here, one can sometimes observe a tendency to 'pin down' the meaning of WTO constitutionalism in 'a rigid fashion'[143] as a one-model-only legitimate shape of WTO law.

The problem is that this isolating carve-out does not encompass the whole concept of existing, potentially emerging or missing constitutional functions of the WTO.[144] The system is looked at in an either-or manner of rigid modelling: the WTO is either a free trade order, mostly disregarding democratic legitimacy and values which are not related to free trade, and claiming its primacy. Or, there is a call for a more legitimate constitutional order tying WTO governance and decisions to human rights, the rule of law, democratic or participatory perspectives, equity

139 R. B. Stewart and M. R. Sanchez Badin, 'The World Trade Organization and Global Administrative Law' (2009) *New York University Public Law and Legal Theory Working Papers* 1; see also B. Kingsbury, N. Krisch and R. B. Stewart, 'The Emergence of Global Administrative Law' (2005) Project Overview Article, available at: www.iilj.org/GAL/documents/TheEmergenceofGlobalAdministrativeLaw.pdf.

140 See for an in-depth analysis Cass, above n 136.

141 See above n 130; Cottier, 'The Legitimacy of the WTO Law', in L. Yueh (ed.), *The Law and Economics of Globalisation. New Challenges for a World in Flux* (Edward Elgar, 2009).

142 M. Krajewski, 'Democratic Legitimacy and Constitutional Perspectives of WTO Law' (2001) 35(1) *Journal of World Trade* 167; R. Howse and K. Nicolaidis, 'Legitimacy and Global Governance: Why Constitutionalizing the WTO is a Step Too Far', in R. B. Porter *et al.* (eds.), *Efficiency, Equity, Legitimacy. The Multilateral Trading System at the Millennium* (Brookings Institution Press, 2001), pp. 236 *et seq.*

143 Cass, above n 136, at p. 18.

144 Cottier, above n 141.

and fairness.[145] In the end, declaring the WTO a constitution or not does not change anything with regard to the political and societal issue areas it touches upon and the fragmentation issues it faces. The debate about 'constitution or not?' thus seems to distract attention from the more fundamental questions of fragmentation calling into question the order's legitimacy and effectiveness, mainly due to the absent 'constitutionalist' considerations of public interest, governance principles and values. Some, therefore, attempt to foster traditional constitutional principles to enhance the effectiveness and legitimacy of the WTO legal order, by defining which constitutional aspects are missing and how they could be integrated or translated into the WTO order.[146]

III. *A third way: The multilayered governance approach – a pragmatic synthesis*

Dealing with questions of fragmentation and coherence in international trade regulation, NCCR scholars elaborated an approach that combines hermeneutics with a constitutionalist perspective. Here, the political order of international law is not limited to the relationships of nation states, but to a system of multilayered governance building upon the traditions of federalism.[147] Under this theory, all relevant governance layers are embedded in an overall international system. Depending on how many layers a vertical governance line involves in a given case, these could vary between a 'two-storey' house (only state and international law as layers) and a 'five-storey' house[148] (layers comprise the municipality, district,

145 E.-U. Petersmann 'Limits of WTO Jurisprudence: Comments from an International Law and Human Rights Perspective', in T. Cottier and P. C. Mavroidis, *The Role of the Judge in International Trade Regulation* (University of Michigan Press, 2006), pp. 81–87; see also E.-U. Petersmann, 'The WTO Constitution and Human Rights' (2000) 3(1) *Journal of International Economic Law* 19; E.-U. Petersmann, 'Human Rights and the Law of the World Trade Organization' (2003) 37 *Journal of World Trade* 241; E.-U. Petersmann, 'Human Rights and International Economic Law in the 21st Century' (2001) 4(1) *Journal of International Economic Law* 3–39.

146 See Chapter 1 of this volume.

147 Cottier and Hertig, above n 128, 264.

148 For the concept see: T. Cottier, 'The Impact from Without: International Law and the Structure of Federal Governance in Switzerland' in T. Cottier, P. Knoepfel and W. Linder (eds.), *Verwaltung, Regierung und Verfassung im Wandel: Gedächtnisschrift für Raimund E. Germann* (Helbing & Lichtenhahn, 2000), pp. 213–230; Cottier and Hertig, above n 128, at 299; see also: T. Cottier, 'The Constitutionalism of International Economic Law', in K. M. Meessen *et al.* (eds.), *Economic Law as an Economic Good. Its Rule Function and its Tool Function in the Competition of Systems* (Sellier de Gruyter,

state, regional cooperation, and international law). Within the house of however many storeys, the state is conceived as a *pouvoir intermédiaire* between the different layers of governance, assuming the role of a central manager of the system. Although embedded in a multilayered system and dethroned as absolute sovereign, the state maintains a supreme authority acting as a guardian over the performances of other layers of governance. Additionally, a principle of supremacy of the upper over the lower layer of governance is advocated, thereby promoting more trans-layer participatory legitimacy to enhance democratic input legitimacy.[149] As multilayered governance has to deal with overlapping systems, cultures and values, there is a special emphasis on procedural instruments and guarantees, which are deemed to play a crucial role in weighing, balancing and arbitrating competing issues and values on all layers. There are differences in degree, but not in principle.[150]

This multilayered model of governance is underpinned by a constitutionalist view which is influenced by the 'first modern and still accepted definition of constitution' by Emer de Vattel[151] which conceives a constitution mainly as a normative order that determines how public authority is to be conducted.[152] On this basis, NCCR Trade Regulation researchers started out from the assumption that 'a constitution (in a normative sense) is the sum of basic (materially most important) legal norms which comprehensively regulate the social and political life of a polity'.[153] This is then applied to the concept of the multilayered system of governance.[154] It allows working with a constitutionalist model separate from an exclusively nation-state type, hierarchical order. The term 'constitutionalism' is thus less a political model than a 'catchword for the continuing process of

2009); T. Cottier, 'Konstitutionalisierungsprobleme im internationalen Wirtschaftsrecht: verfassungsrechtliche Herausforderungen im Rahmen der WTO' (2005, Sonderheft) 50, at 51–52.

149 Others suggest a way to constitutionalise transnational governance, including the WTO, through a three-dimensional conflicts-law approach, based on the model of vertical, horizontal and diagonal legal conflicts in the EU; see C. Joerges, 'The Idea of a Three-Dimensional Conflicts Law as a Constitutional Form', in C. Joerges and E.-U. Petersmann (eds.), *Constitutionalism, Multilevel Trade Governance and Social Regulation* 2nd edn (Hart Publishing, 2010).

150 T. Cottier, *Multi-layered Governance, Pluralism and Moral Conflict* (2008) NCCR Working Paper 2008/23, available at www.nccr-trade.org.

151 Peters, above n 130, at 581.

152 E. de Vattel, *Le droit des gens ou principes de la loi naturelle appliqués à la conduite et aux affaires des Nations et des Souverains,* Book I (Paris, 1758, repr. 1916), at p. 31.

153 Peters, above n 130, at 581.

154 Cottier, above n 150.

the emergence, creation, and identification of constitution-like elements on the international level'.[155]

Against the background of the multilayered governance model, 'constitutionalist' principles, values and instruments can improve the fairness and effectiveness of the international order and/or compensate for the loss of constitutionalist order and protection of people's rights on the national level.[156] Constitutional principles, such as the rule of law, the balance of powers, human rights, or democratic legitimacy,[157] are conceived as principles of good governance that should also be reflected at the international level.[158] For the WTO, this comprises non-discrimination and equal opportunity, the protection of intellectual property, the right to trade, the right to market access, and principles linked to the legalisation of the system, such as the rule of law and good faith.[159] This principle, or right-based approach to the WTO, is linked to other non-trade concerns as part of a wider multilayered governance system, integrating other value-based public interest issues embodied in overlapping international regimes, such as protection of the environment or human rights.

It is important to note that multilayered constitutionalism is not conceived as a 'one-size-fits-all' model or normative skeleton to be imposed on the international order; rather it is intended to serve as a guiding benchmark for norm creation and norm application. The objective is to identify negative impacts of fragmentation in multilayered governance and to address them not only from an analytical, but also from a normative constitutionalist perspective. Multilayered constitutionalism seeks to establish an overall effective and efficient multilayered system of governance by identifying and defining normative benchmarks to allocate power, or by providing appropriate mechanisms to allow for weighing, balancing and decision-making in conflicting cases.

IV. The fundamental critique: missing societal foundations in international relations

All legal approaches that propose methods to address fragmentation have something in common: they are optimistic. They suggest that

155 Peters, above n 130, at 582. 156 *Ibid.*, at p. 583.

157 Cottier and Hertig, above n 128, at 299; Peters, above n 130, at 583.

158 Cottier and Hertig, above n 128, at 296.

159 E.-U. Petersmann, 'Addressing Institutional Challenges to the WTO in the New Millennium: A Long-Term Perspective' (2005) 8 *Journal of International Economic Law* 647, at 650 *et seq.*

conceptual models and technical solutions contribute to mitigating 'bad' fragmentation phenomena and channel or influence them in a positive way. This is what critical voices, mainly from a social science perspective, but also from legal theory, strongly contest. For Teubner and Fischer-Lescano, fragmentation in international law is a real-life phenomenon that – for the most part – has to be accepted as it is. They see fragmentation as intrinsically linked to the fact of deep friction lines marking international society.[160] The multitude of uncoordinated driving forces of public and private actors, and other societal forces determining international action are for them symptoms of conflicting interests, values, and morality, strongly differing among societies and nations. In their eyes, problems of norm collision are highly 'under-evaluated' and 'more dramatic' than generally conceived by lawyers. Teubner and Fischer-Lescano reject any 'meta-level' at which conflicts might be addressed as something 'elusive both in global law and in global society'. Societal frictions do not allow for solid structures of an international legal order.[161]

Clashing systems do not have the same notions of justice and fairness that are conditions of sustainable conflict resolution and acceptance of its outcomes.[162] A normative system of global law is thus estimated as 'doomed from the outset'.[163] Instead, Teubner advocates 'societal constitutionalism' as opposed to state-centred constitutional legal theory. This constitution of world society 'does not come about exclusively in the representative institutions of international politics, nor can it take place in a unitary global constitution' but it 'emerges incrementally in the constitutionalisation of a multiplicity of autonomous sub-systems of world society'.[164] Against the societal fragmentation of the international community, hopes of being able to deal with conflicts and norm collisions through law and procedures have to be abandoned; at best, a 'weak normative compatibility of fragments' is regarded as viable, depending 'on the ability of conflicts law to establish a specific network logic, which can effect a loose coupling of colliding units'.[165] Teubner and Fischer-Lescano propose addressing fragmentation conflicts through 'explicit politicisation'

160 Fischer-Lescano and Teubner, above n 17, at 1017.

161 A. Hurrell, *On Global Order: Power: Values, and the Constitution of International Society* (Oxford University Press, 2007); S. P. Huntington, *The Clash of Civilizations and the Remaking of World Order* (Touchstone Books, 1998).

162 J. Rawls, *The Law of Peoples with 'The Idea of Public Reasons Revisited'* (Harvard University Press, 1999).

163 Fischer-Lescano and Teubner, above n 17.

164 Teubner, above n 7, p. 8.

165 Fischer-Lescano and Teubner, above n 17, at 1003, 1004.

of law by establishing negotiations between relevant collective actors, public debate and collective decisions.

Another school of realist thought, prominently expressed in the writings of Jack A. Goldsmith and Eric A. Posner, holds similarly that legal approaches to international relations are naive. In their eyes, these approaches ignore the rational interests of states as major driving forces on the international level.[166] Systemic approaches find no reflection in the real world.[167] International law is not a 'real' legal order to which states have submitted. It is not effective as law, as it does not imply a state-like monopoly of coercion; this is why international norms cannot have a limiting effect on states' behaviour. States may or may not act regardless of international norms, depending on their power. This is why the validity of international law is always relative to state power.

In response to these objections, it should be noted that they often imply a strong dichotomy between the domestic and the international realm. While the latter is formed by society, international relations operate, in the traditions of the realist school, in terms of conflict and even war. A closer look, underpinning the doctrine of multilayered governance, however, argues that these are differences of degree, and not of principle. Conflicting values and interests common to all human relations, and legal responses to them, therefore can and should share common traits which may vary on different layers of governance, but are not fundamentally different in nature.[168] Recourse to legal theory, beyond the models discussed so far, will confirm this point, offering further and important insights into the issue of coherence versus fragmentation.

E. Insights from legal theory

Every ideal of a political or legal order is linked to the moral or cultural background and perceptions of legitimate governance. When it comes to international relations and culturally rooted ideas on governance, legitimacy and organisation of society, it is difficult to find a common and widely shared basis. In a fragmented international society, values and convictions clash, generating fierce and fundamental debates. But this is not a reason to give up on law as a tool and foundation for the organisation

166 J. L. Goldsmith and E. A. Posner, *The Limits of International Law* (Oxford University Press, 2005).

167 *Ibid.*, at pp. 6–8.

168 See T. Cottier 'Multilayered Governance, Pluralism and Moral Conflict' (2009) 16(2) *Indiana Journal of Global Legal Studies* 647.

of society. To the contrary, it is precisely in this regard that the practical value of law and legal modelling steps in. It provides a tool to establish a normative matrix reflecting benchmarks of conflict prevention and settlement on the basis of overall functional interests in peaceful relations and economic opportunities.

I. The nature and role of law

The law model approach, in this vein, renders less absolute the 'societal fragmentation' argument made by Teubner and Fischer-Lescano. Societal fragmentation does not call into question the idea of law, but rather calls for law as an instrument to deal with conflicts in a peaceful and constructive way.[169] Frictions and conflicts are an expression of different societal dynamics and their interaction. Each nation state, even when based on the most homogeneous society, will comprise different trends and dynamics of clashing societal drifts. In reality, most states are not built upon very homogeneous structures, but face societal frictions of religion, culture or politics, the state being called upon to settle them in a peaceful way.[170] As conflicting currents of society are linked through common interests and have an impact on one another, they cannot exist in isolation. If those entities wish to achieve peaceful and flourishing conditions of human existence and well-being, they need to find ways to collaborate and resolve conflicts in a durable way. This is the structural essence of the legal function, whatever its particular normative contents and underpinnings.

Kelsen considers as a (legally organised) societal order, and, with regard to the law involved, a legal community, any normative order regulating human behaviour, as soon as it directly or indirectly touches upon the life of other human beings.[171] Thus, societal fragmentation constitutes a need to explore means of socially accepted and appropriate regulation and decision-making procedures, rather than avoiding the promotion of common solutions from the outset.[172]

169 See also S. Besson, *The Morality of Conflict* (Hart Publishing, 2005); Cottier, above n 168.

170 T. Cottier, 'Cosmopolitan Values in International Economic Law: Myths and Realities', in B. Sitter-Liver (ed.), *Universality: From Theory to Practice. An Intercultural and Interdisciplinary Debate About Facts, Possibilities, Lies and Myths* (Academic Press Fribourg, 2009), pp. 33–53, at pp. 44 *et seq.*

171 Kelsen, above n 126, at p. 25.

172 P. S. Berman, 'Seeing Beyond the Limits of International Law. Book Review of *The Limits of International Law* by J. Goldsmith and E. Posner' (2006) 84 *Texas Law Review* 1265, at p. 1279.

Constitution is still put by some on a par with a nation-state model and with a notion of law intrinsically linked to the nation-state. Legal theory takes issue with this view. The concept of law, as such, is abstract and thus independent from a 'nation' or a 'people'. The nation-state model and its moral constituents (e.g. people's democracy) belong to one specifically strong and established normative concept: 'the right legal order'. It is not necessarily the one which is most appropriate for the international level. Law, however, is nothing but an instrument to organise societal relations. It is not limited to the nation state.

A closer look at analytical legal theory models of law, in particular those of Hans Kelsen and H. L. A. Hart, is of interest here. These otherwise different models have one trait in common: they see law as a morally neutral instrument; as an analytical sphere or model system, consisting of norms and their various functions.[173] Law is a means to steer human behaviour through coercion and incentive, abstracted from its moral basis. While moral norms are important and influence human behaviour through culturally grown societal norms, which generate social and psychological conviction and pressure or ideas of legitimacy, legal norms primarily stem from a man-made authority system of sanction and incentive accepted by the populace; they are only acting upon and confronted with this moral ground.[174] According to positivist legal theorists, mixing both normative orders or putting law and morality on a par, leads to confusion about the role morality plays in law. This does not reduce the importance of morals and values. At the same time, the method of analysing law separately from morality allows the function of morality in law to be assessed, and, especially with regard to international law, enables one to allocate and analyse the mutual influence and grey zones of law and morality and the norm-generating processes.

In this vein, legal theorists developed 'pure' functional skeletons of law, which assess key elements of law as a societal instrument. Hart distinguishes between 'primary rules', determining the legal 'ought'[175] which has to be observed by law subjects to avoid sanctions or to receive advantages, and 'secondary rules' of law, providing competencies and

173 Even if e.g. Kelsen, sees a 'centralized system' as the most efficient one, his model of law could be applied as a benchmark to other constellations of law; the same is true for the theory of H. L. A. Hart for whom international law does not constitute a legal system, see: H. L. A. Hart, *The Concept of Law*, 2nd edn (Oxford University Press, 1997), at pp. 213 *et seq.*

174 Kelsen, above n 126, at p. 26.

175 Kelsen, above n 126, at p. 202.

organisational structures.[176] The latter are typically reflected in administrative and constitutional norms regulating the mode of creation of law (e.g. a democratic system), competencies (e.g. federal system), substantial guidelines and limits of public power (e.g. human rights),[177] enforcement and compliance (dispute settlement, use of force). To fulfil its function of effectively influencing human behaviour and providing for certainty, security and peace conducive to social action and human welfare, law has to provide clear guidelines and benchmarks, determining which norm is enforceable, which set of norms will be applied, and which sanctions or incentives are at stake.

A major criticism of analytical positivist theory is that it embodies an 'immoral' dictator of legal analysis, rejecting the importance of moral value. Nevertheless, keeping law pure and free from moral content does not mean that moral norms, such as human rights or other morally fundamental principles, are not important, or should not have any legal value. The analytical model skeleton merely frees law as a technical instrument from all moral preconditions, not least that of staying flexible with regard to different forms of law and governance, such as those to be observed in national and international law. Moral norms naturally form part of a legal order if recognised as law according to the pre-established criteria regarding the recognition or creation of law (such as customary law or decision-making competency). In this vein, natural law can be argued to be part of a legal system, as was the case, for example, for the Nuremberg cases addressing crimes committed against humanity, on the basis of customary law.[178] It is not the moral basis which positivist legal theory rejects. Rather, the emphasis is on the analytical composition of law and thus the 'pedigree'[179] of law which ascertains, from a technical viewpoint, legal conciseness, predictability, certainty and formal equality.[180]

At the outset, a positivist model of law blurs value-related aspects of legitimacy, such as democracy; a nation; divine legitimacy (monarchy) or charisma (dictatorship). It is based on another, functional aspect of legitimacy: the rational recognition, both in terms of instruments and values, of the legal order as a means to achieve overall societal

176 Hart, above n 173.
177 See with regard to the 'value' aspect in positivist legal theory below.
178 See K. Ipsen, *Völkerrecht* (Beck, 1990).
179 See for the term Ronald Dworkin, criticising the positivist model of law: R. Dworkin, *Taking Rights Seriously* (Harvard University Press, 1977), at p. 17, pp. 64 *et seq.*
180 For the role of formal justice see N. MacCormick, *Legal Reasoning and Legal Theory* (Clarendon Press, 1978), at p. 73.

goals.[181] Rationality leads to the acceptance and the legitimacy of the legal system. Classifying this aspect into the schemes of input – and output legitimacy, this rational belief[182] can be conceived as an element of input legitimacy, while expectations regarding outcomes with a view to a legal order reflect the aspect of output legitimacy (effectiveness). Deficiencies in achieving rational objectives through the order or in trusting in the order, e.g. expressed through demonstrations against globalisation, would be indicators of a lack of legitimacy, indicating legitimacy gaps on the input (rational belief) and/or output (performance) side.

Against this background, the realist's argument for rejecting the nature and character of international law as law for want of monopolised law enforcement loses ground. Rationality-based legitimacy provides formal validity of the legal system, and thus legitimacy of the norms which form part of it. The effectiveness of the system depends on acceptance and thus compliance 'at large' rather than on an effective ad hoc coercion monopoly. The realist's key argument is in line with those who hold that the principle of effectiveness requires 'that only those claims and situations which are effectively recognised and implemented can produce legal effects'.[183] From a legal viewpoint, this is a critical point. No legal order can constitute a solid and predictable normative benchmark if it lacks effective application and compliance. Effectiveness is largely based upon voluntary compliance. This said, the ability to sanction non-compliance remains crucial, but does not constitute the only key feature of law. Even national systems do not provide absolute effectiveness in terms of automatic sanction; there are always institutional or individual lacunae and failures. Manifold rules depend upon voluntary compliance. Particular failures of enforcement do not affect the legal nature of the norm. One would not, for example, question the legal character of a national order when corruption is hindering its full application and enforcement. The 'soft' perception of legal validity depending on actual effectiveness is one end of a spectrum assuming legal validity on the grounds of pure

181 R. Howse, 'The Legitimacy of the World Trade Organization', in J.-M. Coicaud and V. Heiskanen (eds.), *The Legitimacy of International Organizations* (New York: United Nations University Press, 2001) pp. 355–407, at p. 359 *et seq.*

182 See R. Göhring, 'Shaping the New Europe – Interest Representation in the European Union', Ph.D. dissertation, Otto-Suhr-Institut für Politikwissenschaft der Freien Universität Berlin, 2003, pp. 5 *et seq.*

183 A. Cassese, *International Law in a Divided World* (Clarendon Press, 1986), at p. 26. See similarly, K. Doehring, 'Effectiveness', in R. Bernhard (ed.), *Encyclopedia of Public International Law*, Instalment 7 (North-Holland Publishing, 1984), pp. 70–74, at p. 71.

formality. This 'hard' law validity ignores real-life deficiencies (and thus legitimacy gaps), as well as moral aspects of law which could step in as customary natural law and conviction.

To resolve this dilemma, Hans Kelsen argues that there is legal validity if the legal order is largely recognised as such and generally enforceable.[184] This is an important theoretical bridge for international law: absent any monopoly in the use of force and because implementation depends on power relations, international norms need to be backed up by a legal presumption of voluntary compliance. If international law is merely recognised and applied under conditions of 'absolute effectiveness', it is deprived of its claim to authority which is necessary to ensure its respect. This is why the principle *pacta sunt servanda* constitutes the spine of international law. If there is a call to consider law as non-binding or as void if it is not applied, it cannot fulfil its function as an organisational instrument. Indeed, the same would hold true for every legal order.

II. The benchmark of effective, efficient and legitimate legal systems

From this perspective, legal theory suggests approaching the problem of fragmentation and coherence in terms of a particular systemic model, and developing and relying upon criteria which are related to its qualities. Thus, fragmentation and competition of different legal regimes can be harmful if it affects the proper functioning of the legal regimes concerned and hinders compliance and implementation. Thus, only those aspects with negative effects on the capacity to deal effectively with today's regulatory challenges of international cooperation have to be addressed. Here, analytical recourse could be had to a simple functional benchmark: to what degree and in what ways is the system of specialised and overlapping regimes, states and regions not functioning well? Which are the factors impairing its performance? This is a crucial underlying rationale behind the chapters in this volume.

Three factors will play a role: effectiveness, efficiency and legitimacy of the legal systems concerned. Even though the terms might not be self-evident, as they are linked to various contents and definitions,[185] they can be conceptualised in a way that assists in identifying and dealing with current problems of the fragmentation of international law.

184 Kelsen, above n 126, at p. 218.

185 See H. Krieger, *Das Effektivitätsprinzip im Völkerrecht* (Duncker & Humblot, 2000), pp. 39 *et seq.*

The term 'efficiency' is generally understood in terms of *the relation between effort and performance* with regard to objectives which are to be achieved. *Efficiency means the capacity to perform.*[186] This is related to the capacity of the means (regulation) one chooses. How could one achieve with little effort the best possible performance, or with given means achieve the best possible outcome? With regard to law or institutional performance, treaty provisions would be efficient if they were shaped in such a way as to achieve a high standard and wide range of treaty objectives in a timely and cost-efficient manner.[187] If, for example, the institutional devices and body of norms of the WTO contributed to the goals that are set out in the WTO preamble, it would work efficiently.

The term 'effectiveness' is generally used to describe the *factual state between a given state of how things are and how things should be* (dichotomy between '*Ist- und Sollenszustand*').[188] It relates to the state of performance vis-à-vis a certain aim. If the aim is achieved, the system is working effectively, no matter how, when and at what cost. The term effectiveness can thus designate varying degrees of achievement as to objectives pursued (*Zielerreichungsgrad*).[189] Effectiveness describes the actual *state of performance*, while efficiency stands for the *capacity to perform*. So if a given order (e.g. the WTO) is not effective (state of performance) in terms of its objectives (e.g. sustainable development),[190] it would need institutions that work more efficiently (capacity to perform).

A system's performance in terms of effectiveness and efficiency, and thus aspects of problematic fragmentation, is closely related to questions of legitimacy.[191] Legitimacy as a logic or justification of an authority is not an aspect which can be generally defined. It is closely linked to the acceptance of a political or legal order, i.e. the spinal cord of the functional validity of a legal system. Its perception very much depends on the conceptions of political thought, linked to culture, tradition and history.[192] Complex as this concept is, there are certain theoretical yardsticks that provide traits of legitimacy and help to conceptualise aspects of the logic

186 *Ibid.*, at p. 34; C. de Visscher, *Les effectivités du droit international public* (Editions A. Pedone, 1967), at p. 18.

187 Krieger, above n 185, p. 34. 188 *Ibid.*, pp. 39 *et seq.*

189 *Ibid.*, p. 34; J. Touscoz, *Le Principe d'effectivité dans l'ordre international* (R. Pichon et R. Durand-Auzias, 1964), p. 4.

190 Preamble of the Marrakesh Agreement Establishing the World Trade Organization.

191 F. W. Scharpf, *Governing the European Union, Effective and Democratic?* (Oxford University Press, 1999); R. O. Keohane and J. S. Nye, *Power and Interdependence*, 3rd edn (Longman, 2001), pp. 282–287.

192 Göhring, above n 182.

of a political system.[193] Political scientists have developed schemes which allow aspects of legitimacy to be classified through the notions of input and output legitimacy.[194] Input legitimacy designates normative aspects justifying a system's decision-making authority in terms of its political processes and structures (deliberative decision-making, democratic or pluralistic conceptions). This comprises all normatively anchored sets of criteria upon which a system's authority could logically or factually base its power, e.g. legality or value-rational faith, debate and deliberation (democracy) or recognition of a charismatic leader (dictatorship) and traditional or emotional patterns of authority (e.g. monarchy). Output legitimacy, on the other hand, looks at the 'output' of a political system, its performance with regard to its societal purpose. Relevant questions are: 'What is the public good to be provided and how does the system score in terms of effectiveness and efficiency? What are the costs of action or inaction?'[195] This aspect of legitimacy could be conceived as a corrigendum to mere normative input legitimacy criteria which do not cover a system's performance. A democratic system does not necessarily guarantee welfare and human rights protection; it is only a structural element in their favour. The same is true for a legally well-established order or deliberative decision-making process. Input legitimacy and output legitimacy are two sides of the same coin.

Applying this performance scheme to the fragmentation problem of international law, all interrelated regimes of national and transnational systems and subsystems are based on a set of reasons. All have their individual claim to effectiveness and legitimacy upon which they are based. The object and purpose of an order or regime are frequently anchored in the preamble or explicit objectives of treaties constituting an organisation or legal regime. For the WTO, they are generally to be found in the preamble of the Marrakesh agreement, applicable to all covered agreements, complemented with the specific objectives of specialised issue-areas, such as those laid down in the preamble to or objectives of the WTO agreements. For states, their constitution and culturally shaped understanding of a state's role in organising people's lives would be the general reference

193 *Ibid.*; see also P. Nanz, 'Democratic Legitimacy of Transnational Trade Governance: A View from Political Theory', in C. Joerges and E.-U. Petersmann (ed.), *Constitutionalism, Multilevel Trade Governance and Social Regulation* (Hart Publishing, 2006), pp. 59–82.

194 Scharpf, above n 191; Keohane and Nye, above n 191, pp. 282–287.

195 M. Elsig, 'The World Trade Organization's Legitimacy Crisis: What Does the Beast Look Like?' (2007) 41(1) *Journal of World Trade* 75, at p. 84.

point. Furthermore, a legal order as a technical means to organise societal relations comprises general functional objectives inherent in the purpose of law as an organisational instrument. These include its societal peace-function, dispute settlement according to clear normative benchmarks and decision-making systems, clear competencies of law creation, formal justice, substantial justice, and certainty and predictability in behavioural norms, dispute settlement and decision-making.

In analysing fragmentation features, the starting point would be the effectiveness and efficiency of each individual system involved. Only if there is an actual or potential lack of effectiveness and efficiency of systems, due to overlaps or conflicts regarding their objectives as legal orders and their specific objectives as regulatory entity for a certain issue-area, would there be a problem of fragmentation and lack of coherence which needs to be addressed.

As noted earlier, within the fragmented landscape of international law, this would be the case, if, horizontally, a situation of conflict between issue-oriented international regimes emerges, with one system impinging on the effectiveness of the other. Classical cases may include overlaps between trade-regulating regimes (e.g. the WTO) and the international body of human rights or environmental law. In both cases the effectiveness of one system is potentially called into question by another. Another trade-off with an impact on efficient performance and effectiveness of interrelated systems could occur vertically, in the relationship between international law and other governance layers, such as regional systems or nation states, getting involved in conflict situations. In the horizontal line between overlapping international regimes, as well as in the vertical line between a national, regional or the international order, there is a field of tension and an effectiveness gap in trade-off situations, each system arguing for its individual effectiveness and legitimacy.

If there is no trade-off situation and systems work side by side and are complementary and mutually supportive, there is no problem to be addressed other than how synergies could be created among the inter-related systems to work even more efficiently for the sake of all, and to achieve more overall effectiveness.

With respect to legitimacy, the output legitimacy performance side seems to be an interesting element with which to address the system's legitimacy. This is because, in the sphere of international law, the main source of legitimacy in constructing a system is not democratic will but purpose-related rationality of states and the instrumentality of legalisation. It is increasingly assumed that the 'litmus test for legitimacy is directly linked to the effectiveness of the system'.[196] Elements of democratic participation, in this regard, could play the role of (output) legitimacy-enhancing instruments for the trade system, as they could bridge legitimacy gaps compromising its performance both at home and at the international level. The same is clearly true for other modern principles of constitutionalist legality, aiming at a stable political order, such as the rule of law, or checks and balances. Although output legitimacy might be a starting point, it becomes clear that input legitimacy and output legitimacy are closely linked, and should therefore be balanced in such a way as to sustain the overall performance and long-term stability of the international trade system.[197] Efforts to seek greater coherence would thus be required to re-establish an overall balance and restore overall legitimacy.

III. Coherence as an instrument to enhance effectiveness, efficiency and legitimacy

In legal theory, the degree of effectiveness of a legal order is seen as a matter of institutional density and performance.[198] In conceptualising law from a formal angle of competencies and order, Kelsen generally distinguishes between decentralised 'primitive' legal orders which only allow for self-help retaliation in cases of violation of the law (as is generally the case for international law) and more sophisticated centralised orders with governments, institutions, judicial and administrative bodies to efficiently set and implement law (as is the case for states). In Kelsen's eyes, the more 'centralised' and, thus, legally dense a system of norms and coercion is, the more it allows for stability and peace. Consequently, he argued for establishing a World Federal State internationally.[199] From a very different angle, but equally referring to normative density, Robert Alexy, focusing on the normative content of law expressed through principles underlying a legal order, distinguishes between strong and weak systems of law according to the density of their inner normative logic.[200] Both approaches stand for two concepts referring to an inner systemic logic of 'coherence' or 'consistency'. Coherence is generally defined as a situation

196 *Ibid.*, at 87. 197 *Ibid.*, at 89.

198 H. Kelsen, *Principles of International Law* (Holt Rinehart & Winston, 1967), p. 183.

199 H. Kelsen, *Peace Through Law* (University of North Carolina Press, 1944), p. 5.

200 R. Alexy, 'Juristische Begründung, System und Kohärenz', in O. Behrends *et al.* (eds.), *Rechtsdogmatik und praktische Vernunft: Symposion zum 80. Geburtstag von Franz Wieacker* (Vandenhoeck und Ruprecht, 1990) pp. 95–107, at pp. 96 *et seq.*

in which all parts of something fit together well, while consistency can be described as the absence of conflicting or contradictory parts or aspects or adherence to a regular pattern. Some see consistency as just the flip side of coherence, and thus an aspect of it.[201] Leaving aside terminological branches and theoretical ramifications, we will, in the following, refer to a pattern that can be detected in legal theory to explain different aspects of systemic logic in law in terms of consistency and/or coherence.

1. Formal consistency: the legalistic model of rules

From a legal modelling viewpoint, law has to fulfil the function of setting a clear benchmark of norms, i.e. rules set through a competent and recognised body with decision-making power. If they are breached, a sanction mechanism should be set in motion. If they are followed, an incentive mechanism should step in. For the system to work efficiently in terms of its peace function, societal guidance and compliance, it has to be predictable and concise, and be generally accepted and followed by its subjects. The aspect of consistency is anchored in the validity aspect of law, i.e. *pacta sunt servanda*.[202] This is why conflicts without a proper set of conflict norms (determining how to deal with conflicts) are harmful to a legal system: they make it random, undermining validity and authority.

One way to achieve consistency in law is through a system of rules and competencies as provided by the Kelsenian or Hartian models of law. As mentioned above, the legal system is conceived as an analytical skeleton of rules which contain a legal 'ought' to steer human behaviour (primary rules) and rules regulating competencies of law creation and law application (secondary rules). The legal system's consistency here is mainly achieved through formality: there is a clear order about who decides, which law is valid, and which norms apply. This is achieved mainly through secondary norms determining who is competent to decide or to act and which norm prevails in which context (e.g. through law application norms such as *lex specialis* or *lex posterior*). The density and consistency of the system is thus based on a formal law matrix, regardless of the legal content.

Looking at the fragmentation issue, formal coherence touches upon a trade-off between systems, thus implying the aspect of effectiveness. The legal system cannot fulfil its role as a normative basis for dispute settlement if its norms are random due to lack of coordinative secondary

201 Alexy, above n 200, p. 96. 202 MacCormick, above n 180, p. 195.

law. With regard to legitimacy, the aspect of legal validity is at stake. There is a lack of legitimacy, as it is not clear which norm is valid. In international fragmentation, the aspect of formal coherence steps in when there is a conflict of norms or a question of more coordinated institutional linkages and devices regarding global fields of governance and decision-making. Here, the model of a strict system of 'secondary norms' of institutional elements, which are explicitly determined and 'fit together well' bears mention. The model helps to detect lacunae: where does the international system lack rigidity in secondary-norm coherence? Where do conflicts of law occur and which formal or procedural norms would prevail? Do we have areas of competence overlapping haphazardly? How could these best be resolved and clarified? Here, any kind of mechanism providing for a distinct formality in decision-making competence or hierarchy would be a possible solution, including negotiating bodies or committees, as proposed by Teubner and Fischer-Lescano.[203]

Looking at the above-described legal approaches for dealing with the fragmentation of international law, the hermeneutical as well as the constitutionalist approach draw on techniques of formal consistency of norms. The hermeneutical approach concentrates on existing means and lacunae in norm consistency, analysing which principles could prevent or resolve legal conflicts, or could and should apply as norms of international law. Here, those provisions of the VCLT which determine the applicability of international treaty provisions in cases of conflicting norms become relevant. Constitutionalist approaches have a positivist dimension when seeking a legal skeleton of secondary norm competencies to avoid conflicts through determining clearly who is competent to take which decision and who should decide about competencies, legality and law compliance. Both aspects are reflected in the NCCR approach of multilayered constitutionalism.

2. Substantial coherence: the constitutionalist model of principles

Although the positivist legal models of formal consistency are highly instructive in regard to providing well-fitting elements of governance in modelling a legal order, they suffer from shortcomings when it comes to substantial matters of law.[204] They rely on consistency through formality, strict structures of competencies and procedural predictability, and by this they understand law in an all-or-nothing manner: there is a rule produced

203 Fischer-Lescano & Teubner, above n 17.

204 MacCormick, above n 180, p. 229.

by the competent body, applied by the competent organ, contested in a competent court, and a court's decision based on the competency to create 'individual law' for a given case.[205] If there are open or general norms, containing a 'penumbra of uncertainty' which needs interpretation, it is for the subjective reasoning of the judge ruling on the case. As for law creation and law application, according to Hans Kelsen, the will and motivation of the authority to create the norm should count most. In modern constitutional law, this is underpinned by the importance accorded to the authority of the democratic decision-maker.

These models tend to ignore the value-based substantial grounds of law, input legitimacy aspects, consisting, for example, of the object and purpose of the order or basic standards of human rights, societal peace (governance) and justice, as they form part of modern constitutional law.[206] By this, they do not integrate the potential of these aspects regarding further systemic coherence, analytical strictness and predictability. Law cannot only be tied to a formal skeleton of competencies and application mechanisms, avoiding formal contradiction. The common ground of general law consisting of general principles of law normatively informing (or even binding) law creation and law application needs to be taken into account.[207]

This is why, in legal theory, critical voices have challenged the formal model of rules on the grounds of its failure to integrate the moral or normative basis of law, or to include and work with principles underlying the legal order. One of the most prominent critiques pointing to the positivist rule model was provided by Ronald Dworkin.[208] While positivists leave everything to the subjective discretion of the judge, principle theorists propose that the judges' discretion be tied to a morally anchored, but objectively detectable, structure of law, constituting a kind of normative grammar upon which rules are based. These are basic rights or an order's objectives, reflected in the object and purpose of a legal order, its normative limits and law creation modalities, such as democratic decision-making, the rule of law, human rights, principles of a welfare state and corresponding economic objectives and environmental protection.[209] This 'deep structure code' of a legal order is seen as a

205 H. Kelsen, *Allgemeine Theorie der Normen* (Manz, 1979), pp. 180 *et seq.*

206 MacCormick, above n 180.

207 P. A. Bulloch and J. Raz, 'Postscript', in Hart, above n 173, pp. 238–276.

208 Dworkin, above n 179.

209 R. Alexy, 'Rechtssystem und praktische Vernunft' (1987) *Rechtstheorie* 407, at 412; J.-R. Sieckmann, *Regelmodelle und Prinizpienmodelle des Rechtssystem*, Studien zur

crucial point. Law coherence, understood as the body of law of a certain legal order that forms a system of logically linked content, is achieved through law patterns that 'make sense' in a substantial normative way.[210] Principle theorists thus add to the pattern of consistency (no normative inconsistencies, clear structure of formal competencies and rules) an aspect of substantial coherence (an inner system's logic of normative content).

From a principle theory viewpoint, any norm generation, be it legislative, executive or adjudicative, is to be shaped according to its value-based deep structure code, having an impact on the law-creating (law-makers, judges, authority) discretion of authority.[211] Thus, the normative deep structure not only forms the basis of law creation but also steps in as a layer of general law, when a legal situation runs out of certainty. As a legal basis, general principles and order objectives claim a legal core which could challenge special norms. If the latter are contradicting the former, they should not be valid due to normative inconsistency. Here the law-creating authority fails to respect its mandate, when setting law that is contrary to the normative grounds of the legal order. At this point, the question is which model should prevail: the will of the authority – or contracting parties (as for the model of rules) or the substantial deep structure basis (as for the model of principles), both tied to different aspects of legitimacy (acceptance of authority, rationality and effectiveness of a legal order)?

As international law is not based on a common pole of authority or law-creating body, integrating the normative basis of international law as a common grammar or deep structural code of law could thus be a way to achieve more coherence enhancing legal predictability and legitimacy. A deep structure of international law manifests itself not only through general international law and specialised treaties established according to the Article 38 criteria of the ICJ statute, but also through a normative body of soft-law standards which can be drawn from international societal objectives and commitments. Such standards have been expressed in widely accepted declarations, e.g. under the auspices of the UN. As mentioned above, notwithstanding deficiencies in implementation, these basic principles could still be seen as a generally accepted deep structural

Rechtsphilosophie und Rechtstheorie, vol. 1 (Nomos, 1990), p. 143; H.-J. Koch, 'Zur Methodenlehre des Rechtspositivismus' (1990) 37 *Archiv für Rechts – und Sozialphilosophie* 152, at 156 *et seq.*

210 MacCormick, above n 180.

211 *Ibid.*, p. 101.

normative benchmark, as states have committed to them and should thus be held responsible for their manifested will.[212]

As the principles forming part of a legal order's deep structure are not always in harmony, their normative claims may clash. Principle legal theory seeks to rationally frame conflicts of principles through methodological norms providing criteria for weighing and balancing or allowing for the determination of principle hierarchies in a given case.[213] While conflicts of rules in the sense of a legalistic model of rules can be resolved through interpretative rules such as *lex posterior* or *lex specialis*, assuring as formal secondary norms the consistency of the legal system, conflicts of principles need to be resolved on a case-by-case basis, taking into account various background factors of a case and elements of justice and fairness.

Robert Alexy, a key proponent of principle theory, distinguishes between strong and weak principle theories.[214] The weakest principle theory provides mere patterns of criteria or *topoi* without further indications as to how they should be applied methodologically in relation to each other. As this does not tie the interpretational elements to a deep structure of principles that would determine interpretive mechanisms and 'dimensions of weight', this would be of little additional value as regards the positivist perception of 'random' authority.

The strongest principle theory sets out a dense net of criteria, benchmarks, methodological and hierarchical relations.[215] Here coherence and consistency actually meet, forming two sides of the same coin: principles and rules determining how to apply law and setting dimensions of weight would contribute to secondary norm consistency, while the basis of normative content (deep structure of general law and principles) forms part of the coherence aspect of a normative matrix underpinning a legal system. Dworkin elaborates hierarchies of 'trumps of rights' according to which rights should prevail in instances of conflicting interpretation.[216]

As an example, the deep structure of the WTO preamble contains general objectives and guiding principles, including full employment, enhancement of welfare and the principle of sustainable development which 'has been generally accepted as integrating economic and social

212 See section E. I. above with regard to realists' arguments against these moral implications.

213 E.g. the optimalisation of principles through the application of the proportionality principle as applied in German constitutional law, Alexy, above n 200, p. 100.

214 R. Alexy, 'Zur Kritik des Rechtspositivismus' (1990) 74(37) *Rechtspositivismus und Wertbezug des Rechts, Archiv für Rechts- und Sozialphilosophie* 9, at p. 23.

215 Alexy, above n 200, pp. 96 *et seq.*

216 Dworkin, above n 179, pp. 133 *et seq.*

development and environmental protection'.[217] Behind these very general benchmarks hide deep structural elements which are filled out by international norm standards.[218] By this, WTO law is implicitly tied to other fields of international law. It cannot be instrumentally reduced to trade liberalisation. Interpretation is thus related to a body of substantive benchmarks informing application of WTO law in 'hard cases' of a penumbral character. In this context, the Appellate Body has, for example, with regard to Article XX GATT, provided a handful of standards of law interpretation, such as the benchmark of 'good faith' and the need 'to strike a balance between right and duty' or 'the right of states to determine the level of protection they deem appropriate', when it comes to the interpretation of the *chapeau* of Article XX GATT.[219]

The quest for substantial coherence creates predictable benchmarks. The requirement for normative reflection to be undertaken in each case based on such benchmarks allows for the evolution of a substantially consistent value-based pedigree of law through normative arguments and thus for normative density. In contrast, judicial decisions are mainly grounded in subjective horizons of judges and may impede general principles of equity (e.g. related to good faith) and neglect elements of (conflicting) systems' legitimacy and effectiveness in the process of applying and shaping the law.[220] Decisions of this kind, that may occur particularly in ad hoc settings of jurisdiction, with a loose institutional background and little precedent (e.g. dispute settlement in international investment law), fuel the danger of incoherencies in application of law undermining its credibility and predictability. In this vein, tying law to a common set of not only formal but also methodological or substantial standards of legal interpretation could enhance the structural systemic density of law. But what if similarly solid normative arguments are on the table and are still contradicting each other? Here application of the law encounters the necessarily subjective decision-making which will always persist, and which will demand, in order to avoid inconsistencies, well-founded competence

217 Appellate Body Report, *US – Shrimp*, para. 153.

218 See K. Gehne, *Nachhaltige Entwicklung als Rechtsprinzip, normativer Aussagegehalt, rechtstheoretische Einordnung, Funktionen im Recht* (Mohr-Siebeck, 2010 (forthcoming)).

219 T. Cottier, P. Delimatsis and N. Diebold, 'Article XIV GATS (General Exceptions)', in R. Wolfrum, P.-T. Stoll and C. Feinäugle (eds.), *Max-Planck Commentaries on World Trade Law, Volume 6: WTO-Trade in Services* (Brill Publishers, 2008), p. 287. For the principle-oriented approach to interpretation of WTO law, see ILA, Rio de Janeiro Conference (2008), International Trade Law Committee, para. 20.

220 Alexy, above n 200, p. 106.

structures (formal consistency) to assure formal justice.[221] This is why formal consistency and substantial coherence are complementary.

Those critical of principle theory argue that it is a void attempt to try to put judicial decision-making into categories of substantial law.[222] Such a process reduces law to chitchat and creates something like a 'judicial world-egg' which determines everything from criminal law to the law of clinical thermometers.[223] These critics have a point when principle theory claims to provide normative 'truth' or the 'best justification of law'.[224] Joseph Raz, one of the leading contemporary opponents of deep structure substantial coherence of law, argues that a moral basis of law, even if integrated through secondary law, would be 'inconsistent with the authority based character of law'. For him, law is politics which is expressed through legal norms; and this should be the main guideline for its application. Only strict formality can tie these rules together.[225]

Principle theory, however, does not call into question clear standards of legal application. Rather, it aims at carving out normative guidelines for coherent legal interpretation, generally contributing to legal predictability and rigidity of a legal system. Not every policy or ideology is part of the 'deep structure of law' but only standards which are widely accepted as valid law or at least soft law with a certain repetitive and widely spread background, in particular principles of modern constitutionalism or human rights. Diverse courts around the globe refer to similar legal principles and sources of law and in several instances cross-refer, explicitly or implicitly, to decisions of other international fora.[226] International tribunals do communicate even if only in an uncoordinated manner[227] in that they are aware of the rulings of other tribunals in similar or relevant matters.[228] International courts essentially avoid contradicting

221 *Ibid.*, p. 107.

222 C. Jabloner, 'Wie zeitgemäß ist die reine Rechtslehre' (1998) 29(1) *Rechtstheorie* 1, at pp. 11 *et seq.*

223 E. Forsthoff, 'Die Umbildung des Verfassungsgesetzes', in H. Barion, E. Forsthoff and C. Schmitt (eds.), *Festschrift für Carl Schmitt zum 70. Geburtstag* (Duncker und Humblot, 1989) 35, at p. 41.

224 Alexy, above n 214, p. 23.

225 J. Raz, 'The Relevance of Coherence' (1992) 72 *Boston University Law Review* 273.

226 Cf. Appellate Body Report, *US – Wool Shirts and Blouses*, p. 14; Shany, above n 102, p. 102; also Koskenniemi, above n 10, para. 492.

227 Cf. A. Slaughter, 'A Global Community of Courts' (2003) 44 *Harvard International Law Journal* 191.

228 *Ibid.*

each other.[229] In the end, there is more formal justice through more coherent justification of judicial decisions.[230] Neil MacCormick calls this 'second order justification'.[231] In this sense, reference, application and elaboration of case-law of other international courts could contribute to enhancing the legitimacy (moral and legal) of a given judgment.

H. L. A. Hart, addressing Dworkin's critique in the postscript to the second edition of his 'Concept of Law', shows that principle theory and the moral basis of law could well be included in a formal validity scheme through 'inner system' secondary norms determining interpretation rules.[232] Article 31 VCLT requiring that law interpretation consider the object and purpose of a treaty (thus its deep structure), for example, would constitute such a secondary norm of law interpretation.[233]

F. Promoting coherence through multilayered constitutionalism

The model of multilayered constitutionalism of the 'five-storey house' provides a legal skeleton and a normative foundation allowing fragmentation in international law to be detected and addressed. It does not stand for a 'one-size-fits-all' final solution, but for a continuous process of social technique to shape a well-functioning system, including legal modelling benchmarks of coherence and consistency. This process not only extends to institutional issues of formal coherence in secondary norms, but also to issues of normative, substantial coherence. It responds to the positivist tradition, as it seeks to identify gaps in formal consistency, and allocation of decision-making powers. It looks for coherence in the allocation of competencies, jurisdiction and institutional coordination, both horizontally and vertically. It systematically proposes consistent rules for applicable law and procedures of conflict resolution. The principle theory, on the other hand, steps in in the case of substantive, normative criteria for

229 N. Miller, 'An International Jurisprudence? The Operation of "Precedent" Across International Tribunals' (2002) *Leiden Journal of International Law* 483; also R. Wolfrum, 'Konkurrierende Zuständigkeiten internationaler Streitentscheidungsinstanzen: Notwendigkeit für Lösungsmöglichkeiten und deren Grenzen', in N. Ando, E. McWhinney and R. Wolfrum (eds.), *Liber Amicorum Judge Shigeru Oda*, Vol. 1 (Kluwer, 2002), pp. 651, 659.

230 R. Alexy, 'Coherence and Argumentation or the Genuine Twin Criterialess Super Criterion', in A. Aarnio *et al.* (eds.), *On Coherence Theory of Law* (Juristförlaget I Lund, 1985), pp. 41–49, p. 47.

231 MacCormick, above n 180, p. 119.

232 *Ibid.*, pp. 229 *et seq.*; see also Kelsen, above n 198, p. 305; Hart, fn 173, p. 209.

233 Hart calls this a 'soft positivism' approach.

allocating decision-making powers, determining competencies and establishing methodological norms of law interpretation in that it integrates standards and provides criteria for weighing and balancing conflicting values. The combination of the two aspects, both formal and substantial, within the model of multilayered governance offers a framework of appropriate criteria and standards by which detrimental fragmentation can be overcome to the benefit of coherence, both horizontally within layers, and vertically among layers of governance in an open and continuous process of responding to regulatory challenges. This approach is reminiscent of Karl Popper's critical rationalism or social technique with regard to 'technically' shaping social systems; it implies an open-ended piecemeal perspective, addressing the problems that occur with a view to improving the effectiveness of a social system by appropriate 'social technology'.[234] Popper tied the social technique to his benchmark principles of an 'open society' which for him are the core principles of a well-functioning system of open debate, comprising, in particular, the freedoms of speech and expression, which are equally relevant in the international law context.[235]

Responding to the considerations of legal consistency, the model of multilayered governance offers the possibility of clear determination of the conditions under which norms are to be applied and considered as law. Standards determine which criteria lead to recognition or integration as law, and which governance features are competent to decide in which field, and who is in charge of adjudicating legal cases. Hereby, multilevel constitutionalism widens the perspective to a comprehensive view. Tying law to clear criteria of procedural validity, there is room for all kinds of political instruments or ways of generating norms and for dealing with legal pluralism or phenomena of societal fragmentation. There are various ways, apart from a simple classical law level hierarchy, to organise and allocate competencies and determine level-specific criteria for value limits to law application.[236] Examples include national or regional courts overseeing the protection of basic principles forming the moral basis of their respective legal order,[237] or tying competencies to a deference

234 K. Popper, *Das Elend des Historizismus* (Mohr Siebeck, 2003).

235 See the contributions in Broude and Shany, above n 16.

236 See also P. S. Berman, *Global Legal Pluralism*, Princeton Law and Public Affairs Working Paper No. 08–001; Broude and Shany, above n 16.

237 For a recent example of this, see C-402/05, *Kadi* [2008] ECR I-6351; also G. Pavlakos and J. Pauwelyn, 'Principled Monism and the Normative Conception of Coercion under International Law: From a Hierarchy of Norms to a Competition of Values', in P. Koutrakos *et al.* (eds.), *Beyond the Established Legal Orders* (Hart Publishing, forthcoming).

model, such as the WTO principle providing that the appropriate level of protection in the field of SPS measures is determined by Member States.[238] Responsiveness and sensitivity with regard to societal foundations in law creation, referring to aspects of efficiency and legitimacy, need input from other disciplines, such as economics, social and political sciences, or social anthropology, to find instruments to influence social behaviour and viable solutions on the grounds of empirical data and behavioural analysis (e.g. compliance – or institutional analysis).[239] The hermeneutical approach to fragmentation of the ILC group tends to leave these questions aside, sweeping them under the rug of consistency in law application, presuming that those questions are not part of the legal problem. Here, the social scientists' critique that lawyers often ignore the societal basis of law is justified. With the report of the ILC study group, and related literature, there is considerable guidance when it comes to techniques of consistent law interpretation in international law. There is less consideration of conflicts of jurisdiction or decision-making competence in cases when orders with differing 'ethos' clash, demanding substantial coherence. Such clashes of ethos mainly occur when it comes to interpretation of law regarding diverse points of view due to differing grounds for the views held or institutions involved, for example, when there are conflicts between trade and human rights or trade and environmental norms.[240] In this case, legal modelling on the basis of the multilayered governance approach, together with these techniques for achieving coherence on a formal *and* on a substantial basis, can help to provide a benchmark to inspire new idiosyncratic ways of legal decision-making.

Bibliography

Aaronson, Susan Ariel, *Trade Imbalance: The Struggle to Weigh Human Rights Concerns in Trade Policymaking* (Cambridge University Press, 2008).

Abbott, Kenneth W. and Snidal, Duncan, 'Hard and Soft Law in International Governance' (2000) **54**(3) *International Organization* 421–456.

Alexy, Robert, 'Resisting the Merger and Acquisition of Human Rights by Trade Law: A Reply to Petersmann' (2002) **13** *European Journal of International Law* 815–844.

238 SPS Agreement cases, Art. XX GATT cases (e.g. Appellate Body Reports, *Australia – Salmon*, para. 199; *EC – Hormones*, para. 172; *EC – Asbestos*, para. 168).

239 Peters, above n 36, at 752.

240 See the proposition by IP4 of a Draft Decision on Trade and Human Rights (Chapter 8 in this volume).

'Zur Kritik des Rechtspositivismus' (1990) **74**(37) *Rechtspositivismus und Wertbezug des Rechts, Archiv für Rechts- und Sozialphilosophie* 9–26.

'Juristische Begründung, System und Kohärenz', in O. Behrends *et al.* (eds.), *Rechtsdogmatik und praktische Vernunft: Symposion zum 80. Geburtstag von Franz Wieacker* (Vandenhoeck und Ruprecht, 1990), pp. 95–107.

'Rechtssystem und praktische Vernunft' (1987) *Rechtstheorie* 407–417.

'Coherence and Argumentation or the Genuine Twin Criterialess Super Criterion', in A. Aarnio *et al.* (eds.) *On Coherence Theory of Law* (Juristförlaget I Lund, 1985), pp. 41–49.

Bartels, Lorand, *Applicable Law Before International Courts and Tribunals* (Oxford University Press, 2010, forthcoming).

Bartels, Lorand and Ortino, Federico (eds.), *Regional Trade Agreements and the WTO* (Oxford University Press, 2006).

Beck, Ulrich, 'What is Globalization?', in D. Held and A. McGrew (eds.), *The Global Transformations Reader: An Introduction to the Globalization Debate*, 3rd edn (Cambridge University Press, 2002), pp. 99–103.

Berman, Paul Schiff, *Global Legal Pluralism*, Princeton Law and Public Affairs Working Paper No. 08–001 (2007).

'Seeing Beyond the Limits of International Law. Book Review of *The Limits of International Law* by J. Goldsmith and E. Posner' (2006) **84** *Texas Law Review* 1265–1306.

Besson, Samantha, *The Morality of Conflict* (Hart Publishing, 2005).

Biaggini, Giovanni, 'Die Idee der Verfassung – Neuausrichtung im Zeitalter der Globalisierung?' (2000) **119** *Zeitschrift für Schweizerisches Recht* 445–476.

Bogdandy, Armin von, 'Constitutionalism in International Law: Comment on a Proposal from Germany' (2006) **47**(1) *Harvard International Law Journal* 223–242.

'Globalization and Europe: How to Square Democracy, Globalization, and International Law' (2004) **15**(5) *European Journal of International Law* 885–906.

Broude, Tomer, 'Fragmentation(s) of International Law: On Normative Integration as Authority Allocation', in T. Broude and Y. Shany (eds.), *The Shifting Allocation of Authority in International Law: Considering Sovereignty, Supremacy and Subsidiarity* (Hart Publishing, 2008), pp. 99–120.

Brownlie, Ian, 'Problems Concerning the Unity of International Law', in P. L. Zanardi *et al.* (eds.), *International Law at the Time of Its Codification: Essays in Honour of R. Ago*, vol. II (Giuffrè, 1987), pp. 153–162.

Bulloch, Penelope A. and Raz, Joseph, 'Postscript', in H. L. A. Hart, *The Concept of Law*, 2nd edn (Oxford University Press, 1997), pp. 238–276.

Cameron, James and Gray, Kevin R., 'Principles of International Law in the WTO Dispute Settlement Body' (2001) **50** *International and Comparative Law Quarterly* 248–298.

Cass, Deborah Z., *The Constitutionalization of the World Trade Organization: Legitimacy, Democracy, and Community in the International Trading System* (Oxford University Press, 2005).

Cassese, Antonio, *International Law in a Divided World* (Clarendon Press, 1986).

Conclusions of the Work of the Study Group on the Fragmentation of International Law: Difficulties Arising from the Diversification and Expansion of International Law (United Nations, 2006).

Cossy, Mireille and Marceau, Gabrielle, 'Institutional Challenges to Enhance Policy Co-ordination – How WTO Rules Could be Utilised to Meet Climate Objectives?', in T. Cottier, O. Nartova and S. Z. Bigdeli (eds.), *International Trade Regulation and the Mitigation of Climate Change* (Cambridge University Press, 2009), pp. 371–394.

Cottier, Thomas, 'Multilayered Governance, Pluralism and Moral Conflict' (2009) **16**(2) *Indiana Journal of Global Legal Studies* 647–679.

'Challenges Ahead in International Economic Law' (2009) **12**(1) *Journal of International Economic Law* 3–15.

'Cosmopolitan Values in International Economic Law: Myths and Realities' in B. Sitter-Liver (ed.), *Universality: From Theory to Practice. An Intercultural and Interdisciplinary Debate about Facts, Possibilities, Lies and Myths* (Academic Press Fribourg, 2009), pp. 33–53.

'The Constitutionalism of International Economic Law', in K. M. Meessen *et al.* (eds.), *Economic Law as an Economic Good: Its Rule Function and its Tool Function in the Competition of Systems* (Sellier de Gruyter, 2009), pp. 317–335.

'The Legitimacy of the WTO Law', in L. Yueh (ed.), *The Law and Economics of Globalisation: New Challenges for a World in Flux* (Edward Elgar, 2009), pp. 11–48.

Multi-layered Governance, Pluralism and Moral Conflict (2008) NCCR Working Paper, available at www.nccr-trade.org.

'Konstitutionalisierungsprobleme im internationalen Wirtschaftsrecht: verfassungsrechtliche Herausforderungen im Rahmen der WTO' (2005, Sonderheft) 50–62.

'The Impact from Without: International Law and the Structure of Federal Governance in Switzerland', in T. Cottier, P. Knoepfel and W. Linder (eds.), *Verwaltung, Regierung und Verfassung im Wandel: Gedächtnisschrift für Raimund E. Gernmann* (Helbing & Lichtenhahn, 2000), pp. 213–230.

Cottier, Thomas, Delimatsis, Panagiotis and Diebold, Nicolas, 'Article XIV GATS (General Exceptions), in R. Wolfrum, P.-T. Stoll and C. Feinäugle (eds.), *Max-Planck Commentaries on World Trade Law, Volume 6: WTO-Trade in Services* (Brill Publishers, 2008), pp. 287–328.

Cottier, Thomas and Hertig, Maya, 'The Prospects of 21st Century Constitutionalism' (2003) **7** *Max Planck Yearbook of United Nations Law* 261–328.

Davey, William J., 'Dispute Settlement in the WTO and RTAs: A Comment', in L. Bartels and F. Ortino (eds.), *Regional Trade Agreements and the WTO* (Oxford University Press, 2006), pp. 345–349.

Davey, William J. and Sapir, Andrew, 'The *Soft Drinks* Case: The WTO and Regional Agreements' (2009) **8**(1) *World Trade Review* 5–23.

Delimatsis, Panagiotis, 'Determining the Necessity of Domestic Regulations in Services – The Best is Yet to Come' (2008) **19**(2) *European Journal of International Law* 365–408.

International Trade in Services and Domestic Regulations – Necessity, Transparency, and Regulatory Diversity (Oxford University Press, 2007).

Doehring, Karl, 'Effectiveness', in R. Bernhard (ed.) *Encyclopaedia of Public International Law*, Instalment 7 (North-Holland Publ., 1984), pp. 70–74.

Donnelly, Catherine M., *Delegation of Governmental Power to Private Parties – A Comparative Perspective* (Oxford University Press, 2007).

Dupuy, Pierre-Marie, 'A Doctrinal Debate in the Globalization Era: On the "Fragmentation" of International Law' (2007) **1** *European Journal of Legal Studies*, available at: www.ejls.eu/1/4UK.pdf.

Dworkin, Ronald D., *Taking Rights Seriously* (Harvard University Press, 1977).

Elsig, Manfred, 'The World Trade Organization's Legitimacy Crisis: What Does the Beast Look Like?' (2007) **41**(1) *Journal of World Trade* 75–98.

Fassbender, Bardo, *The United Nations Charter as the Constitution of the International Community* (Martinus Nijhoff, 2009).

Fischer-Lescano, Andreas and Teubner, Gunther, 'Regime-Collisions: The Vain Search for Legal Unity in the Fragmentation of Global Law' (2004) **25** *Michigan Journal of International Law* 999–1046.

Forsthoff, Ernst, 'Die Umbildung des Verfassungsgesetzes', in H. Barion, E. Forsthoff and C. Schmitt (eds.), *Festschrift für Carl Schmitt zum 70. Geburtstag* (Duncker und Humblot, 1989), pp. 35–62.

Gehne, Katja, *Nachhaltige Entwicklung als Rechtsprinzip, normativer Aussagegehalt, rechtstheoretische Einordnung, Funktionen im Recht* (Mohr-Siebeck, 2010 (forthcoming)).

Göhring, Rebekka, 'Shaping the New Europe – Interest Representation in the European Union', D. Phil. dissertation, Otto-Suhr-Institut für Politikwissenschaft der Freien Universität Berlin, 2003.

Goldsmith, Jack L. and Posner, Eric A., *The Limits of International Law* (Oxford University Press, 2005).

Hafner, Gerhard, 'Pros and Cons Ensuing from Fragmentation of International Law' (2004) **25**(4) *Michigan Journal of International Law* 849–864.

'Risks Ensuing from Fragmentation of International Law', in Official Records of the General Assembly, Fifty-fifth Session, Supplement No. 10 (A/55/10), Annex, pp. 143–150, available at: http://untreaty.un.org/ilc/reports/2000/repfra.htm.

Hart, Herbert Lionel Adolphus, *The Concept of Law*, 2nd edn (Oxford University Press, 1997).

Henckels, Caroline, 'Overcoming Jurisdictional Isolationism at the WTO-FTA Nexus: A Potential Approach for the WTO' (2008) **19**(3) *European Journal of International Law* 571–599.

Higgins, Rosalyn, 'The ICJ, the ECJ and the Integrity of International Law' (2003) **52** *International and Comparative Law Quarterly* 1–20.

Higgins, Rosalyn, and Horn, Henrik, 'European Communities – Measures Affecting the Approval and Marketing of Biotech Products' (2009) **8**(1) *World Trade Review* 49–83.

Howse, Robert, 'From Politics to Technocracy – and Back Again: The Fate of the Multilateral Trading Regime' (2002) **96**(1) *American Journal of International Law* 94–177.

'The Legitimacy of the World Trade Organization', in J.-M. Coicaud & V. Heiskanen (eds.), *The Legitimacy of International Organizations* (United Nations University Press, 2001), pp. 355–407.

'Adjudicative Legitimacy and Treaty Interpretation in International Trade Law – The Early Years of WTO Jurisprudence', in J. Weiler (ed.), *The EU, the WTO and the NAFTA: Towards a Common Law of International Trade* (Oxford University Press, 2000), pp. 35–69.

Howse, Robert and Nicolaidis, Kalypso, 'Legitimacy through "Higher Law"? Why Constitutionalizing the WTO is a Step Too Far', in T. Cottier and P. C. Mavroidis (eds.), *The Role of the Judge in International Trade Regulation* (University of Michigan Press, 2006), pp. 307–348.

and Nicolaidis, Kalypso, 'Legitimacy and Global Governance: Why Constitutionalizing the WTO is a Step Too Far', in R. B. Porter *et al.* (eds.), *Efficiency, Equity, Legitimacy: The Multilateral Trading System at the Millennium* (Brookings Institution Press, 2001), pp. 227–252.

Huntington, Samuel P., *The Clash Of Civilizations and the Remaking Of World Order* (Touchstone Books, 1998).

Hurrell, Andrew, *On Global Order: Power, Values, and the Constitution of International Society* (Oxford University Press, 2007).

International Law Association, Rio de Janeiro Conference 2008, International Trade Law Committee.

Ipsen, Knut, *Völkerrecht* (Beck, 1990).

Jabloner, Clemens, 'Wie zeitgemäß ist die Reine Rechtslehre' (1998) **29**(1) *Rechtstheorie* 1–21.

Joerges, Christian, 'The Idea of a Three-Dimensional Conflicts Law as a Constitutional Form', in C. Joerges and E.-U. Petersmann (eds.), *Constitutionalism, Multilevel Trade Governance and Social Regulation*, 2nd edn (Hart Publishing, 2010).

Kelsen, Hans, *Reine Rechtslehre* (Verlag Österreich, 2000).

Allgemeine Theorie der Normen (Manz, 1979).
Principles of International Law (Holt Rinehart & Winston, 1967).
Peace Through Law (University of North Carolina Press, 1944).
Keohane, Robert, and Nye, Joseph S. Jr., *Power and Interdependence*, 3rd edn (Longman, 2001).
Kingsbury, Benedict, 'Foreword: Is the Proliferation of International Courts and Tribunals a Systemic Problem?' (1999) **31** *New York University Journal of International Law and Politics* 679–696.
Kingsbury, Benedict, Krisch, Nico and Stewart, Richard B., 'The Emergence of Global Administrative Law' (2005) Project Overview Article, available at: www.iilj.org/GAL/documents/TheEmergenceofGlobalAdministrativeLaw.pdf.
Koch, Hans-Joachim, 'Zur Methodenlehre des Rechtspositivismus' (1990) **37** *Archiv für Rechts- und Sozialphilosophie* 152–161.
Koskenniemi, Martti, 'The Politics of International Law – 20 Years Later' (2009) **20**(1) *European Journal of International Law* 7–19.
'Fragmentation of International Law: Difficulties Arising from the Diversification and Expansion of International Law', Report of the Study Group of the International Law Commission, United Nations, International Law Commission, A/CN.4/L.682.
Koskenniemi, Martti and Leino, Päivi, 'Fragmentation of International Law? Postmodern Anxieties' (2002) **15** *Leiden Journal of International Law* 553–579.
Krajewski, Markus, *Verfassungsperspektiven und Legitimation des Rechts der Welthandelsorganisation (WTO)* (Duncker und Humblot, 2001).
'Democratic Legitimacy and Constitutional Perspectives of WTO Law' (2001) **35**(1) *Journal of World Trade* 167–186.
Krasner, Stephen D., 'Compromising Westphalia', in D. Held and A. McGrew (eds.), *The Global Transformations Reader: An Introduction to the Globalization Debate*, 3rd edn (Cambridge University Press, 2002), pp. 124–135.
Krieger, Heike, *Das Effektivitätsprinzip im Völkerrecht* (Duncker & Humblot, 2000).
Kwak, Kyung and Marceau, Gabrielle, 'Overlaps and Conflicts of Jurisdiction between the World Trade Organization and Regional Trade Agreements', in L. Bartels and F. Ortino (eds.), *Regional Trade Agreements and the WTO* (Oxford University Press, 2006), pp. 469–470.
Lennard, Michael, 'Navigating by the Stars: Interpreting the WTO Agreements' (2002) **5** *Journal of International Economic Law* 17–89.
Lindroos, Anja, 'Addressing Norm Conflicts in a Fragmented Legal System: The Doctrine of *Lex Specialis*' (2005) **74** *Nordic Journal of International Law* 27–66.
MacCormick, Neil, *Legal Reasoning and Legal Theory* (Clarendon Press, 1978).

Marceau, Gabrielle, 'Fragmentation in International Law: The Relationship Between WTO Law and General International Law – A Few Comments from a WTO Perspective' (2006) **17** *Finnish Yearbook of International Law* 31–47.

'WTO Dispute Settlement and Human Rights' (2002) **13**(4) *European Journal of International Law* 753–814.

'A Call for Coherence in International Law' (1999) **33**(5) *Journal of World Trade* 87–152.

Matz-Lück, Nele, 'Promoting the Unity of International Law: Standard-Setting by International Tribunals', in D. König, P.-T. Stoll, V. Röben and N. Matz-Lück (eds.), *International Law Today: New Challenges and the Need for Reform?* (Springer, 2008), pp. 99–121.

Wege zur Koordinierung völkerrechtlicher Verträge (Springer, 2005).

Mavroidis, Petros C., 'No Outsourcing of Law? WTO Law as Practiced by WTO Courts' (2008) **102**(3) *American Journal of International Law* 421–474.

McRae, Donald M., 'The WTO in International Law: Tradition Continued or New Frontier?' (2000) **3**(1) *Journal of International Economic Law* 27–41.

McGrady, Benn, 'Fragmentation of International Law or "Systemic Integration" of Treaty Regimes: EC – Biotech Products and the Proper Interpretation of Article 31(3)(c) of the Vienna Convention on the Law of Treaties' (2008) **42** (4) *Journal of World Trade* 589–618.

Miller, Nathan, 'An International Jurisprudence? The Operation of "Precedent" across International Tribunals' (2002) *Leiden Journal of International Law* 483–526.

Mitchell, Andrew D., *Legal Principles in WTO Disputes* (Cambridge University Press, 2008).

Möllers, Christoph, *Die drei Gewalten* (Velbrück, 2008).

Muchlinski, Peter, '"Global Bukowina" Examined: Viewing the Multinational Enterprise as a Transnational Law-making Community', in G. Teubner (ed.), *Gobal Law Without A State* (Dartmouth Publishing, 1997), pp. 79–107.

Nanz, Patrizia, 'Democratic Legitimacy of Transnational Trade Governance: A View from Political Theory', in C. Joerges and E.-U. Petersmann (eds.), *Constitutionalism, Multilevel Trade Governance and Social Regulation* (Hart Publishing, 2006), pp. 59–82.

Neumann, Manfred J. M., *Die Koordination des WTO-Rechts mit anderen völkerrechtlichen Ordnungen: Konflikte des materiellen Rechts und Konkurrenzen der Streitbeilegung* (Duncker & Humblot, 2002).

Palmeter, David N. and Mavroidis, Petros C., *Dispute Settlement in the World Trade Organization – Practice and Procedure*, 2nd edn (Cambridge University Press, 2004).

Panizzon, Marion, *Good Faith in the Jurisprudence of the WTO* (Hart Publishing, 2006).

Pauwelyn, Joost, *Fragmentation of International Law*, Max Planck Encyclopedia of Public International Law (Oxford University Press, 2008), available at: www.mpepil.com/subscriber_article?id=/epil/entries/law-9780199231690-e1406.

'Adding Sweeteners to Softwood Lumber: The WTO–NAFTA "Spaghetti Bowl" is Cooking' (2007) **9**(1) *Journal of International Economic Law* 197–203.

'Bridging Fragmentation and Unity: International Law as a Universe of Inter-connected Islands' (2004) **25** *Michigan Journal of International Law* 903–916.

Conflict of Norms in Public International Law: How WTO Law Relates to Other Rules of International Law (Cambridge University Press, 2003).

'The Role of Public International Law in the WTO: How Far Can We Go?' (2001) **95** *American Journal of International Law* 535–578.

Pavlakos, George and Pauwelyn, Joost, 'Principled Monism and the Normative Conception of Coercion under International Law: From a Hierarchy of Norms to a Competition of Values', in P. Koutrakos *et al.* (eds.), *Beyond the Established Legal Orders* (Hart Publishing, forthcoming).

Peters, Anne, 'Membership in the Global Constitutional Community', in J. Klabbers, A. Peters and G. Ulfstein, *The Constitutionalization of International Law* (Oxford University Press, 2009), pp. 153–261.

'Die Zukunft der Völkerrechtswissenschaft: Wider den epistemischen Nationalismus' (2007) **67** *Zeitschrift für ausländisches öffentliches Recht und Völkerrecht* 721–776.

'The Constitutionalist Reconstruction of International Law: Pros and Cons', National Centre of Competence in Research (NCCR) Workshop, 'Compensatory Constitutionalism: Opportunities and Impediments', Hotel Bernerhof Kandersteg, 12.01.2007.

'Compensatory Constitutionalism: The Function and Potential of Fundamental International Norms and Structures' (2006) **19** *Leiden Journal of International Law* 579–610.

Petersmann, Ernst-Ulrich, 'Limits of WTO Jurisprudence: Comments from an International Law and Human Rights Perspective', in T. Cottier and P. C. Mavroidis (eds.), *The Role of the Judge in International Trade Regulation* (University of Michigan Press, 2006), pp. 81–87.

'Justice as Conflict Resolution: Proliferation, Fragmentation, and Decentralization of Dispute Settlement in International Trade' (2006) **27** *University of Pennsylvania Journal of International Economic Law* 273–366.

'Addressing Institutional Challenges to the WTO in the New Millennium: A Long-Term Perspective' (2005) **8** *Journal of International Economic Law* 647–665.

'Human Rights and the Law of the World Trade Organization' (2003) **37** *Journal of World Trade* 241–281.

'Human Rights and International Economic Law in the 21st Century' (2001) **4**(1) *Journal of International Economic Law* 3–39.

'The WTO Constitution and Human Rights' (2000) **3**(1) *Journal of International Economic Law* 19–25.

'National Constitutions, Foreign Trade and European Community Law' (1992) **3** *European Journal of International Law* 1–36.

Popper, Karl Raimund, *Das Elend des Historizismus* (Mohr Siebeck, 2003).

Rawls, John, *The Law of Peoples with 'The Idea of Public Reasons Revisited'* (Harvard University Press, 1999).

Raz, Joseph, 'The Relevance of Coherence' (1992) **72** *Boston University Law Review* 273–321.

Roessler, Frieder, 'Comment: Mexico – Tax Measures on Soft Drinks and Other Beverages' (2009) **8**(1) *World Trade Review* 25–30.

Scharpf, Fritz W., *Governing the European Union, Effective and Democratic?* (Oxford University Press, 1999).

Shany, Yuval, 'Similarity in the Eye of the Beholder: Revisiting the Application of Rules Governing Jurisdictional Conflicts in the Lauder/CME cases', in A. Rovine (ed.), *Contemporary Issues in International Arbitration and Mediation* (Martinus Nijhoff, 2008), pp. 119–138.

The Competing Jurisdiction of International Courts and Tribunals (Oxford University Press, 2003).

Sieckmann, Jan-Reinard, *Regelmodelle und Prinizpienmodelle des Rechtssystem*, Studien zur Rechtsphilosophie und Rechtstheorie, vol. 1 (Nomos, 1990).

Simma, Bruno, 'Universality of International Law from the Perspective of a Practitioner' (2009) **20**(2) *European Journal of International Law* 265–297.

Simma, Bruno and Pulkowski, Dirk, 'Of Planets and the Universe: Self-Contained Regimes in International Law' (2006) **17**(3) *The European Journal of International Law* 483–529.

Slaughter, Anne-Marie, 'A Global Community of Courts' (2003) **44** *Harvard International Law Journal* 191–219.

Spruyt, Hendrik, *The Sovereign State and its Competitors* (Princeton University Press, 1994).

Stewart, Richard B. and Ratton Sanchez Badin, Michelle, 'The World Trade Organization and Global Administrative Law' (2009) *New York University Public Law and Legal Theory Working Papers No. 09–71* 1–30.

Stoll, Peter-Tobias, 'Freihandel und Verfassung. Einzelstaatliche Gewährleistung und die konstitutionelle Funktion der Welthandelsordnung (GATT/WTO)' (1997) **57** *Zeitschrift für ausländisches öffentliches Recht und Völkerrecht* 83–146.

Teubner, Gunther, 'Societal Constitutionalism: Alternatives to State Centered Constitutional Theory?', in C. Joerges, I.-J. Sand and G. Teubner (eds.), *Transnational Governance and Constitutionalism* (Hart Publishing, 2004), pp. 3–28.

'Global Bukowina: Legal Pluralism in the World Society', in G. Teubner (ed.), *Global Law Without a State* (Dartmouth, 1997), pp. 3–28.

Teubner, Gunther, and Korth, Peter, 'Two Kinds of Legal Pluralism: Collision of Laws in the Double Fragmentation of World Society', in M. Young (ed.), *Regime Interaction in International Law: Theoretical and Practical Challenges* (forthcoming).

Touscoz, Jean, *Le Principe d'effectivité dans l'ordre international* (R. Pichon et R. Durand-Auzias, 1964).

Trachtman, Joel P., *The Economic Structure of International Law* (Harvard University Press, 2008).

'The World Trading System, the International Legal System and Multilevel Choice' (2006) **12**(4) *European Law Journal* 469–485.

'Institutional Linkage: Transcending "Trade and . . . "' (2002) **96**(1) *American Journal of International Law* 77–93.

'The Domain of WTO Dispute Resolution' (1999) **40** *Harvard International Law Journal* 333–376.

de Vattel, Emer, *Le droit des gens ou principes de la loi naturelle appliqués à la conduite et aux affaires des Nations et des Souverains*, Book I (Paris, 1758, repr. 1916).

de Visscher, Charles, *Les effectivités du droit international public* (Editions A. Pedone, 1967).

Whitman, Jim, *The Limits of Global Governance* (Routledge, 2005).

Wolfrum, Rüdiger, 'Konkurrierende Zuständigkeiten internationaler Streitentscheidungsinstanzen: Notwendigkeit für Lösungsmöglichkeiten und deren Grenzen', in N. Ando, E. McWhinney and R. Wolfrum (eds.), *Liber Amicorum Judge Shigeru Oda*, Vol. **1** (Kluwer, 2002), pp. 651–663.

Wolfrum, Rüdiger and Matz, Nele, *Conflicts in International Environmental Law* (Springer, 2003).

PART I

Constitutional issues in international trade regulation

1

The constitutionalisation of international trade law

KLAUS ARMINGEON, KAROLINA MILEWICZ, SIMONE PETER AND ANNE PETERS*

KEY MESSAGES

- Empirical research lends support to the idea of a 'multi-speed globe' of differentiated (fragmented) constitutionalisation, rather than a fully-fledged integrative constitutional process. 'Variable geometry' on the global scale could acknowledge irreconcilable differences between nation states.
- A prominent candidate for one fragment of this variable global constitutionalisation is the World Trade Organization (WTO). Constitutionalisation of the WTO means an evolution from constitution to constitutionalism within this organisation.
- A core constitutional issue is the public interest. The concept of 'public interest' can be used in various ways. Exception and limitation clauses play an important role in the constitutionalist reconstruction of international law.
- The WTO is so far only modestly constitutionalised, but could and should be further constitutionalised. Further constitutionalisation of the WTO should comprise the following reforms: upgrading non-trade concerns such as the environment in the treaty language itself, liberalisation in trade sectors in which poor countries can compete, empowerment of individuals by enabling at least indirect participation in secondary law-making (parliamentary dimension) and dispute settlement (direct effect), streamlining of the decision-making and law-making processes by reviving the legally available options for majority voting and judicial review of WTO acts.

A. Introduction

Over the past sixty years, international law has developed from a narrow system of inter-state norms of coexistence into a broader and organised system of cooperation. One of the most essential developments has

* Individual Project No. 1, 'Constitutionalism and multilayered governance'.

been the growing number of multilateral treaties designed not only to set in place legal frameworks but also to promote cooperation in an interdependent world. This growing network of treaties has opened up non-traditional spheres of international law, touching on nearly all aspects of life of contemporary society. And as international law has developed in scope, new actors have been accepted as international legal persons on the international scene.

In recent years, the developments in international law have gained new momentum in the debate on global constitutionalisation. 'Constitutionalisation' is a shorthand term both for the emergence of constitutional law within a given legal order and for the spread of constitutionalism as a mindset. The concept of constitutionalisation implies that a specific type of constitution (or constitutional law), namely a *constitutionalist* constitution, can come into being and develop over time. It also implies that a legal text (or various legal texts) can acquire (or eventually lose) constitutional properties in a positive feedback process. A text can be more (or less) constitution-like and more or less constitutionalist. It may be, in short, a constitution-in-the-making. Also, constitutionalisation is multifactorial. The emerging constitutional profile of the international order might be well developed in one or more areas or even special branches of law, but underdeveloped in others. So the process of global constitutionalisation is not all-encompassing. It is contingent and path-dependent. Patterns of coexistence and cooperation persist even in a generally more constitutionalised world order.

The concept of global constitutionalisation has been mainly studied from a normative angle.[1] First empirical evidence[2] points to the fact that the macro-process of the constitutionalisation of international law does indeed comprise subprocesses of micro-constitutionalisation. Milewicz and colleagues,[3] studying state commitment to so-called *quasi-constitutional* multilateral treaties made between 1945 and 2007 and containing institutional and organisational guidelines for inter-state relations and fundamental human rights provisions for individuals, provide

1 See J. Klabbers, A. Peters and G. Ulfstein, *The Constitutionalization of International Law* (Oxford University Press 2009). See for the different perceptions of constitutionalisation, T. Cottier and M. Hertig, 'The Prospects of 21st Century Constitutionalism' (2003) 7 *Max Planck Yearbook of United Nations Law* 261.

2 A first empirical attempt at the analysis of global constitutionalisation has been made by K. Armingeon and K. Milewicz, 'Compensatory constitutionalisation: A comparative perspective' (2008) 22 *Global Society* 179.

3 K. Milewicz, A. Bächtiger and A. Nothdurft 'Constitutional pluralism or constitutional unity? An empirical study of international commitment (1945–2007)' (2010) 36 *Review of International Studies* 305–336.

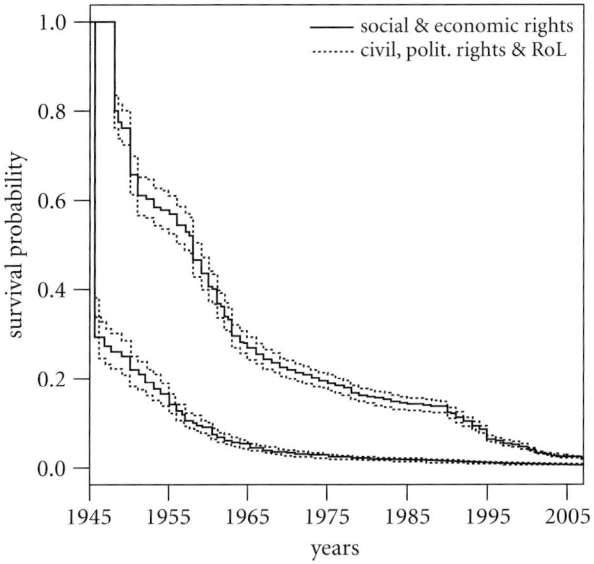

Figure 1.1 Ratification of quasi-constitutional multilateral treaties according to two issue-areas: (1) socio-economic treaties and (2) civil-political and 'rule of law' (RoL) multilateral treaties. *Note:* Survival probability refers to the probability that a state does not ratify a group of treaties.

grounds for the idea of a 'multi-speed globe' of differentiated micro-constitutionalisation, rather than a fully-fledged integrative macro-constitutional process (see Figure 1.1).

Against this background, the present chapter focuses on the development of one sectoral constitution beyond the nation state, in particular within WTO law. The evolution of WTO law presumably constitutes, besides that of the EU, a prominent, but controversial case of micro-constitutionalisation.[4] We begin with a clarification of key concepts. We then discuss the most important aspects of the constitutionalisation of the WTO, notably the problem of democracy. We then focus on one particular aspect of WTO constitutionalism, namely the 'public interest' in WTO law. We argue that exception clauses in international law reflect the tensions between national concerns and international goals. From the point of view of global constitutionalisation these clauses reflect national public interest. We conclude that so far the WTO is only a modestly constitutionalised entity, but should and could be constitutionalised further.

4 See T. Cottier and M. Oesch, *International Trade Regulation: Law and Policy in the WTO, The European Union and Switzerland: Cases, Materials and Comments* (Bern: Staempfli, 2005), Part Two 'Constitutional Principles of the WTO', pp. 346–574.

B. Key concepts and methdodological problems

A constitutionalist vision of the WTO not only considers the world trade regime to have a constitution, but also to possess a constitutionalist constitution-in-the-making. This vision moves significantly beyond the older view that the founding acts of international organisations are 'constitutions'. For instance, long before the creation of the WTO, John Jackson had contemplated the 'constitutional structure of a possible international trade institution'.[5] This vocabulary is in line with the International Court of Justice (ICJ)'s view that '[f]rom a formal standpoint, the constituent instruments of international organisations are multilateral treaties . . . Such treaties can raise specific problems of interpretation owing, *inter alia*, to their character which is conventional and at the same time institutional.'[6] So the founding documents of international organisations have a hybrid character as treaty-constitution.[7]

This more traditional reading of the international organisations' founding documents did not rely on any material, value-laden (constitutionalist) principles, such as the rule of law or fundamental rights, but merely on the fact that the founding treaties established institutional structures, delineated the competences of the organisation, defined the terms of membership and the relations between the members and the organisation, regulated the organisations' core functions of law-making, conflict resolution and law enforcement, and laid down rules for the amendment of the founding treaties themselves. The doctrinal merit of this understanding of the law of international organisations was to

5 J. H. Jackson, *World Trade Law and the Law of GATT*, ch. 30: 4 'The constitutional structure of a possible international trade institution' (Bobbs Merrill, Indianapolis, 1969), pp. 780–785.

6 *Legality of the Use by a State of Nuclear Weapons in Armed Conflict, Advisory Opinion*, ICJ Reports 1996, pp. 66 *et seq.*, para. 19. See in the same sense ECJ, opinion 1/91, *EEC*, ECR 1991-I, 6079, 6102, para. 21. In scholarship notably R. Monaco, 'Le caractère constitutionnel des actes institutifs d'organisations internationales', in *Mélanges offerts à Charles Rousseau: La communauté internationale* (Paris: Pédone, 1974), p. 154, emphasis added.

7 This view has not been accepted by the Appellate Body. See AB, *Japan – Taxes on Alcoholic Beverages* (4 October 1996) WT/DS8/AB/R, WT/DS10/AB/R, WT/DS11/AB/R, p. 15: 'The WTO Agreement is a treaty – the international equivalent of a contract. It is self-evident that in an exercise of their sovereignty, and in pursuit of their own respective national interests, the Members of the WTO have made a bargain. In exchange for benefits they expect to derive as Members of the WTO, they have agreed to exercise their sovereignty according to the commitment they have made in the WTO Agremeent.'

overcome the outdated dichotomy between contract and constitution.[8] But the constitutional view did not introduce a *constitutionalist* approach to the law of international organisations.

A constitutionalist approach – by contrast – seeks to identify and to advocate the application of constitutionalist principles, such as non-discrimination, transparency, the rule of law, checks and balances, human rights protection, and possibly also democracy, to WTO law to improve the effectiveness and the fairness of the international trade order. So global constitutionalism, as applied to the WTO, has both descriptive and prescriptive elements.

We use 'WTO-constitutionalisation' as a shorthand term both for the gradual acquisition of constitutional and constitutionalist features (which overlays, but does not erase the character of the WTO-agreements as international treaties) and for the spread of constitutionalism as a mindset in analysing the WTO regime.

The academic objective of WTO constitutionalism is to identify the constitutional predispositions and indices in WTO law, to encourage reflection on how the process of WTO constitutionalisation might be broadened and intensified, and, in doing so, help to vindicate claims to a more constitutionalised world trade order. It not only purports to analyse the *lex lata*, but also to argue *de lege ferenda*.

This agenda faces objections. The first is that WTO constitutionalism is too apolitical or pretends to be above politics and seeks to place economic freedoms above politics.[9] The constitutionalist reading might be a scholarly attempt to channel or minimise politics. This is what Jeffrey Dunoff has aptly called 'constitutional conceits'.[10] Our response is that law and politics should not be viewed as distinct realms, but rather as structurally coupled systems. In particular, constitutional law and politics are mutually constitutive. In consequence, constitutionalism is *also* political, not simply 'an antidote to trade politics'[11] (although it does

8 See on this dichotomy and its relevance for the debate on the legal nature of the EU Treaties, A. Peters, 'The Constitutionalisation of the European Union – Without the Constitutional Treaty', in S. Puntscher Riekmann and W. Wessels (eds.), *The Making of a European Constitution* (Wiesbaden: VS Verlag für Sozialwissenschaften, 2006), pp. 35–67.

9 R. Howse and K. Nicolaidis, 'Enhancing WTO legitimacy: Constitutionalization or global subsidiarity' (2003) 16 *Governance* 75; J. P. Trachtman, 'The constitutions of the WTO' (2006) 17 *European Journal of International Law* 623.

10 J. Dunoff, 'Constitutional conceits: The WTO's "Constitution" and the discipline of international law' (2006) 17 *European Journal of International Law* 649, pp. 661–665 and p. 672.

11 Dunoff, above note 10, p. 661.

suggest that there is a sphere 'above' everyday politics). Paradoxically, but in our mind laudably, the call for constitutionalism triggers precisely the contestation and politics it is said to pre-empt. The evolutionary dynamics of constitutionalism lead both to the legalisation of trade politics and to a stronger politicisation of trade law. Even if any legalisation of political problems (counting constitutionalisation as a special type of legalisation) modifies the debate surrounding these problems by introducing a different, juridical logic, the underlying issues are only partly depoliticised. Such a relative depoliticisation of international trade relations is not a disadvantage, but a plus. The introduction of legal and even constitutional principles contributes to the stability of expectations, legal certainty and equal treatment of the relevant actors (WTO Members and economic enterprises).

Both proponents and critics of the constitutionalist reading of WTO law agree that the turn towards constitutionalism is to some extent an effort to find a legitimating principle for a system that faces a legitimacy gap: the WTO limits governmental policies without finding sufficient acceptance by the populations affected.[12] However, as a response to the WTO's legitimacy crisis, constitutionalism might be fallacious.[13] Is it only a rhetorical strategy to invest international trade law with the power and authority that domestic constitutional structures and norms possess?[14] Does the constitutionalisation discourse serve to close the door against claims that the WTO has gone too far? If this were the case, the reification of the WTO would indeed backfire. It would only exacerbate the legitimacy crisis or stifle appropriate responses to it. It would also fuel the discontents of globalisation if it simply translated economic liberalism into higher law – irreversible, irresistible and comprehensive.[15]

However, the intrinsic link between constitutionalism and legitimacy works in many ways. Constitutionalism may legitimise the international trade system, but it may also challenge its legitimacy. On the one hand, the danger is that 'things formerly called institutional are being legitimized with the mantle of constitutionalization'.[16] This is unhelpful in analytical

12 See M. Elsig, 'The World Trade Organization's legitimacy crisis: What does the beast look like?' (2007) 41 *Journal of World Trade* 75; D. C. Esty, 'The World Trade Organization's legitimacy crisis' (2002) 1 *World Trade Review* 7; also R. Howse, 'The legitimacy of the World Trade Organization', in J. M. Coicaud and V. Heiskanen (eds.), *The Legitimacy of International Organizations* (Tokyo: United Nations University Press, 2001), pp. 355–407.

13 Howse and Nicolaidis, above note 9, p. 74 and p. 80.

14 Dunoff, above note 10, p. 649.

15 Howse and Nicolaidis, above note 9, esp. p. 74.

16 D. Z. Cass, *Constitutionalization of the WTO* (Oxford University Press, 2005), p. 245.

terms and dangerous from a normative perspective. WTO constitutionalism should not be used apologetically to bestow false legitimacy on international trade law. Nor should the complaint of a lack of legitimacy in international trade law undermine the authority of the WTO. Rather, WTO constitutionalism should and could help rather than hinder the revelation of existing legitimacy deficiencies in world trade law without throwing the baby out with the bath water. There is, as Neil Walker put it, a 'responsibilising' potential in the constitutional discourse and imagination in the development of a polity.[17] Those who wish, for whatever motives, to make a plausible claim to constitutional elements in WTO law, must at least be seen to take these values seriously. So although constitutionalism may be invoked as a way of closing the debate, in practice it often has the opposite effect, namely that of opening up a richer and more productive normative debate. The reason is that the tradition of constitutionalism remains the best-stocked reservoir from which responsible politics may draw and the most persuasive medium in which these politics may be articulated.[18] So WTO constitutionalism deploys, and this is what we deem crucial, a constructive, not an obstructive, critical potential.

C. How far has the WTO been constitutionalised to date?

I. Constitutional principles constraining Members

One indicator and promoter of micro-constitutionalisation is the constitutional rights and principles. Historically, the General Agreement on Tariffs and Trade (GATT) was established on the ground that policies made in one country often adversely affect people in other countries who, in the absence of any institutional framework, have no ability to influence those policies. GATT was supposed to provide a forum in which one member could challenge the protectionist policies of another member.[19] Such protectionist policies are widely seen to result from an undue influence of rent-seeking groups whose lobbyism is apt to damage the domestic democratic processes. Against this background, the WTO's core function is to

17 N. Walker, 'The EU and the WTO: Constitutionalism in a new key', in G. de Burca and J. Scott (eds.), *The EU and the WTO: Legal and Constitutional Issues* (Oxford: Hart, 2001), pp. 53–54.

18 Walker, above note 17, p. 57.

19 P. M. Gerhart, 'The WTO and participatory democracy: The historical evidence' (2004) 37 *Vanderbilt Journal of Transnational Law* 897, p. 933.

neutralise the domestic power of protectionist interests, and the WTO Members have thereby enabled themselves to overcome deficiencies in domestic political processes.[20] This is a typically constitutional function, which is in the domestic realm served by fundamental rights guarantees and by judicial protection through constitutional courts.

In the current WTO, the traditional trade law principles of most-favoured nation and national treatment operate against state failure in the form of protectionism. These principles are constitutive of the system of multilayered governance and thus may be considered as amounting to constitutional principles of the trading system.[21] They constrain the WTO Members and are increasingly viewed as two facets of a constitutional principle of non-discrimination ultimately benefiting the ordinary citizens (such as importers, exporters, producers, consumers and taxpayers).[22] Likewise, the transparency obligations imposed on the WTO Members by provisions such as Article X GATT and Articles III and VI General Agreement on Trade in Services (GATS) also seeek to prevent illegitimate protectionism and to that extent serve a constitutional function.[23]

However, these constitutional principles cannot be enforced by private actors. Although private operators currently have the possibility to influence WTO-related negotiations and also participate informally in WTO dispute settlement,[24] they have no formal legal standing in this regard. Second, private actors are not able to enforce WTO rules in domestic courts, because most domestic courts, the European courts, and a WTO panel reject a direct effect of GATT.[25] Most importantly, that panel

20 J. McGinnis and M. Movsesian, 'The World Trade Constitution' (2000) 114 *Harvard Law Review* 521.

21 Cottier and Oesch, *International Trade Regulation*, above note 4, p. 346.

22 See E.-U. Petersmann, 'Multilevel judicial governance of international trade requires a common conception of rule of law and justice' (2007) 10 *Journal of International Economic Law* 533: 'the WTO guarantees of freedom, non-discrimination and rule of law – by enhancing individual liberty, non-discriminatory treatment, economic welfare, and poverty reduction across frontiers – reflect, albeit imperfectly, basic principles of justice.'

23 P. Delimatsis, *International Trade in Services and Domestic Regulations: Necessity, Transparency, and Regulatory Diversity* (Oxford University Press, 2007).

24 For example the WTO dispute raised by the USA against Japan concerning photographic film and paper has for this reason been perceived as a '*Kodak v Fuji*' dispute: Panel, *Japan – Measures Affecting Consumer Photographic Film and Paper* (31 March 1998) WT/DS44/R. See G. Shaffer, *Defending Interests: Public-Private Partnerships in WTO-Litigation* (Washington, DC: Brookings Institution Press, 2003).

25 Panel, *US – Section 301–310 of the Trade Act of 1974* (27 January 2000) WT/DS152/R (not appealed) para. 7.72: 'Neither the GATT nor the WTO has so far been interpreted by

deliberately distinguished the WTO regime from the EU and the *van Gend & Loos* conception of an autonomous legal order by highlighting that 'the GATT/WTO did *not* create a new legal order the subjects of which comprise both contracting parties or members and their nationals.'[26]

A different aspect of WTO rights-based constitutionalism is the suggestion to integrate human rights concerns into world trade law, not only through the interpretation of existing agreements, but also through the building of new common institutions.[27] In fact, a constitutionalist approach is apt to provide a vocabulary, a theory and institutional building blocks to satisfy the quest for coherence between trade law and human rights law. The rights-based constitutionalist school submits that human rights have become guiding principles of international economic law.[28] Proponents suggest endorsing a general maxim of interpretation of the GATT obligations of WTO Members (and the relevant exception clauses) in the light of human rights guarantees.[29]

The rights-based constitutionalist reading of WTO law has (to some extent erroneously) been perceived as narrow. It has been criticised for marginalising social rights and environmental principles and for focusing on economic and property rights. Early constitutionalist scholarship was therefore criticised as masking a radically economically libertarian free-trade agenda. In fact, the old GATT law neglected social and environmental issues and was geared towards negative integration by eliminating trade barriers. Today, the Agreement on Trade-related Aspects of Intellectual Property Rights (TRIPS), Article VI GATS, the Agreement on Technical Barriers to Trade (TBT Agreement) and the Agreement on the Application of Sanitary and Phytosanitary Measures (SPS Agreement), the Antidumping Agreement and the Agreement on Agriculture seek to achieve positive integration through common standards, even if very few of these standards marginally relate to the environment, and hardly relate at all to social aspects.

GATT/WTO institutions as a legal order producing direct effect [i.e. as creating enforceable rights and obligations for individuals].' It would be better to speak of an 'indirect effect' of GATT (para. 7.78). See also CFI, case T-174/00, *Biret International SA* v. *Council*, ECT 2002 II-17, para. 62.

26 Panel, *US – Section 301*, above note 25, para. 7.72.

27 T. Cottier, 'Trade and human rights: A relationship to discover' (2002) 5 *Journal of International Economic Law* 111.

28 Cottier and Oesch, *International Trade Regulation*, above note 4, p. 513.

29 E.-U. Petersmann, 'Time for a United Nations "Global Compact" for integrating human rights into the law of worldwide organizations: Lessons from European integration' (2002) 13 *European Journal of International Law* 621, pp. 645–46.

In defence of constitutionalism, it can be claimed that the constitutionalist reading of WTO law precisely supports the quest for the adoption of such standards. Moreover, trade liberalisation normally triggers a demand for positive integration. However, the WTO, in contrast to the EU, currently lacks the institutions and means to complement the ongoing negative integration with positive integration.[30] Also, a large part of the membership opposes the WTO having any social agenda. And unlike the EU, the WTO does not have decision-making structures that easily allow for variable geometry. To conclude, the 'constitutional' WTO principles addressed towards the WTO Members seem – for the time being – to be too incomplete to confirm the descriptive claim that the WTO has been constitutionalised along these lines.

II. Democracy

The democratisation of international organisations is a key element of their constitutionalisation.[31] Føllesdal argued 'that we find it conceptually difficult to disentangle legitimacy and democracy: legitimate modes of governance *must* be democratically accountable.' Only democratic systems that advocate the values of liberty and equality deserve the loyalty of their enlightened citizens in modern societies.[32] This is not necessarily applicable to the large number of pre-modern societies, which do not support these values. However, if a global constitutional order needs legitimisation by the citizens in the economically most advanced nation states, only democratic rules pertaining to participation (government of and by the people) and to policy outputs in the common interest of the people (government for the people) may create this legitimacy.

By implication, a global constitutional order needs a democratic decision-making system for producing and developing global constitutional norms, both in general international law and in specific regimes such as that of the WTO. However, as convincingly argued by Michael Zürn,[33] power and resource imbalances impede a system of equal rights

30 Howse and Nicolaidis, above note 9, pp. 84–5.

31 Markus Krajewski, 'International organizations or institutions, democratic legitimacy', *Max Planck Encyclopedia of International Law* (2009), para. 25.

32 A. Føllesdal, 'When "common interests" are not common: Why the "global basic structure" should be democratic' (2009) 16 *Indiana Journal of Global Legal Studies* 585–604.

33 M. Zürn, 'Institutionalisierte Ungleichheit in der Weltpolitik: Jenseits der Alternativen "Global Governance" versus "American Empire"' (2007) 48 *Politische Vierteljahresschrift* 680.

in this constitutional order. There are no such rules as 'one individual – one vote' or 'one nation state – one vote'. It is entirely unclear how preferences of states and preferences of individual citizens have to be aggregated. It is also unclear whether all states should have the same rights and powers. Some nation states have more duties and rights than others. They have different levels of influence on rule formation. They are treated differently. Cases in point are the veto rights of the five permanent members in the UN Security Council; privileges of the US with regard to the International Criminal Court;[34] weighted voting rights in the World Bank; the different risks of nuclear powers compared to other nations with regard to UN interventions; and the fuzziness of procedural rules on the international level and diffuse distributions of competencies among international organisations, allowing for opportunistic behaviour by nation states. Strong nation states have the opportunity of picking the international organisation and the sets of constitutional rules that are most compatible with domestic interests. The global constitution is still basically biased in favour of the most powerful countries, and in particular of the US. In this context Ulrich K. Preuss argued that the principle of sovereign equality of all states may be the first victim of the constitutionalisation of international law.[35]

In conclusion, there is so far no efficient global democratic system concerned with the further development of global norms and the control of their implementation. Even worse, there are no convincing ideas of how such a democratic system – which has to honour the democratic principles on the regional, the national and the international levels and its interactions – could and should look like. Hopes for a deliberative democracy depend on the absence of distributive conflicts and value conflicts – which is hardly realistic. Hopes for a new democracy, which are built on non-governmental organisations as agents and representatives of the people, depend on some democratic accountability of and equality of access to these organisations. At the moment there are no strong empirical arguments suggesting that this may be the case. Hence there is no convincing idea of what a workable and legitimate international democratic system should look like and which rights and powers should be allocated to individuals, regions, private organisations and nation states. On the

34 UNSC Res 1422 (12 July 2002) UN Doc S/RES/1422 and UNSC Res 1487 (12 June 2003) UN Doc S/RES/1487.

35 U. K. Preuss, 'Equality of states – Its meaning in a constitutionalized global order' (2008) 9 *Chicago Journal of International Law* 17.

international level, there may be increasing changes in favour of the rule of the law, but few changes in favour of a combination of rule of law and democracy.

But what is the state of democratisation of the WTO? Here rules and decisions are made following procedures which do not include democratic elements in any meaningful sense. It has therefore been argued that, because of its inherent lack of democratic legitimacy, WTO law cannot serve constitutional functions.[36] The WTO law-making processes can be called democratic only in a transitive way, to the extent that the democratic Members' representatives enjoy a democratic mandate and the domestic parliaments have approved the treaties. However, this type of transitive democratic legitimacy is rather weak, inter alia because not all WTO Members are democracies, and because in those that are democracies the role of parliament is basically limited to an affirmation of treaties concluded by the executives.[37]

III. Rule of law: constitutional principles constraining the WTO

Constitutionalists point out that the WTO itself is based on the rule of law, not only in terms of substance, but also in terms of procedure. While negotiations still largely follow politics and diplomatic traditions, the Dispute Settlement Understanding (DSU) provides for fair procedures in the administration of justice.[38] However, the substantial rules and the dispute settlement procedures currently only work to subject the Members, not the WTO as an organisation, to the rule of law. A more developed rule of law requires that *the WTO itself* is bound by certain principles. Only then are the organisation's powers constitutionally limited. And to be effective, these constitutional limits must be enforceable. The acts of the organisation itself must be subject to judicial review, either by international or by domestic courts. Currently, only the EU possesses this – in our view – crucial constitutionalist feature. The ECJ and the Court of First Instance (CFI) are competent to control the legality of the acts of the organs and institutions themselves. Fully fledged guarantees of human rights infringements by EU acts have been only gradually granted

36 M. Krajewski, 'Democratic legitimacy and constitutional perspectives of WTO law' (2001) 35 *Journal of World Trade* 167.

37 See for the problems of a transitive democratic legitimacy of global governance, A. Peters, 'Dual Democracy', in J. Klabbers, A. Peters, and G. Ulfstein, *The Constitutionalization of International Law* (Oxford University Press, 2009), pp. 263–341.

38 Cottier and Oesch, *International Trade Regulation*, above note 4, p. 543.

in a dialectical process triggered through opposition against European claims of authority by the Member States.[39] A parallel process has been set in motion with regard to the UN Security Council, whose comprehensive sanctions against Iraq since 1991 and more recent targeted sanctions against individuals risk violating social rights, procedural rights and property rights. Again, the threat of non-compliance by outside courts might push the United Nations to clearly acknowledge that the Security Council is bound by human rights standards, to increase the level of human rights protection and to create an institution to monitor compliance. In the WTO, this dimension of constitutionalisation is completely absent. Although it could be argued that certain WTO policies potentially, even if only indirectly, affect or even infringe social or indigenous rights, especially in developing countries, these policies are not subject to any human rights review. Neither are the relevant standards agreed upon, nor are monitoring bodies available. The WTO dispute settlement bodies have no jurisdiction over their institutions. This difference between the (quasi-) compulsory jurisdiction of the WTO dispute settlement mechanism and the EU courts is, from a constitutionalist perspective, crucial.

IV. (Judicial) constitutionalisation of and through WTO dispute settlement

So far, the most viable aspect of micro-constitutionalisation is the judicialisation of dispute settlement. This trend is in the spotlight of the WTO constitutionalisation debate. There are a number of different aspects to this. In institutional terms, quasi-compulsory and quasi-judicial proceedings have been established and progressively entrenched, so that now quasi-binding, judgment-like awards are rendered.

A different constitutional element in dispute settlement is the participation of non-state actors, notably NGOs, which represent the concerns of global civil society. Granting them a voice in the process of judicial law-making allows them to influence the international legal process at least indirectly, and this constitutes a paradigm shift. However, after the *Shrimp* case, the panels and the Appellate Body – following the criticism of the WTO Members – have taken a restrictive posture in this regard,

39 The criticism has still been raised that the ECJ's human rights protection is rather weak, that it gives too much weight to the interests of European integration, and too generously allows human rights restrictions on these grounds.

and admit *amicus curiae* briefs only when they are taken up in the parties' submissions.[40]

In substance, the case law of the panels and the Appellate Body arguably 'is beginning to display some characteristics ordinarily associated with constitutional case-law'.[41] Initially, the role of the panels and the Appellate Body corresponded to a contractual setting in which the institutions mechanically examined whether state conduct was in compliance with the agreements. In contrast, considerations of vertical separation and balance of powers, which have shaped domestic standards of review, were not overtly present in the context of the WTO.[42] The dispute settlement institutions then began to borrow constitutional doctrines, such as the proportionality analysis.[43] They have begun to take into consideration non-trade issues such as human rights and environmental protection, and apply the technique of balancing to determine which of the conflicting interests should prevail in the concrete case. Arguably, the conceptual development of a more constitutional framework would provide room for more nuanced and multilayered standard-of-review principles.[44] Thomas Cottier has called this 'constitutionalism in a modest sense', 'an attitude and a framework capable of reasonably balancing and weighing different, equally legitimate and democratically defined basic values and policy goals'.[45]

But this vision of WTO constitutionalism is subject to strong criticism. One objection is that by taking the principle of trade liberalisation as

40 Panel, *US – Softwood Lumber* (22 March 2004) WT/DS277/R, at 88, n. 75. Here the Panel stated that it would 'consider any arguments raised by *amici curiae* to the extent that these arguments were taken up in the written submissions and/or oral statements of any party or third parties'.

41 D. Z. Cass, 'The "constitutionalization" of international trade law: Judicial norm-generation as the engine of constitutionalization' (2001) 13 *European Journal of International Law* 42.

42 M. Oesch, *Standards of Review on WTO Dispute Resolution* (Oxford University Press, 2003), p. 29 and pp. 241–242.

43 See for a balancing approach to the 'necessity' requirement of Art. XX(d) GATT, which grants an a priori equal rank to the conflicting objectives: AB, *Korea – Measures Affecting Imports of Fresh, Chilled and Frozen Beef* (11 December 2000) WT/DS161/AB/R, WT/DS169/AB/R, para. 162: 'The more vital or important those common interests or values are, the easier it would be to accept as "necessary" a measure designed as an enforcement instrument.'

44 Oesch, *Standards of Review*, above note 42, p. 243.

45 T. Cottier, 'Limits to International Trade: The Constitutional Challenge', in The American Society of International Law (ed.), *International Law in Ferment: A New Vision for Theory and Practice, Proceedings of the 94th Annual Meeting* (Washington, DC, April 5–8, 2000), p. 221.

a constitutional norm, the trade-off between the obligation to liberalise and the protection of non-trade concerns inevitably ends in a preference for free trade. Competing values enter into the picture only as narrow and carefully policed exceptions, and the onus is on the party which invokes the exception, say the critics.[46] However, an important strand of WTO constitutionalism seeks precisely to counter this order of priorities. From that perspective, the competing values are not just exceptions to trade liberalisation, but are provisions to protect legitimate policy goals, which form an integral part of a well-balanced multilateral trading system and which should be acknowledged to have the same status as other constitutional principles.[47]

Also, WTO constitutionalists are accused of falsely dignifying the judicial balancing process, instead of admitting its political character. When a WTO panel invalidates an environmental protection scheme, constitutionalists might view this as the enforcement of higher (namely constitutional) law (of free trade). In reality, however, say the critics, this is a political decision by the panel which is presumably illegitimate because it replaces the policy balancing of domestic democratic institutions with the panel's own policy.

This objection brings us to the heart of the matter. The entire 'constitutionalisation' process has so far been adjudicative rather than deliberative. The WTO's capacity for legislative response to judicial constitutional engineering is muted, last but not least by the consensus practice. This again fuels the fundamental objection against the constitutionalist reading of WTO law mentioned above, namely that this reading condones an impoverished, legalist (judicially made), apolitical conception of constitution. Our conclusion on the constitutional status of WTO is that the WTO is so far only a modestly constitutionalised entity.

D. The WTO: private or public interest?[48]

In 1992, Kenneth W. Abbott addressed the institutional issues of the GATT in terms of 'private' and 'public' interests.[49] He used the term 'private' to

46 Howse and Nicolaidis, above note 9, 75.

47 T. Cottier and M. Oesch, *International Trade Regulation*, above note 4, p. 428 and p. 540.

48 See for a comprehensive study of the ideas and notions of 'public interest' and 'common good' in international law: S. Peter, *'Public Interest' and 'Common Good' in International Law*, forthcoming.

49 K. W. Abbott, 'GATT as a public institution: The Uruguay Round and beyond' (1992) 31 *Brooklyn Journal of International Law* 31.

refer to the 'particular interests of the individual states'. The term 'public' was designed to describe the 'common interests of the nations forming the world trading community'. According to Abbott's paper, GATT members had misconceived the GATT as 'constituting a private interest community'. By way of contrast, the Uruguay round was about institutionalising a 'public interest' approach, characterised by the 'concern for the common interests of the community of trading nations'.

The WTO came into being in 1995. In the following years, 'public interest' groups identified the WTO as the preferred target in their fight against a globalised trade regime and its undesirable effects. From this perspective, the WTO posed a threat to 'public interest' issues and was not seen to be a 'public interest' organisation.[50]

The two uses of 'public interest' show that the term is not a synonym for constitutionalism in international law. Rather, three different approaches to 'public interest' should be distinguished, namely the communal approach, the sovereigntist approach and the constitutionalist approach. This section will focus on the interpretation of exception clauses in international law. These clauses reflect the tension between national public interest and international goals. Accordingly, the different approaches to public interest are mirrored in the way these clauses are interpreted by states or by international adjudication bodies. It is submitted that a constitutionalist understanding of these clauses must accept that they reflect national *public* interests.

I. The communal approach to public interest

1. Public interest and private interest

Abbott used the term 'public interest' to sketch the institutional change of the old GATT. He proposed that this change should imply a 'significantly increased role'[51] for the GATT institutions. Abbott's approach is based mainly on a domestic analogy. States are seen to be individual, unitary actors which pursue their own self-interest (private interest). On the other hand, international organisations adopt a 'public' view when they pursue a community vision, characterised by its independence from the party's visions. They are labelled 'public' because they are supposed to transcend the individual interests of their members. According to Abbott,

50 S. Picciotto, 'Defending the public interest in TRIPS and the WTO', in P. Drahos and R. Mayne (eds.), *Global Intellectual Property Rights* (Basingstoke: Palgrave Macmillan, 2002).
51 Abbott, 'GATT as a Public Institution', above note 49, p. 84.

the GATT was 'created with a vision of the public good, a set of common goals, principles and norms (designed to restrain national autonomy)'.[52] According to this view, the communal core of the GATT would lie in the restraint of 'national autonomy' for the greater good of enabling trade liberalisation. By way of contrast, the traditional (national) public interest 'in a borderless world . . . has become little more than a cloak for subsidy and protection [and] has no meaningful place'.[53]

2. A communal interpretation of Article XX GATT

Let us test a communal approach to Article XX GATT. Roughly speaking, a communal approach would imply that the overall interests of the trading system prevail over the individual interests of the Members. It is possible to see the *Tuna* Panels in this light. The US Marine Mammal Protection Act of 1972 required a general prohibition of the taking and importation into the US of marine mammals. Under the Act, the importation of commercial fish or fish products which resulted in the incidental killing of ocean mammals was prohibited. In *Tuna I*, Mexico claimed that the import prohibition on yellowfin tuna and tuna products was inconsistent with Articles III, XI, and XIII GATT. The US argued that the measure was covered by Articles XX(b) and (g) GATT. The Panel Report in *Tuna I* expressed the fear that any justification under Article XX GATT might lead to 'green protectionism'.[54] Thus, the Panel considerably reduced the scope of this Article by excluding virtually all unilateral measures:

> The Panel considered that if the broad interpretation of Article XX(b) suggested by the United States were accepted, each contracting party could unilaterally determine the life or health protection policies from which other contracting parties could not deviate without jeopardizing their rights under the General Agreement. The General Agreement would then no longer constitute a multilateral framework for trade among all contracting parties but would provide legal security only in respect of trade between a limited number of contracting parties with identical internal regulations.[55]

52 *Ibid.* p. 38.

53 K. Ohmae, *The End of the Nation State: The Rise of Regional Economies* (London: Harper Collins, 1996), p. 64.

54 D. C. Esty, *Greening the GATT: Trade, Environment, and the Future* (Washington, DC: Institute for International Economics, 1994).

55 Panel Report, *United States – Restrictions on the Imports of Tuna (not adopted)* (3 September 1991) BISD 39S/155 para. 5.27.

Although the Panel Reports on the Tuna cases were never adopted, these reports attracted wide attention and marked the beginning of the whole 'trade and environment' debate.[56] The *Tuna* Panels suggested a communal reading of Article XX GATT which would have favoured the GATT values nearly unconditionally over non-trade interests. As a 'public' institution, the GATT system would be able to impose its trade values even against the 'private' interests of an individual Member. However, this communal 'public interest' reading of Article XX GATT did not find approval outside the trade community, which was blamed for having an 'insider understanding'[57] of trade.

In *US – Shrimp*, the Appellate Body rejected the communal approach to the public interest exceptions of Article XX GATT. Measures which fall under the scope of paragraph (a) to (j) of that Article were 'recognized as exceptions to substantive obligations established in the GATT 1994, because the domestic policies embodied in such measures have been recognized as important and legitimate in character'.[58] Further, the Appellate Body has recognised ever since that it is for the Member to determine its own level of protection. However, protectionist measures remain outlawed. Members have to implement these measures in such a way as to satisfy the requirements of the *chapeau* of Article XX GATT.

II. The sovereigntist approach to public interest

1. 'Public interest' in limitation clauses and general exception clauses

States are public entities, inhabited by private individuals. However, Abbott used the public–private distinction in another way. He implicitly compared the behaviour of states to that of individual persons. In the international sphere, state autonomy and state sovereignty thus seem to correspond to the 'private', self-maximising behaviour of individuals.

However, opposing 'public interest' to state sovereignty does not reflect the use of the term in international law. Neither state autonomy nor state sovereignty are opposed to the concept of public interest in international

56 M. Matsushita, T. J. Schoenbaum and P. C. Mavroidis, *The World Trade Organization. Law, Practice, and Policy* (2nd edn, Oxford University Press, 2006), p. 794.

57 R. Howse, 'The Appellate Body rulings in the Shrimp/Turtle Case: A new legal baseline for the trade and environment debate' (2002) 27 *Columbia Journal of Environmental Law* 517.

58 Appellate Body Report, *United States – Import Prohibition of Certain Shrimp and Shrimp Products* (12 October 1998) WT/DS58/AB/R para. 21.

law: quite the contrary. One important use of 'public interest' in international law is closely linked to state sovereignty. The term is explicitly used in Article 8 TRIPS and Article 1 of the First Additional Protocol of the European Convention on Human Rights (ECHR). Article 8 TRIPS allows Members to adopt measures necessary 'to promote the public interest in sectors of vital importance', whereas the peaceful enjoyment of possessions requires that no one 'shall be deprived of his possessions except in the public interest'. 'Public interest' is also an umbrella term for state interests such as the protection of public morals, public policy or safety, public (or national) security or the protection of human, animal or plant life or health. These interests are frequently invoked in international law as *treaty exceptions* such as Articles XX and XXI GATT and Article XIV GATS[59] or Article 30 EC.

2. A sovereigntist interpretation of Article XXI GATT: a self-judging obligation

From a historical perspective, escape clauses, *ordre public* reservations[60] or 'vital interest' clauses[61] reflect the priority claim of state sovereignty.[62] The strong sovereigntist background of these clauses can amount to claims that they are 'self-judging'. 'Self-judging' obligations are considered as being able to block judicial review. The most prominent example of an alleged self-judging obligation is Article XXI GATT, the national security exception. Under GATT 1947, several disputes arose under this Article. The question whether the mere invocation of Article XXI GATT blocks any review process under Article XXIII GATT remained unsettled throughout the GATT years.[63] Although states no longer contest the jurisdiction of panels, recent cases support the view that states prefer to settle disputes which involve national security issues outside the framework of the

59 See also T. Cottier, P. Delimatsis and N. F. Diebold, 'Commentary on Art. XIV GATS' in R. Wolfrum, P.-T. Stoll and C. Feinäugle (eds.), *Max-Planck Commentaries on World Trade Law, Vol. 6: WTO – Trade in Services* (Leiden: Martinus Nijhoff, 2008), pp. 283–328.

60 *Ibid.*

61 M. J. Hahn, 'Vital interests in the law of the GATT: An analysis of GATT's security exception' (1991) 12 *Michigan Journal of International Law* 558.

62 A. Emmerson, 'Conceptualizing security exceptions: Legal doctrine or political excuse?' (2008) 11 *Journal of International Economic Law* 135.

63 P. Lindsay, 'The ambiguity of GATT Article XXI: Subtle success or rampant failure?' (2003) 52 *Duke Law Journal* 1279; S. Rose-Ackermannn and B. Billa, 'Treaties and national security' (2008) 40 *New York University Journal of International Law and Politics* 467.

WTO.[64] By contrast, scholarly writings point to other international treaty organs such as the European Court of Human Rights (ECtHR) or the European Court of Justice to show that national security issues are not per se outside the realm of judicial review. Indeed, in its very first case, the ECtHR established its jurisdiction on Article 15 ECHR, involving the full reviewability of the requirements which allow a state to invoke derogation measures.[65] It rejected thereby the claim of the Irish Government that 'it was for a Government, and for that Government alone, to determine when a state of emergency existed and what measures were required by the exigencies of the situation.'[66]

III. The constitutionalist approach to public interest

1. International adjudication on sovereigntist clauses

The ECtHR *Lawless* ruling has been compared to the seminal judgment of *Marbury* v. *Madison* in which the US Supreme Court asserted its power to review the constitutionality of legislative acts and thus the legitimacy of constitutional judicial review.[67] Indeed, the ECtHR has adopted the view that the Convention was not merely one international treaty among several others but 'a constitutional instrument of European public order (ordre public)'.[68] Similarly, the constitutionalisation of the European Union is closely linked to the ECJ's jurisprudence. Besides the doctrines of supremacy and direct effect of EC law, the Court's case law on the fundamental freedoms has significantly contributed to the constitutionalisation

64 Two disputes have arisen so far under the WTO. In 1996, a dispute arose between the EC and the US on the so-called 'Helms-Burton' Act. The dispute was settled bilaterally in a Memorandum of Understanding although a WTO panel had previously been established. *European Union – United States: Memorandum of Understanding Concerning the U.S. Helms-Burton Act and the U.S. Iran and Libya Sanctions Act (11 April 1997)* 36 ILM 529 (1997). The other dispute involving Art. XXI GATT arose between Nicaragua and Columbia. In *Nicaragua – Measures affecting Imports from Honduras and Columbia*, Columbia requested the establishment of a panel, challenging a Nicaraguan law which imposed sanctions on Columbia and Honduras. The Dispute Settlement Body agreed to the establishment of a panel; however, it appears that it was never constituted. WTO Dispute Settlement Body: Minutes of Meeting held on 18 May 2000, WTO Doc WT/DSB/M/80 (26 June 2000) para 40.

65 *Lawless* v. *Ireland* (App no 332/57) (1961) Series A no. 3 para. 22.

66 *Lawless* v. *Ireland* (App no 332/57) (1959) Report of the Commission pp. 78–79.

67 F. Ni Aolain, 'The emergence of diversity: Differences in human rights jurisprudence' (1995) 19 *Fordham International Law Journal* 111.

68 *Loizidou* v. *Turkey* (Grand Chamber) (App no 15318/89) Series A no. 310 para. 75.

of Community law.[69] Further, much of the debate about the constitutionalisation of the WTO is linked to the strengthened institutional role of the 'judicialised' dispute settlement system in general[70] or more specifically to a suggested approach to the adjudication of Article XXI GATT.[71] The constitutionalist vocabulary is thus closely linked to the existence of international adjudication on clauses which enshrine national public interest concerns.

2. A constitutionalist interpretation of exception clauses: accepting national 'collective preferences'

A constitutionalist interpretation of exception clauses recognises that they reflect 'collective preferences'. The concept of 'collective preferences' was introduced by Pascal Lamy in the context of WTO law as a way in which to address the discomfort felt with free trade rules.[72] He suggested introducing an additional safeguard clause which would allow WTO Members to escape trade obligations provided that they pay compensation in order to adjust the trade system. The problems of such a 'collective preference' safeguard clause are manifold.[73] However, Lamy's term 'collective preferences' merits approval because it makes it clear that states are collectivities. In a state-based system, national communities are forced to speak with one voice and to represent one 'single identity'.[74] It is the State 'which has the exclusive authority to bind the whole community to international law'.[75] But what is the national interest or the public interest of a national community? Lamy advocates domestic procedures which should prove the genuineness of the collective preferences but does not elaborate on the

69 A. Peters, *Elemente einer Theorie der Verfassung Europas* (Veröffentlichungen des Walther-Schücking-Instituts für Internationales Recht an der Universität Kiel. Berlin: Duncker & Humblot, 2001), pp. 406–408.

70 Cass, 'The "constitutionalization" of international trade law' above note 41, 39.

71 H. L. Schloemann and S. Ohlhoff, '"Constitutionalization" and dispute settlement in the WTO: National security as an issue of competence' (1999) 93 *The American Journal of International Law* 424.

72 P. Lamy, 'The emergence of collective preferences in international trade: Implications for regulating globalisation', speech given on 15 September 2004 (available at http://ec.europa.eu/archives/commission_1999_2004/lamy/speeches_articles/spla242_en.htm, 15 April 2009).

73 S. Charnovitz, 'An analysis of Pascal Lamy's proposal on collective preferences' (2005) 8 *Journal of International Economic Law* 449.

74 S. Burchill, *The National Interest in International Relations Theory* (Basingstoke: Palgrave, 2005), p. 47.

75 *Ibid.*, p. 55.

details of such procedures. Steve Charnovitz has rightly shown the difficulties which arise from this 'piercing of the unitary member'.[76] Although the demand for more domestic public deliberation on trade issues merits approval, it is difficult to imagine how the WTO could objectively verify the existence of collective preferences.[77] Further, it is difficult to see why the domestic procedures should only apply in cases relating to trade exceptions and not to the negotiation of trade rules.[78]

The need to verify the genuineness of 'collective preferences' in trade law stems from the fear that the national 'public interest' is protectionism in disguise and that the concept itself is always hijacked by domestic rent-seeking groups. Therefore, international courts engage in a very close textual analysis of the different public interest exceptions when they adjudicate trade rules. The scope of the exception clauses is interpreted rather narrowly[79] whereas the scope of those provisions which can be violated is interpreted rather widely. In EC law, the scope of Article 28 EC was widened to such an extent that the original rules of non-discrimination have developed into rules of de-regulation. However, the widening of the scope of Article 28 EC has occurred alongside the introduction of additional public interest defences, namely the 'mandatory requirements'[80] or the 'overriding requirements of general public importance'.[81] These court-made exceptions are interpreted in a flexible way that has allowed the Court to acknowledge additional public interests such as consumer protection,[82] environmental protection[83] or human rights protection.[84] No additional public interest defences have been introduced so far in WTO law and no exceptions have been developed which could be compared to

76 Charnovitz, 'An analysis of Pascal Lamy's proposal on collective preferences', above note 73, p. 456.

77 *Ibid.*, p. 458.

78 *Ibid.*, p. 456.

79 See for example: Panel Report *EC – Conditions for the Granting of Tariff Preferences to Developing Countries* (1 December 2003) WT/DS246/R paras. 7.207–7.210. The panel found that the European drug arrangements were not covered by Art. XX(b).

80 ECJ, Case 120/78 *Rewe-Zentrale AG* v. *Bundesmonopolverwaltung für Branntwein* [1979] ECR 649 para. 8.

81 ECJ, Case C-34/95 *Konsumentombudsmannen (KO)* v. *De Agostini* [1997] ECR I-3843 para. 46.

82 ECJ, Case 120/78 *Rewe-Zentrale AG* v. *Bundesmonopolverwaltung für Branntwein* [1979] ECR 649.

83 ECJ, Case 302/86 *Commission* v. *Kingdom of Denmark* [1988] ECR 4607 paras. 8–9.

84 ECJ, Case C-112/00 *Eugen Schmidberger, Internationale Transporte und Planzüge* v. *Republik Österreich* [2003] ECR I-5659 para. 74.

the concept of 'mandatory requirements'.[85] Therefore, scholars argue for broad interpretations of the various subparagraphs of Article XX GATT. Article XX(a) GATT, in particular, which provides for the protection of public morals, was considered to allow for the inclusion of concerns such as the protection of human rights.[86]

IV. Preliminary outlook

Far from saying that the international adjudicating bodies are constitutional courts, it can be submitted that their case law on 'public interest' as enshrined in the relevant exceptions or limitation clauses offers important insight into the *legitimacy* of international law adjudication. When exception clauses are interpreted in a communal way, the overall 'public interest' of the treaty system prevails almost unconditionally over the 'public interest' issues which are addressed in these clauses. When they are interpreted in a sovereigntist way, the definition of 'public interest' is left entirely up to the individual parties to the treaty. This may pose a threat to the treaty system because the exception 'ceases to be a rule of law and becomes a maxim of politics'.[87] What is needed, thus, is a way to address the clauses which mediates between the two extremes. European Courts, both the ECtHR and the ECJ, refer to an explicit or implied doctrine of 'margin of appreciation'. This doctrine mitigates the possible impacts of international law on the national public interest, thereby strengthening the Court's own political legitimacy.[88]

The constitutionalist reconstruction of international law should not claim that international law and international institutions always promote 'public interests', whereas States merely act in their own narrowly defined self-interest. The constitutionalist approach to public interest in international law takes into account that public interest exceptions refer to interests which are in principle recognised as legitimate interests of collective actors. Nevertheless, the decision as to whether a Member's measure

85 Cottier, Delimatsis and Diebold, 'Commentary on Art. XIV GATS', above note 59, pp. 283–328.

86 S. Charnovitz, 'The moral exception in trade policy' (1998) 38 *Virginia Journal of International Law* 689; N. F. Diebold, 'The morals and order exceptions in WTO Law: Balancing the toothless tiger and the undermining mole' (2008) 11 *Journal of International Economic Law* 43.

87 H. Lauterpacht, *Private Law Sources and Analogies of International Law* (London: Longmans, Green & Co., 1927), p. 169.

88 D. Shelton, 'The boundaries of human rights jurisdiction in Europe' (2003) 13 *Duke Journal of Comparative & International Law* 95, p. 135.

is covered by the exception is left to an international adjudication body which is charged with the interpretation of these exceptions.

E. Policy recommendations

Further constitutionalisation could be realised by political actors and promoted by doctrinal arguments along the following lines.

I. Constitutional substance

The libertarian inclination of the nascent WTO constitution should be rectified by strengthening the legal relevance of non-trade issues such as environmental and social concerns. The constitutional principle of solidarity should be implemented by promoting liberalisation in sectors in which poor countries can compete.

The so-called 'new, new issues' of the WTO, namely the rule of law, good governance, corruption, corporate responsibility, exchange rates and migration, should be promoted, because these are all issues that deserve the label 'constitutional' on account of their fundamental nature, and are indeed typically dealt with in state constitutions.

Furthermore, it would be appropriate to strengthen the WTO constitutional restraints on Members. This means that direct access of private (business) actors to WTO dispute settlement and the functionally equivalent route, namely traders' access to domestic courts with the complaint that WTO law has been breached by a Member, should be re-examined.

II. Access of private actors to WTO dispute settlement and to domestic courts

Direct access of private parties to the WTO dispute settlement institutions would liberate business actors from the tutelage of their governments, which are often reluctant to institute WTO proceedings. The governmental choice of whether to bring or not to bring a particular WTO case to the dispute settlement forum is often not guided by the importance and meritoriousness of the issue, but is influenced by diplomatic considerations on the general relations with another country, by a desire to leave a legal question undecided, or by the lobbying power or weakness of an industry sector. These policy considerations neglect the rule of law and they lead to unequal treatment of business actors.

The privatisation of WTO dispute settlement would remedy these problems and lead to better respect for the rule of law and equal protection. Because self-interested commercial actors have a strong incentive to sue, it would moreover strengthen the GATT by terminating underenforcement. It would finally relieve governments of the burden of political tensions.

But such privatisation may be a step too far. Given that the military option is largely foreclosed, economic and trade regulation is nowadays the main foreign policy instrument of governments.[89] The regulation of trade flows is intrinsically dualist: it concerns both the public and private interests. Governments litigating before the WTO dispute settlement institutions are therefore often counselled by the interested business actors. This duality should be more clearly acknowledged and regulated under due consideration for the public and private concerns at stake. For instance, one could question the extent to which the interest in business secrecy, which is protected through the non-disclosure of business confidential information by the litigating states parties,[90] really outweighs the public interest in transparency and publicity of the WTO proceedings. Ultimately, it must be kept in mind that the public and the private interests at stake need not coincide. The appropriate constitutional design of WTO dispute settlement therefore seems not to be to remove it completely from governmental control, but to uphold it as a basically inter-state system while greatly increasing and formalising the participatory opportunities of private actors.

In parallel, the direct application of suitable WTO rules should be reconsidered.[91] Admittedly, the direct application of WTO law risks giving undue power to domestic courts to the detriment of the Members' political branches. Also, as long as WTO law has not fully integrated legitimate policy concerns other than trade liberalisation, the 'unfiltered' application of WTO law by domestic courts may threaten those policy

89 T. Cottier, in a panel discussion moderated by P. C. Mavroidis, 'Is the WTO dispute settlement mechanism responsive to the needs of traders? Would a system of direct adjudication by private parties yield better results?' (1998) 32 *Journal of World Trade* 147, p. 154.

90 Panel, *Canada – Measures Affecting the Export of Civilian Aircraft* (14 April 1999) WT/DS70, para 9.68 and Appellate Body, *Canada – Measures Affecting the Export of Civilian Aircraft* (2 August 1999) WT/DS70/AB/R, paras. 141 *et seq.*

91 See T. Cottier, 'A theory of direct effect in global law', in A. von Bogdandy, P. C. Mavroidis, and Y. Mény (eds.), *European Integration and International Co-ordination. Studies in Transnational Economic Law in Honour of Claus-Dieter Ehlermann* (The Hague: Kluwer Law International, 2002), pp. 99–123.

concerns.[92] Finally, it can be argued that the development of WTO law by domestic judges, triggered by private claimants, must be accompanied (and eventually corrected) by WTO rule-making processes in which these private actors can participate.

Ultimately, the constitutionalist agenda encourages a more ready acceptance of the direct effect of suitable provisions of WTO law, because direct effect would enable the domestic judiciary to check the Members' executives, which otherwise enjoy unfettered discretion in applying the rules which were actually designed to restrain these very actors. This is the classic theme of constitutionalism, which seeks to contain political power in order to safeguard the autonomy of the individual. From a constitutionalist perspective, the enactment of a WTO decision that would define the criteria of direct applicability, clarify who is entitled to invoke direct effect, and explicitly allow the direct effect of WTO provisions satisfying the established criteria, is recommended. Provisions suited for direct effect are in essence those whose concretisation can, under a theory of delegation informed by the rule of law, be legitimately delegated to a judge.[93] But because the application of those WTO norms by domestic courts bears the risk of diverging case law, the admission of direct effect would ideally be accompanied by a system of referral to the international adjudicative organs for preliminary rulings in order to harmonise the interpretation of WTO law.

III. A multilevel judiciary

A constitutionalist approach to the judiciary permits us to appraise the WTO dispute settlement institutions and the national courts as forming one multilevel judiciary. From this perspective, the activity at both levels should be informed by constitutionalism and the rule of law, and the intensity of judicial review should be adapted to the degree of integration of their subsystem.[94] The WTO panels' attitude would need to shift to a more constitutionalist approach which would allow for a more refined balancing between market access rights and other legitimate policy concerns. In contrast, national courts should adopt a stricter standard of review for scrutinising the trade policy decisions of their executives.

92 Cottier, 'Direct effect', above note 91, pp.114–115.

93 *Ibid.*, pp. 118–119.

94 T. Cottier and P. Mavroidis, 'Concluding remarks', in T. Cottier and P. Mavroidis (eds.), *The Role of the Judge in International Trade Regulation: Experience and Lessons for the WTO* (Ann Arbor: Michigan University Press, 2003), pp. 349, 353.

IV. Political and legal accountability

In institutional and procedural terms, the accountability of WTO activities should be enhanced. As far as legal accountability is concerned, judicial review of acts of the institutions themselves must be made available in the long run. In terms of political accountability, the involvement of non-state actors in the elaboration of 'secondary' trade law and dispute settlement should be further strengthened in order to increase transparency and to introduce elements of participatory democracy. Concerns about NGOs' legitimacy and accountability and about ineffectiveness of procedures could be allayed by an accreditation scheme which must be as far as possible depoliticised.[95] Besides, a parliamentary dimension could be introduced into the WTO.[96] This should be done both on the national level (liaising better with national parliaments), and on the international level by creating an informal network of national parliaments which might in the long run lead to a standing parliamentary assembly. Members which do not have a parliament could be allowed to send other officials to these meetings.

V. Law- and decision-making

Finally, and most importantly, we face inertia in the creation of primary WTO law (i.e. the amendment of the WTO treaties themselves[97]) and secondary law.[98] More effective WTO rule-making and decision-making

95 See the Guidelines for arrangements on relations with Non-Governmental Organizations, WT/L/162, Decision of 18 July 1996. WTO Director-General Supachi Panitchpakdi established two informal advisory bodies to the WTO Secretariat in 2003, as a platform for dialogue between the DG and business organisations and NGOs. The subsequent Director-General disbanded these informal bodies. See P. van den Bossche, 'NGO involvement in the WTO: A comparative perspective' (2008) 11 *Journal of International Economic Law* 717.

96 Proposals along these lines are supported by the IPU and the European Parliament, but are opposed by the USA and many developing countries. See the parliamentary conference on the WTO convened by the European Parliament and IPU calling for a parliamentary dimension to the WTO (Final declaration of 18 February 2003). See G. Shaffer, 'Parliamentary Oversight of WTO-Rulemaking? The Political, Normative, and Practical Contexts' (2004) 7 *Journal of International Economic Law* 629; E. Mann, 'Parliamentary dimensions in the WTO – More than just a vision?' (2004) 7 *Journal of International Economic Law* 659.

97 See on a 'two tier approach' to negotiations which would allow the influx of outside ideas into WTO negotiations, T. Cottier, 'Structural reform of the WTO' (2007) 10 *Journal of International Economic Law* 497, pp. 505–506.

98 See on this problem Y. Bonzon, M. Elsig, M. Foltea, T. Messerli and A. Ziegler, 'Reflections on Modes of Decision-Making in the WTO', Chapter 2 in this volume.

is needed for two reasons. First, only treaty revision can bring about positive social and environmental integration, which is not yet ingrained in the treaties and which can therefore not be effected by the judiciary alone. Second, the possibility of a legislative response to adjudication is required to counter the problem of a presumably illegitimate government of judges, and to enhance the balance of powers within the WTO.

The current WTO practice for decision-making and rule-making relies on the consensus principle (footnote 1 of the WTO Agreement). Although Article IX WTO Agreement provides for majority voting if a consensus is not reached (with decisions to be adopted upon a simple majority of the votes cast), such voting does not take place. The current consensus practice is ineffective because it risks cementing the status quo. From a constitutionalist perspective, it is even more important that this practice is also illegitimate. It is undemocratic because it allows one WTO Member to tyrannise the others, and allows a small minority or one Member to block collective action.[99] It is also anti-egalitarian, because it gives more weight to the positions of Members who are less likely to give up their resistance, and these tend to be the bigger and richer ones.[100] Finally, the resulting unavailability of a legislative response to the (quasi-) judicial decisions leaves the dispute settlement institutions uncontrolled and thereby undermines the legitimacy of the WTO judiciary.

One possible reform that would enhance the effectiveness and legitimacy of decision-making would be the introduction of weighted voting.[101] Such a reform would make transparent the undeniable preponderance of the powerful Members, while still being more acceptable to the powerful Members than a system of equal votes. However, it is exceedingly difficult to identify the appropriate factors for weighting the votes. From a radically democratic perspective, the decisive criterion would have to be the size of population in order to represent more fairly the world's citizens who are the ultimate unit of global democracy. But other factors reasonably related to the mandate of the WTO, such as shares of world trade and openness of the markets, also seem relevant.

99 Cf. Francisco de Vitoria 'On Civil Power', in *Political Writings* [1528], ed. by A. Pagden and J. Lawrence (Cambridge University Press, 1991), pp. 1–44, p. 30 (para. 14).

100 C. D. Ehlermann and L. Ehring, 'Decision making in the world trade organization: Is the consensus practice of the world trade organization adequate for making, revising and implementing rules on international trade?' (2005) 8 *Journal of International Economic Law* 51, p. 66.

101 T. Cottier and S. Takenoshita, 'The balance of power in WTO decision-making: Towards weighted voting in legislative response' (2003) 59 *Aussenwirtschaft* 171.

An alternative strategy would be to change the decision-making practices without formally amending the decision-making rules. The first option along this route is to eliminate the taboo against voting, and thereby revive the legally available possibility of voting. This 'shadow'of voting would probably induce Members to give up their veto more often and would thus facilitate consensual decision making.[102] Another possibility would be to revitalise the so far underused rule 33 of the various WTO bodies' Rules of Procedure.[103] These rules state that when consensus is not reached in councils, committees, and other subordinate bodies, the decision should be moved up to the General Council. Finally, the option of authentic interpretation under Article IX(2) WTO Agreement could be used more often.[104] A decision defining the authentic interpretation of any WTO law provision can be taken by the Ministerial Conference and the General Council with the votes of three-quarters of the Members and will bind all WTO Members. While Article IX(2) WTO Agreement states that authentic interpretation must not undermine the amendment provisions of Article X WTO Agreement, this limit still leaves considerable leeway for fine-tuning the WTO provisions, and also for correcting an interpretation given by a panel or Appellate Body. While the principal constitutional challenges for the WTO lie in its rule-making and decision-making, we submit that the WTO could and should be constitutionalised further along the proposed lines.

Bibliography

Abbott, Kenneth W., 'GATT as a public institution: The Uruguay Round and beyond' (1992) **31** *Brooklyn Journal of International Law* 31.

Amerasinghe, Chittharanjan Felix, *Principles of the Institutional Law of International Organizations*, 2nd edn (Cambridge University Press, 2005).

Armingeon, Klaus and Milewicz, Karolina, 'Compensatory constitutionalisation: A comparative perspective' (2008) **22** *Global Society* 179.

Van Den Bossche, Pieter, 'NGO involvement in the WTO: A comparative perspective' (2008) **11** *Journal of International Economic Law* 717.

Burchill, Scott, *The National Interest in International Relations Theory* (Palgrave: Basingstoke, 2005).

102 Ehlermann and Ehrig, above note 100, pp. 72–73. See for a discussion on which types of WTO decisions can legitimately be made non-consensually Bonzon *et al.*, above note 98, at section D.III.

103 Ehlermann and Ehrig, above note 100, pp. 73–74.

104 *Ibid.*, pp. 58–59.

Cass, Deborah Z., 'The "constitutionalization" of international trade law: Judicial norm-generation as the engine of constitutional development in international trade' (2001) **12** *Journal of International Economic Law* 39.

Cass, Deborah Z., *The Constitutionalization of the WTO* (Oxford University Press, 2005).

Charnovitz, Steve, 'The moral exception in trade policy' (1998) **38** *Virginia Journal of International Law* 689.

Charnovitz, Steve, 'An analysis of Pascal Lamy's proposal on collective preferences' (2005) **8** *Journal of International Economic Law* 449.

Cottier, Thomas, 'Is the WTO dispute settlement mechanism responsive to the needs of traders? Would a system of direct adjudication by private parties yield better results?' (1998) **32** *Journal of World Trade* 147.

Cottier, Thomas, 'Limits to international trade: The constitutional challenge', in The American Society of International Law (ed.), *International Law in Ferment: A New Vision for Theory and Practice, Proceedings of the 94th Annual Meeting* (Washington, DC, April 5–8, 2000), pp. 220–222.

Cottier, Thomas, 'A theory of direct effect in global law', in A. von Bogdandy, P. C. Mavroidis, Y. Mény (eds.), *European Integration and International Co-ordination. Studies in Transnational Economic Law in Honour of Claus-Dieter Ehlermann* (The Hague: Kluwer Law International, 2002), pp. 99–123.

Cottier, Thomas, 'Trade and human rights: A relationship to discover' (2002) **5** *Journal of International Economic Law* 111.

Cottier, Thomas, 'Structural Reform of the WTO' (2007) **10** *Journal of International Economic Law* 497.

Cottier, Thomas and Takenoshita, Satoko, 'The balance of power in WTO decision-making: Towards weighted voting in legislative response' (2003) **59** *Aussenwirtschaft* 171.

Cottier, Thomas and Mavroidis, Petros, 'Concluding remarks', in T. Cottier and P. Mavroidis (eds.), *The Role of the Judge in International Trade Regulation: Experience and Lessons for the WTO* (Ann Arbor: Michigan University Press, 2003), pp. 349–357.

Cottier, Thomas and Hertig, Maya, 'The Prospects of 21st Century Constitutionalism' (2003) **7** *Max Planck Yearbook of United Nations Law* 261.

Cottier, Thomas and Oesch, Matthias, *International Trade Regulation: Law and Policy in the WTO, The European Union and Switzerland: Cases, Materials and Comments* (Staempfli: Bern, 2005).

Cottier, Thomas, Delimatsis, Panagiotis and Diebold, Nicolas F., 'Commentary on Art. XIV GATS', in R. Wolfrum, P.-T. Stoll and C. Feinäugle (eds.), *Max-Planck Commentaries on World Trade Law, Vol. 6: WTO – Trade in Services* (Leiden: Martinus Nijhoff, 2008), pp. 283–328.

Delimatsis, Panagiotis, *International Trade in Services and Domestic Regulations: Necessity, Transparency, and Regulatory Diversity* (Oxford University Press, 2007).

Diebold, Nicolas F., 'The morals and order exceptions in WTO Law: Balancing the toothless tiger and the undermining mole' (2008) **11** *Journal of International Economic Law* 43.

Downs, George W., Rocke, David M. and Barsoom, Peter N., 'Is the good news about compliance good news about cooperation?' (1996) **50** *International Organization* 3.

Dunoff, Jeffrey, 'Constitutional conceits: The WTO's "constitution" and the discipline of international law' (2006) **17** *European Journal of International Law* 647.

Ehlermann, Claus Dieter and Ehring, Lothar, 'Decision making in the World Trade Organization: Is the consensus practice of the World Trade Organization adequate for making, revising and implementing rules on international trade?' (2005) **8** *Journal of International Economic Law* 51.

Elsig, Manfred, 'The World Trade Organization's legitimacy crisis: What does the beast look like?' (2007) **41** *Journal of World Trade* 75.

Emmerson, Andrew, 'Conceptualizing security exceptions: Legal doctrine or political excuse?' (2008) **11** *Journal of International Economic Law* 135.

Esty, Daniel C., *Greening the GATT: Trade, Environment, and the Future* (Institute for International Economics, Washington, DC, 1994).

Esty, Daniel C., 'The World Trade Organization's legitimacy crisis' (2002) **1** *World Trade Review* 7.

Føllesdal, Andreas, 'When "common interests" are not common: Why the "Global Basic Structure" should be democratic' (2009) **16** *Indiana Journal of Global Legal Studies* 585.

Gerhart, Peter M., 'The WTO and participatory democracy: The historical evidence' (2004) **37** *Vanderbilt Journal of Transnational Law* 897.

Hahn, Michael J., 'Vital interests in the law of the GATT: An analysis of GATT's security exception' (1991) **12** *Michigan Journal of International Law* 558.

Howse, Robert, 'The legitimacy of the World Trade Organization', in Jean Marc Coicaud and Veijo Heiskanen (eds.), *The Legitimacy of International Organizations* (New York: United Nations University Press, 2001), pp. 355–407.

Howse, Robert, 'The Appellate Body rulings in the Shrimp/Turtle Case: A new legal baseline for the trade and environment debate' (2002) **27** *Columbia Journal of Environmental Law* 491.

Howse, Robert and Nicolaidis, Kalypso, 'Enhancing WTO legitimacy: Constitutionalization or global subsidiarity' (2003) **16** *Governance* 73.

Jackson, John H., *World Trade Law and the Law of GATT* (Indianapolis: Bobbs Merrill, 1969).

Jackson, John H., 'Fragmentation or unification among international institutions: The World Trade Organization' (1999) **31** *New York University Journal of International Law and Politics* 823.

Klabbers, Jan, Peters, Anne and Ulfstein, Geir, *The Constitutionalization of International Law* (Oxford University Press, 2009).

Krajewski, Markus, 'Democratic legitimacy and constitutional perspectives of WTO law' (2001) **35** *Journal of World Trade* 167.

Krajewski, Markus, 'International organizations or institutions, democratic legitimacy', *Max Planck Encyclopedia of International Law* (Oxford University Press, online edition [mpepil.com] 2009).

Lamy, Pascal, 'The emergence of collective preferences in international trade: Implications for regulating globalisation', speech given on 15 September 2004 (available at http://ec.europa.eu/archives/commission_1999_2004/lamy/speeches_articles/spla242_en.htm, 15 April 2009).

Lindsay, Peter, 'The ambiguity of GATT Article XXI: Subtle success or rampant failure?' (2003) **52** *Duke Law Journal* 1277.

Mann, Erika, 'Parliamentay dimensions in the WTO – More than just a vision?' (2004) **7** *Journal of International Economic Law* 659–665.

Matsushita, Mitsuo, Schoenbaum, Thomas J. and Mavroidis, Petros C., *The World Trade Organization. Law, Practice, and Policy*, 2nd edn (Oxford University Press, 2006).

McGinnis, John and Movsesian, Mark, 'The World Trade Constitution' (2000) **114** *Harvard Law Review* 511.

Milewicz, Karolina, 'Emerging patterns of global constitutionalization: Towards a conceptual framework' (2009) **16** *Indiana Journal of Global Legal Studies* 2.

Milewicz, Karolina, Bächtiger, André and Nothdurft, Arne, 'Constitutional pluralism or constitutional unity? An empirical study of international commitment (1945–2007)' (2010) **36** *Review of International Studies* 305–336.

Monaco, Riccardo, 'Le caractère constitutionnel des actes institutifs d'organisations internationales', in *Mélanges offerts à Charles Rousseau: La communauté internationale* (Paris: Pédone, 1974), pp. 153–172.

Ni Aolain, Fionnuala, 'The emergence of diversity: Differences in human rights jurisprudence' (1995) **19** *Fordham International Law Journal* 101.

Oesch, Matthias, *Standards of Review on WTO Dispute Resolution* (Oxford University Press, 2003).

Ohmae, Kenichi, *The End of the Nation State: The Rise of Regional Economies* (London: Harper Collins, 1996).

Peter, Simone, *'Public Interest' and 'Common Good' in International Law* (forthcoming).

Peters, Anne, *Elemente einer Theorie der Verfassung Europas* (Veröffentlichungen des Walther-Schücking-Instituts für Internationales Recht an der Universität Kiel (Berlin: Duncker & Humblot, 2001).

Peters, Anne, 'Compensatory constitutionalism: The function and potential of fundamental international norms and structures' (2006) **19** *Leiden Journal of International Law* 579.

Peters, Anne, 'The constitutionalisation of the European Union – Without the constitutional treaty', in S. P. Riekmann and W. Wessels (eds.), *The Making of a European Constitution* (Wiesbaden: VS Verlag für Sozialwissenschaften, 2006), pp. 35–67.

Petersmann, Ernst-Ulrich, 'Time for a United Nations "Global Compact" for integrating human rights into the law of worldwide organizations: Lessons from European Integration' (2002) **13** *European Journal of International Law* 621.

Petersmann, Ernst-Ulrich, 'Multilevel judicial governance of international trade requires a common conception of rule of law and justice' (2007) **10** *Journal of International Economic Law* 529–552.

Picciotto, Sol, 'Defending the public interest in TRIPS and the WTO', in P. Drahos and R. Mayne (eds.), *Global Intellectual Property Rights* (Basingstoke: Palgrave Macmillan, 2002), pp. 224–243.

Preuss, Ulrich K., 'Equality of states – Its meaning in a constitutionalized global order' (2008) **9** *Chicago Journal of International Law* (2008) 17.

Rose-Ackermannn, Susan and Billa, Benjamin, 'Treaties and national security' (2008) **40** *New York University Journal of International Law and Politics* 437.

Schloemann, Hannes L. and Ohlhoff, Stefan, '"Constitutionalization" and dispute settlement in the WTO: National security as an issue of competence' (1999) **93** *American Journal of International Law* 424.

Shaffer, Gregory, *Defending Interests: Public-Private Partnerships in WTO-Litigation* (Washington, DC: Brookings Institution Press, 2003).

Shaffer, Gregory, 'Parliamentary oversight of WTO-Rulemaking? The political, normative, and practical contexts' (2004) **7** *Journal of International Economic Law* 629–654.

Shelton, Dinah, 'The boundaries of human rights jurisdiction in Europe' (2003) **13** *Duke Journal of Comparative & International Law* 95.

Simmons, Beth, *Mobilizing for Human Rights: International Law in Domestic Politics* (Cambridge University Press, 2009).

Trachtman, Joel P., 'The constitutions of the WTO' (2006) **17** *European Journal of International Law* 623.

Vitoria, Francisco de, *Political Writings* [1528], ed. by A. Pagden and J. Lawrance (Cambridge University Press, 1991).

Walker, Neil, 'The EU and the WTO: Constitutionalism in a new key', in Grainne de Burca and Joanne Scott (eds.), *The EU and the WTO: Legal and Constitutional Issues* (Hart: Oxford, 2001), pp. 31–57.

Zangl, Bernhard, 'The rule of law: Internationalization and privatization', in S. Leibfried and M. Zürn (eds.), *Transformations of the State?* (Cambridge University Press, 2005), pp. 73–91.

Zangl, Bernhard, *Die Internationalisierung der Rechtsstaatlichkeit. Streitbeilegung in GATT und WTO* (Frankfurt am Main: Campus, 2006).

Zürn, Michael, 'Institutionalisierte Ungleichheit in der Weltpolitik: Jenseits der Alternativen "Global Governance" versus "American Empire"' (2007) **48** *Politische Vierteljahresschrift* 680.

2

Reflections on modes of decision-making in the World Trade Organization

YVES BONZON, MANFRED ELSIG, MARINA FOLTEA, THOMAS MESSERLI AND ANDREAS ZIEGLER*

KEY MESSAGES

The chapter focuses on selected challenges in decision-making within the WTO, vertical decision-making focusing on firms, and horizontal decision-making addressing the WTO's judicial interactions with other international organisations.

- There are various interpretations of the notions of legitimacy and accountability which in turn have an impact on the way we address the challenges to decision-making.
- The negotiation process needs improvement. Streamlining decision-making could include strengthening the role of the WTO Secretariat.
- There are a variety of decision-making rules in the WTO, but consensus trumps all. Therefore, when reforming consensual decision-making more attention needs to be paid to the different natures of legislative objectives.
- The role of corporations and the effects of domestic political systems are important in understanding current dynamics of WTO negotiations.
- Overlapping authorities pose a challenge for decision-making (horizontal decision-making). Here the fragmentation–coherence issue is most prevalent. Finding the 'institutional sensitivity' to cooperate across international organisations is pivotal.

A. Introduction

International organisations (IOs) have come under increased scrutiny in recent years. Various notions including accountability, legitimacy or performance have characterised the animated public and scholarly debates.

* Individual Project No. 2, 'Decision-making in the WTO and other international organizations'.

There is growing consensus – outside the inner circle of decision-makers within IOs – that reform is necessary to tackle global externalities more swiftly and efficiently. Reform projects mainly relate to designing new mandates and delegating more powers to IOs, as the current crises in the global financial architecture and unfolding summit activities suggest. However, reform needs to go beyond designing new tasks for IOs. Reform should also address governance issues. However, changing the rules on how decision-making works in IOs is a contentious exercise. Three obstacles stand out. First, the existence of veto players, traditional processes that characterise economic diplomacy and the role of dominating ideas on how to manage the system create a high threshold for new ideas for governance to cross before they can persuade stakeholders.[1] Second, powerful actors may choose to engage in partial exit strategies and use other IOs and platforms to negotiate trade should redesign not reflect their interests.[2] Third, the lack of a constitutional moment and existing loyalty to current decision-making processes are creating a bias towards incremental and small reform steps.[3] At the same time, there are a variety of different views about what IOs can and should do, often leading to important expectation–capacity gaps.

This chapter provides a summary of findings from a collaborative research project focusing on decision-making in the WTO. In particular we focus on methods of governance within the WTO and across vertical and horizontal levels. We present selected findings from studying various modes of decision-making. While the individual sections are written by scholars representing international law and international relations, the authors share a common objective. There is an explicit attempt to unpack (and to some degree deconstruct) various normative concepts of decision-making. In particular, the notions of legitimacy and accountability are a recurring theme.[4] In addressing these concepts, the authors suggest that

1 M. Elsig, 'WTO decision-making: Can we get a little help from the secretariat and the critical mass?', in D. Steger (ed.), *Redesigning the World Trade Organization for the Twenty-first Century* (Waterloo, ON: Wilfred Laurier University Press, CIGI and IDRC, 2009).

2 A. Hirschman, *Exit, Voice and Loyalty: Responses to Decline in Firms, Organizations and States* (Cambridge, MA: Harvard University Press, 1970); D. Drezner, *All Politics is Global: Explaining International Regulatory Regimes* (Princeton University Press, 2007).

3 See the recent International Monetary Fund (IMF) reform as an illustration of little outcome after a long reform debate. The external shock of a financial crisis might, however, have created a constitutional moment for IMF reform; constitutional moment as defined by J. Ikenberry, *After Victory: Institutions, Strategic Restraint, and the Rebuilding of Order after Major Wars* (Princeton University Press, 2000).

4 For a discussion on legitimacy, see M. Elsig, 'The World Trade Organization's legitimacy crises: What does the beast look like?' (2007) 41 *Journal of World Trade* 75.

there are different modes of legitimate governance witnessed in competing (and sometimes impossible to reconcile) views as to the objectives and functioning of political and legal systems. These various interpretations also contribute to the fragmentation–coherence debate and pose a certain eye of the beholder problem.[5]

The chapter first introduces the notions of legitimacy and accountability. Then, selected challenges to the WTO from different decision-making angles are discussed: first, we approach the core part of WTO decision-making from a political science perspective. The political science narrative investigates weaknesses in the mantra of a member-driven IO and presents functional arguments for further delegation of negotiation powers to the WTO Secretariat. Second, a legal analysis suggests taking a differentiated approach to improving decision-making and overall legitimacy based on the nature of legislative objectives. Third, starting from the puzzle of missing support from export firms, a framework for vertical decision-making is discussed. Fourth, the issue of overlapping authorities is addressed (horizontal decision-making). Finding the institutional sensitivity to cooperate across IOs is pivotal, as a discussion on law and practice in dispute settlement illustrates. The chapter concludes with selected recommendations related to the challenges presented.

B. Conceptualising a political system: legitimacy and accountability[6]

Legitimacy is a buzzword in the global governance debate. Legitimacy of a political system is related to overall acceptance witnessed most prominently through compliance.[7] Yet, scholars of law and politics widely disagree on the test that needs to be passed for a political system to be called sufficiently legitimate. In this respect it is useful to distinguish four political conceptions of legitimate governance as advocated by Andrew Moravcsik.[8] Depending on the conceptions of what makes a political

5 A. Moravcsik, 'Is there a democratic deficit in world politics?' (2004) 39 *Government and Opposition* 336.

6 This draws on Elsig, above note 4.

7 From this viewpoint, legitimacy 'can be understood as a general compliance of the people with decisions of a political order that goes beyond coercion or the contingent representation of interests'; quoted from P. Nanz and J. Steffek, 'Global governance, participation and the public sphere' (2004) 39 *Government and Opposition* 315.

8 These comprise deliberate, pluralist, libertarian and social-democratic perspectives, see Moravcsik, above note 5. Another debate has developed between constitutionalists/centralists and subsidiarists, see Elsig, above note 4.

system legitimate, the preference mix as to which design elements need to be improved varies. The deliberation school focuses on the political capacity of groups to act and suggests creating platforms to improve open and non-hierarchical debate and access of underprivileged groups to the system. Pluralists highlight mechanisms of accountability based on a competitive view of interest-group politics. For their part, libertarians aim to protect individual liberties and usually advocate limiting the agenda of an IO to its core tasks. Finally, social democrats push for addressing power asymmetries and for designing mechanisms for redistribution. Depending on the preferred model of a political system, adherents to a political perspective will focus differently on process variables or outcome indicators. In the same vein, legitimacy could be distinguished according to the elements that address primarily the input side, including participation, access and transparency (input legitimacy), and to the outputs the organisation produces and how efficiently this is done (output legitimacy).[9] A thorough understanding of philosophical conceptions underlying the calls for more democracy and legitimate governance will help one to understand why some groups demand the creation of a WTO parliament, while others advocate more discretion being given to negotiators to bargain behind closed doors.[10] In addition, the dynamic effects of reforming certain elements of the political system will need to be factored in, as input and output legitimacy are clearly linked (Figure 2.1).[11] The various faces of a legitimate political system are inherently reflected in debate on constitutionalisation.[12] However, depending on the underlying political conception, the baseline for legitimacy (on processes and outcomes) might differ substantially from the dominant ideas of the constitutionalist schools (see Chapter 1).

A second debate that has received greater attention in recent years relates to the question of accountability of IOs. As with the discourse on legitimacy, there is increasing conceptual work on how to make institutions more accountable and how accountability can be measured across

9 F. Scharpf, *Governing in Europe. Effective and Democratic?* (Oxford University Press, 1999).

10 D. Stasavage, 'Open-door or closed-door? Transparency in domestic and international bargaining' (2004) 58 *International Organization* 667; Elsig, above note 4.

11 It could well be that reforming input legitimacy (more access for stakeholders) might strengthen some elements of ouptut legimitacy (acceptance of results), but weaken others (performance).

12 For a discussion on legitimacy, constitutional theory and layers of governance, see also T. Cottier, 'The legitimacy of WTO Law' (2008) *NCCR Working Paper*, No. 2008/19.

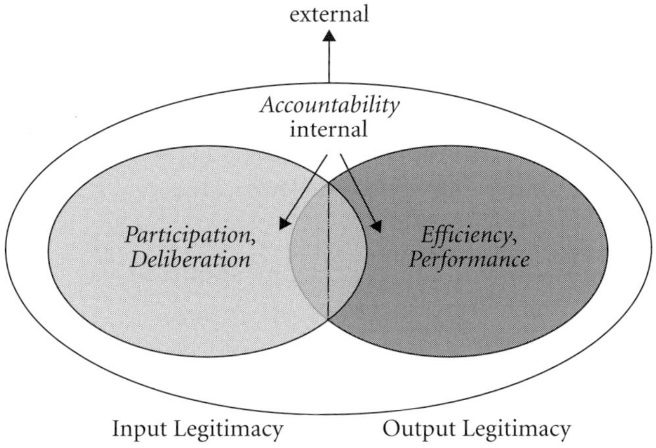

Figure 2.1 The WTO as a legitimate political system

IOs.[13] The notion of 'accountability' has been largely inspired by evolving practice within Anglo-Saxon political systems. However, accountability means different things to different societies and political systems, usually blending elements of control, transparency, responsibility and responsiveness.[14] In an influential contribution to the debate, Grant and Keohane opt for a view that 'at a minimum, institutions of governance should limit and constrain the potential abuse of power.'[15] In relation to the WTO, they argue 'ironically for those who attack the WTO as unaccountable, it represents one of the few attempts in world politics to formalise legal and supervisory accountability over the actions of sovereign states.'[16]

In the IO literature, there is an important conceptual distinction made between *internal* and *external* accountability. Internal accountability reflects the relationship between those that delegate power to international organisations (Member State governments) and those that carry out the tasks (e.g. civil servants). Internal accountability focuses on mechanisms to control the actions of the mandate-takers by creating institutional

13 H. Kovach, C. Neligan and S. Burall, *The Global Accountability Report* (London: One World Trust, 2003).

14 M. Bovens, 'New forms of accountability and EU-Governance' (2007) 5 *Comparative European Politics* 105.

15 R. Grant and R. Keohane, 'Accountability and abuses of power in world politics' (2005) 99 *American Political Science Review* 30.

16 Grant and Keohane, above note 15, p. 39.

control and sanctioning mechanisms.[17] External accountability refers to the possibility for those affected by IO policies to voice their concerns and find ways to influence subsequent policy-making.[18] An important factor in assessing accountability has been the amount of information and transparency within an IO. In this respect, the WTO has improved its internal and external accountability since the end of the 1990s.[19]

C. Decision-making in the WTO from a political science perspective

I. Governance elements: member-driven, consensual and single-package oriented

Decision-making in the WTO includes legislative as well as judicial decision-making. It is widely acknowledged that in recent years, the latter has outperformed the former. At the time of writing this chapter, the legislative decision-making arm of the WTO has again been put on hold. The Doha negotiations have suffered from a number of consecutive failures to make advances. There is ample evidence that the combination of consensus rule, the member-driven nature of the organisation and the single-undertaking approach for trade negotiations have contributed to this situation.[20] All three elements have been largely internalised and accepted by trade diplomats in as much as their discourse is largely driven by disguised 'communicative rationality'.[21]

17 Various sub-models exist from hierarchical to supervisory accountability using a variety of mechanisms including tools such as reporting, re-mandating, re-electing and budget control.

18 The Global Accountability Report focuses on four elements of internal accountability (member control, procedures for the appointment of senior staff, compliance mechanisms and type of evaluations) and four elements of external accountability (stakeholder consultation, complaints mechanisms, corporate social responsibility (CSR) and access to information). Later work has put even more emphasis on measuring participation (participation, transparency, evaluation, complaints and redress), Kovach, Neligan and Burall, above note 13.

19 There is a need for more systematic empirical work on assessing the WTO according to the various accountability mechanisms within a comparative research framework, see also M. Elsig, 'Changing authorities and new accountability in the World Trade Organization: Addressing a research gap', Paper presented at the Conference 'Pathways to Legitimacy – The Future of Global and Regional Governance', Warwick University, 17–19 September 2007.

20 Elsig, above note 1.

21 J. Checkel, 'International institutions and socialization in Europe: Introduction and framework' (2005) 59 *International Organization* 801.

The single-undertaking approach has received a high level of acceptance among the inner circle of the trade community since the successful closure of a difficult trade round (the Uruguay Round). Other approaches, including plurilateral agreements or critical-mass decision-making have not made significant progress and have not (yet) established themselves as credible complementary modes of decision-making. The consensus principle has been strengthened over time while various existing formal rules for adopting decisions by qualified majority voting have never been applied.[22] In particular, many developing countries enjoy the privilege of holding veto power as consensus is needed to close trade rounds. However, de facto decision-making is still dominated by a small (but growing) group of powerful trading nations. Finally, the member-driven nature of the organisation leads to reluctance on the side of contracting parties to delegate additional powers to the WTO and its Secretariat. Increasing membership has not made reform in such a direction more likely given the interest of contracting parties' representatives in playing an important role in various areas of day-to-day decision-making in the WTO.[23]

II. The WTO Secretariat in international negotiations[24]

The member-driven nature of the WTO has been clearly observable in negotiations. The intergovernmental logic has been a trademark of trade rounds since the start of the General Agreement on Tariffs and Trade (GATT)/WTO regime. Managing negotiations with increasing membership and an evolving trade and trade-related agenda has become highly complex. Transaction costs have increased owing to member-driven multilateralism and the effects of growth of potential veto powers have complicated the business of trade diplomacy. In terms of finding agreement by making a multitude of concessions across diverse areas of rules and specific market liberalisation initiatives, parties struggle to find a common 'landing zone' that is acceptable to all. The system increasingly suffers from the absence of a more institutionalised bargaining process. There seems to be a particular problem related to the lack of consolidation of the various positions on the table and parties' inability to move towards

22 N. Shpilkovskaya and D. Steger, 'Internal decision-making and rule-making processes', in D. Steger (ed.), *Redesigning the World Trade Organization for the Twenty-first Century* (Waterloo, ON: Wilfred Laurier University Press, CIGI and IDRC, 2009).

23 M. Elsig, 'Principal-agent theory and the World Trade Organization: Complex agency and missing delegation', forthcoming *European Journal of International Relations.*

24 This section draws on Elsig, above note 23.

real negotiations. In particular, the WTO faces a peculiar version of the 'endless cycling' dilemma. In the absence of clear institutionalised agenda-setting and deal-brokering processes, parties constantly table proposals.[25] In the current negotiation environment, there is insufficient transparency as to the role of various actors in agenda-setting and in overall process management. Decisions are usually taken in small-group settings. However, the growth in number of actors and the lack of institutionalised bargaining affects the likelihood of finding agreement. There exists a dominating strategy for parties not to make concessions until other parties have shown themselves willing to do so. The party that moves first risks ending up with nothing in return, as the signalled concessions are already interpreted as de facto concessions to be obtained.[26] While in certain sub-negotiations Committee chairs (held by permanent representatives of contracting parties) attempt to manage the process and ad hoc powers are usually delegated to the WTO Director-General during Ministerials, existing rules on decision-making seem insufficient to help overcome obstacles to cooperation. While the overall amount of information has increased within the system, and mistrust has been tackled to some degree by ongoing information exchange among contracting parties' representatives, parties collectively fail to conclude negotiations. The Director-General's hands are often overtly tied. This hinders his or her ability to act as deal-broker by tabling negotiations texts. A potential remedy for overcoming endless cycling could be to delegate certain agenda-setting powers to the Secretariat, starting in issue areas that touch less on existing sovereignty concerns. While this move seems counter-cultural, as argued in the Warwick Report,[27] there are a number of functional explanations why a variety of actors should call for a stronger role of the Secretariat. These voices for additional delegation include Members that have preferences similar to the Secretariat, small open economies that share the market-liberalisation doctrine advocated by most WTO officials, or small vulnerable economies that could find an ally in the Secretariat to address a variety of development concerns.[28] However, delegation to the

25 W. Riker, 'Implications for the dis-equilibrium of majority rule for the study of institutions' (1980) 74 *American Political Science Review* 432.

26 The EU has suffered from attempting to provide leadership in small groups and from signalling concessions, see M. Elsig, 'The EU in the Doha negotiations: A conflicted sponsor?', in A. Narlikar and B. Vickers (eds.), *Leadership and Change in the Doha Negotiations* (Leiden: Brill/Martinus Nijhoff, 2009).

27 Warwick Commission, *The Multilateral Trade Regime: Which Way Forward?* (Warwick: University of Warwick, 2007).

28 For other functional reasons to empower the Secretariat, see Elsig, above note 23.

Secretariat will not suffice. Any reform of governance calls for simultaneously addressing the other two mantras that drive decision-making: the single undertaking and the consensus rule.[29] The latter is taken up in the next section. The single undertaking approach seemed to present an optimal choice to conclude the Uruguay Round and commit most Members to a set of common obligations. However, the trade world of the late 1980s looked very different from the emerging multipolar trade world of today. Transatlantic initiatives no longer create sufficient pressures to induce others to follow.

The world economy relies on a trading system that can swiftly take up new regulatory challenges. It cannot wait for the end of a long trade round in which certain regulatory issues will be traded off for something else during the final hours of negotiations. New ways to credibly use variable geometry approaches, including new plurilateralism and critical mass, need to be further explored.[30]

D. Decision-making from a legal perspective

A number of recent proposals for reform of WTO decision-making address the issue of enhancing output legitimacy by focusing on the consensus rule and further delegation.[31] These proposals, which are referred to in this section as 'non-consensual decision-making', include the creation of a system of weighted voting,[32] the idea of critical mass decision-making,[33] strengthening the Secretariat,[34] or the establishment

29 For a contrafactual narrative of empowering the Secretariat and moving away from the consensus principle and the single undertaking, see Elsig, above note 1.

30 Warwick Commission, above note 27; Elsig, above note 1.

31 Formally, the WTO Agreement provides that Members shall resort to voting when the consensus needed to adopt a decision is not achieved. However, Members never resort to voting, which causes inertia of the decision-making process (or a deficit of output legitimacy). On reasons deterring contracting parties from resorting to voting, see C. D. Ehlermann and L. Ehring, 'Decision-making in the World Trade Organization: Is the consensus practice of the World Trade Organization adequate for making, revising and inplementing rules on international trade?' (2005) 8 *Journal of International Economic Law* 51.

32 See T. Cottier and S. Takenoshita, 'The balance of power in WTO decision-making: Towards weighted voting in legislative response' (2003) 58 *Aussenwirtschaft* 171.

33 See J. Jackson, 'The WTO "constitution" and proposed reforms: Seven mantras revisited' (2001) 4 *Journal of International Economic Law* 67.

34 See P. Sutherland *et al. The Future of the WTO: Addressing Institutional Challenges in the New Millennium. Report of the Consultative Board to the Director-General Supachai Panitchpakdi* (Geneva: World Trade Organization, 2004); Elsig, above note 1.

of a consultative body of limited composition.[35] These reform proposals essentially focus on two out of three components of decision-making – the actors and the procedural mode – however, they fail to address the third component: the object (or types of decision at stake).[36] This section attempts to draw a typology of WTO decisions. From a *material* perspective, we refer to general criteria that characterise decisions in terms of their *impact*. From a *formal* perspective, we analyse the powers formally attributed to the WTO and refer to concrete decisions at issue.

Such a characterisation seems useful for addressing the above-mentioned proposals designed to enhance output legitimacy. Indeed, it appears that Members are mostly unwilling to resort to non-consensual decision-making when it comes to decisions with an impact that affects their regulatory autonomy.[37] As will be shown, these concerns are addressed by constitutional requirements at the domestic level that aim at securing input legitimacy in the adoption of international acts. Therefore, reference to material criteria to characterise the impact of WTO decisions might contribute to the identification of decisions for which non-consensual decision-making would be politically feasible. Further, a formal description of WTO decisions should point to those concrete decisions to which non-consensual decision-making would be applied in practice.

I. Material perspective

From a material perspective, the impact of a decision is a function of its *substance* and its *legal nature* (binding character and existence of enforcement mechanisms). In the following, classifications of decisions are considered by reference to several frameworks: general international institutional law, provisions of the WTO Agreement, theories of Swiss

35 See R. Blackhurst and D. Hartridge, 'Improving the capacity of WTO institutions to fulfill their mandate', in E.-U. Petersmann (ed.), *Reforming the World Trading System: Legitimacy, Efficiency, and Global Governance* (Cambridge University Press, 2005).

36 On the three components of decision-making, see A. Ziegler and Y. Bonzon, 'How to reform WTO decision-making? An analysis of the current functioning of the organization from the perspectives of efficiency and legitimacy', in T. Balmelli and J. Chaisse (eds.), *Essays on the Future of the World Trade Organization* (Fribourg: Editions universitaires suisses, 2008).

37 This concern has been analysed using the notion of 'sovereignty': see J. Jackson, 'The Great 1994 sovereignty debate: United States acceptance and implementation of the Uruguay Round results' (1997) 36 *Columbia Journal of Transnational Law* 157.

constitutional law, and other conceptual frameworks in the legal and political science literature.

1. Distinctions in international institutional law

With regard to the legal nature of decisions, legal theory distinguishes between binding and non-binding decisions. Binding decisions are adopted through principal or subsidiary rule-making. Principal rule-making consists of the adoption of primary treaty rules – defined as 'the rights and obligations that bind States as members of an international organisation and as parties to a set of multilateral treaty instruments'[38] – according to general rules of international law (those of the 1969 Vienna Convention on the Law of Treaties (VCLT) in particular) or through procedures established by secondary treaty rules, which in the WTO can take the form of amendments, authoritative interpretations, waivers or decisions on accession.[39] Subsidiary rule-making refers to decisions adopted by an institutional body of an IO that have normative effect.[40] Non-binding decisions include recommendations and declarations, and are sometimes characterised as soft law. In the WTO, the Ministerial Conference has adopted such 'Declarations' that do not refer to Article IV WTO Agreement as their legal basis.[41] From a substantive perspective, legal theory further distinguishes between internal and external decisions.[42] While internal decisions regulate the functioning of an organisation in matters such as the adoption of its budget, the creation of subsidiary bodies or the adoption of staff regulations, external decisions extend beyond the

38 See M. Footer, *An Institutional and Normative Analysis of the World Trade Organisation* (Leiden: Martinus Nijhoff, 2006), p. 184.

39 Secondary rules prescribe specific procedures for generating acts of the organisation.

40 See Footer, above note 38, p. 271. Subsidiary rule-making should have its basis in specific delegations of power. However, some decisions may be based on an implied delegation of power. One example in the WTO is the SPS *Equivalency Decision* (G/SPS/19). It was adopted by the SPS Committee on the basis of Article 12:1 SPS, which generally states that the Committee 'shall carry out the functions necessary to implement the provisions of this Agreement and the furtherance of its objectives [. . .]'.

41 See WT/MIN(O1)/DEC/2 and WT/MIN(O1)/DEC/17, and S. Charnovitz, 'The legal status of the Doha declarations' (2002) 5 *Journal of International Economic Law* 207, who wonders if they are merely political commitments, binding decisions subject to enforcement by the DSB, or a new kind of secondary law emerging from a 'constitutive process' (at p. 211).

42 General classification in internal and external decisions is to be found in H. Schermers and N. Blokker, *International Institutional Law*, 4th edn (Leiden: Martinus Nijhoff Publishers, 2003), p. 752.

organisation to impose obligations upon Members with a possible impact on their legal order.[43]

2. Distinctions in the WTO Agreement

Article X of the WTO Agreement sets different procedural requirements, which are more or less respectful of Members' autonomy, for specific types of decisions. These varying requirements are a function of the specific impact of those decisions. On a gradual scale from low to high impact, one can distinguish between amendments that do not alter the rights and obligations of Members (which can be imposed on those that have not accepted them), authoritative interpretations and waivers (which only require the formal acceptance of a certain majority of Members), and amendments that alter the rights and obligations of Members (which must be submitted to the Members for acceptance).

3. Distinctions elaborated by Swiss constitutional theory

In implementing the democratic principle, Swiss constitutional theory resorts to material criteria that purport to characterise the impact of decisions in order to determine their corresponding legitimisation requirement (input legitimacy). In applying these criteria, the executive branch is in some cases entitled to adopt international acts with no delegation or approval from Parliament.[44] According to legal provisions, these criteria include: the technical nature of an act, the fact that it does not result in new obligations, the fact that it aims at implementing other acts that were previously adopted, and the fact that an act primarily deals with administrative issues that are first and foremost of concern to the public authorities; do not involve any significant spending; and do not impinge on individual interests that are legally protected. *A contrario*, international acts that do not fulfil these criteria are qualified as 'important' and must be approved by the Parliament.[45] The *criterion of importance* has been further defined by legal doctrine and is a function of how serious

43 Examples of external decisions in the WTO include GATS decisions prescribing disciplines for domestic regulations on services.

44 With respect to the adoption of international acts, see : A. Ziegler and Y. Bonzon, 'The domestic making of Member States' Positions in the WTO: The case of Switzerland' (2007) *NCCR Working Paper*, No. 2007/22.

45 On the concept of 'parliamentary reserve' see D. Wüger, 'Die direkte Anwendbarkeit staatsvertraglicher Normen', in T. Cottier, A. Achermann, D. Wüger and V. Zellweger (eds.), *Der Staatsvertrag im schweizerischen Verfassungsrecht* (Bern: Stämpfli Verlag, 2001), p. 197.

the infringement is on individual legal rights, the scope of its addressees, its financial repercussions, and its impact on the Swiss political system.[46] In addition, the period for which the commitment applies and its novel character are also of relevance.[47]

4. Further criteria in the legal and political science literature

The concept of a varying degree of legitimisation requirement according to the impact of decisions has been developed by Markus Krajewski. His criteria include the scope of the matters regulated, the legal density of rules and the existence of compulsory adjudication mechanisms.[48] In addition, Gianfranco Majone, in his work on the EU, proposes criteria that characterise decisions by reference to their impact, and distinguishes between 'efficiency-oriented policies' (legitimised by result) and 'redistributive policies' (that involve value judgments that must be made at the political level). Majone argues that with respect to the former, it is justifiable to delegate decision-making to non-majoritarian bodies, when 'independence and credibility' are required.[49]

II. Formal perspective

The first challenge in drawing up a typology is to delineate the notion of 'WTO decisions'. As we understand it, this notion refers to decisions that are reached according to the processes of the organisation and that, in this sense, are the product of a constitutional structure. These decisions are to be distinguished from the decisions that are reached according to traditional rules of international law (those of the 1969 VCLT in particular), and whose negotiation may take place within the framework of the WTO

46 *Ibid.*, p. 202.

47 Legal commentators further specify that these criteria must be combined with criteria that relate to the characteristics of the decision-making organs, which in some cases will reveal that parliament is not the most appropriate organ to reach the decision at stake. These criteria include a requirement for flexibility and an experimental process, the technical nature and the complexity of the matter at issue, and instances where the regulatory field is subject to rapid changes: see T. Cottier, 'Einleitung und Synthesen', in Cottier *et al.* (eds.), above note 45, p. 19.

48 See M. Krajewski, *Verfassungsperspektiven und Legitimation des Rechts der Welthandelsorganisation (WTO)* (Berlin: Duncker & Humblot, 2001), p. 230.

49 See G. Majone, 'Europe's democratic deficit: The question of standards' (1998) 4 *European Law Journal* 28. In Majone's terminology, non-majoritarian sources of legitimacy refer to expertise, procedural rationality, transparency, accountability by result; it is opposed to majoritarian sources of legitimacy that rely on more democratic representation.

but which are not considered decisions of the Organisation.[50] Article IV of the WTO Agreement describing the 'functions of the WTO' can serve here as a guide. In addition to the function of administering the settlement of trade disputes, for which the procedures are fairly detailed and well-defined, this provision further distinguishes between an 'implementation, administration and operation' function and a 'forum for negotiations' function. Taken together, these functions are often referred to as the functions of the WTO 'political branch'. From this perspective, the 'implementation, administration and operation' function would generate those *institutional decisions* that are the focus of this analysis, while the 'forum function' would refer to negotiations that result in decisions that are not acts of the organisation.[51] Further, this differentiation is matched with a distinction in the object and the mode of adoption of the different types of decisions. While negotiations that are part of the 'forum function' of the WTO are characterised by linkages and cross-concessions as a result of the single undertaking approach, decisions of the organisation tend to focus on a single issue and do not imply cross-concessions.

The WTO's institutional structure is built according to a hierarchical model, at the top of which the Ministerial Conference and the General Council (between meetings of the former) have the power to take binding decisions by virtue of their general 'authority to take decisions on all matters under any of the Multilateral Trade Agreements',[52] and the explicit power to adopt amendments of the agreements, authoritative interpretations, waivers of obligations and decisions on accessions.[53]

50 Such a distinction is made by J. Alvarez, *International Organizations as Law-Makers* (Oxford University Press, 2005). From this perspective, decisions that are not acts of the organisation include all acts that are neither adopted through secondary nor through subsidiary law-making (see above paragraph D. I. 1). In the context of the WTO, these include acts incorporating the results of the multilateral trade negotiations (MTN) process, or Protocols supplementing Schedules (such as the Annexes on Financial Services). Formally, these acts are adopted individually by states as parties to a multilateral treaty, not by an organ of the Organization. Further, on institutional differentiation in the WTO, see Y. Bonzon, 'Institutionalizing public participation in WTO decision-making: Some conceptual hurdles and avenues' (2008) 11 *Journal of International Economic Law* 751, and Y. Bonzon 'Mechanisms of public participation in international free-trade regimes: Insights for the World Trade Organization', in Steger (ed.), above note 22.

51 Some reform proposals make this distinction; see Cottier and Takenoshita, above note 32, who suggest using weighted voting for 'work undertaken in between rounds and in regular business of the WTO'.

52 Article IV of the WTO Agreement.

53 Articles IX and X of the WTO Agreement.

At levels below the Ministerial Conference and General Council, various councils and committees, including the Council for Trade in Goods (CTG), the Council for Trade in Services (GATS Council) and the Council for Trade Related Aspects of Intellectual Property (TRIPS Council), oversee the functioning of their respective agreements. Their authority includes the power to submit proposals and reports to the Ministerial Council regarding authoritative interpretation, amendments and waivers. The WTO decision-making process therefore follows a common institutional pattern according to which lower organs prepare decisions of higher organs, and where a distinction can be made between *preliminary*/non-binding decisions and *final*/binding decisions. Decisions at various levels are interrelated, creating a 'chain of decisions'.

However, some lower bodies are attributed specific powers, which might lead them to adopt binding decisions. These include, for example, the powers to grant special and differential treatment to developing country Members,[54] to concretise notions contained in the Agreements,[55] and interpret them in order to ensure, at a technical level, uniformity in their interpretation and application.

III. Designing flexible, non-consensual decision rules

It appears that consensual decision-making spawns a bargaining process, which implies concessions across topics and results in complex 'package deals', mixing measures focusing purely on tariff barriers with measures on non-tariff barriers that may involve non-trade interests. Furthermore, this bargaining process takes various forms, including informal processes that are hard to frame within the WTO's constitutional structure. By contrast, non-consensual decision-making leads to a focus on single decisions that involve single issues.

With reference to the material criteria listed above, it could be envisaged that some WTO decisions are adopted by the non-consensual mode of decision-making as their impact does not require a high degree of input legitimisation according to Members' constitutional standards. These include internal decisions, such as the appointment of the Director-General, the adoption of the budget and other decisions

54 See, for example, the power of the TBT Committee to grant mini-waivers on the basis of Article 12.8 TBT Agreement.

55 See, for example, the task of the Council on Trade in Goods to concretise the notion of 'parties primarily concerned' or that have a 'substantial interest', in the context of the modification of schedules, at paragraph 1 of the Understanding on the Interpretation of Article XXVIII of GATT 1994.

on procedural issues. For decisions with external effect, non-consensual decision-making could be applied to all preparatory decisions of lower-level bodies, including recommendations and proposals for amendment. In so doing, each Member would retain the option of blocking a decision at the final stage before it becomes binding; nevertheless this would allow the process to move forward with a greater chance of success than is currently the case.[56] In addition, final decisions that do not alter the rights and obligations of Members could be adopted by non-consensual decision-making.[57]

It is difficult to identify further binding decisions with external effect whose impact, according to clear criteria, would be sufficiently low to make them candidates for non-consensual decision-making.[58] One reason is that the constitutional standards of Members vary with more or less stringent requirements of input legitimisation in each case. Another reason is that the impact of a decision on each Member will also vary, depending on its specific commercial interests and regulations.

E. The vertical dimension of decision-making: The role of corporations

This section analyses the role of corporations in the legislative decision-making of the WTO. The difficulties noted in the current multilateral negotiation round serve as a starting point from which to construct an analytical framework that integrates firms into the analysis of trade policy-making. The usefulness of the framework is then illustrated by analysing selected manufacturing industries in the EU and the US. Finally, reference is made to the concepts of input and output legitimacy of the WTO from the perspective of corporations.

I. Demand for trade policy: the missing exporters' coalitions and the changing nature of import-competing group lobbying

The slow progress and bleak prospects for the Doha Round negotiations have been attributed to a number of factors. The lack of leadership,

56 On strengthening the WTO decision-making process in the phases before the final adoption of decisions, see Shpilkovskaya and Steger, above note 22.

57 Decisions that do not alter the rights and obligations of Members mostly deal with technical and minor interpretative matters. They can take the form of amendments (such as mentioned in Article X:4 of the WTO Agreement) or may be adopted by lower-level bodies.

58 The criteria in question would match those set by constitutional rules at the domestic level (see section D. I. 3), relating in particular to the economic impact of a decision or its impact on domestic legal systems.

domestic politics, conflicting views on development concerns, as well as the aforementioned characteristics of legislative decision-making in the WTO, have been proposed as explanations for the standstill in the current multilateral trade negotiations. However, from a decision-making perspective, there is an additional factor that affects the course of negotiations: the interest and support from the business community and its role in national and international trade policy formulation.

The WTO provides a governance platform to tackle concentrated producer interests in the domestic political arena. It creates institutional mechanisms to counterbalance existing alliances of import-competing producers with a coalition of export-oriented producers by means of reciprocal market access commitments between countries.[59] The balance of corporate trade policy interests at the domestic level is thus important since it shapes the politically feasible negotiation solutions at the international level. At present, observations at opposite ends of the spectrum of trade policy interests suggest that the balance of corporate trade policy interests appears to be changing. At the liberal end of the spectrum of trade policy interests, it is puzzling that firms do not voice export-oriented interests more strongly, particularly in the context of rising trade-to-GDP ratios and international production networks. At the protectionist end of the spectrum of trade policy interests, the fact that previously protected industries have apparently modified their trade policy positions also seems to be inconsistent with predictions made following standard politico-economic theories.[60] In view of these observations, closer attention should be paid to analysing the factors shaping corporate trade policy interests as well as to explaining the variation in trade policy positions across industries and countries.

II. Constructing an analytical framework for corporate trade policy interests

Analysing the role and importance of corporations in trade policy-making implies opening the 'black box' of states and focusing attention on domestic actors' interests and domestic institutions. Decision-making on trade policy is thus conceptualised as a 'vertical' system, integrating the

59 See B. Hoekman and M Kostecki, *The Political Economy of the World Trading System: The WTO and Beyond* (Oxford University Press, 2001), p. 28.

60 For an overview of standard politico-economic theories on trade policy, see J. Alt *et al.*, 'The political economy of international trade' (1996) 29 *Comparative Political Studies* 691.

interactions of corporations, business associations and governments into a single analytical framework. At the level of corporations, the focus is on the formation of trade policy interests. Deriving group interests from economic theory alone, however, is not sufficient to explain the trade policy advocated by countries at the international level. The study of institutions is important since individual and group interests are organised and mediated through institutions, fundamentally affecting outcomes.[61] In the domain of trade policy-making, the analysis of the institutional setting essentially includes two different types of 'institution': socio-economic institutions, such as business associations, and the formal political institutions that govern interest aggregation. In order to study outcomes, it is necessary to sequentially analyse interest formation, interest organisation and interest realisation within the political process.[62] The analytical focus thus takes a political input approach, stressing bottom-up interactions and favouring demand-side explanations of trade policy-making. This stands in contrast to supply-side explanations, which conceptualise policy interests as themselves being shaped by institutions, ideas and information in top-down interactions. The political input approach also differs from integrative approaches that model policy-making as a complementary or symbiotic process, in which both bottom-up and top-down aspects combine to produce policy in a complex web of interactions.[63] As the subsequent analysis of the textile industries[64] in the US and the EU suggests, the application of the bottom-up approach is particularly

61 J. Frieden and L. Martin, 'International political economy: Global and domestic interactions', in I. Katznelson and H. Milner (eds.), *Political Science: The State of the Discipline* (New York: W.W. Norton, 2003), p. 131.

62 For additional literature reviewing the political economy of international trade, see D. Rodrik, 'Political Economy of Trade Policy', in G. Grossman and K. Rogoff (eds.), *Handbook of International Economics* (Amsterdam: Elsevier, 1995), vol. 3; H. Milner, 'The political economy of international trade' (1999) 2 *Annual Review of Political Science* 91.

63 See G. Shaffer, *Defending Interests: Public-Private Partnerships in WTO Litigation* (Washington DC: Brookings Institution Press, 2003); C. Woll, *The Politics of Trade Preferences: Business Lobbying on Service Trade in the United States and the European Union*, Dissertation (Institut d'Etudes Politiques de Paris and Wirtschafts- und Sozialwissenschaftliche Fakultät der Universität zu Köln, 2004).

64 The textile industry is part of the aggregate sector composed of natural fibres, textiles, clothing and retailing. Each of these four segments is marked by distinctive characteristics, varying mixes of labour and capital as well as specific adjustment challenges. The case studies in the subsequent section refer only to the textile industry in the narrow sense, in which natural or synthetic fibres are used to produce textiles through manufacturing activities.

relevant to manufacturing industries.[65] The framework also appears to be useful for studying business interest aggregation within a comparative research setting.

III. Comparing textile industries' interest aggregation

Comparing the locus and evolution of recent trade policy interests in the US and the EU's textile industries, we find that trade policy interests in the EU have been modified, whereas they have essentially not changed in the US. In accounting for this observed variance, we focus on the three analytical levels proposed in the research framework. First, at the firm level, textile producers in the US and the EU have faced similar market conditions and developments over time, the most important factor being the progressive elimination of quantitative import restrictions under the WTO Agreement on Textiles and Clothing (ATC). Despite the comparable economic context of the textile sectors, more EU producers than their US textile counterparts have adapted to the increasing competitive pressure by means of technological innovation and product specialisation. In addition, it appears that different adjustment strategies have produced disparate industrial structures.[66]

At the industry level, we find considerable differences within the US and EU textile industries in how they organise and aggregate trade policy interests. In the US, the aggregation of trade policy interests was and is facilitated by relatively unified trade policy positions and increasing industry concentration in the US textile sector. In contrast, the EU textile sector has encountered difficulties in aggregating trade policy interests at the EU level. Considerable variation in factor endowments across Europe has contributed to regional variance in firms' adjustment strategies and trade policy interests, particularly between the textile industries of the more liberal northern Member States and the more protective southern Member States. This intra-industry division has led to compromises in

65 A bottom-up approach for the analysis of trade policy making is particularly relevant if corporations have a clear understanding of their trade policy interests. This is in contrast to supply-side explanations or integrative approaches which might be more relevant in service sectors. See for instance Woll, above note 63.

66 In the US, firms have relied on consolidation, which is reflected in the higher average number of employees per establishment. In contrast, the average number of employees is much lower in the EU where firms have relied more strongly on diversified inter-firm networks to increase production flexibility. Organisation for Economic Co-operation and Development, *A New World Map in Textiles and Clothing – Adjusting to Change* (Paris: OECD, 2004).

the aggregation of trade policy positions at the European level, essentially moving the EU textile industry away from strongly protective trade policy positions.[67]

Finally, at the level of political institutions, we find both similarities and differences between the two cases. One similarity is that the politically feasible trade policy options for the textile industries have changed considerably over time. Both in the US and in the EU, it has become increasingly difficult for the textile industries to demand protective measures, albeit for different reasons. From the 1980s onwards, the US textile industry has been less and less successful in securing additional protection in the face of the more liberal trade policy interests of the political decision-makers.[68] In addition, the textile industry increasingly faced opposition to protective measures from within the textile and clothing supply chains, in particular from organisations representing retailers. In the EU, it was the restructuring of trade policy-making authority at the European level that severely constrained protective trade policy positions for the textile industry, an industry that is characterised by important regional differences in trade policy positions.[69] In addition, the European Commission sought very early on to liberalise trade in lower-value sectors, particularly clothing and textiles, and grew more determined to do so over time.[70] The difference between the two cases is that the modification of the feasible policy options is institutionally grounded in the EU, while this is not the case for the US. We would therefore expect to see more policy stability in the EU, whereas a more restrictive trade policy on textiles is at least not precluded in the case of the US. This may also explain why the US textile industry has not changed trade policy positions whereas the EU textile industry has done so.

This summary of exploratory comparative case studies suggests that the proposed analytical framework is useful in structuring the analysis of decision-making on trade policy from a vertical perspective. Substantively,

67 See J. S. Knudsen, 'Integrating Western and Eastern European markets – Changing trade preferences in traditional manufacturing sectors in the European Union' (1998) 31 *Comparative Political Studies* 188.

68 President Reagan vetoed bills proposed by the Congressional Textile Caucus to control the growth of textile imports to the US. President Carter, before him also vetoed bills to this effect. While congressional support for the textile industry was significant, it was not sufficient to overcome the presidential vetoes, see O. Hathaway, 'Positive feedback: The impact of trade liberalization on industry demands for protection' (1998) 52 *International Organization* 598.

69 Woll, above note 63, pp. 49–52.

70 Knudsen, above note 67, pp. 205–208.

the cases highlight variance in corporate adjustment strategies, intra-industry differences and institutional constraints as particularly important factors shaping the trade policy positions of industries. Conceptually, the identification of three analytical levels and attention to interactions and feedback effects between these levels seems to generate more nuanced explanations than politico-economic theories focusing only on interests or institutions.

With corporations being the ultimate addressees of trade policy, this type of research aims to contribute to a better understanding of important drivers of trade policy-making, an understanding which ultimately relates to more general questions on the role and type of legitimacy of international institutions regulating trade. Even though some limited direct interactions with the WTO Secretariat take place with certain societal actors,[71] the interaction with societal actors on trade policy occurs at the domestic level. Input legitimacy of the WTO thus depends largely on the political system of the Member States and on the institutional mechanisms for interfacing with societal actors such as corporations, as well as the organised interests of civil society. In terms of output legitimacy of the WTO, a major challenge for the future is that the increasingly dynamic world economy needs quick solutions. As indicated above, corporations rely on a trading system that can react promptly to regulatory challenges. In this context, it seems likely that actual or perceived shortcomings in the output legitimacy of the WTO will in the future put even more pressure on legislative decision-making in the WTO and its reform.

F. Decision-making across competing authorities

Challenges also exist in making decisions in areas where there is overlapping authority. This section takes up the subject of the WTO's relations with other IOs in trade governance, in particular with regard to settling trade disputes. While the research frontier on overlapping authorities has been discussed in the field of trade law since the late 1990s, in political science scholars have only recently begun to examine the regime's complexity and how individuals, states and IOs navigate through the various regulatory platforms.[72] This section offers findings from a study

71 See Sutherland *et al.*, above note 34, pp. 41–48.

72 See C. Dupont and M. Elsig, 'Trade-and? The World Trade Organization's fuzzy borders: A framework paper', presented at the Conference on 'Trade-And? The World Trade Organization's Fuzzy Borders', Graduate Institute of International and Development Studies, Geneva, 5–6 February 2009.

that addresses different interactions between various IOs and the WTO adjudicator.

I. The WTO's judicial interactions across intergovernmental organisations

While public international law before World War II was essentially limited to a number of bilateral agreements, the situation has changed in favour of a large number of varied norms to regulate the conduct of both sovereign nations and individuals.[73] The fragmentation of international law which is the result of coexistence of various regimes administered by a number of international organisations, leads to considerable overlap between subject areas, for example in the field of trade and environment, culture, agriculture, health, intellectual property, development and monetary issues. The multitude of different organisations hosting these regimes generally raises a number of questions relating to their coherent functioning and coordination, which necessitates a certain level of reciprocal institutional sensitivity.

In the context of the WTO, critics argue that the organisation is closed to meaningful interaction with other IOs.[74] This also raises legitimacy issues for the WTO dispute settlement system.[75] Other international arrangements and IOs are rather consigned to positions subordinate to that of the WTO by the adjudicating bodies.[76] Although the WTO is increasingly seeking the advice of other IOs, it is clear that it is ill-prepared for these relatively new relationships, either in terms of substantive or procedural law.[77] The input by other organisations in dispute settlement is allegedly

73 See V. Mosoti, 'Law-making: Institutional Cooperation and Norm Creation in International Organizations', in T. Cottier, J. Pauwelyn and E. Buergi (eds.), *Human Rights and International Trade* (Oxford University Press, 2006).

74 *Ibid.*

75 The legitimacy of the WTO adjudication is premised on the contribution of Rob Howse suggesting three factors that legitimate the WTO dispute settlement system: fair procedures, coherence and integrity in legal interpretation; and *institutional sensitivity*. See R. Howse, 'Adjudicative legitimacy and treaty interpretation in international trade law: The early years of WTO jurisprudence' in J. H. H. Weiler (ed.), *The EU, the WTO, and the NAFTA: Towards a Common Law of Economic Integration?* (Oxford University Press, 2000); see also D. Tarullo, 'The relationship of WTO obligations to other international arrangements', in M. Bronckers and R. Quick (eds.), *New Directions in International Law*, Essays in Honour of John H. Jackson (Kluwer Law International, 2000), p. 173.

76 *Ibid.*, p. 171.

77 See T. Cottier, 'Preparing for structural reform in the WTO' (2007) 10 *Journal of International Economic Law* 503.

limited to the giving of factual information upon request which does not fully reflect their normative relevance. Although Article 13 of the Dispute Settlement Understanding (DSU) does not prevent panels from requesting 'legal advice' from other IOs, they have repeatedly shied away from doing so.[78] The WTO provisions that constitute the legal grounds for these interactions contain uneven procedures.[79] Before making a normative judgment on these interactions, we need to analyse to what extent the inputs of other IOs have been taken into account.

In the WTO, there exist several devices by which the adjudicator may link to other intergovernmental institutions. The first device arises explicitly from the WTO treaty reflecting the intention of the negotiators to defer to the jurisdiction of other international arrangements (e.g. the international monetary regime) with the view to avoiding conflicts.[80] The second emanates from the incorporation of other international arrangements in WTO law (e.g. intellectual property); and the third stems from presumptive exceptions from WTO general obligations (or the so-called 'safe harbour' provisions). Let us briefly outline these three linkage mechanisms.

1. Linkage through deference

Deferral to the IMF jurisdiction arises from Article XV GATT which sets out both the principle of consultation with the Fund and its scope, which includes monetary reserves, balance of payments (BOP) and foreign exchange (XV:2).[81] The analysis of this provision and the relevant WTO case law reveal that, while on the balance of payments the Fund provides factual assessments with the GATT retaining its scope of decision on whether this exception applies, its input entails a legal determination with respect to *exchange measures.*[82] An important dimension of this deferral is that a positive finding by the IMF regarding the consistency of 'exchange controls or exchange restrictions' with its Articles of Agreements should

78 For a good example, see *US – Section 211* and *US – Section 110(5) Copyright Act.* See also J. Pauwelyn, 'The use of experts in WTO dispute settlement' (2002) 51 *International and Comparative Law Quarterly* 332.

79 E.g. rules found in General Agreement on Tariffs and Trade (GATT) Art. XV, DSU Art. 13, Sanitary and Phytosanitary Agreement (SPS) Art. 11.

80 The solution devised in the GATT/GATS to avoid conflicts of treaty norms has been described as a form of '*ex ante* coordination'. See J. Pauwelyn, *Conflict of Norms in Public International Law: How WTO Law Relates to other Rules of International Law* (Cambridge University Press, 2003).

81 But also Arts. XII–XIV and XVIII, Section B of GATT.

82 D. Siegel, 'Legal aspects of the IMF/WTO relationship: The Fund's Articles of Agreement and the WTO Agreements' (2002) 96 *American Journal of International Law* 570.

not lead to finding a breach of the WTO Agreements. Article XV GATT has however its own flaws, like the ambiguity on whether the consultation provision can be stretched to the panels and its relationship to Article 13 DSU, which authorises panels to seek information from any source. WTO cases did not lead to a clarification of these points and, given their importance for the institutional sensitivity discussion, these issues should ideally be taken up in a non-judicial context.[83]

2. Linkage through incorporation of other international arrangements

The IMF-GATT/WTO linkage can be contrasted with the relationship of the WTO and WIPO – an international institution administering international property rights. The GATT 1947 makes only sporadic mention of intellectual property rights. This changed during the Uruguay Round (UR) where, with the decision to expand GATT's mandate to regulate trade-related intellectual property rights, trade negotiators suddenly were faced with the challenge of a highly technical and complex field. At the end of the UR, the TRIPS agreement incorporated by reference most obligations of several WIPO treaties.[84] As a result, the TRIPS/WTO dispute settlement provisions apply to any such obligations incorporated into the TRIPS.[85]

Given the former administration of these treaties by WIPO, it emerged as a good example of an organisation possessing superior authority (based on experience) to that of the WTO on a specific subject. In the absence of explicit WTO provisions requiring deference to this organisation, the WTO adjudicator appears to have exercised caution with regard to the treatment of WIPO's input in the disputes.[86] The requests of information addressed to the WIPO were re-emphasising the word 'factual' even if the information sought was allegedly regarding an interpretative issue. On its face, the normative impact of WIPO and the deference thereto by the WTO judiciary appears more limited, if contrasted, for example, to the IMF. Yet, the case law reveals quite a nuanced approach vis-à-vis this institution in that the panels/Appellate Body (AB) deferred to its expert opinion which,

83 The WTO relationship with the IMF has been analysed in *Korea – Beef, Argentina – Footwear, India – Quantitative Restrictions* and *Dominican Republic – Cigarettes.*

84 Paris and Berne Conventions, Rome Convention, and the Treaty on Intellectual Property in Respect of Integrated Circuits; see Art 1.3 TRIPS.

85 TRIPS Art. 64.1.

86 Two cases are relevant for this linkage: *US – Section 211* and *US – Section 110(5) Copyright Act.*

on some points, entailed interpretation of intellectual property norms.[87] This approach was assessed as a good example of institutional sensitivity of the WTO adjudicator.[88]

3. Presumptive exceptions and the adjudication of competing values

With the expansion of the WTO mandate and consolidation of its dispute settlement system at the end of the UR, non-trade values, such as health and environment, are more frequently contrasted to the traditional trade concerns.[89] Thus, a role for the related international arrangements and IOs emerges in the WTO settlement of trade disputes. Specifically, this role stems from GATT Article XX exemptions, as complemented by its variations included in the SPS and TBT Agreements. The SPS Agreement reveals clearly the decision of the negotiators to base the legality of some WTO measures on the standards ensuing from other IOs (like Codex Alimentarius, IOE, IPPC) on a rebuttable presumption.[90] These institutions acquired significance as they are the ones possessing superior knowledge to that of the WTO adjudicator in a specific field regulated by the WTO. Yet, their role in the WTO disputes is nebulous. The relevant case law analyses reveal that their input is limited to the identification of names of the independent scientific experts and provision of technical advice regarding, for example, the operation of their respective institutions (see *EC – Hormones*). Their role in the scientific trade disputes could be further elaborated with the view to contributing to better outcomes. An important question arising in this context is whether the prerogatives of these standard-setting organisations should be expanded to the interpretation of their own standards or whether their role is to be limited to the furnishing of those standards.[91]

87 See *US – Section 211* where the panel asked WIPO to make an assessment as to whether the Paris Convention was regulating the 'determination of the trademark ownership'. See Panel Report, para. 6.41.

88 R. Howse and D. Neven, 'United States – Section 211 Omnibus Appropriation Act of 1998 (WT/DS176/AB/R; DSR 2002:II, 589, DSR 2002:II, 683): A Comment', in H. Horn and P. Mavroidis (eds), *The WTO Case Law of 2002: The American Law Institute Reporters' Studies* (Cambridge University Press, 2005).

89 The adjudication of these values by panels does not only presuppose good legal interpretation techniques but also specific expertise.

90 The TBT Agreement does not name such organisations, contrary to the SPS Agreement.

91 Note should be taken, however, that in some earlier cases the AB tended to consider itself competent to interpret the relevant law of other regimes, including municipal law, as if it were interpreting WTO law itself (provided of course that the other law was properly

The role of these SPS institutions in the WTO disputes should be distinguished from the expert role other IOs (such as health, environment, human rights governmental organisations) have in relation to adjudication of an Article XX exemption. Confronted with such a case, the panel in *Thai – Cigarettes* requested an expert opinion from the World Health Organisation (WHO). While the mere request of an opinion points to the sensitivity of the WTO judiciary, the weight ascribed to this opinion was limited. The panel practically ignored evidence from the latter such as that opening up markets to American cigarettes in Latin American and Asian countries led to an increase in smoking.[92]

II. Various logics of horizontal interaction

IOs have presented information relating to the negotiation records of certain treaties (WIPO); assessments of the balance of payments situation of a Member (IMF); and historical developments of the harmonised system headings (WCO). The WTO adjudicator evidenced an inconsistent treatment of interpretive inputs from other IOs. Examples include *US – Section 211* where the adjudicator deferred to an interpretation by WIPO, and *EC – Bananas* where the AB revealed a tendency to consider itself as competent to interpret the relevant law of other regimes. Thus, a special role would be recognised to these institutions if the interpretative input of the norms falling within their respective regimes is deferred to.

The WTO relationship with the IMF appears to be quite unique in that it is the only organisation whose normative function is recognised in the WTO treaty.[93] Although the WTO adjudicator is encouraged to show higher sensitivity towards other IOs to legitimise itself,[94] the granting of comparable prerogatives to other IOs should not however be left entirely to the discretion of the judiciary. The limits of this sensitivity, which may take a form of 'deference' or 'giving special weight', should be framed by positive law upon a careful analysis of the competence and credibility of each of the institutions concerned.

before it as relevant to the application of a WTO Agreement; *India – Patents, EC – Bananas*). *US – Section 211* qualifies this approach as the WTO adjudicator has allowed the responsible organisation to make an interpretative evaluation of its former regime.

92 Howse, above note 75, p. 392.

93 This can be also claimed with respect to the possible role of the UN as arising from GATT Article XXI security exception.

94 See Howse, above note 75.

Recall, however, that most IOs lack architecture enabling them to provide authoritative interpretations of their own acts (either of their charters or other treaties).[95] Their founding charters do not formally assign this power to any body of IOs.[96] Even the resort to the ICJ in the UN system is hampered by its limited mandate on providing non-binding advisory opinions. Thus, interpretation endeavours in IOs may end up with various institutional bodies of the secretariat – a process which will not stand the legitimacy claims.[97] Some IOs however are different from others in that they specifically provide in their charter for an authoritative interpretation mechanism,[98] elaborating internal alternative dispute-settlement or fact-finding mechanisms which permit interpretation of their charters or other treaties within their administration (e.g. ILO). Thus, the architectural superiority of these institutions over other IOs should not be overlooked by the WTO judiciary. The architectural problem should not, however, prevent the WTO adjudicator from seeking legal opinions from the secretariats of these organisations, which could be attributed weight similar to that of the *amici curiae* briefs.

Seemingly, the role of other IOs in scientific trade disputes can be increased. As case law analysis suggests, there are disputes where the objective assessment of the matter by the panel has been consistently contested before the AB. The most notable example is *EC – Hormones* where the EC claimed and the AB confirmed that errors have been made by the panel in reading the data presented by a scientific expert. However, a number of solutions have been offered to this problem, like the consultation of an expert review group instead of individual experts, as envisaged by the DSU Appendix 4. Thus, one of the solutions to this problem is to ascribe a greater role to the specialised standards-setting organisations referred to in the SPS Agreement in the panel's task of reading

95 An authoritative interpretation will be complementing a provision of the primary law and determine the appropriate interpretation of the relevant provision.

96 J. Alvarez., 'Constitutional interpretation in international organisations', in J.-M. Coicaud and V. Heiskanen (eds.), *The Legitimacy of International Organisations* (United Nations University Press, 2001), p. 111.

97 The main issue here is the representation of the membership to those bodies.

98 This is the case with respect to, for example, the plenary bodies in the Food and Agriculture Organization, the International Maritime Organization, the Organization for African Unity, and the International Civil Aviation Organization. In the case of the IMF and some other financial organizations the interpretative issues are left to the executive directors and to the board of governors.

and understanding the scientific data presented by various individual experts.[99]

G. Conclusions

This chapter has discussed selected decision-making modes and has highlighted a number of the challenges the WTO system is facing. These conclusions briefly develop policy recommendations related to internal decision-making and judicial interactions. On internal decision-making reform, the authors have argued that three elements of decision-making need to be addressed simultaneously. Fixing one aspect will not suffice. We posit that strengthening the WTO Secretariat, developing various modes of qualified majority voting mechanisms and allowing for variable geometry could potentially unblock the current impasse. We suggest creating a working group within the WTO system with the mandate to discuss, elaborate and propose governance reforms (with a view to streamlining decision-making processes). Special emphasis should be placed on the different nature of the decisions, which calls for differentiated approaches to decision-making.

In terms of interaction with other IOs during adjudication, we suggest enhancing the role of other IOs in the WTO. The WTO adjudicator should to the greatest extent possible use the acts stemming from IOs as interpretative elements. Their normative impact will be greater in the WTO disputes if they are considered as context in accordance with the primary rules of interpretation under VCLT Article 31. The possibility of seeking legal opinions from other IOs' secretariats does not clearly arise from DSU Article 13 and therefore such option should be envisaged. The consultative role of the relevant IOs should be expanded in the science-related trade disputes with a view to contributing to the panels' better understanding of the complexities of the scientific expert information. This will contribute to the output legitimacy of the judicial system.

Bibliography

Alt, James, Frieden, Jeffry, Gilligan, Michael, Rodrik, Dani and Rogowski, Ronald, 'The political economy of international trade' (1996) **29** *Comparative Political Studies* 691–699.

99 Despite the fact that the DSU provides for the option of the scientific review groups the panel has opted for individual scientific experts, which led to some criticism. See T. Christoforou, 'Settlement of science-based trade disputes in the WTO: A critical review of the developing case law in the face of scientific uncertainty' (2000) 8 *New York University Environmental Law Journal* 622.

Alvarez, Jose, 'Constitutional interpretation in international organisations', in J-M. Coicaud and V. Heiskanen (eds.), *The Legitimacy of International Organisations* (United Nations University Press, 2001), pp. 104–154.

Alvarez, Jose, *International Organizations as Law-Makers* (Oxford University Press, 2005).

Blackhurst, Richard and Hartridge, David, 'Improving the capacity of WTO institutions to fulfill their mandate', in E.-U. Petersmann (ed.), *Reforming the World Trading System: Legitimacy, Efficiency, and Global Governance* (Cambridge University Press, 2005), pp. 455–468.

Bonzon, Yves, 'Institutionalizing public participation in WTO Decision-Making: Some conceptual hurdles and avenues' (2008) **11** *Journal of International Economic Law* 751–777.

Bonzon, Yves, 'Mechanisms of public participation in international free-trade regimes: Insights for the World Trade Organization', in D. Steger (ed.), *Redesigning the World Trade Organization for the Twenty-first Century* (Waterloo, ON: Wilfred Laurier University Press, CIGI and IDRC, 2009).

Bovens, Mark, 'New forms of accountability and EU-governance' (2007) **5** *Comparative European Politics* 104–120.

Charnovitz, Steve, 'The legal status of the Doha Declarations' (2002) **5** *Journal of International Economic Law* 207–211.

Checkel, Jeffrey, 'International institutions and socialization in Europe: Introduction and framework' (2005) **59** *International Organization* 801–826.

Christoforou, Theofanis, 'Settlement of science-based trade disputes in the WTO: A critical review of the developing case law in the face of scientific uncertainty' (2000) **8** *New York University Environmental Law Journal* 622–648.

Cottier, Thomas, 'Einleitung und Synthesen', in T. Cottier, A. Achermann, D. Wüger and V. Zellweger (eds.), *Der Staatsvertrag im schweizerischen Verfassungsrecht* (Bern: Stämpfli Verlag, 2001), pp. 1–31.

Cottier, Thomas, 'Preparing for structural reform in the WTO' (2007) **10** *Journal of International Economic Law* 497–508.

Cottier, Thomas, 'The legitimacy of WTO law' (2008) *NCCR Working Paper*, No. 2008/19.

Cottier, Thomas and Satoko, Takenoshita, 'The balance of power in WTO decision-making: Towards weighted voting in legislative response' (2003) **58** *Aussenwirtschaft* 171–214.

Drezner, Daniel, *All Politics is Global: Explaining International Regulatory Regimes* (Princeton University Press, 2007).

Dupont, Cédric and Elsig, Manfred, 'Trade-and? The World Trade Organization's fuzzy borders: A framework paper', presented at the Conference on Trade-And? The World Trade Organization's Fuzzy Borders, Graduate Institute of International and Development Studies, Geneva, 5–6 February 2009.

Ehlermann, Claus-Dieter and Ehring, Lothar, 'Decision-making in the World Trade Organization: Is the consensus practice of the World Trade Organization adequate for making, revising and implementing rules on international trade?' (2005) **8** *Journal of International Economic Law* 51–75.

Elsig, Manfred, 'The World Trade Organization's legitimacy crises: What does the beast look like?' (2007) **41** *Journal of World Trade* 75–98.

Elsig, Manfred, 'Changing authorities and new accountability in the World Trade Organization: Addressing a research gap', presented at the Conference on Pathways to Legitimacy – The Future of Global and Regional Governance, Warwick University, 17–19 September 2007.

Elsig, Manfred, 'The EU in the Doha negotiations: A conflicted sponsor?', in A. Narlikar and B. Vickers (eds.), *Leadership and Change in the Doha Negotiations* (Leiden: Brill/Martinus Nijhoff, 2009).

Elsig, Manfred, 'WTO decision-making: Can we get a little help from the secretariat and the critical mass?', in D. Steger (ed.), *Redesigning the World Trade Organization for the Twenty-first Century* (Waterloo, ON: Wilfred Laurier University Press, CIGI and IDRC, 2009).

Elsig, Manfred, 'Principal-agent theory and the World Trade Organization: Complex agency and "missing delegation"', forthcoming *European Journal of International Relations.*

Footer, Mary E. *An Institutional and Normative Analysis of the World Trade Organization* (Leiden: Martinus Nijhoff, 2006).

Frieden, Jeffry and Martin, Lisa, 'International political economy: Global and domestic interactions', in I. Katznelson and H. Milner (eds.), *Political Science: The State of the Discipline* (New York: W.W. Norton, 2003), pp. 118–146.

Grant, Ruth and Keohane, Robert, 'Accountability and abuses of power in world politics' (2005) **99** *American Political Science Review* 29–43.

Hathaway, Oona, 'Positive feedback: The impact of trade liberalization on industry demands for protection' (1998) **52** *International Organization* 598–603.

Hirschman, Albert, *Exit, Voice and Loyalty: Responses to Decline in Firms, Organizations and States* (Cambridge, MA: Harvard University Press, 1970).

Hoekman, Bernard and Kostecki, Michel, *The Political Economy of the World Trading System: The WTO and Beyond* (Oxford University Press, 2001).

Howse, Robert, 'Adjudicative legitimacy and treaty interpretation in international trade law: The early years of WTO jurisprudence', in J.H.H. Weiler (ed.), *The EU, the WTO, and the NAFTA: Towards a Common Law of Economic Integration?* (Oxford University Press, 2000), pp. 35–70.

Howse, Robert and Neven, Damien, 'United States – Section 211 Omnibus Appropriation Act of 1998 (WT/DS176/AB/R; DSR 2002:II, 589, DSR 2002:II, 683): A comment', in H. Horn and P. Mavroidis (eds.), *The WTO Case Law of 2002: The American Law Institute Reporters' Studies* (Cambridge University Press, 2005), pp. 482–522.

Ikenberry, John, *After Victory: Institutions, Strategic Restraint, and the Rebuilding of Order after Major Wars* (Princeton University Press, 2000).

Jackson, John, 'The great 1994 sovereignty debate: United States acceptance and implementation of the Uruguay Round results' (1997) 36 *Columbia Journal of Transnational Law* 157–188.

Jackson, John, 'The WTO "Constitution" and proposed reforms: Seven mantras revisited' (2001) 4 *Journal of International Economic Law* 67–78.

Knudsen, Jette Steen, 'Integrating Western and Eastern European markets – changing trade preferences in traditional manufacturing sectors in the European Union' (1998) 31 *Comparative Political Studies* 188–216.

Kovach, Hetty, Neligan, Caroline and Burall, Simon, *The Global Accountability Report* (One World Trust, 2003).

Krajewski, Markus, *Verfassungsperspektiven und Legitimation des Rechts der Welthandelsorganisation (WTO)* (Berlin: Duncker & Humblot, 2001).

Krasner, Stephen (ed.), *International Regimes* (Ithaca: Cornell University Press, 1983).

Majone, Giandomenico, 'Europe's democratic deficit: The question of standards' (1998) 4 *European Law Journal* 5–28.

Milner, Helen V., The political economy of international trade (1999) **2** *Annual Review of Political Science* 91–114.

Moravcsik, Andrew, 'Is there a democratic deficit in world politics?' (2004) 39 *Government and Opposition* 336–363.

Mosoti, Victor, 'Law-making: Institutional cooperation and norm creation in international organizations', in T. Cottier, J. Pauwelyn and E. Buergi (eds.), *Human Rights and International Trade* (Oxford University Press, 2006), pp. 165–179.

Nanz, Patricia and Steffek, Jens, 'Global governance, participation and the public sphere' (2004) 39 *Government and Opposition* 314–355.

OECD (Organisation for Economic Co-operation and Development), *A New World Map in Textiles and Clothing – Adjusting to Change* (Paris: OECD, 2004), pp. 37–41.

Oesch, Matthias, *Standards of Review in the WTO Dispute Resolution* (Oxford University Press, 2003).

Pauwelyn, Joost 'The use of experts in WTO dispute settlement' (2002) 51 *International and Comparative Law Quarterly* 325–364.

Pauwelyn, Joost, *Conflict of Norms in Public International Law: How WTO Law Relates to other Rules of International Law* (Cambridge University Press, 2003).

Rodrik, Dani, 'Political economy of trade policy,' in G. Grossman and K. Rogoff (eds.), *Handbook of International Economics* (Amsterdam: Elsevier, 1995), vol. 3, pp. 1457–1494.

Riker, William, 'Implications for the dis-equilibrium of majority rule for the study of institutions' (1980) 74 *American Political Science Review* 432–446.

Scharpf, Fritz, *Governing in Europe. Effective and Democratic?* (Oxford University Press, 1999).

Schermers, Henry and Blokker, Niels, *International Institutional Law: Unity Within Diversity*, 4th edn (Leiden: Martinus Nijhoff, 2003).

Shaffer, Gregory, *Defending Interests: Public-Private Partnerships in WTO Litigation* (Washington, DC: Brookings Institution Press, 2003).

Shpilkovskaya, Natalia and Steger, Debra, 'Internal decision making and rule making processes', in D. Steger (ed.), *Redesigning the World Trade Organization for the Twenty-first Century* (Waterloo, ON: Wilfred Laurier University Press, CIGI and IDRC, 2009).

Siegel, Deborah, 'Legal aspects of the IMF/WTO relationship: The Fund's Articles of Agreement and the WTO Agreements' (2002) 96 *American Journal of International Law* 561–599.

Stasavage, David, 'Open-door or closed-door? Transparency in domestic and international bargaining' (2004) 58 *International Organization* 667–703.

Sutherland, Peter *et al.*, *The Future of the WTO: Addressing Institutional Challenges in the New Millennium. Report of the Consultative Board to the Director-General Supachai Panitchpakdi* (Geneva: World Trade Organization, 2004).

Tarullo, Daniel, 'The relationship of WTO obligations to other international arrangements', in M. Bronckers and R. Quick (eds.), *New Directions in International Law, Essays in Honour of John H. Jackson* (The Hague: Kluwer Law International, 2000), pp. 155–174.

Van Den Bossche, Peter and Iveta, Alexovicova, 'Effective global economic governance by the World Trade Organization' (2005) *8 Journal of International Economic Law* 667–690.

Warwick Commission, *The Multilateral Trade Regime: Which Way Forward?* (Warwick: University of Warwick, 2007).

Woll, Cornelia, *The Politics of Trade Preferences: Business Lobbying on Service Trade in the United States and the European Union*, Dissertation (Institut d'Etudes Politiques de Paris and Wirtschafts- und Sozialwissenschaftliche Fakultät der Universität zu Köln, 2004).

WT/MIN(O1)/DEC/2, *Declaration on the TRIPS Agreement and Public Health*, adopted by the WTO Ministerial Conference on 14 November 2001.

WT/MIN(O1)/DEC/17, *Decision on Implementation-Related Issues and Concerns*, adopted by the WTO Ministerial Conference on 20 November 2001.

Wüger, Daniel 'Die Direkte Anwendbarkeit Staatsvertraglicher Normen', in T. Cottier, A. Achermann, D. Wüger and V. Zellweger (eds.), *Der Staatsvertrag im Schweizerischen Verfassungsrecht* (Bern: Stämpfli Verlag, 2001), pp. 93–250.

Ziegler, Andreas and Bonzon, Yves, 'The domestic making of Member States' positions in the WTO: The case of Switzerland' (2007), *NCCR Working Paper*, No. 2007/22.

Ziegler, Andreas and Bonzon, Yves, 'How to reform WTO decision-making? An analysis of the current functioning of the organization from the perspectives of efficiency and legitimacy', in T. Balmelli and J. Chaisse (eds.), *Essays on the Future of the World Trade Organization* (Fribourg: Editions universitaires suisses, 2008), vol. I, pp. 209–232.

3

Regionalism: moving from fragmentation towards coherence

RICHARD BALDWIN AND THERESA CARPENTER*

KEY MESSAGES: THREE FACTS AND AN IMPLICATION

- ***Fact 1***: The world trade system is marked by a motley assortment of discriminatory trade agreements known as the 'Spaghetti Bowl'.
- ***Fact 2***: Regionalism is here to stay. Trade agreements will continue to proliferate even after the current trade round meanders to a conclusion.
- ***Fact 3***: This tangle of trade deals is a sub-optimal way to organise world trade. The discrimination inherent in regionalism is economically inefficient and the costs rise as manufacturing becomes ever more internationalised and supply chains grow across national borders.

Regionalism is also unfair. While the spaghetti bowl is a problem for firms in big nations, it is much more of a problem for firms in poor nations. Rich nations have the resources and negotiating leverage to navigate the tangle's worst effects. The governments of small and poor nations do not. The spaghetti bowl falls much harder on the heads of the world's small and poor nations.

Implication: As the spaghetti bowl's inefficiencies are increasingly magnified, the world must find a solution. Since regionalism is here to stay, the solution must work with existing regional arrangements, not against it. The solution must be to multilateralise regionalism.

A. Introduction

The World Trade Organization (WTO)-centric world trade system is principled and rules-based, yet flexible enough to embrace the vast range of

* Individual Project No. 3, 'Regionalism, Special and Differential Treatment, and Variable Geometry'. We would like to thank the research students who worked on their theses and dissertations under the auspices of IP3, including Pamela Bombarda, Yose Damuri, Elisa Gamberoni, Dany Jaimovich, Vivek Joshi, Andreas Lendle, and Roland Rieder.

realities facing nations across the planet. The key principle – Article I of the General Agreement on Tariffs and Trade (GATT) – is non-discrimination. The rich reality of global trade relations, however, led the founders to allow for disciplined deviations from the non-discrimination principle. Chief among these derogations is the Article XXIV exception for regional trade agreements (RTAs), namely customs unions and free trade agreements (FTAs).

The GATT's treatment of regionalism worked well enough through the 1980s; RTAs were relatively rare and multilateral tariff cutting was the main vehicle for global trade liberalisation. Even as their number began to climb exponentially in the 1980s, RTAs seemed relatively unthreatening. The nations driving effective regionalism were also the stalwarts of the GATT-centric trade system – the United States (US), the United Kingdom (UK), the European Union (EU), the European Free Trade Association (EFTA) nations, Canada, Australia and New Zealand (Japan was the only stalwart which eschewed regionalism). The stalwarts were cutting tariffs both regionally and multilaterally, while other GATT/WTO Members were doing neither.[1]

Regionalism took two important turns from 1990 onwards: (1) the stalwarts started signing effective, reciprocal RTAs with some of their developing country trade partners; and (2) developing nations, which had long since signed RTAs which had little impact on trade flows, started signing and implementing commercially important RTAs among themselves.[2] These changes interacted with shifts in the distribution of global trade flows. The countries of the 'Quad' (EU, US, Japan and Canada), which traditionally were the key drivers of GATT/WTO liberalisation, saw their share of world imports fall gradually from 75 per cent in 1990 to 60 per cent today. The new trade powers – the BRIC countries (Brazil, Russia, India and China), the four tigers (Hong Kong, Singapore, Taiwan, South Korea), together with Indonesia, Mexico, Turkey and South Africa – saw their share rise to almost a quarter of world trade, a share that is rising fast.

These changes have moved regionalism from being a relatively benign phenomenon to one that poses an important challenge to the WTO-centric trade system. To put it crudely, the GATT/WTO 'old guard'

1 See Baldwin and Seghezza (2007), Lendle (2007) and Joshi (2009) for evidence on this correlation of regional and multilateral tariff cutting.

2 Most notably, Mercosur, the Association of Southeast Asian Nations (ASEAN) FTA and the ASEAN+1 FTAs; see Holmes (2005) and Foroutan (1998) for evidence on which RTAs affect trade flows.

is starting to view North–South RTAs as an effective, perhaps superior, means of expanding commercial opportunities for their exporters in the nations that did not open up in the GATT process. At the same time the emerging markets, whose trade volumes suggest they are fast becoming the 'new guard', are showing few signs of making the transition from being the free-riders they were under the GATT to the stalwarts the world needs them to become under the WTO. In particular, the emerging markets – whose exporters have never had to fight for the rules-based, WTO-centric system – are having a worryingly favourable experience with regionalism. Their exporters have good access to rich-nation markets as the result of decades of free-riding under the GATT, and they are gaining good access to their regional developing country partners via RTAs. Both the new guard and the old guard seem to be viewing regionalism as an important complement to multilateralism. The worry is that they will slip into viewing it as a substitute.

The simplest solution to these challenges would be to ban RTAs. This will not work. It is politically impossible for the old guard to give up their well-established RTAs; given the WTO's consensus decision-making, this means that it is politically impossible to convince the new guard to give up theirs.

Regionalism is here to stay. This means that the only way to move from fragmentation to coherence when it comes to RTAs is for the WTO to work with regionalism, not against it. To meet the challenge posed by RTAs, the WTO has to find ways to multilateralise regionalism.

This chapter draws on the research conducted by IP3 on how the WTO could encourage the multilateralisation of regionalism. The paper follows the dictum of the great sleuth, Sherlock Holmes. As he said to Watson in *A Scandal in Bohemia*: 'It is a capital mistake to theorize before one has data. Insensibly one begins to twist facts to suit theories, instead of theories to suit facts.' The next section, section B, presents the facts on regionalism. Section C discusses the implications of these trends for the WTO-centric trading system, and section D discusses ideas for multilateralising regionalism. The final section presents our concluding remarks.

B. The reality of RTAs

The nature of RTAs has changed significantly since the GATT was signed in 1947.[3] We start this section with a brief review of the history of RTAs

3 RTAs is the name used in the WTO even though many are no longer regional. The WTO's working definition of regionalism is any trade agreement notified under the Enabling

(drawing heavily on Carpenter 2009, and Baldwin 1997) and then go on to paint a statistical portrait of today's RTAs.

I. Post-war waves of regionalism

It is useful to distinguish three waves of regionalism. The first occurred in the period prior to 1986.

1. The first wave of regionalism

In the first post-war decades, regionalism was largely a European phenomenon (apart from the pre-existing, colonial-era preferences such as the Commonwealth). All sorts of preferential arrangements appeared in Europe in the 1940s and 1950s, the most important being the European Payments Union (discriminatory liberalisation of bilateral quotas linked to balance of payments problems), the European Coal and Steel Community (ECSC) (preferential tariff and quota treatment among France, Germany and the Benelux nations in coal and steel products), and, of course, the European Economic Community (EEC) which can be thought of as expanding the ECSC to cover all sectors of the economy.

The ECSC was clearly a violation of Article XXIV – specifically the provision that requires a customs union to cover substantially all trade – since it included only two sectors. Despite this, GATT members accepted it (because they agreed that a unified, peaceful Western Europe was in everyone's interest and the ECSC seemed to foster this goal). While the ECSC did not trigger a domino effect, the establishment of the EEC, with its plan to move to a common external tariff, promoted the formation of another West European bloc, the EFTA.[4]

The 1960s saw regionalism spread well beyond Europe. Motivated by South–South solidarity and the prevailing economic doctrine that stressed market size as a key determinant of industrial success, two early RTAs were formed in Latin America: ALALC (Asociación Latinoamericana de Libre Comercio) in 1960, and CACM (Central American Common Market) in 1961. In 1965, North–North regionalism got a double boost when North America joined the RTA club with the US–Canada Auto Pact in 1965, and Australia and New Zealand signed the Closer Economic Relations (CER) treaty.

Clause, or GATT Article XXIV, or General Agreement on Trade in Services (GATS) Article V.

4 The EFTA original seven are Austria, Denmark, Norway, Portugal, Sweden, Switzerland and the UK; it is a plurilateral FTA rather than a customs union.

North–North regionalism took a further big step forward in 1973 when the first EU enlargement in 1973 triggered a domino effect that led to the signing of a bilateral FTA between the EEC and all the remaining EFTA members.[5] As a consequence, Western Europe was one large duty-free zone for industrial goods by the mid 1970s. Another big step came in 1986 when the EU launched a massive, preferential liberalisation of behind-the-border barriers (the Single European Act), and Canada finally reversed its long held opposition to a broadening of US–Canada free trade beyond motor vehicles by proposing an FTA (talks began in 1986). The EU's move triggered a domino effect that brought all the EFTA members into the Single Market (either by EU membership or by membership in the European Economic Area agreement).

From the conclusion of the Kennedy Round in 1967 until the mid-1980s, South–South regionalism expanded rapidly in Africa, Latin America and Asia. Many of the RTAs were ideologically motivated, and did not go far in the way of tariff cutting. For example, the trade concessions embodied in the Tripartite Agreement between Egypt, India and Yugoslavia, whose leaders were the pioneers of the non-Aligned movement, amounted to a 50 per cent tariff reduction for 193 products. However, this period saw the foundations laid for what have become the main regional groupings, including ASEAN, which was formed in 1967 with five members.

The hallmarks of the first wave were: (i) that North–North RTAs were effective while South–South RTAs were not,[6] and (ii) the nations which actually liberalised preferentially were also liberalising multilaterally in the Kennedy and Tokyo Rounds; nations which did not liberalise in the GATT also failed to do so in their RTAs. Regionalism and multilateralism seemed to be driven by a common political economy process that favoured trade openness.

2. The second wave of regionalism

The second wave of regionalism begins in 1990. Rocked by debt crises in the 1980s, many Latin American economies turned their backs on import-substitution industrialisation and started to open up. Mexico was the vanguard. After unilaterally cutting tariffs, joining the GATT and

5 Baldwin (1993, 1997) introduced the domino theory of regionalism; for empirical evidence see Sapir (2001), Baldwin and Rieder (2007), Egger and Larch (2008), and Baldwin and Jaimovich (2009). See Baldwin (1994, 1992, 2008) for detailed historical accounts of these domino effects in Europe.

6 See Holmes (2005) and Foroutan (1998).

implementing domestic economic reforms, Mexican President Salinas suggested that a Mexico–US FTA would lock-in his reforms. When the US accepted and talks began, the result was a massive domino effect throughout the Western Hemisphere, with Canada being the first domino (they asked for US–Canada and US–Mexico to be trilateralised into the North American Free Trade Agreement (NAFTA)).[7] Many Latin American countries expressed interest in FTAs with the US and the Bush Administration responded with the 'Enterprise for the Americas Initiative'.

NAFTA is a landmark in regionalism – the first example of a substantial, reciprocal North–South FTA (previously, North–South preferences tended to be unilateral). Although NAFTA was nowhere near as deep as the Single Market or EEA, it was the first time that Northern partners insisted on disciplines that went far beyond those of GATT.

A second novel element in this second wave was the establishment of effective South–South regionalism as exemplified by Mercosur (Yeats 1998). Here trade preferences initially limited to Brazil and Argentina triggered a domino effect that led to a widening net of Mercosur agreements. A corollary of this was the spread of bilateralism among many Latin American countries that included, notably, cross-regional FTAs (Mexico and Chile were leaders).

The fall of the Berlin Wall unleashed two more domino effects during this wave. The EU rushed to sign FTAs with the newly independent nations in Central and Eastern Europe, and to avoid the emergence of discrimination, the EFTA nations all followed suit. Worried that Central Europe would compete for EU offshoring jobs and investment, the Mediterranean nations pushed for reciprocal FTAs with the EU. This new set of North–South FTAs, like the US–Mexico agreement, involved a high level of discipline for the developing nation partners.

The final novel element of the second wave is what Baldwin (2006a) calls 'spaghetti bowls as building blocs'. By the mid-1990s, Euro-Med trade arrangements were marked by a massive 'spaghetti bowl' of RTAs – a mess that hindered the efforts of EU firms to set up efficient supply chains.[8] In reaction, the EU orchestrated a massive multilateralisation of these RTAs with the 1997 Pan-European Cumulation System (PECS); an effort which soon expanded to include the Mediterranean nations. This system imposed common rules of origin and rules of cumulation on all the trade relations in the Euro-Med area, thus eliminating the spaghetti

7 See Lawrence (1996) or Baldwin (1997) for a detailed account of this domino effect.

8 Bhagwati (1991) coined the term spaghetti bowl to describe the messy state of RTAs.

bowl syndrome throughout the area (see Gamberoni 2008 or Augier *et al.* 2005 for details).

In contrast to the first wave, the line-up of regional and multilateral liberalisers was less exact. While most developed nations were opening up both multilaterally and regionally, many of the developing nations were only liberalising unilaterally or via regional arrangements (they relied on 'special and differential' treatment to avoid important tariff cutting commitments in the Uruguay Round).

3. The third wave of regionalism

The third wave of regionalism was triggered by China's suggestion of negotiating an FTA with ASEAN. In reaction to this domino effect, East-Asian regionalism, which had until then been a rather sleepy affair, took off (Baldwin 2006a, Baldwin and Carpenter 2009). A truly impressive number of FTAs have been concluded since 2000, with many more under negotiation or discussion.

II. Regionalism and multilateralism

As Baldwin (2006c) points out, there is a remarkable correlation of the key multilateral and regional initiatives. Considering in turn the three waves of regionalism mentioned above, during the first wave formation of the EEC triggered the Dillon Round; the Kennedy Round was launched just before the major spread of North–North regionalism in 1965, and the Tokyo Round was launched in the year that Western Europe completed its virtual free trade zone. During the second wave, the Uruguay Round was launched in the same year as the US–Canada FTA talks began and West Europe began the massive deepening of its preferential liberalisation. The Doha Round was launched in 2001, soon after the third wave of regionalism started. More direct evidence for the notion that RTAs are not an enemy of most-favoured nation (MFN) liberalisation can be seen in Lendle (2007), and Estevadeordal, Freund and Ornelas (2008).

III. A snapshot of today's regionalism

Figure 3.1 shows the explosive growth in the number of PTAs in the early 1990s. The numbers are startling. There were just 37 agreements notified to the WTO in 1994; by March 2009 the number of notifications had reached 434, although only 243 are still in force.[9] In some ways, this

9 The enlargement of the EU is responsible for most of the RTAs that became inactive.

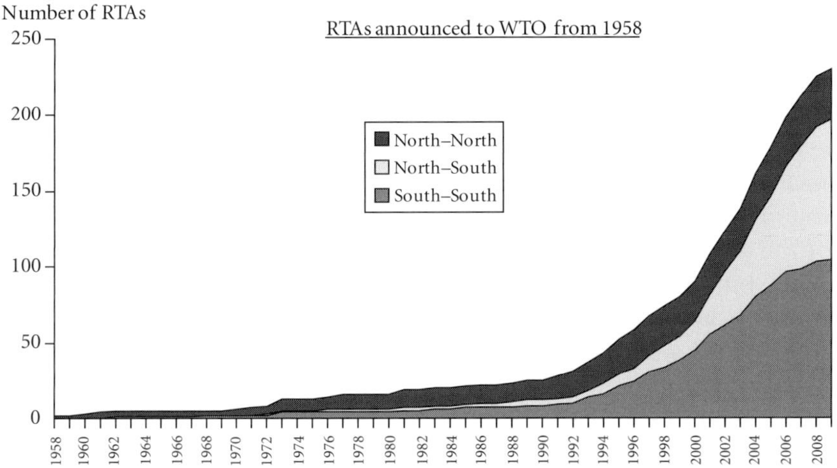

Figure 3.1 Explosion of RTAs, North–North, North–South and South–South, 1958–2009

Source: WTO RTA online database (updated May 2009) and authors' categorisation.

is just an implication of combinatorics; the number of bilateral agreements between 'n' nations is n(n−1)/2, so the number of deals tends to grow with the square of the number of nations playing the bilateralism game. The numbers in Figure 3.1, however, are misleading in at least four ways.

First, the number is mechanically inflated by the fact that since 1994 PTA deals in services and PTA deals in goods have been notified separately.

Second, announcing a PTA to the WTO is much easier than implementing it. For a variety of reasons, many nations sign FTAs that they never implement. While it is impossible to objectively define 'implemented' in a fully satisfactory manner, two studies have attempted just such a categorisation. Holmes (2005) found that only about two dozen of the 150 PTAs in existence at the time had actually created trade in the sense that the PTA dummy in a standard gravity regression was positive and significant. This is especially true for the South–South arrangements. Foroutan (1998) uses a more qualitative approach but arrives at a similar answer.

Third, and more substantially, the nature of the agreements has changed. Before the second wave started, half the agreements were North–North. Since the late 1990s, almost half of the new PTAs are South–South. Although there are exceptions, these tend to cover a lower fraction of the partners' trade with each other and are often not implemented in the sense that commitments to lower tariffs on important items are not carried through. Another important category is the North–South arrangements involving a rich nation and a developing nation, such as the US–Mexico FTA, or Japan–Malaysia Economic Partnership Agreement. These tend to be more fully implemented but often involve very lopsided tariff cutting since most rich nations had already lowered their MFN tariffs in GATT Rounds. In other words, they carry the threat of diverting import sources for the developing nation partner (which typically maintains high MFN tariffs) but much less so for the developed partner.

Fourth, although something like one hundred PTAs have been notified to the WTO since the beginning of the twenty-first century, the total volume of world trade covered by PTAs has hardly changed. The reason is that many of the recent PTAs cover bilateral trade relations that account for only a minor share of world trade. Only six of the 193 PTAs notified to the WTO cover more than 1 per cent of world trade, and only eight surpass the half of one per cent bar. From the twentieth largest on down, the PTAs cover less than one tenth of one per cent and the share rapidly drops to negligible after the first 50. The EU is in a league by itself as it accounts for 27 per cent of world trade, almost four times NAFTA's 7 per cent. Indeed, the EU is a partner in 11 of the 20 biggest PTAs, so in terms of impact on world trade, regionalism still has a strong European accent (the EU has some sort of preferential arrangement with all but nine members of the WTO).

Figure 3.2 shows that, apart from ASEAN and Mercosur, South–South arrangements account for only small amounts of trade from the global perspective.

Every single WTO Member has signed at least one RTA with the sole exception of Mongolia. The top trade powers – the EU, the US, and Japan – are actively pursuing such agreements, and the emerging trading powers – China, Brazil and India are following suit. The newest trend in RTAs is that many of them are no longer regional. Although only 10 per cent of the RTAs in force are extra-regional, around half of the deals currently under negotiation involve nations from different regions (Fiorentino, Verdeja and Toqueboeuf 2007).

IV. Regionalism in the regions

The complexity of RTAs in the Western Hemisphere is legendary, with each wave of regionalism further complicating the picture: the result is a highly complex spaghetti bowl of overlapping, intersecting arrangements.

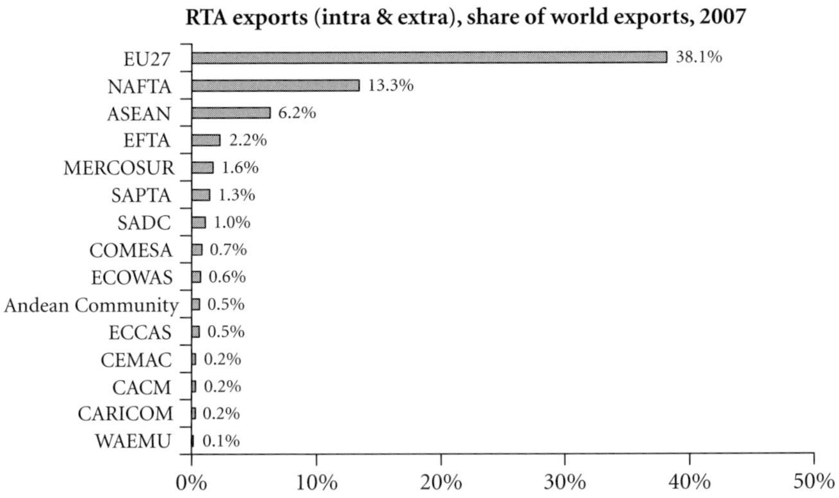

Figure 3.2 Size of RTAs, 2007.
Source: Authors' calculation using COMTRADE data

Regionalism in Africa has a long tradition and is complex on paper, but many agreements are not implemented or only loosely implemented (Draper and Qobo 2009).

Asia, a latecomer to the RTA game, is now the place where regionalism is growing fastest. The number of RTAs in Asia soared from just a handful in the mid 1990s to over a hundred in 2007. There are two natural 'hub' nations in East Asia – China and Japan. For various historical and political reasons, however, neither has taken a strong leadership role. The result has been a particularly messy 'noodle bowl' syndrome with a collection of relatively small nations – the ASEANs – acting as pivot for East-Asian regionalism.

1. Complexity multipliers

The 'spaghetti bowl' inefficiencies are enormously magnified by two types of 'complexity-multipliers': offshoring and rules of origin.

(a) **Offshoring** Starting in 1985, technological and regulatory changes combined to significantly lower the cost of coordinating complex tasks across distance. This, together with falling trade costs – the combination of lower tariffs and lower freight costs – transformed the world of manufacturing and trade along with it. Stages of manufacturing that had previously been performed in close proximity – within walking distance to facilitate face-to-face coordination – could now be dispersed without an enormous drop in efficiency or timeliness. Working methods and product designs were also shifted in reaction to the spatial separation, typically in ways that made production more modular. This is what Baldwin (2006b) calls the 'second unbundling'. Tasks that had had to be performed in adjacent bays in a single factory could now be done in separate factories in separate nations. The increasingly complex trade pattern necessitated by these regional supply chains meant that the spaghetti bowl complexity became more of a problem for firms.

(b) Rules of origin The second 'complexity multiplier' arises from 'rules of origin'. Due to the massive unbundling of manufacturing processes, the true 'origin' of a good is not at all obvious, so these 'rules of origin' that are needed to determine tariffs that would be applied to imports are often highly complex. In turn, this greatly complicates firms' efforts to set up efficient international supply networks.

The two complexity-magnifiers – rules of origin and unbundling – independently worsen the efficiency impact of tariff discrimination. But they also magnify each other's efficiency-dampening effect. Unbundling has made it much harder to determine where a particular good is made; and more complicated rules are needed to determine the origin of items whose ingredients may be sourced from a host of countries.

V. Spaghetti bowl in services and non-tariff barriers

While regionalism in terms of preferential tariff cuts is the easiest to document and measure, regionalism also matters in services and non-tariff barriers.

At the end of 2009, the WTO counted more than 50 services RTAs; only five of these were signed before 1994. Services RTAs fall into three broad categories (Delimatsis 2007). First, services RTAs can provide preferential market access by equalising regulation and tax regimes between domestic and foreign firms (national treatment) and by granting better market access to them, such as recognising foreign professional qualifications (preferential access). Second, services RTAs can rule out discrimination by granting most-preferred access to all members of the RTA. This is known as non-party MFN status in the WTO jargon. Third, services RTAs include rules of origin (ROOs) although they are substantially different from those applied to trade in goods. The issue tends to relate to the origin of the person or firm rather than the services they are supplying. One of the striking features in both areas is the extent to which WTO Members have signed up to services RTAs that include disciplines that they resist at the multilateral level (see Roy, Marchetti and Lim 2006, and Marchetti and Roy 2009).

Given the incidental nature of most service protection – i.e. the political economy of the barriers is aimed at protecting incumbents from competition from all firms, not just foreign firms – and the nature of the barriers (mainly prudential regulation), it is much harder to grant important preferences for services than for goods. It is simply hard to arrange discrimination without the equivalent of ROOs. Baldwin, Evenett and Low (2009) argue that this means that a great deal of the trade liberalisation in RTA services is not discriminatory in the same way that RTAs are on tariffs. Indeed, Fink and Jansen (2009) show that preferential agreements concerning trade in services have not created a 'spaghetti bowl' in the way that tariff preferences have, due to non-discriminatory implementation of RTA commitments, liberal ROOs, and the widespread inclusion of non-party MFN clauses. Moreover, developing nations frequently use RTAs with developed partners to lock in unilateral reform, so there is little intent to discriminate.

Another important feature of many service RTAs – from the perspective of their system implications for the WTO – is the so-called 'non-party MFN clause'. These tend to automatically multilateralise the preferences in each new RTA and thus take the system closer to multilateralism. Here is an example from the Japan–Malaysia Economic Partnership Agreement: 'Each Country shall accord to services and service suppliers of the other Country treatment no less favourable than that it accords to like services and service suppliers of any third State.' Fink and Molinuevo (2008) show that 12 out of 25 services RTAs feature such non-party MFN obligations. Most RTAs negotiated by the EFTA, Japan and the US have incorporated them.

Another important set of non-tariff barriers are the so-called behind-the-border trade barriers. These range from product standards and regulations to the lack of a competition policy that would prevent domestic firms from colluding against their foreign rivals. Baldwin, Evenett and Low (2009) argue that many of the barriers are incidental to the main regulatory justification for the policies. Most are highly technical, making it difficult to ascertain the extent to which they act as a trade barrier.

Baldwin, Evenett and Low (2009) argue that the severity of the spaghetti bowl problem ranged from high for RTAs on government procurement to modest for technical barriers to trade (TBTs) and slight for trade remedies, investment requirements and competition policy. It is noticeable that

ROOs do not contribute to the spaghetti bowl effect in four out of the five groups. The exception is government procurement where it applies to goods in the same way as with general merchandise trade and only slightly for services because it is so difficult to ascertain where a particular service is 'made'.

C. RTAs and the multilateral trading system

The spread of RTAs is one way in which the world trade system has become fragmented in the past few decades. This section discusses the ways in which regionalism threatens the multilateral trade system; it is a prelude to the next section which presents ideas for multilateralising regionalism.

I. What is wrong with regionalism?

Bhagwati (2008) lays out the standard case against discriminatory tariff liberalisation. First, multiple tariff rates introduce economic inefficiency into the trade system. Second, North–South RTAs encourage disciplines that Bhagwati does not believe should be covered by trade agreements (primarily labour and environmental standards). Third, RTAs may hinder multilateral tariff cutting, i.e. they may be stumbling blocks.

1. The threat of pervasive regionalism

These three problems only touch the surface of the threat that pervasive regionalism poses to today's world trading system. The real threat is that regionalism is becoming so pervasive that it may soon be the rule rather than the exception. It could contribute in a forceful way to the erosion of WTO-centricity in the world trade system.

The WTO engages in judicial processes to settle disputes and it organises multilateral trade liberalisation exercises (Rounds). While a wide range of WTO Members support and participate in the dispute settlement part, only a dozen or so have participated in the liberalisation exercises. Special and differential treatment meant that developing nations (as well as Australia and New Zealand for many decades) did not cut their tariffs in GATT Rounds, and yet their exporters benefited from the reduced tariffs in manufactured goods that were agreed by the developed nations and extended under the MFN principle to all GATT members. Typically, the driving forces in these rounds were the US, the EU, Japan and Canada as well as the other smaller nations in Western Europe.

Since the early 1990s, all of these WTO stalwarts have been engaged in systematic regionalism, especially North–South regionalism. They are having a worryingly positive experience. In particular, their exporters find it easier to demand removal of behind-the-border measures when RTAs are negotiated than during multilateral negotiations. Horn and Mavroidis (2009) distinguish two categories of such provisions, WTO+ and WTO-x issues. WTO+ means things like services, that are in principle covered by WTO agreements, but where the RTA goes further (for example, granting US banks access that has not been offered by the partner in the WTO context). WTO-x refers to things that are excluded from the agenda in WTO talks, such as labour and the environment. For both types, an important special interest group – the developed country exporters – has developed. For decades it has been this group that has been the WTO's biggest defender in national polities.

The world of trade, however, is shifting. The advanced nations are becoming less important while the emerging trade powers – China, India and Brazil together with a half dozen other fast growing and trade dependent nations – are accounting for an increasing fraction of world trade. By rights, these emerging markets should start to take their place among the stalwarts of the WTO-centric trade system. But so far they have not stepped up to this role. Indeed, most of them are having a worryingly favourable experience with regionalism in the twenty-first century. This is even more of a problem than it is for the developed nations since the emerging markets have never been thoroughly engaged with the WTO system – special and differential treatment allowed them to pick and choose between the WTO disciplines (this is not so for China which joined after the WTO's Single Undertaking). In short, their commitment to multilateralism is relatively untested. More precisely, the deep and long-standing support that the WTO has among developed country exporters does not exist to the same extent in the emerging markets since they have always taken the WTO for granted. The WTO has never provided them with hard fought increases in market access – either the market access happened or it did not. Participation and support for the WTO was not the key issue.

2. The threat to norms

A good deal of the WTO's centricity stems from the fact that its norms are almost universally accepted. An important aspect of this acceptance rests on the belief that the system is 'fair' to all of its Members. The emergence of RTAs between uneven nations – be it between the trade giants, the US,

EU and Japan and developing nations, or between the new trade giants, India, China and Brazil and developing nations – tend to undermine this 'fairness'.

To date, these changes seem more like challenges than threats. The key players believe the world trade system will continue to be anchored by the WTO's shared values, such as reciprocity, transparency, non-discrimination, and the rule of law. WTO-anchorage allows each member to view its own policies as minor derogations. Yet, at some point derogations become the new norm. The steady erosion of the WTO's centricity will sooner or later bring the world to a tipping point – a point beyond which expectations become unmoored and nations feel justified in ignoring WTO norms since everyone else does.

From this fairness perspective, it is important to note that the spaghetti bowl is actually very well organised for firms located in the US and the EU. These trade giants have used their bargaining power to establish harmonious rules of origin and market access. The confusion and inefficiencies of today's spaghetti bowl of trade preferences is much more of a problem for firms located in poor and/or small nations. In short, the spaghetti bowl falls much harder on the heads of the world's small and poor nations.[10]

There is one final point to make on the threat posed by RTAs to the world trade system.

3. Regionalism as Plan B

Regionalism is now so pervasive that it is seen by many political leaders as an alternative to multilateralism – Plan B for the world trading system, as it were. This is a big switch. The main early-adopters of preferential liberalisation – the West Europeans with their 1958 Treaty of Rome and 1960 Stockholm Convention, the US and Canada with their 1965 Auto Pact, and New Zealand and Australia with their 1965 FTA – were simultaneously ardent supporters of multilateralism. For them, regionalism was an addition to multilateralism, not a substitute. They supported the GATT by (largely) respecting its rules and they eroded the discrimination embodied in all of their regional deals by progressively lowering their multilateral tariffs in the successive GATT Rounds.

10 Research by Damuri (2009) shows that preferences can vary tremendously (using the list of product exclusions as the metric) and presents evidence that the preferences granted seem to be at least in part the outcome of a bargaining process in which market size matters.

Contrast this with the experience of the newly emerging trade powers – Brazil, India and China. These nations were largely free-riders in the tariff-cutting GATT Rounds. There is little sign that Brazil, India and China are switching their attitude towards the multilateral trade system in line with the growing global importance of their trade flows. They are not switching to leadership roles in the WTO. Brazil and China, and to some extent India, are finding that regionalism is an excellent route to getting better market access for their exporters. They are learning that regionalism is the fast, easy and controllable way to liberalise trade; multilateral trade talks are the slow, hard and uncontrollable path. Similar trends are affecting political leaders in the US, the EU, Japan and Canada; they too are starting to find that the regionalism route may be a better, easier and faster way to get improved market access from developing nations.

II. A return to the Great Powers world?

In short, we are approaching a world where regionalism is so pervasive that some nations are starting to view it as a viable Plan B. The problem is that in this case, Plan B does not work without Plan A. That is, regionalism in a world where WTO rules and principles are almost universally respected – as in the first two waves of regionalism – is not really a threat to the world trade system. But when the existing WTO stalwarts are finding bilateralism is an easier way to get what their exporters want out of developing nations, and emerging nations are finding regionalism is more convenient, we risk entering a new regime – a regime where we have regionalism but only sporadic respect for WTO norms. This would be a world where 'might makes right', or more precisely, where nations with large markets have the bargaining leverage they need to ensure the market access their exporters want. Smaller nations would be left to fend for themselves. This would be like a return to the Great Powers era of trade where each powerful nation made the rules in its own sphere of influence.

D. Towards coherence

This section describes a number of ideas that could help reduce the adverse effects of regionalism by moving the present system from one of fragmentation (i.e. uncoordinated RTAs) towards one of coherence where regionalism is multilateralised to the greatest extent possible. Collectively, these ideas form an 'action plan' for enhancing coherence, and are grouped according to whether they are WTO-led or RTA-led.

I. WTO-led ideas enhancing coherence

The EU's PECS initiative shows one way that the global trade system would greatly reduce the fragmentation engendered by regionalism. Although it is unlikely from a political perspective, one could imagine a series of similar exercises where the US and its NAFTA partners induced many Western Hemisphere RTAs to adopt the same set of ROOs, institute regional cumulation and complete the matrix of RTAs. In Asia the same process could start with the ASEAN FTA and its bilateral arrangements with other Asian nations. The final step would then be to move through a combination of lower MFN tariffs, ITA-like sectoral agreements, and harmonisation of ROOs towards a coherent system of global free trade. This outcome, however attractive it is intellectually, would seem unlikely to attract the necessary approval from the nations that would have to undertake the reforms (most notably, the US, Japan, Korea and China). The WTO could, however, undertake a series of more modest steps in the same direction.

As shown above, the number of South–South RTAs is growing rapidly. While it would be almost impossible to stop these, the WTO could help ensure that they are as WTO-friendly as possible. Bilateral agreements are difficult to design, negotiate and implement. Even for rich nations with well-resourced administrations, the bureaucratic stresses of negotiating RTAs can be substantial. For poor nations, where human capital is often the binding constraint, the resource demands of negotiating one or more RTAs alongside multilateral and unilateral trade policy-making are potentially much greater. In such a situation, developing nations may have difficulty fully evaluating specific policy changes that are being demanded in an RTA, especially by developed nation partners. The result is likely to be RTAs that are sub-optimal from the perspective of the developing nations.

Since these problems are faced by developing nations all around the world, the WTO could help by setting up a 'WTO Advisory Service' on RTAs for developing nations.[11] This could help the WTO to assist developing countries to alleviate the disadvantages they face in RTA negotiations. This part of the action plan could include setting up an advisory centre to provide subsidised economic, legal and negotiation services and training. It could be devoted to South–South RTAs alone, or could include North–South ones as well.

11 See Draper and Quobo (2009), Rollo (2009), Hoekman and Winters (2009), Kawai and Wignaraja (2009) and Estevadeordal, Harris and Suominen (2009).

The new Advisory Service's role and – perhaps some of its practical details – could take inspiration from WTO experience on legal issues. The WTO Secretariat has special legal advisers for assisting developing countries in any WTO dispute and for giving them legal counsel. Lessons from the Advisory Centre on WTO could also guide this part of the Action Plan.[12] There are also many local initiatives with similar goals whose experience would be helpful, e.g. the Regional Economic Policy Support Facility ASEAN–Australia Development Cooperation Program. To avoid duplication of effort, the WTO Action Plan initiatives in this area should link up with the regional banks providing similar support to developing nations (e.g. the Inter-American Development Bank and the Asian Development Bank).

1. WTO soft-law disciplines on RTAs

A second line of possible WTO initiatives concerns the negotiation of 'best practice' models. These can be thought of as soft-law initiatives that might work where hard law has failed. WTO hard law has not worked for RTAs since the EU, the US and Canada were granted Article XXIV waivers in the 1950s and 1960s.[13] Moreover, as it is politically implausible that the EU or NAFTA members would accept hard-law reforms that forced them to revise their RTAs, the stronger disciplines would only apply to new RTAs. In practice, this means those of developing countries – an asymmetry that gives such proposals zero chance of being adopted given the political realities of the WTO (developing countries have a clear majority). There is hope, however, on the discipline front.

Soft-law disciplines have in fact worked, in the sense of inducing nations to follow some Article XXIV strictures, even nations that were not obliged to do so. Many RTAs de facto comply or come very close to complying with the provision of Article XXIV that requires nations to reduce tariffs to zero on substantially all trade within a reasonable period. Research by Estevadeordal, Shearer and Suominen (2009) shows that most RTAs cut tariffs to zero on 90 per cent of tariff lines within ten years.

12 First proposed in Baldwin (2006c); see Rollo (2009) for detailed analysis of the possibility.

13 For example, in the GATT years, almost 100 RTAs were examined by working parties for conformity with the rules; consensus was reached in only one case: the Czech–Slovak customs union. Under the WTO, the Committee of RTAs was established to streamline the examination process; no examination report has been finalised since 1995 because of lack of consensus according to the CRTA's website (www.wto.org/english/tratop_e/region_e/regcom_e.htm).

It seems that WTO Members are acting in the spirit of the WTO disciplines on regionalism, but they do not want to tie their hands in legally binding procedures.[14] Building on this idea, the WTO could negotiate more soft-law guidelines on what RTAs should and should not do. Two concrete steps could be included in the Action Plan.

1. Negotiate voluntary best-practice guidelines for RTA disciplines for new RTAs and for modifications of existing RTAs. These would go beyond existing WTO disciplines in an effort to tame the tangle by promoting transparency and cooperation. At the very least, the best-practices exercise can help governments learn lessons from the experience of other countries. The best known effort is the Asia-Pacific Economic Cooperation (APEC) Guidelines and sets of Best Practices on RTAs. There are other initiatives such as those of ASEAN and the new Pacific-11 forum (El Foro sobre la Iniciativa de la Cuenca del Pacifico Latinoamericano, or Forum on the Initiative of the Latin American Pacific Rim). Several of the regional development banks also have more technocratic projects in this area. These projects offer important lessons for the Action Plan. The WTO should seize the initiative here. If nations find it worthwhile to engage in these efforts in regions around the world, why not centralise them in Geneva?

The APEC initiative has yielded 'model chapters' on trade in goods, technical barriers to trade, transparency, government procurement, cooperation, dispute settlement, trade facilitation, ROOs, sanitary and phytosanitary standards, and e-commerce. These model chapters tend to follow chapters of the US–Chile FTA and the US–Australia FTA (Hufbauer and Schott 2009). This is perhaps why APEC members have continued to follow national templates (Hufbauer and Schott 2009). The lesson seems to be that what constitutes a 'model chapter' for the US seems to be suboptimal for ASEAN's members. This suggests the WTO should negotiate a hierarchy of best-practice guidelines for North–North, North–South and South–South RTAs.

2. More ambitiously, negotiate a level of RTA discipline that was in between that of Article XXIV and the Enabling Clause. Nations would be free to declare themselves as subject to this discipline – the benefit to them being that it would provide firmer institutional anchorage for their

14 For instance, efforts to reform Article XXIV during the Uruguay Round never led to firm commitments, only to an 'Understanding'.

commitments and thus provide reassurance to firms considering foreign direct investment.

The past two decades have witnessed a *volte face* by rapidly industrialising developing nations. Trade liberalisation – which used to be viewed as a political 'sacrifice' – is now readily and rapidly undertaken autonomously. Slashing tariffs and opening certain service sectors is seen as a way of enhancing competitiveness, fostering industrialisation and boosting growth. Autonomous reforms, however, only work if domestic and foreign investors believe that they will last long enough to provide a reasonable rate of return on the adoption of new technology, training of new workers and building of new factories. Many developing nations have sought 'anchorage' or credibility by committing to such reforms in RTAs, especially with powerful trade partners.

Why is the WTO unable to provide this sort of commitment device? Anchorage is a *raison d'être* for many WTO disciplines. The WTO could explore interest in establishing an anchorage-building level of discipline that would not require nations to declare themselves as developed nations, but would provide more specific disciplines than the anything-goes approach of the Enabling Clause.

We now turn to WTO-led ideas that might take longer to implement.

2. New sectoral free trade agreements

One other approach that the WTO might take to reduce tariff discrimination would be to propose schemes like the Information Technology Agreement (this lowered bound MFN rates to zero on electronic parts and components) but in new sectors, or better yet in a very broad range of sectors. A bolder initiative that would allow opening the door to more inter-sectoral bargains would be a global free trade agreement for all manufactured goods, or at least parts and components.

BOX 3.1. UNTANGLING THE LEGAL SPAGHETTI: SOME PRESCRIPTIVE IDEAS TOWARDS COHERENCE[15]

1. The WTO should embrace regional agreements both in its research and negotiating activities and, in particular, in WTO dispute settlement. The 'applicable' or 'relevant law' that is considered by both WTO and RTA panels should be explicitly expanded to include all relevant international law consented to by the disputing parties. This does not mean that WTO panels should enforce WTO-plus concessions, but that WTO claims should be read and applied in the context of what

15 The ideas in this box are adapted from Pauwelyn (2009).

the parties themselves (and only those parties) agreed to elsewhere (e.g. forum exclusion clauses in an RTA; retaliation or safeguards approved by an RTA). This measure is a form of 'multilateralising regionalism', and would improve the integration between WTO and regional agreements.

2. The negotiators of regional agreements must be aware of overlaps with the WTO and other regional agreements. To avoid conflicts, they must explicitly regulate questions of overlap. Specific areas of concern are: Agreement on Trade-Related Aspects of Intellectual Property Rights (TRIPS)-plus and the WTO decisions on access to medicines, overlapping dispute settlement procedures, WTO versus regional safeguards, the impact of changes at the WTO on pre-existing RTAs and the relationship among different regional agreements. If RTA negotiators do not regulate these overlaps, RTA and WTO dispute settlement panels might do it for them, with possibly surprising results. Reference by RTA negotiators and RTA dispute panels to WTO provisions and jurisprudence (e.g. when it comes to an RTA dispute over TRIPS-plus provisions) is another form of 'multilateralising regionalism'.
3. Regional agreements should include an 'anti-dual forum' which states that once a matter is brought to the WTO or to an RTA panel, the same matter cannot be litigated a second time in the other forum. This would help avoid repeat proceedings and would protect scarce resources, especially those of developing countries.
4. Where RTA and WTO provisions are substantially equivalent (say, in respect of national treatment or where the RTA does not provide WTO-plus liberalisation), regional agreements should direct potential complainants to bring the dispute to the WTO and not to the RTA. This would help to avoid conflicts and to protect weaker parties.
5. Only in deeply integrated customs unions would an exclusive jurisdiction for the regional courts be justified. That said, WTO-plus obligations would need to be enforced before an RTA panel as, in that case, there is no overlap with the WTO.
6. WTO Members should carefully guard the success of the WTO dispute settlement mechanism. Regional agreements are unlikely to match the effectiveness and legitimacy of WTO dispute settlement. That mechanism alone is likely to preserve the survival of the multilateral trading system.
7. Cross-references in regional agreements to WTO rules should be presumed to be dynamic, that is, to include automatically any updates to WTO rules, unless otherwise provided. This simple step would enhance consistency between regimes.
8. RTA negotiators could consider including an MFN clause in RTAs which would automatically extend any subsequent RTA concessions to all previous and future RTA partners. Such an MFN clause would be an important step towards 'multilateralising regionalism' and could be limited to FTAs (and exclude, for example, preferential treatment under customs unions and unilateral concessions to developing countries).

II. RTA-led ideas

A second set of ideas could be implemented within RTAs with minimal WTO coordination.

1. Plurilateralise rules of origin and cumulation

A good deal of the spaghetti bowl's complexity arises from the highly technical provisions of RTAs called 'rules of origin' (ROOs) (see section B.V above). Overlapping and intersecting ROOs pose problems for businesses in setting up competitive international supply networks and thus for the nations trying to attract such industry. It is thus not surprising that various groups of nations around the world have made or discussed efforts to harmonise ROOs, with the EU's PECS being the most extreme example to date. What is surprising is that the WTO has not been involved in this issue.

The WTO could encourage regions to tame the tangle regionally, i.e. to harmonise their ROOs on a regional basis. A good example can be found in the Western Hemisphere (Figure 3.3). Currently, the region is marked by dozens of different sets of ROOs. Yet, the various sets of rules are not that different, as a detailed analysis in Estevadeordal, Harris and Suominen (2009) shows. The oldest family is the Latin American Integration Association rules that are not very restrictive. A modified form has been embraced by the economically large Mercosur trade bloc. At the other extreme of the scale of complexity and restrictiveness are the NAFTA ROOs and their application to many bilateral agreements signed by the NAFTA members.

The Action Plan could encourage the harmonisation of the dozens of ROOs into just three sets. Presumably the WTO's participation in this activity would guide the harmonisation towards an outcome that was as multilateral-friendly as possible, or at least it would help eliminate avoidable encroachment into the third party interests. Analysis by Kawai and Wignaraja (2009) suggests that a similar regional spaghetti-to-lasagne conversion might also be possible in Asia.[16]

The WTO Action Plan could also encourage extended cumulation within regional sets of ROOs. Evidence shows that ROOs are especially restrictive – and especially trade-dampening – when they tightly restrict the nations where value added counts as far as establishing origin is

16 The analogy is that if spaghetti strands were melded together, the result would resemble the plate-like lasagne pasta.

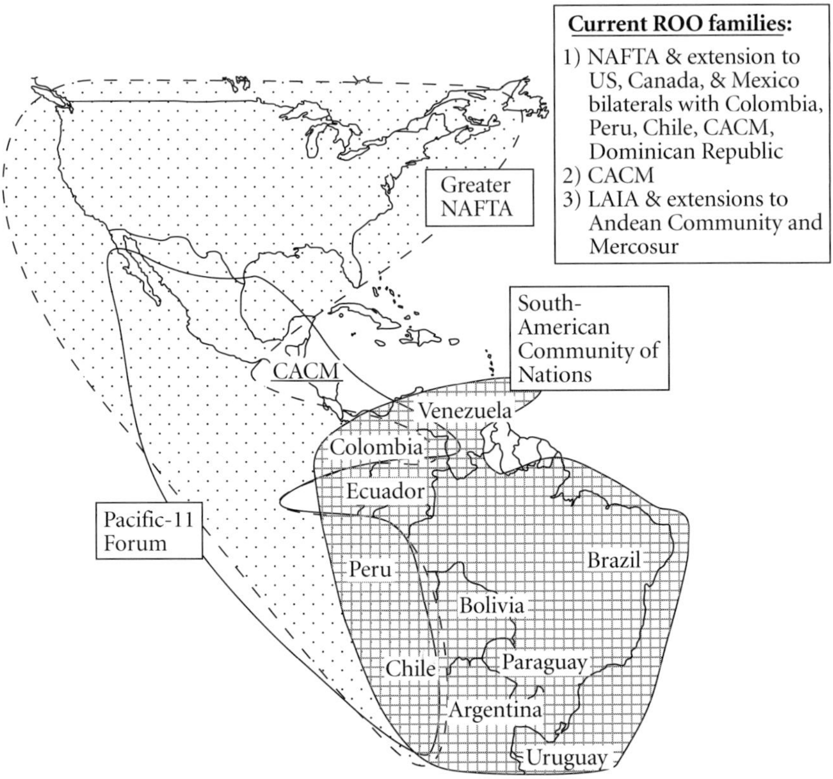

Figure 3.3 Turning the Western Hemisphere spaghetti into three lasagne plates
Source: Authors' diagram based on information in Estevadeordal, Harris and Suominen (2009).

concerned (Bombarda and Gamberoni 2008). Broadening these so-called rules of cumulation can reduce the restrictiveness of regionalism. In particular, it tends to remove ROOs-related barriers to locating industry in small RTA members. Of course, the trade-creating aspects of such initiatives may well imply additional trade diversion for third nations, but such spillovers are exactly why it makes sense to involve the WTO. Discrimination will always be a feature of discriminatory liberalisation, but regional harmonisation of ROOs and extended cumulation are things that are happening or are likely to happen with or without the involvement of the WTO. The WTO Action Plan on Regionalism would be a way to deal with the problem in a manner that makes the final outcomes as WTO-friendly as possible.

2. 'Anti-spaghetti' clauses in RTAs

Estevadeordal, Harris and Suominen (2009) show that many existing RTAs contain what might be called 'anti-spaghetti' clauses. These agreements anticipate that parties to the RTA may sign RTAs with third parties and so set in place automatic adjustments to the original RTA – adjustments that reduce the extent to which any new RTAs will complicate the trade environment for businesses.

The classic examples are 'third-party MFN clauses' observed in some RTAs on trade in services (also called 'non-party MFN'). These say, in essence, 'whatever preference either of us gives to someone else in the future will be automatically extended to each other'. Instead of each new RTA adding a new spaghetti strand, the third-party MFN makes it into an ever-expanding lasagne plate. Currently RTAs only include such clauses for certain preferences, mainly on services and government procurement. The WTO could encourage the adoption of third-party MFN clauses in RTAs.

3. Development friendly ROOs and cumulation

Rules of origin act as protectionist devices, but this is not their official justification. The legitimate reason for ROOs is the need to avoid tariff cheats – to prevent firms in a third nation from exploiting a bilateral FTA by transhipping their good via one of the FTA partners.

Following this line of logic suggests an innovative way of multilateralising regionalism that would be particularly development friendly. The idea, mooted in the paper by Augier, Gasiorek and Tong (2005) is that ROOs should be suspended on imports of all goods where the developing nation maintains a higher MFN tariff. For example, if Kenya has a higher MFN tariff on, say, toaster ovens than does the EU, then unscrupulous firms in third nations would never tranship to the EU via Kenya to avoid the EU's MFN tariff. Logically, if there is no incentive for trade deflection, there is no need to apply ROOs.

Since rich nations have generally cut their MFN tariffs to lower levels than those applied by developing nations, especially those in Africa, this mechanism would apply quite widely. Hence it could be a big step towards making ROOs more 'development friendly'. The WTO could encourage developed nations to suspend or greatly simplify ROOs applied to imports from developing nations that have higher MFN applied rates on the products concerned.

4. Development-friendly cumulation

Rules of cumulation can affect developing countries' trade and thus be pro- or anti-development (Gamberoni 2009). An important part of industrial competitiveness in today's world is an efficient supply chain. For small nations, especially small developing nations, this means importing many of the parts and components used in their manufactured exports. Bilateral cumulation rules hinder efficient sourcing of parts and components and thus discourage industrialisation in small, developing nations. The key concept here is the size of the cumulation zone. All RTAs allow bilateral cumulation, but the WTO could encourage nations with many bilateral RTAs to expand the cumulation zone to all or at least to regional groupings of their bilateral RTA partners.

5. Switching to an 'either/or approach' to rules of origin

Firms located in the world's trade hubs – the US, the EU and Japan – rarely face the problem of conflicting ROOs. It is firms located in the 'spokes' that face the worst problems of ensuring that their exports can comply with multiple ROOs. Research presented in Kawai and Wignaraja (2009) showed that multiple ROOs in East Asia complicate firm businesses and lead to increased costs, either as a result of complicated administrative procedures or of changes to production processes.

The ultimate solution is to harmonise ROOs regionally and globally, as suggested above. But there is something that 'spoke' economies can do themselves to reduce the problem – adopt an either/or approach to ROOs. This idea has been implemented by Central American nations which face NAFTA-like and CACM ROOs depending upon the export destination. Under what is called the 'multilateralism principle', Central American producers may choose between the CACM and CAFTA regimes when exporting to the other markets on the Central American isthmus; a third set of ROOs exists as an option for trade between CACM countries and the Dominican Republic.

The value of adopting such an either/or approach to multiple ROOs depends on a coordinated adoption by many affected nations, so this is the sort of initiative that may take some time for RTAs to implement.

E. Conclusion

When this paper was finalised in summer 2009, the world's most important trade talks – the Doha Round – appeared to have slipped into a coma with key nations playing a waiting game. While Doha has a good chance of coming to fruition eventually, trade liberalisation is not standing still. Nations around the globe are falling over themselves to liberalise trade regionally, bilaterally and unilaterally. The world trade system is labouring under a massive proliferation of RTAs and the problem gets worse month by month. The resulting tangle of trade deals conspire to inject into the multilateral system both inefficiency and discrimination against poor countries.

Amazingly, the WTO has had next to no involvement in this important development. The WTO – and this means the WTO membership since it is a member-driven organisation – has adopted the role of 'innocent bystander'. Key figures in world trade – negotiators, ministers, the WTO Secretariat, academics, civil society and the media – need to look beyond the Doha Round. Doha notwithstanding, countries will continue to strike bilateral and regional deals. Doha will do little or nothing to 'tame the tangle'. The need now is for concrete steps by the WTO to multilateralise regionalism.

IP3 has produced a body of research and a new policy recommendation that might help move the world trade system from fragmentation towards coherence. These are surely not the final words on the matter. Indeed they might not provide the right answer to the question 'What should the WTO do?', but as 'Do nothing' is surely the wrong answer, the tentative solutions offered in this paper might be one place to start.

Bibliography

Augier, P., M. Gasiorek and C. L. Tong (2005). 'The Impact of Rules of Origin on Trade Flows', *Economic Policy*, **20**(43): 567–624.

Baldwin, R. (1992). 'The Economic Logic of EFTA Membership in the EEA and the EC', EFTA Occasional Paper 41.

Baldwin, Richard (1993). 'A Domino Theory of Regionalism', CEPR Discussion Paper 857; NBER Working Paper, 4465. Published in Baldwin, Haaparanta and Kiander (eds.), *Expanding Membership in the European Union*, Cambridge University Press. Republished as Chapter 23 (pp. 479–502) in J. Bhagwati, P. Krishna and A. Panagariya (1999), *Trading Blocs: Alternative Approaches to Analyzing Preferential Trade Agreements*. Cambridge, MA: MIT Press.

Baldwin, Richard (1994). *Towards an Integrated Europe*. London: CEPR.

Baldwin, Richard (1997). 'The Causes of Regionalism', *The World Economy*, **20**(7): 865–88.

Baldwin, Richard (2000). 'Regulatory Protectionism, Developing Nations, and a Two-Tier World Trade System', *Brookings Trade Forum 2000*, 237–80.

Baldwin, Richard (2006a). 'Managing the Noodle Bowl: The Fragility of East Asian Regionalism', CEPR DP 5561, *Singapore Economic Review*, **53**(03): 449–78.

Baldwin, Richard (2006b). 'Globalisation: The Great Unbundling(s)', *Globalisation Challenges for Europe*. Helsinki: Secretariat of the Economic Council, Finnish Prime Minister's Office, Chapter 1, pp. 5–57.

Baldwin, Richard (2006c). 'Multilateralising Regionalism: Spaghetti Bowls as Building Blocs on the Path to Global Free Trade', *The World Economy*, **29**(11): 1451–518.

Baldwin, Richard (2008). 'Sequencing and Depth of Regional Economic Integration: Lessons for the Americas from Europe', *The World Economy*, **31**(1): 5–30.

Baldwin, Richard and Elena Seghezza (2007). 'Are Trade Blocs Building or Stumbling Blocks? New Evidence', CEPR Discussion Paper No. DP6599.

Baldwin, Richard and Roland Rieder (2007). 'A Test of Endogenous Trade Bloc Formation Theory on EU Data', *Journal of International Economic Studies*, **11**(2)(December): 77–111.

Baldwin, Richard and Dany Jaimovich (2009). 'Are Free Trade Agreements Contagious', NCCR Trade Regulation Working Paper 2009/31.

Baldwin, Richard and Theresa Carpenter (2009). 'A 3 Bloc Dance: East Asian Regionalism and the North Atlantic Trade Giants', NCCR Trade Regulation Working Paper 2009/29.

Baldwin, Richard, Simon Evenett and Patrick Low (2009). 'Beyond Tariffs: Multilateralizing Non-tariff RTA Commitments', in Richard Baldwin and Patrick Low (eds.), *Multilateralizing Regionalism: Challenges for the Global Trading System*. Cambridge University Press.

Bartels, Lorand and Federico Ortino (eds.) (2007). *Regional Trade Agreements and the WTO Legal System*. Oxford University Press.

Bhagwati, J. (1991). *The World Trading System at Risk*. Princeton University Press.

Bhagwati, J. (2008). *Termites in the Trading System*. Oxford University Press.

Bombarda, Pamela and Elisa Gamberoni (2008). 'Firm Heterogeneity, Rules of Origin and Rules of Cumulation', HEI Working Papers 09–2008, Economics Section, The Graduate Institute of International and Development Studies.

Carpenter, Theresa (2009). 'A Historical Perspective on Regionalism', in Richard Baldwin and Patrick Low (eds.), *Multilateralizing Regionalism: Challenges for the Global Trading System*. Cambridge University Press.

Cottier Thomas and Marina Foltea (2006). 'Constitutional Functions of the WTO and Regional Trade Agreements', in Lorand Bartels and Federico Ortino (eds.), *Regional Trade Agreements and the WTO Legal System*. Oxford University Press.

Crawford, Jo-Ann and Sam Laird (2000). 'Regional Trade Agreements and the WTO', CREDIT Research Paper, No. 00/3, University of Nottingham.

Damuri, Yose (2009). 'How Preferential are Preferential Trade Agreements? An analysis of Product Exclusions in PTAs', NCCR Trade Regulation Working Paper 2009/30.

Delimatsis, Panagiotis (2007). *International Trade in Services and Domestic Regulations: Necessity, Transparency, and Regulatory Diversity*, Oxford University Press.

Draper, Peter and Mzukisi Qobo (2009). 'Multilateralizing Regionalism: Case Study of African Regionalism', in Richard Baldwin and Patrick Low (eds.), *Multilateralizing Regionalism: Challenges for the Global Trading System*. Cambridge University Press.

Egger, Peter and Mario Larch (2008). 'Interdependent Preferential Trade Agreement Memberships: An Empirical Analysis', *Journal of International Economics*, **76**(2): 384–99.

Estevadeordal, Antoni, Caroline Freund and Emanuel Ornelas (2008). 'Does Regionalism Affect Trade Liberalization toward Nonmembers?', *The Quarterly Journal of Economics*, MIT Press, **123**(4): 1531–75.

Estevadeordal, Antoni, Jeremy Harris and Kati Suominen (2009). 'Harmonizing Preferential Rules of Origin Regimes around the World', in Richard Baldwin and Patrick Low (eds.), *Multilateralizing Regionalism: Challenges for the Global Trading System*. Cambridge University Press.

Estevadeordal, Antoni, Matthew Shearer and Kati Suominen (2009). 'Multilateralizing RTAs in the Americas: State of Play and Ways Forward', in Richard Baldwin and Patrick Low (eds.), *Multilateralizing Regionalism: Challenges for the Global Trading System*. Cambridge University Press.

Fink, Carsten and Marion Jansen (2009). 'Services Provisions in Regional Trade Agreements: Stumbling Blocks or Building Blocks for Multilateral Liberalization?' in Richard Baldwin and Patrick Low (eds.), *Multilateralizing Regionalism: Challenges for the Global Trading System*. Cambridge University Press.

Fink, Carsten and Martin Molinuevo (2008). 'East Asian Free Trade Agreements in Services: Key Architectural Elements', *Journal of International Economic Law*, **11**(2): 263–311.

Fiorentino, Roberto V., Luis Verdeja and Christelle Toqueboeuf (2007). 'The Changing Landscape of Regional Trade Agreements: 2006 Update' WTO Discussion Paper No. 12.

Foroutan, Faezeh (1998). 'Does Membership in a Regional Preferential Trade Agreement Make a Country More or Less Protectionist?' *The World Economy*, **21**(3): 305–35.

Gamberoni, Elisa (2008). 'Do Unilateral Trade Preferences Help Export Diversification? An Investigation of the Impact of European Unilateral Trade

Preferences on the Extensive and Intensive Margin of Trade', HEI Working Papers 17–2007, Graduate Institute of International Studies and Development.

Gamberoni, Elisa (2009). 'Market Access, Imported Inputs and Export Growth: An Analysis of Mauritius Exporting Firms', PhD thesis, Geneva, Graduate Institute, Chapter 3.

Hoekman, Bernard and Alan Winters (2009). 'Multilateralizing Preferential Trade Agreements: A Developing Country Perspective', in Richard Baldwin and Patrick Low (eds.), *Multilateralizing Regionalism: Challenges for the Global Trading System*. Cambridge University Press.

Holmes, Tammy (2005). 'What Drives Regional Trade Agreements that Work?', HEI Working Papers 07–2005, Economics Section, The Graduate Institute of International Studies.

Horn, Henrik, Petros C. Mavroidis and André Sapir (2009). 'Beyond The WTO? An Anatomy of EU and US Preferential Trade Agreements', Centre for Economic Policy Research Discussion Paper No. 7317, available at www.iadb.org/intal/intalcdi/PE/2009/03795.pdf.

Hufbauer, Gary and Jeffrey Schott (2009). 'Fitting Asia-Pacific Agreements into the WTO System', in Richard Baldwin and Patrick Low (eds.), *Multilateralizing Regionalism: Challenges for the Global Trading System*. Cambridge University Press.

Joshi, Vivek (2009). 'Preferential Tariff Formation: The Case of the European Union', CTEI Working Paper 111.

Kawai, Masahiro and Ganeshan Wignaraja (2009). 'Multilateralizing Regional Trade Arrangements in Asia.' in Richard Baldwin and Patrick Low (eds.), *Multilateralizing Regionalism: Challenges for the Global Trading System*. Cambridge University Press.

Lawrence, Robert (1996). *Regionalism, Multinationalism, and Deeper Integration*. Washington, DC, Brookings Institution Press.

Lendle, Andreas (2007). 'The ASEAN Free Trade Agreement: Building Block or Stumbling Block?', NCCR Trade Regulation Working Paper 2007/33.

Marchetti, Juan and Martin Roy (eds.) (2009). *Opening Markets for Trade in Services: Countries and Sectors in Bilateral and WTO Negotiations*. Cambridge University Press.

Pauwelyn, Joost (2009). 'Legal Avenues to "Multilateralising Regionalism": Beyond Article XXIV', in Richard Baldwin and Patrick Low (eds.), *Multilateralizing Regionalism: Challenges for the Global Trading System*. Cambridge University Press.

Rollo, Jim (2009). 'The Challenge of Negotiating RTAs for Developing Countries. What Could the WTO Do to Help?' in Richard Baldwin and Patrick Low (eds.), *Multilateralizing Regionalism: Challenges for the Global Trading System*. Cambridge University Press.

Roy, Martin, Juan Marchetti and Hoe Lim (2006). 'Services Liberalization in the New Generation of Preferential Trade Agreements (PTAs): How Much Further than the GATS?', WTO Staff Working Paper ERSD-2006–07.

Sapir, Andre (2001). 'Domino Effects in Western European Regional Trade, 1960–1992', *European Journal of Political Economy*, **17**(2): 377–88.

Yeats, Alexander (1998). 'Does Mercosur's Trade Performance Raise Concerns about the Effects of Regional Trade Arrangements?', *World Bank Economic Review*, 1–28.

PART II

Reforming specific areas of trade regulation

4

Reframing sustainable agriculture

PHILIPP AERNI, CHRISTIAN HÄBERLI AND BARIS KARAPINAR*

KEY MESSAGES

- 'Sustainability' and 'non-trade concerns' in agriculture are political terms used for different production and trade policies.
- WTO rules and disciplines provide ample policy space for pursuing sustainable agricultural policies, but they must be improved to avoid protectionist misuse.
- The sustainability challenges in least developed countries (LDCs) are high non-tariff trade barriers and lack of investment in agriculture.

A. Introduction

The Agreement on Agriculture (AoA) was arguably one the most significant General Agreement on Tariffs and Trade (GATT) achievements of the 1986–1994 Uruguay Round. It came into effect with the successful establishment of the World Trade Organization in 1995. Yet, while the AoA managed to bring agriculture within the disciplines of the multilateral trading system, Members took advantage of the wide policy space available and exploited many loopholes in the agreement to ensure that they could continue with their highly protectionist policies. While global average tariffs have progressively fallen from above 40 per cent to below 4 per cent during the GATT period, the trend in agriculture seems to be the reverse in many areas. The level of effective protection against the flow of agricultural trade has been rising.[1] Even though a fundamental

* Individual Project No. 5, 'Sustainable Agriculture within WTO Law and Policy'. We would like to thank Allan Rae, Fikret Adaman, Li Ninghui, Yu Wen, Olla Llanto, Ernst Thomke, Sophie Réviron and the many others who contributed to the success of our research.

1 M. G. Desta, *The Law of International Agricultural Trade Products* (The Hague: Kluwer Law International, 2002).

principle of the AoA was the decoupling of support to the farming sector from production decisions, it did not prohibit market price support and other trade-distortive forms of support.

Agricultural protectionism as practised during the Cold War period was mainly based on the justification that national self-sufficiency in food production is necessary due to the potential threat of a new World War. Today however the term 'non-trade concerns' serves as the major argument for maintaining agricultural protectionism. The term covers issues related to environment protection, vibrancy of life in rural areas, food safety, animal welfare and many other consumer and taxpayer concerns.[2] All these concerns are loosely associated with the economic, social and environmental dimensions of sustainable agriculture. However, countries might agree on the overall goal of sustainable agriculture but not necessarily on the means to achieve it. But since the term has largely been shaped by affluent and protectionist developed countries, its implicit assumption that international agricultural trade liberalisation undermines sustainable agriculture is used to justify policies that aim to address such 'market failure' through subsidies and tariff and non-tariff border protection measures.[3] In this article we question this assumption and test the extent to which the term sustainable agriculture is shaped by the dominant perception and interests of domestic stakeholders. For this purpose we conducted four stakeholder perception surveys on sustainable agriculture: in Switzerland, New Zealand, Turkey and China. The results obtained are used to discuss the question of how far the policy space available in the AoA effectively serves the purpose of improving the environment and reducing rural poverty. We believe that the big gaps between rhetoric and reality in domestic debates on sustainable agriculture as well as in agricultural trade negotiations during the Doha Round are not conducive to global efforts to achieve a more sustainable global future in the area of food and agriculture. In this context, we argue in favour of a new perspective on sustainable agriculture that reconsiders the importance of technological innovation and rural entrepreneurship. It would also make sustainable agriculture more compatible with the spirit of the WTO AoA and may make it economically, socially and environmentally more sustainable because it would return more decision-making power to the farmers. Farmers who feel

2 J. R. Simpson, 'Non-trade Concerns in WTO Agricultural Trade Negotiations: Conflict Resolution in the Doha Agenda'. (2005) *Int. J. Agr. Resour. Govern. Ecol.* 4(3/4), 193–202.

3 P. Aerni, 'What is Sustainable Agriculture? Empirical Evidence of Diverging Views in Switzerland and New Zealand' (2009) *Ecological Economics* 68(6), 1872–1882.

in charge of their lives and that they are able to successfully participate in the global economy may contribute to social empowerment in rural areas (social dimension), generate more income and employment in the region (economic dimension) and become more interested in managing their scarce environmental resources in a sustainable way (environmental dimension).

This chapter is structured as follows: Section B discusses the term 'sustainable agriculture'; Section C presents the results of our empirical research on stakeholder attitudes towards sustainable agriculture in developed and developing countries. On the basis of these results, Section D addresses the political economy of sustainable agriculture. Section E deals with the development dimension of sustainable agriculture: it addresses the development impact of Swiss policies, food security issues, preferences for least developed countries, the importance of geographical indications and the role of science and technology in ensuring endogenous growth and food security. We conclude in Section F by looking at the relevant WTO agreements and basic rules, and examine the extent to which available policy space is used – or misused – from a new perspective on sustainable agriculture.

B. What is sustainable agriculture?

The general public in industrialised countries tends to associate 'sustainable agriculture' with a set of post-material values that put emphasis on the conservation of the environment, safe food, and animal welfare.[4] Advocates of sustainable agriculture usually start from the insight that agricultural modernisation in the twentieth century has undermined these values and therefore produced many negative externalities for society and the environment, which must be addressed by recognising the character of agriculture as a public good.[5] The concept of multifunctional agriculture attempts to address this public good character by adopting a systems perspective that takes into account the needs of rural communities and food security,[6] as well as the impact

4 G. W. VanLoon, S. G. Patil, and L. B. Hugar, *Agricultural Sustainability: Strategies for Assessment* (SAGE Publications, 2005).

5 G. Van Huylenbroeck and G. Durand, *Multifunctional Agriculture: A New Paradigm for European Agriculture and Rural Development* (Ashgate, 2003).

6 D. Tilman, K. G. Cassman, P. A. Matson, R. Naylor, and S. Polasky, 'Agricultural Sustainability and Intensive Production Practices' (2002) *Nature* 418, 671–677.

of agricultural practices on local ecosystem services and the global environment.[7]

Legal experts emphasise the important principles of sustainable development as outlined in the three dimensions of sustainability (economic, social and environmental) and entrenched in many multilateral environmental agreements. They argue that a joint effort, again led by governments, is required to manage natural resources in a way that promotes biodiversity as well as agricultural diversity and ensures social and intergenerational equity.[8] The concept of sustainable development is considered to be about balanced development that takes into account short-term and long-term concerns.[9] Applied to sustainable agriculture and international trade, the concept of sustainable development shall highlight the different concerns related to economic development, protection of local markets and environmental management practices. Often there are serious trade-offs involved in efforts to achieve the various objectives and these trade-offs, so it is argued, have to be put on the table.[10]

The concept of multifunctional agriculture is particularly popular among (sub-)urban dwellers in affluent societies and confirmed by surveys on stated preferences for local and organic products and against genetically modified food.[11] The support of this non-agricultural constituency for alternative farming practices and the dislike of modern industrial agriculture may also be related to a nostalgic view of the past when agriculture was hardly affected by global markets and technological change. This emotional dimension of sustainable agriculture helps explain why many governments continue to provide generous financial support and protection for domestic farmers, and why they regulate the introduction of new agricultural technologies in a very restrictive manner – invoking the precautionary principle and non-trade concerns.[12] This type

7 S. S. Prestegard, 'Multifunctional Agriculture, Non-Trade Concerns and the Design of Policy Instruments: Applications to the WTO Agricultural Negotiations' (2005) *International Journal of Agricultural Resources, Governance and Ecology* 4(3/4), 232–245.

8 F. Francioni, *Environment, Human Rights and International Trade* (Oxford University Press, 2001).

9 K. Gehne, 'Nachhaltigkeit als Rechtsprinzip', PhD Thesis (University of Zurich, 2009).

10 E. Bürgi, 'Towards a New Balance of Trade in Agriculture'. NCCR Working Paper No. 2009/17 (World Trade Institute, Bern, 2009).

11 W. S. Chern, K. Rickertsen, N. Tsuboi and T.-T. Fu, 'Consumer Acceptance and Willingness to Pay for Genetically Modified Vegetable Oil and Salmon: A Multiple-Country Assessment' (2002) *AgBioForum* 5(3), 105–112.

12 J. R. Simpson, 'Japan's Non-Trade Concerns: Legitimate or Protectionist?' (2005) *International Journal of Agricultural Resources, Governance and Ecology* 4(3/4), 193–202.

of agricultural policy may be popular with the public and still be legitimate under the present WTO rules and disciplines (depending on a country's schedule of commitments),[13] but there is not much evidence to confirm its effectiveness in view of the real social, economic and environmental challenges of global agriculture.[14] In fact, there is an increasing concern among environmentalists that a strictly value-based approach to sustainable development may not be able to reconcile the increasing global demand for natural resources with the growing pressure to preserve our common cultural and natural resource base.[15]

Moreover, such value-based agricultural policies tend to be very selective about the principles of sustainable development as outlined in Agenda 21 and the Rio Declaration 1992. For example, Principle 9 of the Rio Declaration regards the development, adaptation, diffusion and transfer of technologies, including new and innovative technologies, as an integral part of sustainable development. Principle 12 argues in favour of a supportive and open international economic system, and Principle 21 indirectly emphasises the role of entrepreneurship by pointing to the importance of mobilising the creativity, ideals and courage of the youth of the world. These principles implicitly aim at facilitating change to achieve a sustainable future. Yet they are often not very popular in affluent societies that regard technological and economic change as a risk rather than an opportunity, including for the farming sector.[16]

In developing countries, on the other hand, public perception of the various dimensions of sustainability is markedly different from that of affluent societies. In these countries, the concept faces serious trade-offs and conflicting policy objectives in achieving what is perceived to be 'sustainable'.[17] Existing supply structures, often dominated by small farms, are confronted with the challenge of meeting the demand for a growing volume and changing composition of food. An increasing

13 M. G. Desta, *The Law of International Trade in Agricultural Products* (Kluwer, 2002).

14 D. Kleijn, F. Berendse, R. Smit and N. Gilissen, 'Agri-environment Schemes Do Not Effectively Protect Biodiversity in Dutch Agricultural Landscapes' (2001) *Nature* 423, 723–725.

15 R. Paarlberg, *Starved for Science* (Harvard University Press, 2008).

16 P. Aerni, 'Agriculture in Turkey: Structural Change, Sustainability and EU Compatibility' *International Journal of Agricultural Resources, Governance and Ecology* 6(4/5), 429–439 (2007).

17 V. W. Ruttan, 'The Design of Sustainable Systems of Agricultural Production, in C. K. Eicher and J. M. Staatz' (eds.), *International Agricultural Development* (Johns Hopkins University Press, 1998).

population with rapid income growth, and the subsequent process of diversification from low-value basic staples to high-value secondary products, has led to a transition of demand, requiring a reform of the supply structure, which is often politically difficult to undertake. On the other hand, the agricultural policies of many developing countries have been driven almost exclusively by the priority of maximising economic output, which is now challenged by mounting environmental problems. Land degradation through desertification, salinisation and loss of wetlands, and water depletion through falling ground water levels, pollution and droughts are some of the most pressing environmental challenges which require a shift in policy priorities and a reform of the existing institutions.

I. Doha Round problems with sustainable agriculture

July 2008 saw a third failed attempt to settle the Doha Round initiated in November 2001. Disagreement on the extent of liberalisation in agriculture (but also for industrial goods) was once again the main bottleneck. Advanced developing countries asked for a substantial opening of agricultural markets in developed countries, but without offering market access other than in a manner retractable by extensive safeguards.

In the wake of the 2008 food crisis, the responses of many food exporting developing countries once again reflected a dangerous focus on national food sovereignty that additionally tightened the world food supply.[18] Several European agricultural ministers indirectly endorsed these policies by praising their heavily subsidised agricultural system as the best strategy to ensure food sovereignty, thus avoiding substantial tariff reductions for their own markets. At the same time, the United States enacted a new farm bill in 2008 that foresees spending US$ 307 billion in subsidies over the period 2008–2012, including price and revenue support largely for wealthy farmers. This also includes highly controversial government support for production of corn-derived ethanol. In addition, the legislators once again refused to soften a rule requiring the government to buy foreign food aid from American farmers and transport it on American ships. What all these government actions have in common is the claim that these measures would be necessary to address the economic, the social or the environmental dimension of sustainable agriculture, depending on

18 The topic was addressed at the World Trade Forum in September 2009 on 'Food Crises and the World Trading System', organised by IP5 (www.wti.org/world-trade-forum/world-trade-forum.html).

the issue at stake and the dominant stakeholders involved in the domestic debate. Thus the abuse of this term by the various domestic policy agendas that are associated with it may have prevented a breakthrough for the main issues on the Doha Development Agenda.

The broad policy space presently available in the Green Box to support agriculture also has negative consequences for poor countries. The dependence of African countries on European aid and market access may lead them to accept European structural policies and adopt its high regulatory standards.[19] This not only discourages foreign direct investment, but may also undermine the capacity of local entrepreneurs to set up a successful domestic business in the formal sector.[20] These entrepreneurs in rural and urban areas strive to participate in global trade but do not know how to cope with the complexity and the costs of regulation in industrialised countries. Although European countries spend a lot of money on capacity building programmes in Africa, these programmes are not aimed at enabling local people to set up successful growth-oriented businesses, but rather at instructing government officials on how to implement the regulation they have adopted from Europe.[21] In this context, the term 'capacity building' may require additional scrutiny, because if the purpose is to ensure the successful export of regulation from developed to developing countries it may not be favourable to trade facilitation and endogenous development in poor countries.

To sum up, sustainable agriculture is not only a scientific but also a highly political term that means different things to interest groups with different stakes in the public debate. WTO negotiators and policy-makers need to consider the real meaning when formulating disciplines for implementation measures.

II. The evolving debate on sustainable agriculture, trade liberalisation and food security

If the substantial market access and domestic support concessions envisaged prior to the suspension of the Doha Round negotiations were to be

19 P. Aerni and T. Bernauer, 'Stakeholder Attitudes towards GMOs in the Philippines, Mexico and South Africa: The Issue of Public Trust'. (2006) *World Development* 34(3), 557–575.

20 P. Aerni, 'The Principal-Agent Problem in International Development Assistance and its Impact on Local Entrepreneurship in Africa: Time for New Approaches' (2006) *ATDF Journal* 3(2), 27–33.

21 P. Aerni, 'Agricultural Biotechnology and its Contribution to the Knowledge Economy' (2007) *Adv. Biochem. Engin./Biotechnol.* 107, 69–96.

implemented, the present policy space in rich and well-protected countries would be dramatically reduced. Green Box policies might become the main instrument available for promoting sustainable agriculture. We see two consequences of such a development.

On the one hand, a commitment to substantial cuts in the bound tariff rates and so-called Amber Box measures would not be sufficient to ensure sustainable agriculture. Indeed, governments may be tempted to try 'box shifting', i.e. to reformulate their present production and trade-distorting policies to fit into the present list of allowed practices. The Chair of the Committee on Agriculture has recognised the need to scrutinise Green Box support measures that claim to be minimally trade-distorting and to promote sustainable agriculture.[22] The International Centre for Trade and Sustainable Development (ICTSD) is currently investigating the argument of developing countries that Green Box subsidies neither address their particular needs, nor do they necessarily play a critical role in providing public goods.[23] This underlines the need for a much narrower definition of Green Box measures.

On the other hand, the new parameters – especially with more restrictive definitions – might create sufficient outside pressure for governments to learn from best practices and abandon the tendency to consider agricultural trade negotiations as a mercantilist zero-sum game implying that any concession made in one area needs to be compensated by a counter-concession in another area.

The recent 'food crisis' of 2007–2008 highlighted, once again, the importance of food security for many developing countries. Given that global agricultural markets are still 'thin',[24] which aggravates price volatility, it is risky for policy-makers to rely on international trade for long-term food security. During the early months of 2008, international market prices of major food commodities reached their highest nominal levels in 50 years.[25] One of the most common policy responses to the 'crisis'

22 World Trade Organization, Committee on Agriculture in Special Session, Report to the Trade Negotiations Committee by the Chairman of the Special Session of the Committee on Agriculture, Ambassador Crawford Falconer (JOB(08)/95 dated 11 August 2008).

23 http://ictsd.net/programmes/agriculture/greenbox/ (accessed 24 March 2009).

24 'Thin' in the sense that only a small share of global farm production is traded internationally, and agriculture accounts for only 6 per cent of international trade. K. Anderson. 'Agricultural Policies: Past, Present and Prospective under Doha', in B. Karapinar and C. Häberli (eds.), *Food Crises and the WTO* (Cambridge University Press, 2010).

25 E. Diaz-Bonilla, 'Globalisation of Agriculture and the Food Crises: Then and Now', in B. Karapinar and C. Häberli (eds.), *Food Crises and the WTO* (Cambridge University Press, 2010).

was export restrictions, which were imposed by more than 30 countries including some major exporters of food crops (e.g. Argentina).[26] Since the regulations on export restrictions under WTO law are quite weak, these restrictions, beyond their immediate effects of shrinking the supply and fuelling the rise in prices of food, also undermine trust in the international trading system in general.[27] As a consequence, countries resort to policies aiming at 'self-sufficiency' and 'food sovereignty' in the medium and long run. However, such a policy objective is likely to harm poor food importing countries that simply do not have the means or the appropriate environment to boost agricultural production.[28] Hence, in the context of volatilities in international markets, trade openness versus protectionism, and 'self-sufficiency' versus inefficient allocation of resources and environmental degradation, present a major trade-off for policy-makers.

These challenges and problems, and the need for a multidimensional policy agenda of 'sustainability' to address them are widely recognised by experts, civil society groups, and policy-makers alike.[29] However, there is a need for debate on how the various dimensions – economic, social and environmental – of 'sustainability' are defined in the context of developing countries and on how policy actors (i.e. stakeholders) make difficult choices in the face of conflicting objectives. Hence, investigating the perceptions and policy priorities of relevant stakeholders and seeing how they react to trade-offs is crucial for understanding the policy parameters of 'sustainable' agriculture in developing countries.

C. Empirical research on attitudes towards sustainable agriculture

I. Stakeholder surveys in Switzerland, New Zealand, Turkey and China

National public debates on sustainable agriculture are often framed by the attitudes and interests of the dominant stakeholders involved. They

26 W. Jones and A. Elasri, 'Rising Food Prices: Causes, Consequences and Policy Responses'. in B. Karapinar and C. Häberli (eds.), *Food Crises and the WTO* (Cambridge University Press, 2010).

27 B. Karapinar and C. Häberli (eds.), *Food Crises and the WTO* (Cambridge University Press, 2010).

28 L. Cabanilla and U. E. Rodriguez, 'The Food Versus Fuel Issue: Case of the Philippines' (2008) *ATDF Journal* 5(1/2), 68–74.

29 J. von Braun and E. Diaz-Bonilla, 'Globalization of Agriculture and Food: Causes, Consequences, and Policy Implications', in J. von Braun and E. Diaz-Bonilla (eds.), *Globalization of Food and Agriculture and the Poor* (Oxford University Press, 2006).

simultaneously respond and contribute to the formation of public opinion. In addition, policy-makers associate change with negative externalities that need to be addressed by means of a social planning approach.[30] This often leads to policies reflecting vested domestic interests rather than a genuine concern for sustainable agriculture. Moreover, such views tend to portray trade and exporting countries as harbingers of unsustainable change. This is relevant when considering the use made of the policy space offered by the AoA. If there is evidence that national definitions of sustainable agriculture are related to parochial interests rather than the public interest, then there should be a joint international effort to revise the relevant WTO disciplines. We tested this empirically by conducting stakeholder perception surveys in countries that face different economic, social and environmental challenges in agriculture and respond to these challenges with different agricultural policies. For this purpose we selected Switzerland and New Zealand, two countries with similar affluence and a similar concern for sustainable agriculture but different positions in international agricultural trade. In addition we chose two advanced developing countries with a similar level of income and similar challenges in terms of dealing with economic development, social inequality, and environmental degradation in rural areas.

I. *Stakeholder perception surveys in Switzerland and New Zealand*

1. Agricultural policies in New Zealand and Switzerland

New Zealand decided in the 1980s to embark on a bold agricultural reform by completely dismantling its hitherto heavily protected and subsidised agricultural system. Yet the government did not abandon the farmers but instead supported them in their efforts to become independent and innovative entrepreneurs. The government, however, remained equally committed to sustainable agriculture in order to maintain New Zealand's image of being clean and green. It does so by investing in sustainable and technological change in collaboration with farmers, researchers and the private sector.

Swiss agricultural policy is much more defensive. It is based on the assumption that farming provides public services that are not remunerated by the market and therefore justify government intervention and

30 P. Aerni, 'The Welfare Costs of Not Being Part of the Knowledge Economy: Why Rural Development Needs More Creative Policy Strategies' (2006) *ATDF Journal* 3(4), 27–43.

compensation by way of direct payments. This notion of 'multifunctionality' is even enshrined in the Federal Constitution.[31]

In spite of their different approaches, the two countries share similar social values and levels of affluence. However, it is obvious that stakeholder interests are different in a country like New Zealand, where agriculture is responsible for 50 per cent of the total export receipts and makes up 6.1 per cent of the gross domestic product (GDP) (15.7 per cent if all food and forestry-related businesses are included),[32] from those in a country like Switzerland where agriculture's share of total exports receipts is less than 3 per cent and its contribution to GDP is less than 1 per cent.[33] The different interests of the stakeholders and their attitudes towards sustainable agriculture may also have a significant influence on the construction of social preferences in the two countries.[34]

2. Survey results and interpretation

The stakeholder surveys in Switzerland and New Zealand were carried out in 2007 with a number of selected stakeholders in each country that were considered to be central to the public debate on sustainable agriculture. Roughly 40 stakeholder representatives participated in the survey which corresponds to a response rate of 81 per cent in New Zealand and 86 per cent in Switzerland respectively. The survey results revealed diverging views on the impact of international trade on sustainable agriculture (see Box 4.1). In New Zealand, stakeholders tend to believe that agriculture needs technological and economic change to become sustainable, whereas

31 Article 104 of the Federal Constitution, in relevant parts, provides that: 'The Confederation shall ensure that the agricultural sector, by means of a sustainable and market oriented production policy, makes an essential contribution towards; (a.) the reliable provision of the population with foodstuffs; (b.) the conservation of natural resources and the upkeep of the countryside; (c.) decentralised population settlement of the country.' Furthermore, 'if necessary in derogation from the principle of economic freedom, the Confederation shall support farms that cultivate the land.' And: 'The Confederation shall organise measures in such a manner that the agricultural sector fulfils its multi-functional duties.' What follows is a long list of such measures, including (lit.a) 'supplementing revenues from agriculture by means of direct subsidies in order to achieve fair and adequate remuneration for the services provided, subject to proof of compliance with ecological requirements'.

32 Ministry of Agriculture and Forestry (MAF), 'Agriculture and Forestry in New Zealand: An Overview' (Wellington: MAF, 2003), www.maf.govt.nz/mafnet/rural-nz/overview/nzoverview004.htm.

33 Bundesamt für Landwirtschaft (BLW), Agrarbericht 2006 (Bern, BLW, 2007).

34 S. Lichtenstein and P. Slovic, *The Construction of Preference* (Cambridge University Press, 2006).

BOX 4.1 SUMMARY OF THE EMPIRICAL RESULTS OF THE STAKEHOLDER SURVEYS IN NEW ZEALAND AND SWITZERLAND

Respondents in New Zealand tended to oppose direct payments, the precautionary principle and a tax on food miles as measures to promote sustainable agriculture. They acknowledged the valuable contribution of organic farming and eco-labelling, but thought it was not sufficient to ensure sustainable agriculture on a large scale. They believed it had to be combined with precision agriculture, biotechnology and appropriate policy incentives for farmers, researchers and the private sector to contribute to the character of sustainable agriculture as a public good.

Swiss respondents saw international trade competition as the most important problem of sustainable agriculture, endorsed the concept of multifunctional agriculture and had reservations about the use of new technologies.

The perception pattern analysis revealed that New Zealand also contains one perception group that has more in common with the dominant Swiss view. Yet, there is no Swiss perception group that shares the attitude dominant in New Zealand.

The survey results indicate that political stakeholders tend to make use of affect heuristics in order to gain more influence in the public debate on sustainable agriculture, especially in countries such as Switzerland where most people have jobs outside the agricultural economy.

Despite their many differences, the survey participants in Switzerland and New Zealand tended to agree that free trade, the private sector and technology as such, do not undermine the goals of sustainable agriculture. If this perception were applied to agricultural policy, it would mean that, in addition to monitoring and regulating sustainable agriculture, governments would need to create more incentives for academia, the private sector and the farming community to collaborate more actively in efforts to facilitate sustainable change in agriculture. The case of New Zealand already illustrates how this could lead to better integration of the agricultural sector into the global knowledge economy.[35]

stakeholders in Switzerland tend to believe that any form of change may endanger what they perceive to be the present sustainability of their agriculture.[36] This confirms the assumption that national definitions of sustainable agriculture may be highly dependent on a country's position in the international agricultural trading system. New Zealand is competitive and therefore forced to reconcile agricultural business with sustainable agriculture through innovation and incentive-based policies. The mainly

35 P. Aerni, 'What is Sustainable Agriculture? Empirical Evidence of Diverging Views in Switzerland and New Zealand' (2009) 6 *Ecological Economics* 68(6), 1872–1882.

36 P. Aerni, 'What is Sustainable Agriculture? Empirical Evidence of Diverging Views in Switzerland and New Zealand' (2009) *Ecological Economics* 68(6), 1872–1882.

progressive attitude of stakeholders in the New Zealand survey largely reflects this. It also explains why respondents in New Zealand generally consider new technologies to be an integral part of sustainable agriculture and endorse a bottom-up approach towards agricultural policy which hands over most of the decision-making power to farmers.

Swiss agriculture is less competitive and its stakeholders are therefore more sceptical about technological and economic change. The Swiss network of financial support helps explain the conservative attitude by revealing that the private and the public sector mainly sponsor research projects related to environmental monitoring and organic farming but not the advancement of technological innovation in agriculture.[37]

II. Stakeholder perception surveys in Turkey and China

1. Agricultural policies in Turkey and China

The agricultural sector of Turkey, which is dominated by small farms, around 4 million with an average size of 5 ha, has been stagnant, with almost zero growth over the past five years. In 2007 alone, the sector shrank by 7 per cent.[38] However, during the same period the rest of the economy has been growing relatively rapidly. The industrial sector, for instance, grew by more than 7 per cent on average. As a result, the income gap between rural and urban sectors has been widening. This is reflected in the fact that more than one-third of those employed in the agricultural sector live below the national poverty line, representing by far the highest rate of poverty among all sectors.[39] Hence, the rural society seems to be lagging behind in the process of economic development. As such, the economic dimension of 'sustainability' in agriculture poses a serious developmental challenge. At the same time, environmental degradation presents a major threat to the future viability of farming, especially in ecologically vulnerable areas. Land erosion, desertification and salinisation, falling ground water levels, and increasing frequency and duration of droughts are major problems.[40] However, the integration

37 P. Aerni, A. Rae and B. Lehmann, 'Nostalgia vs. Pragmatism? How Attitudes and Interests Shape the Term Sustainable Agriculture in Switzerland and New Zealand (2009) *Food Policy* 34(2), 227–235.

38 State Planning Organisation, Statistics 2008, availiable at www.dpt.gov.tr/ (accessed in January 2009).

39 World Bank, 'Turkey Joint Poverty Assessment Report', Volume I: Main Report, Report No. 29619-TU (2005).

40 B. Karapinar, F. Adaman and G. Ozertan (eds.), *Rethinking Structural Reform in Turkish Agriculture: Beyond the World Bank's Strategy* (Nova Science Publishers, 2010).

of these environmental concerns into the national political system has been difficult, and the process has been largely driven by external stimuli (e.g. through the EU accession process).[41] Hence it is often argued that, in addressing environmental challenges, the paternalistic state and its public institutions and legislation are ineffective owing to lack of actual implementing power, and to corruption and clientelism.[42]

The Chinese agricultural sector, on the other hand, has largely fulfilled the overarching policy objective of supporting industrialisation by providing reliable supplies of food to the growing population over the past three decades.[43] The substantial growth that it has managed to sustain since the early 1980s has been largely attributed to the shift in the land tenure system from the collective production of the 'People's Commune' to the Household Responsibility System (HRS).[44] However, the agricultural sector has been facing fundamental economic, social and environmental challenges which the HRS was not designed to address. Maintaining productivity growth in the face of rapidly changing diets and consumer preferences, growing income gap between small-farm dominated agriculture and the non-agricultural sectors, international trade competition since the country's accession to the WTO in 2001, mounting pressure on natural resources, and climate change adaptation are the most important of these. In this context, the concept of 'sustainability' may offer an operational and analytical framework for policy-making. However, there are trade-offs and conflicting policy objectives in achieving what might be perceived to be 'sustainable'.

2. Survey Results and Interpretation

The stakeholder surveys in Turkey and China were carried out in 2007. In each country, the respondent group included stakeholders from university and research institutions, government organisations, domestic and international non-governmental organisations (NGOs), the mass media and the private sector. The results of the survey show that although the majority of Turkish and Chinese stakeholders think that agriculture

41 F. Adaman, 'The Political Economy of the Environment in Turkey' (1997) *New Perspectives on Turkey* 17, 129–150.

42 F. Adaman and M. Arsel (eds.), *Environmentalism in Turkey: Between Democracy and Development?* (Ashgate, 2005).

43 J. Y. Lin, 'Agricultural Development and Reform in China', in C. K. Eicher and Staatz (eds.), *International Agricultural Development* (Johns Hopkins University Press, 1998).

44 W. Hu, 'Household Land Tenure Reform in China: Its Impact on Farming Land Use and Agroenvironment' (1997) *Land Use Policy* 14(3), 75–186.

is not 'sustainable', there are marked variations among them regarding priorities on different dimensions of 'sustainability'. There is a general convergence of opinion about the worsening of environmental problems, whereas the stakeholders' perceptions about potential solutions remain divergent. Turkish respondents, regardless of their affiliation, perceive that agriculture is not sustainable in their country.[45] By contrast, in China, although the respondents who represented (domestic and international) NGOs consider that agriculture is not sustainable at all, the respondents representing government and academia think that Chinese agriculture is sustainable (see Box 4.2).[46]

D. The political economy of sustainable agriculture

I. The basic policy insights from comparing the four cases

1. Switzerland and New Zealand

In Switzerland, only 2.4 per cent of the population work in the agricultural sector.[47] The views and values of the large non-farming majority are therefore crucial in explaining Swiss agricultural policy. This majority live in metropolitan areas and regard support for traditional agriculture as an expression of personal values and lifestyle.[48] Their disinterest in the modern business of agriculture and their concern that globalisation will sweep away idyllic Swiss small-scale agriculture makes them very responsive to political stakeholders who claim to defend the values of rural Switzerland and to stop the 'death of farms' (*Bauernsterben*). Thus the public debate becomes highly affect-driven and induces political stakeholders to portray themselves as disinterested actors who only have the public good in mind.[49]

In New Zealand, where agriculture is still perceived to be an important business that creates a lot of employment, the public debate about

45 B. Karapinar, '"Sustainability" in Agriculture: Stakeholders' Perceptions in Turkey', in B. Karapinar, F. Adaman and G. Ozertan (eds.). *Rethinking Structural Reform in Turkish Agriculture: Beyond the World Bank's Strategy* (Nova Science Publishers: 2010).

46 B. Karapinar, '"Sustainability" in Chinese Agriculture: Stakeholders' Perceptions and Policy Trade-offs' (2009), NCCR-Trade Working Paper. 2009/43, University of Bern.

47 Bundesamt für Landwirtschaft (BLW), 'Agrarbericht 2007' (BLW, Bern, 2007).

48 U. Beck, 'Living Your Own Life in a Runaway World: Individualization, Globalization and Politics', in W. Hutton and A. Giddens (eds.), *On The Edge: Living with Global Capitalism* (Jonathan Cape, 2000).

49 P. Aerni, A. Rae and B. Lehmann, 'What is Sustainable Agriculture? Nostalgia Versus Pragmatism in a Climate of Free Trade' (2009) *Food Policy* 34(2), 227–235.

BOX 4.2 SUMMARY OF THE EMPIRICAL RESULTS OF THE STAKEHOLDER SURVEYS IN TURKEY AND CHINA

Stakeholders in both countries are concerned about environmental problems, yet they only acknowledge the potential conflicts between growing intensity of agricultural production and the environment when they are explicitly presented with a trade-off. In Turkey, 'deforestation', 'global warming' and 'water pollution' rank as the most serious environmental threats, whereas in China, stakeholders are primarily concerned about 'water pollution', 'destruction of grassland' and 'land degradation'. In both countries, the respondents are aware of the pressure that agricultural production places on natural resources – as they identify 'excessive water consumption', 'excessive use of plant protection (pesticide, herbicides etc.)', and 'excessive use of nitrogen fertilisers' as 'highly significant contributors' to these problems. Hence the respondents are aware of a trade-off between the growing intensity of agricultural production and protecting natural resources. However, when they were asked if 'in the next 10 years, instead of considering agriculture to be a problem of economic development . . . it should be considered as a problem of environment', most of them disagreed, except the NGOs. In particular, government representatives disagreed with the statement, implying that, for them, economic development is more important than protecting the environment.

In both Turkey and China, the respondents identified international trade competition as a significant contributor to environmental problems. In response to a qualified statement, they agreed (Turkish respondents more strongly than their Chinese counterparts) that 'free trade of agriculture will force farmers to neglect sustainability at the expense of competitiveness'. However, when they were asked about the potential economic benefits of trade liberalisation, they supported the statement that 'from trade liberalization through negotiations in the World Trade Organization (WTO), China/Turkey . . . should benefit'. Hence, albeit perceiving that trade openness would harm the environment, the stakeholders still rate the related potential economic benefits highly.

The statement that achieved the greatest consent in both Turkey and China was that 'the farmer does not just produce food but provides many public services that ensure the ecological, cultural and social sustainability of a society.' This statement epitomises the concept of multifunctionality of agriculture. All stakeholders seem to attribute some additional value to what agriculture entails as an economic activity. However, this perception seems to weaken if respondents are presented with a potential trade-off between economic and environmental priorities. As described above, whenever they were presented with an explicit choice, the majority of the respondents opted for supporting economic objectives. Similarly, the cultural dimension of 'multifunctionality' was not valued highly either – as respondents do not consider 'loss of traditions in farming' a significant problem.

As for the role of new technologies in sustainable agriculture, the respondents both in Turkey and China supported the precautionary principle. However, in response to qualified statements, particularly on genetically modified organisms (GMOs), the results revealed that Turkish stakeholders were more conservative than their Chinese counterparts in their attitudes towards biotechnology in agriculture. As expected, this issue was divisive even in China – as national and international NGOs think that GMOs should be banned altogether, while participants from university and research institutions have more favourable attitudes. Although stakeholders in both countries adopt a relatively risk-averse attitude, perceptions in China are more favourable, also reflecting the growing level of government investment in agricultural biotechnology research. In Turkey, however, the prevailing public perception reflects, or reinforces, the lack of government willingness to invest in new technologies.[50]

sustainable agriculture may be less charged with symbolic value, and more practical. Since a larger portion of the public feels directly affected by the course of the business of agriculture, they are more likely to be intensely involved in the issue.[51] This may allow the important stakeholders to break the value-based meta-discourse down into more concrete problems that have to be addressed in order to make sustainable agriculture compatible with agricultural competitiveness.

The Swiss approach is well embedded in the present international legal framework of sustainable agriculture which tends to frame the sustainability problem as a 'market failure' problem that requires government intervention. The resulting social planning approach is, however, vulnerable to the principal–agent problem in the sense that the agent (the farmer) takes advantage of the situation of asymmetric information by passing on only the information that is required to get the payment from the principal (the government). This means that the enforcement of environmental standards in agriculture is often ineffective.

The Swiss Government could facilitate change by embarking on agricultural trade liberalisation, unilaterally or via an Agricultural Free Trade Agreement with the European Union (EU). This would restrict the policy

50 B. Karapinar and M. Temmerman 'Intellectual Property Rights and Innovation: Promoting New Technologies in Turkish Agriculture', in B. Karapinar, F. Adaman and G. Ozertan (eds.). *Rethinking Structural Reform in Turkish Agriculture: Beyond the World Bank's Strategy* (Nova Science Publishers, 2010); G. Ozertan and P. Aerni 'GM Cotton and its Possible Contribution to Environmental Sustainability and Rural Development in Turkey' (2007) *International Journal of Agricultural Resources, Governance and Ecology* 6(4/5), 552–575.

51 R. E. Petty and J. T. Cacioppo, *Communication and Persuasion: Central and Peripheral Routes to Attitude Change* (Springer, 1986).

space available through border protection. The government would thus be forced to partially abandon its role as caretaker of Swiss farmers. In return, it would open new opportunities for public leadership. The government would act more as a coach assisting farmers in their efforts to become innovation-driven and internationally competitive entrepreneurs and financially encouraging Swiss researchers to collaborate more closely with farmers and the private sector in the development of sustainable technological innovation in agriculture. This is, however, unlikely to happen as long as the New Zealand view of sustainable agriculture is not represented in the public debate in Switzerland. In the 1980s, the New Zealand Federated Farmers felt that the national subsidies system was taking decision-making power away from them without addressing their real concerns. They therefore endorsed radical agricultural reform. In Switzerland, the Swiss Farmers Association (*Bauernverband*), which turned out to be the central player in the Swiss network of information exchange, may eventually decide to move from a defensive to a more bold and offensive strategy. Such a step would reflect a willingness to learn from best practices (in this case New Zealand). It would also make Swiss agriculture more compatible with the spirit of WTO AoA and may make it economically, socially and environmentally more sustainable because it would return more decision-making power to the farmers. Farmers who feel in charge of their lives and able to participate successfully in the global economy may contribute to social empowerment in rural areas (social dimension), generate more income and employment in the region (economic dimension) and become more interested in managing their scarce environmental resources in a sustainable way (environmental dimension).

2. Turkey and China

Both China and Turkey offer good case studies of the relevance of 'policy space' in the context of sustainable agriculture and international trade. Turkey exemplifies how macro-economic instability can quickly induce a government to appeal for outside support and advice, be it from the Bretton Woods Institutions or the European Union. Yet, in periods when Turkey enjoyed relative autonomy, thanks to strong economic growth, it did not fare any better owing to the culture of patronage and clientelism that has created a policy environment which is not conducive to sustainable endogenous growth in agriculture. Their main objective has been to gain electoral support in the rural areas, which are home to more than one-third of the country's electorate, rather than to formulate goals and design new policy tools.[52] This has been reflected in the form of an unsustainable and distorting system of subsidies which have always swung between the highs at parliamentary election times and the lows during financial crises, often followed by 'structural adjustment' programmes.[53] Even in periods when the total support estimate (TSE) reached relatively high levels, the share of spending on major agricultural services remained dismally small.[54] The same trend is also reflected in Turkey's trade policies at the multilateral level. As a leading member of the so-called G33 (a group of developing countries that are relatively less competitive in agriculture) it pursues a protectionist trade policy in agriculture and, as such, exemplifies how 'policy space' is operationalised to seal off vested interests rather than offering public goods to promote inclusive and sustainable growth.

In this context, the case of Turkey illustrates the need for a narrower definition of the term 'policy space' as a tool to facilitate sustainable agricultural development through investing in public goods in infrastructure, environmental protection, education and training, and research and development.[55]

China, on the other hand, exemplifies how highly centralised and authoritarian policies with the main objective of maximising output may fail to address growing environmental problems which require localised solutions and wider participation of stakeholders. However, it also shows the potential benefits of pursuing a common national agenda on agricultural research and technological innovation in efforts to address the growing sustainability challenges of unbridled economic growth.

The Chinese government's reluctance to compromise on its vast 'policy space' and to deregulate markets and to reform its centralised institutions is a major obstacle to addressing the environmental and social challenges

52 H. Akder, 'Policy Formation in the Process of Implementing Agricultural Reform in Turkey' (2007) *International Journal of Agricultural Resources, Governance and Ecology* 6 (4/5), 514–532.

53 E. Cakmak, and H. Akder, '*DTÖ ve AB'deki Gelişmeler Işığında 21. Yüzyılda Türkiye Tarımı' (In the Light of Developments at the WTO and the EU Turkish Agriculture in the 21st century)*, Turkish Industrialists' and Businessmen's Association (TUSIAD), Publication No. T/2005–06/397 (Istanbul, 2005).

54 Organization for Economic Cooperation and Development (OECD), 'Producer and Consumer Support Estimate (PSE-CSE) Database 1986–2005', 2006, available at: www.oecd.org (accessed June 2006).

55 B. Karapinar, 'Managing Rural Transformation in Turkey 1980–2004: Case Studies from three Regions' (2007) *International Journal of Agricultural Resources, Governance and Ecology* 6(4/5), 483–513.

described above. Chinese stakeholders support pro-market and private sector-oriented solutions to promote sustainable agriculture. Apart from the domestic and international NGOs, the majority believes that the role of government in setting agricultural prices should be reduced so that market mechanisms can function properly. They also support higher levels of private sector investment and a stronger intellectual property regime. Similarly, they give preference to other market-oriented solutions to address environmental problems. For instance, they strongly support educating consumers to change their behaviour to send signals to farmers to adopt more environmentally-friendly farming practices. They also believe that sustainable agriculture requires a bottom-up approach. As such, a transition from heavily regulated to more liberal markets which would also support a transition from a top-down social planning approach to more participatory decision-making in achieving sustainable agriculture would mean restricting the government's 'policy space'.

II. Policy space and WTO disciplines

The findings of all four stakeholder surveys reveal that policy space is amply used to pursue agricultural policies that are hardly in line with the spirit of the AoA.

The issue of national 'policy space' versus (international) binding commitments raises questions that are common in most legislative matters. It helps explain why multilateral or bilateral trade liberalisation happens in the form of binding commitments only if a country's export interests are expected to benefit from more global market access. Unilateral dismantling of border protection is one thing. But, while economic wisdom declares that most tariff reductions are beneficial to the national economy, no government will irreversibly commit to such tariff reductions unless its trading partners do likewise.

For agricultural negotiations, the same equation applies, albeit involving more parameters and going far beyond country borders. The WTO AoA became possible only because relatively simple tariff issues were settled together with totally new disciplines on domestic and export subsidies. The mere existence of such disciplines has important systemic implications for the formulation of national agricultural and trade policy. This is why many governments, at the time of ratification, were compelled to modify their policies and their legislation by:

(i) somewhat lowering their maximum border protection;
(ii) at least partially de-coupling farm support from market intervention; and
(iii) reducing export subsidies as a means of surplus disposal.

Each of these disciplines implies a reduction of policy space (regardless of whether or not they had used it at the time of ratification), i.e. of the ability to determine their production and trade policies in full compliance with their international disciplines.

Unlike the results of the Uruguay Round, those envisaged at the end of 2008 would constitute for many countries a much more stringent policy space limitation. Take the 70 per cent tariff reduction possibly applying to the highest tariffs in the developed countries: this figure alone would constitute a commitment never before achieved in any GATT negotiation on a sensitive sector! This not only explains one of the main difficulties in concluding this Round. The underlying issue is that the additional constraints impact in different ways and to different extents on the policy space available to governments, depending on their country's specific situation. For instance, while poor countries insist on tariff flexibility, the US negotiators prefer policy space for future needs in terms of domestic support, and the EU would like to continue to determine the Common Agricultural Policy in accordance with its own objectives. Under these circumstances, the various chairpersons of the agriculture negotiation committee have sought to find solutions inflicting what they called 'equal pain' on each participant, also taking into account their degree of development and even some very specific national situations and domestic policy constraints. Our research shows that 'policy space', more often than not, is a synonym for protecting entrenched sector interests rather than a step towards progressive liberalisation for the good of the national and global economy. Unfortunately, from a systemic point of view, it appears that 'Doha' may leave the door wide open for certain abuses of policy space, especially by advanced developing countries (e.g. Special Products, Special Safeguard Mechanism and export restrictions) but also, albeit in less obvious ways, for the developed countries (e.g. Sensitive Products, various Green Box discretions, food aid and export credits).[56]

The determination of the right balance between policy space limitations (by way of WTO disciplines) and market access benefits (within

56 S. Heri and C. Häberli, 'Can the World Trade Organization Ensure that Food Aid is Genuine?', NCCR Trade Regulation Working Paper 2009/19, May 2009.

and outside agriculture) clearly appears as the linchpin of a successful conclusion of the Doha Round.

E. The development dimension

Sustainability in agriculture has different connotations in different development contexts. This chapter highlights these connotations, starting with a new look at the agricultural trade discipline flexibilities for developing countries. We argue that the Doha Round proposals to promote development largely follow the spirit of existing Special and Differential Treatment provisions (S&D) in the WTO framework even though they have largely proved to be ineffective in promoting development. Based on the shortcomings of existing initiatives we propose to improve the impact assessment methodology for policies aimed at supporting sustainable development. In this context we assess the impact of Swiss agricultural trade policies on access to least developed country markets and conclude that major non-tariff trade barriers explain why least developed countries (LDCs) were unable to take advantage of duty-free quota treatment in Europe. Sustainability in the context of development also relates to the 2008 food crisis and its implications for rural poverty and growth. We believe that the food crisis was mainly the result of old economic theory applied to new policy challenges and argue that a new form of public–private partnership in agriculture and a focus on best practices is necessary to address the current problems and avoid repeating past mistakes.

I. WTO Disciplines

In all WTO Agreements, the development dimension is mostly reflected in so-called S&D provisions. Altogether there are ninety-seven S&D provisions in the whole WTO regulatory framework, thirteen in the AoA alone, the main purpose of these provisions is to take into account the particular situation of food exporting and importing developing countries.[57] Also, based on the experience with the present rules, a number of additional features are to be built into the Doha Development Round results. We briefly describe and comment on both these sets of provisions.

57 WTO, Note by the Secretariat, 'Information on the Utilisation of Special and Differential Treatment Provisions', Document WT/COMTD/W/77/Rev.1/Add.4 dated 7 February 2002.

1. Present rules

In the Uruguay Round, developing countries – a self-elected category! – had to operate lesser tariff, domestic support and export subsidy reductions than industrialised countries. And the now fifty LDCs had no obligations at all, except to bind their agricultural tariffs.

2. Doha

Some would say that the only results so far agreed in the Doha Round address development concerns, for instance the Aid for Trade Programme adopted at the 2005 Hong Kong Ministerial. This being a Development Round, it will be quite natural to see a number of S&D provisions in agriculture. As of July 2008, Special Products and a Special Safeguard Mechanism were the two most prominent examples proposed by the draft modalities.[58]

3. Impact

The question of course is how much these provisions are worth in the real world, in terms of actually furthering the economic and agricultural trade development of developing countries. The WTO Secretariat, when presenting the use made of the various S&D provisions, has to take a neutral view on their effectiveness. But most scholars agree that S&D has not really lived up to expectations, or consider that it has even had outright negative effects on development.[59] It should be noted that policy space enshrined by way of substantive S&D provisions may not only reduce a country's competitiveness but also its rating for investors and creditors.[60]

II. Impact of Swiss trade and agricultural policies on developing countries

1. Trade impact assessments

There is a scientific consensus that the impact of trade liberalisation on agricultural sustainability in developing countries is highly

58 WTO, Committee on Agriculture in Special Session, 'Revised Draft Modalities for Agriculture', Document TN/AG/W/4/Rev.3 dated 10 July 2008.

59 R. Senti, *WTO – System und Funktionsweise der Welthandelsordnung* (Zurich: Schulthess, 2000), p. 257.

60 C. Häberli, 'La Suisse dans les nouvelles négociations agricoles de l'OMC', in *Annuaire Suisse-Tiers Monde*, Institut universitaire d'études du développement (IUED), Geneva, 2001.

significant.[61] However, as our stakeholder attitude surveys have indicated, the questions of how to define the term 'sustainability' and how to measure it are contentious. In an additional study we looked at the potential impact of Swiss trade and agricultural policies on developing countries, building on the existing methodology developed in the EU in the late 1990s, called the Sustainability Impact Assessments (SIAs).[62]

2. Free access for all products of least developed countries?

This impact assessment study considered the substantial opening of the Swiss market for all agricultural products from all LDCs.[63] Following in the wake of the so-called 'Everything But Arms' initiative of the European Union (EBA), this move at first sight appears as one of the boldest unilateral trade liberalisation measures of recent decades, simply because Switzerland is also the country with the highest agricultural tariffs in the world. The initial trade impact, however, turned out to be virtually nil – just like that of the duty-free quota-free treatment now granted to these countries by the European Union. The lack of competitiveness of many LDCs was found to be one reason for this rather surprising result. Some scholars blame over-restrictive rules of origin of the EBA.[64] But sanitary and technical barriers to trade, although applied in a non-discriminatory way, have emerged as a veritable bulwark ('Fortress Europe'), certainly for LDC-based companies: with the exception of some fish industries and four animal casing traders in Bangladesh not one of them was certified for animal product imports into Europe. Added to this, the array of private standards, established mainly by processors, retailers and farmers in developed countries, are clearly discriminatory (even when they are formally identical, they do not affect importers in the same way as domestic producers). It is therefore obvious that agricultural producers and processors continue to face extremely difficult market access conditions. Duty-free treatment of their products has not changed this fact.

61 C. George, and C. Kirkpatrick (eds.), *Impact Assessment for Sustainable Development: European Perspectives and Experience* (Edward Elgar, 2006).

62 C. George, and C. Kirkpatrick, 'Trade and Development: Assessing the Impact of Trade Liberalisation on Sustainable Development' (2004) *Journal of World Trade* 38(3), 441–469.

63 C. Häberli, 'Market Access in Switzerland and in the European Union for Agricultural Products from Least Developed Countries', NCCR Trade Regulation Working Paper 2008/5, July 2008.

64 P. Collier, *The Bottom Billion* (Oxford University Press, 2007).

III. *Food security and trade*

When it comes to the impact of globalisation on food security in LDCs, several questions become relevant. What is the role of international trade? Is the lack of substantial trade liberalisation in agriculture a cause of the latest food crisis? On the other hand, has open trade left some developing countries vulnerable to price shocks? There are also questions about the role of the multilateral trading system and the WTO.[65]

At the country level, there is no simple answer to the question of whether more liberal international trade in agriculture helps or hinders food security. A rigorous analysis by Diaz-Bonilla *et al.* asserted that in addition to the existing categories of developing countries, LDCs and net food importing developing countries (NFIDC), there is a need for more sophisticated categories better capturing the relationship between international trade and food security.[66] The study offered a typology involving twelve different categories of countries, such as trade-stressed countries (those with expenses for food imports being equivalent to over 20 per cent of their total export earnings), food-insecure countries with an urban profile, high-consumption and trade-stressed food-insecure countries (those combining relatively higher levels of average calorie consumption with a substantial level of trade stress), high-consumption and trade-stressed food-neutral countries, net food-importing countries with a dominant tourism industry, and food-insecure countries which are neither LDCs nor NFIDCs. It is clear that the impact of further trade liberalisation would vary substantially based on these profiles at the country level.

In this context, the breakdown in the Doha Round Negotiations of July 2008 came at a time when the impact of the food crisis was unfolding. This raised questions as to whether the Agreement on Agriculture (AoA), or the mandate of the Doha Development Round in general, which were designed for a period of relatively cheap food (including food dumping), would be able to offer an effective legal framework for global trade in radically different market circumstances. After all, one of the fundamental premises of the Doha Round was to eliminate support to farmers in

65 B. Karapinar, 'Food Crises and the WTO', in B. Karapinar and C. Häberli (eds.), *Food Crises and the WTO* (Cambridge University Press, 2010).

66 E. Diaz-Bonilla, M. Thomas, S. Robinson and A. Cattaneo, 'Food Security and Trade Negotiations in the World Trade Organization: A Cluster Analysis of Country Groups', International Food Policy Research Institute (IFPRI) (TMD Discussion Paper, No. 59. 2000).

developed countries, which had been suppressing world prices. Although estimates varied significantly, the downward impact of the OECD domestic support measures on world prices was calculated to be less than 10 per cent, a figure way below the recent price spikes.[67] So the question is whether the fundamentals of the Doha Development Agenda were wrong, or whether WTO rules should be redesigned to make them operative also in an era of high agricultural prices.

As usual, the July 2008 negotiations were politically charged. Yet it was not surprising that both the opponents and the proponents of further liberalisation of agricultural markets used the recent food crisis to justify or strengthen their respective positions.[68] Those arguing for further liberalisation put forward the view that the combination of artificially low world prices and high protection in developed countries had restrained developing countries from investing in higher production and productivity in agriculture, which is also the main reason why these producers now lack the capacity to respond to higher prices. They argue that substantial trade liberalisation would mean that farmers get clear price signals that allow them to invest in the right crops and become less dependent. On the other hand, those arguing against further liberalisation suggested that reducing border protection and agricultural support would lead to additional increases in prices which will hurt consumers in developing countries still more. In the end, the negotiations collapsed seemingly because of a deadlock on the Special Safeguard Mechanism designed to prevent import surges. This was rather ironic – as it came at a time when almost all developing countries had dropped or eliminated their applied tariffs, yet were facing difficulties in importing food crops.

The July 2008 proposal – the final text on the Doha negotiating table – does not seem to offer the right policy tools to promote food security at the multilateral level. It lacks some key elements such as disciplines regulating food aid and biofuels subsidies.[69] More importantly, there is almost nothing to strengthen the rules on export restrictions, such as

67 For instance, B. Dimaranan, T. Hertel and R. Keeney ('OECD Domestic Support and the Developing Countries', paper for the UNU/WIDER project on the impact of WTO on low-income countries, GTAP Center, Purdue University, 2003) estimated that the price impact would be 3.5 to 5 per cent for major agricultural crops such as wheat and oilseeds.

68 Food and Agriculture Organization of the United Nations (FAO), 'The Breakdown of the Doha Round Negotiations: What Does It Mean for Dealing with Soaring Food Prices?', Economic and Social Perspectives Policy Brief 3, Rome, 2008.

69 C. Häberli, 'Food Security and WTO Rules', in B. Karapinar and C. Häberli (eds.), *Food Crises and the WTO* (Cambridge University Press, 2010).

were imposed by many countries during the crisis, and are effectively a major threat to food security in NFIDCs. These export restrictions, beyond their immediate effects, also undermine the notion of trust in the international trading system in general. Hence there is a need for reforming the WTO rules in agriculture to address the new circumstances in commodity markets so that more liberalised trade, regulated by an effective multilateral framework, could play a positive role in improving food security.

IV. The potential of geographical indications for rural development

Geographical indications (GI) are also linked to the development dimension because they are seen as a tool for ensuring higher added value to producers of traditional quality products of a certain region and thus to promote rural development. In a series of case studies we looked into the creation and distribution of economic value in developing countries, based on the same conceptual approach as the systems in force in the EU and in Switzerland and including an overview of the current literature and experiences of what may be expected of a GI system in developing countries. The case studies highlight both a series of recurring conceptual features and considerable diversity of the implementation strategies.[70] Four main results are worth mentioning. First, value is created by consumers' acknowledgement of typicality and uniqueness linked to a territory, which comes from a specific ecosystem and/or the processors' traditional know-how. These products belong to the family of differentiated products according to the economic theory, and value creation comes from product differentiation. Secondly, the results highlight that value distribution to the producers is not guaranteed by the registration process but comes from organisational innovation that emphasises collective action and coordination. But there are limits. For instance, GI systems should not be elaborated for social and environmental purposes. Nevertheless, in many cases the traditional and extensive production processes have positive side effects. Thirdly, a certain degree of intellectual property protection is required because of the ability of GI products to generate price premiums at the consumer level, which leads to usurpation and counterfeiting of famous names. Finally, we also observed that a combination of GI registration and certification marks provided the

70 N. El Benni and S. Réviron, 'Geographical Indications: Review of Seven Case-studies Worldwide', NCCR Trade Regulation Working Paper 2009/15, March 2009.

most efficient protection system in developing countries and on their export markets.

Our research shows that, if placed in an appropriate regulatory, organisational and economic context, GIs can go a long way towards ensuring additional value for small producers even in some of the poorest countries. However, such markets largely depend on fickle consumer preferences in affluent urban areas. It may therefore be risky for farmers to merely respond to an external demand and rely on the continued value attributed to GIs, especially if this leads them to neglect the need to constantly improve quality through innovation.

V. Mobilising science and technology to ensure endogenous growth and food security

1. Facilitating entrepreneurship and technological innovation in agriculture

In Africa, 80 per cent of farms are smaller than 2 hectares.[71] By comparison to Asian countries with a similar agrarian structure, crop yields are extremely low. The overall decline in production per capita of all major food crops can be attributed to the fact that most African farmers do not have access to fertiliser, improved seeds and other inputs, and mechanisation is almost non-existent. In contrast, the large-scale African plantations of cocoa, cotton, peanuts and sugar may be successful exporters to Europe, but they are almost exclusively run by Europeans and stem from the age of colonialism when Europeans still invested in research to improve these speciality crops.

Figure 4.1 shows the dramatic changes in agricultural production per capita in Africa compared to other regions in the world over the past five decades (starting from the period of 1960–65=100). While the numbers increased everywhere else, Africa's per capita production decreased and since 1991 has been stagnating.

In spite of the overwhelming evidence that sub-Saharan Africa needs more public and private sector investment in agriculture and improvements in rural infrastructure to better connect poor farmers to markets, a recent report published by the International Assessment of Agricultural Knowledge, Science and Technology for Development (IAASTD)[72] hardly addresses this urgency. In its global summary for decision makers

71 R. Paarlberg, *Starved for Science* (Havard University Press, 2008).
72 IAASTD (2008), www.agassessment.org/.

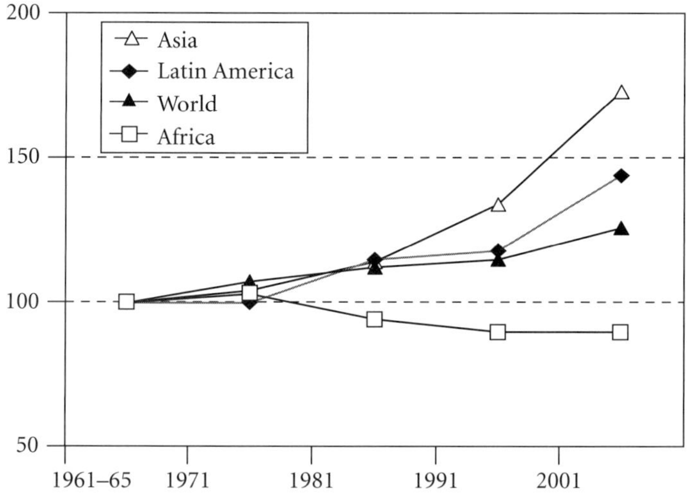

Figure 4.1 Regional differences in the development of agricultural production/capita (Reproduced with permission from Southgate *et al.* 2007: 67)

the World Bank-sponsored IAASTD report implicitly frames open agricultural markets and new technologies as the problem rather than part of the solution to sustainable agriculture.[73]

Even though the report contains a lot of valuable insights gained from agricultural research and correctly identifies the major problems in agriculture with regard to biodiversity, soil degradation and water use, it hardly addresses the challenge of how to produce more food with less land and water. Its recommendations are based on the popular but wrong assumption that hunger is merely a distribution problem and is unrelated to production. If one were to follow this insight and distribute the surpluses from subsidised agricultural systems freely among the people in poor food-importing countries, their farmers would have to abandon farming altogether because they cannot compete with donations. This would thus exacerbate the inability to achieve food self-sufficiency in these countries.

The report was initially meant to highlight the environmental problems of modern agriculture and its impact on smallholders in marginal regions. It was implicitly assumed that food security would not be an issue in a world that produces large food surpluses and consequently depresses food prices everywhere. The food price rises in 2007 and 2008 therefore came

73 E. Stokstad, 'Duelling Visions for a Hungry World' (2008) *Science* 319, 1474–1476.

as a surprise and the IAASTD report had then to be quickly portrayed as a potential solution for the world food crisis as well. Not everyone was buying the conclusions.

Even though the report claims to represent an interdisciplinary approach that involves researchers and experts from all areas, the steering group largely ignored the experts in biotechnology and molecular biology and showed no interest in the potential ability of the private sector to contribute to the global public good character of sustainable agriculture and food security.[74]

The defendants of the right to food and food sovereignty who largely welcomed the IAASTD report[75] tend to ignore the laws of demand and supply that still determine the price of food and consequently access to food. So if access to food is to be improved without further harming the natural environment more food needs to be produced on less land. The IAASTD report is right to argue for more support of multifunctional small-scale agricultural systems that make sustainable use of the local natural resources and thus enable a more integrated approach to farming. But such systems should be combined with promising new agricultural technologies. This would make such agricultural systems more profitable for farmers, less labour intensive (allowing families to send their children to school because they are less needed in the fields) and more efficient in their use of the available natural resources. There are no scientific reasons why a combination of integrated farm management and agricultural biotechnology should not be possible. But unfortunately, the report did not make an effort to go beyond the usual ideological division between small, low-tech farming and big high-tech farming.

2. Best practices

In order to improve agricultural, trade, development and environmental policies in the global economy, and to make more effective use of scarce resources, we need to focus on the production and better use of knowledge, the only non-scarce resource, for the greater public good.

This would require the design of a new national and international institutional environment that is not only concerned with regulation but also provides more incentives for actors to invest in the acquisition of new knowledge. Companies that invest in new knowledge in order to generate new products and solutions not only for the affluent but also for

74 Nature Biotechnology Editorial, 'Off the Rails' (2008) *Nature Biotechnology* 26(3), 247.

75 O. De Schutter, Address by the UN Rapporteur on the Human Right to Food, High-Level Conference on Food Security (Rome 3–5 June 2008).

the poor should be rewarded accordingly. Such a shift from regulation to facilitation in public policy would eventually lead to a transition from a mitigation-based to a more adaptation-based concept of sustainable development.

Increasing knowledge increases the probability that new goods and services will be generated through the commercial use of this knowledge. Knowledge therefore creates opportunities for nearly boundless growth, not by devouring more resources (labour, land, natural resources) but by developing new ways (e.g. instructions, designs) to make more efficient and creative use of existing resources. In other words, 'the raw materials that we use have not changed, but as a result of trial and error, experimentation, refinement, and scientific investigation, the instructions that we follow for combining raw materials have become vastly more sophisticated.'[76]

Knowledge therefore also holds the key to a more sustainable future. Investment in human capital and improved access to knowledge facilitates social empowerment through entrepreneurship and makes economic growth more compatible with environmental sustainability.

Policies that still rely on comparative-static economics have not proved to be very effective when applied to policy strategies to improve the livelihoods and autonomy of the underprivileged in marginal areas. These orthodox policies failed to integrate the rural poor into the global knowledge economy. This has had fatal consequences because it increased the dependence of marginal farmers on outside support and made them more vulnerable to external shocks. The sudden rise in food prices was not their fault, but they suffered most from it due to their lack of response-capacity and purchasing power. Food prices are decreasing again but hunger and starvation are likely to continue, not so much in the cities, where the poor are better organised, but in remote rural areas that are often not even connected to food markets.[77] The inhabitants face an increasing inability to produce sufficient food for themselves because their yields are subject to biotic and abiotic stresses that cannot be controlled. This is because they lack access to means of plant protection and improved varieties that are more resistant to salinity, drought or floods. Moreover, since there has been hardly any investment in the genetic improvement of their orphan

76 P. Romer, 'New Goods, Old Theory, and the Welfare Costs of Trade Restrictions'. (1994) *Journal of Development Economics* 43, 5–38.

77 P. Aerni, 'Public Acceptance of Transgenic Rice and its Potential Impact on Rice Markets in Southeast Asian Countries', PhD Thesis (Zurich: Swiss Federal Institute of Technology, ETH Zurich, Switzerland, 1999).

food crops and their livestock they are facing decreasing yields even in the absence of nature-related stress factors. An additional problem is that temporary yield surpluses often go to waste because of lack of post-harvest facilities and lack of infrastructure to bring the surplus to the market in other regions.[78]

It is not that development organisations involved in North–South collaboration do not see these problems but that their focus on training these people to become self-sufficient rather than growth-oriented is preventing active participation in the new opportunities that are offered by the global knowledge economy and international trade. Trade as such can hardly be blamed for creating poverty where it does not reach the rural poor who are mostly 'self-sufficient' semi-subsistence farmers.

This is in stark contrast to the growing South–South collaborations that are more focused on enabling the poor to participate in globalisation and to improve their situation by combining their traditional knowledge with new knowledge and technologies. The emerging orphan crop research networks such as the Cassava Biotechnology Network show how successful such collaboration can become. Initially this was a classic North–South initiative, but when agricultural biotechnology started to face an acceptance problem in Europe, public funding for this highly interdisciplinary multi-stakeholder network was cut. This weakened the influence of Northern donors and strengthened the role of Southern partners. The research priorities shifted accordingly.[79] Even though funding has become scarcer, these crop networks are offering a new inclusive approach to research by facilitating more exchange between agro-ecologists, social scientists and molecular biologists and by setting research priorities in accordance with local farmer preferences and local private sector activities.[80] The primary goal has become the development of useful products and services for resource-poor farmers that enable them to improve their livelihoods by actively participating in national or even international agricultural markets.

The Cassava Biotechnology Network is only one example of best practices that could be replicated in other areas and guide food policies as well as development and environmental policies. Interestingly, best practices

78 P. Aerni, 'Agricultural Biotechnology and its Contribution to the Knowledge Economy' (2007) *Adv. Biochem. Engin./Biotechnol.* 107, 69–96.

79 A. M. Thro, N. Taylor, K. Raemaker, J. Puonti-Kaerlas *et al.*, 'Maintaining the Cassava Biotechnology Network' (1998) *Nature Biotechnology* 16, 428–430.

80 P. Aerni, '*Mobilizing Science and Technology for Development: The Case of the Cassava Biotechnology Network (CBN)*' (2006) *AgBioForum* 9(1), 1–14.

in combining affordable technological solutions with local knowledge are mostly developed by people in developing countries themselves who have simply more experience and are more familiar with the constraints rural people face in the countryside. Frugal engineering enabled these countries to create entirely new markets that cater to the mass markets of the metropolitan areas of other developing countries rather than to large consumer markets of affluent societies.[81] The frugal engineering approach could now also be promoted through the establishment of institutions of higher learning in rural areas of developing countries.[82] Their livelihoods are different from those in metropolitan areas and they have different needs and face more constraints. Low-tech innovations or successful and cheap combinations of high-tech and low-tech solutions developed by local people in rural areas could meet a demand in other regions and thus create new markets that cater to rural businesses in other developing countries.[83] In this context, the experience in New Zealand indicates that agriculture even in less developed countries could be fully integrated into the global knowledge economy by enabling farmers to take greater advantage of the new knowledge and technologies that are relevant in the business of agriculture. It adopted the principles of the New Growth Theory to reform its agricultural policy in the 1980s.

3. The role of public–private partnerships

Following the era of the 'welfare state' in the 1970s and early 1980s and that of 'neo-liberalism' during the 1990s, there needs to be a significant shift in the political and policy approaches to institutional development. As elaborated above, a state-led centralist approach to scientific research and technological innovation is no longer considered feasible. In many developing countries, public research institutions, which were never designed to be competitive, find it increasingly difficult to obtain adequate resources and expertise to innovate in a rapidly developing field of technology. They lack the market knowledge and entrepreneurial drive to respond to today's world of extremely diversified and sophisticated agricultural markets. On the other hand, the neo-liberal approach, namely, 'let the market decide' has also proven problematic. There are

81 *The Economist*, 'A Bigger World: A Special Report on Globalisation' (20 September 2008).

82 P. Aerni, 'Exploring the Linkages of Commerce, Higher Education and Human Development: A Historical Review' (2007) *ATDF Journal* 4(2), 35–48.

83 S. Rich, A. Gupta and the Honey Bee Network, *World Changing* (21 March 2007), available at www.worldchanging.com/archives/006333.html (accessed 19 November 2008).

serious asymmetry problems causing market failures, indicating that freeing market mechanisms does not automatically create welfare gains. The market-led reforms of the 1980s and 1990s resulted in the privatisation of many state-run agricultural organisations, such as producer cooperatives, credit, purchasing and storing agencies, and research and extension institutions, providing major services to smallholders. In remote rural areas where poverty is particularly prevalent, the withdrawal of the state has left a large vacuum that the private sector is unable or unwilling to fill.[84] Thus it is argued that developing countries need to move away from the conventional institutional approaches that consider scientific research and technological innovation either as explicit 'public goods' which the welfare state has the sole responsibility to provide or as indiscriminate 'private goods' that should fall within the realm of the private sector.[85]

In this context, public–private partnerships (PPPs) offer new institutional opportunities for enhancing sustainable development in agriculture. There are various types of institutional design for PPPs. In the field of technological innovation and research for instance, public institutions and the private sector pool their resources for research, which should then benefit both the private sector and the general public. The private sector usually provides its methodological knowledge, financial resources and marketing expertise, while the public sector provides institutional and infrastructural support, including supportive legislation and the use of testing facilities. In this way, private companies can gain access to large domestic agricultural markets. PPPs can also help public institutions to convert their research outputs into end-user oriented products. They can also promote private sector development in countries with agricultural sectors dominated by state-owned monopolies.[86] Some recent examples show that innovation-driven PPPs can play a major role in making technology both available and accessible to smallholders in low-income developing countries.[87] As such, PPPs should be a strong feature

84 International Fund for Agricultural Development (IFAD), 'Rural Poverty Report: the Challenge of Ending Rural Poverty' (IFAD, Rome 2001), available at www.ifad.org/poverty/ (accessed November 2008).

85 B. Karapinar and M. Temmerman, 'Benefiting from Biotechnology: Pro-poor IPRs and Public Private Partnerships' (2008) *Biotechnology Law Report* 27(3), 189–202.

86 D. J. Spielman, F. Hartwich and K. von Grebmer, 'Sharing Science, Building Bridges, and Enhancing Impact: Public–Private Partnerships in the CGIAR', International Food Policy Research Institute, Discussion Paper 00708, Washington, DC (2007).

87 There have been important examples of PPPs in developing countries. The International Service for the Acquisition of Agri-Biotech Applications (ISAAA) is a significant example of PPPs at the international level. Through its regional operations (in Africa,

of a new institutional thinking promoting sustainable agriculture through innovation and technology.[88]

F. Concluding remarks

Our empirical and legal studies have investigated the role of sustainable agriculture in international trade from different perspectives. The terms 'sustainable agriculture' and 'non-trade concerns' have many different connotations, but they generally tend to reflect the political agendas of the dominant stakeholders involved in the domestic debates on agriculture. There is no agreed definition of either term – but since they reflect objectives rather than measures, there is no need here for us to propose such definitions. Hence our research mainly raises questions regarding the toolbox of governmental 'sustainability' objectives. For example, is it necessary to shield farmers from the process of globalisation or should they be successfully integrated into the global economy? How can we ensure that the term sustainable agriculture addresses the global economic, environmental and social challenges of agriculture rather than merely serving domestic stakeholders seeking to extract protection and subsidies from the state? To what extent would a reduction in policy space in the WTO AoA force countries to design policies that are based on cost-effective best practices – and therefore more sustainable – rather than the result of lobbying by well-organised interest groups? How can developing countries facilitate technological and economic change in rural areas through trade policies that encourage public–private partnerships?

Reflecting on these considerations we can draw three major lessons from our work on the subject of sustainable agriculture and international trade.

Asia and Latin America), it acts as an intermediary between developed country companies and public institutions in developing countries: Patricia Kameri-Mbote, David Wafula and Norman Clark, 'Public/Private Partnerships for Biotechnology in Africa: The Future Agenda' African Centre for Technology Studies', Nairobi, International Environmental Law Research Centre, at 22 (2001), available at www.ielrc.org (last accessed April 2007). The Consultative Group on International Agricultural Research (CGIAR) has also entered into some partnerships with the private sector. For example, its collaboration with a Japanese private company produced the first Bt cassava variety developed in Africa: Gordon C. Rausser, Leo Simon and Holly Ameden, 'Public–private Alliances in Biotechnology: Can they Narrow the Knowledge Gaps between Rich and Poor?' (2000) *Food Policy* 25, 499.

88 B. Karapinar and M. Temmerman, 'Benefiting from Biotechnology: Pro-poor IPRs and Public-private Partnerships' (2008) *Biotechnology Law Report* 27(3), 189–202.

1. *The use of policy space is often non-transparent or outright protectionist.* Our empirical work on stakeholder perception surveys in Switzerland, New Zealand, China and Turkey indicates that the term 'sustainable agriculture' is strongly shaped by a country's position in the international trading system. Consequently, 'constrained flexibility' to promote sustainable agriculture without pre-empting legitimate trade concerns in other countries is key to unblocking the Doha Round. The surveys revealed that it is often not clear whether the term sustainable agriculture really reflects the environmental, social and economic concerns of society at large, or whether it is merely protecting the vested interests of some domestic producers. The Green Box as the main tool for developing agriculture must be revised to provide the necessary policy space while avoiding protectionism. Such a revision will ensure that sustainable agriculture and international trade are not incompatible.
2. *WTO rules and disciplines provide ample policy space for pursuing sustainable agricultural policies, but they must be improved to avoid protectionist abuse.* Our research led us to the conclusion that governments alone can hardly cope with all the challenges of sustainable agriculture because it is not just a question of protecting agriculture from unsustainable change through generous income-support schemes but also of how to facilitate sustainable change through rural entrepreneurship and innovation. For that purpose, governments need to tap the knowledge and experience of the private sector – especially when it comes to the ability to convert knowledge into useful goods and services. Governments should therefore not just regulate but facilitate PPPs that are aimed at producing goods and services with a public good character (be it because they improve the environment or because they support the poor in their effort to make a living). Policy incentives need to be designed to encourage private-sector actors to participate more actively in PPPs, especially in agriculture where such undertakings are still rare and relatively few are successful. Such policy incentives may be perfectly compatible with the AoA but they are seldom applied in domestic policies, especially in affluent societies, because the debates on agriculture are largely dominated by stakeholders that benefit from the status quo and therefore show little interest in change that might threaten incumbent positions. New Zealand provides an exception to the rule, mainly due to bottom-up pressure for change. After more than two decades of experience with the promotion of PPPs in agriculture, New Zealand offers some pointers for governments in developing and developed countries alike:

a. Agricultural trade liberalisation does not have to lead to unsustainable agriculture.
b. There is no such thing as an ideal stage of agricultural sustainability, but rather there is continuous change that needs to be managed through a system of trial and error and addressed by means of innovation in management and technology.
c. Change in agricultural policy will not happen unless there is pressure from the farmers themselves (as in the case of New Zealand) or from the top down in the form of trade agreements that force domestic stakeholders to make changes in the distribution of privileges and subsidies.
d. The successful completion of the Doha Round would contribute to some top-down pressure by reducing trade barriers and product support subsidies. Ultimately, however, farmers themselves must feel the need for a change that would enable them to become more integrated in the global knowledge economy and successfully participate in international trade.

3. *Least developed countries face particularly high de facto trade barriers, but they could also use their own policy space better.* Trade in agriculture is one of the best and yet the least accessible avenues of development, including for the poorest of the poor. Agricultural policy priorities often do not reflect the genuine interests of the rural poor. Moreover, neither foreign aid agencies nor national governments seriously invest in the capacity of farmers to innovate and generate wealth and employment for their own rural region. This failure to enable poor people in rural areas to participate in trade should be addressed by broadening the trade facilitation programmes of the WTO and others. This should include missions by entrepreneurs who have succeeded in benefiting from global trade to tell LDC governments what kind of incentives would be required to induce companies to invest in rural areas and engage in technology transfer and training of local people.

References

Adaman, F., The Political Economy of the Environment in Turkey (1997) *New Perspectives on Turkey* **17**, 129–150.

Adaman, F. and Arsel, M. (eds.), *Environmentalism in Turkey: Between Democracy and Development?* (Ashgate, 2005).

Aerni, P., 'Public Acceptance of Transgenic Rice and its Potential Impact on Rice Markets in Southeast Asian Countries', PhD Thesis, Swiss Federal Institute of Technology, ETH Zurich, Switzerland (1999).

Aerni, P., 'Mobilizing Science and Technology for Development: The Case of the Cassava Biotechnology Network (CBN)' (2006) *AgBioForum* **9**(1), 1–14.

Aerni, P., 'The Welfare Costs of not being part of the Knowledge Economy: Why Rural Development needs more Creative Policy Strategies' (2006) *ATDF Journal* **3**(4):27–43.

Aerni, P., 'The Principal-Agent Problem in International Development Assistance and its Impact on Local Entrepreneurship in Africa: Time for New Approaches' (2006) *ATDF Journal* **3**(2), 27–33.

Aerni, P., 'Agricultural Biotechnology and its Contribution to the Knowledge Economy' (2007) *Adv. Biochem. Engin./Biotechnol.* **107**, 69–96.

Aerni, P., 'Agriculture in Turkey: Structural Change, Sustainability and EU Compatibility' (2007) *International Journal of Agricultural Resources, Governance Ecology* **6**(4/5), 429–439.

Aerni, P., 'Exploring the Linkages of Commerce, Higher Education and Human Development: A Historical Review' (2007) *ATDF Journal* **4**(2), 35–48.

Aerni, P., 'What is Sustainable Agriculture? Empirical Evidence of Diverging Views in Switzerland and New Zealand' (2009) *Ecological Economics* **68** (6), 1872–1882.

Aerni, P. and Bernauer, T., 'Stakeholder Attitudes towards GMOs in the Philippines, Mexico and South Africa: The Issue of Public Trust' (2006) *World Development* **34**(3), 557–575.

Aerni, P., Rae, A. and Lehmann, B., 'Nostalgia vs. Pragmatism? How Attitudes and Interests Shape the Term Sustainable Agriculture in Switzerland and New Zealand' (2009) *Food Policy* **34**(2), 227–235.

Akder, H., 'Policy Formation in the Process of Implementing Agricultural Reform in Turkey' (2007) *International Journal of Agricultural Resources, Governance and Ecology*, **6** (4/5), 514–532.

Beck, U., 'Living Your Own Life in a Runaway World: Individualization, Globalization and Politics', in W. Hutton and A. Giddens (eds.), *On The Edge: Living with Global Capitalism* (Jonathan Cape, 2000).

Braun, J. von and Diaz-Bonilla, E., 'Globalization of Agriculture and Food: Causes, Consequences, and Policy Implications', in J. von Braun and E. Diaz-Bonilla (eds.), *Globalization of Food and Agriculture and the Poor* (Oxford University Press, 2006).

Bürgi, E., 'Towards a New Balance of Trade in Agriculture', NCCR Working Paper No. 2009/17 (World Trade Institute, Bern, 2009).

Cabanilla, L. and Rodriguez, U. E., 'The Food Versus Fuel Issue: Case of the Philippines' (2008) *ATDF Journal* **5** (1/2), 68–74.

Cakmak, E. and Akder, H., *DTÖ ve AB'deki Gelişmeler Işığında 21. Yüzyılda Türkiye Tarımı' (In the Light of Developments at the WTO and the EU Turkish Agriculture in the 21st Century)*, Turkish Industrialists' and Businessmen's Association (TUSIAD), Publication No. T/2005–06/397 (Istanbul, 2005).

Chern, W. S., Rickertsen, N., Tsuboi, N. and Fu, T.-T., 'Consumer Acceptance and Willingness to Pay for Genetically Modified Vegetable Oil and Salmon: A Multiple-Country Assessment' (2002) *AgBioForum* **5**(3), 105–112.

Collier, P., *The Bottom Billion* (Oxford University Press, 2007).

Cottier, T. and Oesch, M., *International Trade Regulation. Law and Policy in the WTO, the European Union and Switzerland* (London: Cameron May, 2005), p. 552.

Davidson, A., 'Dirt Cheap Soil' (2007) *Nature* **447**, 777.

De Gregori, T. R., *The Origins of the Organic Agriculture Debate* (John Wiley, 2003).

De Schutter, O., 'Address by the UN Rapporteur on the Human Right to Food', High-Level Conference on Food Security (Rome 3–5 June 2008).

Desta, M. G., *The Law of International Agricultural Trade Products* (Kluwer Law International, 2002).

Diaz-Bonilla, E., 'Globalisation of Agriculture and the Food Crises: Then and Now', in B. Karapinar and C. Häberli (eds.), *Food Crises and the WTO* (Cambridge University Press, 2010).

Diaz-Bonilla, E., Thomas, M., Robinson, S. and Cattaneo, A., 'Food Security and Trade Negotiations in the World Trade Organization: A Cluster Analysis of Country Groups' International Food Policy Research Institute (IFPRI) (TMD Discussion Paper No. 59, 2000).

El Benni, N. and Réviron, S., 'Geographical Indications: Review of Seven Case-studies Worldwide' NCCR Trade Regulation Working Paper 2009/15, March 2009.

Food and Agriculture Organization of the United Nations (FAO), 'The Breakdown of the Doha Round Negotiations: What Does It Mean for Dealing with Soaring Food Prices?', Economic and Social Perspectives Policy Brief 3, Rome, 2008.

Francioni, F., *Environment Human Rights and International Trade* (Oxford University Press, 2001).

Gehne, K., 'Nachhaltigkeit als Rechtsprinzip', PhD Thesis, University of Zurich (2009).

George, C. and Kirkpatrick, C. (eds.), *Impact Assessment for Sustainable Development: European Perspectives and Experience* (Edward Elgar, 2006).

George, C. and Kirkpatrick, C., 'Trade and Development: Assessing the Impact of Trade Liberalisation on Sustainable Development' (2004) *Journal of World Trade* **38**(3), 441–469.

Häberli, C., 'La Suisse dans les nouvelles négociations agricoles de l'OMC', in *Annuaire Suisse-Tiers Monde*, Institut universitaire d'études du développement (IUED), Geneva, 2001.

Häberli, C., 'Market Access in Switzerland and in the European Union for Agricultural Products from Least Developed Countries', NCCR Trade Regulation Working Paper 2008/5, July 2008.

Häberli, C., 'Food Security and WTO Rules', in B. Karapinar and C. Häberli (eds.), *Food Crises and the WTO* (Cambridge University Press, 2010).

Heri, S. and Häberli, C., 'Can the World Trade Organization Ensure that Food Aid is Genuine?', NCCR Trade Regulation Working Paper 2009/19, May 2009.

Hu, W., 'Household Land Tenure Reform in China: Its Impact on Farming Land Use and Agroenvironment' (1997) *Land Use Policy* **14**(3), 75–186.

International Fund for Agricultural Development (IFAD), 'Rural Poverty Report: The Challenge of Ending Rural Poverty' (IFAD, Rome 2001), available at www.ifad.org/poverty/ (accessed November 2008).

Jones, W. and Elasri, W., 'Rising Food Prices: Causes, Consequences and Policy Responses' in B. Karapinar and C. Häberli (eds.). *Food Crises and the WTO* (Cambridge University Press, 2010).

Karapinar, B., 'Managing Rural Transformation in Turkey 1980–2004: Case Studies from Three Regions' (2007) *International Journal of Agricultural Resources, Governance and Ecology* **6** (4/5), 483–513.

Karapinar, B., '"Sustainability" in Chinese Agriculture: Stakeholders' Perceptions and Policy Trade-offs' (2009), NCCR Trade Regulation Working Paper 2009/43, University of Bern.

Karapinar, B., 'Food Crises and the WTO', in B. Karapinar and C. Häberli (eds.), *Food Crises and the WTO* (Cambridge University Press, 2010).

Karapinar, B., '"Sustainability" in Agriculture: Stakeholders' Perceptions in Turkey', in B. Karapinar, F. Adaman and G. Ozertan (eds.). *Rethinking Structural Reform in Turkish Agriculture: Beyond the World Bank's Strategy* (Nova Science Publishers, 2010).

Karapinar, B. and Temmerman, M., 'Benefiting from Biotechnology: Pro-poor IPRs and Public Private Partnerships' (2008) *Biotechnology Law Report* **27**(3), 189–202.

Karapinar, B., Adaman, F., and Ozertan G., (eds.), *Rethinking Structural Reform in Turkish Agriculture: Beyond the World Bank's Strategy* (Nova Science Publishers, 2010).

Karapinar, B. and Temmerman, M., 'Intellectual Property Rights and Innovation: Promoting New Technologies in Turkish Agriculture', in B. Karapinar, F. Adaman and G. Ozertan (eds.), *Rethinking Structural Reform in Turkish Agriculture: Beyond the World Bank's Strategy* (Nova Science Publishers, 2010).

Kleijn, D., Berendse, F., Smit, R. and Gilissen, N., 'Agri-environment Schemes Do Not Effectively Protect Biodiversity in Dutch Agricultural Landscapes' (2001) *Nature*, **423**, 723–725.

Lichtenstein, S. and Slovic, P., *The Construction of Preference* (Cambridge University Press, 2006).

Lin, J. Y., 'Agricultural Development and Reform in China', in C. K. Eicher and C. M. Staatz (eds.), *International Agricultural Development* (Johns Hopkins University Press, 1998).

Ministry of Agriculture and Forestry (MAF), 'Agriculture and Forestry in New Zealand: An Overview' (MAF, 2003). Available at www.maf.govt.nz/mafnet/rural-nz/overview/nzoverview004.htm (accessed October 2007).

Nature Biotechnology Editorial, 'Off the Rails' (2008) *Nature Biotechnology* **26**(3), 247.

Organisation for Economic Co-operation and Development (OECD), 'Producer and Consumer Support Estimate (PSE-CSE) Database 1986–2005' (OECD, 2006), available at: www.oecd.org (accessed June 2006).

Ozertan, G. and Aerni, P., 'GM Cotton and its Possible Contribution to Environmental Sustainability and Rural Development in Turkey' (2007) *International Journal of Agricultural Resources, Governance and Ecology* **6**(4/5), 552–575.

Paarlberg, R., *Starved for Science* (Harvard University Press, 2008).

Petty, R. E. and Cacioppo, J. T., *Communication and Persuasion: Central and Peripheral Routes to Attitude Change* (Springer, 1986).

Prestegard, S. S., 'Multifunctional Agriculture, Non-Trade Concerns and the Design of Policy Instruments: Applications to the WTO Agricultural Negotiations' (2002) *International Journal of Agricultural Resources, Governance and Ecology* **4**(3/4), 232–245.

Rausser, G. C., Simon, L. and Ameden, H., 'Public– private Alliances in Biotechnology: Can they Narrow the Knowledge Gaps between Rich and Poor?' (2000) *Food Policy* **25**, 499.

Rich, S., Gupta, A. and the Honey Bee Network, *World Changing* (21 March 2007), available at www.worldchanging.com/archives/006333.html (accessed November 2008).

Romer, P., 'New Goods, Old Theory, and the Welfare Costs of Trade Restrictions' (1994) *Journal of Development Economics* **43**, 5–38.

Ruttan, V. W., 'The Design of Sustainable Systems of Agricultural Production', in C. K. Eicher and J. M. Staatz (eds.), *International Agricultural Development* (Johns Hopkins University Press 1998).

Senti, R., *WTO – System und Funktionsweise der Welthandelsordnung* (Schulthess, 2000), p. 257.

Simpson, J. R., 'Adoption of Non-trade Concerns in WTO Agricultural Trade Negotiations: Integration of Human Rights in Resolution of the Conflicts' (2005) *International Journal of Agricultural Resources, Governance and Ecology* **4**(3/4), 193–202.

Simpson, J. R., 'Japan's Non-Trade Concerns: Legitimate or Protectionist?' (2005) *International Journal of Agricultural Resources, Governance and Ecology* **4**(3/4), 344–359.

Spielman, D. J., Hartwich, F. and Grebmer, K. von, 'Sharing Science, Building Bridges, and Enhancing Impact: Public–Private Partnerships in the CGIAR',

International Food Policy Research Institute, Discussion Paper 00708, Washington, DC (2007).

Southgate, D., Graham, D. and Tweeten, L., *The World Food Economy* (Blackwell, 2007).

State Planning Organisation, Statistics 2008, availiable at www.dpt.gov.tr/ (accessed January 2009).

Stokstad, E., 'Duelling Visions for a Hungry World' (2008) *Science* **319**, 1474–1476.

The Economist, 'A Bigger World: A Special Report on Globalisation' (20 September 2008).

Thro, A. M., Taylor, N., Raemaker, K., Puonti-Kaerlas, J., Schöpke, C. *et al.*, 'Maintaining the Cassava Biotechnology Network' (1998) *Nature Biotechnology* **16**, 428–430.

Tilman, D., Cassman, G., Matson, P. A., Naylor, R. and Polasky, S., 'Agricultural Sustainability and Intensive Production Practices' (2002) *Nature* **418**, 671–677.

World Bank, 'Turkey Joint Poverty Assessment Report', vol. 1: Main Report, Report No. 29619-TU (2005).

WTO, Note by the Secretariat, 'Information on the Utilisation of Special and Differential Treatment Provisions' (document WT/COMTD/W/77/Rev.1/Add.4 dated 7 February 2002).

WTO, Committee on Agriculture in Special Session, 'Report to the Trade Negotiations Committee by the Chairman of the Special Session of the Committee on Agriculture', Ambassador Crawford Falconer (JOB(08)/95 dated 11 August 2008).

WTO, Committee on Agriculture in Special Session, 'Revised Draft Modalities for Agriculture', TN/AG/W/4/Rev.3, 10 July 2008.

5

Energy in WTO law and policy

THOMAS COTTIER, GARBA MALUMFASHI,
SOFYA MATTEOTTI-BERKUTOVA, OLGA NARTOVA,
JOËLLE DE SÉPIBUS AND SADEQ Z. BIGDELI*

KEY MESSAGES

- The regulation of energy in international law is highly fragmented and largely incoherent. We submit that pertinent issues should be addressed by a future Framework Agreement on Energy within WTO law.
- Successful regulation of energy requires a coherent combination of rules both on goods and services. Energy services require new classifications suitable to deal coherently with energy as an integrated sector.
- Rules on subsidies relating to energy call for new approaches within the Framework Agreement on Energy. A distinction should be made between renewable and non-renewable energy. Moreover, disciplines need to be developed in the context of emission trading.
- The Framework Agreement should address the problem of restricting energy production and export restrictions.
- Disciplines on government procurement are able to take into account policies on green procurement, but a number of changes to the GPA Agreement will be required to make green procurement more effective and attractive.
- In view of the close interactions between the energy sector and climate change, formulating effective rules to address energy under the WTO system will catalyse coherence and complementarity between the climate and trade regimes.

A. Introduction

Sixty years ago, when the rules of the GATT were negotiated, world energy demand was a fraction of what it is today and so were energy prices.[1]

* Individual Project No. 6, 'Energy in WTO law and policy'.
1 M. A. Adelman, 'World Oil Production and Prices 1947–2000' (2002) 42(2) *Quarterly Review of Economics and Finance* 170.

While energy has always been a crucial factor in geopolitics, at that time liberalising trade in energy was not a political priority. The industry was largely dominated by state-run monopolies and thus governed by strict territorial allocation. International trade in energy resources and products was heavily concentrated, cartelised and controlled by a few multinational companies. This explains why the rules of the General Agreement on Tariffs and Trade (GATT), and now the World Trade Organization (WTO), do not deal with energy as a distinct sector. It was felt that general rules, including the disciplines on state trading, could adequately address trade in energy. Also, no special agreement on trade in energy has emerged in any of the sectorial agreements that have been drawn up since the Kennedy Round. Yet since basic WTO rules are applicable to all forms of trade, they also apply to trade in energy goods and services.[2] Today, these rules can be enforced through the WTO dispute settlement mechanism even if they were not primarily negotiated with energy in mind.[3]

Certain features of the energy sector make it different from other industries in many ways. First, energy goods have peculiar physical characteristics, which influence means of storage, transportation and distribution. Then, particular challenges are associated with the existence of natural monopolies, as well as with the role of state-owned enterprises that dominate some national energy markets. Furthermore, in the Uruguay Round, WTO Members tried but did not manage to address effectively the practice of using dual energy prices and export restrictions.[4] They also undertook very limited commitments to grant access to their energy markets to foreign service operators. Hence, we submit that current WTO rules do not deal properly with trade in energy.

In recent years, energy topics have reappeared on the negotiations agenda. There are several reasons for this:

- Several energy-exporting countries have recently joined the WTO and others are currently negotiating their accession,[5] hence, a substantially larger amount of energy trade is now in the hands of WTO Members.

2 For more see: O. Nartova, 'Trade in Energy Services Under WTO Law: The Impact of Competition Policies', PhD thesis, University of Bern (2009); S. Matteotti, 'Oil Supply Management Practices of OPEC under the World Trade Organization Rules and the National Competition Laws' PhD thesis, University of Bern (2010).

3 P. Lamy, speech at the 20th World Energy Congress on 15 November 2007 in Rome.

4 For more on dual pricing see J. Selivanova, *Energy Dual Pricing in WTO Law* (Cameron May, 2008).

5 Saudi Arabia, Oman and Ukraine have recently become WTO Members, while Russia, several Central Asian countries, Algeria, Libya, Iran and Iraq are currently observers.

- Increasing energy needs have led to a growing interest in competition rules and export restriction practices.
- Progressive unbundling of vertically integrated state-owned entities offers a way for private operators to enter energy markets.
- The relationship of trade and the environment and the debate on sustainable development is strongly bound to energy. The correlations between trade, energy and climate change and the role of biofuels are also bringing attention to the trade in energy under multilateral trade regulation.[6]

Energy has been discussed in the ongoing Doha negotiations. For the first time, Members have been discussing energy as a specific services sector.[7] Energy issues motivate discussions on export taxes and export restrictions on raw materials. Another aspect of the ongoing round of negotiations is a balance between promotion of environmental goods and services and fossil fuel subsidies. Finally, the energy-related negotiations in the current round are focusing on biofuels. When dealing with biofuels there is a need for a balance between climate change and energy security concerns, and their impact on agriculture in order to avoid creating new environmental problems.

Thus, energy and trade is a volatile field. A number of relevant issues were taken up in doctoral research and in working papers within the overall project. They essentially relate to the dilemma whether energy is a good or a service and the issue of classification. They cover energy subsidies, the experience of emissions trading in EC law, the status of the Organization of the Petroleum Exporting Countries (OPEC) in WTO law and the climate change mitigation potentials of energy-efficient government procurement policies. We submit in conclusion that these issues would best be dealt with within a future WTO Framework Agreement on Energy, which would enable greater coherence to be brought about.

B. The current status of energy in WTO law (oil, gas, coal and electricity)

I. Oil, gas and coal

Traditionally, the energy industry has not distinguished between energy goods and energy-related services. This is because energy services were

6 For a comprehensive overview of the interlinkages between trade and climate change see T. Cottier *et al.* (eds.), *International Trade Regulation and the Mitigation of Climate Change: World Trade Forum* (Cambridge University Press, 2009).

7 P. Lamy, speech at the 20th World Energy Congress on 15 November 2007 in Rome.

perceived as a value added to energy goods which could not be dealt with separately. Privatisation and liberalisation of the sector led to market reform which resulted in a conceptual separation of goods and services trade. Hence, the need for a clear legal framework to address this distinction emerged.

Oil and solid fuels such as coal clearly fall within the category of goods; they are easily stored and traded across borders. Crude oil is treated as a global commodity and has been traded internationally since the 1860s. Trade in crude oil represents the key link between the two poles of the industry: upstream and downstream, and crude oil prices give signals to both.[8]

The same applies to natural gas. It is traded across borders via pipelines and although it can be stored in its gaseous form, it is increasingly being liquefied for the purposes of transportation to remote regions and for storage.

It is commonly understood that under the WTO rules, production of energy goods comes within the scope of the General Agreement on Tariffs and Trade (GATT), while energy-related services, including transmission and distribution, fall under the scope of the General Agreement on Trade in Services (GATS).[9]

II. Electricity

Modern society and production methods are inconceivable without electricity. It is a secondary energy source which results from the conversion of primary sources of energy, such as coal, natural gas, oil, nuclear power, wind and solar energy. Unlike oil and gas it is not a physical substance that can be stored easily. Electricity is a physical process which takes place throughout the cables that carry it and it has to be generated more or less at the same time as it is being used.

The invention of the generator capable of producing alternating current is at the heart of the present structure of the power industry – a system which generates electricity in large power stations at remote sites and carries it over long distances to reach its final users.[10] Its value chain consists of four activities: *generation* which converts energy sources into

8 Energy Charter Secretariat, 'Putting a Price on Energy: International Pricing Mechanisms for Oil and Gas' (2007) p. 67.

9 WTO, Energy Services, Background Note by the Secretariat, S/C/W/52 (9 September 1998), para. 36.

10 For more on the functioning of the power industry see W. Patterson, *Transforming Electricity* (Earthscan, London, 1999).

electricity; *transmission* which occurs when electricity is transmitted over high voltage networks to major demand centres; *distribution* which is the process by which transmitted power flows to the final consumers such as factories and homes; and *supply* – the name given to the metering, billing and other services provided to the final consumers.[11]

The WTO law does not contain any specific provisions on electricity. Given the lack of disciplines on services under GATT 1947, electricity was defined as a good irrespective of its peculiar physical properties in the Harmonized System (HS) Nomenclature[12] on the codification of commodities. The definition is followed by the WTO tariff schedules. Electrical energy is classified under the code 2716. Accordingly, electrical energy qualifies as a good under WTO law and is, as such, subject to the rules of the GATT 1994. The same is true for the European Energy Charter and European Community law. Until the end of the 1980s, EC law hardly ever intervened in the organisation of electricity utilities. Although two of the three founding treaties of the EC were specifically directed at regulating energy,[13] electricity was not dealt with explicitly by any of the three treaties. Thus, for a long time, it remained uncertain whether the provisions of the EC Treaty applied to electricity.[14] It was only in the 'Almelo' case in 1994[15] that the European Court of Justice (ECJ) explicitly recognised that the rules on the free circulation of goods of the EC Treaty also applied to electricity.

III. WTO and other instruments of international energy law

WTO law is only a minor fraction of international law addressing energy. A wide range of sources and instruments need to be taken into account. Also, it should be recalled that international trade in energy is mainly based upon contracts subject to international private law and commercial arbitration.[16]

11 For more see M. G. Pollitt, 'The Impact of Liberalisation on the Performance of the Electricity Supply Industry: An International Survey' (1997) 3(2) *Journal of Energy Literature* 3–31.

12 The HS Nomenclature is governed by the Convention on the Harmonized Commodity Description and Coding System, and was elaborated under the auspices of the World Customs Organization (WCO).

13 On the role of EC law in energy regulation see below, section III.5.

14 ECJ Case 6/64, *Costa* v. *ENEL* [1964] ECR 1141.

15 ECJ, Case C-393/92 *Almelo and Others* [1994] ECR I-1477, para. 28.

16 T. Cottier, S. Matteotti and O. Nartova, 'Winterkrieg im Gasgeschäft: Ursachen und Auswirkungen' (2009) 140 *UniPress* 40.

Energy issues around the world today are dealt with in a fragmented manner and some of the energy-specific agreements and institutions are described below.

1. Organisation for Economic Co-operation and Development (OECD)/International Energy Agency (IEA)

OECD is an international organisation, established in 1961, with 30 member countries and a budget of 342.9 million euros (as of 2008). The OECD's affiliate organisation, the IEA is a forum for coordinating the energy policies of 28 industrialised countries. The IEA, which addresses all types of energy sources has the following objectives: 'improvement of the world energy supply and demand structure, more efficient use of energy, development of alternative energy sources to reduce dependence on any one source, assistance in the integration of environmental and energy policies and the promotion of cooperative relations between oil-producing and oil-consuming countries'.[17]

2. Energy Charter Treaty

The Energy Charter Treaty entered into force in 1998; however ratification by some Members is still pending.[18] Several of the WTO Members engage in energy cooperation under this treaty. The ECT covers various issues related to investments and investor relations. The main elements of the ECT include: 'investment protection[19] (e.g. by granting investors non-discriminatory treatment – national treatment and most-favoured nation treatment – compensation in case of expropriation and other losses, free transfer of capital); trade in energy, energy products and energy-related equipment, based on the WTO rules; freedom of energy transit; international dispute settlement, including investor-state arbitration and inter-state arbitration; promotion of energy efficiency, and attempts to minimise the environmental impact of energy production and use'.[20]

17 OECD, Energy: The International Energy Agency, available at www.oecd.org/document/45/0,3343,en_2649_37459_1921517_1_1_1_1,00.html.

18 All Members have ratified the Treaty except for five: Australia, Belarus, Iceland, Norway, and Russia. Belarus and Russia have accepted provisional application of the Treaty, which means that – pending ratification – they have agreed to apply the Treaty to the extent that it is consistent with their own constitutions, laws and regulations.

19 For more on regulation of investment see Chapter 11 in this volume. Unless otherwise specified, investment rules apply to the energy sector.

20 Energy Charter Secretariat, 'The Energy Charter Treaty and Related Documents' (Brussels, 2004).

3. Organization of the Petroleum Exporting Countries

OPEC is a permanent intergovernmental organisation, currently consisting of twelve oil producing and exporting countries, spread across three continents: America, Asia and Africa.[21] The main goals of OPEC are: the coordination and unification of the petroleum policies of its Member Countries, working out ways and means of ensuring the stabilisation of prices in international oil markets with due regard being given to the interests of the producing nations and to the necessity of securing a steady income to the producing countries; an efficient, economic and regular supply of petroleum to consuming nations; and a fair return on capital to those investing in the petroleum industry.[22] When OPEC was founded on 14 September 1960, none of its five founding members[23] was a contracting party to the GATT. This picture has been changing recently.[24]

4. Multilateral environmental agreements

Energy is also addressed by a number of multilateral environmental agreements (MEAs), in particular those relating to climate change, including the United Nations Framework Convention on Climate Change (UNFCCC) and its Kyoto Protocol. Anthropogenic climate change affects the energy sector and threatens the foundations of energy security systems.[25] At the same time, climate change mitigation measures catalyse energy efficiency and motivate energy sustainability policies. Recognising this fact, the climate regimes avoided the approach adopted by a number of earlier MEAs which require parties to those agreements to use trade restrictive rules against non-parties to the agreements.[26]

Reduction of greenhouse gas (GHG) emissions is considered a precautionary measure which must be taken in order to avert what both the

21 www.opec.org/aboutus/.

22 Article 2 of OPEC Statute, 443 United Nations Treaty Series, 248.

23 Kuwait, Iraq, Iran, Saudi Arabia, and Venezuela.

24 Currently 8 out of the 12 current OPEC member countries – Angola, Ecuador, Kuwait, Nigeria, Qatar, Saudi Arabia, UAE, and Venezuela – are WTO Members. Algeria, Iran, Iraq, and Libya have observer status.

25 OECD/IEA, 2007. *Energy Security and Climate Policy: Assessing Interactions* (OECD).

26 See G. I. Malumfashi, '"Green" Public Procurement Policies, Climate Change Mitigation and International Trade Regulation: An Assessment of the WTO Agreement on Government Procurement', PhD Thesis, Centre for Energy, Petroleum and Mineral Law and Policy, University of Dundee, United Kingdom (2009), Chapter 4.

IPCC reports and the Stern Review report of 2006[27] warned would be catastrophic to the future well-being of the ecosystem. While the IPCC reports gave the scientific analysis of the climate change situation, the Stern Review report highlighted the economic costs of inaction or delayed action. Thus, the precautionary principle[28] as an environmental protection strategy is well entrenched in climate change regimes.[29]

The relationship of WTO law to these instruments shares the traits of a complex constellation under the Vienna Convention on the Law of Treaties, addressed in a number of cases in WTO dispute settlement. From the point of view of international law, all instruments find themselves on the same footing, with more specialised or more recent agreements enjoying preferred application vis-à-vis general rules. From the point of view of WTO law, other instruments may only apply to the extent that they influence the application and interpretation of WTO rules. There is even controversy as to whether an agreement to which not all the Members of the WTO are parties can be applied in WTO dispute settlement.

5. Regional level: European Union (EU) and North American Free Trade Agreement (NAFTA)

The European Community (EC) has evolved since the European Coal and Steel Community (ECSC) Treaty of 1952 which covered an energy policy for coal. The ECSC did not address external relations. Indeed, the six initial Member States were free to shape their relations with third countries. In 1957, two other fundamental treaties were signed: those of Euratom and the European Economic Community. In 1967, the Merger Treaty allowed for the unification of the institutions of these Communities, covering all the main economic activities, including the rational use of natural resources. At an international level, the EC is active within the international organisations. Being a full member, alongside its Member

27 See IPCC, 2007: *Climate Change 2007: Synthesis Report. Contribution of Working Groups I, II and III to the Fourth Assessment Report of the Intergovernmental Panel on Climate Change* [Core Writing Team, R. K. Pachauri, and A. Reisinger (eds.)], IPCC, Geneva, Switzerland; N. Stern, *The Economics of Climate Change: The Stern Review* (Cambridge University Press, 2007).

28 The precautionary principle provides that activities threatening to cause serious or irreversible damage should be restricted or even prohibited even before scientific certainty about their impact is established.

29 See T. Cottier and S. Matteotti-Berkutova, 'International Environmental Law and the Evolving Concept of "Common Concern of Mankind"', in T. Cottier *et al.* (eds.), *International Trade Regulation and the Mitigation of Climate Change: World Trade Forum* (Cambridge University Press, 2009).

States, of the WTO, the Energy Charter Treaty and the Kyoto Protocol, the EC has attempted to establish the leadership in promoting international norms of energy trade.

Implementation of NAFTA began on 1 January 1994. The objective of the agreement was to remove trade barriers between the United States, Canada and Mexico. NAFTA covers various issues related to energy trade, including investment, cross-border services, measures related to trade in energy services, limitations and barriers, and measures related to investments in the territories of the parties as well as cross-border trade.[30]

IV. Role of government procurement

Government procurement (GP) is the purchase by a government of the goods and services needed to perform its functions. It is an area of international trade that was previously carved out of the non-discrimination obligations. The Agreement on Government Procurement (GPA) imposes the national treatment and most-favoured nation (MFN) obligations, but it binds only those WTO Members that subscribe to it. Energy-efficient GP was identified by the IPCC as a possible policy tool to address climate change. Accordingly, countries began implementing 'green' public procurement as a part of their policy package for climate change.

In terms of its size, government procurement represents up to 18 per cent of the gross domestic product (GDP) in the OECD countries and, in the EU for instance, it amounts to 10–25 per cent of GDP.[31] This percentage may well be higher in the case of developing countries. GP apparently plays a major role in promoting the use of environmentally friendly products and motivates the market for climate-friendly technology.

V. Unresolved and controversial issues

The interface of trade and climate change mitigation and adaptation is at the heart of contemporary legal developments in energy law. This was the subject of the World Trade Forum in 2007 at which the different angles were extensively addressed. Yet, the challenges of climate change are merely the tip of the iceberg of unresolved and controversial issues relating to the status of energy in international law. The picture is one of fragmentation with multiple instruments involved. The bulk

30 NAFTA Article 603.

31 OECD, *Greener Public Purchasing: Issues and Practical Solutions* (OECD, 2000).

of regulation comes under domestic law and the role of regional and global law in addressing energy and secure production and supplies has remained unclear and unsettled. Doctrines of multilayered governance have hardly been applied to the sector.

The fundamental divide between goods and services does not offer an appropriate basis for addressing and regulating energy in an integrated manner in domestic and international law. Electricity is a case in point. It is traditionally treated as a good, but in fact, by its nature and its dependence upon grids, it is much more like a service, or perhaps a mixture of both. There is no clear perception of defining energy in terms of goods and services, and services relating to energy are not properly defined under GATS.

Different and competing forms of energy are therefore subject to strongly divergent international rules, depending on whether they qualify as a good or a service. The same applies to the operation of trade remedies, in particular because of the absence of disciplines on subsidies in services. Moreover, existing disciplines on subsidies in goods may not be suitable to address a distinction between renewable and non-renewable energy under GATT and the Agreement on Subsidies and Countervailing Measures (ASCM). The Agreement on Agriculture again offers different disciplines. It thus makes a fundamental difference whether a product is classified as an industrial or an agricultural product.

There are also unresolved and basic issues related to competition policy and thus about the relationship of WTO law and OPEC as a producer organisation. The crucial question is whether oil exporters, when they join the WTO, will still be able to support oil prices through the regulation of oil production, or whether they could face challenges on the basis of GATT/WTO rules and provisions.[32] This leads to the question of whether additional WTO rules on competition are required to properly address the relationship between trade and production in the energy sector.

Finally, the relationship of energy and government procurement remains unclear. WTO law disciplines on government procurement seek to facilitate market access and level the playing fields in purchases of goods and services by governments. The current rules on government procurement both within and outside the WTO do not systematically address the linkage to green procurement. There is therefore controversy as to what extent Members are entitled to condition government procurement in the light of goals set out in the Kyoto Protocol.

32 H. Abdallah, 'Oil Exports under GATT and the WTO' (2005) 29(4) *OPEC Review* 267.

WTO law thus leaves a number of basic incoherencies and open questions. They were partly addressed in the papers and the doctoral projects of Individual Project No. 6 of the NCCR Trade Regulation and at the World Trade Forum 2007. The main findings are discussed within the following agenda for reform.

C. Agenda for reform

I. *Towards a WTO Framework Agreement on Energy*

Energy requires an integrated approach and does not lend itself to sectoral negotiations, depending upon different forms of energy applied to competing energy sectors. The sector encompasses fossil and non-fossil fuels and energy including oil, gas, coal, wood, electricity, atomic energy[33] and renewable sources of electrical energy production (solar, wind, wave and tidal), as well as biofuels. All these forms of energy should be subject to the same rules and thus conditions of competition. The production and transmission of energy is a complex operation which often involves both goods and services. It also entails technology and thus is affected by intellectual property rights. The sector shows a high level of governmental involvement which calls for coherent rules on competition and government procurement.

In the effort to enhance coherence and overcome unnecessary fragmentation in regulating trade in energy, the problems and the shortcomings identified above can best be addressed by seeking comprehensive negotiations within the WTO. In much the same way as the Uruguay Round produced a special agreement on agriculture, we submit that future negotiations should turn towards work on a comprehensive sectoral agreement on energy. Negotiations would enable Members to address all the pertinent problems, ranging from issues of classification of goods and services, to disciplines on subsidies, to issues of competition and state trading, as well as intellectual property rights and government procurement. It allows defining authoritatively the relationship to other international agreements, in particular the UNFCCC and the Kyoto Protocol and future global systems of emissions trading. It would allow the relationship

33 Trade in atomic energy is subject to a more stringent set of security regulations and safety standards at both the national and international levels. The experts at the International Atomic Energy Agency (IAEA) warn that the introduction of a nuclear power programme involves a commitment of at least 100 years. See IAEA Staff Report, 10 December 2008.

between trade and regulation of production, and thus of WTO and OPEC, to be defined.

A comprehensive sectoral agreement on energy, encompassing both goods and services, would not render the current structure of the WTO Agreements obsolete. Recourse to a framework convention implies that its provisions may refer to pertinent provisions of other agreements of the WTO, in particular GATT and its instruments, GATS, Agreement on Trade-Related Aspects of Intellectual Property Rights (TRIPS) and the GPA. This is not new and has been done before, for example in defining the relationship of the Agreement on the Application of Sanitary and Phytosanitary Measures (SPS) and GATT, or the agreements on agriculture and on industrial subsidies. They may also incorporate provisions of agreements outside the scope of the WTO, as did the TRIPS Agreement for the Paris and Berne Conventions on industrial property and copyright. Or, they allow reference to other provisions without incorporating them, for example a future and revised UNFCCC or Kyoto Protocol. Both reference and incorporation allow the building of a comprehensive and coherent agreement on energy within the WTO. It is within such a framework that the following issues and proposals for reform should be dealt with.

II. The basic classification of energy and energy services

The basic structure of the proposed Framework Agreement on Energy is to be defined by appropriate classifications of energy and energy services.

Disciplines on goods imply an independent physical property which is distinct from the production process and channels of distribution. Fossil fuels, in particular oil, gas and coal are thus bound to remain goods to be dealt with in accordance with established principles and rules of GATT 1994. However, energy dependent upon networks and grids is, in our view, much closer to a service, albeit physical properties remain to some extent. This is true in particular for gas which can be stored to some extent, and thus detached from a pipeline system. It is, however, different for electricity.

With the advent of disciplines on services, including energy-related services, existing legal definitions of electricity should be reviewed. Electricity is a typical network industry the components of which can best be dealt with following the principles of progressive liberalisation and conditionalities available under the GATS Agreement. It is submitted that electricity should be defined as a service and should no longer be treated as a good. Electricity is not a physical substance, nor is it a fuel. It cannot be stored and must be consumed as it is produced. Accordingly, the use of electricity should not be subject to tariff protection, but to service-related fee structures responding to the need to maintain continuous power production and dissemination. In order to maintain existing levels of market access under definitions of goods, the agreement would secure existing obligations of national treatment under GATT and incorporate them in terms of commitments into the Framework Agreement.

1. Trade in energy services

Energy services are an essential ingredient of any energy market. As markets become more open and competitive, the role of energy services will increase. The major barrier to entry is associated with the significant investments in infrastructure that are necessary.[34] It is well recognised that private-sector participation is frequently necessary to channel the requisite capital and expertise to the sector, and developing countries are stimulated to create 'an attractive enabling environment' and facilitate investment by transnational energy companies.[35]

2. Reform of classification of energy services

The international trading in energy resources and its associated services has always posed special problems, and classification of energy services has been one of the topics of debate among various interest groups. The energy sector has traditionally been dominated by state-owned companies or has been under the direct control of the national government. This situation has resulted in endless negotiations on the classification of energy services and neither the WTO's 'Services Sectoral Classification List' (W/120)[36] nor the United Nations Provisional Central Product Classification (UNCPC)[37] lists energy services as separate categories. Clarifying classification issues is an important precondition to successful negotiations on energy.

34 Energy is also considered to be one of the national security concerns. This reiterates the need in a coherent set of FDI rules to avoid protectionism. See Chapter 11, on investments by sovereign wealth funds and state-owned enterprises.

35 O. Nartova, 'Trade in Energy Services under WTO Law: The Impact of Competition Policies', PhD thesis, University of Bern (2009).

36 WTO, Services Sectoral Classification List MTN.GNS/W/120 (10 July 1991).

37 Department of Economic and Social Affairs, Statistics Division Statistical Papers Series M No. 77, Ver.1.1, UN, New York.

Currently, some of the energy-related products and services are listed under different headings. One is 'transportation of fuel' described in the CPC as 'transportation via pipeline of crude or refined petroleum and petroleum products and of natural gas'.[38] This comes under the broad category of transport services, which is not strictly appropriate. Transportation of energy-related products and services requires very specific and technically complicated procedures. Concerns regarding safety and security are always associated with it. Classifying the energy services sector under a separate category would simplify the process for regulation of transmission and transportation of energy products and services.

The upstream activities for oil and gas fall under the category of 'Other Business Services'. It is 'services incidental to mining' described as 'services rendered on a fee or contract basis at oil and gas fields, e.g. drilling services, derrick building, repair and dismantling services, oil and gas well casings cementing services'.[39] At the same time, the services essential to the energy industry such as oil and gas field exploration and geological surveying services are not covered by this category, but are classified as 'Geological, geophysical and other scientific prospecting services',[40] under 'Engineering related scientific and technical consulting services'.[41] Such a classification does not provide a clear view or complete information in one place and may therefore lead to confusion in commitments.

The third energy-specific entry relates to: 'Services Incidental to Energy Distribution',[42] listed under 'Other Business Services' category. It refers to 'transmission and distribution services on a fee or contract basis of electricity, gaseous fuels and steam and hot water to household, industrial, commercial and other users'.

In practical terms the fragmentation of the various activities relating to the energy service sector, which results from placing them under different subheadings, unnecessarily complicates trade in energy. To understand the various aspects of classification of services under W/120,[43] one has to look under several entirely different subheadings of the schedule. It should be borne in mind that the energy industry is a chain of interconnected activities and often one cannot function without another. Hence, in order to function adequately, an energy service provider requires a set of coherent market access rights in a list of sectors. And, in the current situation in which energy services are spread throughout the classification system,

38 CPC subclass 71310. 39 Division 88. 40 Subclass 86751.
41 Class 8675. 42 CPC 88700.
43 WTO, Services Sectoral Classification List MTN.GNS/W/120 (10 July 1991).

the actual market access conditions may not always be clear, jeopardising both energy security and competition.

With a view to tackling the present confusion in the energy services classification under the W/120, it is therefore advisable to identify the core energy services and confine the negotiations in those areas. One way of identifying core services is to agree that the core services are those which form an essential part of the chain of supply and without which it could not function. In addition, core services would include services that are mainly an input to the energy industry. Such services could be listed under two subcategories on the basis of whether they are upstream or downstream activities.[44]

III. *Energy and the rules on subsidies*

In relation to aspects of energy that are classifiable as goods,[45] the emphasis of research and its findings has been on addressing the relationship between fossil fuels and renewable energy. Both are treated alike under the existing regulation and environmental concerns are neglected. Moreover, a dual regime exists between fossil fuels and biofuels.[46]

1. Renewable energy and the WTO law of subsidies

Subsidies are extensively granted to the energy sector around the world for various reasons. Regardless of their effectiveness in achieving their goal, both the fossil fuel sector and the renewable and alternative energy sectors have benefited from these subsidies. However, the share of fossil fuels in the allocation of energy subsidies worldwide has been disproportionately higher than that for other forms of energy. Moreover while environmental protection has been stated as a policy objective behind promoting renewables through subsidy programmes, these policies have occasionally produced perverse results, for instance in the biofuels sector in some countries.

44 For more detailed proposal for classification reform see O. Nartova, 'Trade in Energy Services under WTO Law: The Impact of Competition Policies', PhD thesis, University of Bern (2009).

45 For discussion on subsidies disciplines in GATS see P. Poretti, 'Waiting for Godot: Subsidy Disciplines in Services Trade' in M. Panizzon *et al.* (eds.), *GATS and the Regulation of International Trade in Services* (Cambridge University Press, 2007), pp. 466–489.

46 See S. Z. Bigdeli, 'Energy Subsidies in International Economic Law: A Trade and Environment Perspective', PhD thesis, University of Bern (2009).

The amount of subsidies available for the renewable energy (RE) sector worldwide is growing as a policy response to energy security concerns and climate change. The introduction of new incentive schemes to promote RE has become increasingly common especially in the US and EU. In this context, the question of the status of RE subsidies in WTO law is highly relevant.[47]

(a) Areas of potential conflict Much of the support provided to the RE sector takes the forms which fit the definition of a subsidy according to Article 1 of the ASCM.[48] These RE subsidies are specific within the meaning of Article 2; if they are contingent upon export – or import-substitution or they cause adverse effects, RE subsidies are likely to result in trade disputes of different kinds and hence are vulnerable under the WTO system.

Yet, under a different scenario, the use of certain trade-distortive subsidies for environmental purposes may be justified. In this context, the absence of a GATT Article XX provision in the ASCM should be given serious consideration.[49] However, it is argued that any attempt to introduce particular environmental exceptions into the SCM Agreement should entail a necessity test similar to GATT Article XX(b) to ensure that such exemptions will not be hijacked by domestic interest groups to the detriment of both trade and the environment.

(b) A case for mutual supportiveness A top-down approach of simply imposing national targets as pursued in the Kyoto Protocol has not worked and will not work unless it is coupled with other reinforcement strategies such as addressing harmful energy subsidies at the multilateral level. In

47 Currently the US is being challenged by Canada's complaint regarding the US subsidies for corn and other agricultural products (see the Request for Consultations by Canada, WT/DS357/1, January 2007). Brazil has further challenged, inter alia, the gasoline and diesel tax exemptions for biofuels (WT/DS365/1, Request for Consultations by Brazil, July 2007). A single panel was established to deal with both cases in December 2007.

48 For the following see also S. Z. Bigdeli, 'Incentive Schemes to Promote Renewable Energy and the WTO Law of Subsidies', in T. Cottier *et al.* (eds.), *International Trade Regulation and the Mitigation of Climate Change: World Trade Forum* (Cambridge University Press, 2009).

49 The applicability of the general exceptions under Article XX of the GATT with respect to subsidies covered by the SCM is still an open question. Many trade lawyers share the view that under the status quo, GATT Article XX does not apply to the ASCM. At the same time, many others argue the opposite. For more on the discussion see L. Rubini, *The Definition of Subsidy and State Aid: WTO and EC Law in Comparative Perspective* (Oxford University Press, 2009), p. 195.

this context, there is a positive and effective role for the WTO to enter into the field of reform of these subsidies.

Dealing with subsidies that are environmentally harmful is not alien to the WTO. The current 'fisheries subsidies' negotiations serve as a good example of cooperation between environmental non-governmental organisations (NGOs), international organisations and the so-called 'Friends of Fish', a group of WTO Members who took the initiative to raise concerns about the contributory effect of these subsidies to fish stock depletion.[50]

There seem to be prospects for following a similar approach for energy subsidies in light of the similarities between these two areas of environmentally harmful subsidies. The stakes are higher in the realm of energy due to the political, social (poverty implications) and energy security issues involved. On the practical level, the first challenge is to collect reliable data on current and future levels of support. The second is to define the criteria for 'harmfulness'; as discussed above, not all fossil fuel subsidies, let alone energy subsidies, increase carbon dioxide (CO_2) levels (consider subsidies to promote fuel switching (e.g. from coal to gas)).

As a first step, the crucial need to fill the gap in the data on energy subsidies might be addressed by establishing a subsidy-watch committee as a subsidiary of the Committee on Subsidies and Countervailing Measures in accordance with Article 24.2 of the ASCM. This new committee's function, in contrast to that of the current Permanent Group of Experts whose duty is more focused on the nature and legality of subsidies, will be to examine whether each Member's energy subsidy notifications sufficiently represent the level of support in this sector. Later, these functions would be assigned to a committee servicing the Framework Agreement on Energy.

After collecting reliable data on all Members' energy subsidies, the second step would be to provide countries with deadlines by which they would have to prepare a national roadmap for subsidy reforms, adapted to their own priorities and intended to phase out 'environmentally harmful energy subsidies' with an appropriate timeline. The committee could have an advisory or compulsory role in identifying which subsidies are indeed 'harmful' and how and over what period of time they should be phased out.

50 For more see S. Z. Bigdeli 'Will the "Friends of Climate" Emerge in the WTO? Applying the "fisheries subsidies" model to energy subsidies' (2008) 2(1) *Carbon and Climate Law Review* 78–89.

Eventually all the roadmaps for subsidy reforms should be submitted to the committee and be approved by Members so that they could become an integral part of the Members' WTO commitments. This whole process from the very beginning should be conducted in full cooperation with the UNFCCC Secretariat and be linked to negotiations on the post-Kyoto Regime.

2. Emissions trading and subsidies: the experience of the European Union

With a view to linking subsidies reform in international trade regulation with climate change mitigation efforts under the UNFCCC, it is helpful to learn from the experience of the EU, by assessing the European Union emissions trading scheme (EU ETS) and its relationship to EC disciplines on subsidies.[51]

The EU ETS was launched in 2005 to cap CO_2 emissions from energy-intensive industry.[52] The key feature is the allocation process, which determines the reduction target within each Member State ('cap') and the way allowances are distributed among the covered operators.[53] In the first two allocation phases – from 2005 to 2012 – Member States had to set up a national allocation plan (NAP), which had to be submitted to the Commission for approval.[54] Member States were granted considerable freedom in fixing the caps.[55] The main restriction was that at least 95 per cent of the allowances had to be allocated for free in the first trading period and 90 per cent in the second.[56]

Most Member States chose to distribute all their allowances for free. For existing installations the amount of allowances was usually calculated according to historical emissions or expected needs, whereas new entrants

51 See for a more thorough analysis of this question and references to case law J. de Sépibus, 'The European Emission Trading Scheme Put to the Test of State Aid Rules', NCCR Working Paper No. 2007/34; J. de Sépibus, *Die Umweltschutzsubvention im Gemeinschaftsrecht: Eine umweltrechtliche Kritik der europäischen Beihilfekontrolle* (Peter Lang, 2003).

52 See the Directive 2003/87/EC establishing a scheme for trading of GHG emission allowances within the Community and amending Council Directive 96/61/EC. Hereafter the 'Directive'.

53 The EU ETS was completed by the Linking Directive. See J. de Sépibus, 'Linking the EU Emissions Trading Scheme to JI, CDM and post-2012 International Offsets', NCCR Trade Regulation Working Paper No. 2008/18.

54 Article 9 of the Directive.

55 See J. de Sépibus, 'Scarcity and Allocation in the European Emissions Trading Scheme: A Legal Analysis', NCCR Working Paper No. 2007/32.

56 Article 10 of the Directive.

were granted allowances with regard to certain benchmarks, which may be fuel-, technology- or output-related. Special rules were also set for closures, early action or co-generation.

As a result, a wide variety of allocation rules existed, which led to considerable distortions of competition. These distortions were exacerbated by a phenomenon called 'windfall profits', which significantly increased the benefits of certain operators, especially CO_2-intensive installations in the power sector that had received the lion's share of the allowances. The reason for these extraordinary profits is that many of the firms concerned could largely pass on the price of the allowance to their customers, even though they had been granted the allowances for free.[57]

The question thus arose whether the large economic rents conferred on certain big players, in particular in the power industry, amounted to state aid prohibited by Article 87 EC Treaty. The relevance of this query is, however, not limited to European law. Many countries, such as the United States, Australia and Japan, which plan to implement emission trading schemes, and also the Member States of the EU and the EU itself, will have to deal with this issue under the law of the WTO, which establishes a regime having many similarities to the provisions of the EC Treaty. Hence the free grant of emission allowances may well not be immune from challenges under the WTO rules.

(a) **The prohibition of state aid (Article 87 para. 1 EC Treaty)** Article 87 EC Treaty ('EC') bans any state aid granted by Member States unless it complies with the derogations provided for it by the Treaty.[58] Generally, it is incumbent on the Commission to verify whether the aid meets the conditions that might exceptionally justify its being granted. Member States are hence requested to notify any proposal to grant aid to the Commission and await its decision before implementing the proposal.

The following conditions must be fulfilled.

(i) The financing by the state or through state resources

Aid must be imputable to the state and be granted directly or indirectly through state resources. When assessing the NAPs, the Commission consistently held that this condition was fulfilled if more than the mandatory amount of allowances was granted for

57 For more see M. Grubb, K. Neuhoff, 'Allocation and competitiveness in the EU Emission Trading Scheme: Policy Overview' (2006) 14 *Climate Policy* 14.

58 See Articles 87(2) and (3) and 88 and 89 EC Treaty.

free[59] and if banking[60] was allowed.[61] The notion of state resources includes not only the direct or indirect transfer of state resources to an undertaking, but also the waiving of revenue, which would otherwise have accrued to the general budget. This is not the case if the financial burden of a measure relies exclusively on private undertakings.

(ii) The existence of a selective benefit for an undertaking

The transfer of state resources must confer an economic advantage on the recipient undertaking. The Commission takes the view that this condition is fulfilled if allowances are granted for free.[62] The revenues in many cases exceed the costs and the 'windfall profits' accrue to the operator without any economic counterpart from the recipient undertaking.

An economic benefit granted by a Member State constitutes state aid only if it displays a certain degree of selectivity. In the case law, this condition entails verifying whether the methods of allocation adopted by Member States favoured certain undertakings over others which are comparable in the light of the objective pursued.

Due to the considerable leeway left to Member States, the amount of allowances allocated to the covered installations varied significantly, not only between sectors, but also within comparable categories of undertakings. As a result, the allocation rules largely favoured certain undertakings at the expense of others, in particular existing operators with respect to new entrants and CO_2-intensive with respect to less emitting installations.[63] These effects were exacerbated in the power sector, where cost abatement differentials are important and operators could largely pass on the price of the allowances to their customers.[64]

(iii) Distortion of competition and effects on trade between Member States

These two conditions are generally considered as fulfilled if the financial aid strengthens the position of an undertaking compared with other undertakings competing in intra-Community trade. Applied to the EU

59 European Commission, Decision on the second Slovakian national allocation plan, 29.11.2006.

60 'Banking' means that allowances issued for one compliance period may be used by the recipient in a later compliance period.

61 European Commission, Decision on the first Danish national allocation plan, 7.7.2004.

62 See European Commission, Decision on the first French national allocation plan, 20.10.2004, para. 5.

63 R. Betz, K. Rogge and J. Schleich, 'EU Emissions Trading: An Early Analysis of National Allocation Plans for 2008–2012' (2006) 6 *Climate Policy* 4.

64 K. Neuhoff *et al.*, 'Implications of Announced Phase II National Allocation Plans for the EU ETS' (2006) 6 *Climate Policy* 411.

ETS, this means that any allocation methodology, which unduly favours some undertakings at the expense of others, is likely to distort competition and to affect trade. In its review of the NAPs the Commission generally considered both criteria as fulfilled.

(b) The derogations of the prohibition of state aid (Art. 87 para. 3 EC) The Commission enjoys a wide, but not unlimited, discretion when evaluating the compatibility of state aid with the common market. It has to examine whether the aid is appropriate to meet one of the objectives mentioned in Article 87 para. 3 EC Treaty and to weigh the beneficial effects of the aid against its adverse effects on trading conditions and the maintenance of undistorted competition.

When appraising the NAPs, the Commission did not conduct a formal state aid investigation, but limited its assessment to provisional evaluations. Primarily, it verified whether the Member States had distributed more allowances than needed to their installations.[65] With respect to the second phase, it considered this condition as fulfilled if the caps set by Member States violated criteria 1–3 of Annex III of the Directive,[66] if individual installations were given more than they needed and if the information provided by Member States was purely subjective. Extending its analysis to specific allocation methodologies, it held a German[67] and a Polish[68] allocation rule to be incompatible with the common market as the former discriminated between comparable installations and the latter used a non-representative baseline with respect to average emissions of installations. The principles established by the Commission when appraising the NAP were by and large confirmed in the recently adopted 'Community guidelines on state aid for environmental protection',[69] which provide the basis for the Commission's assessment until the end of 2012.

(c) Conclusions Despite the accumulating evidence that the EU ETS has conferred large economic rents on CO_2-intensive operators, thereby reducing the economic efficiency of the scheme, the Commission has used

65 European Commission, Decision on the first French national allocation plan, 20.10.2004, para. 5.

66 See European Commission, COM (2006) 725 final.

67 European Commission, Decision on the second German national allocation plan, 29.11.2006.

68 European Commission, Decision on the second Polish national allocation plan, 26.3.2007, para. 23.

69 Official Journal C 82 of 1.4.2008, p. 1.

its powers under the state aid provisions parsimoniously. So far, it has only taken provisional decisions, in which it addressed clearly discriminatory rules and the most patent cases of over-allocation. Somewhat surprisingly, it considers that the free allocation of allowances is compatible with the common market if the amount of allowances does not exceed expected needs, though this amounts to sanctioning business-as-usual practice.

The Commission's concern to ensure the smooth functioning of the scheme is also evident in its practice regarding the complaints of affected operators. As the case *EnBW* v. *Commission* shows,[70] the attempt to challenge an allocation rule that the Commission has evaluated positively in its NAP decision is fraught with difficulties. *In casu*, the Commission merely informed the plaintiff, an operator of a nuclear power station, in a so-called 'service-letter' that there were 'insufficient grounds' for opening a state aid procedure, thus depriving the plaintiff of the option of challenging its act.[71]

The fear that Pandora's box might be opened if operators were given the right to challenge an allocation rule that has been provisionally approved by the Commission, seems to be shared by the Court of First Instance. By considering that EnBW lacked an interest in the annulment of the Commission's decision on the German NAP, inasmuch as the latter had not rejected it, the court effectively forestalled any legal action aimed at challenging an allocation method that the Commission has prima facie considered compatible with the rules on state aid. As a result, the Commission remains the sole gatekeeper of the European state aid rules and its willingness and political clout will be the principle factors in stopping the massive 'windfall' profits of certain operators, which jeopardise the environmental effectiveness of the EU ETS.

Discontented competitors might, however, find a way out of the stalemate by availing themselves of the rules of the WTO. It is a fact that the revenue from the sale of the allowances in many cases exceeds the costs incurred in abating emissions. Accordingly, it may well be argued that the free allocation of allowances amounts to a subsidy actionable under the ASCM.[72] The question hence arises whether a reform of the ASCM should be envisaged in the context of the Framework Agreement

70 CFI Case T-387/04, *EnBW Energie Baden-Württemberg AG* v. *Commission*, 30.4.2007, para. 41 ff.

71 To be challengeable, the letter must come from the College of the Commissioners and be addressed to the Member States, which was not the case here. See Article 25 of Council Regulation No 659/1999.

72 Art. 5 ASCM.

on Energy to take into account the specificities of the introduction and the implementation of emissions trading schemes.

Two aspects should be considered here. On the one hand, the presence of the massive windfall profits of the European electricity industry clearly indicates that to offset the financial burden imposed by the EU ETS only a small quantity of allowances would have to be given for free. On the other hand, the introduction of emissions trading schemes for industry sectors exposed to strong international competition may well be politically possible only if a part of the allowance is initially granted for free. As a result, we recommend that in a reform of the rules on subsidies, a temporary exemption similar to the former green-light category of the ASCM is foreseen, which would allow grandfathering up to 20 per cent of the distributed allowances for industry sectors that are exposed to strong international competition from regions which are not subject to an equivalent regulation of their carbon emissions.

IV. Energy production controls and export restrictions (OPEC)

The Framework Agreement on Energy would also need to deal with the issue of production and export controls, thus clarifying what today is an unresolved and controversial issue in relation to OPEC Members who increasingly are also Members of the WTO.[73] The preamble to the Marrakesh Agreement Establishing the World Trade Organization recognises that expanding the production of and trade in goods and services should be encouraged, thus allowing the optimal use of the world's resources. Recognition of a nation's permanent sovereignty over its own natural resources is another fundamental principle of contemporary international law[74] which OPEC member countries can constantly invoke to explain their supply management practices.

There is a difference of opinion as to the legitimacy of OPEC. The United States government considers the organisation to be contrary to the spirit and objectives of the GATT. The developing countries, which are members of OPEC, rely on Article 5 of the (non-binding) Charter of Economic Rights and Duties of States for the legitimacy of producer organisations such as OPEC. According to most Western countries a

73 See S. Matteotti-Berkutova, 'Oil Supply Management Practices of OPEC under the World Trade Organization Rules and the National Competition Laws', PhD Thesis, University of Bern (2010).

74 Permanent Sovereignty over Natural Resources, GA res. 1803 (XVII), 17 UN GAOR Supp. (No. 17) at 15, UN Doc A/5217 (1962).

producer organisation is not illegitimate as such, although its actions can be.[75] Moreover, there is controversy as to whether production controls violate disciplines of WTO law.

1. Production controls versus export restrictions

Article XI of the GATT 1994 includes a fundamental prohibition of quantitative restrictions: quotas, import and export licences 'or other measures having equivalent effect'. Therefore, it is not the legal form of the measure but its effect on trade which is important.[76] In particular, the GATT Panel in *Canada – Measures Affecting Exports of Unprocessed Herring and Salmon* concluded that provisions of Article XI:1 apply to any measure taken by a contracting state in respect of export restrictions, 'irrespective of the legal status of the measure'. Therefore, the argument that OPEC decisions on production cuts are non-binding[77] will not be sufficient to support an argument that they are outside the scope of Article XI. In *Argentina – Hides and Leather* the Panel discussed the relevance of the actual trade effect of the measure and found that although actual trade effects did not have to be proven in order to establish a violation of Article XI:1, trade effects carried weight, as evidence for establishing the existence of a de facto restriction.[78]

In order to evaluate whether production controls amount to export restrictions, which from the perspective of free trade constitute the most stringent and distortive trade policy instrument,[79] a multi-step test of OPEC's decisions should be performed. A panel would have first to determine whether OPEC practices constitute a 'measure' within the meaning of Article XI:1[80] and then consider if such measures impose a restriction on exportation.[81] OPEC's activities clearly effectuate a quantitative limit

75 H. Van Houtte, *The Law of International Trade* (Sweet and Maxwell, 1995), p. 117.

76 H. Van Houtte, *The Law of International Trade*, 2nd edn (Sweet and Maxwell, 2002), p. 91.

77 According to Article 11C of the OPEC Statute, all decisions of the Conference, other than on procedural matters, require the unanimous agreement of all Full Members and should be made in the form of Resolutions.

78 WTO Analytical Index: GATT 1994, para. 406.

79 T. Cottier and M. Oesch, *International Trade Regulation: Law and Policy in the WTO, The European Union and Switzerland, Cases Materials and Comments* (London, Cameron May, 2005), p. 660.

80 See Panel Report *India – Autos*, paras. 7.318–7.322.

81 See Panel Report *US – Shrimp*, para. 7.16.

on the amount of oil available on world markets. In this regard, OPEC measures generally have the same motivation and effect as quantitative export restrictions. Furthermore, the language of Article XI, in particular the notion of 'other measures', provides broad scope and coverage[82] and allows fitting production restrictions into this category because they are measures that interfere with the free flow to the market of a given product.

Despite the broader reading of Article XI:1, it is submitted that there are limitations. An interpretation of the provision that implies that one WTO Member could have recourse to Article XI:1 in order to commit another Member to producing more of its natural resources to satisfy world demand probably exceeds those limits.[83] This would, in our view, be at odds with the fundamental principle of national sovereignty over natural resources.

2. Restrictions made effective through state-trading operations

Another unresolved issue relates to the nature of restrictions on production. It is well-established in GATT/WTO jurisprudence that only governmental measures fall within the ambit of Article XI:1. 'Past GATT cases demonstrate that the fact that an action is taken by private parties does not rule out the possibility that the action may be deemed governmental if there is sufficient governmental involvement with it. It is difficult to establish well-defined rules in this regard, however. Thus, that possibility will need to be examined on a case-by-case basis.'[84]

In order to identify the restrictive character of a measure in the context of OPEC, it is important to note that this restriction can be made effective through state-trading operations.[85]

The Panel on *India – Quantitative Restrictions* addressed the phrase 'restrictions made effective through state-trading operations'. In its analysis, which was not subsequently reviewed by the Appellate Body,

82 See Panel Report, *India – Quantitative Restrictions*, referring to the panel in *Japan – Semiconductors*.

83 S. Broome, 'A Note on Conflicting Obligations for Oil Exporting Nations? Satisfying Membership Requirements of both OPEC and the WTO' (2006) 38 *George Washington International Law Review* 435.

84 Panel Report, *Argentina – Hides and Leather*, citing the Panel Report on *Japan – Film* in WTO Analytical Index: GATT 1994, para. 405.

85 Note Ad Article XI of GATT.

the Panel emphasised that the fact that imports were effected through state-trading operations did not per se mean that imports were being restricted: 'It should be noted, however, that the mere fact that imports are effected through state-trading enterprises would not in itself constitute a restriction. Rather, for a restriction to be found to exist, it should be shown that the operation of this state-trading entity is such as to result in a restriction.'[86]

3. Available exceptions

The GATT regulation on quantitative restrictions, however, has a limited effect because of the many exceptions. In addition to the ones set out in Article XI:2, further exceptions are contained in Article XII, XX and XXI of the GATT 1994; these exceptions are frequently utilised to pursue other legitimate policy goals.[87]

One exception occasionally cited as meeting the needs of OPEC members is the Article XX(g) exception for measures relating to the conservation of natural resources.[88] Indeed, assuming that a panel determines that production controls are contrary to the principles of GATT Article XI, then Article XX(g) is an exception that OPEC Members could invoke.

4. Lack of competition rules in WTO

In contrast to the situation regarding fundamental WTO principles, there is no unified body of jurisprudence relating to the application of the fundamental principles of competition law and policy at the multilateral level. Rather, the jurisprudence that exists has been developed with reference to diverse national laws and policies.[89]

This is why all the efforts of the United States to challenge OPEC and its member countries to date have been focused on application of American antitrust law to the production restrictions. Civil proceedings against

86 Panel Report *Korea – Various Measures on Beef*, para. 115.

87 T. Cottier and M. Oesch, *International Trade Regulation: Law and Policy in the WTO, the European Union and Switzerland, Cases Materials and Comments* (London: Cameron May, 2005), p. 662.

88 In *Shrimp – Turtle*, the WTO Appellate Body indirectly recognised petroleum as an exhaustible natural resource. See Appellate Body Report, *US – Shrimp*, para. 128.

89 WTO, 'The Fundamental Principles of Competition Policy', Background Note by the Secretariat, WT/WGTCP/W/127, 7 June 1999, para. 4.

OPEC have been launched three times so far.[90] In the first two claims the discussion focused on the privileges OPEC might enjoy, whereas the last proceeding concentrated in detail on questions of US civil procedure rules.[91]

On 22 May 2007, the US House of Representatives passed the No Oil Producing and Exporting Cartels Act of 2007 (NOPEC) and a similar bill was passed in the Senate on 19 June 2007. NOPEC is aimed at OPEC and its oil supply management practices and designed as a response to some unsuccessful legal actions brought against OPEC in the US. It restricts the sovereign rights of states to manage their natural resources and this is why the Bill will also be applicable to other oil exporting countries.

5. Conclusion

Returning to the idea of fragmentation of international trade regulation, it is hard to judge whether OPEC's supply management activities are illegal. To answer this question there should be a coherent set of rules on competition, which the WTO currently lacks. In this sensitive area and in view of the global concerns, which are now on the international agenda, a balance should be found between the right of states to exercise sovereignty over their natural resources, energy security, fair competition and climate change concerns.[92] This challenge can be left to regulatory competition.[93] Competition can be globalised so that the analyst takes a comprehensive world view rather than a nationalistic perspective.[94] We submit that these issues should be addressed in a future Framework Agreement on Energy.

90 See *International Association of Machinists & Aerospace Workers (IAM)* v. *OPEC* (C.D.Cal.1979), which was appealed *IAM* v. *OPEC* (9th Cir.1981), cert. denied, 454 U.S. 1163 (1982). The third case was *Prewitt Enterprises, Inc.* v. *OPEC* 2001 U.S.Dist. Lexis 414 (N.D. Ala. 2001), 2001–1 Trade Cas. (CCH) 73, 246 (N.D. Ala. 2001).

91 J. P. Terhechte, *OPEC und europäisches Wettbewerbsrecht: zugleich ein Beitrag zum Phänomen der Fragmentierung des internationalen Wirtschaftsrechts* (Baden-Baden: Nomos, 2008), p. 119.

92 See T. Cottier and S. Matteotti-Berkutova, 'International Environmental Law and the Evolving Concept of "Common Concern of Mankind"', in T. Cottier *et al.* (eds.), *International Trade Regulation and the Mitigation of Climate Change: World Trade Forum* (Cambridge University Press, 2009).

93 For the notion of regulatory competition and the need for competition rules under the WTO see Chapters 9 and 7 of this volume, respectively.

94 E. M. Fox, 'Competition Law', in Andreas F. Lowenfeld, *International Economic Law* (Oxford University Press, 2003), p. 383.

V. Energy and government procurement as a climate change mitigation policy tool

1. Green public procurement (GPP) in the context of the Kyoto Protocol to the UNFCCC and the WTO Agreement on Government Procurement (GPA): the need for regulatory coherence

Finally, we turn to government procurement. GPP involves the consideration by public authorities of environmental and energy efficiency aspects in the specification of preferred goods and services purchased for governmental functions. An example of this approach is the EU green energy procurement policy.[95] As government procurement is regulated by the GPA,[96] it is pertinent to investigate the extent to which parties to the GPA could pursue their climate change goals using the GPP tool while also safeguarding their non-discrimination obligations under the GPA.[97]

2. GPP and the trade concerns

Trade effects in GPP arise where the description of the goods or services preferred by a procuring authority in a tender notice results in differential treatment between otherwise 'like products', or between local and foreign suppliers. GPP could constitute a non-tariff barrier[98] which may amount to discrimination contrary to the GPA Article VI. This Article permits the use of international standards, technical regulations and other specified sources to define the 'technical specifications' of the products and services, and the service suppliers. The cardinal rule in the GPA is that standards and/or technical regulations 'shall not be prepared, adopted or applied with a view to, or with the effect of, creating unnecessary obstacles to international trade'.[99] Similarly, any technical specifications inserted in the

95 For this see G. I. Malumfashi, 'Procurement Policies, Kyoto Compliance and the WTO Agreement on Government Procurement: The Case of the EU Green Electricity Procurement and the PPMs Debate', in T. Cottier *et al.* (eds.), *International Trade Regulation and the Mitigation of Climate Change: World Trade Forum* (Cambridge University Press, 2009).

96 WTO, *Marrakesh Agreement Establishing the World Trade Organization, Annex 4: Plurilateral Trade Agreements: Agreement on Government Procurement*, done at Marrakesh on 15 April 1994, entered into force 1 January 1996.

97 See Malumfashi G. I., '"Green" Public Procurement Policies, Climate Change Mitigation and International Trade Regulation: An Assessment of the WTO Agreement on Government Procurement, PhD Thesis, Centre for Energy, Petroleum and Mineral Law and Policy, University of Dundee, United Kingdom (2009).

98 See WTO, *World Trade Report 2005: Trade Standards and WTO* (WTO, 2005), p. 46.

99 GPA Article VI.

tender 'shall be in terms of performance rather than design or descriptive characteristics'.[100]

The concern thus lies in the possibility that a procuring entity could insert non-product-related climate-friendly specifications in such a way as to discriminate between like products or services.[101] Similarly, by virtue of the provisions of GPA Article VIII, a condition for participation which requires suppliers to show evidence of compliance with a specific environmental management system may also constitute a barrier to the participation of that supplier in the procurement process. The GPA thus provides that any such requirement should relate only to the technical and/or financial ability of the supplier to perform the particular task in question.[102]

The process and production methods (PPMs) and the 'like' products debates in the WTO jurisprudence are well documented.[103] GPP practices for climate change mitigation are essentially based on environmental and energy-efficiency related considerations, and are therefore essentially in the nature of non-product-related PPMs. Such PPMs are not accepted in the WTO as basis for discrimination between like products, services or service suppliers.

3. GPP and the environmental exceptions

Article XXIII of the GPA, however, provides for environmental exceptions similar to those found under GATT Article XX(b) and (g), to permit otherwise discriminatory measures taken by the parties to address non-trade concerns, including environmental protection. These exceptions can arguably be applied to permit climate-motivated GPP policies. This view is reinforced by the Preamble to the WTO treaty which recognises 'sustainable development' and 'protection of the environment', as being among the objectives of the WTO system.[104] The Preamble was cited by the WTO Appellate Body (AB) in the *US – Shrimp* case in 1998,[105] as a guide to interpreting the environmental exceptions.

100 *Ibid.*

101 See Z. Zhang and L. Assunção, 'Domestic Climate Policies and the WTO' (UNCTAD Discussion Paper series, No. 164 November 2002) pp. 12–13.

102 GPA Article VIII(b).

103 See C. Conrad, 'The Status of Measures Linked to Non-physical Aspects and Processes and Production Methods (PPMs) in WTO Law: A Contribution to the Debate on the Impact of WTO Law on National Regulation Pursuing Social Goals', PhD Thesis, University of Bern (2008).

104 See Recital 1 to the WTO Agreement.

105 Appellate Body Report, US – Shrimp, paras. 12, 18, 153 and 155.

However, in extending this interpretation (of the GATT XX(b) and (g)) to climate-friendly procurement under the GPA Article XXIII, this study raises two concerns: first, there are some textual variations between the wording of the GPA Article XXIII and that of GATT Article XX(b) and (g). One such variation is that the GPA Article XXIII does not contain the equivalent of the words 'relating to conservation of natural resources', namely, the (g) part of GATT Article XX. The question is whether this omission is material enough to make a substantial difference between the GATT and GPA exceptions. The second concern relates to the burden of proof for measures aimed at climate mitigation. Under the conventional WTO jurisprudence, the onus is on the party invoking the GATT Article XX exceptions to prove that the particular measure is not only covered by the exceptions, but is also 'necessary' in the given circumstances to achieve the legitimate objectives, and that it is not applied in a discriminatory manner. Thus, in the event of a challenge, a party to the GPA maintaining climate-motivated procurement policy will have to shoulder this burden of proof.

The authors of this study believe that, in view of the urgent need to deal with the climate change problem and the fact that climate change measures are based on precaution in the face of scientific uncertainty, the GPA should more explicitly recognise climate-motivated GPP and make it a positive norm, rather than an exception. This would mean that the burden of proof in matters related to climate change will shift to the complaining country, which will then have to prove discrimination or that the measure is not targeted at tackling climate change.

The abovementioned approach is not entirely new in the WTO jurisprudence. It is recalled that the Appellate Body in the *EC – GSP*[106] took a view similar to that suggested above when considering that the development motive of the Enabling Clause for developing and least developed countries under the WTO system gave the Clause (which was an exception to GATT Article III) a 'special status'[107] akin to a positive norm. Thus, a developing country complaining against a measure taken by a developed country based on the Enabling Clause should bear the burden of proving discrimination.[108]

The Doha negotiations on liberalisation of environmental goods and services can help in this regard. A specific list should be generated for goods and services and technology, as well as projects and programmes

106 Appellate Body Report, *EC – Tariff Preferences*, paras. 106–111. 107 *Ibid.*

108 See L. Bartels, 'The WTO Enabling Clause and Positive Conditionality in the EC's GSP programme' (2003) 6(2) *Journal of International Economic Law* 518.

targeted specifically at addressing climate change, out of the various lists currently being examined. This list should then be included as an appendix to the GPA so as to form a basis for all GPP measures.

The study notes that the Revised GPA 2007,[109] which is not yet in force explicitly permits the parties to consider environmental factors in their procurement processes.[110] This new provision ostensibly makes up for the GATT Article XX (g) missing in the GPA Article XXIII. To this extent, the new provision does not seem to fundamentally change the status quo, especially as it relates to the burden of proof question.

D. Overall conclusions

Existing WTO rules do not appropriately address all the needs of energy trade today. Ensuring security of supply and addressing climate change mitigation, creating an effective incentives mechanism to reduce CO_2 emissions are the first priorities. Therefore, we recommend a move towards a comprehensive sectoral agreement on energy, which would encompass subsidies reform, introducing a temporary exemption similar to the former green-light category of the ASCM; creation of a check-list of core and related energy services that would facilitate making additional commitments; and redrafting of Article X:6 of the revised GPA 2007 to include a more explicit recognition of climate-related measures.

The WTO, with its currently 153 Members,[111] can make an important contribution to the complex process of energy reform. More predictable and transparent trade rules could benefit both energy-importing and energy-exporting countries, and will contribute to preventing the eruption of energy conflicts.

Bibliography

Abdallah, Hussein, 'Oil Exports under GATT and the WTO' (2005) **29**(4) *OPEC Review* 267–294.

Adelman, Morris Albert, 'World Oil Production and Prices 1947–2000' (2002) **42**(2) *Quarterly Review of Economics and Finance* 169–191.

Bartels, Lorand, 'The WTO Enabling Clause and Positive Conditionality in the EC's GSP Programme' (2003) **6**(2) *Journal of International Economic Law* 507–532.

109 See WTO, Revised GPA 2007, document no. GPA/W/297, available at www.wto.org/english/tratop_e/gproc_e/negotiations_e.htm (last accessed 25/05/09).

110 *Ibid.* Article XI:6

111 As of December 2008.

Betz, Regina, Rogge, Karoline and Schleich, Joachim, 'EU Emissions Trading: An Early Analysis of National Allocation Plans for 2008–2012 (2006) **6**(4) *Climate Policy* 361–394.

Broome, Stephen, 'A Note on Conflicting Obligations for Oil Exporting Nations? Satisfying Membership Requirements of both OPEC and the WTO' (2006) **38** *George Washington International Law Review* 409–436.

Conrad, Christiane, 'The Status of Measures Linked to Non-physical Aspects and Processes and Production Methods (PPMs) in WTO Law: A Contribution to the Debate on the Impact of WTO Law on National Regulation Pursuing Social Goals', PhD Thesis submitted to the Faculty of Law, University of Bern, 2008.

Cottier, Thomas, Nartova, Olga and Sadeq Z. Bigdeli (eds.), *International Trade Regulation and the Mitigation of Climate Change: World Trade Forum* (Cambridge University Press, 2009).

Cottier, Thomas and Matteotti-Berkutova, Sofya, 'International Environmental Law and the Evolving Concept of "Common Concern of Mankind"' in T. Cottier *et al.* (eds.), *International Trade Regulation and the Mitigation of Climate Change: World Trade Forum* (Cambridge University Press, 2009).

Cottier, Thomas and Oesch, Matthias, *International Trade Regulation: Law and Policy in the WTO, The European Union and Switzerland, Cases Materials And Comments* (London: Cameron May, 2005).

Cottier, Thomas, Matteotti, Sofya and Nartova, Olga 'Winterkrieg im Gasgeschäft: Ursachen und Auswirkungen' (2009) **140** *UniPress* 40.

de Sépibus, Joëlle, 'Linking the EU Emissions Trading Scheme to JI, CDM and post-2012 International Offsets', NCCR Working Paper No. 18/2008.

de Sépibus, Joëlle, 'Scarcity and Allocation in the European Emissions Trading Scheme: A Legal Analysis', NCCR Working Paper No. 32/2007.

de Sépibus, Joëlle, 'The European Emission Trading Scheme Put to the Test of State Aid Rules', NCCR Working Paper No. 34/2007.

de Sépibus, Joëlle, *Die Umweltschutzsubvention im Gemeinschaftsrecht: eine umweltrechtliche Kritik der europäischen Beihilfekontrolle* (Bern: Peter Lang, 2003).

Directive 2003/87/EC establishing a scheme for GHG emission allowance trading within the Community and amending Council Directive 96/61/EC.

Energy Charter Secretariat, *Putting a Price on Energy: International Pricing Mechanisms for Oil and Gas* (Brussels, 2007).

Energy Charter Secretariat, *The Energy Charter Treaty and Related Documents* (Brussels, 2004).

European Commission, Communication to the Council and to the European Parliament on the assessment of national allocation plans for the allocation of greenhouse gas emission allowances in the second period of the EU Emissions Trading Scheme, COM (2006) 725 final.

European Commission, Decision on the first Danish national allocation plan, 7.7.2004.

European Commission, Decision on the first French national allocation plan, 20.10.2004.

European Commission, Decision on the second German national allocation plan, 29.11.2006.

European Commission, Decision on the second Polish national allocation plan, 26.3.2007.

European Commission, Decision on the second Slovakian national allocation plan, 29.11.2006.

Fox, Eleanor M., 'Competition Law', in Andreas F. Lowenfeld, *International Economic Law* (Oxford University Press, 2003), pp. 340–390.

Grubb, Michael and Neuhoff, Karsten, 'Allocation and Competitiveness in the EU Emission Trading Scheme: Policy Overview' (2006) **6** *Climate Policy*, 7–30.

Lamy P., speech delivered at the 20th World Energy Congress on 15 November 2007 in Rome.

Lowenfeld A., *International Economic Law* (Oxford University Press, 2003).

Malumfashi, I. Garba, '"Green" Public Procurement Policies, Climate Change Mitigation and International Trade Regulation: An Assessment of the WTO Agreement on Government Procurement', PhD Thesis, Centre for Energy, Petroleum and Mineral Law and Policy, University of Dundee, United Kingdom (2009).

Malumfashi, I. Garba, 'Procurement Policies, Kyoto Compliance and the WTO Agreement on Government Procurement: The Case of the EU Green Electricity Procurement and the PPMs Debate', in T. Cottier *et al.* (eds.), *International Trade Regulation and the Mitigation of Climate Change: World Trade Forum* (Cambridge University Press, 2009).

Matteotti-Berkutova, Sofya, 'Oil Supply Management Practices of OPEC under the World Trade Organisation Rules and the National Competition Laws', PhD Thesis, University of Bern (2010).

Nartova, Olga, 'Trade in Energy Services under WTO Law: The Impact of Competition Policies', PhD thesis, University of Bern (2009).

Neuhoff, Karsten, Ahman, Markus, Betz, Regina, Cludius, Johanna *et al.*, 'Implications of Announced Phase II National Allocation Plans for the EU ETS' (2006) **6**(5) *Climate Policy* 411–422.

OECD, *Greener Public Purchasing: Issues and Practical Solutions* (Paris, 2000).

OECD/IEA, *Energy Security and Climate Policy: Assessing Interactions* (Paris, 2007).

OPEC Statute, United Nations Treaty Series 443, 248.

Patterson, Walt, *Transforming Electricity* (London: Earthscan, 1999).

Pollitt, Michael G., *The Impact of Liberalisation on the Performance of the Electricity Supply Industry: An International Survey* (1997) 3(2) *Journal of Energy Literature*, pp. 3–31.

Poretti, Pietro, 'Waiting for Godot: Subsidy Disciplines in Services Trade', in M. Panizzon, N. Pohl and P. Sauvé (eds.), *GATS and the Regulation of International Trade in Services* (Cambridge University Press, 2007).

Rubini, Luca, *The Definition of Subsidy and State Aid: WTO and EC Law in Comparative Perspective* (Oxford University Press, 2009).

Selivanova, Julia, *Energy Dual Pricing in WTO Law* (London: Cameron May, 2008).

Terhechte, Jörg Philipp, *OPEC und europäisches Wettbewerbsrecht: zugleich ein Beitrag zum Phänomen der Fragmentierung des internationalen Wirtschaftsrechts* (Baden-Baden: Nomos, 2008).

UN Department of Economic and Social Affairs, Statistics Division Statistical Papers Series M No. 77, Ver.1.1 (New York, 2004).

UN General Assembly, Permanent Sovereignty over Natural Resources, GA res. 1803 (XVII), 17 UN GAOR Supp. (No. 17) at 15, UN Doc. A/5217 (1962).

Van Den Bossche, Peter, *The Law and Policy of the World Trade Organization: Text, Cases and Materials* (Cambridge University Press, 2005).

Van Houtte, Hans, *The Law of International Trade* (London: Sweet and Maxwell, 1995).

Van Houtte, Hans, *The Law of International Trade*, 2nd edn (London: Sweet and Maxwell, 2002).

WTO, *Services Sectoral Classification List*, document no. MTN.GNS/W/120, 10 July 1991.

WTO Agreement on Government Procurement, *Marrakesh Agreement Establishing the World Trade Organization, Annex 4: Plurilateral Trade Agreements: Agreement on Government Procurement*, done at Marrakesh on 15 April 1994, entered into force 1 January 1996.

WTO, *The Fundamental Principles of Competition Policy*, Background Note by the Secretariat, WT/WGTCP/W/127, 7 June 1999.

WTO, *World Trade Report 2005: Trade Standards and WTO* (WTO, 2005), 46.

WTO, *Revised Government Procurement Agreement* 2007, document no. GPA/W/297, available at www.wto.org/english/tratop_e/gproc_e/negotiations_e.htm

Z. Bigdeli, Sadeq, 'Will the "Friends of Climate" Emerge in the WTO? Applying the "Fisheries Subsidies" Model to Energy Subsidies' (2008) **2**(1) *Carbon and Climate Law Review* 78–79.

Z. Bigdeli, Sadeq, 'Energy Subsidies in International Economic Law: a Trade and Environment Perspective', PhD thesis, University of Bern (2009).

Zhang, Zhong Xiang and Assunção, Lucas, 'Domestic Climate Policies and the WTO' (UNCTAD Discussion Paper series No. 164, November 2002).

6

Developing trade rules for services: a case of fragmented coherence?

PANAGIOTIS DELIMATSIS, NICOLAS DIEBOLD, MARTÍN MOLINUEVO, MARION PANIZZON AND PIERRE SAUVÉ*

KEY MESSAGES

- Trade in services ranks among the most intractable subject matters in modern trade diplomacy. Confronted with such complexity, diversity, learning by doing and fragmentation are key characteristics of the evolving regimes governing services trade.
- Fragmentation may represent a source of policy and innovation able to inform and shape future directions in multilateral rule-making. It can also offer alternative theatres of collective action able to yield superior outcomes or more politically palatable bargains than those on offer at the World Trade Organization (WTO) or under preferential trade agreements (PTAs).
- The adoption of a necessity test applicable across services sectors and enhanced transparency disciplines would improve the quality of services trade regulation. The absence of a necessity test can devalue regulatory disciplines on domestic regulation.
- The immigration law caveat of the GATS Annex on the Temporary Movement of Natural Persons and flexibilities within the structure for scheduling GATS commitments exacerbate the divide between a global labour migration regime favouring high-skilled workers and bilateral, non-trade migration agreements regulating the flows of low-skilled and potentially irregular migrants. This schism prevents progress towards a coherent global governance of migration.

* Individual Project No. 8, 'Developing trade rules for services: a case of fragmented coherence?'. IP 8 focused on four sectoral research goals: preferentialism (Pierre Sauvé); domestic regulation in services (Panagiotis Delimatsis); non-discrimination in services (Nicolas Diebold); investmest in services (Martin Molinuevo); and labour mobility (Marion Panizzon).

- The interpretation of the 'likeness' concept in the GATS rules on non-discrimination requires an assessment of the competitive relationship between suppliers and services in the marketplace. As trade in services may involve the movement of suppliers and services, consideration must be given to both *service*-related and *supplier*-related factors in order to reach an overall conclusion on the competitive relationship between the types of service transactions under scrutiny.
- Multilateral rules on services and bilateral agreements on foreign investment feature overlapping disciplines that can potentially bring about legal uncertainties regarding the rights and obligations of domestic authorities and foreign investors in services.
- WTO and arbitral panels in the investment field can contribute to a more coherent international framework for investment in services through the interpretation of similar principles in a uniform manner, rather than exacerbating the differences between the two legal systems.

A. Not so straightforward: multilateral coherence and fragmented preferentialism in services trade

I. Context

One of the underlying organising principles of our research on services trade has been a presumed fault line between the innate coherence that is achieved through multilateral rules and commitments, on the one side, and the more inherently fragmented nature of preferential solutions or rules, on the other. Doubtlessly rooted in the way mainstream trade theorists and economists more broadly have long championed multilateralism over its peripheral brethren, such a perception proceeds from the assumed second-best nature of preferential, or non-WTO-centric, policy and rule-making approaches.

Several key questions in services trade are likely to remain unanswered so long as the outcome of the Uruguay Round continues to define the multilateral benchmark against which the more recent preferential movement or alternatives to multilateralism (and indeed to trade agreements all together) are assessed. Chief among such questions is whether the presumed fault line described above offers an analytically meaningful basis for enquiry.

Before describing the main research findings emerging from four years of enquiry in the services field, a few contextual considerations appear warranted. When tracking a 'live' negotiating issue like trade in services, researchers are inevitably caught in negotiating headwinds and their complex political geometry. Recent years have witnessed the coexistence of quasi-paralysis in services negotiations under the WTO's Doha

Development Agenda alongside frenetic negotiating activity under PTAs. It should come as no surprise that such a two-step dance has exerted a significant influence on the direction of our research.

II. Multilateralism

1. Understanding the GATS: legal commentaries

A first major contribution of the project has been to provide legal context to the incipient body of GATS rules. This was done by analysing, in a series of in-depth commentaries published by the Max-Planck Institute of Heidelberg, the legal reach and negotiating intent of several of the most central and potentially contentious provisions of the GATS framework.[1] Such work is aimed to help the epistemic community concerned with trade regulation in services to gain a fuller sense of the meaning and scope of the provisions adopted, situating their development against the broader canvas of the negotiating history of the GATS. This represents a central contribution of the research team, analogous to basic research in the hard sciences. It is also work which no one else has been engaged in to such an extent. It should, accordingly, stand as a major contribution to the understanding and interpretation of a nascent legal order and provide invaluable context and guidance to those called upon to adjudicate contested measures in services trade.

2. Disciplining non-discriminatory regulatory conduct

The Article VI:4 negotiating mandate on domestic regulation is the only element of the unfinished rule-making agenda of the GATS that has generated significant negotiating traction in the Doha Round. The analysis conducted in this area investigated the complex challenges of developing credible disciplines on non-discriminatory regulatory conduct. Such work, described in section B below, centres on the twin challenges of developing a necessity test for services trade and agreeing to a set of enhanced transparency disciplines in services rule-making. Both are areas where a prescriptive, workable, set of solutions have been formulated on what has been a highly sensitive post-Uruguay Round negotiating mandate. Work in this area suggests that Members would ultimately benefit from

1 These include: Articles III (Transparency), III*bis* (Business Confidential Information), V (Economic Integration), XI (Payments and Transfers), XIV (General Exceptions), XIVbis (Security Exceptions), XVI (MA), XIX (Negotiation of Specific Commitments) and XX (Schedules of Specific Commitments). See the contributions in R. Wolfrum, P.-T. Stoll and C. Feinäugle (eds.), *Max-Planck Commentaries on World Trade Law, Volume 6: WTO – Trade in Services* (Brill Publishers, 2008).

embedding a set of clear criteria with which to guide WTO panels tasked with determining whether and how non-discriminatory regulatory conduct can be unduly restrictive of trade and nullify scheduled commitments. Absent such criteria, the WTO judiciary is likely to have little choice but to develop them itself, with potential commensurate downsides in legitimacy terms.

3. Disciplining discriminatory regulatory conduct

Much needed analytical attention was devoted to the issue of 'likeness' in non-discrimination obligations applying to services trade, focusing on how such a concept compares with – and differs from – its treatment under GATT law and the extent to which its interpretation can be informed by the practice of adjudication under investment and competition law and analysis (see Section C below). The question of how to determine when competing services and service providers can be deemed to be '(a)like' or in 'like regulatory or market circumstances' is fundamental to the analysis of whether trade obstacles discriminate between two products or services and service providers. Likeness is indeed key to understanding whether and how non-discrimination – in both its MFN and national treatment (NT) incarnations – is secured or breached through specific regulatory measures governing cross-border trade and investment in services.

4. Investment rules for services

Another strand of research has straddled the domains of WTO and bilateral investment law in exploring the nexus between trade and investment rules governing service industries (see Section D below). Where bilateral investment treaties grant rights to investors and their investments that conflict with the regulatory space afforded to governments under multilateral instruments, or vice versa, legal certainty is diminished, impairing the investment climate of the host countries affected and setting the grounds for possible legal challenges. The key question is whether, and to what extent, bilateral disciplines on foreign investment overlap with multilateral rules on commercial presence and, when such overlaps arise, how potential legal conflicts can be properly contained and mediated.

The key disciplines at play in such an enquiry are the core non-discriminatory principles of MFN and NT, which are embedded in both GATS and bilateral investment treaties (BITs), as well as disciplines on fair and equitable treatment, which are unique to investment law but for which a number of disciplines of equivalent nature can nonetheless be found in Articles III (Transparency) and VI (Domestic Regulation) of the GATS. Work in this area suggests that the solution proposed to avoid conflict of law lies not in the development of uniform multilateral disciplines on investment, for which prospects remain weak in the light of recent, repeated, failures at crafting multilateral rules in the area, but rather in encouraging WTO panels and arbitral tribunals in the investment field to contribute to a more coherent international framework for investment in services through the interpretation of similar principles in a uniform manner. Such interpretative convergence could be achieved through structured dialogue and institutional cooperation between the trade and investment communities.

5. Managed mobility

Cross-border labour mobility ranks among the defining global policy and multilateral rule-making challenges of the day given the underlying demographic and development trends for which no comprehensive collective action solution currently exists. While Mode 4 of the GATS provides a framework for multilateralising the temporary movement of labour incidental to services supply, at the WTO and in PTAs, there is little appetite among the host (labour-receiving) nations for pursuing policy responses in a trade setting. Work here has shed light on a new and highly sensitive frontier in services trade regulation, the murky divide between the treatment of labour movement brokered under trade agreements and the management of flows of temporary workers under a new generation of migration instruments operating outside the trade field (see Section E below). This work has taken stock of recent advances in bilateral migration management agreements (BMMAs) in a Eurafrican context and explored the concept of 'shared responsibility' between sending and receiving countries. We have devised a prescriptive model schedule for Mode 4 commitments that establishes operational linkages between new and improved commitments by host countries against reciprocal commitments by home governments to cooperate in the enforcement of readmission agreements with a view to mitigating the risks of temporary admission schemes (see Table 6.2, p. 276 below).

III. Preferentialism[2]

Beyond conjectures as to the future of multilateral rules for services, significant attention has also been devoted to the question of how

2 We opt for this term rather than regionalism because preferentialism is more precise and encompassing in that it connotes any agreement, be it bilateral, regional or transregional, that grants preferences.

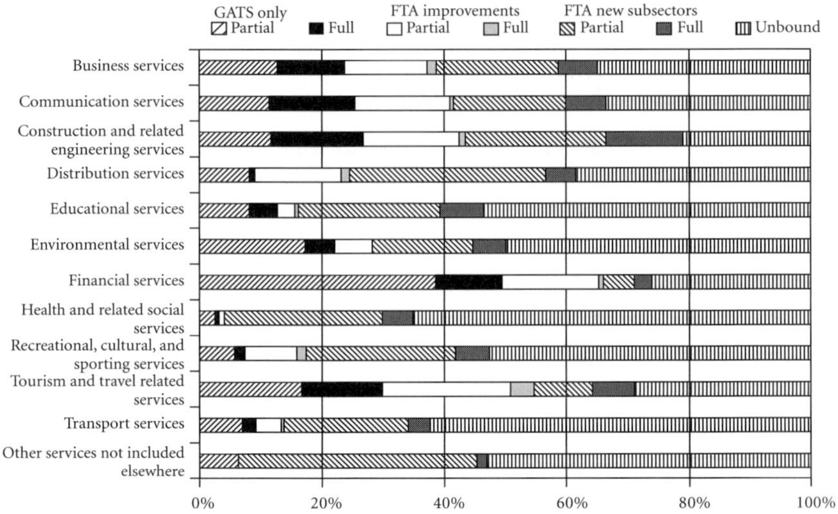

Figure 6.1 GATS+ advances in Asian PTAs covering services: sectoral breakdown
Source: Fink and Molinuevo (2007).

developments under the ever growing number of preferential trade and investment agreements are likely to shape the nascent legal order in services trade.[3]

One focus of the work in this area has been the market opening attributes of PTAs in services, documenting the extent to which current PTA commitments exceed those on offer at the WTO level – be it Uruguay Round commitments or Doha Development Agenda (DDA) offers. Figures 6.1 and 6.2 offer a view of the GATS+ nature of Asian PTA commitments, broken down on both a sectoral (Figure 6.1) and mode of supply basis (Figure 6.2).[4] Research has also focused on evolving legal architectures in services trade, notably in regard to the treatment of investment in services and of financial services in selected PTAs.[5] Such enquiries have revealed a rich tapestry of policy- and rule-making

3 A. Mattoo and P. Sauvé, 'Regionalism in Services Trade', in A. Mattoo, R. M. Stern and G. Zanini (eds), *A Handbook of International Trade in Services* (Oxford University Press, 2007), pp. 221–286.

4 C. Fink and M. Molinuevo, 'East Asian Free Trade Agreements in Services: Roaring Tigers or Timid Pandas?', East Asia and Pacific Region Report No. 40175, The World Bank, http://go.worldbank.org/5YFZ3TK4E0.

5 P. Sauvé and M. Molinuevo, 'Does Architecture Matter? The Treatment of Trade and Investment in Financial Services in Selected Preferential Trade Agreements', NCCR Working Paper, No. 9, May 2008.

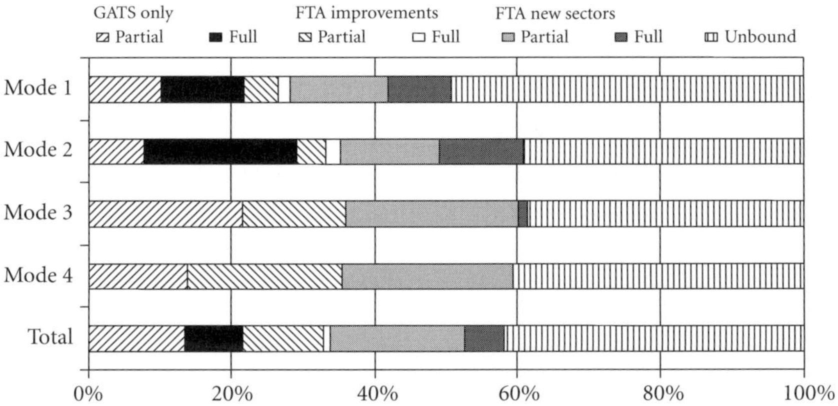

Figure 6.2 GATS+ advances in Asian PTAs covering services: modal breakdown
Source: Fink and Molinuevo (2007).

experimentation, with governments using PTAs to advance new agendas or correct perceived shortcomings in past agreements by refining and clarifying the scope of covered provisions, circumscribing the scope for litigation or addressing new liberalisation challenges.

A third strand of work on PTAs has focused on the treatment of services and investment under the EU-CARIFORUM Economic Partnership Agreement (EPA), chronicling the emergence of a major new model of trade-led integration in services featuring several novel advances. These concern the legal architecture through which trade and investment in services have been addressed, as well as the treatment of new areas of trade regulation or market opening, notably digital trade, trade facilitation, tourism services, cultural cooperation and aid for trade in services, where precedent-setting development provisions have been made operational in ways that are certain to inform the evolution of similar provisions in subsequent PTAs (beyond the EU EPAs) and at the WTO level.

B. Tackling non-discriminatory regulatory conduct in services

Unduly burdensome domestic regulations on non-discrimination constitute the most intractable barriers to trade in services.[6] Members agreed

6 P. Delimatsis, 'Due Process and "Good" Regulation Embedded in the GATS: Disciplining Regulatory Behaviour in Services through Article VI of the GATS' (2007) 10(1) *Journal of International Economic Law* 15–17.

on a negotiating mandate under GATS Article VI:4 ('the mandate') requiring the establishment of regulatory disciplines ('the disciplines') applicable to non-discriminatory measures relating to qualifications, licensing and technical standards, including the procedures for enforcing these standards ('the covered measures'). Domestic regulation has been the area of unfinished GATS rule-making which made the greatest tangible progress over the course of services negotiations. It is also the area in which practice demonstrates that the multilateral avenue is Members' preferred choice. Indeed, regardless of whether they adopt a negative or positive list approach, all PTAs outsource the development of such disciplines at the multilateral level. Thus, in this specific area, Members strive for coherence by favouring multilateral outcomes.

I. *The draft disciplines on domestic regulation*[7]

Regulatory discretion in services is circumscribed by Article VI:4 which considers the creation of effective, enforceable and operationally useful disciplines an appropriate remedy against attempts by Members to circumvent their multilateral commitments.[8] The Draft disciplines aim to facilitate the quest for equilibrium between the collective interest of Members in progressive liberalisation and their individual interest in preserving regulatory autonomy.[9]

The Draft disciplines incorporate provisions that enhance the objectivity and transparency of covered measures and ensure legal certainty as well as the observance of contemporary dictates of due process domestically. *Ratione materiae*, the Draft disciplines only cover measures that affect trade in services in committed sectors and which are not subject to scheduling under Articles XVI (market access) and XVII (NT). Furthermore, the Draft requires that covered measures be *pre-established*, based on *objective* and *transparent* criteria, and *relevant to the supply* of a given service. This provision hints at the overall objective of the disciplines, which is to limit Members' otherwise broad regulatory authority,[10] avert regulatory arbitrariness and unnecessary bureaucracy,

7 Our comments are based on the most recent draft text ('the Draft'). See Working Party on Domestic Regulation (WPDR), 'Disciplines on Domestic Regulation Pursuant to GATS Article VI:4', Room Document, 20 March 2009 (on file with the authors).

8 P. Delimatsis, *International Trade in Services and Domestic Regulations: Necessity, Transparency, and Regulatory Diversity* (Oxford University Press, 2007), p. 167.

9 Cf. Panel Report, *US – Gambling*, para. 6.316.

10 Panel Report, *US – Gambling*, paras. 6.107–109 and 6.314–317.

and ensure the creation of a predictable and trade-facilitating regulatory environment.

Procedural disciplines are the most refined and call for the simplification and streamlining of applicable procedures to avoid restrictions on the supply of services.[11] The procedural novelties in the disciplines are significant and reflect good governance principles. Inter alia, they urge countries to provide a single point of contact to deal with a supplier's application ('one-stop-shops'), process applications and administer application procedures objectively, give reasons when applications are rejected, or ensure the independence of the enforcement authorities.[12]

Regarding licensing requirements, the disciplines call upon Members to reflect on the necessity of using non-discriminatory residency requirements. Under qualification requirements, however, residency requirements are ruled out if they are a precondition for the assessment and verification of the competence of a given service supplier.[13] The disciplines on qualification requirements are fairly detailed and call for a fair and flexible assessment of qualifications and professional experience, also through offering the possibility of fulfilling additional educational requirements in the home or in a third country. The adoption of common or convergent qualification or licensing requirements and procedures are essential prerequisites for any further increase of international labour flows under Mode 4.

On technical standards, the Draft requires that Members take into account relevant international standards, unless these standards would not allow achievement of the national policy objective pursued in an effective and appropriate manner. This provision echoes Article 2.4 of the TBT Agreement, with the important difference that under the WTO Agreement on Technical Barriers to Trade (TBT Agreement) Members are *obliged* to use such standards as a basis for their technical regulations.[14]

Finally, the Draft includes several development-friendly provisions such as phase-in periods for developing countries and the obligation to provide technical assistance to developing countries and least developed countries (LDCs). A new Committee on Domestic Regulation, together

11 The recent EU Services Directive also has similar provisions. See Directive 2006/123 on services in the internal market [2006] OJ L 376/36, Chapter II.

12 Incongruously, this latter requirement applies only to licensing procedures.

13 Cf. Delimatsis, above note 8, pp. 195–6.

14 Cf. Appellate Body Report, *EC – Sardines*, paras. 275, 282, 287.

with the Council for Trade in Services (CTS), would ensure the implementation of prospective disciplines.

II. The unavoidable adoption of a necessity test[15]

Necessity tests have long been used in goods trade as proxies for identifying and disciplining unduly burdensome or protectionist regulatory conduct. Because Article VI:4 mandates the creation of disciplines ensuring that covered measures do not constitute *unnecessary* barriers to trade in services, the creation of a horizontal (i.e. across services sectors) necessity test is embedded in the negotiating mandate.

In deference to the vocal objections expressed by several Members[16] to the adoption of a necessity test under the GATS, the Draft merely requires that covered measures do not constitute 'disguised restrictions on trade in services'. Furthermore, such measures should be 'relevant to the supply of the services to which they apply'. Thus the initially proposed necessity test is replaced by 'relevance' and 'disguised trade restriction' tests. The latter term mirrors the language of the *chapeau* of Articles XX of the General Agreement on Tariffs and Trade (GATT) and XIV GATS. The concept of 'disguised trade restriction' under WTO law is typically associated with discrimination and the manner of application of a certain measure.[17] It includes disguised, arbitrary or unjustifiable discrimination.[18] However, a disguised trade restriction can exist even *without* any overt discrimination.[19] Hence, the intent of negotiators in the Working Party on Domestic Regulation (WPDR) appears to be to cover measures which, while *not* discriminating de jure or de facto, still constitute disguised trade restrictions, i.e. restrictions that are not merely inadvertent or unavoidable, but rather foreseeable violations of WTO obligations.[20] The WTO judiciary will interpret this term according to previous case-law, which classified as disguised trade restrictions several acts or omissions. These include, but are not limited to: the treatment of similarly situated trading partners in a different manner; the lack of good faith consultations with other trading partners;

15 Also P. Delimatsis, 'Determining the Necessity of Domestic Regulations in Services: The Best is Yet to Come' (2008) 19(2) *European Journal of Economic Law* 365–408.

16 Including the United States, Brazil and several developing countries and LDCs.

17 Cf. the *chapeau* of Article XIV GATS or para. 5(d) of the Telecoms Annex; also T. Cottier, P. Delimatsis and N. Diebold, 'Article XIV', in Wolfrum, Stoll and Feinäugle (eds.), above note 1, p. 325.

18 Cf. Appellate Body Report, *US – Gasoline*, p. 25.

19 *Ibid.*

20 *Ibid.*, p. 28.

or the fact that significant costs are only incumbent on the exporters. Hence, just as under a necessity test, the pursuit of less trade-restrictive alternatives and the comparison of regulatory conduct in similar situations will be important evidence under any 'disguised trade restriction' test.

A 'relevance' test could be construed as a 'soft' necessity test. Taking *US – Shrimp* as a yardstick,[21] this means that the adopted measures should be at least 'directly connected' with or 'primarily aimed' at the objective pursued and this connection should be a close and real one. This test would also operate similarly to a necessity test, notably if we consider the judicial restraint in cases involving objectives of vital importance and the description of necessity as a continuum in *Korea – Beef*.[22]

To avoid undue judicial activism and inadequate interpretation from other WTO agreements, Members should consider the adoption of a horizontal necessity test which would be effective and include several concepts that accommodate the demands for regulatory flexibility. While constructive ambiguity has various advantages, clarifying the content of necessity is essential for the long-term viability of the prospective disciplines. We believe that the necessity test proposed in Box 6.1 could enjoy a 'critical mass' of support among Members:

BOX 6.1 PROPOSAL FOR A HORIZONTAL NECESSITY TEST

1. In sectors where specific commitments are undertaken, Members shall ensure that measures relating to qualification requirements and procedures, licensing requirements and procedures and technical standards are not prepared, adopted, applied or administered with a view to creating unnecessary barriers to trade in services. For this purpose, Members shall ensure that these measures are (a) based on objective and transparent criteria, such as competence and the ability to supply a service; (b) not more trade-restrictive than necessary to fulfil a national policy objective,* including to ensure the quality of the service; and (c) in the case of licensing and qualification procedures, not in themselves a restriction on the supply of the service.
2. Members shall endeavour to ensure that measures relating to qualification requirements and procedures, licensing requirements and procedures and technical standards in sectors where commitments have not been undertaken do not constitute unnecessary barriers to trade in services.

21 See Appellate Body Report, *US – Shrimp*, paras. 136–141.

22 Appellate Body Report, *Korea – Beef*, para. 161.

*A measure falling under this provision cannot be considered more trade-restrictive than necessary, unless there is another, reasonably available alternative measure that would equally attain the objective pursued and which is significantly less trade-restrictive. When evaluating the reasonable availability of an alternative measure, panels shall take into account several factors such as economic and technical feasibility, the associated risks, or the creation of any undue burden to the regulating Member, including prohibitive costs, substantial administrative resources, costly technologies or advanced know-how.

The quest for alternatives is intentionally 'managed' in the above test to allow the preservation of regulatory autonomy. The proposed interpretive footnote aims to narrow the pool of potential measures that can be regarded as alternatives and combines previous WTO rulings on necessity.[23]

Not incorporating a necessity test in the disciplines runs against both the letter and spirit of the mandate and prevents effective enforcement of the disciplines.[24] Absent a necessity test, the WTO judiciary will use its own benchmarks or a sort of a necessity-based test, since necessity will creep into the disciplines anyway. Nonetheless, this would mean that Members had missed a unique opportunity to design a necessity test that would encompass concepts and elements expressly allowing for more regulatory flexibility and showing greater deference to domestic regulatory decision-making.

Another argument for the adoption of a necessity test is that the WTO judiciary will interpret both Article VI:4 and the disciplines with a view to giving meaning to both of them harmoniously, consistently with the principle of effectiveness.[25] Disregarding the fundamental objective of the mandate (i.e. ensuring that the covered measures do not constitute *unnecessary* trade barriers) would amount to an interpretation that reduces parts of the GATS to 'redundancy or inutility'.[26] At a minimum, Article VI:4 would be considered as context when interpreting the disciplines. This is corroborated by the first paragraph of the Draft.[27] In sum, necessity will

23 Inter alia, *EC – Asbestos*; *US – Gambling*; and *Brazil – Tyres*.

24 Cf. Australia's intervention in WTO, WPDR, 'Report of the Meeting held on 19 and 20 June 2006', S/WPDR/M/35, 14 August 2006, paras. 7–8.

25 Appellate Body Reports, *Argentina – Footwear (EC)*, para. 81; *Korea – Dairy*, para. 81.

26 Cf. Appellate Body Reports, *Canada – Dairy*, para. 133; *US – Offset Act (Byrd Amendment)*, para. 271.

27 Paragraph 1 of the Draft reads: '*Pursuant to Article VI:4 of the GATS*, Members have agreed to the following disciplines on domestic regulation' (emphasis added). This would mean

become part of the WTO judicial toolbox when applying the disciplines, *regardless* of whether such disciplines incorporate a necessity test.

III. Promoting good governance through disciplines on regulatory transparency

Transparency is another important 'protectionism revelation' proxy. Enhanced transparency is an object and purpose of the WTO in general. The Draft contains detailed provisions aimed at streamlining and guaranteeing transparent application processes. It requires that Members make publicly available detailed information about the covered measures. This information relates, inter alia, to the procedures and the timeframe for processing an application, or the substantive content of the measures. Such information must be published promptly.[28] The disciplines are relatively soft in that they use best-endeavour language to encourage Members to publish the covered measures in advance so as to enable foreign and domestic service suppliers to provide comments prior to their enforcement. Additionally, Members are encouraged to address collectively in writing the substance of these comments. Applied to all levels of regulatory authority, such procedures are conducive to the internationalisation of decision-making and can increase the legitimacy, representativeness and acceptance of proposed measures.[29]

However, the lack of a provision in the Draft requiring that Members explain the rationale behind domestic measures and their connection to a legitimate objective (as in Article 2.5 TBT or the draft accountancy disciplines) weakens its 'bite'. Where the scope for regulatory discretion is virtually unlimited, such a provision would facilitate the distinction between necessary and unnecessary trade impediments.

IV. Concluding remarks and practical issues

On completion of the mandate the GATS will have created multilaterally established private rights against domestic administrators and regulators and added a multilateral level of scrutiny regarding the adherence

that the regulatory disciplines aim to substantiate the criteria of Art. VI:4, including its *chapeau* and sub-paragraph (b).

28 For an analysis of the 'prompt publication' concept, see P. Delimatsis, 'Article III GATS', in Wolfrum, Stoll and Feinäugle (eds.), above note 1, p. 97.

29 Cf. D. Esty, 'Good Governance at the Supranational Scale: Globalizing Administrative Law' (2006) 115 *Yale Law Journal* 1530.

of the competent authorities to the rule of law and due process in a non-discriminatory manner. To avoid the Draft disciplines becoming a dead letter, Members have to ensure that their judicial or other review organs abide by these disciplines when a service supplier has recourse to those organs. As Article VI:2 does not address this situation, Members should allow for the possibility of service suppliers who have been negatively affected directly invoking their rights stemming from the disciplines before national courts. Alternatively, Members could establish a complaint mechanism within the Committee on Domestic Regulation empowering private parties to notify the regulatory barriers they have encountered.

After Doha, the need for national regulatory audits to ensure compliance with the ensuing regulatory disciplines will emerge. Such a 'screening' exercise would induce domestic regulatory reforms, boost regulatory cooperation and ultimately lead to positive integration, minimal harmonisation and/or mutual recognition of quality-enhancing regulations. Viewed from this angle, Article VI complements Article VII (Recognition) of GATS and constitutes an essential trade facilitating vector.

C. Discriminatory regulatory conduct: how to assess 'likeness'

I. The standard of 'likeness' in GATS non-discrimination

The Appellate Body illustrated its approach to the 'breadth' of likeness by stating that the 'concept of "likeness" is a relative one that evokes the image of an accordion', the breadth of which 'must be determined by the particular provision in which the term "like" is encountered as well as by the context and the circumstances that prevail in any given case to which that provision may apply'.[30] The same approach holds true for 'likeness' in GATS. Given the similarities in the non-discrimination provisions of the GATT and the GATS in terms of purpose and structure, it is helpful to define the theoretical breadth of GATS 'likeness' on the basis of the standards developed under GATT.

NT under GATT in regard to *tax measures* distinguishes between a narrow standard of 'likeness', requiring that the products share most physical characteristics (Article III:2, first sentence), and a broad standard of 'directly competitive or substitutable' products, focusing on the

30 Appellate Body Report, *Japan – Alcoholic Beverages II*, pp. 21–23.

competitive relationship in the marketplace (Article III:2, second sentence). In the case that the products are physically identical, even the slightest difference in taxation results in a NT violation. In contrast, if the products are 'only' competitive or substitutable, the difference in taxation must meet a higher threshold ('not similarly taxed') plus the tax measure must be designed 'so as to afford protection'. With regard to the *regulatory measures* of Article III:4, the Appellate Body carefully avoided defining the standard of 'likeness' in light of the two standards under paragraph II.[31] Yet it is argued here that the appropriate breadth for 'like products' under Article III:4 is identical to the standard of 'directly competitive or substitutable' under Article III:2, second sentence.[32]

In order to decide whether these standards can be transposed to GATS NT, it is necessary to determine the differences between the two provisions:[33]

- Under GATT NT, all products are covered, regardless of whether they are subject to tariff bindings. In contrast, GATS NT only applies to services for which a Member has made explicit commitments under its schedule.
- One of the prime goals of GATT NT is the protection of tariff concessions by prohibiting discriminatory internal measures. However, services are in general not subject to tariffs. Hence, GATS NT primarily serves as a broad and general prohibition of discriminatory regulations, similarly to the GATT NT obligations with regard to unbound products that are not subject to tariff concessions.
- Unlike GATT NT, Article XVII GATS stipulates only one standard of service–supplier relationship, namely the one of 'likeness'. At the same time GATS NT neither distinguishes between taxes and regulatory measures, nor does it provide different intensities of less favourable treatment. Article XVII very broadly applies to 'all measures affecting the supply of services'.
- Finally, GATS NT specifically applies to the service and the supplier, whereas GATT NT only applies to the product, not to the producer.

31 Appellate Body Report, *EC – Asbestos*, para. 99.

32 Similarly M. Bronckers and N. McNeils, 'Rethinking the "Like Product" Definition', in T. Cottier *et al.* (eds.), *Regulatory Barriers and the Principle of Non-Discrimination in World Trade Law* (University of Michigan Press, 2000), p. 373.

33 See also M. Cossy, 'Some Thoughts on the Concept of "Likeness" in the GATS', in M. Panizzon *et al.* (eds.), *GATS and the Regulation of International Trade in Services* (Cambridge University Press, 2008), pp. 328–29.

Despite these differences between GATT and GATS NT, it is argued here that the broad market-based standard of 'directly competitive or substitutable' is directly transferable to NT in services for the following reasons:[34]

- The negotiating history shows that earlier drafts referred to 'treatment "no less favourable" than that accorded domestic services [or service suppliers] *in the same market*...]',[35] not applying to the concept of 'likeness' at all. Nothing in the negotiating history of the GATS suggests that the reason for the change in the wording was to depart from the market-based approach.
- GATS Article XVII:2 explicitly states that 'different treatment shall be considered to be less favourable if it modifies the conditions of competition'. It follows that the 'likeness' analysis primarily focuses on the question of competitive relationship in a given marketplace.
- Finally, an overly intrusive application of GATS rules on non-discrimination by means of a broad standard for 'likeness' is prevented because Members may schedule limitations and justify discriminatory measures for reasons of public order (Article XIV(a) GATS).[36]

A comparative analysis of GATT and GATS is more difficult for MFN, given that the concept of 'like products' of Article I GATT has not been subject to a systemic interpretation under GATT/WTO jurisprudence comparable to that for Article III. However, Hudec convincingly argued that a broad 'like product' standard should apply with regard to internal measures, while a narrower standard may be appropriate for border measures.[37] Since services trade is restricted predominantly by internal measures, the same broad market-based standard should apply for MFN under GATS. Moreover, there is no apparent reason why the standard for 'likeness' under MFN should differ from the standard established above for NT.

34 Similarly A. Mattoo, 'National Treatment in the GATS' (1997) 31 *Journal of World Trade* 107, 127.

35 Group of Negotiations on Services, Report to the Trade Negotiations Committee meeting at Ministerial level, December 1988, MTN.GNS/21, 25 November 1988, para 11 (emphasis added).

36 On order exception see N. F. Diebold, 'The Morals and Order Exceptions in WTO Law' (2008) 11 *Journal of International Economic Law* 43, 48 ff.

37 R. E. Hudec, '"Like Product": The Differences in Meaning in GATT Articles I and III', in T. Cottier *et al.* (eds.), *Regulatory Barriers and the Principle of Non-Discrimination in World Trade Law* (University of Michigan Press, 2000), p. 108.

II. *The supplier–service relationship*

In the only two cases pertaining to 'likeness' in GATS, the Panels found that to the extent suppliers provide like services, they are like suppliers,[38] meaning that no supplier-based factors can be taken into consideration for the 'likeness' analysis. However, this interpretation should not be given the force of an authoritative precedent for the following reasons:

- In neither case was 'likeness' contested by the parties and thus it did not require a thorough analysis; the Appellate Body has not yet ruled on this issue. Moreover, in neither case did the measure discriminate on the basis of supplier characteristics.
- The Panels' reasoning is neither supported by the text of the provision nor by the negotiating history. In fact, an earlier draft was formulated exactly along the lines of the Panels' reasoning: 'each Party shall accord . . . to services and service providers of any other Party, treatment no less favourable than that it accords to like services and *providers of like services* of any other country.'[39]
- It is likely that supplier characteristics affect consumer behaviour, a reason why they are relevant to the guiding principle of competitive relationship and substitutability.

Considering that supplier-based and service-based factors may be considered under the 'likeness' analysis, the question arises whether in a specific case 'likeness' must be established between the services, the suppliers, or both.[40] A textual interpretation allows for three different tests:

Cumulative test (two separate and cumulative elements): The cumulative test (see Figure 6.3) requires that one and the same measure treats

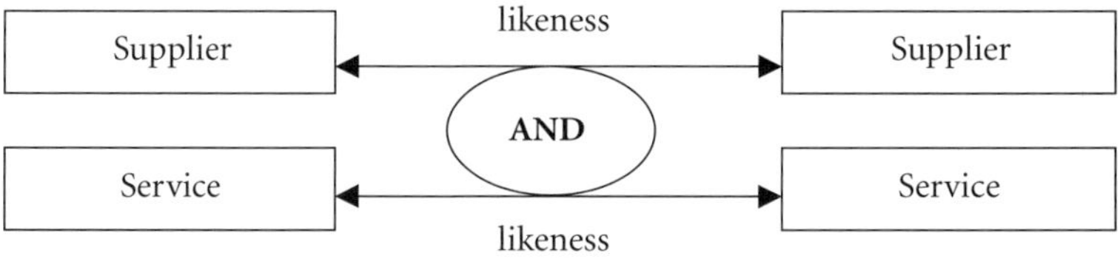

Figure 6.3 Cumulative test of likeness.

38 Panel Reports, *EC – Bananas III*, paras 7.322, 7.346; *Canada – Autos*, para. 10.248.

39 Draft Final Act Embodying the Results of the Uruguay Round of Multilateral Trade Negotiations, MTN.TNC/W/35/Rev.1, 3 December 1990, draft Articles II and XVII (emphasis added).

40 Similarly but less nuanced M. Krajewski, *National Regulation and Trade Liberalization in Services* (Kluwer Law International, 2005), pp. 105–106.

the foreign service *and* the foreign supplier less favourably than the like domestic service *and* the like domestic supplier. Accordingly, likeness must be demonstrated between both suppliers and services, which would considerably restrict the scope of non-discrimination.

Alternative test (two separate and alternative elements): In contrast to the cumulative test, the alternative test (see Figure 6.4) allows for a breach of non-discrimination if the measure *either* treats imported services less favourably than like domestic services *or* if it treats foreign suppliers less favourably than like domestic suppliers. Accordingly, the complainant only needs to demonstrate 'likeness' between either of the two.

The problem with this approach is that it requires the adjudicating bodies to determine whether the suppliers or the services must be like in a given case. Under a *combined approach*, the adjudicating bodies would analyse firstly, whether there is no less favourable treatment between like services and, secondly, whether there is no less favourable treatment between like suppliers. A positive answer to either of the two questions would result in a violation of GATS rules on non-discrimination. Under the *disjunctive approach*, WTO adjudicating bodies limit their scrutiny to either the service or the supplier, which requires determining which of the two is relevant in a given case. Possible criteria could be (i) discretion of the complainant, (ii) addressee of the regulation in question, or (iii) mode of supply. However, under all these criteria the solution is random and not supported by the guiding principle of competitive relationship.

Merged test (one merged element): The merged test (see Figure 6.5) requires considering both supplier-related and services-based factors in order to determine the competitive relationship as a whole.

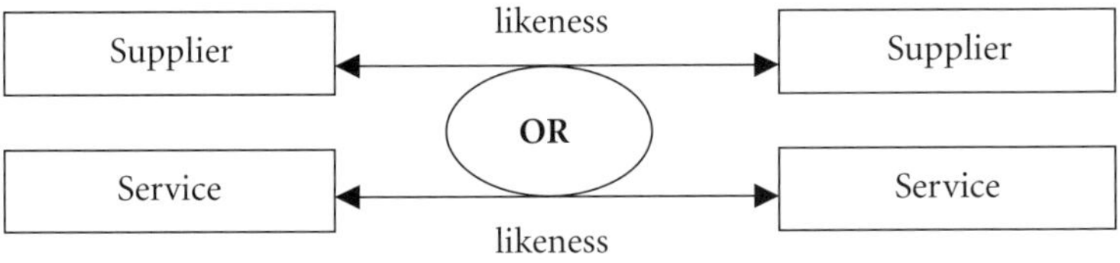

Figure 6.4 Alternative test of likeness.

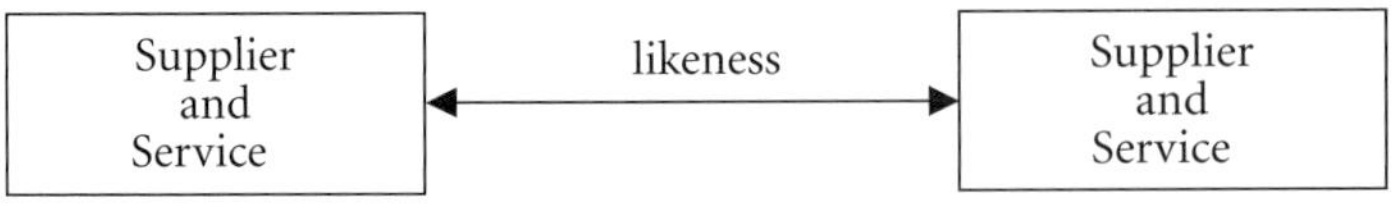

Figure 6.5 Merged test of likeness.

When comparing the three possible interpretations, the merged test prevails as it has numerous advantages over the cumulative and the alternative tests.[41]

- Unlike the cumulative test, it does not unduly restrict the scope of the GATS rules on non-discrimination.
- The alternative test raises additional interpretative questions, namely whether it follows a combined or disjunctive approach and, if the latter, which criterion serves to determine the correct comparative objects.

Only the merged test truly accounts for the guiding principle of competitive relationship, in that it allows the analysis of whether the *foreign supplier and its service* is substitutable with the *domestic supplier and its service.*

III. A Comparative approach to the interpretation of 'likeness' in GATS

In order to develop a test for 'likeness' in GATS, a comparative approach is highly informative. A first comparison is with *other non-discrimination obligations.* A second comparison requires consideration of related concepts *beyond non-discrimination.*

Non-discrimination: The most obvious approach is to transpose the GATT-framework from Border Tax Adjustments – which is designed to assess the competitive relationship – to GATS.[42] Another informative comparison is to consider the concept of 'like circumstances' as it applies, for instance, in non-discrimination clauses pertaining to NAFTA[43] and BITs.[44] However, owing to the different interpretations given to the element of 'less favourable treatment' and the different general exception

41 Similarly W. Zdouc, *Legal Problems Arising under the General Agreement on Trade in Services* (Difo-Druck, 2002), p. 167.

42 Cossy, 'Some Thoughts on the Concept of "Likeness" in the GATS', above note 33, pp. 332 ff.

43 Articles 1202, 1203 (services) and 1102, 1103 (investment) NAFTA; see in particular NAFTA Arbitral Panel Report, *In the Matter of Cross-Border Trucking Services*, USA-MEX-98–2008-01 (Feb. 6, 2001), paras. 246 ff.

44 N. DiMascio and J. Pauwelyn, 'Nondiscrimination in Trade and Investment Treaties: Worlds Apart or Two Sides of the Same Coin?' (2008) 102 *American Journal of International Law* 48, 66 ff; see also section D below. Interestingly, the concept of 'like circumstances' was considered in an early draft of GATS, see Group of Negotiations on Services, Draft on Multilateral Framework for Trade in Services, MTN.GNS/35, 23 July 1990, draft Article on MFN and NT.

clauses in the agreements, the concept of 'like circumstances' – usually taking into account the purpose of a measure – may not be transposed directly to the concept of 'likeness' in GATS.

Market definition: A number of commentators support the argument that 'likeness' in trade should be analysed in accordance with the concept of market definition as it applies in competition law,[45] focusing on demand substitutability. This approach is particularly appropriate with regard to GATS. First, GATS Article XVII:2 specifically refers to 'conditions of competition', thus allowing a market definition analysis. Second, the market definition approach does not have the same deficiencies in the context of services as the Border Tax Adjustments framework. Finally, market definition would resolve the problem related to the service–supplier relationship referred to above.

D. Building coherence in international disciplines on investment in services

I. Introduction

In the eyes of many, the lack of a comprehensive set of multilateral disciplines constitutes an important source of fragmentation in international economic law. International rules governing investment in service industries are spread over 2,600 BITs and more than 100 PTAs featuring investment disciplines applicable to services.[46] The above rules are complemented by those found in the GATS, whose disciplines on 'commercial presence' overlap with those found in BITs and PTAs.

To the extent that GATS Article V allows PTAs to deviate from GATS obligations under certain conditions, the disciplines of PTAs, in principle, do not bring about inconsistencies with WTO rules. The same cannot be said about BITs. Therefore, where BITs grant rights to investors and their investments which conflict with the regulatory space afforded to governments under the WTO agreements, or vice versa, legal certainty is diminished, impairing the investment climate of the host countries and creating the grounds for possible legal challenges. The question remains whether, and to what extent, bilateral disciplines on foreign investment overlap with multilateral rules on commercial presence.

45 See e.g. J. B. Goco, 'Non-Discrimination, "Likeness", and Market Definition in World Trade Organization Jurisprudence' (2006) 40 *Journal of World Trade* 315, 329 ff.

46 UNCTAD, 'Recent Developments in International Investment Agreements' (2008) IIA Monitor No. 2, 8–9.

II. *Substantial disciplines on investment in services*

BIT disciplines overlap with GATS provisions insofar as both apply to 'measures by Members *affecting* trade in services'.[47] Indeed, since the coverage of BITs tends to be broader, applying as it does to portfolio investment and a host of tangible and intangible assets as well as to foreign direct investment, it might be difficult to find measures covered under Mode 3 commitments (commercial presence) of the GATS that are not captured by such instruments.[48]

As summarised in Box 6.1, each of the substantive obligations found at the bilateral level relates to some extent to provisions found in the WTO-GATS context. The case of the MFN and NT obligations provides an example of provisions common to both types of agreements, yet not in a completely equal manner. While the fair and equitable treatment (FET) obligation featured in investment treaties finds no parallel provision under WTO agreements, other GATS provisions can still be seen as affirming obligations embodied in such a provision.[49]

1. MFN and NT

Investment agreements, like the GATS, include obligations on MFN and NT. Through these provisions, the host country undertakes not to discriminate in favour of its own investors and investments, or those from any third country. The scope of these two provisions in investment treaties is broader than that in GATS, since they both apply to a broader set of investments subject to BIT disciplines.[50] However, as regards the foreign direct investments that are covered by both BITs and the GATS (where commitments are scheduled in the case of NT), the operation of the MFN and NT obligations follows the same rationale. Indeed, the object and purpose of preventing discrimination of the MFN and NT obligations has been interpreted in an analogous manner by both WTO and investor–state arbitral panels.[51]

47 R. Adlung and M. Molinuevo, 'Bilateralism in Services Trade: Is there Fire Behind the (BIT-)Smoke?' (2008) 11(2) *Journal of International Economic Law* 369–370.

48 P. Sauvé, 'Qs and As on Trade, Investment and the WTO' (1997) 31(8) *Journal of World Trade* 63–65.

49 For a general review of WTO disciplines on foreign investment, see P. Gugler and V. Tomsik, 'A Comparison of the Provisions Affecting Investment in the Existing WTO Obligations', NCCR Working Paper No. 15, August 2006.

50 UNCTAD, 'Scope and Definition', UNCTAD Series on Issues in International Investment Agreements (United Nations, 1999), pp. 18–23.

51 See Panel Report, *EC – Bananas III*, para. 7.302, and, inter alia, *Feldman* v. *Mexico*, ICSID Case No. ARB(AF)/99/1 (NAFTA) (16 December 2002), para. 181.

Nonetheless, some differences remain when it comes to applying these principles to a specific case. For instance, the WTO Appellate Body has opined that an analysis of the motivations behind a government's decision to take a certain measure – the so-called 'aims and effects test' – is not relevant in determining whether that measure is inconsistent with GATS Articles II and XVII.[52] On the other hand, arbitral panels have resorted to such analysis in assessing compliance with the NT obligation found in the investment chapter of the NAFTA.[53]

The substance of MFN and NT obligations, both being *comparative* treatment standards, depends on the groups or categories of investors and service suppliers that are to be compared. The 'standard of comparison' limits the scope of the MFN and NT provisions by ensuring that such obligations deal with the treatment afforded to essentially comparable subjects – i.e. that they do not compare 'apples to oranges'.[54]

However, the standard of comparison between the GATS and investment agreements is not always identical. The GATS requires a comparison between 'like services and service suppliers' for the MFN and NT obligations to apply.[55] For their part, a number of investment treaties apply the MFN and NT provisions to investors that are in 'like circumstances' or 'like situations'. Moreover, many investment agreements – especially BITs promoted by European countries and most developing countries – set no explicit standard of comparison at all.[56] These seemingly small textual differences may bring about important differences in the scope of the provisions. For example, while the term 'like circumstances' has been interpreted in arbitral decisions similarly to the concept of 'like services and service suppliers' found in the GATS,[57] the phrase 'like situations'

52 Appellate Body Report, *EC – Bananas III*, para. 241.

53 In that sense, the arbitral panel in the Methanex case stated that 'In order to sustain its claim under Article 1102(3), Methanex must demonstrate, cumulatively, that California intended to favour domestic investors by discriminating against foreign investors': *Methanex* v. *United States*, Final Award (3 August 2005), para. 12. See also *Feldman* v. *Mexico*, ICSID Case No. ARB(AF)/99/1 (NAFTA) (16 December 2002), para. 183, and *S.D. Myers, Inc.* v. *Canada*, First Partial Award (13 November 2000) paras. 252–255.

54 T. Weiler, 'Saving Oscar Chin: Non-Discrimination in International Investment Law', in T. Weiler (ed.), *International Investment Law and Arbitration* (London: Cameron May, 2005), p. 561.

55 For a comprehensive analysis of the standard of comparison in the GATS, see Section C above.

56 UNCTAD, 'National Treatment', UNCTAD Series on Issues in International Investment Agreements (United Nations, 1999), pp. 33–34.

57 In the view of the United States, the terms 'like circumstances' which appears in its BITs and the concept of 'likeness' in the GATS do not differ in scope. See statement by the

used in some older BITs concluded by the United Sates has been given a scope that seems to go beyond that of the GATS by allowing comparisons of investors in different economic sectors.[58]

2. Fair and equitable treatment and domestic regulation obligations

In addition to the MFN and NT obligations, investment agreements typically feature a provision that is aimed to ensure a certain level of 'good' treatment to be granted by domestic authorities to foreign investors and their investments – independently of the treatment they afford to their own or other investors and investments. Such an FET obligation has no direct equivalent at the multilateral level under the GATS.

The absence of a provision on FET, however, does not imply that the WTO offers no rights in areas covered by such a principle. The FET provision embodies obligations pertaining to areas such as regulatory transparency, procedural fairness and due process, the absence of discriminatory conduct as well as good faith in the administration of domestic regulations.[59] These are all areas largely covered by the GATS. Multilateral rules on transparency and domestic regulation (Articles III and VI of GATS) provide substantial obligations that effectively ensure a level of treatment comparable to that required under the FET principle – as detailed in Table 6.1.

However, the specific requirements of the FET principle remain elusive and can only be determined on a case-by-case basis. GATS Articles III and VI have not so far been tested in a WTO dispute, leaving unanswered a number of questions regarding the precise meaning of GATS obligations. Furthermore, while the FET principle is a general obligation in investment agreements, Articles III and VI of GATS are in part subject to the scheduling of specific commitments. Such differences in sectoral coverage imply that situations covered by the FET principle under investment agreements may not necessarily fall under the corresponding GATS provisions, and vice versa. This may then heighten the risk of inconsistencies between investment agreements and GATS.

United States in WTO, *Report of the Meeting held on 19 March 2002*, para. 29. See also, S. Murphy, 'US Interpretation of Core NAFTA Investment Standards' (2001) 95 *American Journal of International Law* 882.

58 Adlung and Molinuevo, above note 47, p. 384. *Occidental Exploration and Production Company* v. *Ecuador*, Final Award (1 July 2004) paras. 168, 173 and 176–178.

59 C. Schreuer, 'Fair and Equitable Treatment in Arbitral Practice' (2005) 6 *Journal of World Investment & Trade* 357–386.

Table 6.1 *Main disciplines: bilateral investment treaties versus the GATS*

Bilateral investment treaties (BITS)	Potential equivalent under the GATS	Comments
Most-favoured nation (MFN) treatment	Art. II (MFN)	A number of BITs extend MFN obligation to benefits granted under preferential trade agreements.
National treatment (NT)	Art. XVII (NT)^{SC} Art. XVI:2(e)–(f) (joint venture requirements, foreign equity ceilings)^{SC}	Scope of BIT obligation depends on the standard of 'likeness' used to compare foreign and domestic investors.
Fair and equitable treatment		
Transparency	Art. III:1 (domestic publication) Art. III.3 (notification to WTO)^{CON} Art. IV:2 (contact points for suppliers)	Elements of fair and equitable treatment are dispersed over various GATS provisions.
Procedural fairness and due process	Art. VI:1 (reasonable, objective & impartial administration of measures)^{CON} Art. VI:2 (access to judicial mechanisms) Art. VI:5 (domestic regulatory disciplines)^{CON}	Substantial coverage may not differ significantly.
Absence of arbitrary or discriminatory conduct	Art. VI:1 (reasonable, objective & impartial administration of measures)^{CON}	
Good faith	Art. VI:5 (domestic regulatory disciplines)^{CON}	
Free transfer of funds	Art. XI:1 (current transactions)^{CON} Arts. XI:2, XVII (capital transactions)^{SC} footnote 8 to Art. XVI (capital transfers that are an essential part of a service)^{SC}	No significant differences if sectors have been scheduled under the GATS without relevant limitations.
Expropriation		
Due process	Art. VI:1 (reasonable, objective and impartial administration of measures)^{CON} Art. VI:2 (access to judicial mechanisms)	GATS Art. XVI may capture expropriations that limit the number of service suppliers. However, BIT disciplines seem to be stronger in general.

Compensation	No direct equivalent. Possibly captured by Art. XVII (NT)[SC] and Art. VI:1 (reasonable, objective & impartial administration of measures)[CON]	
Non-discrimination	Art. VI:1 (reasonable, objective & impartial administration of measures)[CON] Art. XVII (NT)[SC]	
Public purpose requirement	Art. XIV (exception for measures necessary to maintain public order)	
Absence of performance requirements	Art. XVII (NT)[SC] Possibly Art. XVI:2(b) (MA)[SC]	
Government procurement NT for foreign companies	None. Arts. II, XVI, XVII are not applicable. However, some 30 WTO Members have assumed obligations under the 'Understanding on Commitments in Financial Services'	BIT disciplines are not 'multilateralised' via GATS Art. II.
Dispute settlement		
State-to-state	Art. XXIII (dispute settlement) WTO Dispute Settlement Understanding	
Investor–State	None	

Note: Unlike the GATS, the coverage of investment treaties extends to minority investments as well.

[CON] Conditional on existence of specific commitments.

[SC] According to the terms, conditions and qualifications provided for in the schedule of specific commitments.

Source: R. Adlung and M. Molinuevo,'Bilateralism in Services Trade: Is there Fire behind the (BIT-)smoke?' (2008) 11(2) *Journal of International Economic Law* 377–378.

III. *Defragmenting international economic rules through coherent interpretation*

Fragmentation in international disciplines on investment in services, as described above, is here to stay. No substitute for the current patchwork of international investment disciplines is likely to appear over the horizon for the foreseeable future.[60] However, a comprehensive multilateral regime for investment may ultimately not be necessary, desirable, or politically feasible.

The possible inconsistencies arising from the overlap of BITs and multilateral disciplines on services could just as easily be tackled on a case-by-case basis through arbitral interpretation. Indeed, as discussed above, bilateral and multilateral agreements tend to pursue similar goals, and possible conflicts between their provisions tend to stem more from dissimilar wording and legal context than from differences in the substantive legal nature of the obligations. The legal challenges posed by bilateral and multilateral provisions are found in the case-by-case application of such rules, rather than in the principles per se.

For this reason, an important tool for promoting greater coherence in the international framework already exists as a result of the work on dispute resolution carried out in the WTO and through investment arbitration. WTO adjudicatory bodies and investment arbitral panels may contribute greatly to a more coherent system of investment rule-making by interpreting multilateral or bilateral disciplines, taking due account of the rules, principles and intent deriving from the other agreements. The WTO Appellate Body has arguably set the scene for fostering coherence in the goods trade context by noting that its rules are 'not to be read in clinical isolation from public international law'.[61]

WTO and investment arbitral tribunals can go one step further by recognising the overlap between the GATS and BITs, each striving to give their principles a coherent meaning, rather than attempting to exacerbate the differences between the two legal systems. Adjudicatory panels may

60 See on this P. Gugler and J. Chaisse, 'Foreign Investment Issues and WTO law: Dealing with Fragmentation while Waiting for a Multilateral Framework', in J. Chaisse and T. Balmelli (eds.), *Essays on the Future of the World Trade Organization* (Geneva: Editions Interuniversitaires Suisses, 2008), pp. 135–171; also A. Beviglia-Zampetti and P. Sauvé, 'International Investment', in A. Sykes and A. Guzman (eds.), *Research Handbook in International Economic Law* (London: Edward Elgar, 2007), pp. 211–270; P. Sauvé, 'Multilateral Rules on Investment: Is Forward Movement Possible?' (2006) 9 *Journal of International Economic Law* 325–355.

61 Appellate Body Report, *US – Gasoline*, 17.

prove that, despite the complex web of bilateral and multilateral rules, a coherent framework for investment in services is within reach – one case at a time.

E. Trade and labour migration agreements: a tale of two speeds

I. Introduction

Most international migration is labour-related, as half of the world's 200 million international migrants in 2005 were economically active.[62] Most economic migration is temporary with between 20 and 50 per cent of immigrants leaving within five years of arriving in a country.[63] Migration for work is accelerating, as trade leads to lower transportation and communication costs and economies globalise. In Spain, the proportion of foreign workers in the labour force rose from 8 to almost 12 per cent between 2005 and 2007 and accounted for about half of the expansion in the active population. In France, levels rose up to 19 per cent between 2004 and 2006.[64] International responsibility for migratory flows is diffuse and incoherently organised. A split treaty landscape substitutes for the 'missing regime of international labour migration'.[65] Bilateral migration agreements regulate migratory flows while trade agreements, including the WTO's GATS, are designed to progressively liberalise the temporary movement of workers. Both sets of agreements – trade and non-trade – incidental to migration exist at all three levels of 'global migration governance', multilateral, regional and national.[66]

II. GATS Mode 4

At the international level, Mode 4 of the GATS represents one of the very few collective action responses in the area of temporary labour migration.

62 GCIM, Migration at a Glance, 2005, p. 4

63 OECD, World Migration Outlook, 2008.

64 OECD, International Migration Outlook, 2008, Country Reports Spain and France.

65 J. F. Hollifield, 'Migration and the "New" International Order: The Missing Regime', in B. Ghosh (ed.) *Managing Migration, Time for a New International Regime* (Oxford University Press, 2000), pp. 100–101; similarly, L. Pritchett, *Let their People Come, Breaking the Gridlock on International Labor Mobility* (Washington, DC: Center for Global Development, 2006).

66 A. Betts and K. Nicolaidis, 'The Trade and Migration Linkage: GATS Mode IV', memo prepared for the Global Trade Ethics Conference, presented at Princeton University, 19 Februrary 2009.

To the extent to which WTO Members have made commitments in Mode 4, the GATS liberalises the temporary movement of natural persons as service suppliers. Levels of liberalisation obtained for Mode 4 of the GATS are rather low and account for only 0–4 per cent of all GATS commitments to date. Mode 4 trade is estimated to account for between 1 and 2 per cent of world services trade, as compared to 39 per cent of services delivered via Modes 1 and 2 (cross-border supply and consumption abroad) and close to 60 per cent for Mode 3 trade (commercial presence or investment-related trade in services).[67] Still, recent figures reveal a near doubling of the share of Mode 4 in world services trade,[68] quasi 'matching' the forecasted doubling of welfare gains predicted to arise from liberalising temporary movement of persons.[69] The trend towards deeper and broader openings in Mode 4 could, theoretically, be expected to continue, not least in light of demographic transitions, the 'global hunt' for talents in OECD countries and in emerging countries, and the equally buoyant skill supply by developing countries.[70] To the disadvantage of developing and least developed countries, which are facing poverty challenges linked with surplus labour in low skills, Mode 4 commitments predominantly target the highly-skilled professionals. WTO Members are more reluctant to offer market access and NT when it comes to persons, who are non-nationals.[71] The liberalisation bias of GATS and its replicas in PTAs, fall short of offering tangible answers to the regulatory challenges posed by the risks associated with labour migration. The weak regulation of migratory flows in the international framework is the exception rather than the rule. The particularity of the GATS scheduling structure, the conditional nature of its NT obligation and the immigration law caveat of the Annex on Movement of Natural Persons Supplying

67 A. Maurer and P. Chauvet, 'The Magnitude of Flows of Global Trade in Services', in B. Hoekman, A. Mattoo and P. English (eds.) *Development, Trade and the WTO, A Handbook* (Washington, DC, World Bank, 2002), pp. 235–246.

68 M. Cali, 'Liberalizing Mode 4 Trade: What Impact on Exporting Countries', Presentation at the WTO Symposium, Mode 4 of the GATS: Taking Stock and Moving Forward, 22–23 September 2008.

69 The World Bank's Global Economic Prospects of 2006 reports that with a 3% increase in labour mobility, world income would be doubled (US$ 356 million).

70 D. Kapur and J. McHale, *Give us Your Best and Your Brightest: The Global Hunt for Talent and Its Impact on the Developing World* (Washington, DC: Center for Global Development, 2005).

71 A. Carzaniga, 'A Warmer Welcome? Access for Natural Persons under Preferential Trade Agreements', in J. A. Marchetti, and M. Roy (eds.), *Opening Markets for Trade in Services Countries and Sectors in Bilateral and WTO Negotiations* (Cambridge University Press, 2009), p. 500.

Services under the Agreement (Annex on MONP) is to create an asymmetric allocation of risk management, whereby industrialised, labour-receiving Members continue to have a free hand to contain what domestic-worker coalitions perceive as negative effects of labour migration: job displacement and downwards wage pressures on domestic workers. On the other hand, the current commitments structure of GATS is inadequately tailored to address the skill depletion of migrant source countries, overstays, unenforced returns, exploitation, smuggling and human trafficking.[72]

1. Immigration law caveat of the Annex on MONP

Pursuant to the Annex on MONP immigration law caveat Members retain almost full sovereignty over visa and work permit policies and are free to apply visa requirements selectively. Unless such visa and work permit requirements are applied in a way that nullifies or impairs the benefits under a specific GATS commitment, a Member could choose to discriminate between Members that cooperate on enforcing readmissions and other Members who refuse to do so.

The rationale for exempting visa procedures from the scope of GATS disciplines on domestic regulation under Article VI:4 stems from the fact that visa procedures provide the right to *enter* a labour or employment market – which, Members have agreed, lies outside the scope of GATS. Visa procedures do not grant the right to *supply* a service.[73] Only if the visa or work permit requirements and/or authorisation procedures are so cumbersome as to constitute a barrier to the right to supply a service, e.g. causing undue delays, could they be considered incidental to the issuance of a licence or work permit and thereby fall under the scope of Articles VI:1, VI:4 or VI:6 of GATS.

The lack of a uniform classification system for service provider categories, the ambiguity of Mode 4 coverage (employee–employer relationship) and the caveat exacerbate the mismatch between national visa and service provider categories.[74] This lack of harmonisation chills the predictability of scheduled commitments.[75] While the Annex on MONP

72 K. Bravo, 'Free Labor! A Labor Liberalization Solution to the Modern Traffic in Humans' (2009) 18 *Transnational Law & Contemporary Problems* 545.

73 Delimatsis, above note 8, p. 198.

74 M. Panizzon, 'Trade and Labor Migration: GATS Mode 4 and Migration Agreements', Friedrich-Ebert-Stiftung, Geneva, Occasional Paper Series, No. 47, 2010.

75 R. Grynberg and V. Qalo, 'Migration and the World Trade Organization' (2007) 41 *Journal of World Trade* 751–782.

exempts the WTO from any responsibility with respect to labour migration, carving out the possibility of a multilateral standard on visa and work permits strips GATS of any inherent mandate to mitigate migratory risks multilaterally.

2. What can GATS Mode 4 learn from new-generation bilateral agreements on the joint regulation of migratory flows?

Absent a coherent architecture of multilateral norms and disciplines, a spaghetti bowl of overlapping provisions has arisen. A new interface emerges in this context between trade agreements (Mode 4 of GATS, labour mobility provisions found in PTAs) and the emerging bilateral migration agreements, spearheaded by France, Spain and Italy with the desire to better manage Eurafrican migratory flows. Bilateral migration agreements cover the regulatory gap left unaddressed by trade agreements.[76]

Since the late 1990s, France, Italy, Spain and Switzerland, which had previously been tolerating migrant overstays and unenforced readmissions,[77] have all sought to tighten controls over temporary migration via immigration law reforms. In this context, the web of national and EU-level readmission agreements was intensified,[78] and the new BMMAs were designed.

To implement such a policy shift, however, host countries have had little choice but to offer quid-pro-quos in exchange for securing source-country cooperation in readmitting migrants who have entered irregularly or overstayed. The preferred tools to reward source-country cooperation, are visa relaxations, development aid and, more controversially, preferential labour market access quotas.[79] Direct recruitment of foreign workers by host country firms is a type of labour mobility which the new bilateral agreements, such as Spain's cooperation agreements on migration, may opt for in order for such preferential recruitment to fall outside the scope of GATS.

76 Carzaniga, note 71 above, p. 500.

77 For Switzerland, see C. De Matos and D. Efionayi-Mäder, 'Bestandesaufnahme von Migrationspartnerschaften in der Schweiz', in IOM Bern (ed.), *Migrationspartnerschaften: Eine Bestandesaufnahme* (IOM Bern, 3rd edn, 2007), p. 36.

78 J.-P. Cassarino, 'Informalising Readmission Agreements in the EU Neighbourhood' (2007) 42 *The International Spectator* 179–196.

79 M. Panizzon, 'Labour Mobility: A Win-win-win Model for Trade and Development: The Case of Senegal', NCCR Working Paper No. 7, June 2008.

III. From request-driven Doha deadlock to a redesigned GATS Mode 4 horizontal schedule

Industrialised countries, which were instrumental in designing the GATS Annex on MONP and its non-interference with domestic immigration law, are paradoxically today the ones bemoaning the lack of 'comfort' stemming from GATS commitments in mitigating migratory risks.[80] To date, these countries have failed to make meaningful offers in response to the requests for more GATS Mode 4 commitments in the sectors and worker categories of interest to developing and least developed countries. Developing countries share some of the blame for the Doha Round's unfulfilled promise, as these countries failed to offer cross-modal or cross-sectoral trade-offs in return for their Mode 4 requests.

1. Regulatory source country obligations on return and reliability of workforce?

The idea of inscribing 'regulatory' *source country* obligations on readmission, voluntary and assisted return and employability of workers into a host country's GATS schedule has been circulating among academics.[81] The suggestion is to replicate, at the multilateral level, the comprehensive packaging of issues as varied as labour mobility, irregular migration, development and migration, with which bilateral migration agreements in their second-generation templates had successfully experimented. Also, the EU's 'global approach on migration'[82] and the concept of 'shared responsibility' propagated by the Global Commission on International Migration,[83] the International Agenda on Migration Management[84] and

80 T. Broude, 'The WTO/GATS Mode 4, International Labour Migration Regimes and Global Justice', Research Paper No. 7–07, May 2007, The Hebrew University of Jerusalem, Faculty of Law, pp. 25–26.

81 Inter alia, Chanda has proposed that these be inscribed into the *additional commitments* column of a host country's schedule via Article XVIII of GATS. See R. Chanda, 'Low-skilled Workers and Bilateral, Regional, and Unilateral Initiatives, Lessons for the GATS Mode 4 Negotiations and Other Agreements', United Nations Development Programme (UNDP) Report, 2008, p. 7.

82 Communication from the Commission to the Council and the European Parliament, 'The Global Approach to Migration one year on: Towards a comprehensive European migration policy', Brussels, 30.11.2006, COM(2006) 735 final.

83 Global Commission on International Migration (GCIM), Final Report, October 2005.

84 IOM Geneva and Swiss Federal Office for Migration, *International Agenda for Migration Management,* p. 29.

Table 6.2 *Model schedule of a horizontal GATS Mode 4 commitment including development-friendly recruitment and guarantees of return*

Sector or sub-sector	Limitations on market access	Limitations on national treatment	Additional commitments
All sectors included in this schedule, all modes	4) unbound, except for measures concerning the entry, temporary stay and return of natural persons, who fall under one of the following categories and on the condition that foreign service suppliers in country X are subject to authorisations (work and residency permit), subject to measures fixing overall number of work permits allocated based on the conclusion of a bilateral migration agreement. For professions set out below, a tri-partite committee (host, source country and immigration association) will consult on scarcity of labour in host country and risk of skill depletion in source country before approving temporary stay abroad.	4) unbound except for measures concerning the categories of natural persons referred to in the market access column, **subject to limitations of national immigration laws** (this immigration law then provides that for foreign service providers a bilateral agreement must be signed) Alternative: **subject to the following limitations and conditions**: 1. **Country Y (source country)** provides guarantee of return and reintegration of TMNP by signing onto a bilateral migration agreement or otherwise. 2. **Firm employing** foreign service provider must sign an MOU and cooperate with authorities of country X [host country] in guaranteeing return. 3. **Foreign service provider** in following sectors (construction, tourism, catering) must be part of a co-development or voluntary and assisted return programme **in force** between country X and country Y.	4) The right to temporary entry of foreign service suppliers in the professions set out below and for the categories set out below is granted on the basis that the foreign service provider is part of a co-development programme or an assisted and voluntary return scheme is **in force** between country X and Y or **will be negotiated** between country X and Y.

the UN High Level Dialogue on Migration and Development,[85] stimulated WTO-GATS negotiators to think creatively about ways and means to increase the comfort levels of the host countries by scheduling regulatory source obligations, such as guarantees on the return of foreign workers once their services contracts are terminated. In this context, we suggest that Members make more creative use of the controversial, 'unbound, except for' formulation typically inscribed in the horizontal section of their GATS schedules. Mode 4 multilateral agreement (MA) commitments could be conditioned by inserting into *national* immigration laws a return obligation for the source country.[86] In addition, a Mode 4 commitment could multilateralise the trend initiated by France and Spain,[87] which is to offer a preferential MA quota on condition that a source country agrees to negotiate or conclude a bilateral (readmission) agreement ensuring the return of unauthorised temporary workers.[88]

Developing countries could seek a guarantee – via host country Mode 4 commitments – against the undue depletion of scarce highly-skilled human resources (e.g. medical doctors). A development-friendly (e.g. anti-brain drain) recruitment scheme would require a joint selection commission, consisting of host and source country representatives as well as a representative from an immigration association or from the International Organization for Migration (IOM). Its task would be to screen would-be service suppliers moving abroad under a Mode 4 commitment against the risk of skill depletion.

Arguably, the GATS, and its reliance on MFN treatment, undermines the relative success of newer-generation migration management agreements in controlling migratory flows. Firstly, the unconditional nature of the MFN obligation does *not offer sufficient flexibility* for Mode 4 to allow for tactical-issue linkages to be made between irregular and lawful labour migration. Yet, these are exactly the tools which make BMMAs today's preferred policy tool for managing lawful and irregular migration. Secondly, most of today's most successful BMMAs do not comply with Articles V and Vbis of the GATS. They would thus need to be

85 UN Resolution 61/208 International Migration and Development, adopted by the 61st UN General Assembly on 20 December 2006, UN Doc. A/RES/61/208 of 6 March 2007.

86 See Table 6.2.

87 France, loi n°2006–911 du 24 juillet 2006 relative à l'immigration et à l'intégration; Spain, Law 4/2000 (Ley orgánica or Ley de extranjería).

88 As unauthorised migrants are 'unlike' the temporarily moved service supplying natural persons falling under the purview of the GATS, this potential deviation from MFN does directly affect the market access of temporarily moved natural persons.

'waived' pursuant to Article XI:3 Marrakesh Agreement.[89] Thirdly, there is *too much flexibility* under the GATS scheduling approach not allowing the WTO to occupy the centre stage of an emerging multilateral governance of migration. Inherent flexibility in GATS, such as NT limitations, does little to limit the disproportionately high prevalence of wage and working conditions parity, prohibitive residency and equivalency requirements, relating to professional training, education and qualifications in Mode 4, which further erodes the value of Mode 4 commitments.[90] Such NT limitations exacerbate the divide between low- and high-skill economic migration. Industrialised countries can continue to discriminate de facto against low-skilled workers by protecting domestic workers from industrialised countries against Mode 4 temporary movement and so prevent labour-sending Members from reaping the full benefits of their comparative advantage in supplying services.

F. Concluding remarks

More than twenty years after the launch of the Uruguay Round, trade in services continues to rank among the most intractable subject matters in modern trade diplomacy. It is an area where fragmentation, whether of rule-making architectures or liberalisation outcomes typically defines the norm. Yet fragmentation is something one can live with and learn from. It may well represent a source of policy- and rule-making innovation able to inform future directions in multilateral rule-making (a process one could call 'infant industry' preferentialism) or offer alternative theatres of collective action able to yield outcomes superior to those on offer at the WTO (so-called 'subsidiary' preferentialism). Fragmentation, policy experimentation and cosmopolitanism in services trade regulation may thus not only define the norm but could actually be particularly welcome.

Such musings are in line with the overall directions our research has taken.[91] Our findings have confirmed that fragmentation in services trade regulation is pervasive and that, whether in policy design, institutions, legal architectures, approaches to the conduct of market opening negotiations or market access outcomes, it most likely represents a form of coherence in the design of workable rules in the services field.

89 LDC Group Request on Mode 4, JOB(06)/155, 24 May 2006.

90 Delimatsis, above note 6, p. 35.

91 P. Sauvé, 'Been There, not Yet Done That: Lessons and Challenges in Services Trade', in M. Panizzon, N. Pohl and P. Sauvé (eds.), *GATS and the Regulation of International Trade in Services* (Cambridge University Press, 2008), pp. 599–631.

Our research has also highlighted the iterative, mutual learning-by-doing, relationship characterising multilateral and preferential approaches to services trade regulation. There can be little doubt that a fair share of recent PTA activism in services can be traced to the frustration many governments have experienced over the slow pace of progress at the multilateral level. But much peripheral rule-making also originates in the quest to shape an emerging legal order and to do so in novel ways that move policy and open markets beyond WTO approaches, rules and architectures.

PTAs, including those governing trade in services, are not just reactions to the state of play at the WTO. They have their own *raison d'être*, and perhaps more so in services than in goods trade. This is so as domestic regulation represents the very currency of services negotiations and because of the greater ease with which regulatory convergence can be promoted and MFN leakage contained in the narrower confines of PTAs.

Our research has provided a useful sense of the scale of the liberalisation gap that now exists between the WTO and PTAs, a gap Members should be aiming to close post-DDA. Future research should focus on gauging the scope that exists for 'multilateralizing regionalism' and exploring the political economy of preference erosion in services trade.

Work on preferential approaches to services liberalisation has recalled how PTAs can serve as useful rule-making laboratories, affording Members space in which to experiment with – and create legal precedence on – issues not yet on the multilateral agenda or help pave the way for needed amendments to existing WTO disciplines or negotiated commitments. Among the topics analysed over the past four years, this is most vividly the case for labour mobility and investment rule-making and its nexus with services disciplines and commitments. Our work has also revealed the difficulties that arise from applying the principle of non-discrimination in services trade, notably with regard to the standard of 'likeness'. While non-discrimination has proven highly effective for the elimination of border measures in goods trade, its limits are plain to see in the services field where trade is inhibited predominantly by non-discriminatory domestic regulatory measures. While a broad interpretation of de facto discrimination may strongly interfere with countries' regulatory autonomy, a lenient interpretation may prove ineffective for the liberalisation of trade in services. In addressing this dilemma, our research focused, on the one hand, on developing an appropriate standard for the concept of non-discrimination in services trade and, on the other hand, a fuller set of disciplines on transparency and domestic regulation. At the same time, our findings have revealed the clear limits of peripheral experimentation in key areas of services rule-making, with increasing deference of PTA negotiations towards negotiating breakthroughs brokered at the WTO level in regard to much of the GATS' unfinished rule-making agenda.[92]

Bibliography

Adlung, Rudolf and Martín Molinuevo, 'Bilateralism in Services Trade: Is there Fire behind the (BIT-)smoke?' (2008) **11**(2) *Journal of International Economic Law* 365–409.

Beviglia-Zampetti, Americo and Pierre Sauvé, 'International Investment', in Alan O. Sykes and Andrew Guzman (eds.), *Research Handbook in International Economic Law* (London: Edward Elgar, 2007), pp. 211–270.

Bravo, Karen 'Free Labor! A Labor Liberalization Solution to the Modern Traffic in Humans' (2009) 18 *Transnational Law & Contemporary Problems* 545.

Bronckers, Marco and Natalie McNeils, 'Rethinking the "Like Product" Definition in GATT 1994: Anti-Dumping and Environmental Protection', in T. Cottier, P. C. Mavroidis and P. Blatter (eds.), *Regulatory Barriers and the Principle of Non-Discrimination in World Trade Law: Past, Present, and Future* (University of Michigan Press, 2000), pp. 345–385.

Broude, Tomer, 'The WTO/GATS Mode 4, International Labour Migration Regimes and Global Justice', Research Paper No. 7–07, May 2007, The Hebrew University of Jerusalem, Faculty of Law.

Cali, Massimiliano, 'Liberalizing Mode 4 Trade: What Impact on Exporting Countries?', Presentation at the WTO Symposium, 'Mode 4 of the GATS: Taking Stock and Moving Forward', 22–23 September 2008.

Chanda, Rupa, 'Low-skilled Workers and Bilateral, Regional, and Unilateral Initiatives, Lessons for the GATS Mode 4 Negotiations and other Agreements', UNDP Report, 2008.

Carzaniga, Antonia, 'A Warmer Welcome? Access for Natural Persons under Preferential Trade Agreements', in J. A. Marchetti and M. Roy (eds.), *Opening Markets for Trade in Services Countries and Sectors in Bilateral and WTO Negotiations* (Cambridge University Press, 2009), pp. 475–502.

Cassarino, Jean-Pierre, 'Informalising Readmission Agreements in the EU Neighbourhood' (2007) **42**(2) *The International Spectator*, 179–196.

Castles, Stephen, 'Guestworkers in Europe: A Resurrection?' (2006) **40**(4) *International Migration Review*, 741–766.

92 Indeed, with the partial exception of government procurement in services, governments involved in PTA negotiations increasingly affirm their desire to incorporate by reference any future disciplines agreed by WTO Members in the areas of domestic regulation, subsidy disciplines for services as well as emergency safeguard measures.

Cossy, Mireille, 'Some Thoughts on the Concept of "Likeness" in the GATS', in M. Panizzon, N. Pohl and P. Sauvé (eds.), *GATS and the Regulation of International Trade in Services* (Cambridge University Press, 2008), pp. 327–357.

Cottier, Thomas, Panagiotis Delimatsis and Nicolas Diebold, 'Article XIV GATS' (General Exceptions), in R. Wolfrum, P.-T. Stoll and C. Feinäugle (eds.), *WTO-Trade in Services: Max-Planck Commentaries on World Trade Law* (Brill Publishers, 2008), pp. 287–328.

Delimatsis, Panagiotis, 'Due Process and "Good" Regulation Embedded in the GATS: Disciplining Regulatory Behaviour in Services through Article VI of the GATS' (2007) **10**(1) *Journal of International Economic Law* 13–50.

International Trade in Services and Domestic Regulations: Necessity, Transparency, and Regulatory Diversity (Oxford University Press, 2007).

Article III GATS, in R. Wolfrum, P.-T. Stoll and C. Feinäugle (eds.), *Max-Planck Commentaries on World Trade Law, Volume 6: WTO-Trade in Services* (Brill Publishers, 2008), pp. 92–107.

'Determining the Necessity of Domestic Regulations in Services: The Best is Yet to Come' (2008) **19**(2) *European Journal of International Law* 365–408.

De Matos, Claudia and Denise Efionayi-Mäder, 'Bestandesaufnahme von Migrationspartnerschaften in der Schweiz', in IOM Bern (ed.), *Migrationspartnerschaften: Eine Bestandesaufnahme* (IOM Bern, 3rd edn, 2007).

Diebold, Nicolas F., 'The Morals and Order Exceptions in WTO Law: Balancing the Toothless Tiger and the Undermining Mole' (2008) **11** *Journal of International Economic Law* 43–74.

DiMascio, Nicholas and Joost Pauwelyn, 'Nondiscrimination in Trade and Investment Treaties: Worlds Apart or Two Sides of the Same Coin?' (2008) **102** *American Journal of International Law* 48–89.

Esty, Daniel, 'Good Governance at the Supranational Scale: Globalizing Administrative Law' (2006) **115** *Yale Law Journal* 1490–1562.

Fink, Carsten and Martín Molinuevo, 'East Asian Free Trade Agreements in Services: Roaring Tigers or Timid Pandas?', East Asia and Pacific Region Report No. 40175, The World Bank, http://go.worldbank.org/5YFZ3TK4E0.

Goco, Jonell B., 'Non-Discrimination, "Likeness", and Market Definition in World Trade Organization Jurisprudence' (2006) **40** *Journal of World Trade* 315–40.

Grynberg, Roman and Veniana Qalo, 'Migration and the World Trade Organization' (2007) **41**(4) *Journal of World Trade* 751–782.

Gugler, Philippe and Julien Chaisse, 'Foreign Investment Issues and WTO Law: Dealing with Fragmentation while waiting for a Multilateral Framework', in Julien Chaisse and Tiziano Balmelli (eds.), *Essays on the Future of the World Trade Organization* (Geneva: Editions Interuniversitaires Suisses, 2008), pp. 135–171.

Gugler, Philippe and Tomsik Vladimir, 'A Comparison of the Provisions Affecting Investment in the Existing WTO Obligations', NCCR Working Paper No. 15, August 2006.

Hollifield, James H. 'Migration and the "New" International Order: The Missing Regime', in B. Ghosh (ed.), *Managing Migration, Time for a New International Regime* (Oxford University Press, 2000), pp. 100–101.

Hudec, Robert E., '"Like Product": The Differences in Meaning in GATT Articles I and III', in T. Cottier, P. C. Mavroidis and P. Blatter (eds.), *Regulatory Barriers and the Principle of Non-Discrimination in World Trade Law: Past, Present, and Future* (University of Michigan Press, 2000), pp. 101–23.

Kapur, Devesh, and John McHale, *Give us Your Best and Your Brightest: The Global Hunt for Talent and Its Impact on the Developing World* (Washington, DC: Center for Global Development, 2005).

Krajewski, Markus, *National Regulation and Trade Liberalization in Services: The Legal Impact of the General Agreement on Trade in Services (GATS) on National Regulatory Autonomy* (Kluwer Law International, 2005).

Martin, Lisa, 'The Rational State Choice of Multilateralism,' in D. Ruggie (ed.), *Multilateralism Matters* (Columbia University Press, 1993), pp. 91–121.

Mattoo, Aaditya, 'National Treatment in the GATS – Corner-Stone or Pandora's Box?' (1997) **31** *Journal of World Trade*, 107–135.

Mattoo, Aaditya and Pierre Sauvé, 'Regionalism in Services Trade', in Aaditya Mattoo, Robert M. Stern and Gianni Zanini (eds.), *A Handbook of International Trade in Services* (Oxford University Press, 2007), pp. 221–286.

Maurer, Andreas and Philippe Chauvet, 'The Magnitude of Flows of Global Trade in Services', in B. Hoekman, A. Mattoo and P. English (eds.), *Development, Trade and the WTO, A Handbook* (World Bank, 2002), pp. 235–246.

Murphy, Sean D., 'US Interpretation of Core NAFTA Investment Standards' (2001) 95 *American Journal of International Law* 882.

Panizzon, Marion, 'Trade and Labor Migration: GATS Mode 4 and Migration Agreements', Friedrich-Ebert-Stiftung, Geneva, Occasional Paper Series No. 47 (2010).

'Labour Mobility: A win-win-win model for Trade and Development: The Case of Senegal', NCCR Working Paper No. 7, June 2008, available at: www.nccr-trade.org/ip-8/labour-mobility-as-a-win-win-win-model-for-trade-and-development-in-the-case-of-senegal-2.html (24 November 2008).

Pauwelyn, Joost, 'Comment: The Unbearable Lightness of Likeness', in M. Panizzon, N. Pohl and P. Sauvé (eds.), *GATS and the Regulation of International Trade in Services* (Cambridge University Press, 2008), pp. 358–69.

Pritchett, Lant, *Let their People Come, Breaking the Gridlock on International Labor Mobility* (Washington, DC: Center for Global Development, 2006).

'Been There, Not Yet Done That: Lessons and Challenges in Services Trade', in Marion Panizzon, Nicole Pohl and Pierre Sauvé (eds.), *GATS and the Regulation of International Trade in Services* (Cambridge University Press, 2008), pp. 599–631.

'Multilateral Rules on Investment: Is Forward Movement Possible?' (2006) **9**(2) *Journal of International Economic Law* 325–355.

'Qs and As on Trade, Investment and the WTO' (1997) **31**(8) *Journal of World Trade* 55–79.

Sauvé, Pierre and Martin Molinuevo, 'Does Architecture Matter? The Treatment of Trade and Investment in Financial Services in Selected Preferential Trade Agreements', NCCR Working Paper, No. 9, May 2008.

Schreuer, Christoph, 'Fair and Equitable Treatment in Arbitral Practice' (2005) **6**(3) *Journal of World Investment & Trade* 357–386.

Sommerville, Will and Madelein Sumption, 'Immigration in the United Kingdom, The Recession and Beyond', Report for the Equality and Human Rights Commission, March 2009.

Trachtman, Joel, *The International Law of Economic Migration: Toward the Fourth Freedom* (W. E. Upjohn Institute, 2009).

Weiler, Todd, 'Saving Oscar Chin: Non-Discrimination in International Investment Law', in T. Weiler (ed.), *International Investment Law and Arbitration* (London: Cameron May, 2005).

Zdouc, Werner, Legal Problems Arising under the General Agreement on Trade in Services: Comparative Analysis of GATS and GATT (Difo-Druck, 2002).

Documents

Communication from the Commission to the Council and the European Parliament, The Global Approach to Migration one year on: Towards a comprehensive European migration policy, Brussels, 30.11.2006, COM(2006) 735 final.

Draft Final Act Embodying the Results of the Uruguay Round of Multilateral Trade Negotiations, MTN.TNC/W/35/Rev.1, 3 December 1990.

Global Commission on International Migration (GCIM), Final Report, October 2005, available at: www.gcim.org/attachements/gcim-complete-report-2005.pdf.

Group of Negotiations on Services, Report to the Trade Negotiations Committee meeting at Ministerial level, December 1988, MTN.GNS/21, 25 November 1988.

UNCTAD, 'Recent developments in international investment agreements', IIA Monitor No. 2 (2008), (United Nations, 2008).

'National Treatment', UNCTAD Series on Issues in International Investment Agreements (United Nations, 1999).

'Scope and Definition', UNCTAD Series on Issues in International Investment Agreements (United Nations, 1999).

WPDR, Disciplines on Domestic Regulation Pursuant to GATS Article VI:4, Room Document, 20 March 2009.

7

Challenges of biotechnology in international trade regulation

SUSETTE BIBER-KLEMM, MICHAEL BURKARD, THOMAS COTTIER, SUFIAN JUSOH AND MICHELANGELO TEMMERMAN*

KEY MESSAGES

Biotechnology and multilayered governance

- Biotechnology offers an interesting case study in multilayered governance. While some regulatory aspects are best dealt with by harmonisation, other areas are best left to regulatory competition in light of diverging ethical perceptions and attitudes towards the potential risks of the technology.
- Coherent regulation combines harmonised and decentralised regulation in the field, depending upon the regulatory area.

Human rights and biotechnology

- Human rights cut both ways in substantive terms, with the exception of a clear ban on biological warfare. They both support and limit recourse to biotechnology. Human rights shape the process of balancing interests and values but do not offer clear guidance in the field.
- Human rights are of prime importance in procedural terms. They help in shaping appropriate legal avenues and participation in assessing biotechnology in research and commercial use.

Intellectual property rights and biotechnology

- Appropriate regulation of intellectual property rights in biotechnology varies and is not uniform.

Human genetic engineering is best dealt with by domestic regulation on the basis of broadly harmonised principles of intellectual property rights. Pluralist values and

* Individual Project No. 9, 'Genetic engineering in international trade regulation and policy: Intellectual property, technical regulations and the impact of human rights'.

diverging ethical and moral perceptions of genetic engineering, and the advantages of making progress by trial and error, outweigh the advantages of harmonised rules and enhanced market access in international law.

- Animal genetic resources (AnGR) are key to modern breeding and biodiversity. They call for a new and appropriate regime. Analogies to plant genetic resources need to be looked at with caution as animal-related regulation functions against a fundamentally different background.
- Intellectual property will play an increasing role in animal breeding. Patent law reverses the normally applicable ownership rule over animal progeny. *Sui generis* IP rights can enable new breeds to gain a sufficiently strong position to enter the highly concentrated and monopolised AnGR market. The market in animal genetic resources must be shaped to actively encourage marketed biodiversity.
- In all areas of biotechnology, a strong research exemption will facilitate innovation and reduce the risk of patent-thickets.

Biotechnology and risk management

- The narrow focus of the SPS Agreement on quarantine risks is not appropriate to address new risks deriving from biotechnology.
- Risk assessment and risk management in biotechnology need to be clearly separated.
- Risk assessment as a scientific assessment should be assigned to international organisations or be effected in international networks of qualified institutions under the auspices of international organisations.
- Risk management is the core function of domestic governance. It allows the taking into account of socio-economic considerations which inherently vary due to diverging attitudes to risk and needs in different societies.
- A clear distinction between risk assessment and risk management in WTO law will strengthen the precautionary approach and strengthen procedural rules in assessing and managing new risks.
- Risk communication is a third and key component and needs development in legal terms. The right to information obliges governments and international organisations to provide full and prompt transparency of the potential risks of biotechnology. They need to allow for full and fair debate.

Biotechnology and liability rules

- Liability rules in biotechnology reflect diverging perceptions of the technology, its advantages and risks. As countries have different needs and perceptions, liability rules are not suitable for harmonisation in international law. Liability is best left to regulatory competition. Model laws may assist countries, and harmonisation may be possible at the regional level.

- Harmonisation is possible and suitable in terms of access to justice and courts. International law should provide appropriate minimal standards to this effect.
- Transboundary conflicts do not seem to call for further harmonisation but can be dealt with on the basis of existing international law.

A. Introduction

The advent of biogenetic engineering in the late twentieth century was met with optimism and scepticism alike. A new potential to improve nutrition, medicine and renewable energy emerged. Yet, the recombination of DNA triggered ethical and moral concerns. The debates engendered by this technology and its applications are well known.[1] Moreover, those using conventional methods of production feared competition and reverted to protection. Approaches to and domestic regulation of genetic engineering or modern biotechnology thus vary considerably between countries depending on the strategies adopted.

Biotechnology regulation must deal with a number of traits which render it inherently more complex than for other topics. The scientific nature of the technology, the pace of its evolution, the uncertainty as to the long-term effects, the pressing and diverging public opinion, ethical concerns and the risks and difficulties of assessing them, and the fostering of research in the field are some of the factors that need to be taken into account in regulating biotechnology and how it should be addressed in international law and trade regulation.

This background defines the approach chosen by the researchers involved in this project: at the outset, the relevant ethical questions as incorporated in the human rights are examined with regard to their normative value to inform the creation of new regulations. Secondly, questions regarding the informational character of innovation in genetics are considered. Central to this discussion is how a balance between the protection of innovation by intellectual property rights (IPRs) and access to innovation can be struck; and whether an adaptation of the Agreement on Trade-Related Aspects of Intellectual Property Rights (TRIPS Agreement)[2] ought to be envisaged. The basic questions concern the scope

1 T. Cottier, 'Genetic engineering, trade and human rights', in F. Francioni, Studies in International Law No. 13, *Biotechnologies and International Human Rights* (Oxford: Hart Publishing, 2007), p. 279.

2 Agreement on Trade-Related Aspects of Intellectual Property Rights, Annex IC to the Agreement Establishing the World Trade Organization, Marrakesh, 15 April 1994, 33 *International Legal Materials* 1197 (1994), hereafter the 'TRIPS Agreement' or 'TRIPS'.

of protection at the interface with the regulation of unfair competition.[3] The third section of this chapter addresses the question of assessment and management of risk in the law of the World Trade Organization (WTO); and in the fourth section, the international order of liability for damage caused by genetically engineered organisms in international trade is investigated.

B. The impact of human rights

Human rights standards embodied in the UN Covenants and regional instruments are an important ingredient to be taken into account in international trade regulation in order to achieve viable and acceptable interfaces between diverging perceptions. Together with constitutional law, they influence the appropriate shaping of intellectual property law and trade regulation, notwithstanding that they are not formally incorporated into WTO law.

Human dignity is of particular significance in the context of biotechnology, especially with respect to the debate concerning the possible applications of human-DNA-related technology in medicine.[4] Yet there are a number of other core individual rights that are likely to influence the legal environment of genetic engineering. They encompass the right to life, the right to adequate standards of living including the right to medical care, the right to food, the right to property and the right to protection for moral and material interests resulting from scientific production. Other rights might also be relevant such as the generic right to development that may be included in the principle of sustainable development.

An extensive examination of different human rights standards, however, shows that they are neither unanimously in favour nor unanimously against application of this technology. Moreover, human rights are not absolute, but subject to restrictions and the balancing of competing interests. Recourse to human rights depends upon a contextual analysis. It neither allows for generalisation nor offers uniform and simple answers. The ban on use of genetic engineering for the purposes of warfare and mass destruction is the only area where clear-cut answers are possible.

3 Cf. T. Cottier, M. Temmerman, S. Jusoh and A. Dolotbaeva, *The Research Exemption in Patent Law*, work in progress, on file with authors.

4 See International Law Association (ILA), *International Law on Biotechnology: Conference Report Rio de Janeiro 2008.*

Nevertheless, human rights criteria should be employed in assessing specific regulatory problems and in the process of applying and interpreting appropriate rules. Ultimately, the balance of interests inherent to an assessment of human rights will primarily depend upon the utility and the risks of the specific technology in a particular context. Yet, judgements about utility and long-term impact of genetic engineering vary. The framework may, nevertheless, substantially contribute to the process of finding appropriate solutions by weighing all the pros and cons.[5]

Regulation of biotechnology strongly depends upon appropriate procedures. This is true on all layers of government, both domestic and international. Informed decisions depend upon comprehensive fact finding and analysis, and a voice being given to all concerned. Substantive and procedural human rights therefore are of unequivocal importance. Yet, in taking account of the regulatory ambiguity and vagueness of normative guidance under human rights standards, it is important to stress the relevant procedural requirements in regulating genetic engineering. Procedural due process, entailing the right to be informed and heard before a determination is made, an obligation to argue and justify decisions in a rational and non-arbitrary manner, a right to appeal, and judicial review provide essential elements based upon which procedures for regulating genetic engineering should be shaped. Complementary rights, to freedom of speech, freedom of the press, freedom of association and the right to obtain information from government are of paramount importance in enabling an informed political debate on the subject. They lie at the foundation of risk communication. This is of particular importance in regulating scientific research, in patent law and procedures, in risk assessment and management and matters relating to liability for harm incurred.

Another question in this field is whether these principles are to be applied to the issue of prior informed consent (PIC) of the donors of human genetic material to patenting the results of the research based on this material. Unlike consent to medical intervention and consent to research, which are widely established in international law, this requirement is not yet established under utilitarian concepts of intellectual property protection.[6] The burden imposed on research and access to material by eventual additional patentability requirements such as PIC has so far been found to be more important than the human dignity aspect.

5 See Cottier, above, note 2.

6 See for instance *John Moore* v. *the Regents of the University of California (et al.)*, 9 July 1990, No. S006987, 51 Cal. 3d 120.

Analysis has shown that the *right to property* does not call for a PIC requirement in relation to patenting human genetic material. Since, under the UNESCO Declaration on Bioethics and Human Rights, the human body cannot be used for financial gain, the right to property cannot cover the material interest of an individual in sharing in financial profits generated by marketing a patent based on research with material from his or her body. *Privacy rights*, however, by preventing the state from collecting personal information about an individual without his or her consent, would provide an appropriate human rights basis for PIC in relation to patenting. Deciding to grant a patent has an impact on how personal information on an individual (in this case genetic information) will be used and should therefore be viewed in the light of privacy rights.[7]

Although PIC of human donors of genetic material might hence appear necessary in respecting the human right to privacy or even in certain interpretations of the concept of human dignity, human rights arguments must be balanced against the interest in having recourse to genetic information in medical research and treatment, and the practicalities of obtaining PIC. This is a matter of balancing affected interests, also in a particular setting of urgency, and overriding public interests.

The procedural implications of human rights protection thus extend to the acquisition of IPRs. In addition, in light of the regulatory ambiguity and vagueness of normative guidance under human rights standards, the relevant procedural requirements for regulating genetic engineering must be stressed.

To sum up, human rights are important factors in informing both the shaping of appropriate rules, and – importantly – the interpretation of existing procedural rules.

C. Intellectual property and competition

In the context of trade regulation, protection of (IPRs) – in this case patents – is of paramount importance for the legal status of biotechnology.

Much of the debate on modern biotechnology has indeed focused on the issue of patenting. This may be rooted in the specific characteristics of biotechnology – dealing with self-propagating living material and the multitude of functions gene sequences can have.

7 M. Schefer, 'Human rights and patenting the results of research on human material', paper presented at the NCCR Workshop 'Human Rights in the Patent Procedure', Bern, 28 March 2007, p. 4.

Patents are IPRs that, in order to create incentives for innovation, grant their owners a time-limited monopoly for excluding others from the use of the owner's innovation. In order to further innovative research and progress, the applicant is obliged to disclose his or her innovation, thus enabling others to use it for further research.

The status of biotechnology in patent law so far is essentially defined by domestic law and practice. Levels of protection and the scope of rights vary in different jurisdictions, commensurate with levels of social and economic development. While protection is strong in industrialised countries, in particular the United States and the European Union, developing countries have been less inclined to create strong systems.

The TRIPS Agreement makes patents obligatorily available for any type of new, inventive, industrially applicable and sufficiently disclosed inventions, whether products or processes, in all fields of technology; for a minimum term of 20 years, and without discrimination as to the field of technology, the place of invention, or whether products are imported or locally produced.[8] As the TRIPS Agreement is embedded in the WTO dispute settlement system, it enjoys a strong enforcement mechanism. In fact, for the first time in history, disputes over IPRs are now brought before an international court. In relation to living matter, however, the TRIPS Agreement allows for considerable flexibility. The TRIPS Agreement does not embody a general exclusion of inventions in the sphere of animate nature, neither does it set strong obligations to the contrary. Under Article 27, we read that [WTO] Members *may* exclude from patent protection *plants*[9] or *animals*[10] other than *micro-organisms* as well as *essentially biological processes* for the production of plants (again, other than microbiological ones). Furthermore, the TRIPS Agreement neither excludes nor obliges the grant of patents for *plant varieties*, but nevertheless requires plant varieties to be protected either by patent protection or by a *sui generis* system.[11] No such rule has been included in relation to animal varieties. Finally, the Agreement allows for the exclusion from patentability of inventions whose commercial exploitation would be

8 Article 27 of the TRIPS Agreement in conjunction with Article 30 (term of protection).

9 See M. Temmerman, 'The Patentability of Plant Genetic Inventions', NCCR Trade Regulation Working Paper 2007/04 (Bern, 2007).

10 Countries such as Canada have made use of this flexibility (cf. Supreme Court of Canada, *Harvard College* v. *Canada (Commissioner of Patents)*, 5 December 2002, 4 Supreme Court Reports (Canada) 45 (2002)).

11 Article 27 § 3 (b) TRIPS Agreement. The openness of this provision has led to a rather disharmonised situation regarding patentability of plants throughout WTO Members.

contrary to the *ordre public* or morality.[12] Consequently, TRIPS only compels member countries to qualify micro-organisms, microbiological processes and non-biological processes as patentable.[13]

Patents are intrinsically linked to trade and investment. Therefore, international harmonisation of patent rules may be generally advisable – at least among developed countries – in order to further the establishment of equal conditions for trade and thereby also to ensure the legal security and predictability necessary to encourage investment. A lack of stable and predictable conditions for patenting, particularly in the biotechnology industry, which is very sensitive to investment protection, amounts to a disincentive to investment, and hence also to innovation.

But the specifics of biotechnology lead to several questions such as how the scope of the rights is to be defined in order to optimise competition and innovation and to prevent the negative implications of unduly strong monopolies, concentrations and too little inter-firm rivalry.[14] Competition is vital to provide optimal incentives for innovation and efficiency in a knowledge-based economy.[15] Patents, however, exclude competition over protected inventions for the very same purpose of stimulating innovation: they correct a market failure situation of underinvestment in research if the market is left to regulate itself. A careful balance between both players, patents and competition, must therefore be sought so as to optimise incentives for innovation.

In the process of globalisation, the issue of harmonisation of patentability of biotechnology will arise. In this debate, ethical issues and local sensitivities need to be considered. Furthermore, harmonisation of patent law often appears fraught with pitfalls. Firstly, the patent system is not so much a system regulated by the patent *laws* but rather one governed by jurisprudence and the patent office's guidelines for examination. 'Harmonised' legal provisions often fall to pieces given the differing jurisprudential decisions of the national courts.

12 Article 27 § 3 TRIPS.

13 It is unclear from the wording of the TRIPS Agreement whether it requires microbiological processes in general to be patentable or only microbiological processes for the production of plants or animals. See M. Temmerman, 'Die Patentierbarkeit von gentechnischen Erfindungen auf internationaler Ebene' (August 2006) *Die Volkswirtschaft* 13–17.

14 J. A. Schumpeter, *Capitalism, Socialism and Democracy* (New York: Harper and Row, 3rd edn, 1950), p. 106.

15 R. D. Anderson and N. T. Gallini, 'Competition policy, intellectual property rights and efficiency: An introduction to the issues', in Robert D. Anderson and Nancy T. Gallini (eds.), *Competition Policy and Intellectual Property Rights in the Knowledge-Based Economy* (Cambridge University Press, 1998).

Secondly, patent laws are fairly abstract and need this feature for the proper, smooth, functioning of the system: technologies develop fast; enacting new, technology-specific legislation every time there is a new development would be extremely burdensome and would slow down the functioning of the patent system while political compromises were being sought. Its adaptation to fresh technologies and inventions hence primarily depends on the ability of patent examiners to assess prior art and to correctly determine the level of sufficient disclosure and non-obviousness needed, so as to prevent the grant of patent monopolies to minor contributors to the state of the art, or overly rewarding attributions that block further innovation. This may lead to a problem with the quality of patents in new technologies. Yet this is usually corrected over time: the ability of patent examiners to find the correct state of the art and to assess inventiveness increases as the technology progresses and time passes. For technologies that attract high levels of investment, such as biotechnology, the question is whether the cost of this evolutionary process might not be too high.

I. Human genetic inventions and the harmonisation of patent rules

Inventions based upon human DNA sequences or other human biological material are seen in various fields including agriculture, where for instance rice has been engineered with a human-based DNA sequence. Its major field of application, however, is the pharmaceutical sector. The focus is on therapeutic antibodies and vaccines, including the controversial field of stem cells and cloning, and the inventions in the medical sector relating to diagnostics, gene therapy and modern transplantation methods.

Trends in human biotechnology point to an increased interest in the post-genomic, i.e. the proteomics age.[16] The entire human genome has been sequenced and human genetic sequences are now in sight for researchers, pharmaceutical companies and those with an interest in tailor-made medicine. The increasing use of information technologies will change the research and patenting landscape. Biomedical databases and search tools allow the identification of almost any DNA – or protein-based sequence. Yet only mathematical probabilities are given for each output. This raises the question whether a previously unknown sequence which can be easily assigned to its function via the usage of biomedical databases and search tools is an invention that can be patented.

16 'Proteomics age' is a fixed term in modern biology. Proteomics is a branch of genetics that studies the full set of proteins encoded by a genome.

Technical patent law issues immediately arise, and the application of the patent system in this field, together with the corresponding technology, faces stronger ethical objections than any other branch of biotechnology. The application of the essentially utilitarian-based patent system must be set in this context. Patents covering human genetic inventions have indeed been challenged in many systems, including in Europe, where the *Edinburgh*[17] and *WARF*[18] cases, have seen fierce debates on the application of the morality exception to patentability.[19] Although the patent system as such does not regulate access to commercialisation, and cannot prevent or allow controversial research to be undertaken, it nonetheless needs to take into account certain ethical guidelines.

Patents, research and commercialisation are intrinsically linked through the fact that the commercialisation of patented inventions, with the advantage of monopolistic prices, is the only way the inventors can be rewarded for their heavy investments in research and development. The differences in regulation in terms of market access, research authorisation, public funding and patenting must be adjusted so that they complement each other, among other reasons to avoid strategic patenting.

On the international level, both the 1883 Paris Convention,[20] stemming from the 'pre-biotechnology era' and the TRIPS Agreement are silent on the issue of human genetic inventions. However, in scientific terms the word 'animal' encompasses 'human'. Therefore there is a need for international clarification, and an explicit exclusion of the human body from patentability.[21]

Among the intellectual property concerns relating to patenting inventions based on human genes is the question whether a large number of patents on genes and their diverse owners would make it difficult to acquire the rights to all necessary research inputs and thus result in the

17 EPO, Opposition Division, *Edinburgh University*, EP 0 695 351, not published; appeal withdrawn.

18 EPO, Technical Board of Appeal, *Wisconsin Alumni Research Foundations*, T 1374/04.

19 Convention on the Grant of European Patents, Munich, 3 October 1973, text as amended by the act revising Article 63 EPC of 17 December 1991 and by decisions of the Administrative Council of the European Patent Organisation of 21 December 1978, 13 December 1994, 20 October 1995, 5 December 1996 and 10 December 1998, 1065 United Nations Treaty Series 199 (with parts of the EC Directive 98/44 incorporated into the 'Implementing Rules' 23b to 23e).

20 Convention for the Protection of Industrial Property, Paris, 20 March 1883, as amended on 28 September 1979, 828 *United Nations Treaty Series* 303, administered by WIPO (Hereafter 'Paris Convention').

21 See ILA, above, note 4.

underuse of valuable technologies.[22] The scope of patents is controversial in relation to biotechnology. This seems even more important in the human genetic context. Evidence suggests that research is effectively hindered to an unjustifiably large extent by patents in the field of diagnostic testing.[23]

A balancing of scope of rights and breadth of patent claims with the disclosure requirement appears essential in this context.[24] To varying degrees in the US and the EU, the disclosure obligation precludes applicants from obtaining rights to subject matter they have not fully conceived, and further guarantees that the public is enabled to recreate the invention after expiration of the patent. The principle of disclosure is an underinvestigated, pre-grant, scope-rebalancing tool.

Comparing the approaches to disclosure employed by the US, the EU and some EU nations reveals significant differences in the extent to which human gene sequence patents are protected. The policies of the European Patent Office (EPO), which apply to contracting EU countries, have encouraged a liberal atmosphere with respect to assessing scope and what constitutes sufficient disclosure specific to human gene sequence patents. However, a more vigorous ethics-based scope limitation is to be recognised in most European countries.[25]

Difficulties arise from these divergent regulations. Efforts to harmonise approaches to bioethical issues on the international level have failed so far. This in turn influences any possible harmonised set of patent rules in relation to inventions based on human genetics.[26] This situation gives rise to some questions: What are the international regulatory needs in the field of human biotechnology or genetic engineering applied to humans? What are the arguments and needs for diverging (or harmonised) rules in relation to trade in human genetic inventions?

The reports of the Nuffield Council and the Human Genome Organisation (HUGO) provide perhaps the most legally and scientifically based

22 T. Caulfield *et al.*, 'Evidence and anecdotes: an analysis of human gene patenting controversies' (2006) 24 *Nature Biotechnology* 1091.

23 B. Verbeure, G. Matthijs and G. Van Overwalle, 'Analysing DNA patents in relation with diagnostic genetic testing' (2006) 14 *European Journal of Human Genetics* 26.

24 See United States Patent & Trademark Office, *Manual of Patent Examining Procedure*, § 2163.02 (September 2007); European Patent Office, *Guidelines for Examination*, June 2005, at C-II § 4.

25 See for instance, A. Thorstenson, 'Patentability of human genetic stem cells: Finding the balance between the moral hazard in Europe and the wide scope in US', University of Lund (Spring 2007).

26 ILA, above note 4, p. 16.

analyses of the treatment of human genetic patents in the current IP regimes. While the United Nations Educational, Scientific and Cultural Organization (UNESCO) and the European Group on Ethics in Science and New Technologies (EGE) are significantly founded on humanistic concerns of human dignity and ethics, the Nuffield Council and HUGO reports incorporate existing international and regional regulations for a more realistic treatment of the potential concerns regarding DNA patents. While human dignity and ethics are certainly relevant to the application of these laws, it is arguably unrealistic to expect patent systems based on the TRIPS, the EU Biotechnology Directive, common law, statutory law, and constitutional law, or on the significant trade and investment interests involved, to amend gene patent regulations based purely on these more intangible concerns.

Efforts to harmonise international standards in the field of human genetics show that the world community is far from reaching a consensus. No common rules even on a ban on cloning could be found within the United Nations.[27] The same is likely to be seen in the field of patenting human genetic inventions. Members of the WTO are unlikely to agree on matters of such sensitivity. Improving the situation may be less a matter of harmonising the rules on patenting of biotechnology, than one of harmonising general patent law. In the EU, the introduction of a Union-wide unitary patent – in particular in the field of genetic engineering – has been suggested. Moreover, Members are entitled to invoke moral exceptions under the current agreement, and practice is likely to result in considerable diversity even if a common standard were to be adopted. The importance of case-by-case assessment renders harmonisation possible only to the extent that common bodies of adjudication and judicial review exist. It is therefore appropriate to leave harmonisation to regional integration, to gain experience and perhaps to expand protection on the global scale once experience in the field has been gained. In conclusion, this matter is most suitable for regulatory competition and restrictions on trade in goods and services need to be taken into account. At any rate, future efforts at harmonisation will need to include flanking measures, in particular more effective transfer of technology and knowledge, and incentives to engage in private–public partnerships as means to enhance benefits for developing and emerging economies.[28] To this effect, new and more

27 M. Arsanjani, 'Negotiating the UN Declaration on Human Cloning' (2006) 100 *American Journal of International Law* 164.

28 B. Karapinar and M. Temmerman, 'Benefiting from biotechnology: Pro-poor IPRs and public-private partnerships' (2008) 27 *Biotechnology Law Report* 189.

efficient models and modes of transfer of technology and knowledge need first to be developed and designed.

II. Animal genetic resources, IPRs and genetic diversity

Animal genetic resources (AnGRs) have seen a fundamental change with the introduction of biotechnology and its recent developments. The past decades witnessed the first successful cloning of animals and the creation and commercialisation of genetically modified animal organisms.[29] Biotechnological research in AnGRs has been slower in its development than, for instance, research on plant genetic resources, but it now produces transgenic animal organisms ready to be applied in different commercial activities, including agriculture.[30] The legal framework in this context has also developed more slowly than that for plants, also in IP law; yet it is today in the process of overtaking.

With the TRIPS Agreement leaving the choice of patentability of animals open to domestic regulation, countries have opted for different approaches. Most so-called developed countries have established animal patentability. This includes European countries, even if they show a reluctant attitude towards the technology. Developing and least developed countries appear more reluctant to do so. Yet they are increasingly pressured to introduce animal patentability in bilateral treaty negotiations. An opportunity for local investment is said to be lost in many cases because of this,[31] and it is recommended that TRIPS flexibilities are fully used so as to tailor locally adapted IPRs and patent regimes.[32]

Whereas biotechnological innovation is subject to patent rights in many systems, traditional progress is often not able to reach the patentability

29 The first development of a genetically modified animal was reported in 1982 (R. D. Palmiter, H. Y. Chen and R. L. Brinster, 'Differential regulation of metallothionein-thymidine kinase fusion genes in transgenic mice and their offspring' (1982) 29 *Cell* 701–710). The first patent on a transgenic animal was issued in the US in 1988: the Harvard Oncomouse (US Patent 4 736 866, Harvard College, 12 April 1988).

30 See H. Nieman, W. Kues, J. W. Carnwath, 'Transgene farm animals: Current status and perspectives for agriculture and biomedicine' in M. Engelhard, K. Hagen and M. Boysen (eds.), *Genetic Engineering in Livestock: New Applications and Interdisciplinary Perspectives* (Berlin/Heidelberg: Springer, 2009).

31 For instance, J. Straus, 'Genomics and the food industry: Outlook from an intellectual property perspective', in D. Vaver and L. Bently (eds.), *Intellectual Property in the New Millennium, Essay in Honour of William R. Cornish* (Cambridge University Press, 2004), p. 134.

32 S. Biber-Klemm and T. Cottier (eds.), *Rights to Plant Genetic Resources and Traditional Knowledge: Basic Issues and Perspectives* (Oxford: CABI, 2006).

threshold. Unlike for plant varieties, no separate IP regime has been established for low-tech innovation in animal breeding.[33] Patents will thus only have their effect on the biotech market, yet a clear border between biotechnology and traditional markets cannot be drawn. Breeds are increasingly a result of both biotechnology and what is considered 'traditional' breeding. Only animals that are the result of recombinant DNA procedures are so far largely rejected on agricultural markets (although widespread for research purposes). Biotechnological *tools*, however, are widely used, including in traditional breeding.

Debate in patent law is focused on several issues, circling around the alleged broad 'scope' of patents in biotechnology.[34] On the one hand, the boundaries of the patent system are disputed in relation to its (possible) extension over 'traditional' methods as opposed to biotechnology.[35] The discussion in Europe, for instance, boils down to the question whether the exclusion from patentability of essentially biological processes for the production of animals or plants is or is not applicable from the very moment the said process makes *one* biotechnological step.[36] On the other hand, the scope of patents in relation to AnGR must be investigated in relation to progeny and patent protection over subsequent, and eventually auto-reproducing, generations of initially patent-protected breeds.[37] Extension of rights might appear the general rule in most cases. This approach is aimed at placing patents over animate subject matter at the same level as those granted for inanimate matter, where the right to produce remains with the patent holders. However, this reverses the traditional ownership rule that allows purchasers of animals to freely use their progeny. Finally, an ethical question often arises in setting the borders between inventions excluded in relation to human material and similar ones allowed in relation to animals, yet which in theory

33 Cf. International Convention for the Protection of New Varieties of Plants, Union internationale pour la protection des obtentions végétales, 2 December 1961, as last revised on 19 March 1991, 1861 *United Nations Treaty Series* 281, hereafter: 'UPOV Convention'.

34 See: S. Bostyn, 'Patenting DNA sequences (polynucleotides) and scope of protection in the European Union: An evaluation, background study for The European Commission', Office for Official Publications of the European Communities (2004).

35 This discussion is closely linked to the notion of essentially biological processes and whether or not, and to what extent, these are set patentable.

36 Technical Board of Appeal to the European Patent Office, *Brassica*, T 0083/05, 22 May 2007 (appeal pending before the Enlarged Board of Appeal, case number G2/07).

37 See: M. V. Tvedt and M. Finckenhagen, 'Scope of process patents in farm animal breeding' (2008) 11 *Journal of World Intellectual Property* 3 203–228.

are applicable by analogy to humans. In general, the lack of jurisprudence in relation to AnGR is striking; notably in comparison to plant-related inventions.[38]

Rules and regulations affecting AnGR, including IPRs, must be placed in the light of the erosion of animal genetic resources, which is causing the loss of one livestock breed per month.[39] Assessing the impact of the market on the erosion of livestock breeds appears essential in this context. It is indeed the market that is designing agricultural diversity and is hence of essential impact on the conservation of livestock. Commercialisation can be the predominant 'saviour' of agricultural breeds from extinction: in the absence of commercial value and a market, conservation often runs out of direct incentives. AnGR markets however tend to work against conservation. With a focus on productivity traits, genetically uniform high-yield breeds designed in developed countries will usually outcompete less productive, but locally adapted breeds.[40] This is especially the case in developing countries, where the erosion of animal genetic resources strikes the hardest.[41] This engenders the loss of livestock breeds often carrying adaptive traits whose conservation might appear essential in the future, notably in times of climate change.

The market of genetic supply in animal breeds appears highly concentrated in certain sub-sectors such as poultry and swine. For example, the control over genetic material for commercial layer hens, broilers and turkeys is globally left to four companies only.[42] The market in traditional AnGR was not shaped by IP-based monopolies, but instead by the use of secrecy jointly with hybridisation leading to monopolies unlimited in time and scope.

Oligopolisation, concentration of a few businesses controlling a market section, is, however, not problematic as such: competition can be

38 T. Sommer, 'Patenting the animal kingdom? From cross-breeding to genetic make-up and biomedical research' (2008) 39 *International Review of Intellectual Property and Competition Law* 2.

39 Food and Agriculture Organization of the United Nations, *The State of the World's Animal Genetic Resources for Food and Agriculture* (Rome: Commission on Genetic Resources for Food and Agriculture, 2007), p. xxxv.

40 S. Anderson and R. Centonze, 'Property rights and the management of animal genetic resources' (2007) 35 *World Development* 1529–1541, at 1537.

41 S. Anderson, 'Animal genetic resources and livelihoods' (2003) 45 *Ecological Economics* 331–339.

42 See S. Gura, *Livestock Genetics Companies: Concentration and Proprietary Strategies of an Emerging Power in the Global Food Economy* (Ober-Ramstadt: League for Pastoral Peoples and Indigenous Livestock Development, 2007).

fierce in an oligopolised structure as well.[43] Moreover, this situation does not seem to stand in direct connection with market mechanisms leading to extinction of local breeds: more competitors in the field will not necessarily lead to (more) genetic diversity on the market. The market mechanisms seem to be more fundamental and to solely root in the demand for productive breeds.

The offering of locally non-adapted breeds carries however two features that might be tackled from a competition law point of view as abuse of monopoly and/or unfair competition. Offering high-yield yet non-locally adapted breeds can be considered to be inappropriate if it is apparent that adjusted industrial production systems are lacking. With the case study of AnGR, unfair competition can be tested on its theoretical limits, in relation to consumers and outside a direct competitive relationship – taking into account 'third' factors such as biodiversity. The same is true for the concept on abuse of monopoly position, for those (sub-)sectors where monopoly positions are at the root (e.g. poultry and swine, at least).

For the relationship between AnGR diversity and IPRs, a distinction must be made between the effect they have on conservation on the one side, and innovation on the other. In livestock both seem to be sharply influenced by the shape of the market, and IPRs therefore do have a role to play.

On the *conservation* side, an essential tool to keep locally adapted breeds (indirectly) on the market is to create incentives for (export) niche markets for products derived from such breeds.[44] On the *innovation* side, it is important to create a framework which offers incentives to new breeders to enter the market using genetic engineering in animal breeding. The lack of diversity on the AnGR market requires not only an encouragement of innovative production; it also requires innovations to enter the market in a position strong enough to be able to compete with the existing monopoly/oligopoly players.

In addressing these challenges, two options are available. Firstly, it is possible to extend patent protection to AnGR. On the international level, this implies a removal of the general exception for animals in Article 27 of the TRIPS Agreement. Secondly, as with plant varieties, it is possible to design a system of *sui generis* rights.[45] While existing players may not

43 See R. Whish, *Competition Law* (Oxford University Press, 6th edn, 2009) pp. 544–570.

44 See S. Biber-Klemm, 'Trade in breeds at risk', NCCR Trade Regulation Working Paper, forthcoming, on file with author.

45 See, for instance, W. Lesser, 'Animal variety protection: a proposal for a US model law' (1993) 76 *Journal of Patent and Trademark Office Society* 697–715.

be motivated to use newly created IP protection systems for AnGR and instead continue to pursue a secrecy-based strategy, new players may consider it as an essential tool for entering the market successfully and as an intangible asset necessary for obtaining the necessary financial credits. It may also accompany livestock breeders and pastoralist communities[46] with official (IP) ownership rights and recognition of their contribution to the creation and conservation of locally adapted breeds and biodiversity.

A separate question, governed by different rationales, concerns the appropriate level of implementation and whether the settings described above call for changes at the *international* level. An example is the limitation of the scope of patent rights applied to AnGR. Is this scope limitation needed at the international level, within the TRIPS Agreement, as certain authors claim?[47]

The international level might appear, and is often claimed to be, intrinsically the most appropriate regulatory platform in relation to AnGR.[48] However, investigating intellectual property harmonisation must be done with a view to the removal of trade barriers, and either be rooted in a necessity common to all WTO Members, or in a need to be applied top-down from the international level to domestic regulation. Taking into account the factual and legal situations, three aspects in particular need to be analysed.

First, it is necessary to decide whether animals should be excluded from patentability or made compulsorily patentable. This question must be analysed on the basis of eventual trade-distorting effects of the disharmonised system as it currently exists.[49]

Second, the scope of patents needs to be examined. This is closely linked to the question whether the AnGR experience supports the TRIPS Agreement moving into ceiling provisions, as opposed to ruling minimum standards only, for instance by explicitly deciding over the extension of patent protection over subsequent generations of progeny, or by ruling a compulsory farmer's privilege in the field as has been done in

46 I. Köller-Rollefson, 'Keepers of genes: The interdependence between pastoralists, breeds, access to the commons, and livelihoods', Sadri Rajasthan, the LIFE Network (2007).

47 See for instance M. V. Tvedt, *et al. Legal Aspects of Exchange, Use and Conservation of Farm Animal Genetic Resources*, Fridtjof Nansens Institutt, FNI Report 1/2007, 188: 'The scope of protection in the TRIPS Agreement is not adapted to the field of animal breeding – so these consequences are probably not foreseen in the WTO.'

48 See § 16 of the Global Action Plan for Animal Genetic Resources.

49 See ILA, above, note 5.

Europe.[50] The scope of patents in biotechnology is an issue of relevance to international trade regulation: an unjustifiably broad scope of patents may distort the balance between the advantages and disadvantages of the system.[51]

Third, it will be necessary to investigate whether an international anchoring in the TRIPS Agreement should be created for a *sui generis* system of IP protection for animal breeds, in parallel with the one for plant varieties. This can be rooted in the internationally relevant need to further AnGR diversity, eventually combined with a necessity for imposing top-down enforcement so as to avoid, for instance, bilateral negotiations taking the lead on the issue.

III. Research and patent law: an international research exemption?

Biotechnology strongly depends upon scientific research. Defining a proper relationship between research and patents granted is crucial to securing progress and avoiding a situation in which exclusive rights hamper research. Both product and process patents require a careful analysis of how far they affect research in biotechnology by competitors. This matter, the so-called 'research exemption', is primarily addressed in domestic law, and gives rise to the question of the extent to which the status of research should be harmonised in the TRIPS Agreement.

Research exemption is a legal avenue to allow researchers to conduct follow-on research in areas affected by patents. The WTO law does not prescribe standards which Members are obliged to comply with. Accordingly, the rules guiding exemption for research are highly fragmented.

Although not directly tested under WTO case law, the research exemption (within certain borders) arguably falls under TRIPS Article 30, allowing exceptions to patent rights under a 'three step test': the exceptions must be limited, the exceptions must not unreasonably conflict with

50 Cf. Article 11 § 2 Directive 98/44/EC: 'By way of derogation from Articles 8 and 9, the sale or any other form of commercialisation of breeding stock or other animal reproductive material to a farmer by the holder of the patent or with his consent implies authorisation for the farmer to use the protected livestock for an agricultural purpose.'

51 As to levels of protection, the doctrine of graduation and phasing in of obligations commensurate with levels of economic development of a WTO Member will be of assistance here as it is in shaping obligations in the field of intellectual property rights in general (see T. Cottier, 'From progressive liberalisation to progressive regulation in WTO Law' (2006) 9 *Journal of International Economic Law* 779–821).

the normal exploitation of the patent, and the exceptions must not unreasonably prejudice the legitimate interests of the patent owner.[52]

Research exemption provisions at the national level may vary. Many European countries provide for research exemption in the national law, either for 'scientific experimentation' or 'experimental research'. The EU countries also provide for regulatory approval exemptions in relation to medicinal products for human and veterinary use.[53] The new Swiss Patent Act, through Article 9, establishes a whole range of patent infringement exemptions and a regulatory approval exemption, whereas the US Federal Courts have developed a limited defence under the common law tradition. In the *Madey* v. *Duke University* case[54] the Federal Circuit explained that the experimental use privilege '[d]oes not immunise any conduct that is in keeping with the alleged infringer's legitimate business, regardless of commercial implications.' Developing countries such as India, Malaysia and Peru provide for both the research exemption and the regulatory approval exemptions.[55] The issue is whether the laws in the developing countries are properly understood and implemented. Developing countries are encouraged to take the necessary measures to explain to the stakeholders, including the research communities, about the flexibility afforded by the research exemption provisions.

D. Analysis of biotechnology risks

Biotechnology is subject to several international agreements. The transfer, handling and use of living modified organisms (LMO) is addressed in the Convention on Biological Diversity (CBD) and the Cartagena Protocol on Biosafety (Cartagena Protocol). Trade in biotechnology products is subject to GATT/WTO law. The picture is one of fragmentation where different standards, if they exist, apply to risk assessment and risk management and no uniform perceptions exist as to the role and scope of the precautionary principles in the field. We suggest a review of the standards of risk management and risk assessment and a focus on reform of the

52 Panel Report, *Canada – Patent Protection*, para. 7.34–7.38.

53 Directive 2001/83/EC of the European Parliament and of the Council of 6 November 2001 on the Community code relating to medicinal products for human use, as amended by Directive 2004/27/EC of the European Parliament and of the Council of 31 March 2004 amending Directive 2001/83/EC on the Community code relating to medicinal products for human use.

54 307 F.3d 1351 (Fed. Cir. 2002).

55 For ASEAN countries see S. Jusoh, *Biotechnology Law and Regulation: The ASEAN Perspective* (London: Cameron May, 2006).

Agreement on the Application of Sanitary and Phytosanitary Measures (SPS Agreement) in the WTO with a view to bringing about better coherence. The proposal is essentially based upon the idea that risk assessment, risk management and risk communication should be clearly separated and allocated to different levels of multilayered governance.

I. Risk analysis in general

The theory of risk analysis distinguishes three components: risk assessment, risk management and risk communication. This triad emerged mainly in the field of financial risks, but equally applies to technology, including biotechnology.[56] There are two potential risks linked to genetic modification: one is the risk posed by the release of genetically modified organisms into nature which may affect, on the one hand, biological diversity in general and, on the other, neighbouring conventional crops and the production of organic and natural food. The second risk is that posed to human and animal health. Both aspects have informed restrictive legislation which has given rise to serious tensions in international trade relations.

The disciplines of risk assessment and management are not uniform. Different regulatory approaches employ different definitions, and the relationship between assessment and management varies. Moreover, different regulatory instruments apply to divergent threats. The Cartagena Protocol addresses the problem of release into the environment at large, while WTO, in particular the SPS Agreement, deals with trade restrictions based upon health and environmental concerns. The Panel in *EC – Biotech* found that neither the CBD nor the Cartagena Protocol was applicable to the case at hand as the Panel interpreted Article 31(3)(c) of the Vienna Convention on the Law of Treaties (VCLT) in a way that international treaties only apply between WTO Members which are also party to the international treaty in question.[57] Hence, the SPS Agreement takes centre stage in regulating trade in biotech products involving countries which are not party to the CBD and the Cartagena Protocol, in particular the big biotech producers, namely the US, Canada and Argentina.

56 See Cartagena Protocol Articles 15, 16, 23 and Annex III; and R. Andrén and B. Parish 'Risk assessment', in Christoph Bail, Robert Falkner and Helen Marquard (eds.), *The Cartagena Protocol on Biosafety: Reconciling Trade in Biotechnology with Environment & Development?* (London: Earthscan, 2002), pp. 335, 336.

57 Panel Report, European Communities – Measures Affecting the Approval and Marketing of Biotech Products, WT/DS291/R, WT/DS292/R, WT/DS293/R, paras. 7.74, 7.75.

II. Main approaches and differences

In theory, risk assessment depicts a scientific analysis of risk and is distinguished from risk management which exercises governmental functions on the basis of appropriate levels of risks being adopted, which may take into account economic and other factors.[58] The US has a long tradition of separation between the 'scientific' process of risk assessment and the policy-driven process of risk management. In Europe, however, the dividing line between risk assessment and risk management is more blurred.[59] The challenge of integrating 'scientific soundness' with economic, societal and environmental concerns sheds light on the iterative nature of scientific risk assessment procedures, on the one hand, and policy-driven risk management considerations, on the other.

The Codex Alimentarius Commission (Codex) suggests a functional separation of risk assessment and risk management. This is to ensure the scientific integrity of the risk assessment, to avoid confusion over the functions to be performed by risk assessors and risk managers, and to reduce any conflict of interest. The Codex also recognises that risk analysis is an iterative process where interaction between risk managers and risk assessors is essential.[60]

By contrast to the approach in the Cartagena Protocol that distinguishes risk assessment and risk management, the SPS Agreement does not distinguish between the two. The SPS Agreement also requires authorities to include economic and other factors within a single operation called risk assessment. Equally, precaution is given a minor status by the SPS Agreement compared to the Cartagena Protocol.

The SPS Agreement was designed to address 'quarantine risks' to human, animal or plant life or health, e.g. plant pests, animal diseases and risks to human health from additives, contaminants and toxins. It is ill-suited to deal effectively with increasing scientific requirements in assessing risks deriving from the application of new technologies in food production and agriculture, e.g. biotechnology and nanotechnology. Problems relating to an unclear or missing functional separation of risk assessment and risk management as identified by the Codex Alimentarius Commission, i.e. corruption of scientific integrity, confusion over the role of risk assessors and risk managers, and conflicts of interests can be

58 R. Fairman, C. Mead and P. Williams *Environmental Risk Assessment: Approaches, Experiences and Information Sources* (Copenhagen: European Environmental Agency, 1998), p. 20.

59 *Ibid.*

60 Codex Alimentarius Commission, Procedural Manual 2007, p. 113.

observed in SPS case law. In the case *Australia – Salmon*, scientific integrity was corrupted by the Australian Department of Primary Industries and Energy reversing the scientific findings of its Quarantine and Inspection Service for protectionist motives.[61] Confusion over the functions of risk assessors and risk managers became apparent in the *EC – Hormones* case.[62] Conflicts of interests were identified by the Appellate Body in the *Continued Suspension* cases, considering that institutional affiliations of scientific experts with the Joint FAO/WHO Expert Committee of Food Additives 'compromised the adjudicative independence and impartiality of the Panel'.[63]

Experience with biotechnology assessment in foodstuffs had not yet been gained when the SPS Agreement was negotiated. The Cartagena Protocol, negotiated later, embodies wider experience in the field which in turn should find its way into the SPS Agreement, at least for the purpose of assessing biotechnology, but possibly in more general terms. It is difficult to see why the two agreements should operate a different standard when it comes to risk assessment and risk management. We suggest that the methods and procedures should be aligned and based upon a clear operational distinction between risk assessment and risk management. Scientific work is not free from value judgements, but it would nevertheless seem possible to allocate societal factors exclusively to risk management. We insist on the fundamental distinction for yet another reason, which is that it also serves as a criterion for allocating regulatory powers among different layers of multilayered governance.

III. *Reforming the SPS Agreement*

1. Internationalising risk assessment

Experience, such as that gained in *Australia – Salmon,* shows that a clear institutional separation of risk assessment and risk management is difficult to achieve at the national level.[64] This is particularly true when it comes to biotechnology as a politically sensitive area. Moreover, many

61 Panel Report, *Australia – Salmon*, para. 8.154; finding upheld by the Appellate Body, Appellate Body Report, *Australia – Salmon*, paras. 170, 173.

62 Appellate Body Report, *EC – Hormones*, para. 206.

63 Appellate Body Reports, *US/Canada – Continued Suspension*, paras. 456–482, in particular para. 481; reversing Panel's findings in *US – Continued Suspension*, paras. 6.22, 6.62–6.63 and 7.85, also *Canada – Continued Suspension*, paras. 6.21, 6.57–6.58 and 7.83.

64 Panel Report *Australia – Salmon*, above note 62, para. 8.154; finding upheld by the Appellate Body, above note 62, paras. 170, 173.

countries are not in a position to support highly specialised scientific institutions able to undertake reliable and sound risk assessment. As risk assessment is a highly specialised activity, which depends on expertise and experience, it is appropriate to seek a system of risk assessment to be carried out by networks of institutions under the auspices of the relevant international organisations. We recommend, based on the doctrine of multilayered governance, engagement in a clear vertical separation of powers and placing risk assessments with those international bodies already concerned with the elaboration of international standards in the relevant fields, i.e. the Codex, the World Organisation for Animal Health (OIE), and the International Plant Protection Convention (IPPC). The task of providing risk assessments in individual cases could be assigned to bodies already established by Codex, OIE and IPPC which could be used as nuclei for establishing an international network for risk assessments on an individual basis, mandated by the specific Member State wishing to introduce an SPS measure. We are aware that scientific risk assessment is not free of value judgement, but we think that subjective elements here and elsewhere will best be addressed by providing full transparency with regard to the background, funding and interests of the research institutions and researchers involved. We do not consider these problems to be different at the national and international levels. In fact, we think that transparency and independence from vested interests in risk assessment can be more efficiently achieved by working within an international network of accredited institutions. Internationalisation of risk assessments would also favour developing countries and least developed countries, which are prevented from participating fully in SPS procedures owing to limited scientific resources.

BOX 7.1 PROPOSAL TO AMEND ARTICLE 5 OF THE SPS AGREEMENT

Article 5: [*Risk Assessment*]
Members shall ensure that their sanitary or phytosanitary measures are based on an [*international*] assessment, as appropriate to the circumstances, of the risks to human, animal or plant life or health [*based upon determination of respective international organisations and accredited specialised scientific research institutions*].

2. Domestic risk management

The theory of risk analysis emphasises the fundamental role of risk management and its iterative relationship to risk assessment. In particular, risk managers have to provide a risk assessment policy for risk assessors, defining, inter alia, the appropriate level of protection (ALOP). Risk is defined by Codex as '[A] function of the probability of an adverse effect and the severity of that effect, consequential to a hazard(s) in food'.[65] By formulating a risk assessment policy, risk managers essentially have to define the factor of probability deemed necessary to achieve the ALOP in the sense of Article 5 of the SPS Agreement.

The definition of ALOP, as well as taking into account economic and other factors in managing risk is inherently a task for domestic authorities. Based upon the results of the risk assessment, appropriate measures are adopted commensurate with the defined appropriate level.

Therefore, it has to be laid down explicitly in the SPS Agreement that risk management is an exercise distinct from risk assessment and that it has to be carried out at the appropriate national levels.

It is proposed that risk management should be defined in the SPS Agreement. Technically, the proposal suggests that Articles 5.3–5.6 SPS Agreement shall be carved out into a separate Article, entitled '*Risk Management* and Determination of the Appropriate Level of Sanitary or Phytosanitary Protection'. In terms of substance, the wording of the previous Articles 5.3–5.6 SPS may remain unchanged.

BOX 7.2 PROPOSAL TO AMEND ARTICLES 5.3, 5.4, 5.5 AND 5.6 OF THE SPS AGREEMENT

[*Risk Management*] and Determination of the Appropriate Level of Sanitary or Phytosanitary Protection

3. In [*managing*] the risk to animal or plant life or health and determining (. . .).
4. Members should, when determining (. . .).
5. With the objective of achieving consistency (. . .).
6. Without prejudice (. . .).

3. Socio-economic considerations as part of risk management

Socio-economic considerations are an important part of defining ALOP and adopting appropriate measures. These factors should not be considered in scientific risk assessment, but find their proper place in what amounts to a political and legal regulation of the risks involved. Article 5.3 of the SPS Agreement only accepts the need to take into account direct economic damage from animal diseases or plant pests.

65 Codex Alimentarius Commission, *Procedural Manual*, p. 44.

Indirect effects, such as the risk of developing countries being denied access to EU markets when adopting GM technology, are not sufficiently covered by the narrow definition of quarantine risks in the sense of Annex A(4) of the SPS Agreement.

We therefore submit that a new provision, addressing socio-economic concerns as part of the legitimate risk management considerations should be introduced in the SPS Agreement. This will be in line with Article 26 of the Cartagena Protocol. In particular, the proposal takes into account the need for addressing socio-economic considerations in cases where WTO Members are not party to the Cartagena Protocol, but biotechnology is at issue.

BOX 7.3 PROPOSAL TO INSERT SOCIO-ECONOMIC PROVISION INTO THE SPS AGREEMENT

[*Socio-Economic Considerations*
In managing risks to human, animal and plant life or health, Members may take into account socio-economic considerations arising from the impact of novel plants and novel animal breeds, in particular with regard to sustainable agriculture and food security.]

4. Strengthen the precautionary approach in the SPS agreement

The proposed separation of powers between international risk assessment and domestic risk management is complemented by a review and reform of the precautionary approach in the SPS Agreement. We submit a proposal to revise Article 5.7 SPS accordingly. The requirement 'to obtain the additional [*scientific*] information [. . .] within a reasonable period of time' would rest upon international scientific expert bodies. The proposal would enable developing countries and least developed countries with insufficient means for carrying out complex risk assessments to make use of provisional measures in the same way as industrialised countries.

5. The interplay of international risk assessment and domestic risk management

The doctrine of multilayered governance allows clarification of the interplay of risk assessment and risk management within existing international organisations and national authorities. The adoption of international standards by Member States of relevant international bodies implies that Members agree on a common and shared perception of ALOP, providing,

BOX 7.4 PROPOSAL FOR NEW PROVISION ON PROVISIONAL MEASURES IN THE SPS AGREEMENT

[*Provisional Measures*] (previously Article 5.7)
In cases where relevant scientific evidence is insufficient, a Member may provisionally adopt sanitary or phytosanitary measures on the basis of available pertinent information, including that from the relevant international organisations as well as from sanitary or phytosanitary measures applied by other Members. In such circumstances, Members shall seek to obtain the additional [*scientific*] information necessary for a more objective assessment of risk [*from the relevant international organisations*] and review the sanitary or phytosanitary measure accordingly within a reasonable period of time.

together with the risk assessment, a common basis for an equally shared risk management. Adoption of international standards of this kind, however, does not bar a Member from seeking a higher level of protection, i.e. adopting its own separate ALOP in accordance with the principles set out in Article 3 of the SPS Agreement. In this case, national risk managers turn to international risk assessment to be undertaken on the basis of the level of risk defined by these authorities. Scientific assessment will then be undertaken taking the defined level into account. In extremis, and provided consistency is assured, it may amount to a zero risk policy, and restrictions may only be excluded in such cases where no scientific risk at all can be found and identified. The same approach applies, subject to precautionary measures, in areas where no international standard exists and individual countries do not wish to wait for the elaboration of an international standard. Based upon the ALOP defined, or the options defined, a risk assessment would be undertaken by the appropriate accredited institution within the international scientific network. Under this proposal, the role of national risk assessment, properly speaking, would be limited to cases of emergency and monitoring compliance. The main contribution of Members consists of making available the services of specialised laboratories serving, in specialised areas, all Members of the system alike.

6. Introducing risk communication

Finally, it is appropriate to introduce disciplines relating to risk communication into the SPS Agreement. Inspired by information principles developed by the Convention on Access to Information, Public Participation in Decision-Making and Access to Justice in Environmental Matters (Aarhus

Convention), the SPS Agreement should enable consumers to gain access to information necessary for making informed judgements.

Labelling is a way of addressing consumers' concerns with minimal trade-distorting effect. However, in cases where no risks have been scientifically established, reference to the Agreement on Technical Barriers to Trade (TBT Agreement) is of no avail. The TBT Agreement also requires the existence of some kind of objectively assessable risk (Article 2.2 TBT). Therefore, it is proposed to introduce a provision into the SPS Agreement addressing subjective consumers' concerns, e.g. information about hormones or biotechnological modifications, or on ecological[66] and ethical issues.[67] The proposed labelling schemes should inform consumers about positive features of relevant products (positive labelling). The relevant product sensitivities should be established through recognised scientific techniques, e.g. opinion polls. The following wording is suggested:

BOX 7.5 PROPOSED NEW PROVISION ON RISK COMMUNICATION IN THE SPS AGREEMENT

[*Risk Communication*
Members shall enable public access to adequate product information about risks to human, animal and plant life or health, taking into account consumers' perceptions, as assessed by the relevant social scientific disciplines, and the objective of minimising negative trade effects.]

Reform of the SPS Agreement is a viable option, in line with the gradual reform of other WTO Agreements. Aligning the SPS Agreement to the disciplines and methods expounded in the Cartagena Protocol will result in more coherent regulation built upon vertical separations of powers and principles of multilayered governance. A reformed SPS Agreement will be better equipped to distinguish genuine concerns for safety from creeping economic protectionism often inherent in today's practices of domestic regulations.

E. Liability rules in biotechnology

This section discusses the fragmentation of rules on liability for transboundary damage caused by biotechnology. The release of GMOs has the potential to cause harm to neighbouring crops. The problem is inherently

66 E.g. organic produce. 67 E.g. animal welfare and cloning.

one of international transboundary harm, as well as of domestic liability rules.

Liability rules in this area involve both substantive liability rules and procedural rules. Substantive liability rules may differ depending upon the type of liability, namely state responsibility, state liability or civil liability, whereas procedural rules in transboundary liability relate to the application of private international law. The question here is, whether such liability rules should and could be harmonised.

I. The fragmentation of liability rules in biotechnology

Fragmentation in the liability rules in biotechnology is due to several factors: firstly, the existing international rules applicable to such damage are based on the general rules applicable to all other types of damage. Secondly, although there are national liability rules for damage caused by biotechnology, such as those in Germany and Switzerland, these rules do not address the issue of transboundary damage. Thirdly, there are several available courses of action: a state may be 'liable' under the rules of state responsibility, which is part of public international law, or alternatively under the rules of state liability, which is based on national administrative law. Further, private parties may stake a transboundary claim against another private party under civil liability.

1. Fragmentation in state responsibility

Rules on state responsibility are applicable when a state claims against another state for transboundary damage caused by biotechnology. These rules are based on international customary law, where a state is under a general obligation not to cause injury to another state, based on the good neighbour principle.[68] One of the factors contributing to the fragmentation of state responsibility in biotechnology is the generality of this rule, which does not correspond to the complexities of modern biotechnology.

For instance, uncertainty may arise due to the International Court of Justice's decision not to hold a party liable when that party announced that it would cease to commit the act that was the cause of the complaint.[69] Applied to liability in transboundary damage caused by a GMO, this

68 *Trail Smelter Arbitration Tribunal,* Award II (1941) 3 RIAA 1905, at 1963.

69 The Nuclear Tests case (*New Zealand* v. *France*), [106 ILR 1] International Court of Justice, 20 December 1974.

would mean that a state that has contributed to the damage will not face any consequence if it takes steps to stop the activities causing the damage. In addition, there is uncertainty as to the applicable standard of liability. The question here is whether fault-based or strict liability is applicable. Fault-based liability requires proof of fault or negligence on the part of the person accused of causing the damage. Strict liability is the legal responsibility for damages even if the person found strictly liable was not at fault or negligent. Although international customary law normally imposes fault-based liability, treaties such as the Convention on International Liability for Damage Caused by Space Objects 1972 may impose strict or absolute liability.[70]

2. Fragmentation in state liability

Rules on state liability will be applicable when a private party claims against the state for damage caused by biotechnology. Yet, as state liability is normally a matter of domestic administrative law, it is not clear whether state liability will also be applicable in the case of transboundary damage caused by biotechnology. Nevertheless, the ECJ has held that Member States are obliged to pay compensation for harm caused to individuals when there are 'sufficiently serious breaches of Community law which focuses on the conduct of the Member State and its relationship to the norm established by Community Law'.[71] This means that an EU national can bring an action against another EU Member State for breach of community law, such as failure to implement the EU Biotechnology Directives.[72]

3. Fragmentation of international civil liability rules

Civil liability rules are applicable to transnational litigation between private parties in different jurisdictions. Yet, different legal cultures and different treatment of biotechnology in the individual states may lead to

70 Convention on International Liability for Damage Caused by Space Objects 1972, Article III.

71 Joined Cases C–6/90 & C–9/90, *Francovich* v. *Italy*, 1991 ECR I–5357, para. 37, read together with Joined Cases C–46/93 & C–48/93, *Brasserie du Pêcheur SA* v. *Germany* and *R.* v. *Secretary of State for Transport, ex parte Factortame Ltd and others*, [1996] ECR I-1029.

72 Directive 2001/18/EC of the European Parliament and of the Council of 12 March 2001 on the deliberate release into the environment of genetically modified organisms and repealing Council Directive 90/220/EEC, OJ L 106 17.4.2001, pp. 1–39.

fragmentation of the national liability rules which affects transboundary civil litigation. This is true especially in setting the standards of liability.

Leading exporters of GMOs such as Canada and the US treat GM crops as 'substantially equivalent' to their conventional counterparts; accordingly they are assumed not to pose any special risks.[73] Many common law countries such as Australia, Canada and the US and countries that accept GM crops as 'substantially equivalent' lean towards fault-based liability. This includes the United Kingdom, although as an EU Member State, it has to implement the EU Environmental Liability Directive which imposes strict liability for environmental damage caused by operators of GMOs.[74]

On the other hand, some countries such as the EU Member States and Switzerland use 'the process oriented approach' which considers the products resulting from genetic engineering as different from conventional products.[75] These countries classify GMOs as posing increased risks, and therefore impose strict liability.

Different jurisdictions, such as the EU and the US, have different procedural rules which may have an impact on access to justice and the enforcement of a judgment in any international biotechnology-related litigation. For example, the Brussels Convention imposes an inflexible *lis pendens* rule whereas the courts in the US use the 'minimum contacts' test and the 'purposeful availment' test.[76]

Fragmentation also exists in the way countries treat recovery of economic loss. In many countries only consequential economic loss is recoverable; this means the loss resulting from a physical injury to the plaintiff's own person or property. But the Swiss and the German laws on genetic engineering allow for recovering the economic loss that has been incurred as a result of having to pay for restoration of the environment.[77]

Recoverability of any redress for any liability in biotechnology is aggravated by the difficulty in obtaining insurance cover due to various factors

73 B. R. Furrow, 'Governing science: Public risks and private remedies' (1983) 131 *University of Pennsylvania Law Review* 1403, 1466.

74 Directive 2004/35/CE of the European Parliament and of the Council of 21 April 2004 on environmental liability with regard to the prevention and remedying of environmental damage, OJ L 143, 30.4.2004, p. 56–75.

75 P. Newell, and D. Glover, 'Business and biotechnology: regulation and the politics of influence', (July 2003), IDS Working Paper 192, p. 4.

76 See *International Shoe Co.* v. *Washington* 326 US 310 (1945) and *Asahi Metal Industry Co.* v. *Superior Court of California* 480 US 102 (1987).

77 See B. Feldthusen, *Economic Negligence* (Ottawa, Carswell, 2nd edn, 1989) pp. 199–280.

such as lack of actuarial data for calculation of premium, and the application of strict liability.[78]

II. Harmonisation of liability rules?

The above-mentioned fragmentation of the liability rules on transboundary damage caused by biotechnology leads to the question of whether there should be harmonised rules.

The parties to the Cartagena Protocol have been elaborating liability rules on transboundary movement of LMO since 2004. In their draft rules, the Friends of the Co-Chairs under Article 27 of the Cartagena Protocol express a preference for an internationally binding instrument. The draft rules state that the existing rules on state responsibility remain applicable[79] and the parties are still undecided on the civil liability rules. As it stands, the draft only proposes guidelines and thus leaves many issues such as the standards of liability to the national laws.[80]

There are also concerns about the relationship between the Cartagena Protocol and the WTO Agreements, especially in relation to the application of the liability rules to non-parties. This is because the Cartagena Protocol deals with both the environment and the transboundary movement of GMOs which may involve international trade.[81] As mentioned above, the WTO Panel in *EC – Biotech* decided that the Cartagena Protocol was not applicable as the US, Canada and Argentina are not parties to it.[82] One way to resolve the potential conflict between the two frameworks is to treat them as mutually supportive with room for systematic integration under Article 31(3)(c) VCLT.

III. Conclusions and recommendations

The above discussion shows that liability rules on transboundary damage caused by biotechnology are highly fragmented. The fragmentations

78 T. Epprecht, *Cartagena Protocol on Biosafety: Insurance Industry and Art. 27 (Liability and Redress) of the Cartagena Protocol* (Zurich: Swiss Reinsurance Company, 2002), p. 3.

79 Draft Decision on the Liability and Redress as recommended by the Groups of the Friends of the Co-Chairs, 1st meeting, Mexico City, 23–27 February 2009, UNEP/CBD/BS/GF-LR&R/1/3.

80 Texts of the Friends of the Co-Chair under Article 27 of the Cartagena Protocol, UNEP/CBD/BS/COP-MOP/4/18.

81 T. Cottier, 'Implications for trade law and policy: Towards convergence and integration', in Christoph Bail, Robert Falkner and Helen Marquard (eds.), *The Cartagena Protocol on Biosafety – Reconciling Trade in Biotechnology with Environment and Development* (London: Earthscan, 2002), p. 467.

82 Panel Report, *EC – Biotech*, above note 57, paras. 7.74–7.75.

arise from the availability of different causes of actions such as state responsibility and civil liability. There are also differences in the approach towards the standards of liability and the recovery of economic loss by different countries. At the same time, most of the existing rules are of general application and not unique to transboundary damage caused by biotechnology.

Thus, any attempt to harmonise liability rules in biotechnology is a difficult task. This may be illustrated by the work of the parties to the Cartagena Protocol, which started with high ambitions and ended up with a draft that leaves most of the issues to the national level. This establishes the strong role the national policy objectives play in deciding on liability rules in biotechnology, which will be based on the overall national policy objectives in this area.

As an alternative to an internationally harmonised system countries may opt for regional harmonisation measures such as those taken in the EU, under the Environmental Liability Directive which provides for a strict liability rule for GMO operators.[83] In addition, countries may also opt to adopt laws or court judgments from other countries, through mutual recognition. For example, the EU Product Liability Directives have been adopted, with modifications, by many countries such as Switzerland and Australia. Model laws may also be developed to suit the situation in a regional environment, for example, the African Model Law on Safety in Biotechnology 2003, which provides for liability and redress in Article 14. Countries may also adopt the ILC works on 'International liability for injurious consequences arising from acts not prohibited by international law' and the draft principles on the allocation of loss in the case of transboundary harm arising out of hazardous activities.

On the matter of redress and insurance, one possible solution is for countries to set up a mutual fund where countries suffering from transboundary damage caused by biotechnology could file a claim. In addition, private biotechnology exporters could establish their own compensation mechanism similar to the mechanism for marine oil pollution.

Any harmonisation process should take the interests of developing countries into account, especially regarding access of these countries to technology.[84] Any strict rules could hinder the development of such technology as researchers could take an easy way out by not conducting research in areas where they could be exposed to potential liability.

83 Directive 2004/35/CE, above note 74.

84 See S. Jusoh, 'Developing biotechnology legal system in developing countries: The case for Malaysia' (1983) 3 *Journal of International Biotechnology Law* 161–183.

F. Conclusion

The subject of biotechnology regulation in international law brings a widely mixed conclusion. International or global law is able to play an important, but not exclusive role in regulating biotechnology. While some areas are and should be harmonised, others are and should be left to domestic regulation and regulatory competition. Coherence can be improved as the interaction between the different regulatory areas and the relationship between international and domestic regulation becomes more finely tuned and better coordinated.

Human rights offer a clear foundation for the ban on biological warfare and weapons. Beyond this, human dignity and related rights do not allow for conclusions to be drawn one way or the other on balancing the pros and cons of genetic engineering. Human rights offer an important foundation for participation in decision-making relating to biotechnology in all proceedings related to the grant of intellectual property protection or marketing approval. New international disciplines are called for in the field of animal and plant genetic resources, with a view to generating and supporting biodiversity and to enhancing competition in a field which today is highly concentrated. The TRIPS Agreement should be amended with a view to creating minimal standards on access to protected resources for the purposes of research. The TRIPS Agreement should no longer be limited to minimal standards, but should also set ceilings with a view to enhancing competition and bringing about an appropriate balance between intellectual property and competition in the field. A reform of the SPS Agreement and international disciplines on risk assessment and risk management would be a mainstay of future international law in the field. It offers the potential to enhance coherence by placing risk assessment on the international level while leaving risk management and communication to domestic government. Provisional measures as defined in international law will offer sufficient room for governments to address genuine concerns.

Other areas are, in our view, best left to domestic law and thus regulatory competition. We do not see a need for harmonisation in the field of human genetics beyond general disciplines of intellectual property law. The matter is subject to highly diverging ethical and moral perceptions and ample policy space should be left to the individual states. This may result in restrictions on access to therapies and treatment. Finally, we conclude that liability rules in agricultural biotechnology are best left to domestic standards as they too reflect differing perceptions as to the use of and recourse to biotechnology in social and economic developments. Transboundary liability under international law, on the other hand, is addressed by the Cartagena Protocol and the general principles of international environmental law.

Bibliography

Anderson, Robert and Gallini, Nancy, 'Competition policy, intellectual property rights and efficiency: An introduction to the issues,' in R. D. Anderson and N. T. Gallini (eds.), *Competition Policy and Intellectual Property Rights in the Knowledge-Based Economy* (Cambridge University Press, 1998).

Anderson, Simon, 'Animal genetic resources and livelihoods' (2003) **45** *Ecological Economics* 331–339.

Anderson, Simon and Centonze, Roberto, 'Property rights and the management of animal genetic resources' (2007) **35** *World Development* 1529–1541.

Andrén, Robert and Parish, Bill, 'Risk assessment', in Christoph Bail, Robert Falkner and Helen Marquard (eds.), *The Cartagena Protocol on Biosafety: Reconciling Trade in Biotechnology with Environment & Development?* (London: Earthscan, 2002).

Arsanjani, Mahnoush, 'Negotiating the UN Declaration on Human Cloning' (2006) **100** *American Journal of International Law* 164.

Biber-Klemm, Susette, 'Trade in breeds at risk' *NCCR Trade Regulation Working Paper*, forthcoming, on file with author.

Biber-Klemm, Susette and Cottier, Thomas (eds.), *Rights to Plant Genetic Resources and Traditional Knowledge: Basic Issues and Perspectives* (CABI Publishing, 2006).

Bostyn, Sven, 'Patenting DNA sequences (polynucleotides) and scope of protection in the European Union: An evaluation, background study for the European Commission', Office for Official Publication of the European Communities, 2004.

Caulfield, Timothy, Cook-Deegan, Robert, Kieff, Scott and Walsh, John, 'Evidence and anecdotes: An analysis of human gene patenting controversies' (2006) **24** *Nature Biotechnology* 1091–1094.

Codex Alimentarius Commission. *Procedural Manual* (Rome: Food and Agriculture Organization of the United Nations, 17th edn, 2007).

Convention on Access to Information, Public Participation in Decision-Making and Access to Justice in Environmental Matters, adopted 1998 by the Fourth Ministerial Conference of the United Nations Economic Commission for Europe (UNECE) in Aarhus, Denmark.

Convention on Biodiversity. 'Report of the Fourth Meeting of the Conference of the Parties to the Convention on Biological Diversity Serving as the

Meeting of the Parties to the Cartagena Protocol on Biosafety' (25 June 2008), UNEP/CBD/BS/COP-MOP/4.

Cottier, Thomas, 'Implications for trade law and policy: Towards convergence and integration', in Christoph Bail, Robert Falkner and Helen Marquard (eds.) *The Cartagena Protocol on Biosafety: Reconciling trade in Biotechnology with Environment and Development* (London: Earthscan, 2002).

Cottier, Thomas, 'From progressive liberalisation to progressive regulation in WTO law' (2006) **9** *Journal of International Economic Law* 779–821.

Cottier, Thomas, 'Genetic engineering, trade and human rights', in F. Francioni (ed.), *Studies in International Law No. 13, Biotechnologies and International Human Rights* (Oxford: Hart Publishing, 2007), pp. 275–314.

Cottier, Thomas, Temmerman, Michelangelo, Jusoh, Sufian and Dolotbaeva, Aida, *The Research Exemption in Patent Law* (forthcoming).

Epprecht, Thomas, *Cartagena Protocol on Biosafety: Insurance Industry and Art 27 (Liability and Redress) of the Cartagena Protocol* (Zurich: Swiss Reinsurance Company, 2002).

European Patent Office, *Guidelines for Examination*, June 2005, available at www.epo.org/patents/law/legal-texts/html/guiex/e/c_ii_4_1.htm (last accessed 29 April 2008).

Fairman, Robyn, Mead, Carl and Williams, Peter, *Environmental Risk Assessment. Approaches, Experiences and Information Sources* (Copenhagen: European Environmental Agency, 1998).

Feldthusen, Bruce, *Economic Negligence* (Ottawa: Carswell, 2nd edn, 1989).

Food and Agriculture Organization of the United Nations, *The State of the World's Animal Genetic Resources for Food and Agriculture* (Rome: Food and Agriculture Organization of the United Nations, 2007).

Furrow, Barry, 'Governing science: Public risks and private remedies' (1983) **131** *University of Pennsylvania Law Review* 1403, 1466.

Gura, Susanne, *Livestock Genetic Companies: Concentration and Proprietary Strategies of an Emerging Power in the Global Food Economy* (Ober-Ramstadt: League for Pastoral Peoples and Indigenous Livestock Development, 2007).

International Law Association, *International Law on Biotechnology: Conference Report Rio de Janeiro 2008*, available at: www.ila-hq.org/en/committees/draft_committee_reports_rio_2008.cfm (last accessed 9 February 2009).

International Law Commission, Report of the Study Group on Fragmentation of International Law, 54th Session of the International Law Commission, Geneva, 29 April–7 June and 22 July–16 August 2002, CN.4/L.628.

Jusoh, Sufian, *Biotechnology Law and Regulation: The ASEAN Perspective* (London: Cameron May, 2006).

Jusoh, Sufian, 'Developing biotechnology legal system in developing countries: The case for Malaysia' (2006) **3** *Journal of International Biotechnology Law* 161–183.

Karapinar, Baris and Temmerman, Michelangelo, 'Benefiting from biotechnology: Promoting small-farm competitiveness and intellectual property rights' (2007) **4** *African Technology Development Journal* 3.

Karapinar, Baris and Temmerman, Michelangelo, 'Benefiting from biotechnology: Pro-poor IPRs and public-private partnerships' (2008) **27** *Biotechnology Law Report* 189.

Köller-Rollefson, Ilse, 'Keepers of genes: The interdependence between pastoralists, breeds, access to the commons, and livelihoods', Sadri Rajasthan, the LIFE Network (2007), available online at: www.pastoralpeoples.org/docs/keepersofgenes_web.pdf (last accessed 22 February 2009).

Lesser, William, 'Animal variety protection: A proposal for a US model law' (1993) **76** *Journal of Patent and Trademark Office Society* 697–715.

Molinuevo, Hector, *Genética bovina y producción en pastoreo* (Buenos Aires: INTA, 2005).

Newell, Peter and Glover, Dominic, 'Business and biotechnology: Regulation and the politics of influence' (July 2003), IDS Working Paper 192.

Nieman, Heiner, Kues, Wilfried and Carnwath, Joseph, 'Transgene farm animals: Current status and perspectives for agriculture and biomedicine', in M. Engelhard, K. Hagen and M. Boysen (eds.), *Genetic Engineering in Livestock. New Applications and Interdisciplinary Perspectives* (Berlin/Heidelberg: Springer, 2009).

Palmiter, Richard, Chen, Howard and Brinster, Ralph, 'Differential regulation of metallothionein-thymidine kinase fusion genes in transgenic mice and their offspring' (1982) **29** *Cell* 701–710.

Schefer, Markus, 'Human Rights and Patenting the Results of Research on Human Material', Paper presented at the NCCR Workshop 'Human Rights in the Patent Procedure', Bern, 28 March 2007.

Schumpeter, Jose, *Capitalism, Socialism and Democracy* (New York: Harper and Row, 3rd edn, 1950).

Sommer, Tine, 'Patenting the animal kingdom? From cross-breeding to genetic make-up and biomedical research' (2008) **39** *International Review of Intellectual Property and Competition Law* 2.

Straus, Joseph, 'Genomics and the food industry: Outlook from an intellectual property perspective', in D. Vaver and L. Bently (eds.), *Intellectual Property in the New Millennium: Essays in Honour of William R. Cornish* (Cambridge University Press, 2004), p. 134.

Temmerman, Michelangelo, 'Die Patentierbarkeit von gentechnischen Erfindungen auf internationaler Ebene' (August 2006) *Die Volkswirtschaft* 13–17.

Temmerman, Michelangelo, 'The patentability of plant genetic inventions' NCCR Trade Regulation Working Paper 2007/04 (Bern, 2007), available at: www.nccr-trade.org and at http://www.ssrn.com/

Thorstenson, Anna, 'Patentability of human genetic stem cells: Finding the balance between the moral hazard in Europe and the wide scope in US', University of Lund, Spring 2007 available at: www.essays.se/essay/2f3a87a000.

Tvedt, Morten and Finckenhagen, Magnus, 'Scope of process patents in farm animal breeding' (2008) **11** *Journal of World Intellectual Property* 203–228.

Tvedt, Morten, Hiemstra, Sipke, Drucker, Adam, Louwaars, Niels *et al.*, *Legal Aspects of Exchange, Use and Conservation of Farm Animal Genetic Resources*, Fridtjof Nansens Institutt, FNI Report 1/2007, available at: www.fni.no/doc&pdf/FNI-R0107.pdf.

United States Patent & Trademark Office, *Manual of Patent Examining Procedure* (September 2007).

Verbeure, Birgit, Matthijs, Gert and Van Overwalle, Geertrui, Analysing DNA patents in relation with diagnostic genetic testing (2006) **14** *European Journal of Human Genetics* 26.

Verrier, Etienne, Tixier-Boichars, M., Bernigaud, R. and Naves, M., 'Conservation and value of local livestock breeds: usefulness of niche products and/or adaptation to specific environments', *FAO Animal Resources Information* (2005), available online at: www.fao.org/docrep/008/a0070t/a0070t07.htm.

Whish, Richard. *Competition Law* (Oxford University Press, 6th edn, 2009).

PART III

'Trade and . . . ' linkages

8

A call for a WTO ministerial decision on trade and human rights

BARNALI CHOUDHURY, KATJA GEHNE, SIMONE HERI, FRANZISKA HUMBERT, CHRISTINE KAUFMANN AND KRISTA NADAKAVUKAREN SCHEFER*

KEY MESSAGES

- International trade law and human rights share a common origin as mutually supportive bodies of law to protect individual freedom. Yet, to a large extent they developed in isolation from each other. As a result, the two regimes are now part of the fragmented landscape of international law. On the one hand, human rights protect individual rights that are essential for international trade, such as rights to freely pursue economic activities or freedom of expression. On the other hand, trade rules may jeopardise the realisation of human rights, especially social rights.
- In order to avoid negative impacts of this fragmentation, mechanisms for solving conflicts between the two regimes are necessary. We argue that such mechanisms require neither a rigid concept of hierarchy of norms nor new substantive obligations to be imposed on states. Instead, we call for appropriate procedures and coordination. This general procedural approach is illustrated for specific human rights and their relation to international trade law.

A. Introduction

At first glance, human rights[1] and trade regimes do not have much in common. Human rights' primary focus on ensuring human dignity for each individual is absent from trade's commitment to ensuring that nations can flourish economically. Separate in their legal development in the

∗ Individual Project No. 4, 'Human Rights and Trade'.

1 The term 'human rights' in this document refers to existing human rights norms as enshrined in core international human rights treaties.

twentieth century,[2] human rights and trade regimes are, however, as offspring of an international post-world war order, both instruments of the same overall global interest, which is to promote peace and human welfare. As different sides of the same coin, they are mutually complementary. The objective of the World Trade Organization (WTO) of increasing human welfare with an open trading system that fosters employment and development at the same time requires and promotes individual freedom and human rights.[3] Human rights serve trade interests because they enhance economic potential (e.g. human resources and education) and protect economic freedoms. Defining procedures and parameters to strike a careful balance when, in a fragmented international order, systemic overlaps occur, is thus crucial to assure the effectiveness of both regimes. In addition, the sustainable development provision as anchored in the preamble of the WTO Marrakesh Agreement requires balancing WTO economic objectives against social and environmental concerns.[4] As human rights standards form part of the social factor of the concept[5] the task of efficiently coordinating human rights and WTO law is implicitly expressed in the sustainability objective to which WTO Members have committed.

However, after almost fifteen years of existence of the WTO, this mandate has still not been fulfilled. WTO bodies have not reacted to the human rights approach to trade proposed by the UN High Commissioner for Human Rights. The Doha Agenda does not refer to human rights.[6] New initiatives for coordinating international trade law and human rights seem unlikely in the near future.[7] Hence, WTO policy is not only committed to coordinate both systems, but is also under

2 T. Cottier, 'Trade and human rights, a relationship to discover' (2002) 5 *Journal of International Economic Law* 111.

3 T. Cottier, 'Legitimacy of the WTO law' (2008) NCCR Working Paper 2008/19, 6; S. A. Aaronson, 'Seeping in slowly: How human rights concerns are penetrating the WTO' (2007) 6 *World Trade Review* 413.

4 Appellate Body Report, *US – Shrimp*, para. 129, at footnote 107; International Law Association, Report of the 70th Conference, New Delhi, Committee on Legal Aspects of Sustainable Development (Cambrian Printers, 2002), pp. 385–398.

5 K. Gehne, 'Nachhaltige Entwicklung als Rechtsprinzip: normativer Aussagegehalt, rechtstheoretische Einordnung, Funktionen im Recht', PhD thesis, University of Zürich (2008).

6 R. Howse and R. G. Teitel, 'Beyond the divide: The Covenant on Economic, Social and Cultural Rights and the World Trade Organization' (2007) 30 *Dialogue on Globalization*, available at: http://library.fes.de/pdf-files/iez/global/04572.pdf (visited 14 April 2009), p. 5.

7 International Law Association, 'Report of the 73rd Conference', Rio de Janeiro, (2008), Committee on International Trade Law, para. 39.

pressure to react. No legal system will operate effectively if the solution of potential conflicts of norms is left to legal uncertainty and the related legitimacy concerns are being ignored. Neither the human rights nor the trade regime can function effectively if they are not promoted in such a way as to mutually assure their objectives. If the WTO remains silent on overlapping trade and human rights issues, it loses credibility which may jeopardise its status as a key actor in international governance.[8] Legal instruments to coordinate both regimes, as proposed in this chapter, could contribute significantly to a more coherent and predictable legal structure, improve international decision making and sustain the Organization's legitimacy. The goal is not to establish a hierarchy of one regime over the other based on ideological concepts or to freeze legal options into a fixed system of rules. Rather, we aim at an ongoing process of creating flexible legal and institutional mechanisms which allow the careful balancing and coherent development of both systems on a case-by-case basis. The systemic necessity for coherently interpreting trade and human rights rules has already been acknowledged by the International Law Association Trade Law Committee in its 2008 Report which submitted a Draft ILA Declaration on International Trade Law and Human Rights.[9] This chapter will go beyond this approach by suggesting a general framework as well as recommendations for specific human rights.

In the following we are advocating a Multilateral Agreement on Trade and Human Rights to be annexed to the WTO Marrakesh Agreement. With a view to creating such a commitment and launching the necessary political process, we propose a WTO Ministerial Decision to prepare the agreement. In this vein, we first present an annotated Draft Decision on Trade and Human Rights (B). Second, based on our research, we set out elements of a Multilateral Agreement on Trade and Human Rights (C). Third, we elaborate on regulatory initiatives in specific areas which could be considered as annexes to the Multilateral Trade and Human Rights Agreement or other WTO agreements (D).

8 E.-U. Petersmann, 'The "Human Rights Approach" advocated by the UN High Commissioner for Human Rights and by the International Labour Organization: Is it relevant for WTO law and policy?' (2004) 7 *Journal of International Economic Law* 611; J. Pauwelyn, 'The Sutherland Report: A missed opportunity for genuine debate on trade, globalization and reforming the WTO' (2005) 8 *Journal of International Economic Law* 331.

9 International Law Association, Report of the 73rd Conference, Rio de Janeiro (2008), Committee on International Trade Law, available at www.ila-hq.org/en/committees/index.cfm/cid/24 (visited 14 April 2009), para. 35.

B. Creating the commitment: a decision on trade and human rights as a starting point and normative guideline

The following draft Decision on Trade and Human Rights together with short comments transmits some of our key research findings and their potential policy implications. It is intended as a commitment for coordinating trade law and human rights by the Ministerial Conference which can take decisions on all matters under any of the multilateral trade agreements.[10]

BOX 8.1 DRAFT DECISION ON TRADE AND HUMAN RIGHTS

DECISION ON TRADE AND HUMAN RIGHTS

Ministers,

- Recognising that human rights concerns are inextricably linked to free trade;
- Reaffirming our commitment to respect, protect and promote the dignity of all humans;
- Acknowledging our legal obligations under international human rights law;
- Convinced that trade liberalisation can foster the practical advancement of human rights;
- Concerned that international trade's impact on some individuals has lessened rather than increased their enjoyment of basic human rights and that trade rules may form a hindrance to the progressive development of human rights law;
- Aware that private actors can significantly affect dignified conditions for work and life and reaffirming the duty of the State to protect all human rights from abuses by, or involving, business enterprises;
- Accepting the United Nation's human rights approach to trade, that 'seeks to devise trade law and policy to take into account the rights of all individuals, in particular vulnerable individuals and groups' and 'requires a constant examination of the impact of trade liberalisation on the enjoyment of human rights';
- Noticing the Singapore Declaration's 'commitment to the observation of internationally recognised core labour standards' as well as the statement in the Declaration on Social Justice for a Fair Globalization of the International Labour Organization that the 'violation of fundamental principles and rights at work cannot be invoked or otherwise used as a legitimate comparative advantage';

10 We deliberately opt for the political and not the judicial body to decide on trade and human rights issues. This is not only in line with the general character of the WTO as a member-driven organisation but also ensures participation and public discussion of this controversial field of law. See, e.g., M. A. Glendon, *Rights Talk: The Impoverishment of Political Discourse* (New York, The Free Press, 1993), pp. 171, 182.

- Noting that carefully drafted trade incentive regimes may advance the cause of human rights

Decide,

- that the World Trade Organization shall fully respect the international law of human rights and support their full enjoyment;
- that the protection of human dignity shall be a guiding principle of the Organization;
- that a Multilateral Agreement on Trade and Human Rights is to be negotiated, providing appropriate instruments to foster mutually supportive regimes and institutional and legal coherence to promote the full effectiveness of both regimes.

I. ... Recognising that human rights concerns are inextricably linked to free trade and convinced that trade liberalisation can foster the advancement of human rights

As mentioned above, human rights and international trade law are interdependent legal regimes. Trade policy and rules can positively influence employment, competitive advantage, and living conditions, but can also – if competition is detrimental or production toxic – destroy income sources and livelihoods and thus compromise human rights, such as the rights to food, to health, to work or to be free from discrimination.[11] Likewise, free markets depend on human rights; such as access to information, free movement, economic freedom, and judicial rights. As a result, a free trade regime can foster human rights at the same time as human rights are fostering trade.[12] This is conceptually expressed in a constitutionalist approach to the WTO, according to which human rights form part of a constitutional horizontal layer of law which serves as a guiding principle for law creation and law application.[13]

11 See, e.g. 'Globalization and its impact on the full enjoyment of human rights', Report of the High Commissioner for Human Rights submitted in accordance with the Commission on Human Rights Resolution 2001/32. UN Doc. E/CN.4/2002/54 (15 January 2002).

12 E.-U. Petersmann, 'The "Human Rights Approach" advocated by the UN High Commissioner for Human Rights and by the International Labour Organization: Is it relevant for WTO Law and Policy?' (2004) 7 *Journal of International Economic Law* 613; International Law Association, 'Report of 73rd Conference', Rio de Janeiro (2008), Committee on International Trade Law, para. 42.; R. Howse and R. G. Teitel, 'Beyond the divide: The Covenant on Economic, Social and Cultural Rights and the World Trade Organization' (2007) 30 *Dialogue on Globalization*, available at: http://library.fes.de/pdf-files/iez/global/04572.pdf (visited 14 April 2009).

13 See the contribution of the Individual Project No. 1 to this book, 'Constitutionalism and Multilayered Governance'.

II. . . . Reaffirming our commitment to respect, protect and promote the dignity of all humans

The concept of human dignity constitutes the root of all human rights. Since human rights also form part of the sustainability objective of the WTO,[14] human dignity belongs to the 'basic principles' and 'objectives underlying this multilateral trading system', which WTO Members are committed to 'preserve' and 'foster'.[15] In order to raise the awareness of Members and WTO arbitrators this Declaration emphasises and reaffirms human dignity as a key conceptual element in coordinating the human rights and trade regime.

III. . . . Acknowledging our legal obligations under international human rights law

Besides their trade treaty obligations, WTO Members are bound by human rights law. All 192 UN Member States have human rights obligations under the UN Charter.[16] Each WTO Member has ratified at least one of the eight core international human rights treaties.[17] In addition, parts of the Universal Declaration of Human Rights (UDHR) have become customary international law.[18] States cannot refrain from meeting their human rights obligations by adhering to other legal regimes with lower standards of human rights protection.[19]

IV. . . . Concerned that international trade's impact on some individuals has lessened rather than increased their enjoyment of basic human rights and that trade rules may form a hindrance to the full enjoyment of human rights and progressive development of human rights law

Studies on the WTO Agreement on Agriculture, the General Agreement on Trade in Services, on trade and investment, and the

14 See above, Introduction.

15 Preamble of the WTO Marrakesh Agreement, para. 5.

16 See Articles 55 and 56 of the UN Charter.

17 See for the core agreements: www2.ohchr.org/english/law/index.htm#core (visited 8 December 2008), for ratification statistics www2.ohchr.org/english/bodies/ratification/ (visited 14 April 2009).

18 See P. Alston, 'Ships passing in the night: The current state of the human rights and development debate seen through the lens of the Millennium Development Goals' (2007) 27 *Human Rights Quarterly* 754–828.

19 See European Court of Human Rights, *Matthews* v. *the United Kingdom*, case No. 24833/94, § 28, ECHR 1999-I.

principle of non-discrimination show that international trade has the potential for compromising human rights.[20] Such potential negative impacts became apparent and were confirmed during our project through doctoral research exploring the impact of international trade law on the right to food and public services:

1. Example: The right to food

Several studies which have examined the impact of trade liberalisation on the right to food found violations of this right[21] by a government vis-à-vis its people. Such violations occur, for example, through not stabilising farm gate prices at an adequate level, not sufficiently targeting support to poor farmers and not reacting to dumping.[22] The studies assessed the impact of trade liberalisation on the right to food by combining macro-level analysis of domestic food production, foreign importation and related state policies with micro-analysis at the community level. The main challenge of such studies is the verification of causalities between trade policies and the violation of the right to food. The effects of natural disasters, civil wars, changes in land tenure arrangements, deterioration in access to infrastructure, farm input, credits or extension services are additional factors that need to be carefully assessed.[23]

The 2008 food crisis illustrates that international trade significantly influences the food situation. A panel organised with scholars from the NCCR Trade Regulation research group on agriculture (IP5) found that from a food security perspective, export restrictions and regulation of biofuels need to be addressed in the Doha Round.[24]

20 C. Breining-Kaufmann, 'The legal matrix of human rights and trade law: State obligations versus private rights and obligations', in T. Cottier, J. Pauwelyn and E. Bürgi (eds.), *Human Rights and International Trade* (Oxford University Press, 2005), p. 118; C. Dommen, 'Human rights and trade: Two practical suggestions for promoting coordination and coherence', in T. Cottier, J. Pauwelyn and E. Bürgi (eds.), *Human Rights and International Trade* (Oxford University Press 2005), p. 200.

21 The right to food is enshrined in Article 11(1) of the International Covenant on Economic, Social and Cultural Rights. For an overview of the different state obligations to respect, protect and fulfil the right to food, see C. Kaufmann and S. Heri, 'Liberalizing trade in agriculture and food security: Mission impossible?' (2008) 40 *Vanderbilt Journal of Transnational Law* 1039-1070, 1051–55.

22 For an example see A. Paasch, F. Garbers and T. Hirsch, *Trade Policies and Hunger: The Impact of Trade Liberalisation on the Right to Food of Rice Farming Communities in Ghana, Honduras and Indonesia* (Geneva, Ecumenical Advocacy Alliance, 2007).

23 *Ibid.*, p. 113.

24 World Trade Organization, 2008 Public Forum Proceedings (25–26 September), Session 16: 'World Food Crisis: Are trade rules a problem or a way forward?' Organised by NCCR Trade Regulation, World Trade Institute and the International Centre for Trade and

During the Uruguay Round, negotiators were already concerned that agricultural reform could have negative effects on least developed and net food-importing developing countries, since several analyses had shown that the reform process was likely to increase food import bills as world prices of basic foodstuffs were expected to increase.[25] The response was the Marrakesh Decision on Measures Concerning the Possible Negative Effects of the Reform Programme on Least-Developed and Net Food-Importing Countries.[26] The Marrakesh Decision included four response mechanisms:

1. food aid;
2. short-term financing of normal levels of commercial imports;
3. favourable terms for agricultural export credits; and
4. technical and financial assistance to improve agricultural productivity and infrastructure.[27]

Although it was an integral part of the negotiations on agricultural trade liberalisation in the Uruguay Round,[28] and despite its incorporation in Article 16 of the Agreement on Agriculture, the Marrakesh Decision has not been satisfactorily implemented. Since the main obligation to respect, protect and fulfil the right to adequate food to the maximum of available resources remains with the national governments, further efforts to implement and update the Marrakesh Decision to buffer negative and promote positive impacts are needed.

2. Example: Public services

Public services are of crucial importance to human life as they meet key needs such as health, education and water.[29] Their provision is often a

Sustainable Development. Report written by S. Heri and C. Häberli (Geneva: WTO Publications, forthcoming); C. Kaufmann and M. Grosz, 'Poverty, hunger and international trade: What's law got to do with it? Current mechanisms and the Doha Development Agenda' (2008) 51 *German Yearbook of International Law* 79–109.

25 Food and Agriculture Organization of the United Nations, *The Right to Food Guidelines: Information Papers and Case Studies* (FAO, 2005), pp. 66–67.

26 World Trade Organization, Decision on Measures Concerning the Possible Negative Effects of the Reform Programme on Least-Developed and Net Food-Importing Developing Countries (15 April 1994), Marrakesh Agreement Establishing the World Trade Organization, Decisions adopted by the Trade Negotiations Committee, 1867 UNTS 60 (1994).

27 *Ibid.*, para. 3–5.

28 R. Howse and R. G. Teitel, 'Beyond the Divide. The Covenant on Economic, Social and Cultural Rights and the World Trade Organization' (2007) 30 *Dialogue on Globalization*, 26.

29 Report of the High Commissioner, UN Commission on Human Rights, Liberalization of Trade in Services and Human Rights, E/CN.4/Sub.2/2002/9, 13 (25 June 2002).

precondition for the realisation of human rights.[30] Public services are needed both economically and socially to propel growth and development.[31] From a human dignity perspective, they need to be provided on an equitable basis and regardless of an individual's ability to pay for them.[32] Thus, problems with the provision of public services can have particularly detrimental effects on human rights. In the context of agreements facilitating investment, such as GATS, liberalisation of these services may increase in the future.[33] Experience shows that in some instances, liberalisation has led to improved quality or gains in efficiency. In other cases, however, the privatisation of water services has had a negative impact on the quality or quantity of the water provided, on the cost of water services, and on access to water. As a result, the three core entitlements of the human right to water have been infringed.[34] Similar effects have been reported for the right to education[35] and the right to health.[36]

Problems resulting from liberalising essential services have also led to detrimental effects having a disproportionate impact on women's human rights. Due in part to the gendered nature of the economy or to the division of labour in many countries, correcting the deficiencies in the provision of essential services can become 'women's work'.[37] Compromises in the provision of water services can force women to become responsible for the

30 Human rights with regard to public services are, e.g., expressed through the right to water, the right to education, or to health, enshrined in Articles 11, 12, 13 and 14 of the Covenant on Economic, Social and Cultural Rights, see www2.ohchr.org/english/bodies/cescr/comments.htm.

31 UNCTAD Secretariat, Universal Access to Services, Note by the UNCTAD Secretariat, TD/B/COM.1/EM.30/2, 18 September 2006, para. 5.

32 *Ibid.*

33 See, e.g., M. Mashayekhi, M. Julsain and E. Tuerk, 'Strategic considerations for developing countries: The case of GATS and health services', in C. Blouin, N. Drager and R. Smith, (eds.) *International Trade in Health Services and the GATS* (World Bank, 2005), p. 21.

34 General Comment No. 15, The Right to Water (Articles 11 and 12 of the International Covenant on Economic, Social and Cultural Rights), E/C.12/2002/11 (26 November 2002), para. 12.

35 United Nations, Economic and Social Council, The Right to Education (Art. 13), General comment No. 13, E/C.12/1999/10 (8 December 1999), para. 6.

36 See generally United Nations Committee on Economic, Social and Cultural Rights, The Right to the Highest Attainable Standard of Health, Substantive Issues Arising in the Implementation of the International Covenant on Economic, Social and Cultural Rights, General Comment No. 14 (2000), E/C.12/2000/4 (11/08/2000).

37 United Nations, 'World survey on the role of women in development: Globalization, gender and work' (1999), 56–62; D. Joshi, 'Misunderstanding gender in water', in A. Coles and T. Wallace (eds.), *Gender, Water and Development* (Oxford, Berg Publishers, 2005), p. 138.

gathering and collection of water from other sources.[38] This, apart from affecting their health, has caused a loss of women's economic opportunities and their ability to pursue education. Additionally, they may suffer from problems with hygiene, due to deficiencies in services, or become victims of sexual assault or harassment, e.g. on their way to and from the places where they collect water.[39]

V. ... Aware that private actors can significantly affect the conditions necessary for fulfilling human dignity and reaffirming the duty of the State to protect all human rights from abuses by, or involving, business enterprises

Private actors are generally not directly bound by human rights because they are not considered full subjects of international law.[40] Efforts to hold private actors responsible thus need to relate to the state's horizontal obligation to protect human rights. Yet, the activities of private actors can have a significant impact on human rights, mainly if states do not have at their disposal sufficient legal frameworks to protect human rights. On the international level, the UN, ILO and OECD have adopted various non-binding instruments regarding 'Corporate Social Responsibility', such as the ILO Tripartite Declaration and the OECD Guidelines. The former UN Sub-Commission on the Promotion and Protection of Human Rights drafted the 'Norms on the Responsibilities of Transnational Corporations and Other Business Enterprises with Regard to Human Rights' which extended human rights obligations to corporations. The document was not adopted because of strong opposition by states and the business community. It led, however, to the appointment of a Special Representative to the UN Secretary General on the issue of human rights and transnational corporations and other business enterprises in July 2005. Since then, a new approach has been developed, based on a bottom-up process exploring attitudes of the business community to the issue. The approach starts out from the horizontal duty of states to protect human

38 United Nations Development Programme, Human Development Report 2006 'Beyond Scarcity: Power, Poverty and the Global Water Crisis' (2006), p. 87.

39 *Ibid.*; V. Roaf, A. Khalfan and Malcolm Langford, 'Monitoring implementation of the right to water: A framework for developing indicators' (2005) 14(1) *Global Issues Papers* 34.

40 See C. Breining-Kaufmann, 'The legal matrix of human rights and trade law: State obligations versus private rights and obligations', in T. Cottier, J. Pauwelyn and E. Bürgi (eds.), *Human Rights and International Trade* (Oxford University Press, 2005), p. 99.

rights from being violated by private actors. It defines a framework to be implemented by states which requires companies to respect human rights and calls for the development of effective remedy mechanisms. The next step will be to further develop this framework into a viable and effective regime for international business and human rights.[41] This approach overcomes the conceptual deficit in general international law with regard to private actors by defining a clear framework for states on how to comply with their horizontal obligations under international human rights law. The suggested draft decision follows this avenue and applies it to potential conflicts of international trade law and human rights in the business context.

VI. ... Accepting the United Nations' human rights approach to trade, that 'seeks trade law and policy that take into account the rights of all individuals, in particular vulnerable individuals and groups' and 'requires a constant examination of the impact of trade liberalization on the enjoyment of human rights'

The UN High Commissioner for Human Rights asks for policies which:

(a) Set the promotion and protection of human rights among the objectives of trade liberalization;
(b) Examine the effects of trade liberalization on individuals and seek trade law and policy that take into account the rights of all individuals, in particular vulnerable individuals and groups;
(c) Emphasize the role of the State in the process of liberalization – not only as negotiators of trade law and setters of trade policy, but also as the primary duty bearer for the implementation of human rights;
(d) Seek consistency between the progressive liberalization of trade and the progressive realization of human rights;
(e) Require a constant examination of the impact of trade liberalization on the enjoyment of human rights;
(f) Promote international cooperation for the realization of human rights and freedoms in the context of trade liberalization.[42]

41 See for all available material www.business-humanrights.org/SpecialRepPortal/Home (visited 16 August 2009).

42 Report of the High Commissioner for Human Rights, Liberalization of Trade in Services and Human Rights, E/CN.4/Sub.2/2002/9; see also www2.ohchr.org/english/issues/globalization/trade/index.htm (visited 14 April 2009).

Against this background, policy evaluations are necessary to measure the impact of trade policies on human rights and mutually supportive synergies. Impact assessment methodologies are currently being developed by international organisations (UNHCHR and UNEP) as well as by WTO Members (EU) and academia,[43] with human rights impact assessment being mainly addressed within the UN framework.[44]

VII. . . . Noticing the Singapore Declaration's 'commitment to the observation of internationally recognized core labour standards' as well as the statement in the Declaration on Social Justice for a Fair Globalization of the International Labour Organization that the 'violation of fundamental principles and rights at work cannot be invoked or otherwise used as a legitimate comparative advantage'

During the WTO Ministerial Conference held in Singapore in 1996, states renewed their commitment to internationally recognised labour standards.[45] The ILO was defined as the competent body for addressing and developing international labour standards.[46] In 1998, the International Labour Conference adopted the today widely accepted ILO Declaration on Fundamental Principles and Rights at Work that all members of the ILO are required to respect, promote and realise.[47] These fundamental rights at work comprise the prohibition of forced labour and child

43 M. Gehring, *Nachhaltigkeit durch Verfahren im Welthandelsrecht. Umwelt – und Nachhaltigkeitsprüfungen und die WTO* (Berlin, Duncker & Humblot, 2007); Communication from the Commission on Impact Assessment, 5.6.2002, COM(2002)276; Communication from the Commission, A Sustainable Europe for a Better World: A European Union Strategy for Sustainable Development, 15.5.2001, COM(2001)264; C. George and C. H. Kirkpatrick, *Impact Assessment and Sustainable Development: European Practice and Experience* (Cheltenham, Edward Elgar, 2007); L. Turner, N. Nguyen and K. Bird, *Fighting Poverty, An Overview of Ex Ante Tools for Assessing the Impact of Trade Liberalisation on the Poor* (Overseas Development Institute, 2008); for UNEP methodology see www.unep.ch/etb/areas/IntTraRelPol.php (visited 14 April 2009).

44 S. Walker, 'Human rights impact assessments of trade-related policies', in M. W. Gehring and M.-C. Cordonier Segger (eds.), *Sustainable Development in World Trade Law* (The Hague, Kluwer, 2005), p. 227.

45 WTO, Singapore, Ministerial Declaration, WT/MIN(96)/DEC/W, 13 December 1996, para. 4.

46 *Ibid.*

47 Adopted by the International Labour Conference, 86th session, 18 June 1998, ILC, Record of Proceedings, Nos. 20 and 22 (86th Session, Geneva 1998); C. Kaufmann, *Globalisation and Labour Rights* (Oxford, Hart, 2007), pp. 67–77.

labour, freedom of association, the right to organise and bargain collectively, equal remuneration for men and women for work of equal value and non-discrimination in employment.

One of the most controversial issues in the trade and labour debate is the effect of labour standards on terms of trade. As early as 1919, the Preamble of the Constitution of the International Labour Organization (ILO) stated that 'the failure of any nation to adopt humane conditions of labour is an obstacle in the way of other nations, which desire to improve the conditions in their own countries'.[48] Likewise, the Havana Charter of 1948 mentioned that unfair labour conditions can create difficulties in international trade and provided for cooperation with the ILO.[49] Yet, when the World Trade Organization (WTO) was established in 1995, it did not provide for a formal linkage of trade and labour standards. The ILO Declaration on Fundamental Principles and Rights at Work of 1998 confirmed the approach of the WTO in Singapore holding that 'labour standards should not be used for protectionist purposes',[50] thus securing the competitive advantage of the developing countries. However, the Declaration did not address the reverse situation where low labour standards are used to lower production costs.

The recently adopted ILO Declaration on Social Justice for a Fair Globalization of June 2008 balanced this statement by holding that the:

> violation of fundamental principles and rights at work cannot be invoked or otherwise used as a legitimate comparative advantage.[51]

This constitutes a fundamental shift in the trade and labour debate, putting labour standards on the same level as trade and even calling on other organisations to cooperate.[52] In fact, with this statement, the ILO is going back to the Philadelphia Declaration of 1944 where it had emphasised the need for mainstreaming labour rights into the work of financial

48 International Labour Organization, Part XIII (Labour) of the Treaty of Versailles of 28 June 1919, Section I.

49 Art. 7 of the Havana Charter, Final Act and related Documents, UNCTAD, Interim Commission for the International Trade Organization, Havana, 1948, E/Conf.2/78.

50 Para. 5 of the ILO Declaration of Fundamental Principles and Rights at Work.

51 Para. I. A. (iv) of the ILO Declaration on Social Justice for a Fair Globalization, ILO, Provisional Record 13 A/B, International Labour Conference, 97th session (Geneva, International Labour Office, 2008).

52 See F. Humbert, *The Challenge of Child Labour in International Law* (Cambridge University Press, 2009).

and economic organisations.[53] Thus, a 'new' form of social clause may be back on the global agenda for the trade and labour debate, as is already the case at the regional and bilateral levels.[54] Accordingly, the new Declaration calls upon the ILO to assist its Members to promote the ILO's strategic objectives within the framework of bilateral or multilateral agreements.[55] In conclusion, the new ILO Declaration represents a building block in the trade and labour debate because it not only refers to the rationale of unfair competition for the trade and labour linkage but also highlights the potential for trade agreements to advance the objectives of the ILO.

By invoking the most recent ILO Declaration, the draft decision follows the approach chosen by the Singapore Declaration in reaffirming Members' commitments.

VIII. . . . Noting that carefully drafted trade incentive regimes may advance the cause of human rights

Carefully drafted social clauses in trade agreements such as the US and EU Generalized Systems of Preferences (GSPs) or the US–Cambodia Textile Agreement can advance the cause of human rights. Such clauses have contributed towards improving the implementation of labour standards and human rights in some countries.[56] Therefore, they might be explored as a model for multilateral agreements. Since the application of such social clauses has shown that their unilateral adoption and application carries the risk of being politically and economically arbitrary,[57] criteria

53 Adopted at the 26th General Conference of the ILO in Philadelphia on 10 May 1944 as Annex to the ILO Constitution, Art. II(d). See C. Kaufmann, *Globalisation and Labour Rights* (Oxford, Hart, 2007), pp. 50–52.

54 See for example the partnership agreement between the members of the African, Caribbean and Pacific Group of States, and the European Community, signed in Cotonou on 23 June 2000 – Protocols – Final Act – Declarations, OJ 2000 No. L 317/3; Agreement between the United States of America and the Hashemite Kingdom of Jordan on the Establishment of a Free Trade Area, available at: www.ustr.gov/assets/Trade_Agreements/Bilateral/Jordan/asset_upload_file250_5112.pdf (visited 14 April 2009).

55 Para. II. A. (iv) of the ILO Declaration on Social Justice for a Fair Globalization, ILO, Provisional Record 13 A/B, International Labour Conference, 97th session (Geneva, International Labour Office, 2008).

56 See F. Humbert, *The Challenge of Child Labour in International Law* (Cambridge University Press, 2009), chapter 4; F. Humbert, 'Do social clauses in generalized systems of preferences advance the cause of women?' (2008) NCCR Working Paper 2008/4.

57 See F. Humbert, *The Challenge of Child Labour in International Law* (Cambridge University Press, 2009), chapter 4.

for a multilateral framework for GSPs under the WTO agreements will be suggested below.[58]

1. Lessons from the US GSP

Under GSPs, developed countries grant reduced or zero tariff rates to selected products originating in developing countries. Under the Trade Act of 1984, the US GSP was re-authorised and labour rights conditionality was introduced, requiring beneficiary countries to observe 'internationally recognized worker rights'. An applicant country is ineligible if it is not taking steps to implement a certain set of unilaterally determined labour rights such as the right to association and collective bargaining, the prohibition on the use of any form of forced or compulsory labour, a minimum age for employment of children, acceptable conditions of work with respect to wages, hours of work and occupational health and safety.[59] A country is also ineligible if it has not complied with its commitments to eliminate the worst forms of child labour.[60] Generally, it would be preferable to explicitly refer to the relevant ILO Conventions in order to provide a clear applicable standard.

Under the national interest clause, the President may however determine that the economic interests of the US preclude a country from being designated as a beneficiary.[61] This opens the door for arbitrary application and non-transparent criteria. Nevertheless, the reporting, petition and review process of the US GSP has achieved good results for the labour rights situation in some countries.[62] Still, the application of the social clause could be made more objective and effective through a review mechanism overseen by trade *and* human rights experts at the decision-making level, by introducing guidelines for the acceptance and rejection of petitions and by mainstreaming it with regard to the international level, e.g. through subjection to a special multilateral appeal mechanism.[63]

58 See III, 3, c. 59 19 United States C. Sec. 2462 (b)(2)(G).

60 19 United States C. Sec. 2462 (b)(2)(H). 61 19 United States C. Sec. 2462(b)(2).

62 See for example F. Humbert, *The Challenge of Child Labour in International Law* (Cambridge University Press, 2009), chapter 4; F. Humbert, 'Do social clauses in generalized systems of preferences advance the cause of women?' (2008) NCCR Working Paper 2008/4.

63 While the WTO dispute settlement mechanism may already take on a complaint relating to the GSPs, there should be a special appeal mechanism consisting of trade and human rights experts and allowing for a timely and effective handling of disputes on GSPs. For a more thorough analysis, see *ibid.*

2. Lessons from the EU GSP including the case of Sri Lanka

The current EU GSP provides for general arrangements and, inter alia, a special incentive arrangement for sustainable development and good governance that refers to several human rights treaties.[64] Under the special incentive arrangements, additional incentives are granted to beneficiary countries if they have ratified and effectively implemented sixteen human rights conventions and at least seven conventions from a choice of conventions on the environment and governance principles.[65] Under its withdrawal procedure, the EU may withdraw the special incentive arrangement if the beneficiary country ceases to implement human rights or labour rights.[66]

A Sri Lankan case study has shown that if the granting and withdrawal procedure is effectively implemented and cooperation with trade unions and civil society groups takes place, the EU GSP can be a useful tool for improving human rights performance, including the introduction of administrative measures such as equal wage rates for men and women or new guidelines for a broader application of trade union rights.[67] In particular, the EU should review the human rights situation before granting special preferences including in situ visits, should exert continued pressure on a non-complying country, introduce an effective complaints mechanism and closely cooperate with ILO and UN bodies as well as with trade unions and civil society.[68]

IX. . . . that the World Trade Organization shall fully respect the international law of human rights and support their full enjoyment

Those responsible for WTO policy should be aware of potential negative impacts of WTO law on human rights in their daily practice. In this regard, sufficient policy space for Members to meet their human

64 Council Regulation (EC) No. 980/2005 of 27 June 2005 applying a scheme of generalized tariff preferences, OJ 2005 L 169/1, extended by Council Regulation (EC) No. 732/2008 of 22 July 2008 applying a scheme of generalized tariff preferences for the period from 1 January 2009 to 31 December 2011 and amending Regulation (EC) No. 557/97, (EC) No. 1933/2006 and Commission Regulations (EC) No. 1100/2006 and (EC) No 964/2007, OJ 2008 L 211/1.

65 Art. 9(1) lit. a to e of Council Regulation (EC) 980/2005.

66 Art. 16(2) of Council Regulation (EC) No. 980/2005.

67 F. Humbert, 'Do social clauses in generalized systems of preferences advance the cause of women?' (2008) NCCR Working Paper 2008/4, pp. 26–37.

68 *Ibid.*, pp. 36–7.

rights obligations[69] as well as technical assistance and flanking measures to support developing countries in complying with their human rights obligations are essential. Such a mainstreaming approach requires cooperation with competent human rights bodies.

X. . . . *that the protection of human dignity shall be a guiding principle of the Organization*

Human dignity as a guiding principle in resolving conflicts between human rights and international trade law requires a 'dimension of weight'[70] or 'importance'[71] to be attributed to it, e.g. in a conflict between the prohibition of subsidies and assuring the right to food.

XI. . . . *that a Multilateral Agreement on Trade and Human Rights is to be negotiated, providing appropriate instruments to foster the cause of mutually supportive regimes, institutional and legal coherence and the full enjoyment of all human rights*

We came to the conclusion that a full agreement, annexed to the Marrakesh Agreement, and thus with a legal relevance equal to that of GATT, GATS or TRIPS, is preferable to other possible regulatory forms, such as a side-agreement, a political declaration, an authoritative interpretation (Article IX:2 Marrakesh Agreement), or a plurilateral agreement with phase-in provisions. As mentioned above, all WTO Members are bound to specific human rights. Furthermore, the objective of sustainable development requires a balance between human rights and trade. Establishing appropriate legal instruments to coordinate both regimes is thus not optional or a mere interpretative issue, but a genuine systemic task to be performed. Given that human rights are a horizontal issue affecting the whole body of WTO law and not a sub-category of international trade law or conflict rules, they need to be enshrined at the same regulatory level as the WTO Agreements.

69 C. Dommen, 'Human rights and trade: Two practical suggestions for promoting coordination and coherence', in T. Cottier, J. Pauwelyn and E. Bürgi (eds.), *Human Rights and International Trade* (Oxford University Press 2005), p. 199.

70 R. Dworkin, *Taking Rights Seriously* (Harvard University Press, 1977).

71 See for a 'dimension of weight' regarding values of 'vital importance to the highest degree', Appellate Body Report, *EC – Asbestos*, paras. 169–172.

C. Fulfilling the task: elements of a multilateral agreement on trade and human rights

As an instrument of effective coordination, a multilateral agreement on trade and human rights has to provide procedures and mechanisms to develop criteria and principles which address the intersection of trade and human rights, not only with regard to dispute settlement but also policies and decision-making procedures.

I. Policy coordination

An effective balance between trade and human rights regimes requires an exploration of the potential positive and negative impacts of both fields on each other and a search for appropriate means to prevent and counter the negative effects. In line with the UNHCHR human rights approach to trade,[72] this calls for systematic impact assessments scanning existing WTO law as well as future provisions on the agenda, including monitoring and follow-up. Accordingly, adequate institutional devices, mechanisms, procedures and criteria are needed, with inter-institutional cooperation between the WTO and human rights institutions being a central condition. Avenues to be pursued include mutual observer status and exchange of information, inter-institutional agreements,[73] memoranda of understanding and common committees.[74] A Committee on Trade and Human Rights could be mandated to establish and monitor policies and to create a cooperative link to other international bodies competent to deal with human rights questions, such as the UNHCHR, the ILO[75] the OECD, UNESCO, the World Bank or the FAO.

For more information on trade and human rights, to be 'fed' into impact assessment analysis and methodology, broadening the mandate of the Trade Policy Review Mechanism (TPRM), to address not only trade policy per se but also its impact on human rights, may be an avenue to pursue. Such a mandate would enable a multilateral assessment of the

72 See note 43 above.

73 See J. Neumann, *Die Koordination des WTO Rechts mit anderen völkerrechtlichen Ordnungen* (Berlin, Duncker & Humblot, 2002).

74 See for an overview V. Mosoti, 'Institutional cooperation and norms creation in international organizations', in T. Cottier, J. Pauwelyn and E. Bürgi (eds.), *Human Rights and International Trade* (Oxford University Press, 2005).

75 See for the current state of WTO/ILO cooperation, www.wto.org/english/thewto_e/coher_e/wto_ilo_e.htm (visited 14 April 2009).

positive and negative effects that WTO norms may have on human rights and policies.

The suggested assessment would correspond better to the WTO's sustainable development objective than the existing mechanism does.[76] It could build on current TPRM transparency obligations which already comprise Members' 'wider economic and developmental needs, their policies and objectives'.[77]

II. Dispute settlement

A multilateral framework on trade and human rights should clarify WTO law interpretation with regard to human rights and provide for more coherence and predictability. Existing rules of treaty interpretation (such as the VCLT)[78] require WTO dispute settlement bodies to consider human rights obligations and to apply WTO law in conformity with existing human rights obligations.[79] This implies that WTO bodies should exercise judicial restraint if human rights claims are based on measures that are necessary to protect human rights and are thus applied on a good faith basis and not in an arbitrary or discriminatory manner.[80] WTO bodies have, in the light of Article 3.2 DSU and Article 31(3)(c) VCLT, recognised that the WTO is embedded in the international legal system and that provisions outside WTO law should clarify rights and obligations under the WTO covered agreements.[81] There is still dispute, however, over the extent to which 'relevant rules of international law' should be 'applicable

76 R. Howse and R. G. Teitel, 'Beyond the divide. The Covenant on Economic, Social and Cultural Rights and the World Trade Organization' (2007) 30 *Dialogue on Globalization* 18, available at: http://library.fes.de/pdf-files/iez/global/04572.pdf. (visited 14 April 2009).

77 See TPRM Agreement, Annex 3, Trade Policy Review Mechanism, A. Objectives (ii).

78 Preamble, para. 6; Art. 31.

79 With regard to human rights obligations of international organisations, see the decision by the European Court of Human Rights in *Behrami and Behrami* v. *France* and *Saramaty* v. *France, Germany and Norway* (dec.) [GC], Nos. 71412/01 and 78166/01, 2 May 2007.

80 See in terms of a human rights caveat for the national level, *Yassin Abdullah Kadi and Al Barakaat International Foundation* v. *Council of the European Union and Commission of the European Communities*, cases C-402/05P and C-415/05P, [2008] ECR I-(nyr); K. Ziegler, 'Strengthening the rule of law, but fragmenting international law: The Kadi decision of the ECJ from the perspective of human rights (2009) 9 *Human Rights Law Review* 288–305.

81 Appellate Body Report, *US – Gasoline*, p. 17; Appellate Body Report, *US – Shrimp*, para. 130; Appellate Body, *EC – Asbestos*, para. 172; J. Pauwelyn, *Conflict of Norms in Public International Law: How WTO Law Relates to Other Rules of International Law* (Cambridge University Press, 2003), pp. 443–472.

in relation between the parties'.[82] Here, three interpretations are possible: first, only binding rules applicable between *all* member parties are to be considered;[83] second, only binding rules applicable between the *parties to the dispute* are to be taken into account;[84] and third, *all relevant rules* 'in relation between the parties' are to be applied, regardless of their binding effects[85] – or more restricted, if at least one party to the dispute is bound.[86] In 2003, the International Court of Justice convincingly argued for a broader interpretation.[87]

The narrow interpretations could lead to a de facto priority of WTO provisions and thereby hinder coherence and consistency with norms in other areas of international law. Based on the principles of good faith and *pacta sunt servanda*, states are simultaneously and equally bound by their international law obligations. Except for *ius cogens* and obligations derived from the UN Charter, there is no priority of any specific body of international law.[88] As the Appellate Body stated, the WTO is not a self-contained regime, therefore its provisions are not to be read in 'clinical isolation' from public international law.[89] The WTO system is forming part of an international multilayered system of governance,[90]

82 Fragmentation of International Law: Difficulties Arising from the Diversification and Expansion of International Law. Report of the Study Group of the International Law Commission (Koskenniemi Report), A/CN.4/L.682 (2006), para. 37; C. McLachlan, 'The principle of systemic integration and Article 31 (3) (c) of the Vienna Convention' (2005) 54 *International and Comparative Law Quarterly* 279–319; J. Pauwelyn, 'Bridging fragmentation and unity: International law as a universe of inter-connected islands' (2004) 25 *Michigan Journal of International Law* 913.

83 Panel Report, *EC – Biotech*, para. 7.68.

84 J. Pauwelyn, 'Bridging fragmentation and unity: International law as a universe of inter-connected islands' (2004) 25 *Michigan Journal of International Law* 910; J. Pauwelyn, 'Human rights in WTO dispute settlement', in T. Cottier, J. Pauwelyn and E. Bürgi (eds.), *Human Rights and International Trade* (Oxford University Press, 2005), p. 216.

85 R. Howse and R. G. Teitel, 'Beyond the divide: The Covenant on Economic, Social and Cultural Rights and the World Trade Organization' (2007) 30 *Dialogue on Globalization* 28–29, p. 39, available at: http://library.fes.de/pdf-files/iez/global/04572.pdf. (visited 14 April 2009).

86 B. McGrady, 'Fragmentation of international law or "systemic integration" of treaty regimes: EC-Biotech products and the proper interpretation of Article 31 (3) (c) of the Vienna Convention on the Law of Treaties' (2008) 42 *Journal of World Trade* 594.

87 International Court of Justice Case, Oil Platforms (*Islamic Republic of Iran* v. *United States of America*) ICJ Reports 2003, p. 161.

88 European Court of Human Rights *Matthews* v. *the United Kingdom*, case No. 24833/94, § 28, ECHR 1999-I.

89 Appellate Body Report, *US – Gasoline*, p. 17.

90 T. Cottier, 'Legitimacy of the WTO law' (2008) NCCR Working Paper 2008/19, 8.

which should be shaped in such a way as to allocate competencies appropriately and to coordinate 'inter-connected islands' of law.[91] With regard to coordinating overlapping regimes, legal standards of interpretation and conflict resolution, providing guidelines for weighing and balancing rights and obligations (e.g. the 'importance' of values, or good faith standards[92]), could clarify legitimate rights and obligations within the broader context of international law. Developed systematically, in collaboration between relevant institutions, such standards could enhance overall legitimacy of WTO law and foster coherence in international law. Although real conflicting cases regarding human rights may be rare,[93] it is a matter of time until the WTO bodies are confronted with delicate challenges to be resolved within the existing framework of WTO law. The WTO waiver for the 'Kimberley Process' on the control of conflict diamonds and the WTO dispute settlement rulings on conditional trade preferences for developing countries point in this direction.[94]

The approach we propose here is procedural in nature, focusing on cooperation between international standard-setting bodies and judicial bodies, seeking competencies to provide expertise and establishing decision-making mechanisms to find viable solutions.[95] Such an approach would, for instance, allow WTO bodies to be involved in cases with political impact. Article 3(9) DSU and Article IX:2 WTO Agreement already foresee recourse to the Ministerial Conference and the Council to issue binding interpretations of WTO law. Yet, so far this mechanism has never

91 For the model of multilayered governance see the Introduction to this book; J. Pauwelyn, 'Bridging fragmentation and unity: International law as a universe of inter-connected islands' (2004) 25 *Michigan Journal of International Law* 903–916.

92 Appellate Body Report, *EC – Asbestos*, para. 172; Appellate Body Report, *US – Shrimp*, paras. 158 *et seq.*

93 See G. Marceau, 'WTO dispute settlement and human rights' (2002) 13 *European Journal of International Law* 758.

94 K. Nadakavukaren Schefer, 'Stopping trade in conflict diamonds: Exploring the trade and human rights interface with the WTO waiver for the Kimberley Process', in T. Cottier, J. Pauwelyn and E. Bürgi (eds.), *Human Rights and International Trade* (Oxford University Press, 2005), p. 391.

95 See in this respect, Report (Sutherland Report) of the Consultative Board to the Director-General Supachai Panitchpakdi, *The Future of the WTO: Addressing Institutional Challenges in the New Millennium* (WTO, 2004). The Report does not tackle coordinative challenges and effective coordination with other regimes, but concentrates on 'old' WTO issues not facing further coordinative challenges and conflicts; see for critique Joost Pauwelyn, 'The Sutherland Report: A missed opportunity for genuine debate on trade, globalization and reforming the WTO' (2005) 8 *Journal of International Economic Law* 329.

been applied. Making use of this mechanism, WTO Members could clarify the meaning of WTO norms with regard to human rights in given cases. The instrument could be further developed, e.g. by establishing a quorum or procedures to allow for temporary violation, suspension or direct amendment of WTO provisions in the case of conflicts with human rights obligations. Other procedural instruments include systematic cooperation with international legal bodies in WTO arbitration, e.g. the obligation to apply, or to actively take into account, the opinion of UN treaty bodies or the ILO. In this context, hierarchy, or 'dimensions of weight' in international law, as well as criteria to resolve conflicts of norms could be explored on a more legitimate basis, e.g. by inter-institutional cooperation. Another instrument could be to establish a burden of proof favouring human rights, similar to cases under the WTO Agreement on the Application of Sanitary and Phytosanitary Measures (SPS) where the Appellate Body placed the burden of proof on the applicant,[96] or expert commissions in specific dispute settlement fields, as provided for in paragraph 4 of the Annex to the GATS on Financial Services, or improve civil society participation through greater transparency in decision-making, e.g. by granting public access to WTO Committees under an appropriate regime (Article V:2 Marrakesh Agreement), thus securing the functioning and effectiveness of the political bodies.

D. Specific annex agreements – some examples

In order to foster mutual supportiveness of human rights and trade law in specific fields, the multilateral framework should encourage the negotiation of specific agreements. Such agreements can take the form of an annex to a multilateral agreement on trade and human rights or to other WTO agreements. Our research included the development of rules for specific areas of potential conflicts between trade law and human rights.

I. Trade law and the right to food

Increased integration of international markets has raised concerns that openness to agricultural trade may jeopardise food security in developing

96 Appellate Body Report, *EC – Hormones*, para. 97. G. Marceau and J. P. Trachtman, 'The Technical Barriers to Trade Agreement, the Sanitary and Phytosanitary Measures Agreement, and the General Agreement on Tariffs and Trade. A map of the World Trade Organization law of domestic regulation of goods' (2002) 36 *Journal of World Trade* 831.

countries.[97] However, empirical evidence does not confirm that engaging in (international) agricultural trade is necessarily associated with high levels of undernourishment.[98] The impact of agricultural trade liberalisation on the right to food is mediated by many factors such as domestic policy reform that enhances positive effects of trade and cushions negative impacts.

From a right to food perspective, it is problematic that empirical studies typically refer to aggregates and say little about the distributional effects among and within countries.[99] Even if trade reform is likely to reduce poverty in the long run, economic theory recognises that some of the poor may be worse off.[100] Human Rights Impact Assessments (HRIAs) of trade-related rules and policies that are being developed as part of the doctoral research conducted in our project constitute an instrument to ensure coherence between human rights and international trade law obligations by identifying those complementary measures that may be required by human rights law to address adverse consequences of international trade.

Human rights law provides a conceptual framework for analysing trade rules and undertaking impact assessments, the latter implying that they should be public and participatory and focus on disadvantaged and vulnerable groups as well as gender effects of trade rules. It is important from both a legal and a political point of view that Human Rights Impact Assessments do not mean or imply conditionalities, monitoring or measuring human rights performance of states in any way that they have not agreed to. In particular, HRIAs are aimed to:

- help people identify and assess their rights;
- understand how trade reform can affect the enjoyment of those rights;
- identify ways in which governments can improve trade policies to fulfil human rights obligations; and

97 See B. Karapinar and C. Häberli (eds.), *Food Crises and the WTO* (Cambridge University Press, 2010).

98 Food and Agricultural Organization of the United Nations, 'The state of food and agriculture 2005: Agricultural trade and poverty – can trade work for the poor?' (2005) 36 *FAO Agriculture Series* 82–84.

99 C. Kaufmann and S. Heri, 'Liberalizing trade in agriculture and food security: Mission impossible?' (2008) 40 *Vanderbilt Journal of Transnational Law* 1041–1042.

100 S. Matusz and D. Tarr, 'Adjusting to trade policy reform', in A. O. Krueger (ed.), *Economic Policy Reform: The Second Stage* (University of Chicago Press, 1999), p. 389.

- identify ways in which governments can cooperate with the international community to fulfil human rights obligations.[101]

BOX 8.2 POLICY ADVICE ON TRADE LIBERALISATION AND THE RIGHT TO FOOD

Draft guiding principles on Trade and the Right to Food

- With regard to the Marrakesh Ministerial Decision on Measures Concerning the Possible Negative Effects of the Reform Process on Least-Developed and Net Food-Importing Developing Countries[102] further efforts must be undertaken to operationalise the response mechanisms listed in the Decision: (1) food aid, (2) short-term financing of normal levels of commercial imports, (3) favourable terms for agricultural export credits, and (4) financial assistance to improve agricultural productivity and infrastructure. A Ministerial commitment in the Doha Final Act to update and implement the Marrakesh Decision would be a first step in this regard.
- Efforts to reach a compromise between policy space and market access on Special Products and on the Special Safeguard Mechanism should be strengthened. The Agreement on Agriculture's preamble stipulates that 'commitments under the reform programme should be made in an equitable way among all Members, having regard to non-trade concerns, including food security [. . .]'. The draft modalities' illustrative list of indicators for the designation of special products currently being discussed points in this direction.[103]
- In line with the long-term objective in the preamble of the WTO Agreement on Agriculture 'to establish a fair and market-oriented agricultural trading system', important issues such as biofuels and disciplines for export restrictions should be addressed in future negotiations.
- Recalling the preambular paragraph of the Marrakesh Agreement that 'there is a need for positive efforts designed to ensure that developing countries, and especially the least developed among them, secure a share in the growth in international trade commensurate with the needs of their economic development', more efforts in the agricultural field are necessary. The Enhanced Integrated Framework should increasingly be used to build productive agricultural sectors. The evaluation criteria for the success of Aid for Trade should not only be growth in

101 S. Walker, 'Human rights impact assessments of trade-related policies', in M. W. Gehring and M.-C. Cordonier Segger (eds.), *Sustainable Development in World Trade Law* (The Hague, Kluwer, 2005), p. 227.

102 15 April 1994.

103 Draft Modalities for Agriculture, Doc. TN/AG/W/4/Rev.4 (6 December 2008), paras. 129–131, Annex F.

trade volumes but the impact of Aid for Trade on poverty reduction, the Human Development Index, and its contribution to the Millennium Development Goals.

- A feasibility study on whether a violation or a threat thereof by a WTO Member to respect, protect, and fulfil the right to food could serve as a criterion for different forms of special and differential treatment shall be undertaken. Causality involving a genuine and substantial relationship of cause and effect between the violation of the right to adequate food or the threat thereof, and the trade rule for which special and differential treatment is sought will be a necessary element. Whether there is a violation by a WTO Member of their obligation to respect, protect and fulfil the right to food will be determined by the Committee on Economic, Social and Cultural Rights. The WTO Secretariat will cooperate in this endeavour with the Office of the High Commissioner for Human Rights, the UN Special Rapporteur on the Right to Adequate Food and the Advisory Committee of the Human Rights Council.
- Following the missions to the WTO of the UN Special Rapporteur on the right to health in 2004[104] and the UN Special Rapporteur on the right to adequate food in 2008, a standing invitation of the WTO Membership to Missions of UN Special Rapporteurs should be considered to enable such exchanges to become more common.
- Members should be encouraged to report on food security-related trade policies in their trade policy review by e.g. structuring the food security-related trade policy review along the trade-relevant guidelines of the FAO Voluntary Guidelines to Support the Progressive Realization of the Right to Adequate Food in the Context of National Food Security. Usage of the Voluntary Guidelines in the TPRM shall not be construed as recognising any change in the current state of conventional or customary international law regarding rights related to food.
- Aid for Trade and Food Aid Commitments shall become binding by inclusion in Members' schedules.

II. *Trade in services and human rights*

A specific Annex to the GATS on trade-related aspects of human rights and essential services could underline the need for human rights impact assessment in the services sector. WTO rules can only provide regulatory space for WTO Members to protect human rights; concrete regulation or flanking measures for protecting affected people remain the responsibility of the individual Member. Regarding the WTO's specific commitment to

104 Report of the Special Rapporteur on the right of everyone to the enjoyment of the highest attainable standard of physical and mental health, Mission to the World Trade Organization, UN Doc. E/CN.4/2004/49/Add. 1 (1 March 2004), para. 2.

developing countries, the WTO could assist as a consultative body in the technical design of flanking measures or cooperation with development institutions (World Bank, foreign technical assistance) in the countries concerned. Institutionally, establishing a specialised Coordinating Committee in the WTO could facilitate cooperation.

III. Corruption, trade and human rights

The rationale for a specific Agreement or Protocol on Corruption annexed to a multilateral agreement on trade and human rights begins with the significance of corruption in individuals' enjoyment of their fundamental rights. It is underlined by the impacts of corruption on trade liberalisation that distort the human rights of traders and citizens.

1. The relationship between corruption and human rights

The links between corruption and human rights are the focus of significant research efforts.[105] While looking at corruption's impacts on specific human rights can illuminate the severe violations of human rights protection, analysis of how corruption affects the willingness or ability of a state to respect, protect, and promote such rights is more apparent by an examination of three aspects of human rights obligations on the state: duties of non-interference, substantive duties to act, and procedural duties of the administrative and court systems. To these three aspects a discussion of corruption's effects on the right to democratic participation as a right that is especially put at risk by corrupt state structures can be added. In the area of duties of non-interference, corruption can have the result of spurring violations in order to benefit the official who authorises the interference. Here, actions to block political opposition, whether through restraints on speech, press, or gatherings, can arise from corrupt political systems or be maintained by power-holders who keep their control through illicit transactions.

Where substantive duties to act are necessary to comply with a state's human rights obligations, such as in the provision of social and economic goods, corruption's impacts are even clearer. Losses of state moneys through embezzlement or nepotism-driven overpayment on

105 E.g. J. Bacio-Terracino, Corruption as a Violation of Human Rights (2008) http://ssrn.com/abstract=1107918 (visited 14 April 2009); B. Rajagopal, 'Corruption, legitimacy and human rights: The dialectic of the relationship' (1999) 14 *Connecticut Journal of International Law* 495.

contracts or corruption-induced laxness in enforcing quality controls reduces the state's ability to provide citizens with access to health, education, and food, and can endanger the lives of labourers and consumers of state-built infrastructure. Procedure-based human rights can be negated by corruption as principles of non-discrimination and fair treatment are ignored in favour of self-interest. Judicial corruption, too, puts individual's rights to be presumed innocent, to be judged in accordance with the law, and subject to proportionate sanctions in competition with the court's personal interests.

Despite the severity of corruption's infringements of the above-mentioned human rights, the systemic nullification of rights to democratic participation necessarily arising from any significant level of corruption in a state may be the most damaging effect of corruption in the long term.[106] Extreme corruption, such as existed in states like Indonesia under the leadership of Suharto, can effectively blend the personal interests of the leader with the public interest. Even moderate levels of corruption, however, damage democracies. When state officials, whether bureaucrats, legislators, or leaders, act in their own personal interest, rather than that of the state and its population, the electorate is effectively denied its right to participate in the governance.

2. Corruption's effects on trade

Evidence offered by empirical studies shows how trade is affected by (and affects) levels and types of corruption.[107] The review and analysis of such studies for their human rights implications makes clear that – using the framework set out above – those general effects of corruption on human rights have specific parallels within the trade administration, in particular where the state has procedural duties (in the administrative and court

106 The right to participate in public affairs, voting rights and the right of equal access to public service is anchored in Article 25 of the International Covenant on Economic, Social and Cultural Rights, see General Comment No. 25, available at www.unhchr.ch/tbs/doc.nsf/(Symbol)/d0b7f023e8d6d9898025651e004bc0eb?Opendocument (visited 5 August 2009).

107 See, e.g., S. Bandyopadhyay and S. Roy, 'Corruption and trade protection: Evidence from panel data' (2007) Fed. Res. Bank of St. Louis Working Paper 022A (available at: http://research.stlouisfed.org/wp/2007/2007-022.pdf); R. Damania, P. G. Fredriksson, J. A. List, 'Trade liberalization, corruption, and environmental policy formation: Theory and evidence' (2003) 46 *Journal of Environmental Economics & Management* 490–512; H. Sung, 'Between demand and supply: Bribery in international trade' (2006) 44 *Crime, Law & Social Change* 111.

systems) and where trade liberalisation requires the approval of the citizenry to be legitimate.[108] In even the simplest case of corruption in the trading system, for instance bribery of an official for an import licence, the corruption itself can violate the trader's right to fair and non-arbitrary administrative procedures. Other cases of corruption, where government procurement contracts are granted to relatives of an official despite a lower quality or higher cost end-product than other bidders could have delivered, for example, may have even more serious human rights implications – such as violating citizens' rights to health if the contract was to supply medicines to the national healthcare system. And, as stated above, corruption's frequent violation of the right to democratic participation can have clear impacts on the legitimacy of trade liberalisation. Where legislated openings of markets are passed due to illicit influences on law-makers by foreign industry, the citizens are denied their voice in government. The liberalisations are therefore equally illegitimate – procedurally, even if not always substantively.

3. Corruption's effects on the trade and human rights relationship

Finally, a WTO text on corruption, trade and human rights is necessitated by the fact that corruption has an influence on whether or how trade liberalisation could be affecting human rights. That is, corruption impacts areas where there are 'trade and human rights' problems, at times making the liberalisation of such areas more threatening to human rights (such as when corrupted legislators pass laws that allow highly efficient foreign competitors to enter a market previously dominated by small-scale producers who lived at the margins of existence and who now face serious violations of their economic rights to work, shelter, food and health; or when the access of foreign service providers of education to a market results in a factual division of the school system into public schools and private schools, with the poor forced to attend increasingly under-resourced institutions while the wealthy attend private schools) and at other times making the non-liberalisation of certain areas threatening to human rights (if corrupt officials with an interest in maintaining a monopoly market refuse to permit competition in a food staple, for example, poor urban dwellers may be denied access to sufficient nutrition). It is even possible that corruption has prevented some negative

108 See K. Nadakavukaren Schefer, 'Corruption and human rights' (2009) 43 *Journal of World Trade* 737–770.

changes to the level of particular human rights enjoyed by some while nevertheless failing to support an overall system of human rights protection (when, for instance, a particular export industry is sheltered from foreign competition due to the monetary benefits from such protection going to the law-maker, the employees are ensured further work, but suffer in their rights to an answerable government).

BOX 8.3 DRAFT AGREEMENT ON CORRUPTION, TRADE, AND HUMAN RIGHTS

Members,

- *Acknowledging* the impact of corruption on all governments and at every level of administration;
- *Recognising* the multiple opportunities for corruption in trade regulation provided by the high volume of transactions and the economic value of these transactions;
- *Stressing* the need to continually strive to develop new methods to counter corruption;
- *Deploring* the massive misallocation of public resources (financial, personnel) that corruption causes;
- *Concerned about* the grave consequences of corruption on the willingness and ability of a state to fulfil its human rights obligation, and in particular about the inevitable demise of effective rights of democratic participation that accompanies corruption;
- *Determined* to address corruption in trade administrations as a human rights problem,

Hereby agree as follows:
Article 1 – Coverage
This Agreement applies to Members' efforts to address corruption as it relates to trade and human rights;

Article 2 – Definition of Corruption
For purposes of this Agreement, corruption shall include any acts or omissions by a public official of a Member to give an illegitimate benefit or to refrain from issuing a punishment or disadvantage to another individual in exchange for something of value to that official.

Article 3 – Minimum Standard of Corruption-Control Efforts
1. Members shall comply with the United Nations Convention against Corruption.
2. A Member may require higher standards of corruption control, should it consider it feasible to do so.

Article 4 – Transparency

1. Members shall ensure the transparency of their trade administrative procedures, in particular by:
   a) ensuring that decision-making is reasoned and made available to affected traders, and
   b) providing judicial review of administrative decisions by independent judges.
2. Members shall make detailed public accounts open and available to interested persons.

Article 5 – Non-Discrimination

Members shall perform their corruption control activities within a framework of non-discrimination as set forth by Articles I and III GATT 1994 and Articles 3 and 4 TRIPS.

Article 6 – Dispute Settlement

1. The provisions of Articles XXII and XXIII of GATT 1994, as elaborated and applied by the Dispute Settlement Understanding shall apply to consultations and the settlement of disputes under this Agreement.
2. Members shall refrain from using corruption charges as an instrument of negotiating pressure.

Article 7 – Developing and Least-Developed Country Members

1. Members shall accept a commitment to extend financial support to developing and least-developed Members in their efforts to reduce public corruption.
2. Members shall accept a commitment to extend technical support to developing and least-developed Members in their efforts to reduce public corruption.

Article 8 – Committee on Corruption

1. A Committee on Corruption will be established that will act as a point of enquiry as well as a provider of technical assistance and international cooperation with other intergovernmental and non-governmental organisations.
2. Committee members will meet not less than twice a year and otherwise at the request of any Member.
3. The Committee's function will include the furthering of research on the topic of this Agreement.

IV. Trade incentive regimes for human rights

Carefully drafted social clauses in trade incentive regimes such as GSPs may not only foster human rights but also contribute to achieving coherence between human rights and international trade law.

1. The status quo of GSPs under WTO law

Under the status quo, GSPs are compatible with WTO law if they meet the criteria of the Enabling Clause.[109] According to the Appellate Body, schemes that provide for objective criteria and are available to all similarly situated developing countries with the same developing needs meet these conditions.[110] Examples of such objective criteria include international human rights protected under UN and ILO Conventions as mentioned in the EU GSP. By contrast, interest clauses such as those used by the US are unlikely to meet the standards established by the Appellate Body.[111] Thus, future social clauses should be framed along the lines of the EU GSP taking into account the recommendations made above.

2. Developing criteria for GSPs under a multilateral framework

Criteria for future social clauses in trade incentives should be incorporated into the WTO Agreement building upon the criteria of the Enabling Clause. From a substantial point of view they should be drafted along the following guiding principles:

- They should provide for cooperation with UN and ILO bodies.
- The relevant standards should be the ILO and UN human rights conventions.
- The procedures for granting and withdrawing tariff preferences should include human rights assessments, in situ visits by trade and human rights experts, ideally in cooperation with civil society and trade unions, and should provide detailed application guidelines ensuring effective monitoring and should set out the consequences in case of non-compliance with human rights.[112]

The decisions on granting and withdrawing should be made subject to an effective review mechanism. Such a review mechanism should in

109 GATT Contracting Parties, Decision of 28 November 1979, 'Differential and More Favourable Treatment, Reciprocity and Fuller Participation of Developing Countries', BISD 26/203 (1980).

110 Cf. Appellate Body Report, *EC – Tariff Preferences.*

111 F. Humbert, 'Do social clauses in generalized systems of preferences advance the cause of women?' (2008) NCCR Working Paper 2008/4, 45.

112 See also the Draft Proposal for a 2008 ILA Resolution on 'International trade law and human rights' in International Law Association, Rio Conference (2008), International Trade Law, pp. 15–17, which submits that respect for human rights increases civil society support for the WTO.

turn be subjected to a special appeal mechanism under the WTO, open for WTO Members.

Bibliography

Aaronson, Susan Ariel, 'Seeping in slowly: How human rights concerns are penetrating the WTO' (2007) **6** *World Trade Review* 413–449.

Alston, Philip, 'Ships passing in the night: The current state of the human rights and development debate seen through the lens of the millennium development goals' (2007) **27** *Human Rights Quarterly* 754–828.

Bacio-Terracino, Julio, 'Corruption as a violation of human rights' (2008), available at: http://ssrn.com/abstract=1107918 (visited 14 April 2009).

Bandyopadhyay, Subhayu and Roy, Suryadipta, 'Corruption and trade protection: Evidence from panel data' (2007) 022A Fed. Res. Bank of St. Louis Working Paper, available at: http://research.stlouisfed.org/wp/2007/2007–022.pdf (visited 14 April 2009).

Breining-Kaufmann, Christine, 'The legal matrix of human rights and trade law: State obligation *versus* private rights and obligations', in T. Cottier, J. Pauwelyn and E. Bürgi (eds.), *Human Rights and International Trade* (Oxford University Press, 2005), pp. 95–136.

Cockcroft, Laurence, 'Corruption and human rights: A crucial link' (1998) Transparency International Working Paper.

Cordonier Segger, Marie-Claire and Gehring, Markus, 'Introduction', in M.-C. Cordonier Segger and M. Gehring (eds.), *Sustainable development in world trade law* (Kluwer Law, 2005), pp. 1–24.

Cottier, Thomas, 'The legitimacy of WTO law' (2008) NCCR Working Paper 2008/19.

Cottier, Thomas, 'Trade and human rights, a relationship to discover' (2002) **5** *Journal of International Economic Law*, pp. 111–132.

Damania, Richard, Fredriksson, Per G. and List, John A., 'Trade liberalization, corruption, and environmental policy formation: theory and evidence' (2003) **46** *Journal of Environmental Economics & Management* 490–512.

Dommen, Caroline, 'Human rights and trade: Two practical suggestions for promoting coordination and coherence', in T. Cottier, J. Pauwelyn and E. Bürgi (eds.), *Human Rights and International Trade* (Oxford University Press, 2005), pp. 199–204.

Dommen, Caroline, 'Raising human rights concerns in the World Trade Organization – actors, processes and possible strategies' (2000) **24** *Human Rights Quarterly* 1–50.

Dworkin, Ronald, *Taking Rights Seriously* (Harvard University Press, 1977).

Fine, Chop, 'The human rights impact of local government corruption and mismanagement in Rivers State' (2007) Human Rights Watch Report **19**(2A).

Gehne, Katja, 'Nachhaltige Entwicklung als Rechtsprinzip: normativer Aussagegehalt, rechtstheoretische Einordnung, Funktionen im Recht', PhD thesis, University of Zurich (2008).

Gehring, Markus, *Nachhaltigkeit durch Verfahren im Welthandelsrecht: Umwelt- und Nachhaltigkeitsprüfungen und die WTO* (Berlin, Duncker & Humblot, 2007).

Gehring, Markus, Hepburn, Jarrod and Cordonier Segger, Marie-Claire, *World Trade Law in Practice* (Globe Law & Business, 2006).

George, Clive and Kirkpatrick, Colin H., *Impact Assessment and Sustainable Development: European Practice and Experience* (Cheltenham, Edward Elgar, 2007).

Gilgen, Elisa, 'The case of conflicts in diamonds: An analysis of regime theories and regime interaction' (2007) NCCR Working Paper 2007/1.

Glendon, Mary Ann, *Rights Talk: The Impoverishment of Political Discourse* (New York, The Free Press, 1993).

Grewlich, Klaus W., *Transnational Enterprises in a New International System* (Sijthoff & Noordhoff, 1980).

Grunwald, Armin and Kopfmüller, Jürgen, *Die Nachhaltigkeitsprüfung, Kernelement einer angemessenen Umsetzung des Nachhaltigkeitsleitbilds in Politik und Recht* (Forschungszentrum Karlsruhe, 2007).

Harrison, James, *The Human Rights Impact of the World Trade Organization* (Hart Publishing, 2007).

Heri, Simone and Häberli, Christian, 'World food crisis: Are trade rules a problem or a way forward?', in World Trade Organization, 2008 Public Forum Proceedings 25–26 September 2008 (Geneva: WTO Publications, 2009).

Howse, Robert and Ruti G. Teitel, 'Beyond the divide: The Covenant on Economic, Social and Cultural Rights and the World Trade Organization' (2007) 30 *Dialogue on Globalization*, available at: http://library.fes.de/pdf-files/iez/global/04572.pdf (visited 14 April 2009).

Howse, Robert and Mutua, Makau, 'Protecting human rights in a global economy. Challenges for the World Trade Organization' (2000) Working Paper, International Centre for Human Rights and Democratic Development, Rights & Democracy, available at: www.ichrdd.ca/english/commdoc/publications/globalization/wtoRightsGlob.html (visited 14 April 2009).

Humbert, Franziska, *The Challenge of Child Labour in International Law* (Cambridge University Press, 2009).

Humbert, Franziska, 'Do social clauses in generalized systems of preferences advance the cause of women?' (2008) NCCR Working Paper 2008/4.

Jessen, Henning, 'Trade and development law', in M. Gehring and M.-C. Cordonier Segger (eds.), *Sustainable Development in World Trade Law* (Kluwer Law, 2005), pp. 77–101.

Joshi, Deepa, 'Misunderstanding gender in water', in A. Cole and T. Wallace (eds.), *Gender, Water and Development* (Oxford, Berg Publishers, 2005).

Karapinar, Baris and Häberli, Christian (eds.), *Food Crises and the WTO: World Trade Forum* (Cambridge University Press, 2010).

Kaufmann, Christine, 'Globalisation and Labour Rights: The Conflicting Relationship between Core Labour Rights and International Economic Institutions' (Oxford, Hart, 2007).

Kaufmann, Christine, 'The right to food and trade in agriculture', in T. Cottier, J. Pauwelyn and E. Bürgi (eds.), *Human Rights and International Trade* (Oxford University Press 2005), pp. 341–381.

Kaufmann, Christine and Grosz, Mirina, 'Poverty, hunger and international trade: What's law got to do with it? Current mechanisms and the Doha Development Agenda' (2008) **51** *German Yearbook of International Law* 75–109.

Kaufmann, Christine and Heri, Simone, 'Liberalizing trade in agriculture and food security: Mission impossible?' (2008) **40** *Vanderbilt Journal of Transnational Law* 1039–1070.

Kaufmann, Christine and Laura Meyer, 'Trade and human rights' (2007) **1** *Human Rights and International Legal Discourse* 61–93.

Kaufmann, Daniel, 'Human rights and governance: The empirical challenge', in P. Alston and M. Robinson (eds.), *Human Rights and Development: Towards Mutual Reinforcement* (New York University Law School, 2004).

Larsen, Kurt, Martin, John P. and Morris, Rosemary, 'Trade in educational services: Trends and emerging issues' (2002) OECD Working Paper.

Marceau, Gabrielle and Trachtman, Joel P., 'The Technical Barriers to Trade agreement, the Sanitary and Phytosanitary Measures Agreement, and the General Agreement on Tariffs and Trade. A map of the World Trade Organization law of domestic regulation of goods' (2002) **36** *Journal of World Trade*, pp. 811–881.

Marceau, Gabrielle, 'WTO dispute settlement and human rights' (2002) **13** *European Journal of International Law* 753–814.

Marceau, Gabrielle, 'A call for coherence in international law: Praises for the prohibition against "clinical isolation" in WTO dispute settlement' (1999) **33** *Journal of World Trade* 87–152.

Mashayekhi, Mina, Martine, Julsain, and Tuerk, Elisabeth, 'Strategic considerations for developing countries: The case of GATS and health services', in C. Blouin *et al.* (eds.), *International Trade in Health Services and the GATS: Current Issues and Debates* (World Bank, 2005).

Matusz, Steven and Tarr, David, 'Adjusting to trade policy reform', in A. O. Krueger (ed.), *Economic Policy Reform: The Second Stage* (University of Chicago Press, 1999).

McGrady, Benn, 'Fragmentation of international law or "systemic integration" of treaty regimes: EC-Biotech products and the proper interpretation of Article 31 (3)(c) of the Vienna Convention on the Law of Treaties' (2008) **42** *Journal of World Trade* 589–618.

McLachlan, Campbell, 'The principle of systemic integration and Article 31 (3)(c) of the Vienna Convention' (2005) **54** *International and Comparative Law Quarterly* 279–319.

Mosoti, Victor, 'Institutional cooperation and norms creation in international organizations', in T. Cottier, J. Pauwelyn and E. Bürgi (eds.), *Human Rights and International Trade* (Oxford University Press, 2005), pp. 165–179.

Nadakavukaren Schefer, Krista, 'Corruption and human rights' (2009) **43** *Journal of World Trade* 737–770.

Nadakavukaren Schefer, Krista, 'Corruption and the WTO legal system' (2008) NCCR Working Paper 2008/15.

Nadakavukaren Schefer, Krista, 'Chilling the protection of human rights: What the Kimberley Process Waiver can tell us about the WTO's effect on international law' (2007) NCCR Working Paper 2007/3.

Neumann, Jan, *Die Koordinierung des WTO Rechts mit anderen völkerrechtlichen Ordnungen* (Berlin, Duncker & Humblot, 2002).

Nowrot, Karsten, '*UN-Norms on the Responsibility of Transnational Corporations and other Business Enterprises with Regard to Human Rights*: Gelungener Beitrag zur transnationalen Rechtsverwirklichung oder das Ende des Global Compact?' (2003) *Beiträge zum transnationalen Wirtschaftsrecht*, vol. 21.

Paasch, Armin, Garbers, Frank and Hirsch, Thomas, *Trade Policies and Hunger – The Impact of Trade Liberalisation on the Right to Food of Rice Farming Communities in Ghana, Honduras and Indonesia* (Geneva, Ecumenical Advocacy Alliance, 2007).

Pauwelyn, Joost, 'Human rights in WTO dispute settlement', in. T. Cottier, J. Pauwelyn and E. Bürgi (eds.), *Human Rights and International Trade* (Oxford University Press, 2005), pp. 205–231.

Pauwelyn, Joost, 'The Sutherland Report: A missed opportunity for genuine debate on trade, globalization and reforming the WTO' (2005) **8** *Journal of International Economic Law* 329–346.

Pauwelyn, Joost, 'Bridging fragmentation and unity: International law as a universe of inter-connected islands' (2004) **25** *Michigan Journal of International Law* 903–916.

Pauwelyn, Joost, *Conflict of Norms in Public International Law: How WTO Law Relates to Other Rules of International Law* (Cambridge University Press, 2003).

Petersmann, Ernst-Ulrich, 'Human rights and international trade law: Defining and connecting the two fields', in T. Cottier, J. Pauwelyn and E. Bürgi (eds.), *Human Rights and International Trade* (Oxford University Press, 2005), pp. 29–94.

Petersmann, Ernst-Ulrich, 'The "human rights approach" advocated by the UN High Commissioner for Human Rights and by the International Labour

Organization: Is it relevant for WTO law and policy?' (2004) **7** *Journal of International Economic Law* 605–626.

Petersmann, Ernst-Ulrich, 'The WTO Constitution and human rights' (2000) **3** *Journal of International Economic Law* 20–24.

Qureshi, Asif, 'International trade and human rights from the perspective of the WTO', in F. Weiss, E. Denters and P. de Waart (eds.), *International Economic Law with a Human Face* (Kluwer Law, 1998), pp. 159–173.

Rajagopal, Balakrishnan, 'Corruption, legitimacy and human rights: The dialectic of the relationship' (1999) **14** *Connecticut Journal of International Law* 495–507.

Roaf, Virginia, Khalfan, Ashfaq and Langford, Malcolm, 'Monitoring implementation of the right to water: A framework for developing indicators' (2005) **14** *Global Issues Papers.*

Robertson, Christopher, Gilley, K. M. and Crittenden, William F., 'Trade liberalization, corruption, and software piracy' (2007) *Journal of Business Ethics* 623–634.

Rose-Ackerman, Susan, *Corruption and Government* (Cambridge University Press, 1999).

Skogly, Sigrun I., *Beyond National Borders: States' Human Rights Obligations in International Cooperation* (Intersentia, 2006).

Stiglitz, Joseph E., *Globalization and Its Discontents* (Norton & Company, 2002).

Stillwell, Matthew, 'Sustainable development and trade law: Overview of key issues', in, M-C. Cordonier Segger and C. G. Weeramantry (eds.), *Sustainable Justice: Reconciling Economic, Social and Environmental Law* (Martinus Nijhoff Publishers, 2005), pp. 87–119.

Sung, Hung-En, 'Between demand and supply: Bribery in international trade' (2006) **44** *Crime, Law & Social Change* 111–132.

Turner, Liz, Nguyen, Ngoc and Bird, Kate, *Fighting Poverty, An Overview of Ex Ante Tools for Assessing the Impact of Trade Liberalisation on the Poor* (Overseas Development Institute, 2008).

Varghese, N. V., *GATS and Higher Education: The Need for Regulatory Policies, International Institute for Educational Planning* (UNESCO, 2007).

Walker, Simon, 'Human rights impact assessments of trade-related policies', in M. W. Gehring and M.-C. Cordonnier Segger (eds.), *Sustainable Development in World Trade Law* (The Hague, Kluwer, 2005), pp. 221–255.

Winters, L. Alain, McCulloch, Neill and McKay, Andrew, 'Trade liberalization and poverty: The evidence so far' (2004) **24** *Journal of Economic Literature* 72–115.

Ziegler, Katja S., Strengthening the rule of law, but fragmenting international law: The Kadi Decision of the ECJ from the perspective of human rights (2009) **9** *Human Rights Law Review* 288–305.

9

The protection and promotion of cultural diversity in a digital networked environment: mapping possible advances towards coherence

MIRA BURRI-NENOVA, CHRISTOPH BEAT GRABER AND THOMAS STEINER*

KEY MESSAGES

- Neither the WTO nor UNESCO currently offers appropriate solutions to the trade and culture predicament that would allow for efficient protection and promotion of cultural diversity.
- The trade and culture discourse is over-politicised and owing to the related path dependencies, a number of feasible solutions presently appear blocked.
- The digital networked environment has profoundly changed the ways cultural content is created, distributed, accessed and consumed, and may thus offer good reasons to reassess and readjust the present models of governance.
- Access to information appears to be the most appropriate focus of the discussions with a view to protecting and promoting cultural diversity in the new digital media setting, both in local and global contexts.
- This new focal point also demands broadening and interconnecting the policy discussions, which should go beyond the narrow scope of audiovisual media services, but cautiously take account of the developments at the network and applications levels, as well as in other domains, most notably protection of intellectual property rights.
- There are various ways in which the WTO can be made more conducive to cultural policy considerations and these include improved and updated services classifications; enhanced legal certainty with regard to digitally transferred goods and services; and incorporation of rules on subsidies for services and on competition.

* Individual Project No. 7, 'eDiversity: The Protection of Cultural Diversity in a Digital Networked Environment'. Thanks for insightful comments are owed to Manfred Elsig, Thomas Messerli, Thomas Cottier and Panagiotis Delimatsis.

A. Introduction

Cultural diversity as a concept and as a distinct public policy objective has substantially gained in significance in the past decade and its role is likely to be augmented in the years to come. While there is no single understanding of what cultural diversity is, and perhaps fortunately so, we have observed the emergence of a clear set of policy choices and decisions at all levels of governance that could be subsumed under this rather novel public policy goal. Particularly interesting have been the developments at the international level because of the battle – intrinsic to economic globalisation – between 'trade' and 'non-trade' values, of which cultural diversity is one. The trade and culture quandary has also been intriguing because of its political charge and because the cultural proponents have been successful in forum-shifting cultural policy matters (at least partially) from the World Trade Organization (WTO) to the United Nations Educational, Scientific and Cultural Organization (UNESCO). Adding a level of complexity to these discussions, but also offering exciting challenges and possibilities for reform, is the fact that the regulatory environment, where any trade and culture debate is to be resolved, has been profoundly changed due to the advent and wide spread of digital technologies.

It is the purpose of this chapter to account for these changes in the global media landscape and while recalling the main tenets of the trade and culture discourse, to advance proposals for its reformulation. We conjecture that there is no 'one-size-fits-all' solution to the trade and culture predicament but many that need to be coherently fitted together. The digital networked environment that utterly transforms the ways in which cultural content is produced, distributed, accessed and consumed, has potentially also created a number of opportunities to abandon (as far as politically possible) the current strong path dependencies, to reassess and to amend the international trade rules accordingly, making them more conducive to the pursuit of domestic cultural policies, while at the same time avoiding blatant protectionism. The international community may also need to take into account a host of new issues that are emerging – issues that require additional regulatory intervention in order to ensure a sustainable and thriving cultural environment.

B. The discourse of trade and culture

The discourse of trade and culture at the international level is an example *par excellence* of fragmented regulatory regimes. Many institutions and organisations (e.g. WTO, UNESCO, the World Intellectual Property Organization (WIPO); the World Summit on the Information Society (WSIS); and the International Telecommunications Union (ITU)) adopt rules of both a hard and a soft nature that affect cultural diversity to different degrees, and these decisions are taken without any meaningful coordination or even any attempt at dialogue between them. Multiple decisions with strong impact and spill-over effects are also taken at the regional, bilateral and domestic levels. To reduce this complexity and going back to the original roots of the trade and culture predicament, we reconstruct it primarily in the framework of the WTO and that of UNESCO.[1]

The discussions on the relationship between trade and culture started in a context of international trade after World War I when the initial predominance of European cinema came to an end and Hollywood was established as the new centre of global filmmaking.[2] As a reaction to this shift of power, many European governments introduced measures to protect their domestic film industries, including import and screen quotas. The US State Department coming to the aid of Hollywood exerted pressure on European governments to overturn the protective measures. Both antagonists were relieved when in 1947 the newly established General Agreement on Tariffs and Trade (GATT) managed to provisionally resolve the conflict.[3] With the emergence and wide spread of television as a lucrative mass medium in the second half of the twentieth century, European and Canadian airtime quotas for domestic television programmes fuelled the debate anew. The flexibility mechanisms introduced after the Uruguay Round under the auspices of the newly founded WTO in 1994 only managed to put the conflict on ice rather than providing for an enduring solution. No such solution is anticipated in the Doha Trade Talks either.

Interestingly, it was only in the 1990s that UNESCO took a concrete interest in protecting cultural diversity from the alleged negative effects of

1 C. B. Graber, 'The New UNESCO Convention on Cultural Diversity: A Counterbalance to the WTO?' (2006) 9 *Journal of International Economic Law* 553, p. 554.

2 N. Gabler, *An Empire of Their Own: How the Jews Invented Hollywood* (New York: Anchor, 1988); R. Sklar, *Film: An International History of the Medium* (Upper Saddle River, NJ: Prentice Hall, 1993), p. 95.

3 The GATT prohibited quantitative restrictions on imports in Article XI GATT but provided for an exception from the obligation of national treatment for cinematograph films in Articles III(10) and IV GATT. See C. B. Graber, *Handel und Kultur im Audiovisionsrecht der WTO* (Bern: Staempfli, 2003), pp. 125–128.

international trade and economic globalisation,[4] and in this way one can clearly discern the pattern of conflict in the matters of trade and culture (in this sense, often framed as 'trade versus culture'). Key steps in this process were the publication of the seminal report 'Our Creative Diversity' by the World Commission on Culture and Development in 1995 and the 1998 Stockholm Conference on Cultural Policies for Development, recommending, inter alia, a recognition that cultural goods and services should be 'treated as being not like any other form of merchandise'.[5] In November 2001, UNESCO adopted a non-binding declaration on cultural diversity and on 18 March 2007, the binding UNESCO Convention on the Protection and Promotion of the Diversity of Cultural Expressions entered into force[6] as a culmination of these efforts.

In the next section, we look in more detail into the respective frameworks of the WTO, in particular at the rules applicable to trade in goods and services, and of UNESCO, in particular at the legal and policy impact of the UNESCO Convention on Cultural Diversity. We expose the lack of appropriate solutions catering for cultural diversity protection and promotion in both of these fora, which offers fruitful soil for suggesting new perspectives, adjustments and reforms.

C. Incompleteness of the trade and culture discourse

I. The WTO framework

As already noted, the GATT 1947 provided for a provisional solution to the film dispute between the US and Europe by conceding screen quotas in Article IV GATT while prohibiting import quotas for films pursuant to Article XI GATT. Over time, screen quotas have lost much of their practical significance and South Korea is probably the only state left that still insists on this instrument for assuring a strong presence of domestic films on cinema screens.[7] Besides the leeway for screen quotas expressly

4 I. Bernier, 'A UNESCO International Convention on Cultural Diversity', in C. B. Graber, M. Girsberger and M. Nenova (eds.), *Free Trade versus Cultural Diversity: WTO Negotiations in the Field of Audiovisual Services* (Zurich: Schulthess, 2004), pp. 65–76, p. 72.

5 See Objective 3, para. 12 of the Action Plan adopted at the Stockholm Conference.

6 UNESCO, Convention on the Protection and Promotion of the Diversity of Cultural Expressions, adopted 20 October 2005, entry into force 18 March 2007. For a detailed discussion of this process, see Graber, above n. 1, pp. 556–558.

7 After the US made the conclusion of a free trade agreement contingent on the partial abolishment of the screen quota scheme, South Korea halved the requirement for exhibitors to screen Korean films as of 1 July 2006 from 40% to 20% of the total screening time. Today

devised in Article IV GATT, plenty of other norms scattered throughout the body of the WTO law can be found relevant and allow some flexibility as far as trade in cultural goods and services is concerned.[8] In particular, the General Agreement on Trade in Services (GATS) offers more wriggle room than the GATT,[9] since the GATS framework involves primarily a 'bottom-up' (or 'positive list') approach. Thereby Members can choose the services sectors and sub-sectors in which they are willing to make national treatment or market access commitments,[10] and can define the modalities of these commitments. In contrast, obligations under GATT regarding national treatment and quantitative restrictions apply across the board, subject to specified exceptions.

The scope for domestic measures regarding trade in culture was however never found sufficient.[11] The inner tension between trade and culture has always been there, even within the GATT 1947, the WTO's less far-reaching institutional predecessor.[12] This tension led to an explosion during the Uruguay Round (1986–1994), when France and Canada fought the 'exception culturelle' battle with the goal of exempting cultural services (in particular audiovisual ones) from the newly created agreement on services.[13] The infamous 'Agreement to Disagree' was a sort of ceasefire in the trade versus culture quandary. Thereby, it was established

Korean cinemas have to screen locally produced films for 73, rather than the 146 days necessary under the previous regime. See W. Choi, 'Screen Quota and Cultural Diversity: Debates in Korea–US FTA Talks and Convention on Cultural Diversity' (2007) 2 *Asian Journal of WTO and International Health Policy* 267.

8 For an overview of all relevant provisions, see C. B. Graber, 'Audiovisual Media and the Law of the WTO', in Graber *et al.*, above n. 4, pp. 47–56.

9 Graber, above n. 1, pp. 555 and 569.

10 Articles XVI and XVII GATS.

11 S. Cahn and D. Schimmel, 'The Cultural Exception: Does it Exist in GATT and GATS Frameworks? How Does It Affect or Is It Affected by the Agreement on TRIPS? (1997) 15 *Cardozo Arts and Entertainment Law Journal* 281, pp. 287–289.

12 See e.g. GATT, *EEC – Directive on Transfrontier Television: Response to Request for Consultations under Article XXVII:I by the United States*, DS4/4, 8 November 1989. Later WTO cases worth mentioning are WTO, *Turkey – Taxation of Foreign Film Revenues: Request for Consultations by the United States*, WT/DS43/1, 17 June 1996; WTO, *Turkey – Taxation of Foreign Film Revenues: Request for Establishment of a Panel by the United States*, WT/DS43/2, 10 January 1997; WTO Panel Report, *Canada – Certain Measures Concerning Periodicals (Canada – Periodicals)*, WT/DS31/R and Corr.1, adopted 30 July 1997, as modified by the Appellate Body Report, WT/DS31/AB/R, DSR 1997:I, 481 14 March 1997 and WTO Appellate Body Report, *Canada – Certain Measures Concerning Periodicals (Canada – Periodicals)*, WT/DS31/AB/R, adopted 30 July 1997, DSR 1997:I, 449WT/DS31/AB/R, adopted 30 June 1997.

13 See C. B. Graber, 'Audio-visual Policy: The Stumbling Block of Trade Liberalisation', in D. Geradin and D. Luff (eds.), *The WTO and Global Convergence in Telecommunications and*

that GATS covers all services sectors but permits substantial commitment flexibilities.[14] Taking advantage of these, many states had listed no or only minimum commitments with regard to national treatment and market access and exempted sensitive sectors (in particular audiovisual services) from most-favoured-nation (MFN) obligations.[15]

However, the 'Agreement to Disagree' was not a real solution and cultural proponents were well aware of this. The further liberalisation commitment[16] was impending and the MFN exemptions made were at least theoretically limited in time.[17] A particularly hard blow to the backers of the cultural exception was the *Canada – Periodicals* case,[18] decided by the Panel and the Appellate Body to the benefit of the US and despite the fact that the Canada–US Free Trade Agreement (CUSFTA)[19] envisaged a cultural exception clause.[20] Furthermore, as *Canada – Periodicals* showed exemplarily, the system of exceptions to GATT obligations, including the

Audiovisual Services (Cambridge University Press, 2004), pp. 165–214; M. Roy, 'Audiovisual Services in the Doha Round: Dialogue de Sourds, The Sequel?' (2005) 6:6 *Journal of World Investment and Trade* 923, p. 941.

14 See C. M. Bruner, 'Culture, Sovereignty, and Hollywood: UNESCO and the Future of Trade in Cultural Products' (2008) 40 *International Law and Politics* 351, p. 374; F. S. Galt, 'The Life, Death, and Rebirth of the "Cultural Exception" in the Multilateral Trading System: An Evolutionary Analysis of Cultural Protection and Intervention in the Face of American Pop Culture's Hegemony' (2004) 3:3 *Washington University Global Studies Law Review 909*, p. 914; Cahn and Schimmel, above n. 11, pp. 291–301.

15 Almost all Members, with the notable exception of the US, Japan and New Zealand, have been reluctant to commit and have listed substantial MFN exemptions. See Roy, above n. 13, p. 927.

16 See Part IV GATS. Article XIX therein states: 'In pursuance of the objectives of this Agreement, Members shall enter into successive rounds of negotiations, beginning not later than five years from the date of entry into force of the WTO Agreement and periodically thereafter, with a view to achieving a progressively higher level of liberalization.'

17 The GATS Annex on Article II Exemptions states (para. 6) that, '[i]n principle, such exemptions [to MFN] should not exceed a period of 10 years. In any event, they shall be subject to negotiation in subsequent trade liberalizing rounds.' The exemptions made theoretically expired in 2005.

18 See above n. 12.

19 Canada–US Free Trade Agreement, 22 December 1987–2 January 1988, 27 ILM 281 (1988).

20 In CUSFTA, the culture exception was coupled with a retaliation provision. Article 2005 CUSFTA provides that, '[c]ultural industries are exempt from the provisions of this Agreement', but also that either party could 'take measures of equivalent commercial effect in response to [such] actions'. The North American Free Trade Agreement (NAFTA; 17 December 1992, 32 ILM 289 (1993)) incorporated by reference to CUSFTA this cultural exception. It exists only between Canada and both the US and Mexico, but not between the US and Mexico. In practice, this provision offering comfort to the Canadian cultural sector had little effect. See Cahn and Schimmel, above n. 11, p. 30.

general exceptions provided by Article XX GATT, does not sufficiently respond to cultural concerns in domestic policy making.[21] The only provision available for cultural issues is Article XX(f) GATT providing for an exception to GATT disciplines for the protection of 'national treasures of historic, artistic, or archaeological value'. However, this concept does not include artefacts of contemporary creative production.[22] Following the design of GATT, the GATS' general exceptions[23] to the obligations of national treatment, market access and MFN fall short of providing for a safeguard for cultural diversity purposes.

Moreover, because of the deadlock in negotiations, neither the GATT nor the GATS has been substantially updated as far as the modalities of committing are concerned. In particular, the existing GATS nomenclature for services classification (the W/120 with reference to the United Nations Central Product Classification (CPC)[24]) has been outpaced by the rapid technological developments of the past few years. It has not adapted to the digital turn, which has profoundly changed the ways in which audiovisual media are created, produced, distributed and consumed and is ill-prepared to appropriately classify a number of new services associated with electronic commerce.[25]

To exemplify this lack of appropriate and up-to-date responses in WTO law, we discuss here the instance of digital games. Digital games, in particular in their online versions, are increasingly becoming not only a major attraction for the new generation of media consumers but also an important economic and cultural asset. Governments have been assuming that certain types of digital games are a form of cultural expression and have put in place support programmes for the production of new games.[26]

21 Although Canada argued, inter alia, that the disputed customs tariff discriminating split-run periodicals was necessary for protecting the Canadian periodicals industry and cultural policy goals, the WTO dispute settlement authorities did not consider this to be an issue of Article XX(f) GATT. See above n. 12.

22 Graber, above n. 1, p. 568.

23 See Article XVI GATS.

24 WTO, Services Sectoral Classification List, WTO Doc.MTN.GNS/W/120, 10 July 1991, referring to UN Provisional Central Product Classification (CPC), UN Statistical Papers, Series M, No 77, Ver.1.1, E.91.XVII.7, 1991. The classification problem is similar for goods and the applied Harmonized System, created and regularly amended by the World Customs Organization. See D. Yu, 'The Harmonized System: Amendments and Their Impact on WTO Members' Schedules' (2008) WTO Economic Research and Statistics Division Staff Working Paper No. 2, pp. 1–23.

25 Graber, above n. 13, pp. 208–209.

26 For a detailed analysis, including examples for government support programmes, see C. B. Graber, 'State Aid for Digital Games and Cultural Diversity: A Critical Reflection in the Light of EU and WTO Law', in C. B. Graber and M. Burri-Nenova (eds.), *Governance*

From a trade law perspective, however, these media are under conditions of legal uncertainty. It stems above all from the difficulty of classifying digital games into a certain category of goods or services. Such a classification is related to distinct (and often starkly different) legal consequences (in particular with regard to the leeway a state may have to adopt for targeted cultural measures), because of the different depth of liberalisation under GATT or GATS, and because of the uneven commitments for different types of services under the GATS.

While ideally the classification of digital games between GATT and GATS should be resolved through political consensus, such a decision is currently not anticipated, mostly because of the diverging positions of the US and the EU.[27] While awaiting such an agreement, the fact that the GATT does not provide a tariff number for digital games' content may be an indication for a GATS classification.[28] However, even if GATS appears applicable, it is unclear whether the appropriate sub-classification is that of computer and related services; value-added telecommunications services; entertainment; or audiovisual services[29] (which are further divided into more sub-categories).[30]

II. The UNESCO Convention on Cultural Diversity

Only a couple of years after its entry into force almost 100 countries had ratified the UNESCO Convention on Cultural Diversity

of Digital Game Environments and Cultural Diversity (Cheltenham: Edward Elgar, 2010), pp. 170–201.

27 M. Burri-Nenova, 'Trade versus Culture in the Digital Environment: An Old Conflict in Need of a New Definition' (2009) 12 *Journal of International Economic Law* 17, pp. 52–54.

28 Whereas the physical carrier medium on which digital games' software is stored may be classified under either Heading 85.24 or 9504.10, the HS does not seem to provide for a classification for the digital games' content itself. See T. Steiner, 'Online Games under WTO Law: Unresolved Classification Issues' (2009) NCCR Trade Regulation Working Paper 2009/3 pp. 13–15.

29 S. Wunsch-Vincent, *The WTO, the Internet and Trade in Digital Products* (Oxford: Hart, 2006), p. 71.

30 In this regard, we would tend to nominate audiovisual services in particular the subcategory of 'other' as the most relevant since this is most likely to reflect the essential character of the digital games as a multimedia service. The classification of digital games as GATS 'other' audiovisual services would have important implications for the treatment of digital games as presumably cultural products. In view of the low level of commitments in the audiovisual services sub-sector, it may be established that existing obligations of the WTO agreements do not seem to prevent governments from supporting the development and production of digital games. See Steiner, above n. 28, and Graber, above n. 26.

(CCD).[31] Whereas the ratification process is a success and an important precondition for the CCD being able to play its intended role as a counterbalance to the WTO, it cannot disguise the serious flaws that disturb the beauty of the new instrument.

The CCD builds on two cornerstones. The first is the recognition of the cultural sovereignty of the Parties, encompassing the right to adopt measures on cultural policy.[32] The second is the recognition of the dual nature of cultural goods and services as objects of trade and as cultural artefacts.[33] Since cultural goods and services are not only objects of trade but have a distinctive cultural nature as 'vehicles of identity, values and meaning',[34] the CCD calls upon governments to take appropriate measures to adjust imbalances in the relationship between trade and culture. The CCD provides no explicit definition of culture but rather adopts a discursive approach to culture, referring to 'the manifold ways in which the cultures of groups and societies find expression'.[35] Hence, this definition permits one to analyse cultural diversity in terms of the markets where it is represented. As the discursive approach to cultural diversity opens the door for statistical measurement and for political economic analysis, it has been considered to be an important contribution towards rationalising the debate on trade and culture at the international level.[36] This positive aspect of the CCD is, however, nearly nullified by the fact that most of its provisions – including those in its core chapter IV on rights and obligations – are rather fuzzy.[37] The UNESCO Convention has precious few obligations and these are primarily formulated as mere stimuli for the Parties to adopt measures for the protection and promotion of the diversity of cultural expressions at the national[38] and international[39] levels, rather than as genuine duties.[40] The only provision of binding

31 As of 2 July 2009, 99 countries had ratified the UNESCO Convention (see http://portal.unesco.org/la/convention.asp?KO=31038&language=E; last accessed 29 July 2009).

32 Article 5 CCD.

33 Recital 18 of the Preamble and Article 1(g) CCD.

34 Article 1(g) CCD.

35 Article 4 CCD.

36 Graber, above n. 26.

37 For a detailed analysis see C. B. Graber, 'Substantive Rights and Obligations under the UNESCO Convention on Cultural Diversity', in H. Schneider and P. van den Bossche (eds.), *Protection of Cultural Diversity from an International and European Perspective* (Mortsel: Intersentia, 2008), pp. 141–162.

38 CCD, at Articles 7–11.

39 CCD, at Articles 12–19, excluding Article 16, which is of binding nature.

40 Graber, above n. 37, p. 6.

nature[41] resembles the WTO's Enabling Clause[42] and relates to the preferential treatment for developing countries, whereby developed countries must facilitate cultural exchanges with developing countries by granting preferential treatment to artists and other cultural professionals and practitioners, as well as to cultural goods.[43] The fuzziness of many provisions[44] and the limited obligations make the CCD vulnerable to accusations of being an instrument of protectionism.

A further shortcoming is related to the centrality of state sovereignty which is intrinsic to the CCD. Indeed, the sovereignty of the State Parties in the cultural field is included as one of the eight guiding principles underpinning the Convention (Article 2(2)[45]) and all rights and obligations stemming from the Convention are attributed to states. This is particularly disturbing with regard to the relationship between indigenous peoples and the governments of the territory where they live. While the Convention does mention indigenous peoples and traditional cultural expressions a few times,[46] the relevant provisions remain declarative in nature and address not the rights of the indigenous peoples themselves but those of the states whose territory is affected. Consequently, the CCD does not respect the rights of indigenous peoples for cultural self-determination and self-governance, which are the

41 *Ibid.* p. 8, footnote 59. Another provision that qualifies as an obligation relates to the cooperation in providing assistance, in particular to developing countries, in situations of serious threat to cultural expressions (Article 17 CCD). Burri-Nenova, above n. 27, p. 22.

42 See GATT, Decision of 28 November 1979 (L/4903), Differential and More Favourable Treatment, Reciprocity and Fuller Participation of Developing Countries ('Enabling Clause'). See also B. Hoekman, 'More Favorable Treatment of Developing Countries: Ways Forward', in R. Newfarmer (ed.), *Trade, Doha, and Development: Window into the Issues* (Washington, DC: World Bank, 2006), pp. 213–221; S. W. Chang, 'WTO for Trade and Development Post-Doha' (2007) 10 *Journal of International Economic Law* 553.

43 CCD, at Article 16; Burri-Nenova, above n. 27, p. 22. On the probably limited effect of Article 16 CCD, see K. Nurse, Expert Report on Preferential Treatment (Article 16) in the UNESCO Convention on the Protection and Promotion of the Diversity of Cultural Expressions, 10 October 2008, p. 24.

44 H. Ruiz Fabri, 'Reflections on Possible Future Legal Implications of the Convention', in N. Obuljen and J. Smiers (eds.), *UNESCO's Convention on the Protection and Promotion of the Diversity of Cultural Expressions: Making It Work* (Zagreb: Institute for International Relations, 2006), pp. 73–87, p. 80.

45 Burri-Nenova, above n. 27, p. 25. See also R. Craufurd Smith, 'The UNESCO Convention on the Protection and Promotion of Cultural Expressions: Building a New World Information and Communication Order?' (2007) 1 *International Journal of Communication* 24, p. 37.

46 CCD, Preamble at recitals 8, 13 and 15, Articles 2(3) and 7(1)(a).

fundament of the recently adopted Declaration of the United Nations on the Rights of Indigenous Peoples.[47] Finally, the CCD falls short of clarifying its relationship to the international system of intellectual property rights protection,[48] which is deplorable, since, as we show below, intellectual property rights play a vital role in promoting and sustaining creativity.

This innate defect of normative incompleteness of the CCD is aggravated by the lack of institutional or adjudicatory mechanisms that could procedurally clarify and complete the contract. The Convention's exponents still hope that the Intergovernmental Committee and the Convention's own dispute resolution will fill some of the existing gaps, since both allow evolutionary advances, depending upon the willingness of the Parties. It should be noted however that the dispute settlement is ultimately not compulsory[49] and the tasks of the Intergovernmental Committee, as defined in Article 23(6) CCD, may not provide a solid legal basis for it to engage in interpretation of the Convention beyond commenting on the State Parties' reports.[50]

Against the above backdrop, it is evident that neither of the institutional domains of the trade and culture discourse, i.e. the WTO and UNESCO, provide appropriate solutions for the underlying trade–culture quandary. Nor do they ensure a workable interface between the two regimes, as the recent *China – Publications and Audiovisual Products case* confirmed.[51] What is instead observable is a continuing disconnect between the issues of trade and culture, which has been strongly politically driven and

47 The Declaration was adopted on 13 September 2007. See UN General Assembly, 'General Assembly Adopts Declaration on Rights of Indigenous Peoples', Press Release GA/10612, 13 September 2007.

48 Burri-Nenova, above n. 27, pp. 55–58.

49 See M. Hahn, 'A Clash of Cultures? The UNESCO Diversity Convention and International Trade Law' (2006) 9 *Journal of International Economic Law* 515, p. 533, who critically remarks that the UNESCO Convention's dispute settlement is 'worth mentioning only as being reminiscent of the very early days of modern international law'.

50 See Article 23(6)(c) CCD.

51 WTO Appellate Body Report, *China – Measures Affecting Trading Rights and Distribution Services for Certain Publications and Audiovisual Entertainment Products (China – Publications and Audiovisual Products)*, WT/DS363/AB/R, adopted 21 December 2009, confirming in most essential points WTO Panel Report, *China – Measures Affecting Trading Rights and Distribution Services for Certain Publications and Audiovisual Entertainment Products (China – Publications and Audiovisual Products)*, WT/DS363/R, adopted 12 August 2009. For an analysis, see M. Burri, 'Trade and Culture in International Law: Paths to (Re)conciliation' (2010) 44 *Journal of World Trade* 49.

widely accepted but which may obstruct the formulation of coherent solutions.[52]

D. Need to broaden the picture due to the new digital reality

The above system of institutional and substantive relationships between issues of trade and culture emerged under the conditions of analogue/offline media. The hornets' nest in these developments has primarily been around audiovisual media and the diverse measures that states have adopted to protect and promote the national industries producing them.[53] Such initiatives have been politically strengthened by the perceived adverse effects of globalisation, in particular upon culture,[54] as well as by the presumption that technological advances negatively affect the diversity of cultural expressions and demand more rather than less regulatory intervention.[55]

The media landscape has however not remained static and in the past two decades has experienced profound changes, which have led to a decidedly different information and communication environment.[56] We argue that under these new conditions, whose salient features will be sketched here,[57] there is a need to broaden the trade and culture debate and seek a new focal point of these deliberations that more appropriately

52 M. Burri-Nenova, 'Trade and Culture: Making the WTO Legal Framework Conducive to Cultural Considerations' (2008) 5 *Manchester Journal of International Economic Law* 3.

53 The underlying 'axioms' of state intervention have been that some sort of additional regulation is needed because of the failures inherent to media markets and that these market failures can be corrected through state measures. Failures typical of the markets for cultural goods and services can be identified as failures due to: (i) economies of scale in production and distribution; (ii) the nature of competition in products with substantial public goods aspects; (iii) the impact of externalities on the pricing of cultural products; and (iv) collective action problems. See P. Sauvé and K. Steinfatt, 'Towards Multilateral Rules on Trade and Culture: Protective Regulation or Efficient Protection?', in Productivity Commission and Australian National University, *Achieving Better Regulation of Services* (AusInfo, 2000), pp. 323–346, p. 325.

54 Against such undifferentiated arguments, see A. Giddens, *Runaway World: How Globalisation Is Reshaping Our Lives* (Oxford: Routledge, 2002), p. xxiv. See also T. Cowen, *Creative Destruction: How Globalization Is Changing the World's Cultures* (Princeton, NJ: Princeton University Press, 2002), p. 146 and T. Cowen, *In Praise of Commercial Culture* (Cambridge, MA: Harvard University Press, 1998), pp. 15–43.

55 For a discussion, see Graber, above n. 1, p. 570.

56 Y. Benkler, *The Wealth of Networks: How Social Production Transforms Markets and Freedom* (New Haven, CT: Yale University Press, 2006), p. 2.

57 For a full analysis, see M. Burri-Nenova, 'The Changing Environment of Audiovisual Media: New Technologies, New Patterns of Consumer/Business Behaviour and Their Implications for Audiovisual Media Regulation' (2007) 12 *medialex* 171.

reflects the changed reality of media. Translating this into the policy space may also demand a re-evaluation of the policy tools for the achievement of the objective of cultural diversity.

At the core of the sweeping changes on the media canvas is the process of digitisation, which enables any type of information (be it text, audio, video, or image) to be expressed in a line of zeroes and ones. This coded data can also be easily stored and transported at the speed of light, and this, as the experience of the past fifteen years shows, takes place at an ever decreasing price.[58] This basic matrix combined with the wide spread of optical fibre networks and exponentially increasing computational power, has led to a variety of transformations in the information and communications environment, which have become palpable in different facets of societal practices. Filtering in context these transformations, we can identify as particularly relevant: (i) the proliferation and diversity of content; (ii) its accessibility; (iii) the empowerment of the user; and (iv) the new modes of content production, where the user is not merely a consumer but is also an active creator, individually or as part of the community. While some of these developments are still in their infancy, they are already entering a phase that permits observations of immediate relevance for the discussion on protecting and promoting cultural diversity. Some of these observations hint at opportunities for better, more efficient and flexible accommodation of the goal of cultural diversity, while others are to be viewed as challenges, perhaps calling for additional regulatory intervention.

In the latter category, one may list the anticipated drastically fragmented media environment, as content consumption moves from a 'push' to a 'pull' mode (i.e. from broadcasting to on-demand).[59] The split between digital and analogue households, which is already a reality, will also be exacerbated, and while this widening gap between the digital 'haves' and 'have-nots' is noticeable within developed societies, it is all the more striking between the developed and the developing and least developed societies.[60] In terms of competition, the effects of the digital

58 See e.g. C. Marsden *et al.*, *Assessing Indirect Impacts of the EC Proposals for Video Regulation* (RAND Europe, 2006), pp. 72 ff.

59 J. Naughton, 'Our Changing Media Ecosystem', in E. Richards *et al.* (eds.), *Communications: The Next Decade* (Ofcom, 2006), pp. 41–50. See also D. Graham *et al.*, Impact Study of Measures Concerning the Promotion of Distribution and Production of TV Programmes Provided for under Article 25(a) of the TV without Frontiers Directive, Final Report prepared for DG Information Society, 2005, at section 3.5.1.

60 E. S. Nwauche, 'African Countries' Access to Knowledge and the WIPO Digital Treaties' (2005) 8 *Journal of World Intellectual Property* 361.

networked environment are multi-directional. On the positive side, it is conceivable that the reduced barriers to entry will allow new market players to position themselves and make use of niche markets, which have become economically viable in the digital ecosystem due to the dramatically falling storage, distribution and search costs (the so-called 'long tail' effect[61]). The digital setting may also have reduced the significant entrepreneurial risk inherent in launching new cultural goods and services[62] (at least for some of them), while making the visibility of cultural goods and services greater and empowering the consumer in terms of choice and actual consumption.

On the other hand, a concentration among the diverse players in media markets, both horizontally and vertically, may also be expected, because of their pursuit of better utilisation of all available channels and platforms[63] and the related benefits from economies of scale worldwide. The development of truly ubiquitous global market players may have a number of grave effects upon cultural diversity, among others, certainly leading to magnified importance of a very small number of languages (in particular English). Nonetheless, the digitally facilitated abundance of content, its dissemination and accessibility without real location restrictions undoubtedly lead to more content and to new content[64] being generated and spread individually or by groups.[65] Some of this user created content (UCC) reflects the key media policy components of diversity,

61 See C. Anderson, *The Long Tail: Why the Future of Business Is Selling Less of More* (New York: Hyperion, 2006). The name 'long tail' has to do with the image of a demand curve that gets longer and longer and covers more and more niche 'non-hit' products. Anderson's theory builds upon previous and parallel economic research. See E. Brynjolfsson, Y. Hu and M. D. Smith, 'From Niches to Riches: The Anatomy of the Long Tail' (2006) 47 *Sloan Management Review* 67; E. Brynjolfsson, Y. Hu and D. Simester, 'Goodbye Pareto Principle, Hello Long Tail: The Effect of Search Costs on the Concentration of Product Sales', MIT Center for Digital Business Working Paper (2007).

62 Germann argues that this specificity of cultural goods and services is the main issue that commands intervention. See C. Germann, 'Culture in Times of Cholera: A Vision for a New Legal Framework Promoting Cultural Diversity' (2005) 6 *ERA–Forum* 109, p. 116.

63 For instance, by placing a single video on mobile and digital TV networks, on content platforms and social networking websites such as YouTube, MySpace and Facebook.

64 D. Weinberger, *Everything Is Miscellaneous* (New York: Henry Holt, 2007) and OECD, Participative Web: User-Created Content, DSTI/ICCP/IE(2006)7/FINAL, 12 April 2007.

65 'Changes in the way users produce, distribute, access and re-use information, knowledge and entertainment potentially give rise to increased user autonomy, increased participation and increased diversity. These may result in lower entry barriers, distribution costs and user costs and greater diversity of works as digital shelf space is almost limitless.' OECD, *ibid.*, p. 5.

localism and non-commercialism[66] and in this sense harnessing the UCC processes could be critical for achieving cultural diversity objectives.[67] Beyond these 'amateur' creations,[68] the digital environment has also had a strong impact upon how artists and culture-makers express themselves, how they communicate with one another and with the public, how cultural content is presented and made accessible and how it is consumed. In short, digitisation, both as a tool of expression and as a new cultural communication space 'affects the entire spectrum of culture production, distribution and presentation . . . [and] brings with it the promise of cultural renewal'.[69]

The new dynamics of the markets for digital cultural content may also impact upon the market failures conventionally associated with 'analogue' media markets, mostly because of the changed notion of scarcity in the digital space. In this context, the idea of protecting some 'shelf-space' for culturally or nationally distinctive productions makes little sense since the 'shelf-space' is virtually unlimited. Furthermore, it may also become *im*possible to 'reserve' space for a certain purpose, since it is the consumer herself or himself who decides about the content, its form and time of delivery.

E. Access as a new focal point of the cultural diversity debate

Following the above arguments, one may legitimately question any cultural policy measure that restricts trade by putting up barriers to incoming foreign cultural goods and services.[70] One may also have

66 E. P. Goodman, 'Media Policy Out of the Box: Content Abundance, Attention Scarcity, and the Failures of Digital Markets' (2004) 19 *Berkeley Technology Law Journal* 1389, pp. 1395–1399.

67 For a specific analysis of UCC in virtual worlds, see M. Burri-Nenova, 'User Created Content in Virtual Worlds and Cultural Diversity', in Graber and Burri-Nenova, above n. 26, pp. 74–112.

68 A. Keen, *The Cult of the Amateur: How Today's Internet Is Killing Our Culture* (New York: Doubleday, 2007).

69 Netherlands Council for Culture, From ICT to E-Culture: Advisory Report on the Digitalisation of Culture and the Implications for Cultural Policy, submitted to the State Secretary for Education, Culture and Science, 2003 (English edn, 2004), p. 8. See also T. O'Regan and B. Goldsmith, 'Emerging Global Ecologies of Production', in D. Harries (ed.), *The New Media Book* (British Film Institute Publishing, 2004), pp. 92–105.

70 Such as the EC TV quotas for European content, as we have argued elsewhere. See M. Burri-Nenova, 'The New Audiovisual Media Services Directive: Television without Frontiers, Television without Cultural Diversity' (2007) 44 *Common Market Law Review* 1689.

reservations about the extremely narrow concentration of the trade and culture debate upon audiovisual media.[71] The changed modalities of the digital space and the overall transformed environment call for a broader perspective when examining the pertinent issues of trade and culture and, as we argue in the following, for a new focal point of the cultural diversity debate. We suggest 'access' as the new focus of deliberations and construe it in the widest of contexts and as informed by the values of the freedom of speech and information.[72] We argue that while the above-sketched effects of the new digital ecology may have positive repercussions and even promise a vital and diverse cultural environment sustainable without supplementary regulatory intervention, most of these effects would not unfold unless certain conditions of access, of practical, economic, societal and legal nature, are fulfilled.

I. Access to infrastructure

At the most basic level, increased diversity, distribution and access to the so-created information environment are strongly dependent upon access to infrastructure, hardware, software, and increasingly, access to media literacy. In a development discourse, this matrix is often used to identify the digital divide between the developed and the developing and least developed societies, although, as we signalled above, such gaps are the reality of industrialised societies too. We approach the matrix from a legal perspective here, however, and seek to unveil the legal constraints to this type of access. These legal limitations abound, especially as the digital networked environment matures, spreading 'at all levels of the information environment: the physical infrastructure layer – wires, cable, radio frequency spectrum – the logical infrastructure layer – software – and the content layer',[73] and making decisions previously peripheral to the cultural debate now move towards its centre. Thus, regulatory choices related to content cannot be analysed in isolation and any enquiry needs to incorporate and cautiously consider all choices made at all layers of the information and communication model.

71 Burri-Nenova, above n. 27.

72 J. M. Balkin, 'Media Access: A Question of Design' (2008) 76 *George Washington Law Review* 101.

73 Y. Benkler, 'From Consumers to Users: Shifting the Deeper Structures of Regulation toward Sustainable Commons and User Access' (2000) 52 *Federal Communications Law Journal* 561.

The infrastructural level falls within the domain of telecommunications law and this has traditionally been totally disassociated from media (content) regulation because of the inherent strict divide between content and networks that existed in the pre-convergence era.[74] Such a divide is no longer apposite, especially as networks (in particular broadband) have become critical to accessing online media, or broadly speaking to entering the Information Society.

In this sense, the tremendous evolution of the telecommunications sector over the past two decades, its opening up to competition and undergoing substantial deregulation, are to be assessed as highly beneficial.[75] The WTO rules have played a vital role in this process securing a level playing field and spreading the profits of deeper liberalisation among states. The GATS Annex on Telecommunications and the Reference Paper on Basic Telecommunications[76] are particularly worthy of mention as instruments that go beyond the conventional services sector commitments and offer a progressive and suitable framework for advancing competition in telecommunications services.[77] While there are a number of ways in which the Reference Paper could be improved to provide more clarity and stability of legitimate expectations,[78] such improvements are highly unlikely to occur during the current Doha Round.[79] After *Mexico – Telecommunications*,[80] which exposed some of the drawbacks of the

74 Convergence is a complex process that can be briefly described as the coming together of media, telecommunications and information technologies markets and sectors. The process began in the mid-1980s and has been widely acknowledged as having deep regulatory implications in all policy circles. For an overview of stakeholders' positions, see M. Burri-Nenova, *EC Electronic Communications and Competition Law* (London: Cameron May, 2007), pp. 28–31.

75 *Ibid.*, pp. 10–16.

76 Attached as an additional commitment (Article XIX GATS) to the Members' individual schedules of commitments.

77 For a detailed analysis, see M. Bronckers and P. Larouche, 'A Review of the WTO Regime for Telecommunications Services', in K. Alexander and M. Andenas (eds.), *The World Trade Organization and Trade in Services* (Leiden: Martinus Njihoff, 2008), pp. 319–379 and M. Burri-Nenova, 'The Law of the World Trade Organization and the Communications Law of the European Community: On a Path of Harmony or Discord?' (2007) 41 *Journal of World Trade* 833.

78 See e.g. D. Geradin and M. Kerf, 'Levelling the Playing Field: Is the WTO Adequately Equipped to Prevent Anti-Competitive Practices in Telecommunications?', in Geradin and Luff, above n. 13, pp. 144–157.

79 S. Peng, 'Trade in Telecommunications Services: Doha and Beyond' (2007) 41 *Journal of World Trade* 293.

80 WTO Panel Report, *Mexico – Measures Affecting Telecommunications Services (Mexico – Telecoms)*, WT/DS204/R, adopted 1 June 2004.

Reference Paper, what also became especially palpable is the lack of competition rules within the WTO frame.[81] The need for antitrust supervision is in fact stronger in the post-liberalisation period where sectoral regulation is gradually withdrawn and national competition agencies take over to ensure fair competition conditions,[82] and it is unfortunate that any advance in the direction of incorporating competition rules within the WTO is far from becoming real at this stage.[83]

Yet, to reiterate with some optimism, the current telecommunications provisions at the international level do on the whole provide a fairly good basis for securing access to infrastructure. This is partly because their negotiation has been excluded from the politically laden 'trade versus culture' debates and has instead been driven by economic interests. Notwithstanding this economic rationale, it should be noted that the present regime also allows for the accommodation of national measures aimed at public interest objectives, since these can be subsumed under the universal service provision of the Reference Paper.[84] The Reference Paper is formulated in a flexible manner and one may even argue that states can use this leeway to include content-related universal service obligations that secure not only access to infrastructure but also access to *information*.[85] Indeed, there are numerous initiatives under way, both national and regional, aimed at securing 'broadband for all'[86] as a first step along this avenue.

81 E. M. Fox, 'The WTO's First Antitrust Case – *Mexican Telecom*: A Sleeping Victory for Trade and Competition' (2006) 9 *Journal of International Economic Law* 271, p. 290.

82 Burri-Nenova, above n. 74.

83 Although the synergies between trade and competition have been repeatedly acknowledged, there has been little progress since Singapore and the issue was dropped from the Doha agenda. See WTO, Doha Work Programme: Decision Adopted by the General Council on 1 August 2004, WT/L/579, 2 August 2004, para. (g). For a comprehensive analysis, see P. Marsden, *A Competition Policy for the WTO* (London: Cameron May, 2003).

84 With respect to universal service, the Reference Paper allows Members to define the type of universal service obligation they wish to maintain and states that such obligations will not be regarded as anti-competitive per se, provided that they are administered in a transparent, non-discriminatory and competitively neutral manner and are not more burdensome than necessary: Reference Paper, at section 3.

85 M. Burri-Nenova, 'The New Concept of Universal Service in a Digital Networked Communications Environment' (2007) 3 *I/S: A Journal of Law and Policy for the Information Society* 117.

86 See e.g. 'Empowering Users: The Key to the Development of the Information Society', speech by V. Reding, Member of the European Commission responsible for Information Society and Media at the BEUC Annual General Assembly, Brussels, 13 November 2008.

Looking into the future and bearing in mind some developments at national level (mostly in the US and EC), what may be critical to ensuring access to infrastructure, broadly construed, will be all decisions that influence the interoperability of networks and code,[87] the control of the network,[88] as well as those pertinent to the principle of net neutrality.[89] In respect of these, the lack of antitrust rules at the global level and the failure to recognise the principle of technological neutrality in the WTO realm[90] are especially deplorable.

II. Access to content

1. The availability and organisation of information

As noted above, under the conditions of the digital networked environment, content abounds. Yet, this does not automatically mean that information is readily accessible and if it is, it may not be easy to find. The fact that any type of data can be expressed in digital format has changed the rules for organising information.[91] So whereas the Dewey decimal classification used to be used for organising libraries and alphabetical order was used for name registers and genre categories in CD shops, the digital environment enables an encompassing, global, extremely miscellaneous and dynamic information archive that can be searched through a single entry point according to virtually unlimited criteria. This has been made technologically possible through the availability and continuous improvement of search engines that serve as linchpins of the Internet.[92] As the importance of these technological facilitators, which are essentially under private property and control, grows, it will become necessary

87 U. Gasser and J. G. Palfrey. 'Breaking Down Digital Barriers: When and How ICT Interoperability Drives Innovation' (2007) Berkman Center Research Publication No. 08.

88 J. G. Palfrey, Jr. and R. Rogoyski, 'The Move to the Middle: The Enduring Threat of "Harmful" Speech to the End-to-End Principle' (2006) 21 *Washington University Journal of Law and Policy* 31.

89 The principle of net(work) neutrality holds that the network should be neutral to the content being passed and that intermediaries should pass all packets, while the intelligence is located at the edges of the network where necessary See S. P. Crawford, 'Network Rules' (2007) 70 *Law and Contemporary Problems* 51; T. Wu, 'Network Neutrality, Broadband Discrimination' (2003) 2 *Journal on Telecommunications and High Technology Law* 141.

90 P. Larouche, 'Dealing with Convergence at the International Level', in Geradin and Luff, above n. 13, pp. 390–422.

91 Weinberger, above n. 64.

92 J. Grimmelmann, 'The Structure of Search Engine Law' (2007) New York Law School Research Paper Series 23, p. 2. See also J. Battelle, *The Search* (Portfolio, 2005).

to ensure that precision, universal access and non-discrimination are guaranteed.[93] Possible impediments to gaining access to content due to either filtering by the incumbent company or by the state (through commercial intermediaries[94]) have also an essential human rights dimension in that they may infringe the freedoms of expression and information, association or privacy.[95] While the scope of this chapter does not allow a full analysis, it is apparent that there is a host of new issues arising in this context that the international legal framework is not yet prepared to reflect appropriately.[96]

2. Intellectual property rights

In contrast, intellectual property rights (IPR) protection has long been secured at the international level and the contemporary IPR architecture[97] has evolved over time and elaborated a broad palette of sophisticated and flexible intellectual property (IP) tools 'to protect both traditional and new forms of symbolic value produced in particular places as they circulate in global commodity markets'.[98] When talking about trade and

93 Vaidhyanathan, for instance, questions the role of Google as ubiquitous search engine and asks whether public libraries may be more appropriate to administer knowledge. See S. Vaidhyanathan, 'The Googlization of Everything and the Future of Copyright' (2007) 40 *UC Davis Law Review* 1207, p. 1220. For a more optimistic vision, see L. A. Kurtz, 'Copyright and the Human Condition' (2007) 40 *UC Davis Law Review* 1233, pp. 1250–1251.

94 J. Rosen, 'Google's Gatekeepers', *New York Times*, 30 November 2008.

95 Internet filtering has been practised by many states with different degrees of intervention, China being the most prominent example. See R. J. Deibert *et al.*, *Access Denied: The Practice and Policy of Global Internet Filtering* (MIT Press, 2007).

96 There have been some private initiatives to remedy the situation, at least partially. For instance, the Center for Democracy and Technology and Business for Social Responsibility, together with leading human rights groups, academic institutions and ICT companies, including Google, Vodafone, France Telecom, Microsoft and Yahoo! have launched a project to protect and advance individuals' rights to free expression and privacy on the Internet through the creation of a set of principles and supporting mechanisms for ICT companies. See www.globalnetworkinitiative.org/.

97 Under IPR as a general category, one understands the rights granted to creators and inventors to control the use made of their productions. They are traditionally divided into two main branches: (i) 'copyright and related (or neighbouring) rights' for literary and artistic works and (ii) 'industrial property', which encompasses trademarks, patents, industrial designs, geographical indications and the layout designs of integrated circuits. In the following, we discuss primarily the first category.

98 R. J. Coombe, S. Schnoor and M. Ahmed, 'Bearing Cultural Distinction: Informational Capitalism and New Expectations for Intellectual Property' (2007) 40 *UC Davis Law Review* 891, p. 916.

culture, IPR are particularly vital for (at least) two reasons: the first has to do with the foremost rationale for IPR protection, which is to foster creativity;[99] this is also essentially the most important prerequisite for a flourishing and diverse cultural environment. The second reason has to do with the way IPR protection is granted, whereby authors receive a temporary monopoly over their creations and thus exclude the rest of the public from having access to the protected works.[100] Within both of these rationales, which are essentially interrelated, a series of critiques from the perspective of protecting and promoting cultural diversity can be formulated.

First, the IPR system is far from perfect and some of its deficiencies relate to the inherent centrality of authorship, originality and mercantilism in the 'Western' IP model, which leaves numerous non-Western, collaborative or folkloric modes of production outside the scope of IP protection.[101] It is furthermore not certain whether the existent IP model appropriately reflects – especially under the conditions of the digital ecology, which have magnified the value of copyright law[102] and expanded its reach[103] – the precarious balance between the private interests of authors and the public interest in enjoying broad access to their productions,[104]

99 As the US Constitution (at Article I, Section 8, para. 8) beautifully puts it: '[t]o promote the Progress of Science and useful Arts, by securing for limited Times to Authors and Inventors the exclusive Right to their respective Writings and Discoveries'.

100 It should also be mentioned here that while this monopoly was initially vested in the creators, presently 'these rights are routinely assigned away to the distributor of the work in order to gain access to the channels of distribution and their audience'. See R. Ku, 'Promoting Diverse Cultural Expression: Lessons from the US Copyright Wars' (2007) 2 *Asian Journal of WTO and International Health Law and Policy* 369, p. 377, referring also to N. W. Netanel, 'Market Hierarchy and Copyright in Our System of Free Expression' (2000) 53 *Vanderbilt Law Review* 1879, p. 1889.

101 See the contributions to C. B. Graber and M. Burri-Nenova (eds.), *Intellectual Property and Traditional Cultural Expressions in a Digital Environment* (Cheltenham: Edward Elgar, 2008), in particular those of F. Macmillan, W. B. Wendland, C. B. Graber and M. Burri-Nenova.

102 J. E. Cohen, 'Pervasively Distributed Copyright Enforcement' (2006) 95 *Georgetown Law Journal* 1.

103 L. Lessig, '(Re)creativity: How Creativity Lives', in H. Porsdam (ed.), *Copyright and Other Fairy Tales: Hans Christian Andersen and the Commodification of Creativity* (Cheltenham: Edward Elgar, 2006), pp. 15–22, p. 19.

104 See e.g. Committee on Economic, Social and Cultural Rights, General Comment No. 17: The Right of Everyone to Benefit from the Protection of the Moral and Material Interests Resulting from Any Scientific, Literary or Artistic Production of Which He Is the Author (Article 15(1)(c)), UN Doc. E/C.12/2005, 21 November 2005, para. 35.

and whether this balance offers the best incentives to promote creativity. The content industries are quite sure of copyright's virtues and have convinced most governments that strong and enforceable IPRs are the *sine qua non* for a vibrant culture. Through race-to-the-top strategies, this strong protection has been emancipated to the international level in the framework of the Agreement on Trade Related Aspects of Intellectual Property Rights (TRIPS Agreement) and in the even further-reaching free trade agreements.[105]

Yet, while IP protection certainly fulfils essential economic functions in production and distribution of cultural materials,[106] evidence of a direct correlation between IPR and creativity is equivocal and IP protection may even trigger systemic harm.[107] Furthermore, some copyright scholars observing the process of creativity more closely argue that it is the 'creative play' that is of primary importance for artistic and intellectual innovation.[108] The existing copyright models do not reflect such arguments. Especially under the conditions of the digital networked environment, these models are often too rigid to allow full realisation of the possibilities of the digital mode of content production and distribution, or render them illegal, possibly chilling a considerable amount[109] of creative activities and creative potential.[110] These deficiencies have been exposed by the emergence of new hybrid models for the protection of authors' rights, such as the Creative Commons (cc) licence,[111] which short of a

105 N. W. Netanel, 'Why Has Copyright Expanded? Analysis and Critique', in F. Macmillan (ed.), *New Directions in Copyright Law*, vol. 6 (Cheltenham: Edward Elgar, 2007), pp. 3–34.

106 W. M. Landes and R. A. Posner, *The Economic Structure of Intellectual Property Law* (Cambridge, MA: Belknap Press of Harvard University, 2003), pp. 11–123.

107 J. E. Cohen, 'Creativity and Culture in Copyright Theory' (2007) 40 *UC Davis Law Review* 1151, pp. 1193–1194. In *Grokster*, the US Supreme Court did recognise the possible harm, noting that, '[t]he more artistic protection is favored, the more technological innovation may be discouraged': see US Supreme Court, *Metro-Goldwyn-Mayer Studios, Inc. v. Grokster, Ltd.*, 125 S. Ct. 2764 (2005), referring to *Sony Corp. of America v. Universal City Studios, Inc.*, 464 U. S. 417 (1984), at 442.

108 See Cohen, above n. 107, and J. E. Cohen, 'The Place of the User in Copyright Law' (2005) 74 *Fordham Law Review* 347.

109 Vaidhyanathan notes in this regard: 'Copyright in recent years has certainly become too strong for its own good. It protects more content and outlaws more acts than ever before. It stifles creativity and hampers the discovery and sharing of culture and knowledge': see Vaidhyanathan, above n. 93, p. 1210. See also S. Vaidhyanathan, *Copyrights and Copywrongs: The Rise of Intellectual Property and How It Threatens Creativity* (New York: New York University Press, 2003).

110 Burri-Nenova, above n. 67.

111 See http://creativecommons.org/.

comprehensive copyright reform, allow content to be managed and spread under a 'some rights reserved' mode.[112]

Such developments have also been partly a reaction to the particularly troublesome mechanisms of Digital Rights Management systems (DRM) and other technological protection measures, which under the guise of protecting digital content from uncontrolled distribution and unlawful use, have had pernicious effects, thereby eroding some fundamental rights of consumers[113] and restricting usages traditionally allowed under copyright.[114]

To wrap up the above argument, the initial *raison d'être* for copyright[115] may need to be restated in the newly formed environment, and this is not simply a matter of yielding to the media industries' lobbying, but of weighing anew private interests against public values.[116] Ensuring sustainable access to cultural goods and sustainable production of culturally diverse content[117] would thus not mean that everything is accessible in the romantic sense of the public domain[118] but would involve a complex balance between openness and discretion.[119]

112 Under a cc-licence, the creator/licensor may shape her or his package of rights applying different conditions to the licensed work (attribution; non-commercial; no derivatives; or share alike). Such models have also proven to feed back positively into the user-created content creation and dissemination, thereby enhancing content diversity (see OECD, above n. 64, p. 14).

113 C.B. Graber, 'Copyright and Access – a Human Rights Perspective', in C.B. Graber *et al.* (eds.), *Digital Rights Management: The End of Collecting Societies?* (Bern: Staempfli, 2005), pp. 71–110.

114 N. Lucchi, 'Countering the Unfair Play of DRM Technologies' (2007) 16:1 *Texas Intellectual Property Law Journal* 91.

115 R. Deazley, *Rethinking Copyright: History, Theory, Language* (Cheltenham: Edward Elgar, 2008).

116 See L. Lessig, *Free Culture* (New York: Penguin, 2004).

117 R. J. Coombe, 'Protecting Cultural Industries to Promote Cultural Diversity: Dilemma for International Policy-Making Posed by the Recognition of Traditional Knowledge', in K. E. Maskus and J. H. Reichman (eds.), *International Public Goods and Transfer of Technology under a Globalized Property Regime* (Cambridge University Press, 2005), pp. 559–614, p. 613.

118 See A. Chander and M. Sunder, 'The Romance of the Public Domain' (2004) 92 *California Law Review* 1331.

119 See R. J. Coombe, 'Fear, Hope, and Longing for the Future of Authorship and a Revitalized Public Domain in Global Regimes of Intellectual Property' (2003) 52 *DePaul Law Review* 1171. Various proposals have already been advanced. With regard to liability rules, see J. H. Reichman and T. Lewis, 'Using Liability Rules to Stimulate Local Innovation in Developing Countries: Application to Traditional Knowledge', in Maskus and Reichman, above n. 117, pp. 337–366. See also the work of NCCR Individual Project No. 9, as highlighted in this volume.

The World Intellectual Property Organization (WIPO) itself has admitted that certain amendments to the existing IP architecture and a search for new forms are necessary because of the need for: (i) the preservation and safeguarding of intangible cultural heritage; (ii) the promotion of cultural diversity; and (iii) the promotion of creativity and innovation, including tradition-based forms.[120] The WIPO Development Agenda, adopted by the WIPO General Assembly in September 2007[121] equally rejects a purely IP-centric view. 'It posits that strong intellectual property protection does not consistently promote creative activity, facilitate technology transfer, or accelerate development' and 'places the benefits of a rich and accessible public domain, national flexibilities in implementing IP treaty norms, access to knowledge, UN development goals, curbing of IP-related anti-competitive practices, and the need to balance the costs and benefits of intellectual property protection firmly within WIPO's central mission.'[122] It remains to be seen how these initiatives will be implemented and linked to the TRIPS framework and what their overall effect upon the international trade system will be.[123]

F. Conclusions: from fragmentation to coherence?

The area of trade and culture reveals extreme fragmentation and 'no homogenous, hierarchical meta-system is realistically available to do away with such problems of [conflicting rules and overlapping legal regimes]'.[124] In addition, and typical of 'trade and culture' issues, it is not only the regulatory framework that is profoundly fragmented but also the policy discussions.

Such fragmentation and the increasing politically driven disconnect between the issues of trade and culture complicate and partly obstruct

120 WIPO Intergovernmental Committee on Intellectual Property and Genetic Resources, Traditional Knowledge and Folklore, Consolidated Analysis of the Legal Protection of Traditional Cultural Expressions, WIPO/GRTKF/IC/5/3, 2 May 2003, Annex, para. 8.

121 WIPO Doc. A/43/16, at Annex A.

122 N. W. Netanel, 'The WIPO Development Agenda and its Development Policy Context', in N. W. Netanel, *The Development Agenda: Global Intellectual Property and Developing Countries* (Oxford University Press, 2009), pp. 1–32, p. 2.

123 In the same vein, see J. de Beer (ed.), *Implementing the World Intellectual Property Organization's Development Agenda* (Waterloo, ON: Wilfrid Laurier University Press, 2009).

124 United Nations, Fragmentation of International Law: Difficulties Arising from the Diversification and Expansion of International Law, Report of the Work of the Study Group of the International Law Commission, finalised by Martti Koskenniemi, A/CN.4/L.682, 13 July 2006, para. 493.

the process of identifying coherent solutions. While under 'coherent' we certainly do not mean uniform 'one-size-fits-all' regulatory solutions, we believe that there are a number of ways in which the existing framework can be improved to make it both more trade enhancing and more conducive to cultural considerations.

The modified market mechanisms for content and the changed conditions for creativity, as well as for production, distribution and consumption of cultural content in the digital networked environment, can be viewed as an opportunity in this regard, allowing (if not indeed demanding) a re-evaluation. First it is necessary to acknowledge that we are now faced with a situation that is 'significantly different from the audiovisual sector of the Uruguay Round when negotiations focused primarily on film production, film distribution, and terrestrial broadcasting of audiovisual goods and services'[125] and that is even different from the conditions prevailing at the outset of the Doha Round in 2001, when the Internet was in its infancy and the implications of this network of networks were largely unknown.

We do not, however, suggest that cultural policy measures should be abandoned and that the free flow of goods and services alone will cater for a diversity of expressions in the newly formed environment. Yet the benefits of the existing trade restrictions may very well prove not to outweigh their costs and indeed may be detrimental to the goal of cultural diversity.[126] One may even argue that it is within the mandate of the UNESCO Convention, the scope of which certainly goes beyond the plain reservation of 'shelf-space for domestic productions in television programs and cinemas',[127] to encourage the ratifying parties to dismantle some trade barriers.

Whereas the emergence of a global digital environment and some of its effects have increasingly been acknowledged, it has yet to become an essential issue of policy-making or to be sufficiently integrated into any of the 'old' rule-making domains, notably trade and culture. We argue that access, taken in its broadest sense, offers the appropriate focus in the cultural diversity deliberations. This would most probably call for actions outside the extremely constrained domain of audiovisual services

125 WTO, Communication from the United States: Audiovisual and Related Services, S/CSS/W/21, 18 December 2000, para. 2.

126 J. P. Singh, 'Culture or Commerce? A Comparative Assessment of International Interactions and Developing Countries at UNESCO, WTO, and Beyond' (2007) 8 *International Studies Perspectives* 36, p. 42.

127 Hahn, above n. 49, p. 533.

and require adjustments in other regulatory fields, most notably that of intellectual property protection.

In the concrete terms of a WTO reform and in view of the changing media environment, an important avenue for improving the WTO framework could be the redesign of the existing services classification. A clearer, better-structured and up-to-date classification, especially with regard to the sectors pertinent to culture and the rapidly changing audiovisual and telecommunications areas, can be put high on the list of desiderata.[128] Such an improved system could, most importantly in the present context, allow finer-tuned scheduling rather than the existing 'all-or-nothing' approach. It could also facilitate deeper market access commitments not only in the services sectors (such as computer and telecommunications services), where this may reasonably be expected. Achieving a level of legal certainty with regard to the classification may also contribute to resolving the dilemma of classifying digitally transferred products and services, as outlined above in the context of digital games.

As a more comprehensive improvement plan, there is a good deal that can be achieved by taking up the unfinished business of the Uruguay Round. The 'framework of GATS rules and disciplines is still very much under construction'[129] and, as well as the progressive liberalisation through more and deeper commitments (Article XIX GATS), the GATS structure needs to be completed with rules on: (i) emergency safeguard measures (Article X:1); (ii) subsidies (Article XV:1); (iii) government procurement (Article XIII:2); and (iv) domestic regulation (Article VI:4).[130] While all of these projects[131] would make the rules of the GATS finer-grained, thereby also allowing better-tuned commitments,[132] new rules

128 The need for careful scheduling has been stressed by the *US – Gambling* rulings. See WTO Panel Report, Panel Report, *United States – Measures Affecting the Cross-Border Supply of Gambling and Betting Services (US – Gambling)*, WT/DS285/R, 10 November 2004, as modified by the Appellate Body Report, WT/DS285/AB/R and WTO Appellate Body Report, *United States – Measures Affecting the Cross-Border Supply of Gambling and Betting Services (US – Gambling)*, WT/DS285/AB/R, adopted 20 April 2005.

129 Pierre Sauvé, 'Completing the GATS Framework: Addressing Uruguay Round Leftovers' (2002) 3 *Aussenwirtschaft* 301, p. 302.

130 *Ibid.*, pp. 302–303.

131 For an analysis of these undertakings, see Sauvé, *ibid.*, as well as P. Sauvé, 'Been There, Not Yet Done That: Lessons and Challenges in Services Trade', in M. Panizzon, N. Pohl and P. Sauvé (eds.), *GATS and the Regulation of International Trade in Services* (Cambridge University Press, 2008), pp. 599–631.

132 We noted above that GATS allows substantially more flexibility than the GATT. It should however be borne in mind that if Members do make unlimited commitments under GATS, they may in fact be more restricted than under GATT since within the fairly new

on subsidies[133] are to be viewed as particularly appropriate in the context of trade and culture. The audiovisual sector is one of the traditionally subsidised ones[134] and 'often subsidies are the most efficient instrument for pursuing noneconomic objectives',[135] possibly also for the protection and promotion of local or national culture. Furthermore, the US has noted in this respect that, 'Members may also want to consider developing an understanding on subsidies that will respect each nation's need to foster its cultural identity by creating an environment to nurture local culture',[136] so there may be some tolerance already.

Finally, one should mention the possibility of inserting competition rules within the WTO legal framework[137] that would deal with market distortions by private undertakings.[138] Such rules could be particularly helpful considering that digital media are by default global in their distribution and new media providers operate regardless of borders. This is, however, perhaps the least feasible of avenues, bearing in mind the little progress made since Singapore[139] and that the issue was dropped from the Doha agenda.[140]

construct of the agreement on services no rules on subsidies, safeguards or an equivalent to GATT Article IV for screen quotas exist.

133 Although the current GATS framework contains no specific rules on subsidies, subsidies are not excluded from GATS' scope of application. As 'measures by Members affecting trade in services' within the meaning of Article I:1, subsidies are fully covered by the provisions of the GATS. There are a number of GATS provisions that restrict governments' ability to provide services subsidies or to offer a remedy to those Members harmed by their negative effects. See P. Poretti, 'Waiting for Godot: Subsidy Disciplines in Services Trade', in Panizzon *et al.*, above n. 131, pp. 466–488.

134 Sauvé, above n. 129, p. 325.

135 B. Hoekman, 'Toward a More Balanced and Comprehensive Services Agreement' in J. J. Schott (ed.), *The WTO after Seattle* (Washington, DC: Institute for International Economics, 2000), pp. 119–135, p. 129.

136 WTO, Communication from the United States, above n. 125, para. 10(iii). The US has already accepted some leeway for subsidies in its FTAs with Singapore and Australia.

137 Marsden, above n. 83; M. E. Janow, 'Trade and Competition Policy', in P. F. J. Macrory, A. E. Appleton and M. G. Plummer (eds.), *The World Trade Organization: Legal, Economic and Political Analysis*, vol. 3 (Berlin: Springer, 2005), pp. 487–510.

138 Germann, above n. 62, p. 111; Graber, above n. 3, pp. 317–328, 343.

139 WTO, Singapore Ministerial Declaration, WT/MIN(96)/DEC/W, 13 December 1996. The Singapore Declaration (para. 20) mandated the establishment of 'a working group to study issues raised by Members relating to the interaction between trade and competition policy, including anti-competitive practices, in order to identify any areas that may merit further consideration in the WTO framework'.

140 WTO, Doha Work Programme: Decision Adopted by the General Council on 1 August 2004, WT/L/579, 2 August 2004, para. (g).

To conclude, one needs to acknowledge that there is a growing understanding of the potency of digital technologies as tools and a corresponding flurry of declaratory messages stating that digital technologies could and should be operationalised[141] for the pursuit of diverse public interest objectives, including cultural diversity. Yet, a concrete approach encompassing all pertinent regulatory fields is still lacking. It is perhaps reasonable to start such an exercise at the national level, where a deeper and finer-grained understanding of the effects of the digital networked environment upon creativity, cultural content production, dissemination and consumption can be gained. This knowledge might prompt the formulation of new priorities,[142] which, without compromising cultural diversity as a valid regulatory objective, may lead to a readjustment of the tools of cultural policy regulation at diverse levels of governance. As we have argued, this may mean that barriers, both of legal and of practical nature, relating to the movement of content and to access to content, need to be lifted, while well-targeted subsidies systems, for instance for productions in local languages, for infrastructural support or efforts at bridging the digital divide, are put in place. The WTO law has the potential to accommodate such changes if the political will is there.

Bibliography

Anderson, Chris, *The Long Tail: Why the Future of Business is Selling Less of More* (New York: Hyperion, 2006).

Balkin, Jack M., 'Media Access: A Question of Design' (2008) **76** *George Washington Law Review* 933–951.

Battelle, John, *The Search* (New York: Portfolio, 2005).

Benkler, Yochai, 'From Consumers to Users: Shifting the Deeper Structures of Regulation toward Sustainable Commons and User Access' (2000) **52** *Federal Communications Law Journal* 561–580.

Benkler, Yochai, *The Wealth of Networks: How Social Production Transforms Markets and Freedom* (New Haven, CT: Yale University Press, 2006).

Bernier, Ivan, 'A UNESCO International Convention on Cultural Diversity', in C. B. Graber, M. Girsberger and M. Nenova (eds.), *Free Trade versus Cultural Diversity: WTO Negotiations in the Field of Audiovisual Services* (Zurich: Schulthess, 2004), pp. 65–76.

141 For an overview, see T. McGonagle, 'The Promotion of Cultural Diversity via New Media Technologies: An Introduction to the Challenges of Operationalisation' (2008) 6 *IRIS: Legal Observations of the European Audiovisual Observatory* 1.

142 With specific regard to audiovisual media, see Burri-Nenova, above n. 57.

Bronckers, M. C. E. J. and Larouche, Pierre, 'A Review of the WTO Regime for Telecommunications Services', in K. Alexander and M. Andenas (eds.), *The World Trade Organization and Trade in Services* (Leiden: Martinus Njihoff, 2008), pp. 319–379.

Bruner, Christopher M., 'Culture, Sovereignty, and Hollywood: UNESCO and the Future of Trade in Cultural Products' (2008) **40** *International Law and Politics* 351–436.

Brynjolfsson, Erik, Hu, Yu Jeffrey and Smith, Michael D., 'From Niches to Riches: The Anatomy of the Long Tail' (2006) **47** *Sloan Management Review*, pp. 67–71.

Brynjolfsson, Erik, Hu, Yu Jeffrey and Simester, Duncan, 'Goodbye Pareto Principle, Hello Long Tail: The Effect of Search Costs on the Concentration of Product Sales' (2007) MIT Center for Digital Business Working Paper.

Burri-Nenova, Mira, *EC Electronic Communications and Competition Law* (London: Cameron May, 2007).

Burri-Nenova, Mira, 'The New Concept of Universal Service in a Digital Networked Communications Environment' (2007) 3 *I/S: A Journal of Law and Policy for the Information Society* 117–146.

Burri-Nenova, Mira, 'The New Audiovisual Media Services Directive: Television without Frontiers, Television without Cultural Diversity' (2007) **44** *Common Market Law Review* 1689–1725.

Burri-Nenova, Mira, 'The Law of the World Trade Organization and the Communications Law of the European Community: On a Path of Harmony or Discord?' (2007) **41** *Journal of World Trade* 833–878.

Burri-Nenova, Mira, 'The Changing Environment of Audiovisual Media: New Technologies, New Patterns of Consumer/Business Behaviour and Their Implications for Audiovisual Media Regulation' (2007) **12** *medialex* 171–177.

Burri-Nenova, Mira, 'Trade and Culture: Making the WTO Legal Framework Conducive to Cultural Considerations' (2008) **5** *Manchester Journal of International Economic Law* 3–39.

Burri-Nenova, Mira, 'The Long Tail of the Rainbow Serpent: New Technologies and the Protection and Promotion of Traditional Cultural Expressions', in C. B. Graber and M. Burri-Nenova (eds.), *Intellectual Property and Traditional Cultural Expressions in a Digital Environment* (Cheltenham: Edward Elgar, 2008), pp. 205–236.

Burri-Nenova, Mira, 'Trade versus Culture in the Digital Environment: An Old Conflict in Need of a New Definition' (2009) **12** *Journal of International Economic Law* 17–62.

Burri-Nenova, Mira, 'User Created Content in Virtual Worlds and Cultural Diversity', in C. B. Graber and M. Burri-Nenova (eds.), *Governance of Digital Game Environments and Cultural Diversity* (Cheltenham: Edward Elgar, 2010), pp. 74–112.

Burri-Nenova, Mira, 'Trade and Culture in International Law: Paths to (Re)conciliation' (2010) **44** *Journal of World Trade* 49–80.

Cahn, Sandrine and Schimmel, Daniel, 'The Cultural Exception: Does It Exist in GATT and GATS Frameworks? How Does It Affect or Is It Affected by the Agreement on TRIPS?' (1997) **15** *Cardozo Arts and Entertainment Law Journal* 281–314.

Chander, Anupam and Sunder, Madhavi, 'The Romance of the Public Domain' (2004) **92** *California Law Review* 1331–1374.

Chang, Seung Wha, 'WTO for Trade and Development Post-Doha' (2007) **10** *Journal of International Economic Law* 553–570.

Choi, Won M., 'Screen Quota and Cultural Diversity: Debates in Korea-US FTA Talks and Convention on Cultural Diversity' (2007) **2** *Asian Journal of WTO and International Health Policy* 267–286.

Cohen, Julie E., 'The Place of the User in Copyright Law' (2005) **74** *Fordham Law Review* 347–374.

Cohen, Julie E., 'Pervasively Distributed Copyright Enforcement' (2006) **95** *Georgetown Law Journal* 1–48.

Cohen, Julie E., 'Creativity and Culture in Copyright Theory' (2007) **40** *UC Davis Law Review* 1151–1206.

Coombe, Rosemary J., 'Fear, Hope, and Longing for the Future of Authorship and a Revitalized Public Domain in Global Regimes of Intellectual Property' (2003) **52** *DePaul Law Review* 1171–1192.

Coombe, Rosemary J., 'Protecting Cultural Industries to Promote Cultural Diversity: Dilemma for International Policy-Making Posed by the Recognition of Traditional Knowledge', in K. E. Maskus and J. H. Reichman (eds.), *International Public Goods and Transfer of Technology under a Globalized Property Regime* (Cambridge University Press, 2005), pp. 559–614.

Coombe, Rosemary J., Schnoor, Steven and Ahmed, Mohsen, 'Bearing Cultural Distinction: Informational Capitalism and New Expectations for Intellectual Property' (2007) **40** *UC Davis Law Review* 891–918.

Cowen, Tyler, *In Praise of Commercial Culture* (Cambridge, MA: Harvard University Press, 1998).

Cowen, Tyler, *Creative Destruction: How Globalization Is Changing the World's Cultures* (Princeton, NJ: Princeton University Press, 2002).

Craufurd Smith, Rachael, 'The UNESCO Convention on the Protection and Promotion of Cultural Expressions: Building a New World Information and Communication Order?' (2007) **1** *International Journal of Communication* 24–55.

Crawford, Susan P., 'Network Rules' (2007) **70** *Law and Contemporary Problems* 51–90.

Deazley, Ronan, *Rethinking Copyright: History, Theory, Language* (Cheltenham: Edward Elgar, 2008).

de Beer, Jeremy (ed.), *Implementing the World Intellectual Property Organization's Development Agenda* (Waterloo, ON: Wilfrid Laurier University Press, 2009).

Deibert, Ronald J. *et al.*, *Access Denied: The Practice and Policy of Global Internet Filtering* (Cambridge, MA: MIT Press, 2007).

Fox, Eleanor M., 'The WTO's First Antitrust Case – *Mexican Telecom*: A Sleeping Victory for Trade and Competition' (2006) **9** *Journal of International Economic Law* 271–292.

Gabler, Neal, *An Empire of Their Own: How the Jews Invented Hollywood* (New York: Anchor, 1988).

Galt, Frederick S., 'The Life, Death, and Rebirth of the "Cultural Exception" in the Multilateral Trading System: An Evolutionary Analysis of Cultural Protection and Intervention in the Face of American Pop Culture's Hegemony' (2004) **3** *Washington University Global Studies Law Review* 909–936.

Gasser, Urs and Palfrey, John G., 'Breaking Down Digital Barriers: When and How ICT Interoperability Drives Innovation' (2007) Berkman Center Research Publication No. 08.

Geradin, Damien and Kerf, Michel, 'Levelling the Playing Field: Is the WTO Adequately Equipped to Prevent Anti-Competitive Practices in Telecommunications?', in D. Geradin and D. Luff (eds.), *The WTO and Global Convergence in Telecommunications and Audiovisual Services* (Cambridge University Press, 2004), pp. 144–157.

Germann, Christophe, 'Culture in Times of Cholera: A Vision for a New Legal Framework Promoting Cultural Diversity' (2005) **6** *ERA-Forum* 109–130.

Giddens, Anthony, *Runaway World: How Globalisation Is Reshaping Our Lives* (Oxford: Routledge, 2002).

Goodman, Ellen P., 'Media Policy Out of the Box: Content Abundance, Attention Scarcity, and the Failures of Digital Markets' (2004) **19** *Berkeley Technology Law Journal* 1389–1472.

Graber, Christoph Beat, *Handel und Kultur im Audiovisionsrecht der WTO* (Bern: Staempfli, 2003).

Graber, Christoph Beat, 'Audiovisual Media and the Law of the WTO', in C. B. Graber, M. Girsberger and M. Nenova (eds.), *Free Trade versus Cultural Diversity: WTO Negotiations in the Field of Audiovisual Services* (Zurich: Schulthess, 2004), pp. 47–56.

Graber, Christoph Beat, 'Audio-visual Policy: The Stumbling Block of Trade Liberalisation', in D. Geradin and D. Luff (eds.), *The WTO and Global Convergence in Telecommunications and Audiovisual Services* (Cambridge University Press, 2004), pp. 165–214.

Graber, Christoph Beat, 'Copyright and Access – a Human Rights Perspective', in C. B. Graber *et al.* (eds.), *Digital Rights Management: The End of Collecting Societies?* (Bern: Staempfli, 2005), pp. 71–110.

Graber, Christoph Beat, 'The New UNESCO Convention on Cultural Diversity: A Counterbalance to the WTO?' (2006) **9** *Journal of International Economic Law* 553–574.

Graber, Christoph Beat, 'Using Human Rights to Tackle Fragmentation in the Field of Traditional Cultural Expressions: An Institutional Approach', in C. B. Graber and M. Burri-Nenova (eds.), *Intellectual Property and Traditional Cultural Expressions in a Digital Environment* (Cheltenham: Edward Elgar, 2008), pp. 96–120.

Graber, Christoph Beat, 'Substantive Rights and Obligations under the UNESCO Convention on Cultural Diversity', in H. Schneider and P. van den Bossche (eds.), *Protection of Cultural Diversity from an International and European Perspective* (Mortsel: Intersentia, 2008), pp. 141–162.

Graber, Christoph Beat, 'State Aid for Digital Games and Cultural Diversity: A Critical Reflection in the Light of EU and WTO Law', in C. B. Graber and M. Burri-Nenova (eds.), *Governance of Digital Game Environments and Cultural Diversity* (Cheltenham: Edward Elgar, 2010), pp. 170–201.

Grimmelmann, James, 'The Structure of Search Engine Law' (2007) New York Law School Research Paper Series 23.

Hahn, Michael, 'A Clash of Cultures? The UNESCO Diversity Convention and International Trade Law' (2006) **9** *Journal of International Economic Law* 515–552.

Hoekman, Bernard, 'Toward a More Balanced and Comprehensive Services Agreement' in J. J. Schott (ed.), *The WTO after Seattle* (New York: Institute for International Economics, 2000), pp. 119–135.

Hoekman, Bernard, 'More Favorable Treatment of Developing Countries: Ways Forward', in R. Newfarmer (ed.), *Trade, Doha, and Development: Window into the Issues* (Washington, DC: World Bank, 2006), pp. 213–221.

Janow, Merit E., 'Trade and Competition Policy', in P. F. J. Macrory, A. E. Appleton and M. G. Plummer (eds.), *The World Trade Organization: Legal, Economic and Political Analysis*, vol. 3 (Berlin: Springer, 2005), pp. 487–510.

Keen, Andrew, *The Cult of the Amateur: How Today's Internet Is Killing Our Culture* (New York: Doubleday, 2007).

Ku, Raymond S. R., 'Promoting Diverse Cultural Expression: Lessons from the US Copyright Wars' (2007) **2** *Asian Journal of WTO and International Health Law and Policy* 369–398.

Kurtz, Leslie A., 'Copyright and the Human Condition' (2007) **40** *UC Davis Law Review* 1233–1252.

Landes, William M. and Posner, Richard A., *The Economic Structure of Intellectual Property Law* (Cambridge, MA: Belknap Press of Harvard University, 2003), pp. 11–123.

Larouche, Pierre, 'Dealing with Convergence at the International Level', in D. Geradin and D. Luff (eds.), *The WTO and Global Convergence in Telecommunications and Audiovisual Services* (Cambridge University Press, 2004), pp. 390–422.

Lessig, Lawrence, *Free Culture* (New York: Penguin, 2004).

Lessig, Lawrence, '(Re)creativity: How Creativity Lives', in H. Porsdam (ed.), *Copyright and Other Fairy Tales: Hans Christian Andersen and the Commodification of Creativity* (Cheltenham: Edward Elgar, 2006), pp. 15–22.

Lucchi, Nicola, 'Countering the Unfair Play of DRM Technologies' (2007) **16** *Texas Intellectual Property Law Journal* 91–124.

Macmillan, Fiona, 'Human Rights, Cultural Property and Intellectual Property: Three Concepts in Search of a Relationship', in C. B. Graber and M. Burri-Nenova (eds.), *Intellectual Property and Traditional Cultural Expressions in a Digital Environment* (Cheltenham: Edward Elgar, 2008), pp. 73–95.

Marsden Chris *et al.*, *Assessing Indirect Impacts of the EC Proposals for Video Regulation* (RAND Europe, 2006).

Marsden, Philip, *A Competition Policy for the WTO* (London: Cameron May, 2003).

McGonagle, Tarlach, 'The Promotion of Cultural Diversity via New Media Technologies: An Introduction to the Challenges of Operationalisation' (2008) **6** *IRIS: Legal Observations of the European Audiovisual Observatory* 7.

Naughton, John, 'Our Changing Media Ecosystem', in E. Richards *et al.* (eds.), *Communications: The Next Decade* (London: Ofcom, 2006), pp. 41–50.

Netanel, Neil W., 'Market Hierarchy and Copyright in Our System of Free Expression' (2000) **53** *Vanderbilt Law Review* 1879–1932.

Netanel, Neil W., 'Why Has Copyright Expanded? Analysis and Critique', in F. Macmillan (ed.), *New Directions in Copyright Law*, vol. 6 (Cheltenham: Edward Elgar, 2007), pp. 3–34.

Netanel, Neil W., 'The WIPO Development Agenda and Its Development Policy Context', in N. W. Netanel (ed.), *The Development Agenda: Global Intellectual Property and Developing Countries* (Oxford University Press, 2009), pp. 1–32.

Nwauche, E. S., 'African Countries' Access to Knowledge and the WIPO Digital Treaties' (2005) **8** *The Journal of World Intellectual Property* 361–382.

OECD, Participative Web: User-Created Content, DSTI/ICCP/IE(2006)7/FINAL, 12 April 2007.

O'Regan, Tom and Goldsmith, Ben, 'Emerging Global Ecologies of Production', in D. Harries (ed.), *The New Media Book* (London: British Film Institute Publishing, 2004), pp. 92–105.

Palfrey, John G., Jr. and Rogoyski, Robert, 'The Move to the Middle: The Enduring Threat of "Harmful" Speech to the End-to-End Principle' (2006) **21** *Washington University Journal of Law and Policy* 31–66.

Peng, Shin-yi, 'Trade in Telecommunications Services: Doha and Beyond' (2007) **41** *Journal of World Trade* 293–317.

Poretti, Pietro, 'Waiting for Godot: Subsidy Disciplines in Services Trade', in M. Panizzon, N. Pohl and P. Sauvé (eds.), *GATS and the Regulation of International Trade in Services* (Cambridge University Press, 2008), pp. 466–488.

Reichman, Jerome H. and Lewis, Tracy, 'Using Liability Rules to Stimulate Local Innovation in Developing Countries: Application to Traditional Knowledge', in K. E. Maskus and J. H. Reichman (eds.), *International Public Goods and Transfer of Technology under a Globalized Property Regime* (Cambridge University Press, 2005), pp. 337–366.

Rosen, Jeffrey, 'Google's Gatekeepers', *New York Times*, 30 November 2008.

Roy, Martin, 'Audiovisual Services in the Doha Round: Dialogue de Sourds, The Sequel?' (2005) **6** *Journal of World Investment and Trade* 923–952.

Ruiz Fabri, Hélène, 'Reflections on Possible Future Legal Implications of the Convention', in N. Obuljen and J. Smiers (eds.), *UNESCO's Convention on the Protection and Promotion of the Diversity of Cultural Expressions: Making It Work* (Zagreb: Institute for International Relations, 2006), pp. 73–87.

Sauvé, Pierre and Steinfatt, Karsten, 'Towards Multilateral Rules on Trade and Culture: Protective Regulation or Efficient Protection?', in Productivity Commission and Australian National University, *Achieving Better Regulation of Services* (Canberra: AusInfo, 2000), pp. 323–346.

Sauvé, Pierre, 'Completing the GATS Framework: Addressing Uruguay Round Leftovers' (2002) **3** *Aussenwirtschaft* 301–341.

Sauvé, Pierre, 'Been There, Not Yet Done That: Lessons and Challenges in Services Trade', in M. Panizzon, N. Pohl and P. Sauvé (eds.), *GATS and the Regulation of International Trade in Services* (Cambridge University Press, 2008), pp. 599–631.

Singh, J. P., 'Culture or Commerce? A Comparative Assessment of International Interactions and Developing Countries at UNESCO, WTO, and Beyond' (2007) **8** *International Studies Perspectives* 36–53.

Sklar, Robert, *Film: An International History of the Medium* (Upper Saddle River, NJ: Prentice Hall, 1993).

Steiner, Thomas, 'Online Games under WTO Law: Unresolved Classification Issues' (2009) NCCR Trade Regulation Working Paper 2009/3.

Vaidhyanathan, Siva, 'The Googlization of Everything and the Future of Copyright' (2007) **40** *UC Davis Law Review* 1207–1231.

Vaidhyanathan, Siva, *Copyrights and Copywrongs: The Rise of Intellectual Property and How It Threatens Creativity* (New York University Press, 2003).

Weinberger, David, *Everything Is Miscellaneous* (New York: Henry Holt, 2007).

Wendland, Wend B., '"It's a Small World (after all)": Some Reflections on Intellectual Property and Traditional Cultural Expressions', in C. B. Graber and M. Burri-Nenova (eds.), *Intellectual Property and Traditional Cultural Expressions in a Digital Environment* (Cheltenham: Edward Elgar, 2008), pp. 150–181.

Wu, Tim, 'Network Neutrality, Broadband Discrimination' (2003) **2** *Journal on Telecommunications and High Technology Law* 141–174.

Wunsch-Vincent, Sacha, *The WTO, the Internet and Trade in Digital Products* (Oxford: Hart, 2006).

Yu, Dayong, 'The Harmonised System: Amendments and Their Impact on WTO Members' Schedules' (2008) WTO Economic Research and Statistics Division Staff Working Paper No. 2.

10

Development and stability in the nexus between trade and finance

ERNST BALTENSPERGER AND NILS HERGER*

KEY MESSAGES

- The international regulation of asset trade differs substantially from that of trade in goods and services. In particular, since the breakdown of the Bretton Woods system, multiple authorities including the International Monetary Fund (IMF), the World Bank, the Bank for International Settlements (BIS), and the Organisation for Economic Co-operation and Development (OECD) have retained partly overlapping responsibilities for regulating asset trade.
- There are enormous differences between countries in their level of financial development which, by and large, coincide with the differences in economic development. Financial underdevelopment appears to be primarily the result of an incomplete protection of property rights, which manifests itself in aggravated risks for financiers of being expropriated by the political elite or a corrupt bureaucracy.
- Financial crises are recurrent and have, at least temporarily, affected most countries during recent decades. Owing to financial globalisation, distress within the financial system tends to be transmitted more rapidly across national borders.
- A coherent system of international financial regulation ought to create favourable results in terms of fostering the development and improving the stability of the financial system. Such a framework is most likely to find support from the relevant stakeholders.
- Owing to the aggravated level of uncertainty in financial transactions, coherence in international financial regulation necessitates a framework that is at the same time open to regulatory competition and based on commonly shared experiences, and which stipulates some mutually recognised minimum standards. Amid the complexities underlying the international exchange in assets, such an approach is the most suitable to identify and embody the rules that foster the development and stability of the financial system.

* Individual Project No. 10, 'Finance and Trade'. We would like to thank Roland Hodler for valuable comments.

A. Introduction and motivation

Aside from the most rudimentary barter economies, goods are typically not directly traded against each other, but rather paid for with financial instruments such as money or credit, which in turn generate a widely recognised claim for imminent or future purchases of goods (or services) of equivalent value from a wide array of possible trade partners. Owing to additional frictions and risks that arise when trading goods over long distances and in different currencies, the internationalisation of trade and finance share a particularly close historical interrelationship. Indeed, without access to financial markets or the services of the banking and insurance industry, firms would barely be able to undertake cross-border exchanges at manageable cost. Thereby, trade credit and trade insurance provide the most prominent example of a financial instrument enabling exporters to fund the delays between producing, transporting and delivering goods, and collecting the corresponding payments. It is therefore not surprising that in Europe the usage of trade credit dates back to early forms of international exchange at medieval fairs.[1] Meanwhile, the evolution of the financial system itself provides an impetus for international trade. The financial sector played a crucial role in the development of early trade centres such as Florence, Venice, Antwerp, Amsterdam, and London. Another example for the trade and finance nexus can be found in the establishment of financial intermediaries by the merchant industry in seventeenth-century England.[2]

Subsequently, the international financial system evolved far beyond the mere funding of trade. In particular, mutual exchanges of assets that are unrelated to the cross-border exchange of goods and other services today account for the majority of international financial transactions. The origins of financial institutions that are not related to trade can be traced back to banks that, rather than emerging from the trade of merchants, did so from that of goldsmiths and started to issue receipts on deposited gold that rapidly began to serve as a broadly accepted and convenient medium of exchange and, thus, almost accidentally, introduced a financial

1 See M. Obstfeld and A. M. Taylor, *Global Capital Markets: Integration, Crisis, and Growth* (Cambridge University Press, 2004), pp.17ff. For an overview of the trade implications of state-guarantees issued by many countries on such export credits, see E. Baltensperger and N. Herger, 'Exporting against Risk? Theory and Evidence from Public Export Insurance Schemes in OECD Countries' (2009) 20 *Open Economies Review* 545–563.

2 For an overview see C. H. Kindleberger, *A Financial History of Western Europe* (London: George Allen and Unwin, 1984).

service unrelated to trade. Even compared with the recent growth in international goods trade, the international financial system has witnessed a dramatic expansion that has given rise to a set of closely interrelated markets on which banks, multinational enterprises, and public agencies trade massive amounts of assets such as bonds, shares, or currencies. The reasons for this marked development lie primarily in the dismantling of public controls and regulations formerly impeding the free movement of capital across borders. Furthermore, by broadening the information about foreign markets and cutting the cost and time required to undertake international capital transactions to insignificant levels, innovations in information technology have greatly contributed to this surge. Such is the importance of international financial transactions that in Switzerland, for example, the value of cross-border trade in assets is about three times the corresponding value of trade in goods and services.

The development of international finance has never been smooth, but has witnessed marked cycles of booms and crashes. Most notably, an age of economic and financial integration came to an abrupt end with the Great Depression, during which tariff barriers were raised and the international movement of capital was met with increasing political scepticism. Among other things, this probably contributed to a separate development of international trade and finance regulation after the Second World War despite their historical interdependencies. In particular, while the General Agreement on Tariffs and Trade (GATT) and, more recently, the World Trade Organization (WTO) have been set up to foster the unimpeded international exchange in goods and services, stringent barriers to international capital movement were erected under the so-called Bretton Woods system, which devised the International Monetary Fund (IMF) and the World Bank as principal international organisations. Their primary task was to prevent the exploitation of international differences in financial returns. Owing to the detachment from funding trade in goods and services, such arbitrage involving short-term flows of financial assets was deemed destabilising and speculative, since it could deplete countries of the foreign reserves that were necessary to maintain fixed exchange rates. However, in our opinion, postulating a fundamental difference between the welfare gains of free trade in goods or services and assets does not withstand a careful analysis. There is indeed a good theoretical case that the liberalisation of asset trade creates benefits similar to those being used by advocates of free trade to justify the dismantling of artificial trade barriers such as tariffs. In particular, removing, for example, capital controls permits the investment of funds in those countries that promise the highest expected rates of return and diversification of risks across a larger number of international markets. Further benefits arise insofar as an internationally integrated financial system fosters competition between domestic and foreign financial intermediaries forcing them to enhance their services and develop innovative products, which, in turn, might facilitate cross-border transactions. Finally, rather than contributing to international financial stability, rigid controls on trade in international assets provided an important ingredient of the speculative attacks that eventually brought down the Bretton Woods system, when central banks were no longer able, or willing, to use their reserve to offset the diverging returns between the leading international currencies at the beginning of the 1970s. Since then, many of the restrictions formerly impeding international capital transactions have been lifted and exchange rates are primarily determined on the international currency market rather than according to multilateral agreements.[3] Inevitably, the liberalisation of the international financial market has transformed the role of the IMF and the World Bank, which today have fewer possibilities for intervening in the international financial system and, furthermore, share this responsibility with other authorities such as central banks, the Bank for International Settlements and the Organisation for Economic Co-operation and Development (OECD). Furthermore, the recent global financial crisis provides a further impetus for this transformation.

Against the cumbersome overlaps and differences between trade and finance, the present chapter endeavours to discuss some implications as regards international regulation and, following the enveloping theme of the present book, seeks to uncover potential measures which could achieve more policy coherence. As discussed in more detail in section D, we adopt a rather pragmatic approach to the notion of 'coherence', which is here understood as a policy framework that produces favourable results and is thus supported by major stakeholders. Within the current context, the quality of a regulatory regime manifests itself primarily in

3 However, fixed exchange rates have not disappeared as a large number of developing countries and emerging markets continue to peg their national currency against a leading currency such as the US dollar. The monetary integration of some European countries even goes a step further, culminating in the adoption of the euro as a common currency. Arguably, a common currency tends to expand trade (see Andrew Rose, 'One Money, One Market: Estimating the Effect of Common Currencies on Trade' (2000) 30 *Economic Policy* 7–46), though the magnitude of this effect remains controversial (see Torsten Persson, 'Currency Unions and Trade: How Large is the Treatment Effect?' (2001) 31 *Economic Policy* 434–448).

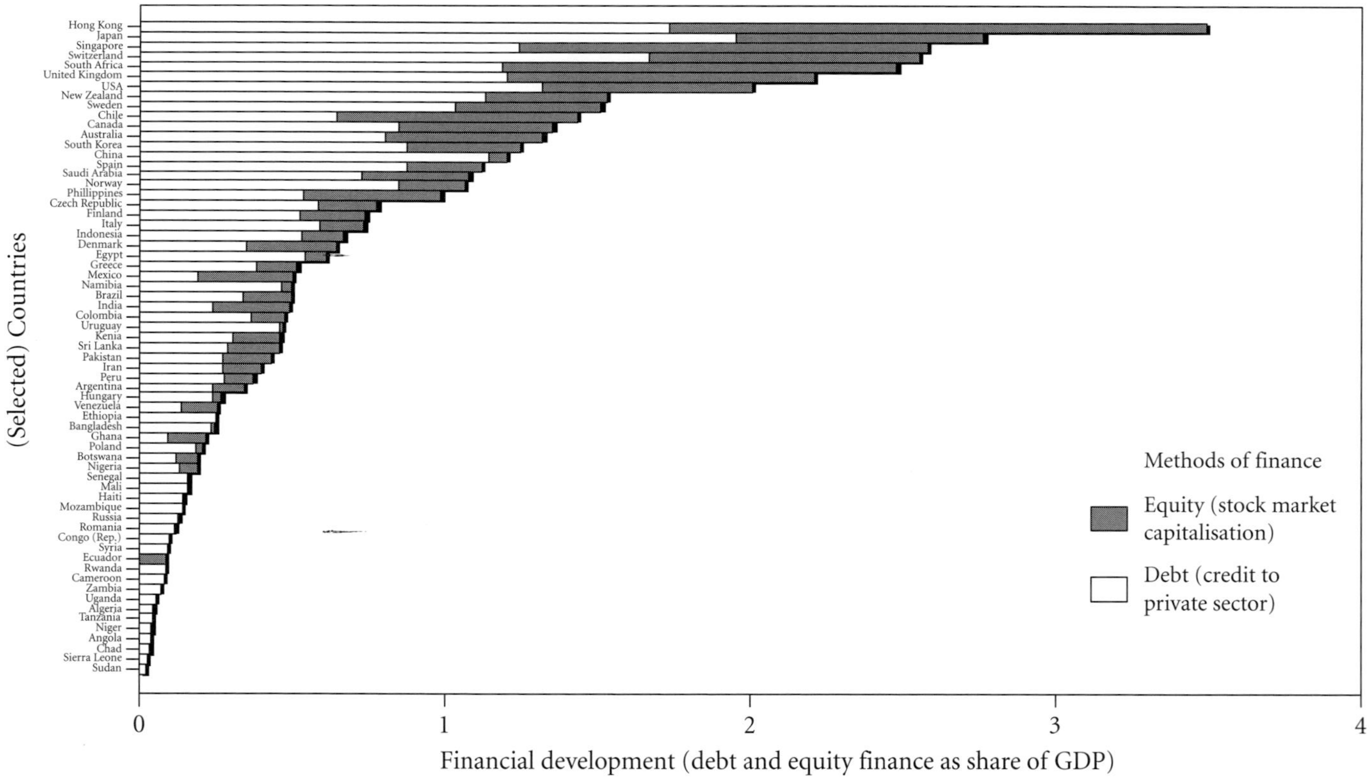

Figure 10.1 Financial development across countries

its capacity to foster financial development and proliferate stability in the sense of abating excessive swings and avoiding panics and crises (or at least reducing the fallout from them). To prepare the field, sections B and C will therefore compare the current conditions in financial development and stability around the world. Section E discusses some aspects of the current global financial crisis in greater detail; section F summarises and concludes.

B. Financial development

Despite the ongoing globalisation in the financial system, substantial differences in levels of financial development persist. For selected countries and the years between 1990 and 1999, Figure 10.1 illustrates these differences by comparing the average size of the financial systems relative to a country's gross domestic product (GDP). To disentangle the usage of equity and debt as method of finance, the gross figure has been broken down according to the total stock market capitalisation and the credit allocated by financial intermediaries such as banks to the private sector. It is noteworthy that while the financial system provides funds in excess of 200 per cent of the GDP in countries such as Hong Kong, Japan, Singapore, and Switzerland,[4] financially least developed countries such as Chad, Sierra Leone, and Sudan merely allocate a small fraction of their already modest GDP in the form of credit to the private sector. Furthermore, many of the countries at the bottom of Figure 10.1 lack institutions such as stock markets where entrepreneurs can sell an ownership stake of their companies to raise funds.

A ranking of countries according to their financial development coincides by and large with a corresponding ranking by economic development. Apparently, a financial system facilitating the mobilisation of savings and the channelling of funds to investors constitutes an important component for countries wishing to alleviate poverty. This ostensibly necessitates financial support to enable a plethora of private and public

4 The countries with the largest financial industries obviously benefit from their specialisation in the international provision of financial services. Furthermore, market size does not necessarily coincide with a financial system efficiently channelling funds from savers to investors. However, considering alternative measures of financial development such as net interest rate differences between deposits and credits, or relative turnover ratios on stock markets results in similar differences with broadly the same ranking of countries' financial development.

projects to enter new markets, develop new products, enhance the public infrastructure, and invest in education among others.[5]

Protectionism can arguably disrupt this interrelationship between financial and economic development. In particular, to foster economic growth, some countries have tried to create clusters of high technology industries by initially sheltering them from foreign competition, thinking that they would be able to enter the global market and generate large export revenues once they had learnt to compete effectively with foreign rivals. For several reasons, industrial policies erecting trade barriers for industries in their infancy have proved to be quite an unsuccessful development strategy. Firstly, governments have had a poor record in identifying national industries with great development potential. Secondly, particularly in countries with modest domestic markets, protectionism creates monopoly rents together with the associated hazards such as the retarding of innovation, and political lobbying for the retention of appropriated economic privileges.[6] Against this background, a financial system surrendering sufficient long-term funds to a large number of promising ventures probably offers a better way for countries wishing to bridge the time between building up new industries and reaping the corresponding benefits if firms start earning profits on the world market.[7] In addition to funding investments in new industries, the financial system serves further purposes such as the generation of information about possible investment or the identification and management of credit and liquidity risks. Owing to an aggravated level of frictions and risks, international trade relies even more on the support of a sound financial system easing the exchange of goods and services.

Although financial systems are crucial for economic development, financially underdeveloped countries apparently cannot directly replicate the economic, legal and political structure necessary to foster the raising of often desperately needed funds on the domestic or global capital market. Several explanations have been put forward as to why this does not happen:

5 See R. Levine, 'Finance and Growth: Theory and Evidence', in P. Agihion and S. Durlauf (eds.), *Handbook of Economic Growth* (Amsterdam: Elsevier, 2005).

6 For a textbook overview of trade policies and economic development see P. R. Krugman and M. Obstfeld, *International Economics: Theory and Policy* (New York: Addison-Wesley, 2006) ch. 10.

7 See R. Hodler, 'Specialization and Welfare in the Presence of Imperfectly Integrated Capital Markets and Learning-by-Doing' (2008) 19 *Open Economies Review* 391–402.

1. Financial transactions are embedded in a set of institutionalised rules and procedures.[8] In particular, financiers will typically be reluctant to surrender funds without the safeguards of entrenched property rights that mitigate the threat of preventable delays in payment, or of fraud or embezzlement. Thereby, the peril of expropriation might not only arise from the counterparties to a financial transaction, but also from a malevolent political elite dedicated to extracting rents from financiers, for example, by engaging in corruption or excessive red tape rather than providing public services to safeguard financial transactions. In sum, even in the face of highly profitable investment opportunities, the evolution of a financial system might be severely hampered in countries lacking sufficient economic and political institutions to safeguard the future return on current financial transactions.
2. For several reasons, countries that are open to international trade might have larger, and more efficient financial systems. As noted at the beginning of the chapter, cross-border trade involves longer delays between the delivery of and payment for goods and is exposed to additional commercial and political risk increasing the demand for financial services.[9] Furthermore, although financial development typically benefits most sectors of an economy, it might not necessarily contribute to the vested interests of an elite dedicated to retaining economic privileges and which is, thus, hostile to a financial system that funds economic innovations and change. However, internationally open markets inevitably expose inefficient industries to the market discipline of foreign rivals and thus undermine the incentives for domestic elites to retard financial development for their own benefit.[10]
3. Finally, cultural heritage might uphold values and beliefs that hinder financial development. The most prominent example of this are religions that have historically imposed numerous rules on moral conduct prohibiting, for example, the charging of interest on financial transactions.[11]

8 For a seminal contribution on the importance of institutional quality in economics, see D. North *Institutions, Institutional Change and Economic Performance* (Cambridge University Press, 1990).

9 See Q. T. Do, and A. A. Levchenko, 'Comparative Advantage, Demand for External Finance, and Financial Development' (2007) 86 *Journal of Financial Economics* 796–834.

10 See R. G. Rajan and Luigi Zingales, 'The Great Reversals: The Politics of Financial Development in the Twentieth Century' (2003) 69 *Journal of Financial Economics* 5–50.

11 See R. M. Stulz and R. Williamson, 'Culture, Openness, and Finance' (2003) 70 *Journal of Financial Economics* 313–349.

Confronting such theories with the global pattern of financial development as depicted in Figure 10.1 provides evidence that underdevelopment is caused by poor institutions, in particular when public misconduct and political instability undermine the proliferation of secure property rights.[12] There is also some support for the view that countries more open to trade tend to have a more efficient financial sector. Conversely, cultural differences, for example, in the form of religious beliefs appear not to be systematically related to the substantial differences in the capacity of financial systems to channel funds from savers to investors.

C. Financial stability

For the following reasons, the international financial system, within which the trade of assets occurs, exhibits a greater propensity towards instability than markets on which goods and other services are exchanged.[13] Firstly, the essence of any financial transaction lies in an inter-temporal exchange between a lender, who surrenders funds for a certain period of time, and a borrower, who promises to service his financial obligations in terms of paying interest and refunding the principal at a specified future date. As with any statement about future events, uncertainty is inherent in such promises and manifests itself most prominently in the risk of default. Secondly, the incentives to fully and honestly disclose relevant financial information inevitably differ between borrower and lender, which often inhibits the accurate establishment of the creditworthiness of a financial partner. Incomplete information about financial risks introduces an important friction and can foreclose a direct exchange of funds on financial markets.[14] Intermediaries such as banks can offset some imperfections on financial markets by specialising in the simultaneous holding of different assets that satisfy the short-term liquidity needs of depositors and the long-term capital needs of investors and drawing on their experience when it comes to monitoring credit risks.[15] The white section of the bar

12 For more details on this, see Nils Herger, Roland Hodler, and Michael Lobsiger, 'What Determines Financial Development? Culture Institutions or Trade, (2008) 144 *Review of World Economics* 558–587.

13 For a more detailed discussion of this see Frederic S. Mishkin, 'Global Financial Instability: Framework, Events, and Issues' (1999) 13 *Journal of Economic Perspectives* 3–20.

14 For a thorough theoretical discussion of incomplete information on financial markets see Joseph E. Stiglitz and A. Weiss 'Credit Rationing in Markets with Imperfect Information' (1981) 71, *The American Economic Review* 393–410.

15 For seminal contributions discussing the competitive advantages of banks over financial markets see D. W. Diamond, 'Financial Intermediation and Delegated Monitoring' (1984) 51 *The Review of Economic Studies* 393–414 and D.W. Diamond and P. H. Dybvig, 'Bank Runs, Deposit Insurance, and Liquidity' (1983) 91 *Journal of Political Economy* 401–419.

in Figure 10.1 shows that in virtually every country of the world, indirect methods of finance, which rest on the exchange of funds via debt instruments issued by banks, exceed the volume of direct methods of finance where an equity stake is sold on the stock market as represented by the grey section of the bar. However, to satisfy the needs of lenders and borrowers alike, banks must typically simultaneously hold short-term and highly liquid liabilities in the form of deposits against long-term and highly illiquid assets in the form of bank credits, and thereby cover only a part of their current liabilities with reserves. As long as lenders (or depositors) withdraw only a fraction of their liabilities during a certain period, this is unproblematic. However, any banking system operating with fractional reserves is intrinsically exposed to sudden losses in confidence that result in a correlated pattern of unexpectedly high withdrawals by nervous depositors and investors. A vicious cycle between high withdrawals of a bank's liquid liabilities, the resulting drying up of reserves, and a loss of confidence in a bank's ability to honour its future liabilities, can push essentially every financial intermediary into bankruptcy.

Against this background, the contemporary financial system typically enters into a state of crisis when increasing financial distress and imminent bankruptcies hit the banking industry, often accompanied by downturns on the stock market. Taking the example of the years 1990 to 1999, Figure 10.2 shows that episodes of systemic banking crises occurred in many countries, in particular, a substantial fraction of the developing world as well as emerging and transition economies. Ostensibly, financial underdevelopment and instability constitute a partly intertwined phenomenon. However, systematic banking crises have also occurred in the developed world, with Scandinavia and Japan providing prominent examples during the 1990s.

The ongoing internationalisation of financial markets has ambiguous implications for financial stability. On the one hand, international financial flows enable investors to diversify the associated risks across a larger number of countries and gain access to foreign funds in times of reduced confidence in the stability of the domestic financial sector. Within a globalised world, recent examples of severe financial crisis demonstrate that this international risk-sharing can benefit developed and developing countries alike. On the other hand, since investors typically possess more knowledge about local than about foreign market conditions, international capital transactions typically suffer from an aggravated degree of incomplete information about liquidity, credit or default risks that provide an important ingredient to instability. Furthermore, the regional or even global integration of the financial system implies that crises on

Data Source: Caprio and Klingebiel (1999)

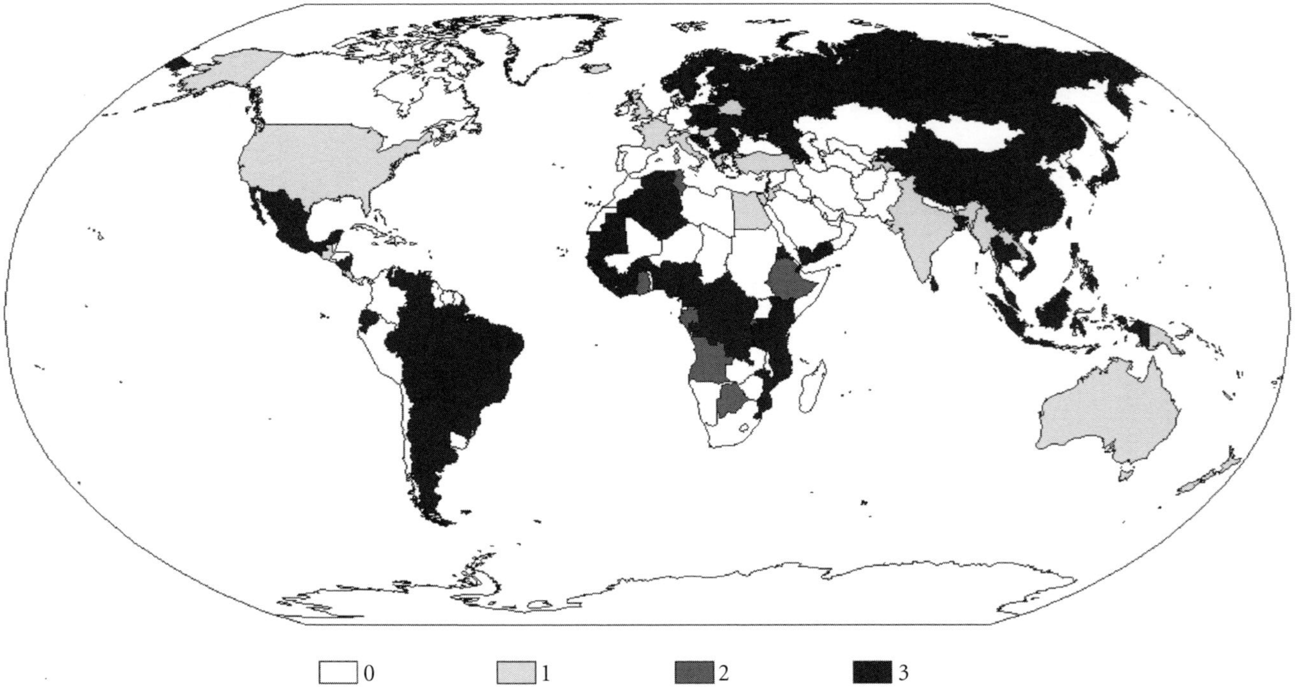

0 = no crisis; 1 = individual cases of bank failures; 2 = episodes of borderline and smaller banking crisis; 3 = episodes of systemic banking crisis

Figure 10.2 Banking crises during the 1990s

financial markets and in the banking system are increasingly tending to affect entire regions rather than individual countries. Figure 10.2 shows an apparent clustering of systematic banking crises in South America, South-East Asia and transition economies. More recently, the financial instability during the second half of 2007 in the US resulted in an almost global destabilisation of the financial sector.[16] In sum, although financial internationalisation offers important benefits when it comes to shifting funds to countries with the highest expected return or diversifying the corresponding investment risks across a larger number of markets, the drawback of such international integration lies in the peril of the rapid transmission of a financial crisis across national borders.

Systemic instabilities within the financial system entail substantial economic costs. For example, recent episodes of systemic banking crisis have typically absorbed around 10 to 20 per cent of a country's annual GDP.[17] In times of crisis, the financial system does not fully shape up to its functions such as providing short-term liquidity, facilitating long-term investments by means of issuing credit, or managing financial risks. Specifically, when it comes to financing cross-border trade, payment risks, which are typically higher in countries with a history of financial crisis, continue to act as important impediments to internationally open markets.[18] This result coincides with the casual observation that the export sector has been severely affected by episodes of financial instability occurring, for example, in South-East Asia in 1997 and 1998 as well as by the worldwide financial crises of 2008 and 2009, which resulted in the biggest global decline in world trade since the Second World War.

D. Coherence in the regulation of the international financial system

Based on the previous observations about financial development and stability, this section provides some thoughts about the coherence of the current rules guiding the international exchange of assets. Inevitably, the application of a broad theoretical concept such as regulatory coherence[19]

16 See section E for more on this.

17 Gerard Caprio, and Daniela Klingebiel 'Bank Insolvency: Bad Luck, Bad Policy, or Bad Banking?' (1996) Annual World Bank Conference on Development Economics.

18 See E. Baltensperger and N. Herger, 'Exporting against Risk? Theory and Evidence from Public Export Insurance Schemes in OECD Countries' (2009) 20 *Open Economies Review* 545–563.

19 The introductory chapter to this book provides a comprehensive discussion on the concept of coherence.

to the specific and actual conditions on, for example, the international financial market is prone to lead to relatively vague statements. Following the findings discussed above in sections B and C, we respond to this by adopting a rather pragmatic interpretation of the concept of coherence in the sense that we will judge the rules governing the international exchange of assets against the degree to which they appear to have fostered development and contributed to the stability and instability within the financial system. Hence, we deem a regulatory framework as coherent when it produces favourable results and is therefore accepted by a broad range of stakeholders.

A coherent policy framework need not necessarily be uniform across countries. Indeed, the breakdown of the Bretton Woods system, which provided a commonly shared framework operating with capital controls to maintain a system of fixed exchange rates, has undoubtedly given a significant impetus to the development of the global financial system. Specifically, the ensuing liberalisation of financial markets during the following decades has given rise to an unprecedented growth in the trade of assets. Today, the international financial system is still characterised by the lack of an overarching authority charged with overseeing the cross-border exchange of assets. Instead, several international organisations such as the IMF, the World Bank, the WTO, the BIS, the OECD and even informal coalitions of major central banks have taken responsibility for developing and stabilising the international financial system (see Box 10.1 for a brief summary of their respective roles). This multiplicity of regulators with several international authorities stands in sharp contrast to the regulatory framework of the international trade in goods, where the WTO has adopted by far the most prominent role.

A framework within which multiple domestic and international authorities retain partly overlapping responsibilities for fostering financial development and stability, offers several advantages. Firstly, the complexity of global market relations, which has been exacerbated by recent innovations in information technologies that have transformed the processing of financial transactions in particular, creates significant uncertainties about the effect of public interventions and changing rules. There are a number of widely cited examples where intervention in the international financial system has produced surprising and sometimes even counterproductive results.[20]

20 The development of the euromarkets to circumvent the capital controls imposed by financial regulators provides the most prominent example for this. Recall that the primary

BOX 10.1 INTERNATIONAL REGULATORS AND THEIR ROLE IN THE INTERNATIONAL FINANCIAL SYSTEM

The **Bank for International Settlements (BIS)** is an international organisation set up to foster monetary and financial cooperation and to serve as a bank for central banks. The BIS fulfils this mandate, e.g. by means of providing a forum for the discussion of policies and standards between central banks and the financial industry, acting as a counterparty for central banks in their financial transactions, or as trustee in international financial transactions. One of the most prominent activities is the setting of minimal regulatory standards in commercial banking by the Basel Committee on Banking Supervision.

The **Organisation for Economic Co-operation and Development (OECD)** brings together countries committed to the principles of democratic rule and the market economy. A primary task of the OECD is to conduct research on a broad range of economic subjects including financial topics such as the stability of financial markets, monetary policy, the role of exchange rates etc.

The **International Monetary Fund (IMF)** endeavours to foster global monetary cooperation and to secure financial stability. The primary policy instrument of the IMF is to provide loans and technical assistance to countries in financial crisis, which are therefore confronted with imminent international payments, problems that cannot otherwise be solved by accessing from other sources sufficient financing on affordable terms.

The **World Bank** was set up to provide funds at preferential interest rates to developing countries to finance a wide array of projects including investments in education, health, public administration, infrastructure, financial and private sector development, agriculture, and environmental and natural resource management.

The **World Trade Organization (WTO)** deals primarily with the facilitation of international trade in goods and services by reducing tariffs and non-tariff barriers. Thereby, the liberalisation of trade in financial services falls within the realm of the General Agreement on Trade and Services (GATS). The corresponding financial services annex recognises the peril of financial instability and gives governments substantial possibilities for prudential measures, such as those for the protection

motive for adopting rigid capital controls after the Second World War was to uphold the stability of the domestic and international financial system. However, during the 1960s, banks began to bypass such rules by accepting deposits and loans denominated in currencies other than that of the country in which the corresponding financial transactions took place (e.g. a bank located in London offers services denominated in US$). During the subsequent decades, these so-called euromarkets expanded rapidly, both geographically and in terms of currencies. Today the euromarkets are globally interrelated, cover even financial instruments such as bonds, are essentially open 24 hours per day and offer funds at virtually identical conditions worldwide. Instead of insulating domestic financial markets from foreign influences, the rigid capital controls of the 1950s and 1960s have ended up creating one of the most internationalised markets for financial instruments.

of investors, depositors and insurance policy holders, and to ensure the integrity and stability of the financial system. The annex also excludes from the agreement services provided when a government is exercising its authority over the financial system, for example central banks' services.

A world where regulatory authorities are not in a position to anticipate many of the consequences of their interventions calls, in our opinion, for a contestable regulatory system retaining some degree of openness to alternative and potentially competing measures. Within an international system where customers, firms and, in particular, assets have become highly mobile internationally, regulatory competition puts pressure on legislators and public authorities to abandon outdated, unnecessary, or inefficient rules. Secondly, regulators entrusted with public authority do not always serve the common good but inevitably also pursue their private, vested interests.[21] In practice, this might manifest itself in the adoption of initiatives and rules that enhance the popularity of a financial regulator but barely further the stability or efficiency of the financial system, or even in outright abuses of the delegated public power for private benefits, for example through fraud, corruption or nepotism. The decentralisation of public power across multiple regulatory authorities provides an obvious remedy against such misconduct. In sum, under the assumptions of incomplete information and the existence of vested interests, policy coherence is typically not achieved by means of centralised decision-making by a powerful authority, but more often than not the result of a historical process that remains open to trial and error and competitive pressure to remove dysfunctional regulation.[22] Incidentally, since the disintegration of the Bretton Woods Institutions during the 1970s, international financial regulation has broadly followed this approach, which has resulted in an increase of global financial integration that by far exceeded the corresponding developments in the international trade of goods.

The proposition of regulatory competition is often confronted with demands for a 'level playing field', or the anxiety that multiple authorities would try to undermine each other and sacrifice regulatory standards by entering a 'race to the bottom'. For the following reasons, we do not share these concerns: as shown in sections B and C, across countries,

21 For this view, see in particular G. Stigler, 'The Theory of Economic Regulation' (1971) 3 *Bell Journal of Economics and Management Science* 3–18.

22 Compare Friedrich August von Hayek, 'Der Wettbewerb als Entdeckungsverfahren', in F. A. von Hayek, *Freiburger Studien* (Tübingen, 1969), pp. 249–265.

considerable differences exist in the degree of financial underdevelopment and stability, which are closely interrelated with heterogeneous political and economic conditions. Levelling the playing field in terms of advocating a uniform set of rules that guide international financial transactions might not adequately reflect the different degree of development, historical experiences, or disparate political priorities that arise, for example, between developing and developed countries. Furthermore, insofar as public regulation ought to produce socially desirable results in terms of improving the ability of the financial system to mobilise savings and finance investment in a stable manner, it is not clear why adequate international or domestic rules would be sacrificed on the altar of international regulatory competition.

Caveats against a complete nationalisation of financial regulation lie rather in the rapid transmission of crisis within an internationally integrated financial system. Then, the stability of the financial sector depends not only on the quality of the domestic supervision but also on decisions taken in countries that are closely interrelated financially. The peril of transmitting a crisis calls for minimum standards of financial regulation in countries that are closely integrated in the international financial system. Such an agreement between major national authorities has been reached, for example, within the framework of the BIS, where some countries with internationally integrated banking sectors have formed the Basel Committee on Banking Supervision to develop common capital adequacy requirements to introduce more stability into the international banking system. Financial innovations and the cycles within the international financial system imply that such a process is never complete and must respond, in particular, to dramatic events such as major international financial crises.

E. The global financial crisis and possible areas of reform

A large number of financial crises occurred in previous decades (see Figure 10.2 for examples during the 1990s). However, with a geographical dispersion that is maybe not even matched by the Great Depression of the 1930s,[23] the recent global financial and economic crisis has exhibited an unprecedented degree of international contagion. Furthermore,

23 When making comparisons with the Great Depression, it should not be forgotten that the social implications of the economic and financial turbulence of the 1930s were more severe in Western countries, since e.g. social security schemes were far less advanced and the general level of economic welfare was much lower.

compared with the financial crises of the 1990s, the developed countries were more affected than emerging markets. The development of events of the recent global financial crisis can perhaps be summarised by the following stages: first, despite developing into a global issue, the crisis can initially be traced back to a relatively narrow segment of the US mortgage market where there was an aggravated risk of default. The bundling of sub-prime mortgages into tradable financial instruments exposed the banking system to correlated credit risks when US house prices started to decline nationwide during 2007, undermining the ability of an unexpectedly large number of homeowners to service their debt.[24] Although this 'sub-prime' crisis was originally associated with mortgages and mortgage-backed securities, in the second stage the patchy information on exposure to such financial instruments made banks reluctant to lend funds, in particular within the interbank market. Owing to the international integration of the financial system, as well as the global importance of the US financial system, this led to a rapid transmission of adverse developments in banking from the national to an international level. For some financial intermediaries, the combination of writing down bad debt and the worsening conditions for accessing liquid funds gave rise to the imminent risk of insolvency resulting in a wave of acquisitions, nationalisations, and eventually even bankruptcies[25] that further undermined the confidence in the international financial system. In particular, the failure of Lehman Brothers, a US investment bank, in September 2008, lifted the sub-prime crisis to a different level underscoring the so called too-big-to-fail issue insofar as this bankruptcy imperilled the functioning of the entire financial system. The end of 2008 and the beginning of 2009 were indeed characterised by a severe credit crunch. Insofar as the corresponding effects could be felt beyond the financial industry, this might be considered as a third stage of the crisis during which worldwide economic growth started to slow down and virtually every developed country found itself confronting the start of a recession. Even global trade, which has witnessed positive growth rates every year since 1982, was declining during 2009.[26]

24 Similar problems occured in other countries that were experiencing a housing boom including the United Kingdom, Ireland and Spain.

25 Some important examples for this are the takeovers of Bear Stearns and Merill Lynch, the public bailouts of the City Group, the Bank of America, Fannie Mae and Freddie Mac, Lloyds TSB, the Royal Bank of Scotland and AIG, the nationalisation of Northern Rock, and the failure of Lehman Brothers.

26 For a more detailed discussion of effects of financial crises and international trade, see Nils Herger, 'Trade Finance and Financial Crises' (2009), Paper presented at the

Governments acted, partly in a coordinated manner, with several monetary and fiscal interventions to limit the consequences of this global financial and economic crisis. In particular, central banks increased their provision of liquid funds to avoid the collapse of the entire banking and payment system. Furthermore, in several countries, so-called bad banks have been created. These are publicly owned schemes towards which financial intermediaries can transfer non-performing assets (such as mortgage-backed securities) from their balance sheets as a measure to restore the confidence in the financial system. Finally, to alleviate the effects of recessions, monetary measures have been complemented with fiscal policy in terms of increases of government spending to counter the decline in macroeconomic demand. To support international trade, these stimulus packages included the provision of additional funds to support trade credit and export insurance policies.[27] In particular in developed countries, the adoption of these measures was associated with increases in public debt resulting in some cases in a fiscal crisis. Public debt reduction is likely to provide one of the most important future economic challenges resulting from the global financial crisis.

The use of such expansionary monetary and fiscal policies amid the worsening global crisis reflects the experiences of the Great Depression, during which the lack of such measures was blamed for the virtual collapse of the international financial and economic exchange.[28] Nevertheless, as with any crisis, the adverse economic events worldwide will almost certainly transform the regulatory framework for international trade and finance. The debate about regulatory reform has begun and is increasing in intensity. Though we are still far from identifying past regulatory failures and, thus, from reaching a consensus on the necessary changes, as far as international trade and finance regulation is concerned, discussions are likely to deal with interrelated issues concerning the role of internationally operating banks and the peril of protectionism:[29]

NCCR Workshop on 'Financial Services Regulation: Challenges and New Directions', Bern, Switzerland.

27 *Ibid.*

28 For a classical discussion see M. Friedman and A. Schwarz, *A Monetary History of the United States, 1867–1960* (Princeton University Press, 1963). A more recent discussion can be found in A. H. Melzer, *A History of the Federal Reserve, Volume 1: 1913–1951* (University of Chicago Press, 2002).

29 The global financial crisis involves areas of rather domestic regulatory reform. Examples include the design of effective systems of deposit insurance, the arrangement of management compensation (bonus payments) and enhancing consumer protection by supervising financial products.

- In globally integrated financial systems, big and internationally operating banks constitute probably the most important channel through which financial crises are transmitted across borders. This gives rise to several areas of regulatory challenge including:
  - The review of the role of regulation of international bank capital and, in particular, the appropriate design of risk weighting, the removal/containment of pro-cyclical effects, and finding ways to account for systemic risk.
  - How to discipline financial institutions that are too-big-to-fail. Note that a substantial fraction of systemically relevant banks and insurance companies operate in several countries.
  - Appropriate international cooperation when it comes to supervising banks that operate internationally.
  - Designing mechanisms to allow orderly liquidation of big international banks.
- Historically, economic and financial crises have tended to increase the appeal of protectionism, which in turn can aggravate a crisis.[30] Since multilateral and bilateral trade agreements limit the scope of increasing tariffs, protectionism today tends to arise primarily in the form of non-tariff barriers. The global financial crisis has probably increased such risks by opening opportunities to:
  - abuse financial regulation by providing liquidity supports or granting public bailouts to domestic, but not foreign financial institutions. Furthermore, nationalised financial institutions could serve political purposes by being urged to provide credit to domestic companies under distortionary conditions.
  - adopt fiscal stimulus measures that could likewise give rise to competitive distortion when restricting the support to national companies or attaching conditions, for example, the need to produce or buy locally.
  - increase public expenditure to combat economic recessions. The resulting public deficits and debt is likely to call for future tax increases. As regards international tax regulation, this has created tensions between high and low tax (in particular so-called tax haven) countries. Part of this effort is dedicated to limiting tax evasion and fraud. However, a harmonisation of international standards could also be a device used by high-tax countries to reduce international fiscal competition.

30 See M. K. Fingerrand and L. Schuknecht (1999), 'Trade, Finance and Financial crises', *WTO Special Studies* 3 (Geneva: World Trade Organization).

There is widespread agreement today that the existing system of international regulation of financial markets is in need of considerable revision. However, in spite of initial calls for an immediate and fundamental overhaul, few concrete international measures have so far been agreed on, let alone implemented. Rather, most of the salient issues, e.g. as regards capital adequacy requirements, the redesign of international institutions and cooperation between financial regulators, or the way in which non-bank financial institutions such as hedge funds can coherently be dealt with, remain at the stage of initial review and discussion. Concrete international decisions are as yet restricted to minor issues. These developments lend some support to the view proposed in section D, in that uncertainties about the effectiveness and effects of interventions in international finance result in a slowly progressing debate and to experimenting with specific measures using a process of trial and error and, hence, a discretionary rather than a fundamental reform of international financial regulation. We believe that the success of this process depends crucially on whether policy-makers are sufficiently aware of the uncertainties in balancing the beneficial and harmful effects of public interventions in the international financial system. Otherwise, intervention risks impeding financial and economic development and thereby going against the interest of relevant stakeholders. Furthermore, it is crucial that the discussions focus on what is, in our view, the core issue of how to mitigate the cross-border contagion of a crisis within an internationally integrated financial system.

F. Summary and conclusion

This chapter has endeavoured to discuss some of the regulatory implications of the international integration of the financial system. Compared with the international regulation of the trade in goods, which falls primarily within the realm of the WTO, multiple authorities such as the IMF, the World Bank and the BIS have retained important and partly overlapping responsibilities when it comes to supervising the international trade in assets. Concerns about a harmful 'race to the bottom' are often raised in discussions of this framework. However, in our view, the quality of a regulatory regime manifests itself primarily in its capacity to produce favourable results, which include in particular the facilitation of the access to financial services and the maintenance of a minimum level of stability when it comes to assessing financial regulation. Against this benchmark, there is no evidence that the existence of multiple regulatory authorities has retarded the level of financial development. Quite the opposite, because since the relatively uniform system of Bretton Woods disintegrated at the beginning of the 1970s the growth in international asset trade has outperformed the corresponding growth in international trade by far.

Financial transactions provide a means for inter-temporal trade between a borrower receiving funds today against the promise of future returns in terms of interest, dividends and repayments of the principal. This inevitably gives rise to the risk of default when unexpected events adversely affect the creditworthiness of a borrower. Owing to the frictions that arise when financiers or financial intermediaries such as banks possess only limited information about the future behaviour of their borrowers, or the political and economic conditions in general, financial markets exhibit an intrinsic tendency towards fragility. Indeed, crises and crashes are almost as old as the financial system and are known to have occurred well before the recent growth in cross-border financial transactions took off. The internationalisation of the financial system has, however, aggravated the risk that a financial crisis will transmit rapidly across countries. The recent global financial crisis suggests that, aside from furthering financial development, mitigating the effects of so-called contagion poses the biggest challenge to international financial regulation.

Incomplete information that has resulted in recurrent misjudgements by professional investors and banks likewise affects international regulators trying to foresee the sources of instability in the international financial system. With a large number of unexpected political and economic events occurring in the world every day, it would be naive to assume that an omniscient regulator could be created to forestall most financial crises, and protect citizens from the resulting damage. The relevance of uncertainty has important implications when it comes to bringing about the favourable results that are expected from coherent regulation of the international financial system. Above all, in our view, a certain degree of contestability is warranted to allow domestic and international regulators to pursue partly different approaches to remedy, for example, an erupting financial crisis. We think that the benefits of such openness are twofold: first, an open system permits financial regulators and other stakeholders to gain experience with the costs and benefits of several alternative approaches when dealing with the risk and fallout of a financial crisis. This opens up the possibility of confronting the uncertainty of the effects of specific measures by means of engaging in a process of trial and error. Secondly, within a globalised financial system, competition between financial markets generates pressure to abandon inefficient and unnecessary measures. Conversely, even though the creation of an overarching authority for international financial regulation would probably contribute to 'levelling the playing field', the corresponding centralisation is likely to suffer from overly rigid reactions to changing financial conditions – an important caveat when considering the impact of market change and financial innovation during recent decades. Finally, let us not forget that the countries of this earth constitute the 'playing field' of the international financial system. In our experience (bearing in mind that both authors of this chapter live in mountainous Switzerland) in many areas of this planet the 'playing field' just happens not to be flat. With considerable confidence, we also believe that this situation will prevail for the foreseeable future.

Bibliography

Baltensperger, Ernst, and Nils Herger, 'Exporting against Risk? Theory and Evidence from Public Export Insurance Schemes in OECD Countries' (2009) 20 *Open Economies Review* 545–563.

Caprio, Gerard and Daniela Klingebiel, 'Bank Insolvency: Bad Luck, Bad Policy, or Bad Banking?' (1996) Annual World Bank Conference on Development Economics.

Caprio, Gerard and Daniela Klingebiel, *Episodes of Systemic and Borderline Financial Crisis* (Washington, DC: World Bank, 1999).

Diamond, D. W., 'Financial Intermediation and Delegated Monitoring' (1984) **51** *The Review of Economic Studies* 393–414.

Diamond, D. W., and P. H. Dybvig, 'Bank Runs, Deposit Insurance, and Liquidity' (1983) **91** *Journal of Political Economy* 401–419.

Do, Q. T., and A. A. Levchenko, 'Comparative Advantage, Demand for External Finance, and Financial Development' (2007) **86** *Journal of Financial Economics* 796–834.

Fingerrand, M. K. and L. Schuknecht, 'Trade, Finance and Financial Crises', *WTO Special Studies* 3 (Geneva: World Trade Organization, 1999).

Friedman, M., and A. Schwarz, *A Monetary History of the United States, 1867–1960* (Princeton University Press, 1963).

Hayek, Friedrich August von, 'Der Wettbewerb als Entdeckungsverfahren', in F. A. von Hayek, *Freiburger Studien* (Tübingen, 1969), pp. 249–265.

Herger, Nils, 'Trade Finance and Financial Crises' (2009), Paper presented at the NCCR Workshop on 'Financial Services Regulation: Challenges and New Directions', Bern, Switzerland.

Herger, Nils, Roland Hodler, and Michael Lobsiger, 'What Determines Financial Development? Culture Institutions or Trade (2008) **144** *Review of World Economics* 558–587.

Hodler, Roland, 'Specialization and Welfare in the Presence of Imperfectly Integrated Capital Markets and Learning-by-Doing' (2008) **19** *Open Economies Review* 391–402.

Kindleberger, Charles P., *A Financial History of Western Europe* (London: George Allen and Unwin, 1984).

Krugman, P., and M. Obstfeld, *International Economics: Theory and Policy*, 7th edn (New York: Addison Wesley, 2006.).

Mishkin, Frederic S., 'Global Financial Instability: Framework, Events, and Issues' (1999) **13** *Journal of Economic Perspectives* 3–20.

Melzer, A. H., *A History of the Federal Reserve, Volume 1: 1913–1951* (University of Chicago Press, 2002).

North, Douglass, Institutions, Institutional Change and Economic Performance (Cambridge University Press, 1990).

Levine, R., 'Finance and Growth: Theory and Evidence', in P. Agihion and S. Durlauf (eds.) *Handbook of Economic Growth* (Amsterdam: Elsevier, 2005).

Persson, Torsten, 'Currency Unions and Trade: How Large is the Treatment Effect?' (2001) **31** *Economic Policy* 434–448.

Obstfeld, Maurice and A. M. Taylor, *Global Capital Markets: Integration, Crisis, and Growth* (Cambridge University Press, 2004).

Rajan, R. G., and Luigi Zingales, 'The Great Reversals: The Politics of Financial Development in the Twentieth Century' (2003) **69** *Journal of Financial Economics* 5–50.

Rose, Andrew, 'One Money, One Market: Estimating the Effect of Common Currencies on Trade' (2000) **30** *Economic Policy* 7–46.

Stigler, George, 'The Theory of Economic Regulation' (1971) **3** *Bell Journal of Economics and Management Science* 3–18.

Stiglitz, Joseph E., and A. Weiss, 'Credit Rationing in Markets with Imperfect Information' (1981) **71** *The American Economic Review* 393–410.

Stulz, R. M., and R. Williamson, 'Culture, Openness, and Finance' (2003) **70** *Journal of Financial Economics* 313–349.

11

The regulatory framework of international investment: the challenge of fragmentation in a changing world economy

BERTRAM BOIE, JULIEN CHAISSE AND PHILIPPE GUGLER*

KEY MESSAGES

- International investment regulation is fragmented since this field is multilayered and multifaceted, made in substance of obligations differing in geographical scope and coverage and constituting an intricate web of commitments that partly overlap and partly supplement one another. The increasing importance of foreign direct investment (FDI) makes the current legal situation unsatisfactory.
- Multilateral failures to negotiate an investment agreement may rather be considered an indication of the importance of multilateral regulations on investment and of the fact that governments have not yet identified an appropriate negotiating agenda.
- Several initiatives have been contemplated such as the Policy Framework for Investment (PFI) proposed by the Organisation for Economic Co-operation and Development (OECD). The PFI may contribute to a more coherent international policy framework on investment.
- Despite the ongoing globalisation process, FDI (still) seems to have a rather regional dimension instead of a truly global one. FDI flows and multinational enterprises' (MNEs) strategies are regional by nature.
- MNEs from emerging markets change the political economy game of negotiating International Investment Arrangements (IIAs) and are increasingly becoming key stakeholders. The presence of MNEs from developing countries, such as Chinese FDI, may also influence the expectations and the attitudes of the civil society towards IIAs.
- The rise of state-owned enterprises (SOEs) and of sovereign wealth funds (SWFs) from emerging countries, such as China, have effects on the political responses (protectionism on the rise), at the national level as well as at the international ones (control of protectionism).

* Individual Project No. 11, 'International Rules on Investment'.

- The fragmented, incomplete and complex system of Treaty rules enabling the European Community to take external action on foreign investment illustrates the need for establishing an explicit legal basis for foreign investment and provides the necessary background for scrutinising the controversial aspects of the new FDI competence.
- The Sino-European legal framework for investment regulation needs renewal on the grounds of new expectations and the recognition that greater coherence in law has positive effects for effectiveness and efficiency of the regulation.
- The European Union's supranational approach towards SWFs helps to advert national tendencies of protectionism.

Capital throughout the world has become increasingly mobile in recent decades and international trade has been exploding. Advances in information and communication technology and the accelerated pace of international distribution in recent years have promoted the growth of foreign investment, which divides the various processes of research and development (R&D), procurement, production, manufacturing and sales, among others, between a number of countries.[1] As a result, international investment regulation is one of the fastest-growing areas of international economic regulation. Corporate investment decisions depend to some extent on the legal framework governing international capital flows as well as on proactive policy measures to assist companies in their internationalisation process. In addition, IIAs offer to help regulate investment and thus constitute an important tool for national policy-makers. As a result, international investment regulation is an example *par excellence* for fragmentation in an important area of international economic law.

A multiplicity of instruments serves the purpose of investment protection and promotion, and illustrates a structural fragmentation. Treaties, bilateral, regional and plurilateral, have increasingly become the basic source of international investment law. At the same time, new cases are being lodged at an exponential rate not always resulting in converging interpretation of substantive provisions. This fragmentation in the substance of the norms is confirmed by the fact that even if the network of Bilateral Investment Treaties (BITs) is expanding it is still heavily one-sided. They are mainly agreements between developed and developing countries. This multifaceted fragmentation does not only depict a status quo. On the contrary, fragmentation has a dynamic character since it has grown over time with a continuously increasing number of treaties,

1 UNCTAD, *World Investment Report 2008* (New York and Geneva: United Nations, 2008).

actors and fora dealing with international investment issues. These several indicators underline the increase of fragmentation in international investment regulation.

When the research team brought together under the 'Individual Project 11 (Investment)' of the National Centre of Competence in Research (NCCR) – Trade Regulation took up its work in Autumn 2005, the blockage for forward movement on investment matters seemed to lie rather on the side of political will than disaccord over the agenda items to be discussed and negotiated in the field of investment. Investment had been included in the work of the World Trade Organization (WTO) in 1996 as one of the 'Singapore Issues', and the WTO's Working Group on Trade and Investment (WGTI) had since then carried out work on the topic. Yet, in the WTO's General Council July 2004 Decision, it was decided to exclude 'investment' from further negotiations within the Doha Development Round (DDR). With this, negotiations on investment were halted, and experts on investment regulation felt (once more) that the important topic was set aside for giving priority to other subject matters. Other international organisations such as United Nations Conference on Trade and Development (UNCTAD) and the Organisation for Economic Co-operation and Development (OECD) continued at the time their valuable, research-oriented work on investment with a focus on the fragmentation and growing numbers of bilateral agreements, known under the catchword 'spaghetti-bowl'. With the stop in negotiations at the WTO, investment received, however, overall less attention by researchers and trade diplomats, since the community felt that the topic would remain of lower importance until other topics under the DDR were successfully settled.

This appraisal proved right and wrong at the same time. It proved right in the sense that since then the world has seen little – if any – progress towards coherent international regulation for foreign investment in terms of finding the political will in favour of it or a forum for its negotiation. It proved wrong, however, with regard to the development of investment in terms of the substance of a future agreement. Indeed, during the last years, the landscape for international investment has undergone a number of significant developments that undoubtedly reshape the agenda for any future negotiations.

- Historically conceived as an instrument to be used by developed countries to protect their firms' investments against political risks, over the years the role of IIAs has undergone a significant mutation. With more and more emerging and developing countries finding themselves as both recipients and sources of foreign direct investment (FDI), these countries now have to consider not only the role of such agreements in facilitating inward FDI, but also in creating better opportunities for the internationalisation of their firms. The immediate result is that with growing FDI flows, investment disputes involving investors from emerging economies are becoming increasingly important.

- More and more preferential trade agreements (PTAs) are currently being concluded in areas of the world with developing economic activity. As Asian developing countries, in particular, remove restrictions and implement policies to attract FDI inflows, trade and investment have become increasingly intertwined. This favours the negotiation and establishment of new PTAs.
- The year 2008 marked the end of a growth cycle in global FDI, with worldwide flows down by more than 20 per cent. Due to the global financial crisis, the capacity of companies to invest has been weakened. One of the challenges is now to think of possible regulation which will take into account the need for the state to control FDI without implying protectionism.

In light of this, we decided after an initial stock-taking exercise to focus the Individual Project's work on a number of these crucial developments, instead of reworking basically known fragmentation, or proposing an overall solution to international fragmentation in investment regulation, which in any case remains a political decision to be taken by the relevant international stakeholders. We thus worked towards the identification of the relevant new issues, analysed a number of them in detail, and assessed – to the extent possible – what these developments meant for future multilateral rules on investment from a perspective of fragmentation and coherence. In our work, we have been particularly glad to collaborate with colleagues of the NCCR working on 'regionalism' and 'services', as well as with researchers of the University of Fribourg, researchers located all over the world and within international organisations such as UNCTAD. What follows now, describes some of the most important research outcomes of the Project.

This chapter offers a view of the legal as well as the economic development occurring in the field of the international regulatory framework on foreign investment. Its aim is also to underline the key challenges and developments which will play a significant role in the future discussion occurring at the WTO as well as within other international fora such as the European Union (EU). It contains three sections: the first depicts the significant fragmentation of the current framework on investment; the second analyses the new economic developments which may have a significant importance in the future discussion and negotiations regarding market access and national treatment granted to foreign investment at the national, regional, plurilateral and multilateral levels; finally, the third section analyses the situation under the EU lens.

A. The regulatory developments in international investment regulation

International investment agreements, instruments of cooperation for the promotion, protection and liberalisation of foreign investment, have all increased in the last years. In 2007, UNCTAD listed 44 new BITs that were signed, bringing their total number to 2,608 at the end of the year.[2] Still in 2007, 12 new IIAs other than BITs and double taxation treaties (DTTs) were concluded, bringing the total of such agreements comprising substantive investment provisions that have been concluded in this period to 254. Most of the treaty-making activity in 2007 involved Asian countries. The legal framework of investment agreements has also evolved significantly and the growing package of jurisprudence raises new questions about interpretation and implementation for governments and investors in both developed and developing countries.[3] The number of international investment disputes arising from investment agreements has increased sharply. Likewise, the cases brought to dispute settlement have become increasingly complex, creating various interpretations of their provisions and generating huge debates among governments, academics and practitioners.

We had to analyse these issues in three ways and provide a regular update of the data and statistics. The first section of the analysis takes stock of the current situation. The second part examines the various multilateral initiatives undertaken in the field of international investment. Finally, an exploration of some possible next steps is undertaken in the third section of this chapter as a means of contemplating a more coherent international normative framework governing FDI.

2 UNCTAD, IIA Monitor No. 2 (2008): Recent developments in international investment agreements (2007–June 2008), 01/09/08 (UNCTAD/WEB/DIAE/IA/2008/1), pp. 2 and 8.

3 P. Gugler and J. Chaisse, 'Foreign Investment Issues and WTO Law – Dealing with Fragmentation while Waiting for a Multilateral Framework', in J. Chaisse and T. Balmelli, *Essays on the Future of the World Trade Organization (Volume 1)* (Geneva: Editions Interuniversitaires Suisses, 2008), p. 135.

I. The spaghetti bowl at work

Comprehensive multilateral rules governing international economics are currently limited to trade issues. Even though the WTO agreements contain major loopholes, multilateral rules on trade constitute a broad umbrella of rights and obligations under which regional, plurilateral and bilateral agreements as well as national laws all regulate trade issues. Although FDI has increased significantly over the last two decades, outpacing the already significant expansion of trade during the same period, the current international legal framework for FDI is highly fragmented. The current framework consists of a wide variety of national and international rules and principles that differ in form, strength, and coverage.[4] The result is an increasingly complex international setting for international investment in which governments must ensure consistency between differing sets of obligations. An important advantage of bilateral investment treaties and regional agreements is that they can be tailored to the specific circumstances of the parties concerned, such as to their development issues.[5] However, as the number of bilateral investment treaties and regional agreements continue to expand, different standards and disciplines are beginning to be exerted over foreign investments. This might create confusion for MNEs operating on a global scale.

The sources of international law are international treaties, custom, general principles of law, and national law (Article 38 (1) of the Statute of the International Court of Justice). Customary international law treats FDI as a matter of national law in accordance with the principle of national sovereignty. Conversely, it is recognised that each state has an interest in the proper treatment of its nationals and their property abroad. A state may therefore invoke the rules concerning the responsibility of states for injuries to aliens and their property that have occurred in violation of customary international law (principle of nationality).

Although national laws and policies still constitute the most concrete and detailed part of the legal framework of FDI, the current system has become increasingly dependent upon international treaties. The attempt to create a multilateral organisational framework for FDI in the Havana Charter failed to enter into force in 1948, with the result that the legal situation since then has become a patchwork of bilateral, regional,

4 P. Gugler and V. Tomsik, 'General Agreement on Investment: Departure from the Investment Agreement Patchwork', in J. H. Dunning and P. Gugler (eds.), *Foreign Direct Investments, Location and Competitiveness* (Oxford: Elsevier, 2008), p. 229.

5 P. Gugler, 'Foreign Investment and Poverty Reduction', paper presented at the NCCR Trade Regulation Annual Conference, Bern, 3–4 July 2007.

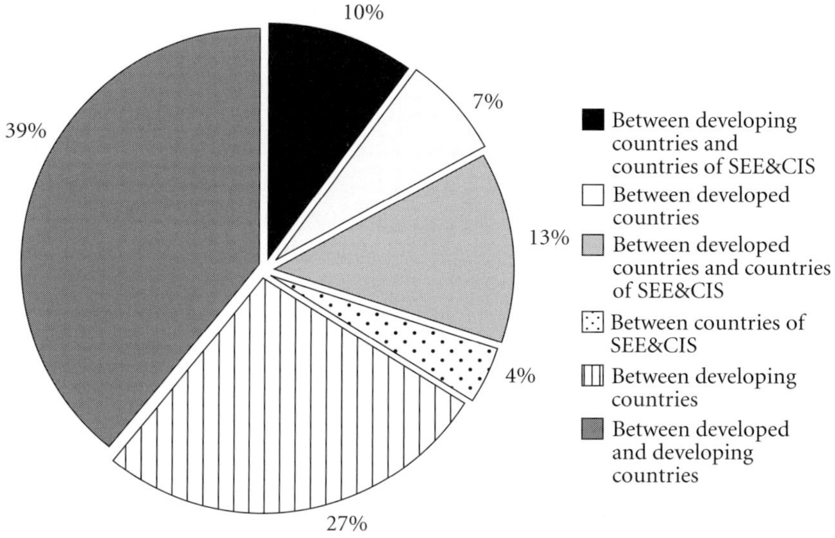

Figure 11.1 Total BITs concluded, *by the end of 2007*, by country group
Note: SEE&CIS: South East Europe and Commonwealth of Independent States
Source: UNCTAO, IIA Monitor No. 2 (2008): Recent developments in international investment agreements (2007–June 2008), 01/09/08 (UNCTAD/WEB/DIAE/IA/2008/1), p. 4

plurilateral and multilateral treaties. The early 1960s witnessed the early process of negotiating bilateral investment promotion and protection agreements between countries. The proliferation of these agreements set up two competing themes within international investment rules, notably that although an increasing number of developing countries were willing to subscribe to basic standards for investment protection and treatment, they were unwilling to do so at the multilateral level. BITs have since become the core of the current framework for FDI. More than 2,600 bilateral agreements have been concluded since the early 1960s, most of them in the 1990s. The trend for enhanced South–South economic cooperation continued in 2007 (Figure 11.1). Of the 44 new BITs signed in 2007, 13 were between developing countries, which represented more than 26 per cent of the total number of BITs. China alone accounted for a large share of those South–South agreements.[6] About 60 per cent of the

6 J. Xiao, 'Chinese Bilateral Investment Treaties in the 21st century: Protecting Chinese Investment', in J. Chaisse and P. Gugler, *Expansion of Trade and FDI in Asia: Strategic and Policy Challenges* (London: Routledge, Contemporary Asia Series, 2009), p. 122.

Chinese BITs concluded from 2002 to 2007 were with other developing countries, mainly in Africa.

Regional and plurilateral agreements are also popular means of formalising international rules on investment. Regional and plurilateral agreements comprise, by definition, a limited number of countries. Among OECD Members, for example, two Liberalisation Codes cover capital movements and current invisible operations respectively. Their degree of integration and cooperation differs depending upon the treaty and the member states. The EU model is the most integrated of these regional agreements and is characterised by the strong impact it has on FDI among member states and investment in and from third countries. Other regional integration agreements involve lower degrees of integration than that displayed by the EU, but nonetheless have a noticeable effect upon FDI regulation. The North American Free Trade Agreement (NAFTA) is a good example of such an agreement. Although NAFTA is formally neither a 'free trade zone' nor a common market or economic union, the agreement does pertain to FDI. Another example is the recently negotiated Framework Agreement on the Association of Southeast Asian Nations (ASEAN) Investment Area, which focuses exclusively on FDI.[7] This agreement seeks to promote the liberalisation of investment regulations in the region by enhancing cooperation between countries in the Asia-Pacific.

The policy space left behind by the failure of a multilateral set of rules on investment has been filled to some extent by international organisations and institutions. Among the relevant multilateral agencies in existence, several deal with issues that are important for FDI, such as the Agreement of the International Monetary Fund and the General Agreement on Tariffs and Trade (GATT). The international organisations created as part of these agreements, e.g. the WTO and the World Intellectual Property Organization (WIPO), constitute the sole international institutional structure that is indirectly or directly relevant to FDI. Other multilateral agreements, although they may not address the FDI process in its entirety, nonetheless pertain to important aspects of it (e.g. the Convention on the Settlement of Investment Disputes between States and Nationals of other States). A draft Code of Conduct on transnational companies (TNCs) has been developed by the United Nations. Finally, several WTO agreements are related to foreign investment issues such as the General Agreement

7 J. Chaisse and P. Gugler, 'The ASEAN in a New Era: Unveiling the Promises', in P. Gugler and J. Chaisse, *Competitiveness of ASEAN countries: Corporate and Regulatory Drivers* (Cheltenham: Edward Elgar, New Horizons in International Business series, 2010).

on Trade in Services (GATS), the Agreement on Trade-Related Investment Measures (TRIMs) and the Agreement on Trade-related Aspects of Intellectual Property Rights (TRIPS).[8]

Following the failure to install a multilateral framework on foreign investment within the OECD as well as within the WTO, opinions diverge as to whether approaches to regulate FDI through multilateral regulations should continue. These failures should not be read as a signal to abandon the search for multilateral rules. They may rather be considered an indication of the importance of multilateral regulations on investment and of the fact that governments have not yet identified an appropriate negotiating agenda.[9]

Indeed, the increasing importance of FDI makes the current legal situation unsatisfactory. A comprehensive multilateral legal framework for FDI would help to reduce transaction costs and thereby enhance the economic benefits of FDI. A renewed impetus to create such a framework has begun to gain momentum.

A comprehensive set of consistent multilateral rules on foreign investment could allow for a stable, transparent and consistent environment for firms operating internationally, whatever their ownership structure or place of incorporation. The global application of broadly the same investment disciplines would remove the complexity arising for investors from the existing framework of bilateral and regional investment treaties and agreements and thus facilitate compliance.

II. Key issues for achieving a coherent international framework on foreign investment

Multilateral action may still be necessary and may still be addressed to regulating MNE activity. Among the key issues to tackle in such an agreement should be the degree of liberalisation of rules governing the entry of foreign investment, the treatment in force in the post-establishment phase, the macroeconomic effects of FDI, the environmental concerns as well as the protection of social and human rights.[10]

8 P. Gugler and J. Chaisse, 'Foreign Investment Issues and WTO Law – Dealing with Fragmentation while Waiting for a Multilateral Framework', in J. Chaisse and T. Balmelli, *Essays on the Future of the World Trade Organization (Volume 1)* (Geneva: Editions Interuniversitaires Suisses, 2008), p. 140.

9 S. Brunner and D. Folly, 'The Way to a Multilateral Investment Agreement' (2007), NCCR Working Paper No. 24.

10 *Ibid.*

Liberalisation, in the context of FDI, involves the diminution of restrictions on the entry of foreign companies. Today, screening of investments is still common although it tends not to be strict and demanding. It may be assumed that such screening is subject to considerable influence by political pressure groups. Such restrictive, and thereby market-distorting, governmental measures need to be removed. The catchphrase here should be fair competition in contestable markets. However, developing countries in particular may prefer to retain screening powers in order to protect infant industries.[11]

Of the two basic model BITs, only the treatment provisions of the 'North American model' BIT apply to the pre-establishment phase, while the 'European model' merely covers investment post-establishment.[12] The choice of one of these two rival models in a multilateral framework will generate a lot of debate. The existence of two competing models may prolong negotiations about a possible future framework. A second principal category of issues concerns 'investment protection'. Positive standards of treatment, particularly directed at the elimination of discrimination against foreign investors, are common. In certain treaties the standards of treatment are also applied to the pre-entry phase. The most common standards of treatment are the 'most-favoured-nation' (MFN) standard, the 'national treatment' standard and the standard of 'fair and equitable' treatment. In the case of developing countries the question that arises is whether they can preserve sufficient policy space to promote their development. Therefore, most provisions allow for exceptions (e.g. referring to public order and health). As the extent of these exceptions and their impact are subject to interpretation, a substantial amount of uncertainty remains both for the investor and for the host state. This often results in unwieldy agreements in which the exceptions complicate the application. Another topic steeped in controversy is the amount of compensation due for breach of the provisions of the agreement. Opinions range from full compensation (including future profits) to no compensation at all. Several BITs contain references to adequate compensation. All these issues give rise to scores of legal problems that may lead to disputes. Investor-state dispute settlement methods are hence necessary to translate the standards

11 J. Chaisse, D. Chakraborty and A. Guha, 'India's Multilayered Regulation of Foreign Direct Investment: Between Resistance to Multilateral Negotiations and Unilateral Proactivism', in J. Chaisse and P. Gugler, *Expansion of Trade and FDI in Asia: Strategic and Policy Challenges* (London: Routledge, Contemporary Asia Series, 2009), p. 255.

12 P. Gugler and V. Tomsik, 'The North American and European Approaches in the International Investment Agreements' (2007) 4(5) *Transnational Dispute Management Review.*

into action. The potential costs of adhering to an investment agreement for host states are a limitation of their sovereignty and the risk of financial crises. In order to protect investors, many BITs enlarge the notion of 'expropriation' to cover so-called 'regulatory takings'. All government measures that are seriously detrimental to an investor's interests or affect foreign investors in a disproportionate way entail compensation.

Obviously, this raises the risk of unduly limiting generally acknowledged regulatory powers of the host state. The multilateral agreement on investment (MAI) was designed as a pure investor-protection instrument and was therefore considered an anachronism which failed to reflect the recent transformation in political discourse. This discourse did not challenge the importance of free private enterprise as such but rather its legitimacy as a potential violator of human rights, an abuser of market power, a corruptor and a polluter. Civil society stressed the need for standards for TNC conduct and criticised the MAI for the imbalance between investor rights and obligations. It has been argued that foreign investors could secure additional property rights which would be more substantial than many host states had anticipated. This could lead to problems of moral hazard and adverse selection as these provisions could be used as an insurance against 'normal' business risks. Another point of controversy concerns the macroeconomic aspects of FDI. Capital account liberalisation was initially thought to lead to the efficient allocation of savings in the global economy and to allow citizens to diversify their portfolios.

However, it can be argued that this liberalisation has instead led to an increase in economic and financial crises, with subsequent implications for economic meltdown. Although FDI is generally regarded to be much more stable, this view seems to be contradicted by empirical evidence. On the opposite side, full liberalisation can be seen as entailing considerable foreign exchange liabilities and may lead to a liquidity crisis especially in the case of developing countries. Therefore, the government must screen the amount and timing of inward FDI. It is important to keep in mind that financial crises are sometimes brought about within the context of sound economic fundamentals due to a process of self-fulfilling expectations. Constraints on capital movements might channel the conduct of investors into a more development-friendly direction. Considering these risks, it seems that further evidence on the causal link between financial liberalisation, banking crises and currency crises is necessary. Otherwise, the economic and social costs of financial crises may end up surpassing the potential benefits of liberalisation.

Initiatives have recently been undertaken under the auspices of the UN, as well as by some research institutes in order to address those issues within the framework of a multilateral agreement on investment. Given the complexity of all the dimensions to be taken into account, the progress toward a less fragmented framework will need further analyses. Studies on the key dimensions of rules governing foreign investments should be designed to promote both the firms' efficiency and the economic development and competitiveness of host and home countries. Furthermore, the challenge is not only to 'open' the framework to new issues but also to consider it in a dynamic perspective. The interaction between governments and MNEs is a dynamic and iterative process.

B. The economic development in the international investment arena since 2000

While negotiation efforts for the conclusion of a multilateral agreement failed, the development of FDI continued and, as one of the shaping factors of globalisation, increased in importance rather than decreased. New characteristics of FDI emerged; new players showed up and set the scene for future discussions on a multilateral agreement, which is substantially different from what it was a number of years ago. An important effort of our work has been to focus on these issues and create a new yearly conference in Asia and to make it a perennial event in association with local leading institutions.[13] This initiative largely contributed to give our research project a pivotal role in the research on the latest developments on Asia and FDI.

Most of the world's FDI is made by MNEs in the 'triad'. The triad is a group of three major trading and investment blocs in the international area: North America, Europe and the Asia-Pacific regions. About 80 per cent of the world's total FDI is conducted in the triad, and the world's 500 largest MNEs account for about 90 per cent of the world's stock of FDI as demonstrated by research led by Professor Alan Rugman. Moreover, most of these firms within the triad have the vast majority of their sales within their home region. Therefore, understanding the importance of the triad and the strong intra-regional dimension of MNE activities is a

13 IP 11 International Conference, Expansion of FDI in Asia and Implications for the Development of International Rules on Investment, 18 January 2008, National Institute of Development Administration (NIDA), Bangkok; and IP 11, University of Fribourg Annual Conference, NIDA Bangkok, Competitiveness of ASEAN Economies – Investment and Trade Issues, 8–9 January 2009, National Institute of Development Administration (NIDA), Bangkok.

prerequisite for our analysis of possible multilateral investment regulation (section I below). Besides, new characteristics of FDI emerged with the BRIC countries (Brazil, Russia, India and China) as new players appeared (section II). We also need to look at outward investments from state-capitalist countries via state-owned enterprises (SOEs) and sovereign wealth funds (SWFs) (section III).

I. The regional dimension of FDI

The discussion about fragmentation and any possible harmonisation of international investment regulation is based on the understanding of increasingly global investment flows. This understanding assumes that globalisation brings along a flattened world, where MNEs operate their business activities worldwide, follow business opportunities and are hardly hindered in their approach by any national borders. Outsourcing is a key concept that allows for unhindered internationalisation and globally integrated production and distribution chains.[14] It is on this idea of globalisation that a discussion on the harmonisation of the currently fragmented international rules available for international investment is based, since the assumed international activities of MNEs should be responded to by coherent international rules.

Research by various experts (discussed by researchers of our group in a workshop with other academic NCCR staff and external researchers in Geneva in December 2008),[15] however, presents evidence of a different characterisation of globalisation. Indeed, as pointed out by Rugman, evidence exists that investment flows are today much more regional than global.[16] His empirical studies on regionalisation show that globalisation as popularly understood does not exist. For example, there is no evidence that US firms operate globally. Instead, these companies produce and sell on a home region basis, which is equally true for MNEs from Europe and Asia.[17] A 'triad rivalry' seems to exist in all of the triad regions, in which

14 P. Gugler and J. Chaisse 'L'Asie dans l'économie politique mondiale contemporaine', in P. Gugler and J. Chaisse , Les économies asiatiques face aux défis de la compétitivité internationale (2009) 67(1) *Revue Economique et Sociale* 7–20.

15 Joint workshop of NCCR research groups, 'Is the World Flat or Mountainous? Implications for International Rules on Trade and Investment', 28 November 2008, Graduate Institute of International and Development Studies (HEID), Geneva, Switzerland.

16 A. Rugman, 'How Global are TNCs from Emerging Markets?', in K. Sauvant (ed.), *The Rise of Transnational Corporations from Emerging Markets* (Northampton: Edward Elgar, 2008), pp. 86–106.

17 P. Gugler and J. Chaisse, 'L'Asie dans l'économie politique mondiale contemporaine', in P. Gugler and J. Chaisse, Les économies asiatiques face aux défis de la compétitivité internationale (2009) 67 (1) *Revue Economique et Sociale* 7–20.

the world's corporate giants compete, but with a continuously strong intra-regional effect.

Thus, despite the ongoing globalisation process, FDI (still) seems to have a rather regional dimension instead of a truly global one. The implications of these findings for the regulation of investment await a definite answer, but the question of the need for global rules compared to the need for more regional rules comes up. Perhaps any multilateral framework for investment is irrelevant, because FDI flows and MNEs' strategies are regional by nature. Evidence shows that countries to date follow a path of regional integration agreements with investment provisions. In a similar vein to the European Union's far-reaching integration in many areas of politics, regional integration with a more trade and investment focus has been seen in the US (NAFTA), Asia (ASEAN),[18] and is about to emerge in South America as well. Regionalisation of investment flows and regionalisation of investment regulation thus seem to go hand-in-hand. This constitutes an important development in today's investment landscape, which any future attempt to develop a (multilateral) investment agreement will have to take into consideration.

II. The increase of FDI from emerging countries

Flow of FDI has grown faster over the recent past. Global flow of FDI reached a record level of US$ 1,306 billion in the year 2006. Increase in FDI was largely fuelled by cross-border mergers and acquisitions. FDI in 2006 increased by 38 per cent as compared to the previous year. This growth of global FDI inflows was shared by countries at various stages of development, particularly in Asia. FDI inflows to South, East and Southeast Asia maintained their upward trend last year, rising by 19 per cent to reach a new high of US$ 200 billion. South and South-East Asia saw a sustainable increase in FDI flows, while growth in East Asia was slower. However, FDI in East Asia is shifting towards more knowledge-intensive and high value-added activities. Another important point we underlined in our research is that a large share of the FDI inflows into Asia originated from other Asian countries. Of the US$ 138 billion of FDI inflows into South, East and South-East Asia in 2004, approximately 40 per cent is estimated to have originated from other Asian countries.

18 J. Chaisse, 'L'ANASE et les défis du multilatéralisme émergent en Asie', in P. Gugler and J. Chaisse, Les économies asiatiques face aux défis de la compétitivité internationale (2009) 67(1) *Revue Economique et Sociale* 89–105.

China, Hong Kong, Indonesia, the Philippines and Thailand stand out as having inward FDI that is dominated by Asian investors.[19] As indicated in Box 11.1 below, numerous factors have driven the increasing levels of intra-Asian FDI.[20]

BOX 11.1 MAIN DETERMINANTS OF INTRA-ASIAN FDI

- *Competitiveness:* a large component of international competitiveness for Asian firms is achieved through intra-regional sales within the home region. International competitiveness should not be confused with globalisation.[21] Asian firms do not compete globally; instead, they mainly operate regionally.
- *Need for global presence*: MNEs are undergoing an attitudinal change, realising that they operate in a global economy in which Asia is a rising force. In addition, developing country MNEs are investing in other countries to reduce the risk of overdependence on the home market. Offshore centres of excellence, such as India's data recovery centres in Singapore, are examples of this trend.
- *Costs of production*: Labour costs are of concern to most MNEs, especially those from more developed nations. Production has increasingly been relocated to developing economies where costs are lower. This practice is commonplace in industries such as electrical and electronics, and garments and textiles – FDI in the electrical and electronics industry has a strong regional focus while FDI in the garments industry is more geographically dispersed.
- *Market access*: Production and distribution centres are eventually set up close to consumer markets. This reduces the problems of transportation of perishable goods such as agricultural food products and processed food. The Indonesian-owned Indofood Corporation, for instance, has located production in China where a large part of its market resides.
- *Favourable FDI regulatory trends in Asian host countries*: Changes in government policy have facilitated FDI through creating greater openness to foreign investors, reducing taxes, simplifying procedures and enhancing incentives. In host economies, liberalisation policies have created many investment opportunities, such as the privatisation of state-owned enterprises and assets. The investment promotion agencies now consider developing Asia as a key FDI source region.

19 P. Gugler and J. Chaisse, 'Patterns and Dynamics of Asia's Growing Share of FDI', in J. Chaisse and P. Gugler, *Expansion of Trade and FDI in Asia: Strategic and Policy Challenges* (London: Routledge, Contemporary Asia Series, 2009), pp. 1–21.

20 *Ibid.*

21 P. Gugler and S. Brunner, 'Foreign Direct Investments Effects on National Competitiveness: A Cluster Approach' (2007) 13(3) *International Advances in Economic Research* 268.

FSAs / CSAs	**Weak**	**Strong**
Strong	1	3
Weak	2	4

Figure 11.2 The FSA–CSA matrix
Source: Alan Rugman, 2008, p. 14

We have analysed this development of Asian FDI from interdisciplinary perspectives. On the legal side, attention to Chinese BITs and the ASEAN has focused on approaches to investment and the emergence of Chinese BITs concluded since 2000, which contain some significant improvements denoting a high degree of investment protection.

In relation to economic theories explaining FDI developments, we have applied known theories (foremost Dunning, 1981), as well as very recent concepts developed by leading international scholars. Rugman has pointed out firm-specific advantages (FSAs) and country-specific advantages (CSAs) (see Figure 11.2).[22]

Analysing the competitiveness of Chinese MNEs on this model, we found that the CSAs play a far greater role than FSAs. Major features of FSAs include expertise and technology-based advantages of Chinese companies, early adoption of new technologies, sustainable investment in research and development and other resources. It is only a few Chinese MNEs that have recently shown a catch-up compared to leading international MNEs on these issues. Important CSAs of Chinese MNEs, in contrast, consist of relatively cheap labour, and an unsophisticated – but growing – demand in its domestic market. Further, developing and

22 A. Rugman and C. Hoon Ho, 'The International Competitiveness of Asian Firms' (2008) 1(1) *Journal of Strategy and Management* 57–71.

transition economies typically see an active involvement of their home governments in business, both through ownership and through regulation. This is the case for China, and the consequences for the internationalisation of Chinese firms are significant.[23] In this sense, CSAs play a crucial role for any Chinese company wishing to engage in global investment. It is not always evident whether these state activities are beneficial or detrimental to the companies' activities, but applied strategically for selected activities they may in a given situation be detrimental to a level playing field and fair competition amongst international MNEs. These factors will include capital market imperfections, and interference by government bodies and authorities in shaping the form and activities of Chinese MNEs. As an example, the emergence of Chinese 'national champions' as first-ranking global players is a clear goal of the Chinese government and is an expression of considerable activity on the side of investment regulation categorised as CSA.[24] China invested heavily in strategic asset seeking FDI in order to upgrade the FSAs. This operation mainly took the form of mergers and acquisitions in the developed economies, causing political concerns that may be reflected in future agreements on investment.

Further, an important aspect in FDI that we researched is the growing importance of the concept of CSR, and its possible impact on the competitiveness of developing countries' and economies' SMEs and MNEs in globalisation. We reviewed the traditional wisdom of the concept of strategic CSR developed in the North and the role that CSR engagement can play in corporate competitiveness, and compared it with the competitive advantage the South has through supply chains.[25] We pointed out that among the many factors that could explain the 'CSR divide', the negative impact of CSR on comparative advantage is the final resort where developing countries are resistant and defensive toward western-style CSR. The research concluded with two policy proposals that aim to bridge the CSR gap, the first is to improve CSR standard-setting participation from both

23 J. Nie, 'Towards China's Greater Influence on the World's Finances: A Legal Analysis of Chinese Overseas Direct Investment', in J. Chaisse and P. Gugler, *Expansion of Trade and FDI in Asia: Strategic and Policy Challenges* (London: Routledge, Contemporary Asia Series, 2009), p. 99.

24 P. Gugler, 'How are Chinese Multinational Enterprises Different?', VoxEU online, 23 August 2008.

25 P. Gugler and J. Shi, 'Corporate Social Responsibility for Developing Country Multinational Corporations: Lost War in Pertaining Global Competitiveness?' (2009) 87 *Journal of Business Ethics* 3–24 (see comment in the bibliography).

sides, and the second to search for solutions in the international investment legal framework which will define corporate obligations in relation to CSR in a more explicit way.

III. The rise of FDI by state-controlled entities

Despite trends of market liberalisation and privatisation seen over the last years,[26] the role of states has in this period of time arguably grown in importance on some particular aspects of investment.[27] Most importantly, investments of emerging countries went up, mostly executed by state-owned enterprises (SOEs) and sovereign wealth funds (SWFs). Both forms of investments originate from state ownership and state activity, and are thus regularly referred to as investments by 'state-controlled entities' (SCEs).[28] In light of this phenomenon, policy-makers in a number of countries have started to rethink their own regulatory frameworks for investment. Engaging in this research and discussion, our research group coorganised a conference in October 2008 in collaboration with Columbia University,[29] gathering outstanding scholars and representatives from international organisations. The following provides synthesising key ideas on both SOEs and SWFs.

SOEs are particularly important in emerging and transition markets such as China, India, Vietnam, Singapore, Malaysia, Czech Republic and Russia. Some SOEs are listed among the Fortune Global 500. Chinese SOEs are the most numerous in this listing, making up 24 firms. Due to the significance of Chinese SOEs' FDI, we have studied those firms in particular.[30] Indeed, by far the largest outward investments by Chinese MNEs are made by SOEs, and all investment projects follow a scheme that ensures that they are strictly in line with government policies. The

26 The recent economic crisis may change the picture again.

27 See Chapter 5 in this volume on energy regulation.

28 The legal difference between SWFs and SOEs is obvious: it is the same as that between any type of investment fund and any type of company. However in reality the difference is not that obvious, since there are SOEs that are used as a conduit for their respective state's sovereign wealth, as part either of a longer channel involving an SWF or of a shorter channel between the foreign reserve manager and the target company.

29 NCCR IP11 and Columbia Center on Sustainable International Investment, 3rd Columbia International Investment Conference, 'Foreign Direct Investment by State-Owned Entities: Do the rules need changing?' 1–2 October 2008, Columbia University, New York, USA.

30 P. Gugler and B. Boie, 'The Rise of Chinese Multinational Enterprises', in J. Chaisse and P. Gugler, *Expansion of Trade and FDI in Asia: Strategic and Policy Challenges* (London: Routledge, Contemporary Asia Series, 2009), pp. 25–57.

motivations of Chinese firms to internationalise and the government interest in this are to a large extent aligned and institutionally intertwined.

Both Chinese state-owned enterprises and private enterprises are engaged in FDI, and no clear breakdown has been published on the shares of SOEs and private enterprises in the total number (5000) of investment projects. However, certain characteristics of Chinese investors give a strong indication that the role the Chinese Government is playing in Chinese FDI is tremendous. Most of the large-scale investment projects that weigh heavy in Chinese FDI statistics have so far been executed by Chinese SOEs. The largest FDI players substantially overlap with the most profitable SOEs in China. The bulk of FDI is thus executed by the Chinese SOEs which are the large domestic players in major industries in China. They are often backed up with an officially sanctioned monopoly in their industry, such as natural resources, telecommunications or infrastructure.

Investment projects are expected to follow the catalogue of encouraged FDI, and may be rejected or restricted, for example via foreign currency exchange limitations. With these instruments, the government ensures that all investment activities, even if executed by privately owned companies, are strictly in line with government policies. Clearly, this needs to be taken into consideration when analysing the motivations and strategies of Chinese MNEs that are becoming international. Chinese particularities are so strong and the motivations of government, state and business so deeply integrated and interlinked, that it is doubtful that Chinese MNEs emerge with traditional motivations, but Chinese characteristics. Indeed, the emergence of Chinese MNEs is an expression of a broader development in the sphere of today's international business landscape: it is the People's Republic of China going global.

The second type of state-controlled entities are SWFs and we analysed many issues they raise in terms of international regulation.[31] SWFs played an important role in the economic crisis of 2007–2009, incidentally acquiring large stakes in some financial giants. Yet that role has also raised questions about the influence of these state-owned investment vehicles. The United States and the European Union have expressed concerns that SWFs have more than just commercial aims. In particular, there are concerns that SWFs seek political and strategic leverage on top of financial gain. Such anxieties have been exacerbated by the relative opacity of these

31 J. Chaisse and P. Gugler, 'Sovereign Wealth Funds: What Should the European Union Do?', in K. Sauvant (ed.), *Sovereign Wealth Funds: Do We Need New Rules?* (Cheltenham: Edward Elgar, 2010).

large investors. The rise of SWFs is one sign of the shift in the balance of power in the world economy from Western industrialised countries to new emerging market giants like China and the oil-rich Middle East.[32]

Sovereign wealth funds have come into the spotlight (Table 11.1), especially since 2007 when China declared its intention to invest US$ 3 billion of its fund reserves in private holding companies. The SWFs have raised concerns about: financial stability, corporate governance, and political interference and protectionism. The importance of SWFs in global capital markets is expected to grow, mainly because of high oil prices, the relative weakness of the US dollar and persistent current account surpluses in China and certain other Asian countries.

The International Working Group (IWG) of sovereign wealth funds in the International Monetary Fund (IMF) tried to see how the conduct of the SWFs themselves can be influenced. IMF negotiations mainly covered issues of transparency and governance. The result is a set of Generally Accepted Practices and Principles (GAPP) for SWFs which were developed directly in cooperation with the owners of the SWFs. These GAPP or 'Santiago Principles' were released on 11 October 2008. The principles encourage the funds to explain their investment criteria, and recommend that they avoid buying stakes in sensitive companies, such as Western defence contractors. They also voted on setting up a standing committee that will update the guidelines and liaise with Western governments and institutions such as the World Bank and IMF on issues of concern. But the principles stop short of requiring an explicit pledge not to invest for political ends. The principles include a call for funds to abide by local rules and regulations and base their investments on financial and economic grounds. They even call on funds to disclose any investment decisions 'subject to other than economic and financial considerations'. Above all, the IMF guidelines are based on a standard definition of SWFs. They do not cover SOEs as made clear by a footnote. Consequently, they could find themselves in the pointless situation of being rigorously adhered to by, for example, Norway's Government Pension Fund – Global, while Russia's Gazprom felt no need to take any notice of them. If so, the SWF guidelines will serve little more than a public relations purpose should they encourage sovereign investment to flow through other investment vehicles not covered by the guidelines.

32 J. Ruet, 'The reshaping of Global Capitalism by MNEs from Emerging Countries', in J. Chaisse and P. Gugler, *Expansion of Trade and FDI in Emerging Asia: Strategic and Policy Challenges* (London: Routledge, Contemporary Asia Series, 2009).

Table 11.1 *Top sovereign wealth fund merger and acquisition transactions 2007–2009**

Target	Target nation	Sovereign wealth fund	Value (US$m)
Citigroup	United States	Kuwait Investment Authority (KIA), GIC (Singapore)	12,500
UBS	Switzerland	GIC (Singapore)	11,535
Citigroup	United States	Abu Dhabi Investment Authority (UAE)	7,500
Merrill Lynch	United States	KIA (Kuwait), Korea Investment Corp	6,600
Merrill Lynch	United States	Temasek Holdings (Singapore)	5,600
Morgan Stanley	United States	China Investment Corp (China)	5,000
Laureate Education	United States	Caisse de Depot et Placement (Canada)	3,677.5
OMX	Sweden	DIFC (UAE)	3,551.4
Barclays	United Kingdom	China Development Bank (China)	2,980.1
Budapest Airport	Hungary	Caisse de Depot et Placement (Canada)	2,610.4
London Stock Exchange	United Kingdom	DIFC (UAE)	1,648.0
Related Cos	United States	Mubadala Development Co (UAE)	1,400.0
Carlyle Group	United States	Mubadala Development Co (UAE)	1,350.0
Och-Ziff Cap Mgmt Group	United States	Dubai International Capital (UAE)	1,258.6
Alliance Medical	United Kingdom	Dubai International Capital (UAE)	1,248.7
Mauser	Germany	Dubai International Capital (UAE)	1,159.8
OMX	Sweden	DIFC (UAE)	1,100.6
Bharti Infratel	India	Temasek Holdings (Singapore)	1,000
Chapterhouse Holdings Ltd	United Kingdom	GIC Real Estate (Singapore)	954.2
Barneys New York	United States	Istithmar PJSC (UAE)	942.3

(*cont.*)

Table 11.1 *(cont.)*

Target	Target nation	Sovereign wealth fund	Value (US$m)
Pearl Energy	Singapore	Mubadala Development Co (UAE)	877.5
Cevahir Shopping Mall Istanbul	Turkey	Kuwait Investment Authority (Kuwait)	750
Sturegallerian	Sweden	Abu Dhabi Investment Authority (UAE)	580
Euronext of France	France	DIFC (UAE)	370
Manchester City	United Kingdom	Abu Dhabi United Group (UAE)	£200m
AIG Private Bank	Switzerland	Aabar Investments (UAE)	253

Source: University of Fribourg/database of our research group.

* The methodology for gathering data is centred on a search of publicly available data, particularly: SWF reports when they exist, government reports on the activities of SWFs, official reports by public and private financial institutions on SWFs, media reports on the activities of SWFs. Although we are trying to be rigorous and systematic in our evaluation of each entity and its shares in an invested company, some degree of subjectivity necessarily is present in our procedure.

It might then make sense to go on to redefine SWFs along broader lines. Robert Kimmit, the former Deputy Secretary of the Department of the US Treasury, suggests that SWFs could be conceived as 'large pools of capital controlled by a government and invested in private markets abroad',[33] rather than as the funds that serve exclusively as investment vehicles for these pools. With 'sovereign wealth fund' defined in this way, a code of conduct for SWFs would cover sovereign wealth at its source, regardless of the route it then took to reach any foreign investment target. Because of the limited outcome of IMF work, we took the initiative throughout 2008 to study the efforts led by the European Union to highlight protectionist tendencies in its economy. This complementary aspect of our research on SWFs is developed below.

33 R. Kimmitt, 'Public Footprints in Private Markets: Sovereign Wealth Funds and the World Economy' (2008) 87(1) *Foreign Affairs* 119–130.

C. Trade and investment developments under the European Union lens

Some of the most relevant developments in international investment matters in the last decade have been witnessed in Europe. As part of the triad in investment matters (next to North America and East Asia), Europe is one of the most relevant sources and destinations for investment. Yet, Europe as a player in investment matters is only about to emerge. Until today, a number of relevant competences in the field of investment regulation remain with the Member States of the European Union. Internationally, it is therefore the European states that are still perceived as regulators of investments to and from their territories within Europe.

This view only partially reflects the current reality of investment regulation in Europe. Investment regulation in Europe is today a patchwork of various national, European, and multilateral rules, applicable to different issues and involving various stakeholders. It is important to underline that the challenge investment regulation in Europe is facing is not limited to a question of competences and actors. Regulatory power, substantive agendas and interests of various stakeholders are intrinsically intertwined, and together they form the European 'jumble' of investment regulation. As such, Europe constitutes a key example of fragmentation in international investment regulation, and a case with special characteristics going even beyond the known international fragmentation of law.

In our work we identified the developments in European investment regulation as relevant for, and relating to, developments in the international framework of investment regulation. Work carried out by our research team covers some of the upcoming issues. It treated in particular the question of the European competence on investment (section I below), substantive elements of investment regulation between the European side (by whomever represented) and China, one of the most important external investment partners (section II), and aspects of the emerging European position with regard to a regulation of investments by SWFs (section III), a topic that caught great attention during the working period of the NCCR. By following these recent developments we created a lot of interest amongst international researchers with similar views, which led to the co-organisation of a conference together with Columbia University on the regulation of investments undertaken by state actors.[34] A subsequent joint workshop was organised with the Czech National Bank, which reviewed major outcomes of the former conference and discussed ways forward for Europe's internal market.[35]

I. Towards a European Union external investment policy

Since December 2009, the new legal regime entailed in the Lisbon Treaty promotes a new and coherent Common Commercial Policy (CCP). Thus, for the first time, investment may become the exclusive competence of the European Union, and Europe may speak with one voice in any negotiations on international investment regulation. The change in competence may reverse the growing and unnatural substantive divide between investment-related provisions in FTAs (as concluded by the EU), and those of traditional, national BITs (concluded by EU Member States). Today, these bilateral treaties of EU Member States remain important for their investment protection characteristics. Globally, the immediate result of a common European investment policy would be a cut in the number of bilateral agreements in the world, since Europe would step by step replace the members' agreements with third countries. Today, more than 50 per cent of worldwide BITs are concluded by European Member States.

As initially planned by the Constitutional Treaty, the Treaty of Lisbon extended the CCP to the second most important field of international economic relations,[36] namely foreign investment (Articles 206 and 207 of the Treaty on the Functioning of the European Union – TFEU). The new Article 207 TFEU expressly includes, and for the first time, 'foreign direct investment' under the Common Commercial Policy Title II of the TFEU. This is of great importance since the European Union will therefore gain a legal basis to act in its external relations with respect to most aspects of foreign investment regulation.[37] The innovation brought

34 NCCR IP11 and Columbia Center on Sustainable International Investment, 3rd Columbia International Investment Conference, 'Foreign Direct Investment by State-Owned Entities: Do the rules need changing?' 1–2 October 2008, Columbia University, New York, USA.

35 IP11 Workshop, 'SWFs in an Evolving Global Financial System: Regulatory Challenges in the European Union', 30 January 2009, Czech National Bank (CNB), Prague, Czech Republic.

36 J. Chaisse, 'Adapting the European Community Legal Structure to the International Trade' (2006) 17(6) *European Business Law Review* 1615–1635.

37 J. Chaisse and P. Gugler 'Sovereign Wealth Funds: What Should the European Union Do?', in K. Sauvant (ed.), *Sovereign Wealth Funds: Do We Need New Rules?* (Cheltenham: Edward Elgar, 2010).

about by the EU Treaty will largely contribute to greater coherence of European policies in the field of FDI. The main purpose of the new Article 207 TFEU is to provide the EU with a single legal basis to deal with all FDI issues. It seems to us that EC and international law give the same meaning to the concept of FDI and it is a first and significant step for the external policies of the EU. We, however, underscore that the scope of European Union competence to regulate foreign investment under the Lisbon Treaty is not totally identified and circumscribed. Does Article 207 TFEU confer competence to take action with respect to all aspects of FDI regulation?

The new Article 207 TFEU unifies rules on establishment in all sectors of foreign investment. This Article is placed under the CCP, which is based on principles of uniformity and liberalisation. As a result, admission of foreign investment, in both services and goods, falls within the scope of a given competence on the regulation of FDI. The new Article confers powers on all foreign-established persons, irrespective of whether they meet the requirements of Article 54 TFEU. Furthermore, the FDI competence is broad since it explicitly includes all standards of treatment of FDI, in particular 'fair and equitable treatment'. The FDI competence covers the treatment of EU-controlled or -managed undertakings in third countries which do not straightforwardly fall within the scope of a European Union competence by virtue of establishment rules. A third major issue relates to the protection of foreign investors against expropriation, and we analyse whether it falls under EU competence. At first sight it may be argued that Article 207 TFEU cannot extend to measures of investment protection. We do not think such a narrow interpretation could be adopted. The fact that Article 207 TFEU does not distinguish between trade in goods and other aspects of the CCP, as Article 133 of the Treaty on the European Community (TEC) does, illustrates that the Lisbon Treaty is moving further away from the traditional trade orientation of the CCP, which is expanding towards other fields of economic activity.

Article 207 TFEU gives the EU new powers and a broad scope of action at the international level in the field of FDI. More precisely, the EU should (probably after a transition period) be able to entirely substitute the EU Member States in investment regulation. This significant change raises many issues since more than 1200 bilateral investment treaties (BITs) have been concluded by EU Member States. Indirectly, the emergence of a new role in the field of investment regulation for the EU gives some means to address the issue of fragmentation. Possibly, the national European BITs will be replaced by a limited number of European BITs. It is for the time being unclear when and under which conditions the EU could substitute Member States' activities and enter into new BITs with third countries. We believe that the history of the common market could give some clues. In order to achieve a common market between the Member States, a twelve-year transitional period up to 31 December 1969 was introduced. Up to 1970, it was for Member States to coordinate their trade relations with non-Community countries. Since the transitional period ended 40 years ago, the Community has had the sole competence for the commercial policy: the so-called CCP.

The EU external action is about to experience a new important development since the Lisbon Treaty establishes for the first time an express competence over foreign investment by including it within the scope of the CCP. Bringing into the same hands trade and investment matters contributes to ensuring the development of a strong, coherent and efficient external economic policy for the EU. It contributes at the same time to reducing the fragmentation of international investment regulation, since it will initially reduce the number of existing international instruments, which will reinforce the need for ensuring a greater homogeneity of the contents of these rules.

II. The Sino-European framework for investment

The legal framework of Sino-European investment regulation gives expression to some of the latest developments in Europe's investment regulation both with regards to competences and an emerging formulation of common European policies on investment regulation. On the Chinese side, it highlights the development of China's investment policy, following the needs of the country as an outbound investor and underlining a general shift of China towards integration into the international investment law landscape. PhD research undertaken within our research project has analysed the currently fragmented legal basis of investment law applicable in bilateral agreements between Europe and China and the options for improvements of substance in light of existing multilateral rules.

A comparative analysis of the 25 bilateral agreements that currently exist with China reveals light and shadow. As a point of major criticism, the fragmentation finds expression in important differences in the substance of the agreements. No standard wording is commonly applied in the substantive or procedural provisions. The lack of uniformity will create different legal rights for European investors in China or Chinese investors in different EU Member States. Tribunals interpreting these provisions in possible investor-state dispute settlement cases will also review the precise wording critically and may come to different conclusions on the basis of the different wording used. Further, shortcomings in law in some of the mostly older agreements highlight that individual European governments may lack sufficient resources, will or initiative to keep their agreements up-to-date. It is difficult to see how agreements concluded with China before the revolutionary opening of China to foreign direct investment, such as agreements for Denmark (1985), France (1984), or Italy (1985) remain equally effective tools for investment regulation today.

On the positive side, the most advanced agreements European countries have negotiated with China in recent years have a rather high general level of investment protection as compared to international standards. Agreements such as those for Germany (2003), the Netherlands (2001) and Finland (2004) enshrine an assortment of standards and disciplines, including fair and equitable treatment, full protection and security, MFN treatment, national treatment, protection against uncompensated expropriation and umbrella clauses. These standards and disciplines together make up all major aspects of what can be considered standard treaty practice in approximately 2,600 BITs worldwide.[38]

The novelty in these provisions relates most importantly to the national treatment and dispute settlement provisions. National treatment for established investment is available (limited by a grandfather clause for existing investments, unrestricted in one single agreement). Comprehensive investor-state dispute settlement is now provided for, usually to take place under the Convention on the Settlement of Investment Disputes between States and Nationals of Other States (ICSID). The relevance of this dispute settlement provision lies mostly in offering enforcement to the already established treatment and protection standards, which considerably improves the legal standing of foreign investors in China against expropriation. It is, however, doubtful if the inclusion of such provisions can be attributed to a negotiation success of European governments. Rather, it must be seen in the context of the emergence of China as an outbound investor. Having traditionally been critical towards the rule of international law in affairs considered domestic Chinese, the introduction of such clauses mirrors China's need for legal certainty and protection of

38 S. Schill, 'Tearing Down the Great Wall: The New Generation Investment Treaties of the People's Republic of China' (2007) 15 *Cardozo Journal of International Comparative Law* 73, 76.

its own outward investments. A number of legal aspects of the bilateral agreements between European countries and China are set out in more detail in Box 11.2.

BOX 11.2 A COMPARATIVE ANALYSIS OF EUROPEAN–CHINESE BITS: KEY OBSERVATIONS

Definitions of 'investor' and 'investment': The definitions applied in different agreements are broad. There should be clarification on questions that typically arise in relation to China, i.e. joint-ventures, investors without legal personality, or indirect investments (via third countries).

National treatment: The BITs range from agreements without any national treatment standard to recent BITs with full national treatment standard (limited by a grandfather clause) for established investments. Surprisingly, a single, older agreement provides for full national treatment (post-establishment), but it is doubtful if this reflects Chinese policy today.

MFN treatment: Agreements reviewed include an MFN clause, with the Finnish BIT being the only agreement to cover the pre-establishment phase. It may be recommendable to consider the Finnish model for all agreements, and to clarify the scope of MFN treatment in more detail (most importantly with regard to dispute settlement).

Expropriation: Agreements reviewed differ considerably in detail. The overall scope of the clauses in the agreements is, however, similar. Legal work therefore seems necessary to find an acceptable formula, taking into consideration crucial issues such as direct and indirect expropriation and fair market value.

Umbrella clause: Some agreements reviewed include umbrella clauses, others do not. This reflects different legal traditions in Europe on the use of such a clause, and suggests a need for clarification amongst the European stakeholders.

Dispute settlement: China has via several steps updated its BIT practice towards full dispute settlement (not solely questions of quantum), limited only by an administrative review process. No agreement should today remain below this legal threshold, and a critical eye should be kept on the questions of local remedies and, in particular, the practical effect of administrative review.

While the need for a more coherent approach to investment regulation between Europe and China becomes evident in light of the differences existing amongst Sino-European BITs, international fragmentation of investment law and unclear competences on the European side may be a reason that a number of more fundamental issues in investment regulation are today hardly addressed at all. Most importantly, current BITs concluded and administered by national governments apply to established investments only, and thus leave open the question of market access to other fora and other actors. For the creation of a level playing field amongst investors worldwide, market access is, however, a crucial topic. The rather restrictive approach of the Chinese side, carefully regulating market access of foreign investors, is often seen as being in contradiction to a generally liberal investment climate, and may thus be a key concern to European investors. Further, parallel structures in investment law in bilateral and multilateral agreements (mainly the GATS and TRIMs) are a phenomenon of international investment regulation with implications for the European-Sino context. Last but not least, differences in the perception of human rights, corporate social responsibility and environmental concerns must be assumed to exist in China and Europe.

III. The European Union approach toward sovereign investments

Unlike the other freedoms guaranteed by the Treaty, the free movement of capital extends beyond the frontiers of the Community. It is not an instrument of the internal market but a measure which expresses economic openness towards the whole world. Article 56 may thus be thought to be based not on notions of reciprocity but on the concept that free movement of capital brings benefits even when it is unilateral.

During the year 2008 SWFs emerged as an important issue to be tackled at the European level as opposed to national levels.[39] The Commission expected Member States to send a strong signal regarding their readiness to take joint action to avoid a repeat of the financial turmoil that hit the global economy after the US mortgage crisis in 2007. As the resulting financial turmoil has demonstrated, financial liquidity is vital for Western economies. Their finance was needed to allow companies to fulfil their strategic aims. Even Russian sovereign funds have not attempted to buy into any strategic assets; they are taking very limited stakes in some companies and the European Commission and the national governments are watching this activity. But there is no evidence at the moment that these sovereign funds are being used for any nefarious purpose.

Over the years, the free movement of capital has contributed to growth in Europe and in the world as a whole. It should not endanger the future through overregulation and protectionism, but rather should abide by free market principles. These funds have provided capital just when it was

39 J. Chaisse and P. Gugler, 'Sovereign Wealth Funds: What Should the European Union Do? ', in K. Sauvant (ed), *Sovereign Wealth Funds: Do We Need New Rules?* (Cheltenham: Edward Elgar, 2010).

most desperately needed. The purpose of SWFs is to invest surplus state reserves to yield profits. The investing countries may well be entitled to seek the best way to invest their reserves in foreign currency. The funds improve the liquidity of the financial markets and create growth and jobs. They also contribute to investment in the longer term. They create stability for the companies they invest in. Hence two clear conclusions can be drawn at this stage:

- It appears that a new wave of protectionism against foreign ownership represents a reincarnation of protectionism from years past.[40]
- Any domestic or European regulation would send the wrong signal as to the EU (or individual Member countries) being a good place in which to invest.

Europe must remain an attractive place for investment. Sovereign wealth funds are the by-products of increasing globalisation and of the benefits of international trade. They have so far always proved to be good shareholders. They are interested in the long-term, positive development of their business and hence in obtaining a good, long-term rate of return on their investment. If Europe were to restrict the activities of sovereign funds within its borders, it might find itself at an economic disadvantage, with important investment dollars going to other parts of the world.

There is a risk of seeing a strategy being implemented in each of the Member States that, ultimately, would not help to tackle the reality. There is a need to make clear at the European level which sectors should be protected from foreign takeovers and to go beyond the vague criteria of public order and public security. Such a list of EU strategic sectors could be drafted and would isolate energy, technologies etc. from standard competition. In addition, public mistrust of overseas investment and isolationist sentiment could cause an overreaction to the question of regulation. This could have far-reaching consequences not only financially, but in terms of diplomatic and economic relationships with other nations. To that extent, European leaders do not have the same policy towards Russia as they do towards the US. There is a need to clarify the interpretation of Article 58 ECT, which provides for restrictions on the free movement of capital on grounds of public order. Because it has not been applied until now in the context of SWFs, it is worthwhile to ensure that Member States will not be tempted to make extensive use of it.

40 P. Gugler and S. Brunner, 'Les défis du patriotisme économique en matière d'investissements étrangers en Europe: l'apport possible d'une approche multilatérale' (2008) 66 *Revue Economique et Sociale* 1–11.

D. Conclusions

A search for a coherent general framework for investment has so far been the major concern of international organisations and institutions. A comprehensive set of multilateral rules on FDI (multilateral agreement on investment) could allow for stable, transparent, and consistent environments for multinationals, whatever their ownership structures and locations of foreign production. The global application of broadly similar investment disciplines would remove the complexity arising for investors from the existing framework of bilateral and regional agreements on investment and would facilitate compliance. Having researched some of the most recent economic developments and the regulatory framework for investment, we can draw conclusions that shed some light on the 'fragmentation versus coherence debate'.

The multilateral approach has significant advantages over bilateral treaties and regional agreements, as it provides a level playing field for all firms, independent of their origin, and, consequently, improves allocative efficiency. But economic analysis demonstrates that FDI flows are regional by nature. This regionalism calls for a regional regulatory framework. As a social phenomenon law is always slower than real facts. It is because FDI will develop regionally that adequate frameworks will appear in these regions.

The European Union is a good example in this sense. The legal reality has come much later than the reality. Since its beginning, the EC has had to change and develop its institutional law, which defines the concept and the scope of the CCP, to follow as much as possible the protean mutations of the international trade system governance. This augmented the commercial policy to a significant sector of the EC external action, and led to a progressive evolution of its legal competences in this field. As an expected step of high importance, the proposed Lisbon Treaty today suggests changing the competences on investment regulation in Europe in an unprecedented manner. Although various interpretations of the legal text are possible (and will most probably be tested and clarified over time by the European Court of Justice), it is certain that the competences of the European Union will overall increase. The need for a more coordinated approach to investment regulation becomes obvious through analysis of the fragmented legal framework of Sino-European investment regulation.

Once the EU is able to develop a coherent external economic policy, this will have an impact on third countries. The bilateral relations will be largely reinforced and perhaps the EU integration will be a source of inspiration for other regional integrations such as the Mercosur or the Gulf Council which could develop external policies contributing at the regional level to the de-fragmentation of international regulation for investment.

Because of the financial crisis we cannot conclude without taking this context into account. As a matter of fact, FDI flows decreased significantly on a global scale in 2009 and this will continue in the short-to-medium term. This will impact the economies of many countries be they developed or developing countries. What is now very important for policy-makers is to identify the appropriate policy responses. The usual attitude is to make use of protectionist measures. Fears have come up in mainly Western countries with regard to this development. The 'new' host countries care about the ownership of the investing entities. Unease is usually not so much based on the fact that an investment fund is getting engaged, but rather derives from the implications of national ownership and control. In this sense, concerns are the same for financial investments, or for SOEs acquiring corporations or assets in the country. More precisely, concerns arise mostly over national security issues, subsidisation of the state-entities, and a general lack of transparency. Our studies of SWF regulation in the EU were a case in point. The role of international bodies or the EU itself is to seek to prevent such bad reflexes by controlling the establishment of new rules that could encourage protectionism. Governments around the world need to resist the temptation of protectionism. The challenges are to restore the credibility and stability of the financial system, to provide the 'right' stimulus for investment, and to renew the commitment to an open economy.

Also, investment matters are and will be affected by international crises such as the ongoing financial and economic crisis and ecological developments such as climate change. These reinforce, inter alia, ongoing discussions about the social side of FDI and its regulation in hard and soft law. In view of the standstill at the WTO, preferential trade agreements see a growing importance being added to the traditional role of bilateral investment protection treaties.

Bibliography

Brunner, Serge and Folly, David, 'The Way to a Multilateral Investment Agreement' (2007) NCCR Working Paper No. 24.

Chaisse, Julien, 'Adapting the European Community Legal Structure to the International Trade' (2006) **17**(6) *European Business Law Review* 1615–1635.

Chaisse, Julien, Chakraborty, Debashis and Guha, Arup, 'India's Multilayered Regulation of Foreign Direct Investment: Between Resistance to Multilateral

Negotiations and Unilateral Proactivism', in J. Chaisse and P. Gugler (eds), *Expansion of Trade and FDI in Asia: Strategic and Policy Challenges* (London: Routledge, Contemporary Asia Series, 2009), pp. 240–268.

Chaisse, Julien, 'L'ANASE et les défis du multilatéralisme émergent en Asie', in P. Gugler, and J. Chaisse (eds.), Les économies asiatiques face aux défis de la compétitivité internationale (2009) **67**(1) *Revue Economique et Sociale*, pp. 89–105.

Chaisse, Julien and Gugler, Philippe, 'Sovereign Wealth Funds: What Should the European Union Do? ', in K. Sauvant (ed), *Sovereign Wealth Funds: Do We Need New Rules?* (Cheltenham: Edward Elgar, 2010).

Chaisse, Julien and Gugler, Philippe, 'The ASEAN in a New Era: Unveiling the Promises', in P. Gugler and J. Chaisse, *Competitiveness of ASEAN Countries: Corporate and Regulatory Drivers* (Cheltenham: Edward Elgar, New Horizons in International Business series, 2010).

Cheng, Shaoming and Stough, Roger R., 'The Pattern and Magnitude of China's Outward FDI in Asia', ICRIER Working Paper, Indian Council for Research on International Economic Relations (2007).

Dunning, John H., *Multinational Production and the Multinational Enterprise* (London: Allen & Unwin, 1981).

Dunning, John H., 'The Eclectic Paradigm as an Envelope for Economic and Business Theories of MNE Activity' (2000) **9** *International Business Review* 163–190.

Dunning, John H. and Gugler, Philippe (eds.), *Foreign Direct Investments, Location and Competitiveness* (Oxford: Elsevier, 2008).

Dunning, John H. and Lundan, Sarianna M. (eds.), *Multinational Enterprises and the Global Economy* (Cheltenham: Edward Elgar, 2nd edn, 2008).

Gugler, Philippe, 'Foreign Investment and Poverty Reduction', paper presented at the NCCR Trade Regulation Annual Conference, Bern, 3–4 July 2007.

Gugler, Philippe, 'How are Chinese Multinational Enterprises Different?', VoxEU online, 23 August 2008 http://ssrn.com/abstract=1372031.

Gugler, Philippe and Ben Hamida, Lamia, 'How the PFI May Contribute to a More Coherent International Policy Framework on Investment' (2007) NCCR Working Paper No. 27.

Gugler, Philippe and Boie, Bertram, 'The Rise of Chinese Multinational Enterprises', in J. Chaisse and P. Gugler (eds.), *Expansion of Trade and FDI in Asia: Strategic and Policy Challenges* (London: Routledge, Contemporary Asia Series, 2009), pp. 25–57.

Gugler, Philippe and Brunner, Serge, 'Foreign Direct Investments Effects on National Competitiveness: A Cluster Approach' (2007) **13**(3) *International Advances in Economic Research* 268–284.

Gugler, Philippe and Brunner, Serge, 'Les défis du patriotisme économique en matière d'investissements étrangers en Europe: l'apport possible d'une approche multilatérale' (2008) **66** *Revue Economique et Sociale* 1–11.

Gugler, Philippe and Chaisse, Julien, 'Foreign Investment Issues and WTO Law: Dealing with Fragmentation while Waiting for a Multilateral Framework', in J. Chaisse and T. Balmelli (eds.), *Essays on the Future of the World Trade Organization (Volume 1)* (Geneva: Editions Interuniversitaires Suisses, 2008), pp. 135–171.

Gugler, Philippe and Chaisse, Julien, 'L'Asie dans l'économie politique mondiale contemporaine', in P. Gugler and J. Chaisse (eds.), Les économies asiatiques face aux défis de la compétitivité internationale (2009) **67**(1) *Revue Economique et Sociale* 7–20.

Gugler, Philippe and Chaisse, Julien, 'Patterns and Dynamics of Asia's Growing Share of FDI', in J. Chaisse and P. Gugler (eds.), *Expansion of Trade and FDI in Asia: Strategic and Policy Challenges* (London: Routledge, Contemporary Asia Series, 2009), pp. 1–21.

Gugler, Philippe and Shi, Jacylyn, 'Corporate Social Responsibility for Developing Country Multinational Corporations: Lost War in Pertaining Global Competitiveness? ' (2009) **87** *Journal of Business Ethics* 3–24.

Gugler, Philippe and Tomsik, Vladimir, 'The North American and European Approaches in the International Investment Agreements' (2007) **4**(5) *Transnational Dispute Management Review.*

Gugler, Philippe and Tomsik, Vladimir, 'General Agreement on Investment: Departure from the Investment Agreement Patchwork', in J. H. Dunning and P. Gugler (eds.), *Foreign Direct Investments, Location and Competitiveness* (Oxford: Elsevier, 2008), pp. 229–254.

Nie, Jianqiang, 'Towards China's Greater Influence on the World's Finances: A Legal Analysis of Chinese Overseas Direct Investment', in J. Chaisse and P. Gugler (eds.), *Expansion of Trade and FDI in Asia: Strategic and Policy Challenges* (London: Routledge, Contemporary Asia Series, 2009), pp. 99–121.

Rugman, Alan M. 'How Global are TNCs From Emerging Markets?', in K. Sauvant (ed.), *The Rise of Transnational Corporations from Emerging Markets* (Northampton: Edward Elgar, 2008), pp. 86–106.

Rugman, Alan M. and Hoon Oh, Chang, 'The International Competitiveness of Asian Firms' (2008) 1(1) *Journal of Strategy and Management* 57–71.

Rugman, Alan M. and Verbeke, Alain, 'Towards a Theory of Regional Multinationals: A Transaction Cost Economics Approach' (2005) **45**(1) *Management International Review* 3–15.

Sauvant, Karl, 'New Sources of FDI: The BRICS – Outward FDI from Brazil, Russia, India and China' (2005) **6**(5) *Journal of World Investment and Trade* 639–710.

Schill, Stephan W., 'Tearing Down the Great Wall: The New Generation Investment Treaties of the People's Republic of China' (2007) **15** *Cardozo Journal of International Comparative Law* 73, 76.

UNCTAD, Investment Brief 2007, UNCTAD/PRESS/PR/2007/001.

UNCTAD, *World Investment Report 2006: FDI from Developing and Transition Economies: Implications for Development* (New York and Geneva: United Nations, 2006).

UNCTAD, *World Investment Report 2007: Transnational Corporations* (New York and Geneva: United Nations, 2007).

UNCTAD, *World Investment Report 2008: Transnational Corporations and the Infrastructure Challenge* (New York and Geneva: United Nations, 2008).

Xiao, Jun, 'Chinese Bilateral Investment Treaties in the 21st Century: Protecting Chinese Investment', in J. Chaisse and P. Gugler (eds.), *Expansion of Trade and FDI in Asia: Strategic and Policy Challenges* (London: Routledge, Contemporary Asia Series, 2009), pp. 122–137.

12

Low-income countries and commodity price volatility

HANNAH BARGAWI, ELVA BOVA, BENNO FERRARINI AND SUSAN NEWMAN*

KEY MESSAGES

- Low-income countries (LICs) are highly vulnerable to fluctuations in commodity prices. Excessive price volatility complicates macroeconomic management and can worsen long-run growth and development prospects.
- Financial speculation has caused price volatility in the international markets beyond what could possibly be explained on the grounds of fundamentals of supply and demand alone.
- Field studies of the cotton and coffee sectors in Tanzania and Uganda show that sound market structures and institutions need to be in place for producers, households and villages to cope with price shocks.
- The case study of copper in Zambia highlights the extraordinary difficulties LICs encounter in devising appropriate monetary and exchange rate policies over the commodity price cycle.
- Overall, we reach the conclusion that LICs' vulnerability to commodity price volatility requires international support targeting supply-side constraints, together with the establishment of a financing scheme compensating the effects of price shocks. Of course, it is crucial that international support be premised on the pursuance of sound governance and macroeconomic policy at the domestic level.

* Individual Project No 12, 'Trade in Primary Commodities and Exchange Rates'. This chapter was put together with the individual contributions of the IP12 Alternate Leader, Dr Benno Ferrarini, World Trade Institute, Switzerland, and of the three IP12 PhD candidates based at the School of Oriental and African Studies, University of London. Section B was contributed by Susan Newman, Section C by Hannah Bargawi, and Section D by Elva Bova. Section E draws from the journal publications by Benno Ferrarini in relation to this NCCR project.

- In support of our argument for an increased role of foreign aid as a temporary device to counter excessive price volatility, we outline the main features of our proposal for such a compensatory financing mechanism and show, in the case of Uganda, that its application would be highly effective and relatively cost-efficient in achieving the goal of increased protection from price volatility and trade shocks more in general.

A. Introduction

The difficult circumstances facing the poor, primary-commodity-exporting countries have long been enshrined in the legislative body of the General Agreement on Tariffs and Trade (GATT)/World Trade Organization (WTO). The Enabling Clause, introduced in 1979, reproduced the idea of non-reciprocity first embedded in Article XXXVI:8, allowing for preferential treatment in favour of developing countries, in particular of least developed countries (LDCs).[1] The Uruguay Round later accorded the LDCs a number of special treatment clauses by means of specific provisions in the WTO agreements, most notably the right to opt out of these agreements on the grounds of special development needs and capabilities. For instance, the Agreement on Agriculture allowed for special and differential treatment of developing countries, and LDCs in particular, through fewer obligations and the easing of rules and time frames of implementation.[2]

It has long been acknowledged that the benefits and long-term prospects for LDCs' participation in the world markets are undermined by their vulnerability to commodity price fluctuations and the special financing needs arising from dependence on a narrow basket of primary export crops. Indeed, Article XXXVI of GATT 1947, one of the Kennedy Round results, already contained a special reference to the circumstances of its weakest Contracting Parties. Even if statements of principle, it is remarkable that this legal text continues to provide an accurate description of the plight many of these countries are still facing today, sixty

1 See also Appellate Body Report, *EC – Tariff Preferences*, paras. 106ff.

2 For instance, Article 15 of the Agreement on Agriculture allows lower reduction commitments and longer periods for the implementation of these commitments, while LDCs are not required to undertake any reduction commitments pursuant to Article 15:2. Additional flexibilities exist notably in the areas of market access, domestic support and export competition. See J. McMahon, *The WTO Agreement on Agriculture: A Commentary* (Oxford University Press, 2006), p. 173.

years later.[3] However, while issues of agriculture and special and differential treatment provisions continued to feature in the Uruguay and Doha rounds, the issue of fluctuating commodity prices has been omitted from negotiations since the late 1970s.

This omission was largely a consequence of a number of multilateral interventions that were put in place during the 1970s that acted to stabilise commodity export incomes for developing countries. Interventions included the International Commodity Agreements (ICAs) for the maintenance of minimum prices for a number of commodities, as well as the Compensatory Finance Facility of the International Monetary Fund (IMF) and Système de Stabilisation des Recettes d'Exportation (STABEX) scheme of the European Community (EC) that were set up to ameliorate the adverse effects of export instability that arose from fluctuating commodity prices.[4] Many of these multilateral interventions have since broken down. Political and economic factors culminated in the collapse of the ICAs, none of which survived the 1980s.

Against this background, and in light of the increasing frequency and amplitude of commodity price fluctuations since the early 1990s, we argue that the issue of commodity price volatility ought to receive greater recognition in WTO negotiations – and in the debates about the development

3 GATT, Part IV, Article XXXVI: Principles and Objectives, paragraphs 4 and 6 stipulate that (emphasis added):

> 4. Given the continued dependence of many less-developed contracting parties on the exportation of a limited range of primary products, there is need to provide in the largest possible measure more favourable and acceptable conditions of access to world markets for these products, and wherever appropriate to *devise measures designed to stabilise and improve conditions of world markets in these products, including in particular measures designed to attain stable, equitable and remunerative prices, thus permitting an expansion of world trade and demand and a dynamic and steady growth of the real export earnings of these countries so as to provide them with expanding resources for their economic development.*
>
> 6. Because of the chronic deficiency in the export proceeds and other foreign exchange earnings of less-developed contracting parties, *there are important inter-relationships between trade and financial assistance to development. There is, therefore, need for close and continuing collaboration between the contracting parties and the international lending agencies so that they can contribute most effectively to alleviating the burdens these less-developed contracting parties assume in the interest of their economic development.*

4 In fact, Article XX GATT incorporated an exception in favour of obligations under ICAs. Ad Article XX extends the exception to any ICA conforming to the principles approved by the UN Economic and Social Council in its resolution 30(IV) of 28 March 1947. The latter invokes the principles of chapter VI of the Havana Charter.

challenges facing LDCs, more generally – if the international community's assistance is to be more effective. Within the context of the National Centre of Competence in Research (NCCR) focus on international trade regulation, the goal of this research project has thus been to provide better insights into the origins and implications of commodity price volatility in relation to LDCs and low-income countries (LICs) more generally, in order to lay the grounds for the design of a more coherent and equitable multilateral trading system.

Our research into the processes of price formation and the structure of commodity markets, and of the effects of volatile commodity prices on producers in LDCs, was conducted on the basis of selected commodity case studies (coffee, cotton and copper) and fieldwork in Africa (Tanzania, Uganda and Zambia). We have further focused on the relationship between aid and trade in the context of commodity price volatility, yielding a proposal for a compensatory financing framework to bring about more coherence between the multilateral trade and aid frameworks in dealing with the special financing needs of shock-prone economies. A third and final focus of our research has been on the issue of exchange rate management, both in the context of the broader macroeconomic management difficulties facing resource-rich economies along the commodity price cycle, and in support of an argument in favour of intermediate exchange rate regimes for the case of emerging economies.

The structure of this chapter reflects the contributions by the individual researchers working on a specific topic of relevance to the research project overall. Each section provides a summary of the author's key findings in relation to his or her research, with a final section outlining the main conclusions reached.

Section B analyses the processes of price formation in the coffee market along the global value chain and against the background of alternative institutional settings, influencing the distribution of returns and exposure to price volatility. We find that the growing presence of new financial players and speculative activities on international exchanges has led to a loosening in the relationship between prices and supply and demand conditions for coffee. Upstream coffee market actors, with limited ability to utilise futures markets for the purposes of hedging against price risks, depend on the types of price risk management strategies employed by downstream actors. This has important implications for price transmission and income generation at different stages of the coffee value chain and, ultimately, for the sustainability of the production and local marketing systems.

Section C focuses on the effects of volatile commodity prices on producers in LDCs, following widespread domestic liberalisation of export sectors. Our case studies of the coffee and cotton markets in Tanzania highlight the complexity of social and historic aspects determining the impact of commodity price volatility, and point to a limited ability of both commodity producers and domestic institutions to cope with the effects of sudden price changes. We conclude that the effects of commodity price instability and LDCs' poor integration with the world trading system are compounded by the existence of severe supply-side constraints in export sectors. For effective assistance, the international community – including the WTO – would have to recognise the challenges in the LDCs' institutional production and marketing environments.

Section D takes issue with the management of resource-based economies over the commodity price cycle. More than any other economies, LDCs are strongly affected by the boom–bust price cycles of major primary export commodities and by external market conditions more generally. To avoid externally induced balance-of-payments crises, it is necessary for these countries to implement an effective macroeconomic management strategy over price cycles, a task fraught with many complexities. Focusing on the experience of Zambia in the management of the current copper boom, we identify the key elements and the economic conditions conducive to successful macroeconomic management. We formulate a framework for the analysis of fiscal, monetary and exchange rate policies, as an indicator of countries' vulnerability and of governments' capacity to respond to terms of trade shocks.

Section E outlines the main implications of our proposal for a multilateral aid framework to compensate LICs against commodity price volatility and trade shocks. In light of LICs' reliance on foreign aid to support their balance of payments and fiscal positions, we argue that a revision of the extant multilateral aid framework would be conducive to reducing the impact of macroeconomic vulnerability on long-run growth and trade performance. In support of our proposal for a so-called contingency debt sustainability framework, we outline the findings of an econometric assessment of the relationship between economic vulnerability and the sustainability of LICs' balance of payments and external debt, and go on to present the core elements of a debt contract that would tailor the amount and type of financial assistance to the nature and magnitude of trade shocks experienced by LICs.

B. International coffee markets and price volatility

We investigate the extent to which portfolio investment on international commodity exchanges drives the behaviour of prices, not only on the exchange itself, but also prices at which physical commodities are exchanged on the ground. It is shown that the growing presence of new financial players on international exchanges has led to a loosening in the relationship between prices and supply and demand conditions for the commodity. In addition we find that increased price volatility is associated with the entry of financial investors onto the international exchange.

Since coffee market actors differ in their ability to utilise futures markets for the purposes of hedging against price risks we find that the extent to which prices are transmitted along the supply chain, as well as the outcome in terms of income generation at different stages of the chain, depend crucially on the types of price risk management strategies employed by downstream actors. The resultant pattern of price has serious implications on the sustainability of the production and local marketing system.

I. Portfolio investment and price behaviour on futures markets

This part of our research explores the changes in composition of traders on the coffee exchange of the New York Board of Trade (NYBOT) and the implications of these on the behaviour of the price of coffee futures.[5] Using data from the NYBOT, for the period 1986–2006, it is shown that increases in the total volume of futures trading have been attributed mainly to the entry of new institutional investors such as hedge and pension funds. Their entry onto the market does not necessarily reflect supply and demand conditions in the international market; rather, they respond to changes in the global economic context more widely. For example, the dot-com crash of 2000 saw a massive shift in funds from equities to commodities, including coffee. Structural break tests identified a jump in the volume of portfolio investment on the coffee exchange that is associated with a break in the relationship between prices and supply and

5 A more detailed exposition of methods and results for this part of the research can be found in S. Newman, 'The New Price Makers: An Investigation into the Impact of Portfolio Investment on Coffee Price Behaviour', paper presented at the international workshop, 'Challenges and Prospects for Commodity Markets in the Global Economy', The School of Oriental and African Studies, University of London, 19–20 September 2008.

BOX 12.1 FINANCIAL INVESTMENT AND PRICE VOLATILITY – THE COFFEE 'C' CONTRACT

- The Coffee 'C' futures contract – traded on the New York Coffee Exchange – is the hedging instrument most widely used by international trading houses that deal in Arabica coffee.
- The traded volume of Coffee 'C' contract has been increasing since the 1970s. The main component of this increase has been an inflow of financial investment from portfolio investors. The extent to which the market is composed of financial investors can be seen in the ratio of non-commercial to total open interest on the exchange (see Figure 12.1).
- Movements in the price of the coffee 'C' futures contract have increased in both amplitude and frequency (see Figure 12.2).

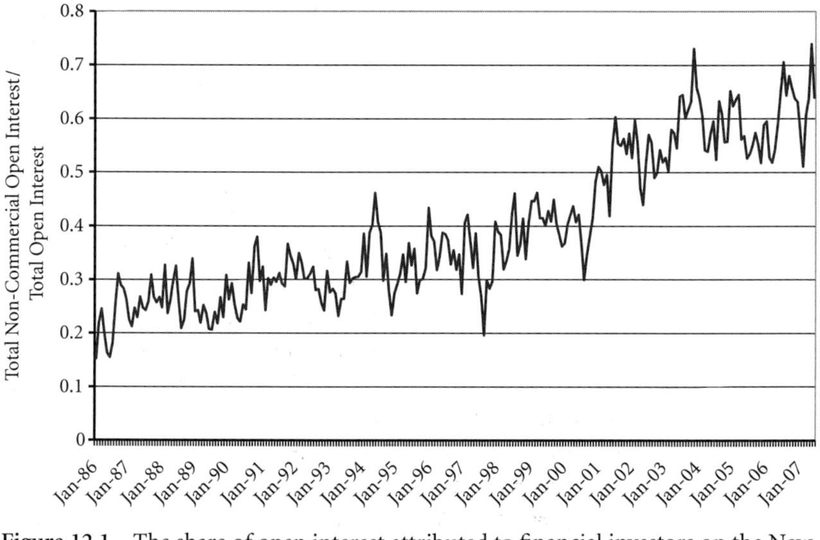

Figure 12.1 The share of open interest attributed to financial investors on the New York Coffee Exchange 1986–2007

demand conditions. Prices became less responsive to changes in supply and demand conditions following the entry of hedge funds in 1993/4.

We examined the relationship between the volume of contracts traded by non-physical traders and a monthly price volatility index for the period 1972–2006. Two breaks in the relationship were identified (April 1994 and October 2002). The period that followed the break in 1994 is characterised by heightened price volatility that supports the argument

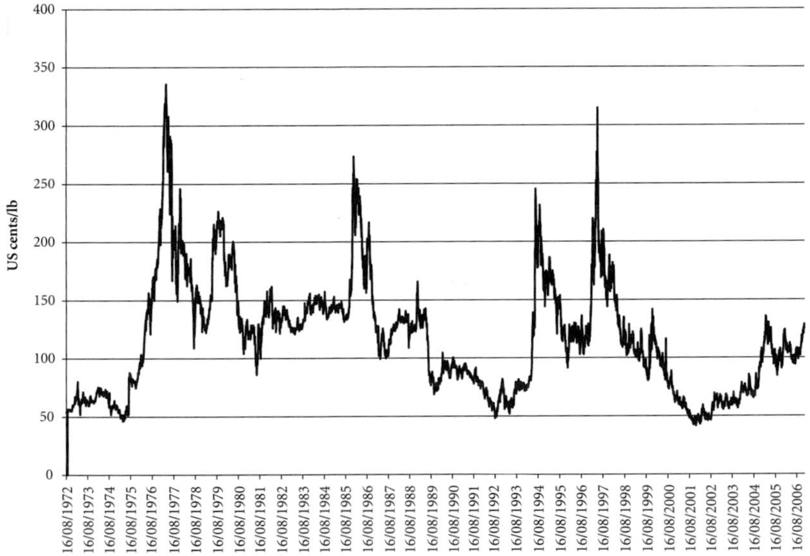

Figure 12.2 Daily closing coffee prices on the New York Coffee Exchange 1972–2006

that financial investment increased price volatility for coffee futures. In contrast, the period after the break in 2002 did not see an increase in price volatility despite the large inflow of funds from financial investors. This apparent contradiction in the relationship between financial investment on commodity exchanges and volatility can be explained if we consider the type of participants in the market, their motivations for trading and consequently, the nature of the trading activities.

The structural break in the relationship between price volatility and financial investment on the NYBOT coffee exchange in 1994 is explained by the inflow of funds associated with the inclusion of commodities by a number of large hedge funds. Hedge funds can profit from price volatility on commodities markets in a way that other financial investors cannot and provide commodity markets with a large proportion of the liquidity in them. An estimated 80 per cent of funds in commodity markets are looking for higher-than-market-following returns (alpha).[6] This alpha money is short-term and moves quickly into and out of the market. The volatility of fund in- and out-flows has implications on short-term price

6 E. Doyle, J. Hill and I. Jack, 'Growth in Commodity Investment: Risks and Challenges for Commodity Market Participants' (2007), FSA Markets Infrastructure Department, Financial Services Authority, London.

movements on commodity exchanges where large flows can rapidly drive prices away from the price warranted by world supply and demand.

The motivations of financial investors entering commodities markets in 2000 differed from the inflows of money due to hedge funds in the 1990s. Falling returns on equity and bond markets, together with the anticipation of inflation led to an inflow of funds seeking an inflation hedge and looking to diversify their bond and equity heavy portfolios. The period since 2000 has thus been accompanied by greater variety in the types of financial investors and investment strategies in commodity markets.[7] In particular, passively managed investment and portfolio products have been growing. Rather than trading on volatility, this group of investors profit from long-run price increases. Rather than enhanced price volatility, the period between 2001 and 2006 has seen an upturn in commodity prices that has been largely driven by financial investors with longer-term horizons.

II. Price transmission along coffee chains

Our research also looked at the implications of changes on prices experienced by different actors along coffee chains that have taken place on international exchanges.[8] Since futures markets are relied upon for price discovery, departures from price movements that are warranted by physical market conditions can impact upon the supply and demand decisions of physical market players.

The international coffee system has undergone significant restructuring following the collapse of the International Coffee Agreement in 1989 and the liberalisation of coffee marketing systems in many coffee-producing countries under structural adjustment. As a result, all market actors became exposed to risks associated with price volatility. Revisiting early theories of futures markets shows that futures markets are inherently biased against producers and local exporters owing to the asymmetry between long- and short-hedgers in terms of opportunities to profit from price movements.[9] Moreover, since coffee market actors differ in their ability to utilise futures markets, the extent to which prices

7 D. Domanski and A. Heath, 'Financial Investors and Commodity Markets' (2007) *BIS Quarterly Review.*

8 A detailed account of this part of the research can be found in S. Newman, 'The Role of International Commodity Exchanges in Price Formation and Transmission of Prices and Price Risk along International Coffee Chains' (2008) NCCR Trade Regulation Working Paper No. 2008/12.

9 B. A. Goss and B. S. Yamey, *The Economics of Futures Trading* (London, Macmillan, 1978).

are transmitted along the supply chain depends crucially on the types of price risk management strategies employed by downstream actors, as illustrated in the case of Tanzanian and Ugandan coffee chains. These in turn depend crucially on the organisation of the market as well as access to finance, information, warehousing and brokerage services. Where there is no access to futures markets or cooperative risk management strategies, producers tend to sacrifice price level for the sake of stability, and local traders take on the risk but do so for a price. The resultant pattern in terms of price has serious implications on the sustainability of the production and local marketing system. At the international level, trading companies seized the opportunities to profit on futures markets, engaging in forms of speculative hedging. The spread of such business practices has resulted in further industrial concentration. Smaller firms are wiped out in the event of a perverse market movement whilst the largest, diversified, commodity trading companies expand their market share.

C. The effects of price volatility on producers

This part of our research agenda focused on primary commodity markets in least developed countries and the effects of volatile commodity prices on producers, following widespread domestic liberalisation of export sectors. A case study approach considered coffee and cotton markets in Tanzania and highlighted complex, social and historic aspects. This work has drawn attention to the asymmetric effects of commodity price volatility over time and space across the country. Commodity producers' ability to cope with the effects of sudden price changes have become more complicated and blurred as other effects of domestic liberalisation have moulded these sectors. Domestic institutions at all levels have attempted to adapt and transform in the wake of these experiences but their ability to do this effectively remains partial and uneven. The research highlighted the crucial supply-side constraints in the export sectors of LDCs such as Tanzania in overcoming the effects of commodity price instability and in meeting WTO objectives of greater integration of LDCs in the world trading system. Greater recognition and appreciation of the challenges in the domestic institutional production and marketing environments is therefore urgently needed.

I. Tanzania coffee and cotton fieldwork: main findings

It is evidently important to address some of the impediments to the fulfilment of LDCs' full trade potential and our research contributes to this understanding by considering the adverse impacts of commodity price volatility on producers. The research was focused on producers of cotton and coffee in Tanzania, an LDC which has undergone widespread domestic liberalisation and has been a member of the WTO since 1995. Cotton and coffee are important crops for Tanzania, in terms of export revenue but also in terms of rural poverty and employment. However, whilst other LDCs have been experiencing growth and expansion in their export sectors, such as Vietnam in the case of coffee and West Africa in the case of cotton, Tanzania's cotton and coffee sectors have been retracting. At the same time Tanzania's cotton and coffee producers have been exposed to increasing commodity price volatility arising from greater domestic liberalisation and integration into world markets.

The research relied on information gathered first-hand from producers of cotton and coffee in three regions of Tanzania to uncover the detailed effects of price volatility on these producers. This work was complemented by interviews with other institutional players in the domestic cotton and coffee markets to gain a better understanding of the post-liberalisation institutional set-up. The frameworks for delivering inputs and research and extension services as well as price-setting structures for cotton and coffee were analysed.

Research results showed that producers were unevenly affected by price fluctuations and that cotton producers were more exposed to price changes than coffee producers. Furthermore, the nature of price fluctuations was complicated across time and space. Producers were doubly hit by sudden price changes, firstly through changes in prices between years and secondly by within-season price changes. Differences between crops, across areas and within villages could be best understood by the differential impacts of domestic liberalisation on these crops. Supply and production of cotton and coffee were therefore constrained both by the effects of unstable prices and by the lack of supportive institutional structures for producers. Often unstable prices for cotton and coffee acted as the final deciding factor in pushing producers out of cotton and coffee production and towards rural and non-rural alternatives, with detrimental poverty outcomes.[10]

10 H. Bargawi, 'Cotton Price Fluctuations at the Ground-level: Assessing the Difference in Impact in Rural Tanzania' (2008) NCCR Trade Regulation Working Paper No. 2008/11.

BOX 12.2 KEY FINDINGS ON THE IMPACT OF A DECLINE IN COFFEE PRICES IN KILIMANJARO REGION, TANZANIA

The extent of the coffee price drop between 1999 and 2002 varied between producers, although most received less than TSH 400 per kg (about US$ 0.3) at the lowest point, under one third of the nominal 2006/07 producer price. The impact of this decline in prices and income was diverse with only the wealthiest producers, reliant on other income sources, stating that they had not been affected. In general the impacts were felt across households with most producers lowering their consumption and expenditure in response to the drop in prices.

Spending reductions affected the entire household through cuts in expenditure on housing, clothing, school fees and other essential school-related equipment. A further area mentioned by the poorest was the search for employment and to a limited extent the sale of livestock assets in response to the income shortfall. Finally, the fall in prices over 1999–2002 was also a deciding factor in shaping agricultural decision-making and changes to coffee production in the area. A large number of producers, particularly the poorest, stopped applying the correct amounts of labour and non-labour inputs in response to lower prices. Wealthier producers on the other hand relied on alternative income sources to purchase inputs for coffee.

Despite varying degrees of dissatisfaction with current institutional structures surrounding coffee production, many producers continued producing coffee. For producers across wealth categories the revenue raised through coffee production remained a vital part of household income. Only through the income raised from coffee sales could households afford to make major cash investments in their children's education as well as allowing them to invest in more diversified production and income-raising opportunities.

Wider analysis of the cotton and coffee sectors revealed the vast institutional void left by the domestic liberalisation of these sectors in Tanzania. Furthermore, our work highlighted the unequal outcomes of institutional change on the ground, with ad hoc private sector, non-governmental organisation (NGO) or village society arrangements taking on new responsibilities. In some cases, particularly in the coffee sector, these new institutions have had limited success, although underlying village dynamics appear intrinsic to locating those most able to benefit from new institutional structures. Both the cotton and coffee sector in Tanzania have suffered greatly from a lack of coherent structures that ensure the effective and widespread delivery of information on prices, research and extension services (assistance) to producers. Furthermore, frameworks for accessing inputs and for delivering output to market are also lacking, leading to unequal outcomes in terms of market access within Tanzania.[11]

D. Exchange rate policy and macroeconomic management: the case of Zambia

This study examines the complexities of the macroeconomic management in commodity dependent countries whose balance of payments and fiscal budget move pro-cyclically to the commodity price cycle. As highlighted by the 'resource curse' literature,[12] cyclical balance of payments and budget deficits complicate macroeconomic and investment planning. Moreover, as exposited by the 'Dutch disease' literature,[13] the positive prospects envisaged by a commodity boom may easily be reverted by an exchange rate appreciation which negatively impacts on the country's external competitiveness. These are some of the factors that explain the tight connection between commodity dependence and underdevelopment, often defined by the concept of 'commodity trap' or 'resource curse'. Historical evidence demonstrates that to overcome the 'curse', i.e. to promote a long and sustainable development process based on export diversification, macroeconomic management plays an overriding role.[14]

In the light of the Zambian experience in the management of the current copper boom this study tries to identify what are the key

11 H. Bargawi, 'Tanzania's Agricultural Institutions in Flux: Lessons from Coffee and Cotton Producing Villages' (2008) NCCR Trade Regulation Working Paper No. 2008/14.

12 P. Collier, 'Managing Commodity Booms: Lessons of International Experience' (2007) CSAE Working Paper, Department of Economics, University of Oxford; R. Auty (ed.), *Resource Abundance and Economic Development* (Oxford University Press, 2001); J. Sachs and A. Warner, 'Natural Resource Abundance and Economic Growth' (1997) CID Working Paper, Harvard University.

13 M. Corden, 'Booming Sector and Dutch Disease Economics: Survey and Consolidation' (1984) 36 *Oxford Economic Papers* 359–380; M. Corden and P. Neary, 'Booming Sector and De-Industrialisation in a Small Open Economy' (1982) 92 *The Economic Journal* 825–848; S. Van Wijnbergen, 'The "Dutch Disease": A Disease After All?' (1984) 94 *The Economic Journal* 41–55.

14 P. Collier, 'Primary Commodity Dependence and Africa's Future' (1992) *mimeo World Bank*; P. Collier and J. Willem Gunning, 'Trade Shocks: Theory and Evidence', in P. Collier and J. Willem Gunning (eds.), *Trade Shocks in Developing Countries* (Oxford University Press, 1999); D. Bevan and P. Collier, 'Anatomy of a Temporary Trade Shock: The Kenyan Coffee Boom of 1976–79', in P. Collier and J. Willem Gunning (eds.), *Trade Shocks in Developing Countries* (Oxford University Press, 1999).

elements and the necessary economic conditions for a successful macroeconomic management. We formulate a framework for the analysis of fiscal, monetary and exchange rate policies, which assesses the actual capacity of governments to respond to terms of trade shocks and identifies countries' degree of vulnerability. Our research has three components. The first part examines the implications of mine ownership on the extent of fiscal and exchange rate policy, looking at and comparing the management of the recent copper boom in Chile and Zambia. The second part assesses the suitability of a flexible exchange rate regime with inflation-stabilising monetary frameworks for commodity dependent countries. The third part explores alternative exchange rate arrangements and puts forward a proposal for a commodity currency, an arrangement for commodity dependent countries applied to the Zambian economy.

I. Relevance of mine ownership[15]

Evidence from Zambia and Chile in managing the current copper boom highlights the role played by the ownership structure and taxation regime of the commodity industry. In Chile, the state-owned enterprise Codelco owns almost 40 per cent of the total assets of the mines while the remaining 60 per cent is owned by transnational corporations. In Zambia, the sector went through an almost complete privatisation and is now fully controlled and managed by transnational corporations, which benefited from minimal royalties and large tax exemptions and deductions until 2008.[16] As far as fiscal policy is concerned, such ownership structures meant large inflow of revenues to the Chilean budget and negligible inflow to the Zambian government (Figures 12.3, 12.4, 12.5, 12.6). The surge in revenues in Chile has been saved in accounts held abroad with the possibility to access part of these funds every five years.

When the government gets the inflow of export receipts, spending may be more easily phased out and postponed to periods when the country

15 Due to space limits, the comparison between the implications of mine ownership in Chile and Zambia presented in this section abstracts from important qualifications made in relation to these countries' very different levels of economic development, governance and accountability. For a fuller discussion, the reader is referred to E. Bova, 'The Implications of Mine Ownership for the Management of the Boom: A Comparative Analysis of Zambia and Chile' (2009) NCCR Trade Regulation Working Paper No. 2009/13.

16 A. Fraser and J. Lungu, 'For Whom the Windfalls: Winners and Losers in the Privatisation of Zambia's Copper Mines' (2007) www.minewatchzambia.com. J. Craig, 'Putting Privatisation into Practice: The Case of Zambia Consolidated Copper Mines Limited' (2001) 39(2) *Journal of Modern African Studies* 389–410.

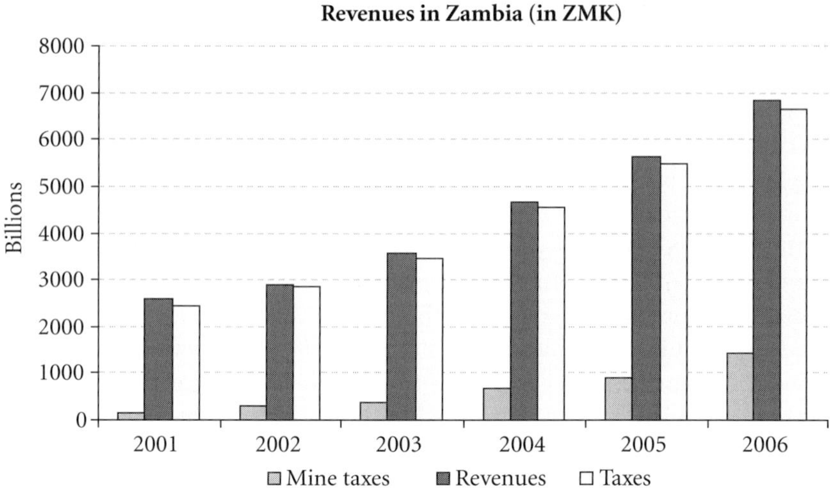

Figure 12.3 Revenues, general taxes and mine taxes in Zambia
Sources: The World Bank, World Development Indicators and Zambian Revenue Authority.

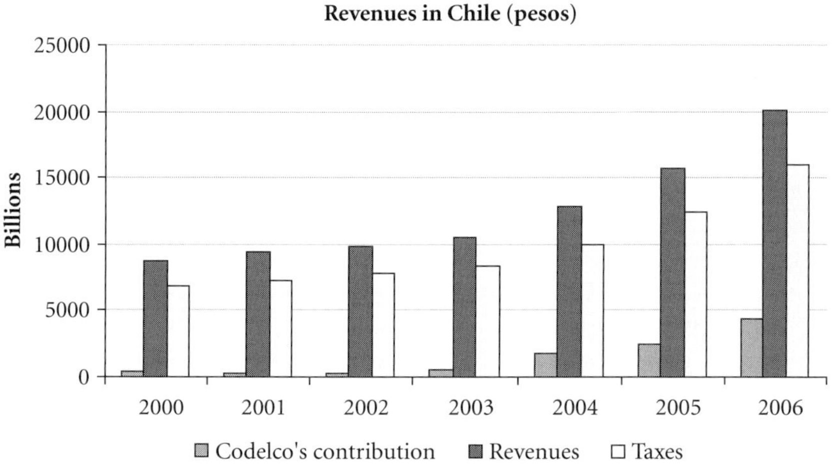

Figure 12.4 Revenues, general taxes and mine taxes in Chile
Sources: The World Bank and World Development Indicators.

is more able to absorb new investments. This allows avoiding low-return investments, which were common in the first commodity boom during the 1970s and 1980s when countries were caught by a spending euphoria so that their economies became heavily indebted even before the boom

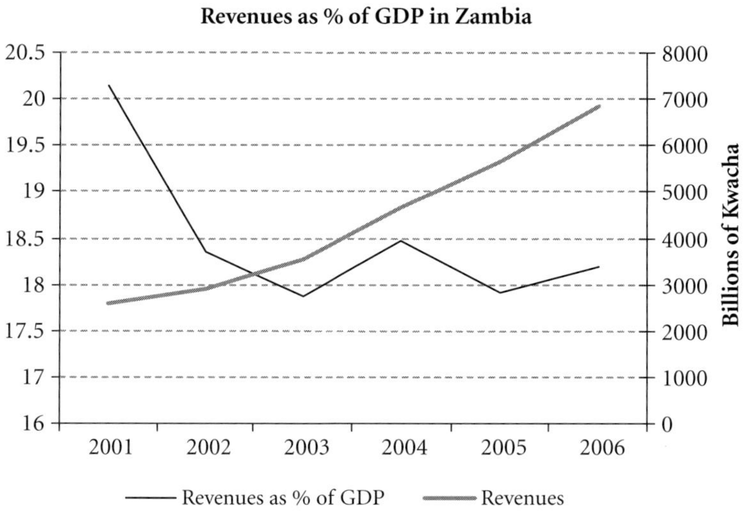

Figure 12.5 Total revenues and revenues as % of GDP in Zambia
Sources: The World Bank, World Development Indicators.

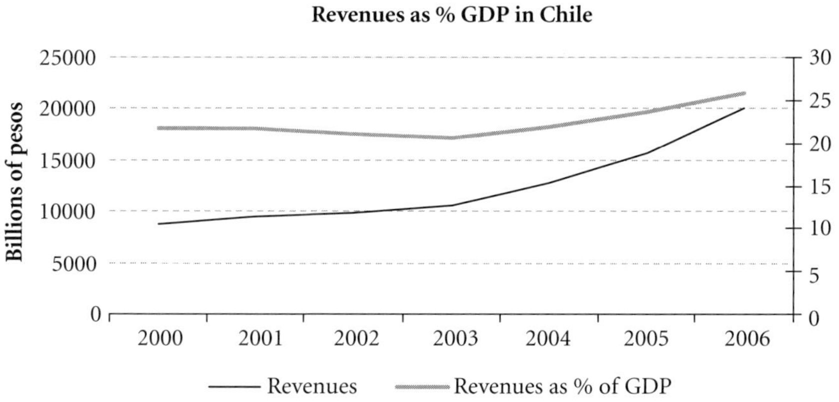

Figure 12.6 Total revenues and revenues as % of GDP in Chile
Sources: The World Bank, World Development Indicators.

was over.[17] Furthermore, saving avoids incurring into a real exchange rate appreciation that may result from an increase in spending. In Zambia, the inflow of foreign exchange has been spent by the domestic market whose propensity and possibility to save are smaller and this has determined a real

17 A. Hewitt, *Economic Crisis in Developing Countries: New Perspectives on Commodities, Trade and Finance* (London: Pinter Publishers, 1993), pp. 56–78.

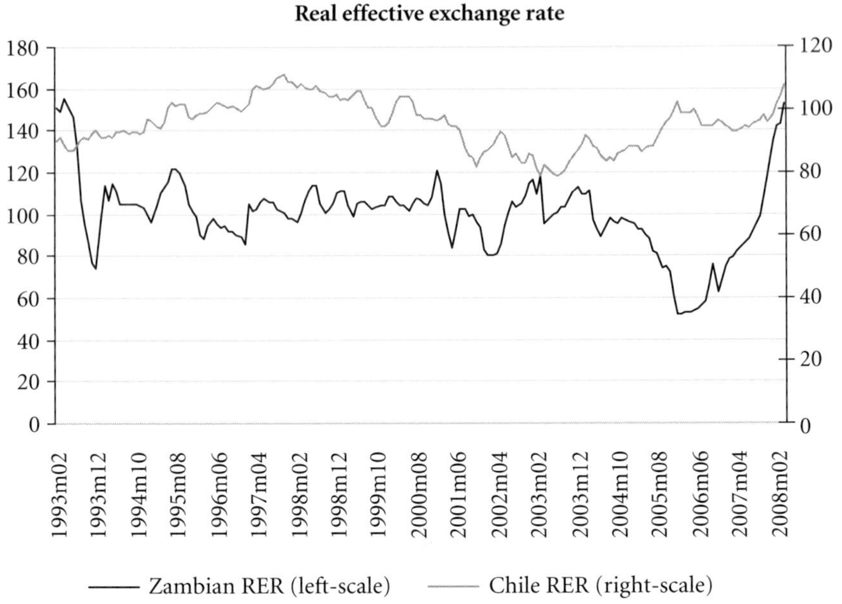

Figure 12.7 Real exchange rates in Zambia and Chile
Sources: International Monetary Fund, International Financial Statistics.

exchange rate appreciation (Figure 12.7) which has negatively impacted on the non-traditional exports.

All in all, public mine ownership may expand the possibilities of macroeconomic management, notably fiscal and monetary responses to commodity shocks and this refers not only to direct ownership as such but also to the taxation regime, often negotiated in conditions of low prices with very little bargaining power on the side of the government.

II. Exchange rate management

The second part of the research explores the implications of different kinds of exchange rate regimes in the context of commodity dependence and shows how exchange rate management can be a useful tool to offset commodity shocks and enhance sustainable development through export diversification. An analysis of the exchange rate management of the Zambian copper boom illustrates how floating regimes may determine exchange rate appreciations which are harmful for export competitiveness. In Zambia the increase in the export receipts has determined a sharp

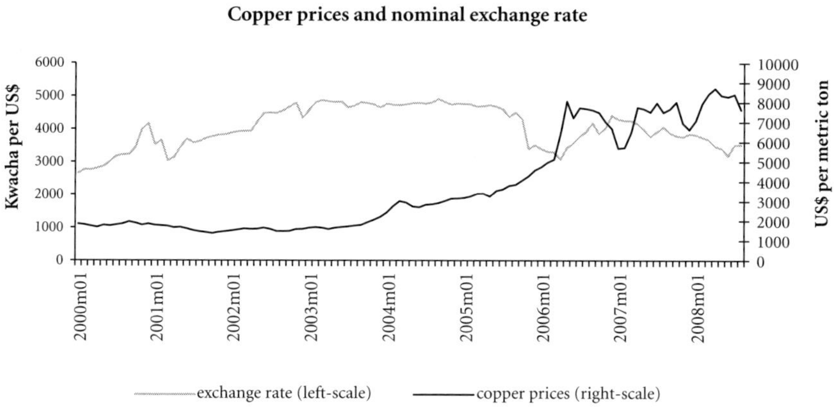

Figure 12.8 Exchange rate appreciation and copper prices in Zambia
Sources: International Monetary Fund, International Financial Statistics, and Bank of Zambia, Zambia Export Growers Association.

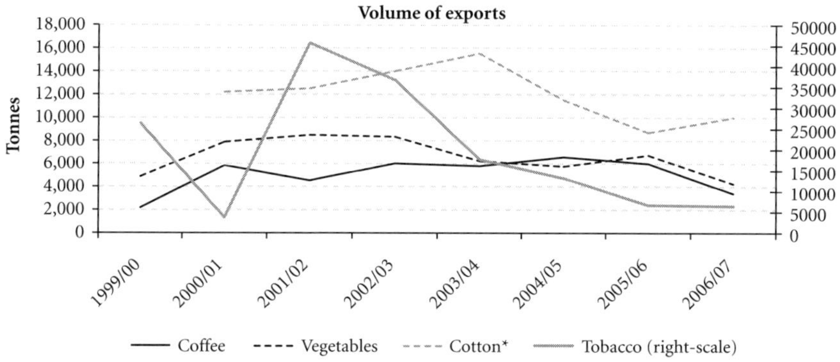

Figure 12.9 Non-traditional export performance in Zambia
Note: the value for cotton has been multiplied by ten. *Sources:* International Monetary Fund, International Financial Statistics, and Bank of Zambia, Zambia Export Growers Association.

appreciation of the Kwacha and this, in turn, determined a contraction of some key non-traditional exports (Figures 12.8 and 12.9).

Applying vector autoregression (VAR) we find that the risk of an increase in inflation which usually results from a more managed exchange rate is relatively low in Zambia, as in most developing countries, where domestic prices are heavily dominated by food prices which depend more on supply than demand conditions. However, due to a high imported component in the Zambian Consumer Price Index (CPI) – mainly imported food, oil and fertilisers – exchange rate management may impact on the economy via devaluations which increase the prices of imported goods. This complicates monetary policy since, to avoid an appreciation, prices of food and fertilisers[18] may actually increase with serious implications for poverty reduction and for the profitability of other export sectors, like agriculture. This kind of import dependence limits the extent of macro management and highlights an additional element of developing countries' vulnerability.

III. Commodity currency

Further to Frankel's 2002 proposal[19] on a commodity currency this part of our research examines different arrangements for commodity countries and then formulates an exchange rate mechanism which takes into account both the interest of maintaining competitive exports and the concern for high inflation. Through macro simulations applied to the Zambian economy we assess the impact of an arrangement that is counter-cyclical to movements in the main commodity price but at the same time pro-cyclical to shifts in the terms of trade net of the copper exports (Figure 12.10).

The arrangement will then de-link the economy from the copper price cycle and at the same time promote non-traditional exports, which are the

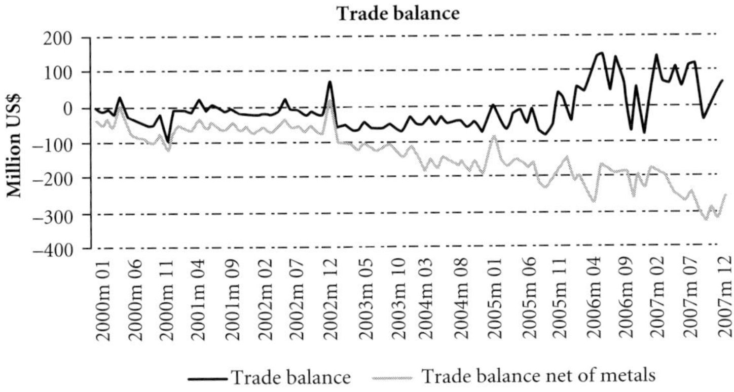

Figure 12.10 Trade balance and trade balance net of metal exports in Zambia
Source: Bank of Zambia.

18 Although oil prices are a large component of CPI, they are set by the government and thus are not too sensitive to changes in the exchange rate.

19 J. Frankel, 'Should Gold Exporters Peg their Currency to Gold?' (2002) World Gold Council, Research Study No. 29.

stepping stone for the diversification process. Given the large imported food component, the mechanism has a lower bound for the domestic currency set so as to avoid excessive increases in the CPI through exchange rate devaluations.

IV. Towards a sustainable macroeconomic framework

In the context of mineral-based economies a sustainable macroeconomic framework is one that will de-link the economy from the commodity price cycle, so as to avoid pro-cyclicality in the balance of payments and fiscal budget, and that will promote export diversification, avoiding excessive fluctuations in the exchange rate. From the analysis of the Zambian management of the copper boom in comparison with Chile, this research identifies the following elements for a sound macroeconomic system. First is the extent of fiscal policy space, which is essentially related to how the commodity industry is managed and controlled. The reason for this is that with a large share of public ownership and high taxation of the mines a commodity boom will increase government revenues. Assuming sound public governance, when mine revenues accrue to the public sector rather than to private companies, these could be more effectively used in a way to spur long-term investment and to avoid real appreciation which may be harmful for non-traditional exports. A second key element is the exchange rate regime and, precisely, its degree of flexibility, since this regulates central banks' intervention and sets how successfully central banks can achieve a real target, i.e. export competitiveness, but also a nominal target, i.e. price stability, which are key for the long-term development of the economy. The study indicates that highly flexible arrangements with the sole objective of price stability may indeed maintain the pro-cyclicality of the economy, while a more managed float will be more appropriate in promoting export diversification and setting specific patterns of trade.

E. Commodity price volatility, trade shocks, and compensatory finance

This section outlines our work on a proposal for a contingency aid framework, compensating LICs for external shocks affecting their trade balance. In view of the difficulties LICs experience in macro-managing their economies in the face of commodity price volatility and external shocks to the balance of payments more generally, compensatory finance has – under certain conditions and within a limited time horizon of application – the potential to circumvent the negative effects of macroeconomic vulnerability on these countries' long-run growth and development performance.

Our work on compensatory finance followed a three-pronged approach: (1) an empirical assessment of the role of economic vulnerability in explaining debt distress episodes; (2) the definition of an accounting method to identify and measure the impact of exogenous shocks, and the proposal of a so-called contingency debt sustainability framework to adjust the amount, timing and grant element of aid flows in compensation of qualifying shocks; (3) the simulation of the proposed framework to the case of Uganda. What follows is a brief overview of the findings described in the three articles arising out of this research component.

BOX 12.3 LOW-INCOME COUNTRIES AND THE FOCUS ON AID

Our work on compensatory finance has mainly evolved within the field of foreign financial aid and debt sustainability, as a reflection of the crucial importance official aid has had in financing LICs' persistent current account and fiscal deficits. Unfortunately, in the case of most recipient countries over the last three decades, aid has proven largely ineffective in promoting economic development and repayment capacity. The occurrence of debt distress, which is essentially a borrowing country's incapacity to service its debts, became the normal state for LICs and the donor community to find themselves in. The relationships between sovereign borrowers and lenders, like those concerning the donor community within itself, became increasingly complex. Lending policy experienced important shifts over time, from defensive roll-over lending, to Paris Club rescheduling and relief operations, to the multilateral debt relief initiatives of the late 1990s and early 2000s. Along came a progressive change in the scope and depth of the strings attached to official aid, constraining the set of policy options open to borrowing nations. The liberalisation of trade and capital accounts, and sweeping privatisation across economic sectors were part of the donors' standard prescription package, both bilaterally and multilaterally.

To the extent that LICs' policy and development has been shaped by their dependence on official aid, any question of coherence of international policy pertains to the realm of aid as much as it does to WTO. One aspect of coherence has been addressed with the emerging 'aid for trade' debate, recognising the role for aid in targeting specific bottlenecks impeding LICs' exploitation of market access opportunities. Another aspect concerns the role of contingency finance as a new instrument of targeted aid. Few would contest the evidence that volatility of commodity prices and the occurrence of trade shocks constitute a major causal factor underlying LICs' economic vulnerability and their incapacity to reap the full benefits from trade. Our work on contingency finance addresses the potential for a multilateral solution in this regard.

I. *Policy, vulnerability, and the new debt sustainability framework*[20]

We investigate the factors undermining low-income countries' sustainability of external debt and of the balance of payments more broadly.[21] We assess the findings of the two studies constituting the empirical foundation of the lending and debt sustainability assessment framework currently adopted by the International Development Association (IDA) and the IMF[22] for their lending policies toward low-income countries.[23] Applying probabilistic analysis across a panel of low-income countries, we find that economic vulnerability indicators[24] are reliable predictors of debt distress episodes, while policy and governance indicators are generally not.[25] The empirical investigation casts doubts on the benefits from relying on the World Bank Country Policy and Institutional Assessment (CPIA) as a guiding principle for multilateral aid. Instead, it finds support in what appears to be an emerging consensus, namely that the effectiveness of foreign aid is increased when it is guided by concerns about poor countries' economic vulnerability, and particularly when it is disbursed in timely response to the price and trade shocks these countries experience.

II. *Proposal for a contingency debt sustainability framework*[26]

In an attempt to redress these shortcomings of IDA aid allocation, we outline the basic features of a proposal for a Contingency Debt Sustainability

20 B. Ferrarini, 'Policy, Vulnerability and the New Debt Sustainability Framework' (2009) 21(7) *Journal of International Development* 895–914.

21 A. Kraay and V. Nehru, 'When is External Debt Sustainable?', World Bank Policy Research Working Paper WP3200 (World Bank, Washington, DC, 2004).

22 IMF and IDA, 'Debt Sustainability in Low-Income Countries – Proposal for an Operational Framework and Policy Implications' (International Development Association and International Monetary Fund, 2004) www.imf.org/external/np/pdr/sustain/2004/020304.pdf, 3 February 2004.

23 These policies are enshrined in the New Debt Sustainability Framework, as well as the 14th replenishment of the International Development Association: IDA, 'Additions to IDA Resources: Fourteenth Replenishment Report from the Executive Directors of the International Development Association to the Board of Governors' (International Development Association, 2005), http://siteresources.worldbank.org/IDA/Resources/14th_Replenishment_Final.pdf

24 For further information about the United Nations Economic Vulnerability Index, see United Nations Environment Programme (UNEP): www.vulnerabilityindex.net/

25 B. Ferrarini, above note 20.

26 B. Ferrarini, 'Proposal for a Contingency Debt Sustainability Framework', (2008) 36(12) *World Development* 2547–2565.

Framework (CDSF).[27] The core analytical component of the framework is an accounting mechanism based on counterfactuals, suitable to identify and measure the impact of exogenous disturbances on LICs' balance of payments (BOP).

With the exception of well-defined shocks, such as sharp fluctuations in world market prices of traded commodities, it is typically not possible to clearly identify, ex-post, the exogenous nature of factors determining a country's BOP. To overcome this indeterminacy, the author builds on an accounting method introduced by Bela Balassa,[28] to specify trend deviations and hypothetical BOP flows that would have prevailed in the absence of certain events. The formal derivation of the method is described in the articles presenting the full results.[29] For the purpose of this discussion, it should suffice to note that the accounting mechanism provides the evidential basis for the CDSF to distinguish factors influencing an LIC's BOP sustainability under the control of country authorities from those which are not, and to compensate a country accordingly, through adjustments to the amount, timing and type of official aid disbursements. Figure 12.11 outlines the basic intuition and the financial instruments underlying the contingency framework.

With reference to some period of assessment (t),[30] compensation for the liquidity and debt stock implications of qualifying events occurs essentially through two financial instruments: a contingent credit line, to compensate for the direct liquidity effects of exogenous shocks through timely adjustments of aid flows, and an automatic debt relief facility, to lower the external debt burden in light of unfavourable trend effects. Jointly, the credit line and the relief facility operate in function of an underlying, state-contingent, debt contract, which defines the policy conditions (conditionality) multilateral lenders attach to the loans.[31]

27 Of course, the major emphasis of any such analysis has to ensure that such an insurance scheme is incentive compatible, in order to minimise the moral hazard (and adverse selection) implications it has with regard to the actions (and the type) of debtor countries involved. For an exposition of the key issues involved, the interested reader is referred to Ferrarini, above note 26.

28 B. Balassa, 'Structural Adjustment Policies in Developing Economies' (1982) 10(1) *World Development* 23–38.

29 Ferrarini, above note 26, and B. Ferrarini, 'Compensatory Aid and Debt Relief: A Case Study of Uganda' (2009) 45(7) *Journal of Development Studies* 1134–1149.

30 The length of the reference period is determined by the minimum amount of time necessary for the verification of the occurrence and implications of exogenous shocks.

31 Optimally, such policy conditionality would be the outcome of a process of negotiation between the parties to the contract, and involve the stakeholders and civil society of the recipient country.

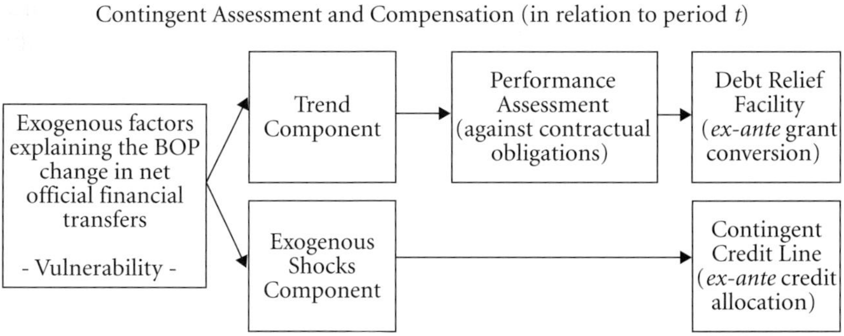

Figure 12.11 The Contingency Debt Sustainability Framework (core elements)
Sources: B. Ferrarini, 'Proposal for a Contingency Debt Sustainability Framework' (2008) 36(12) *World Development.*

Operating as a buffer against liquidity excesses or shortages, contingency credit involves the automatic disbursement – or amortisation,[32] for the case of positive shocks – of interest-free top-up funds in proportion to the net magnitude and sign of qualifying events. To avert the long-term repercussions of liquidity shocks, such disbursements occur automatically at the end of each period of assessment (*t*). Shocks are modelled as random realisations around trends, hence mean-reverting with no particular justification for the contingency mechanism to disburse grants, instead of operating as an unconditioned and fully concessional credit line.

By contrast, trend effects are only in part exogenous to LIC, since their internalisation in policy enactments influence macroeconomic resilience – and outcomes more generally – over time. To circumvent the intrinsic identification problem arising from trend effects' endogeneity, the contingency framework validates any such measures according to their conformity with donor conditionality. To the extent that a recipient country's compliance with policy obligations is ascertained, it qualifies for the automatic grant-conversion of official credit flows in proportion to the net amount of BOP effects.[33]

32 Amortisation refers to the repayment of outstanding debt. An acceleration of amortisation amounts to a detraction of excess liquidity from the debtor country.

33 The conversion of loans in grants is equivalent to providing debt relief to the debtor country.

III. A case study of Uganda[34]

As a final step of analysis, we simulate the implications of the contingency framework for the case of Uganda during the period 1988–2002. The CDSF accounting method is applied to extrapolate, ex post, the shock and trend effects experienced by Uganda. Accordingly, official loans and external debt stocks are adjusted by application of the credit and debt relief facilities, as outlined above.

A comparison between the liquidity and debt stock implications of the CDSF and the outcome of the Paris Club and heavily indebted poor countries (HIPC) debt relief initiatives that actually involved the country during the period of analysis reveals that the contingency framework would have been highly effective in countering the severe disturbances to the country's trade balance, with beneficial debt stock effects. Indeed, Figures 12.12 and 12.13 display sharp liquidity corrections in loan disbursements and amortisations of existing debt over the entire period of analysis. For example, during years of extreme price fluctuations marked by the coffee price peak around 1995 – or during its dip, later in 2001 – the credit line would have detracted or added up to US$ 200 million of loan disbursements to Uganda per year (Figure 12.12). Against the background of Uganda's close adherence to policy conditionality, additional benefits would have accrued to the country in the form of compensatory debt amortisations in the face of negative trend factors observed (Figure 12.13). As a result, the total external debt stock is

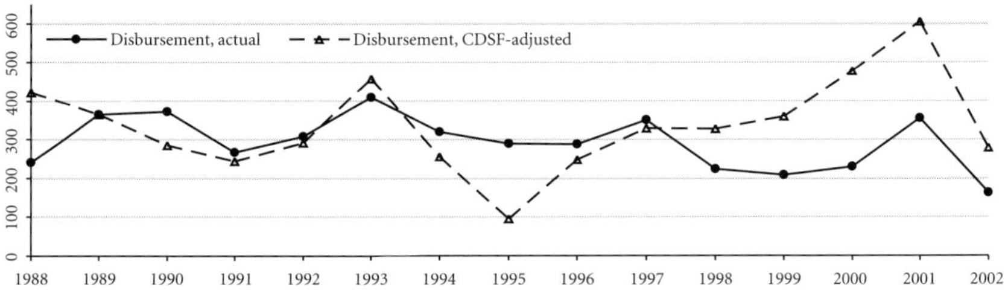

Figure 12.12 Contingent Credit Line – CDSF simulation: Uganda, 1988–2002, million US$

Sources: adapted from B. Ferrarini, 'Proposal for a Contingency Debt Sustainability Framework' (2008) 36(12) *World Development*, Graph 2 and B. Ferrarini, 'Compensatory Aid and Debt Relief – A Case Study of Uganda' (2009) 45(7) *Journal of Development Studies*, Figure 3.

34 Ferrarini, 'Compensatory Aid and Debt Relief: A Case Study of Uganda', above note 29.

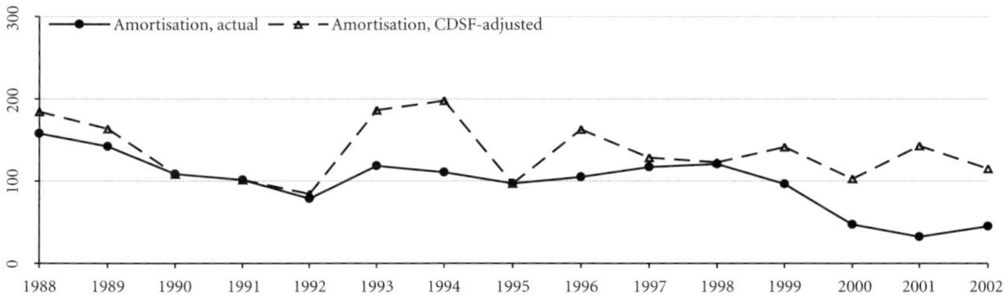

Figure 12.13 Debt Relief Mechanism – CDSF simulation: Uganda, 1988–2002, million US$
Sources: adapted from B. Ferrarini, 'Proposal for a Contingency Debt Sustainability Framework' (2008) 36(12) World Development, Graph 2 and B. Ferrarini, 'Compensatory Aid and Debt Relief – A Case Study of Uganda' (2009) 45(7) *Journal of Development Studies*, Figure 3.

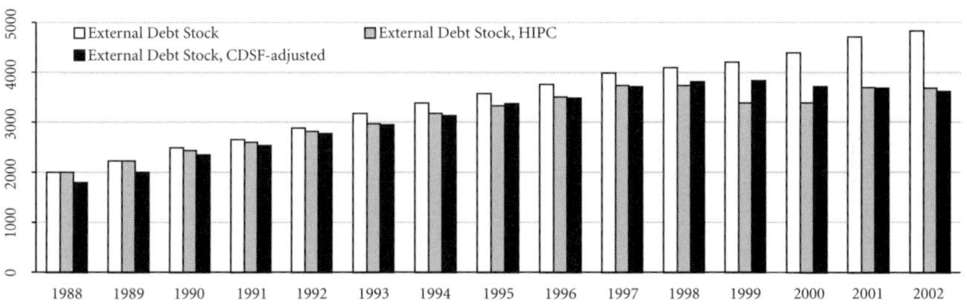

Figure 12.14 Debt Stock Reduction – CDSF simulation: Uganda, 1988–2002, million US$
Sources: adapted from B. Ferrarini, 'Proposal for a Contingency Debt Sustainability Framework' (2008) 36(12) *World Development*, Graph 2 and B. Ferrarini, 'Compensatory Aid and Debt Relief – A Case Study of Uganda' (2009) 45(7) *Journal of Development Studies*, Figure 3.

simulated to shrink at a level comparable to that associated with the Paris Club and HIPC debt relief initiatives (Figure 12.14). Without these ad hoc relief operations providing any of the insurance benefits associated with the contingency framework, their overall transfer costs of US$ 1,161 million are shown to be of similar magnitude to those associated with the CDSF, estimated at US$ 1,216 million.[35]

35 *Ibid.*

F. Concluding remarks

The research pursued within this NCCR project highlights the need for greater recognition of the difficulties price volatility poses for LICs' macroeconomic management and of the institutional gaps in these countries' domestic markets. The main policy implication is the importance of concerted efforts at the multilateral level towards targeted development assistance for LICs to overcome excessive vulnerability to commodity price fluctuations. This would require greater consistency between the current focus of the 'aid for trade' initiative and the broader question about the effectiveness of aid programmes involving the international financial institutions and the donor community more generally.

Our work on international coffee markets and local marketing structures in African countries highlights the fact that the current policy agenda of the WTO has not taken into account the specificities characterising today's international commodity markets. In order for the world trading system to engender development through export it is crucial for it to take into account the way in which commodity exporting developing countries are integrated into the world economic system, not just through direct trade relationships but also in terms of the way in which developing country actors are related to the international financial system through the international commodity exchanges. The negotiations around aid for trade in the current Doha round provide a possible opportunity for supporting stable export earnings for developing countries. However, this should not simply be in terms of providing technical assistance to enhance the access of developing country actors to hedging instruments on the international commodity exchanges, as has been promoted by the World Bank's Commodity Task Force, owing to the instabilities that originate from the futures exchanges themselves. Under the existing institutional framework at the international level, there is a need for cooperation between the regulators of international commodity exchanges and the International Financial Institutions in tackling the problems associated with market distortions that arise from financial investment on commodity exchanges. Otherwise, any technical assistance aimed at improving the risk management strategies for developing country actors will be futile and can exacerbate income inequalities already present along commodity chains.

Our study of the effects of volatile commodity prices on producers shows that the current policy agenda on agriculture and rural development in Tanzania and other LDCs has often failed to recognise the centrality of coherence in rural institutional structures and instead focused on price transmission and market integration alone.[36] It is evident from our work that these will not be sufficient for bringing about the desired agricultural supply response in the Tanzanian context and in other LDCs. The WTO and other international bodies therefore need to work together to reconsider the institutional problems of commodity producing LDCs as central to the commodity question and beyond. Again, we see scope for the WTO's delivery of technical assistance and new aid for trade modalities, as an opportunity for the WTO to act alongside other development organisations to confront the institutional weaknesses in LDC commodity markets. In order for LDCs such as Tanzania to truly take advantage of the international trading system, the institutional structures surrounding the provision of information, inputs, extension services and marketing in agricultural commodity markets will need strengthening. Recognition of these institutional gaps in domestic markets can act as an important area in which the WTO can create policy coherence with other development organisations and ensure that its trade-related capacity building and technical assistance is consistent with programmes and objectives of other international bodies, such as the World Bank, the IMF and the United Nations agencies.

Finally, we see scope for the establishment of a contingency financing mechanism, as a temporary element of international assistance against the effects of price shocks, complementing the long-run objectives of improving LICs' resilience to shocks through technical assistance and capacity building. The key implication of our work is that international development assistance, including aid for trade, will only be effective if supported by a major multilateral effort devoted to the provision of compensatory finance. A coherent approach to multilateral policy towards LICs requires a concerted effort by WTO Members, also in relation to their role as members of the international donor community.

Bibliography

Anderson, Kim and Martin, Will, 'Agricultural Trade Reform and the Doha Development Agenda' (2005) **3607** World Bank Policy Research Working Paper.

Auty, Richard (ed.), *Resource Abundance and Economic Development* (Oxford University Press, 2001).

36 K. Anderson and W. Martin, 'Agricultural Trade Reform and the Doha Development Agenda' (2005) 3607 World Bank Policy Research Working Paper; A. Keck and P. Low, 'Special and Differential Treatment in the WTO: Why, When and How?' (2004) 3 ERSD Staff Working Paper.

Balassa, Bela, 'Structural Adjustment Policies in Developing Economies', (1982) **10**(1) *World Development* 23–38.

Bargawi, Hannah, 'Cotton Price Fluctuations at the Ground-level: Assessing the Difference in Impact in Rural Tanzania' (2008) NCCR Trade Regulation Working Paper No. 2008/11.

Bargawi, Hannah, 'Tanzania's Agricultural Institutions in Flux: Lessons from Coffee and Cotton Producing Villages' (2008) NCCR Trade Regulation Working Paper No. 2008/14.

Bevan, David and Collier, Paul, 'Anatomy of a Temporary Trade Shock: The Kenyan Coffee Boom of 1976–79', in P. Collier and J. Willem Gunning (eds.), *Trade Shocks in Developing Countries* (Oxford University Press, 1999).

Bova, Elva, 'The Implications of Mine Ownership for the Management of the Boom: A Comparative Analysis of Zambia and Chile' (2009) NCCR Trade Regulation Working Paper No. 2009/13.

Cashin, Paul and McDermott, John C., 'The Long-Run Behavior of Commodity Prices : Small Trends and Big Volatility', Working Paper WP/01/68 (International Monetary Fund: Washington, DC, 2001).

Cassese, Antonio, 'L'immunité de juridiction civile des organisations internationales dans la jurisprudence italienne' (1984) **30** *Annuaire français de droit international* 555–580.

Collier, Paul, 'Managing Commodity Booms: Lessons of International Experience' (2007) CSAE Working Paper, Department of Economics, University of Oxford.

Collier, Paul, 'Primary Commodity Dependence and Africa's Future' (1992) mimeo World Bank.

Collier, Paul and Dehn, Jan, 'Aid, Shocks, and Growth', Development Research Group Policy Research Paper No. 2688 (The World Bank, Washington, DC, 2001).

Collier, Paul and Gunning, Jan W., 'Trade Shocks: Theory and Evidence', in P. Collier and J. Willem Gunning (eds.), *Trade Shocks in Developing Countries* (Oxford University Press, 1999).

Collier, Paul and Gunning, Jan W., *Trade Shocks in Developing Countries* (Oxford University Press, 1999), vols. 1 and 2.

Corden, Max, 'Booming Sector and Dutch Disease Economics: Survey and Consolidation' (1984) **36** *Oxford Economic Papers* 359–380.

Corden, Max and Neary, Peter, 'Booming Sector and De-Industrialisation in a Small Open Economy' (1982) **92** *The Economic Journal* 825–848.

Craig, John, 'Putting Privatisation into Practice: The Case of Zambia Consolidated Copper Mines Limited' (2001) **39**(2) *Journal of Modern African Studies* 389–410.

Deaton, Angus, 'Commodity Prices and Growth in Africa' (1999) **13**(3) *Journal of Economic Perspectives* 23–40.

Deaton, Angus and Miller, Ron, 'International Commodity Prices, Macroeconomic Performance and Politics in Sub-Saharan Africa' (1996) **6**(5) *Journal of African Economies* 99–191.

Domanski, Dietrich and Heath, Alexandra, 'Financial Investors and Commodity Markets' (2007) *BIS Quarterly Review.*

Doyle, Emmet, Hill, Jonathan and Jack, Ian, 'Growth in Commodity Investment: Risks and Challenges for Commodity Market Participants' (2007), FSA Markets Infrastructure Department, Financial Services Authority, London.

Ferrarini, Benno, 'Compensatory Aid and Debt Relief: A Case Study of Uganda' (2009) **45**(7) *Journal of Development Studies* 1134–1149.

Ferrarini, Benno, 'Policy, Vulnerability and the New Debt Sustainability Framework' (2009) **21**(7) *Journal of International Development* 895–914.

Ferrarini, Benno, 'Proposal for a Contingency Debt Sustainability Framework', (2008) **36**(12) *World Development* 2547–2565.

Frankel, Jeffrey, 'Should Gold Exporters Peg their Currency to Gold?' (2002) World Gold Council, Research Study No. 29.

Fraser, Alastair and Lungu, John, 'For Whom the Windfalls: Winners and Losers in the Privatisation of Zambia's Copper Mines' (2007), www.minewatchzambia.com.

Gordley, John, 'Good Faith in Contract Law', in R. Zimmerman and S. Whittaker (eds.), *Good Faith in European Contract Law*, 2nd edn (Cambridge University Press, 2000), pp. 80–95.

Goss, B. A. and Yamey, B. S., *The Economics of Futures Trading* (London: Macmillan, 1978).

Hewitt, Adrian, 'Economic Crisis in Developing Countries: New Perspectives on Commodities, Trade and Finance' (London: Pinter Publishers, 1993), pp. 56–78.

IDA, 'Additions to IDA Resources: Fourteenth Replenishment Report from the Executive Directors of the International Development Association to the Board of Governors' (International Development Association, 2005), http://siteresources.worldbank.org/IDA/Resources/14th_Replenishment_Final.pdf

IMF and IDA, 'Debt Sustainability in Low-Income Countries – Proposal for an Operational Framework and Policy Implications' (International Development Association and International Monetary Fund, 2004) http://www.imf.org/external/np/pdr/sustain/2004/020304.pdf, 3 February 2004.

Keck, Alexander and Low, Patrick, 'Special and Differential Treatment in the WTO: Why, When and How?' (2004) **3** ERSD Staff Working Paper.

Kraay, Aart and Nehru, Vikram, 'When is External Debt Sustainable?', World Bank Policy Research Working Paper WP3200 (World Bank, Washington, DC, 2004).

McMahon, Joseph, *The WTO Agreement on Agriculture: A Commentary* (Oxford University Press, 2006).

Newman, Susan, 'The New Price Makers: An Investigation into the Impact of Portfolio Investment on Coffee Price Behaviour', paper presented at the international workshop, 'Challenges and Prospects for Commodity Markets in the Global Economy', School of Oriental and African Studies, University of London, 19–20 September 2008.

Newman, Susan, 'The Role of International Commodity Exchanges in Price Formation and Transmission of Prices and Price Risk along International Coffee Chains' (2008) NCCR Trade Regulation Working Paper No. 2008/12.

Sachs, Jeffrey and Warner, Alex, 'Natural Resource Abundance and Economic Growth' (1997) CID Working Paper, Harvard University.

Solis, Leopoldo and Zedillo, Ernesto, 'The Foreign Debt of Mexico', in G. W. Smith, and J. T. Cuddington (eds.), *International Debt and the Developing Countries* (Washington, DC: World Bank, 1985).

UNCTAD, *Economic Development in Africa 2008 – Export Performance Following Trade Liberalization: Some Patterns and Policy Perspectives* (United Nations Publication, 2008).

Van Wijnbergen, Sweder, 'The 'Dutch Disease': A Disease After All?' (1984) **94** *The Economic Journal* 41–55.

Williamson, John, 'Policies to Reduce the Vulnerability of Low-Income Countries', in J. J. Teunissen and A. Akkerman (eds.), *Protecting the Poor: Global Financial Institutions and the Vulnerability of Low-Income Countries* (The Hague, FONDAD, 2005), pp. 14–34.

WTO, Doha Ministerial Declaration, Geneva (WTO, 2001).

WTO, Hong Kong Ministerial Declaration, Hong Kong (WTO, 2005).

WTO, 'Aid for Trade Task Force: Recommendations of the Task Force on Aid for Trade', WT/AFT/1 (WTO, Geneva, 2006).

INDEX